PRACTICAL PHYSICS
AT A LEVEL

PRACTICAL PHYSICS AT A LEVEL

TREVOR CROSS
Great Sankey High School, Warrington

COLLINS EDUCATIONAL
London

ACKNOWLEDGEMENTS

The author would like to thank Great Sankey High School for their help and the use of their equipment, and also his family for their patience and support.

The publishers would like to thank the following suppliers for the photographs of equipment and apparatus:

Philip Harris, pp. xii–xvii, 82;
Acorn Computers Ltd., p. xvii;
Economatics (Education) Ltd., p. xv;

Educational Electronics, pp. xvi, 4;
Research Machines Ltd., p. xvii;
Unilab, pp. xii, xv, xvi.

The author and publishers would also like to acknowledge the use of tables, in the section on 'Useful Information', obtained from the *Science Data Book*, R. M. Tennent (ed.), 1971, Oliver and Boyd.

© Trevor Cross 1985

All rights reserved.
No part of this publication may be reproduced, stored in a retrieval system, or transmitted, in any form or by any means, electronic, mechanical, photocopying, recording or otherwise, without the prior permission of the owner.

ISBN 0 00327763-1

First published 1985
by Collins Educational
8 Grafton Street
London W1X 3LA

ISBN 0-03-27763-1

Designed, typeset and illustrated by
Sharp Print Management, Manchester

Printed in Great Britain by R. J. Acford Ltd., Chichester

1 2 3 4 5 6 7 8 9 10

British Library Cataloguing in Publication Data
Cross, Trevor
  Practical physics at A level.
  1. Physics—Laboratory manuals.
  I. Title
  530'.028   QC35

CONTENTS

The experiments in this book are grouped under four main headings:

Experimental techniques (1 to 25)
Investigating relationships (26 to 52)
Deductions, applications and data analysis (53 to 80)
Measuring quantities and investigating laws (81 to 100)

A classification of the experiments is also given at the end of the book under the following headings:

1. Experimental techniques
2. Short or sectioned experiments
3. Electrical experiments
4. Magnetism and electromagnetism
5. Forces and mechanics
6. Waves, light and sound
7. Atomic and nuclear experiments
8. Molecular movement and heat
9. Experiments with data analysis sections
10. Practice for practical examinations
11. Experiments which use a computer, a data memory or a microprocessor-controlled recording instrument.

INTRODUCTION	xi
TYPICAL EQUIPMENT IN AN A LEVEL PHYSICS LABORATORY	xii
TAKING MEASUREMENTS AND FINDING PROBABLE ERRORS	1
RECORDING, DISPLAYING AND ANALYSING THE RESULTS	12
WRITING EXPERIMENTAL REPORTS	22

EXPERIMENTAL TECHNIQUES

1. **Measurement of length and mass** — 38
   A variety of experiments giving practice in the use of:
   - Vernier calipers
   - Micrometer
   - Spherometer
   - Balances for measuring mass and force

2. **Using the travelling microscope** — 42
   To measure
   - The pitch of a screw
   - The separation of lines on a diffraction grating
   - The spacings on an interference pattern
   - The thickness of tracks on a microcircuit

   and to take measurements so that the refractive index of a liquid can be calculated.

3. **Measuring times** — 44
   - Using a stopwatch
   - Using electronic timers
   - Using microprocessor based methods

4. **Timing oscillations** — 47
   Experiments based round measuring the periods of the following:
   - Springs
   - A compound pendulum
   - Swinging chains
   - Thin beams clamped at one end
   - A Y-shaped pendulum
   - Suspended beam
   - Beams oscillating on a curved surface
   - Coupled oscillators

5. **Some experiments involving density** — 51
   - Deduction of the density of unknown solids hidden in Plasticine
   - The identification of clear liquids
   - Investigation of the pressure due to a column of liquid
   - Making and using a simple hydrometer

6. **Using the principle of moments** — 53
   - Using a balanced beam to deduce mass and to identify liquids
   - Making and calibrating a simple current balance
   - Investigating the angle of a force needed to support a beam

7. **Detecting electromagnetic radiation** — 55
   - Plotting an amplitude against frequency spectrum across the frequency band of a radio
   - Methods of detecting infrared radiation
   - General details about detecting other frequencies

8. **Plotting rays and image positions with pins** — 56
   - Virtual image in a plane mirror
   - Path of a ray through a glass block
   - Focal length of a convex lens
   - Real image in a convex lens
   - Maxima seen through a diffraction grating

9. **Using an illuminated object with lenses and mirrors** — 58
   - Finding a sharp image accurately and estimating the error
   - Measuring the focal length of a concave mirror
   - Measuring the focal length of a concave lens
   - Finding the position of a hidden convex lens

10. **The paths of rays through a prism** — 60

11. **Stroboscopic and photographic methods of measuring changing position with time** — 61

12. **Bending beams** — 62
    Investigation on the deflection under load of:
    - A beam loaded centrally
    - A cantilever

13. **Measuring frequency** — 64
    Various experiments on the techniques of measuring frequency using:
    - Beats
    - The time-scale on an oscilloscope
    - Lissajous' figures
    - A stroboscope
    - Direct electronic counting
    - Resonance

14. **The forced vibration of a wire** — 67

15. **The spectrometer** — 69

16. **Measuring potential difference** — 72
    Direct voltages using:
    - A moving coil meter
    - A moving coil meter with an operational amplifier as a voltage follower
    - An oscilloscope
    - A potentiometer
    - Digital electronic methods

    Alternating voltages using:
    - Rectification and a moving coil meter
    - An oscilloscope
    - A moving iron meter
    - Calibration of a moving coil a.c. meter

17. Measuring the e.m.f. produced by a thermocouple — 76
    Using a potentiometer with a high resistance in series
    By direct measurement using an operational amplifier to produce amplification

18. Using moving-coil ammeters and voltmeters to measure resistance — 77
    An investigation into the choice of instruments, their positions in circuits and the accuracy of the value of resistance calculated

19. Wheatstone bridge and metre bridge — 79

20. Finding the resistivity of a resistance wire using a metre bridge — 81

21. Displaying and drawing waveforms on an oscilloscope — 82

22. Measuring impedance — 85

23. Methods of measuring magnetic fields — 88
    Search coil and ballistic galvanometer
    Search coil and integrator
    Hall effect probe
    A.c. induction

24. Using the computer and data memories as measuring instruments — 94
    Timing free fall
    Investigating the change in resistance against time after a lamp is switched on
    Damped s.h.m. of a compound pendulum
    Investigating how the temperature changes as two liquids mix

25. Detecting nuclear particles — 98
    Measuring the background radiation
    Safety in the use of radioactive sources
    Adjusting the Geiger–Müller tube to measure the activities of sources
    Using a cloud chamber
    Using photographic paper

INVESTIGATING RELATIONSHIPS

26. Frictional forces — 102
    An investigation of the static and sliding friction between two surfaces

27. Fluid friction — 103
    An investigation of the forces on ball bearings moving through a fluid

28. Springs and damping — 104

29. Energy absorbed by a bouncing ball — 105

30. Air resistance on a falling object — 106

31. Efficiency of an electric motor — 107

32. Energy stored in a flywheel — 108

33. Heat losses from a wire under different pressures — 109

34. Variation of boiling point with pressure and s.v.p. with temperature — 110

35. The general gas law — 111

36. Bernouilli's principle — 112

37. The parallel plate capacitor — 113

38. Energy stored in a capacitor — 115

39. Charge and discharge of a capacitor — 116

40. Electrical resistivity and conductivity — 119

41. Conduction in liquids and gases — 121

42. Investigating the operation and applications of a transistor — 123

43. Plotting the characteristic curves for a transistor (common-emitter mode) — 127

44. Characteristics of light-sensitive devices — 129

45. E.m.f. induced as a magnet passes through a coil — 131

46. Magnetic field produced by a pair of co-axial coils — 133

47. Resonances of a vibrating wire — 134

48. Interference pattern produced by double slits — 137

49. The behaviour of microwaves — 139
    Width of the beam
    Reflection
    Refraction
    Double slit interference pattern

50. Interference pattern of sound waves — 142

51. Phase angles in a.c. circuits using a capacitor and resistor in series — 144

52. Series LCR resonant circuit — 147

DEDUCTIONS, APPLICATIONS AND DATA ANALYSIS

53. Circuit deductions — 149
54. Deducing hidden components — 150
55. Investigations with a magnet — 153
56. Controlling a current — 153
    Switches, thermistor, reed switch, relay, resistor
57. Diodes: junction, zener, LED and lambda — 155
58. The operational amplifier — 157
    Inverting, amplification, feedback and switching applications
59. Potential dividers — 160
    Using resistors, light dependent resistors and capacitors
    The application of potential dividers to logic gates
60. The effect of temperature on resistance — 162
    The behaviour of various components
    The temperature coefficient of resistance
61. Thermometers — 164
    Calibration of a thermistor thermometer and its use in temperature control
    A thermometer using resistance wire
62. Logic circuits and logical control — 166
63. Investigations using TTL 7400 NAND gates and a 7493 counter — 169
64. Pneumatic control — 173
65. Internal resistance and Kirchhoff's laws — 176
    Measuring the internal resistance
    Investigating the conditions for maximum power transfer
    Investigating Kirchhoff's laws
66. Electric field patterns — 178
67. Electrical forces — 180
68. Optical instruments — 182
    Camera
    Astronomical telescope
    Microscope
69. Using reflection and refraction of light — 185
70. Thickness measurement using the absorption of radioactivity — 187
71. Simulation of a mass spectrometer — 188
72. Analogue computing — 191
73. Digital control by computer — 195
74. Analysis of spectra — 200
75. Analysis of projectiles — 202
76. Analysis of the collisions of objects — 203
77. Designing experiments — 204
78. Analysis of melting points — 206
79. Analysis of sound waves — 206
80. Polarisation of light and the analysis of stress — 208

MEASURING QUANTITIES AND INVESTIGATING LAWS

81. Finding information about atoms and molecules — 211
    Oil film experiment
    Brownian motion
    Specific latent heat of vaporisation and bonding energy
    Bombarding the atom with particles
82. Elasticity and Young's modulus — 216
83. Equilibrium of a body under coplanar forces — 218
84. Falling sand: Newton's second law — 219
85. Does force equal mass times acceleration? — 220
86. Conservation of linear momentum with an air track — 222

CONTENTS

87. The force produced by a current-carrying wire in a magnetic field — 224

88. Investigating laws for gamma radiation — 226
    Absorption and half-value thickness
    The inverse square law with no absorber

89. Measurement of half-life — 228

90. Finding the energy of β^- particles — 230

91. Measurement of the ratio e/m for a beam of electrons — 233

92. Millikan's experiment to measure e, the fundamental unit of charge — 234

93. Measuring the permittivity of air and Perspex — 238

94. The photoelectric effect and the measurement of Planck's constant — 240

95. Measuring the speed of waves
    Sound, microwaves and light — 241

96. Measuring the wavelength of light using Newton's rings — 244

97. Focal length and focal plane of a convex lens — 245

98. Measuring the resolution of your eye — 247

99. Resonance of an air column — 249

100. Heat energy transfer — 251
    Newton's Law of cooling
    Thermal conductivity

USEFUL INFORMATION — 257
CLASSIFICATION OF EXPERIMENTS — 261

INTRODUCTION

The purpose of practical work in physics at A level is to develop your skills in manipulating apparatus, recording and displaying the results and in making deductions and conclusions from those results. As a result, it is hoped that you will understand the theory more fully. In this book there are also experiments which give you practice in planning experiments, widen your experience of physics and associated fields, and enable you to apply the information you find.

The apparatus used has changed rapidly over the last few years, with the introduction of data memories and microcomputers, allowing new types of investigations. The examination syllabi have changed, placing more emphasis on experimental techniques and the analysis of recorded data, and placing less emphasis on 'set' experiments. The experiments cover a wide range of content, and attempt to be self-contained and not over-dependent on theory already covered. More experiments are included than can normally be covered in an A level course, to give your teacher choice. They are grouped not by topic but by the areas of skill developed. Experiments range from those using basic techniques, such as you might find in a practical examination, to investigations where there may be no clear-cut conclusions. Many experiments will promote discussion.

I am assuming that you will read the experiments *carefully* and *think about* what you are doing before you start.

Always remember to work safely. Remember also that the equipment in the diagrams may not be exactly the same as the equipment you have in front of you. The equipment may be made by a different manufacturer or alternative items substituted. There are some experiments where it will be necessary for your teacher to explain how to use the particular equipment involved. Some experiments make use of computer programs to extend the investigations, so it would be a good idea to find out how to load and run a program and even how to type in a program from the keyboard.

T. J. Cross

TYPICAL EQUIPMENT IN AN A LEVEL PHYSICS LABORATORY

THE BASIC MEASUREMENTS Length

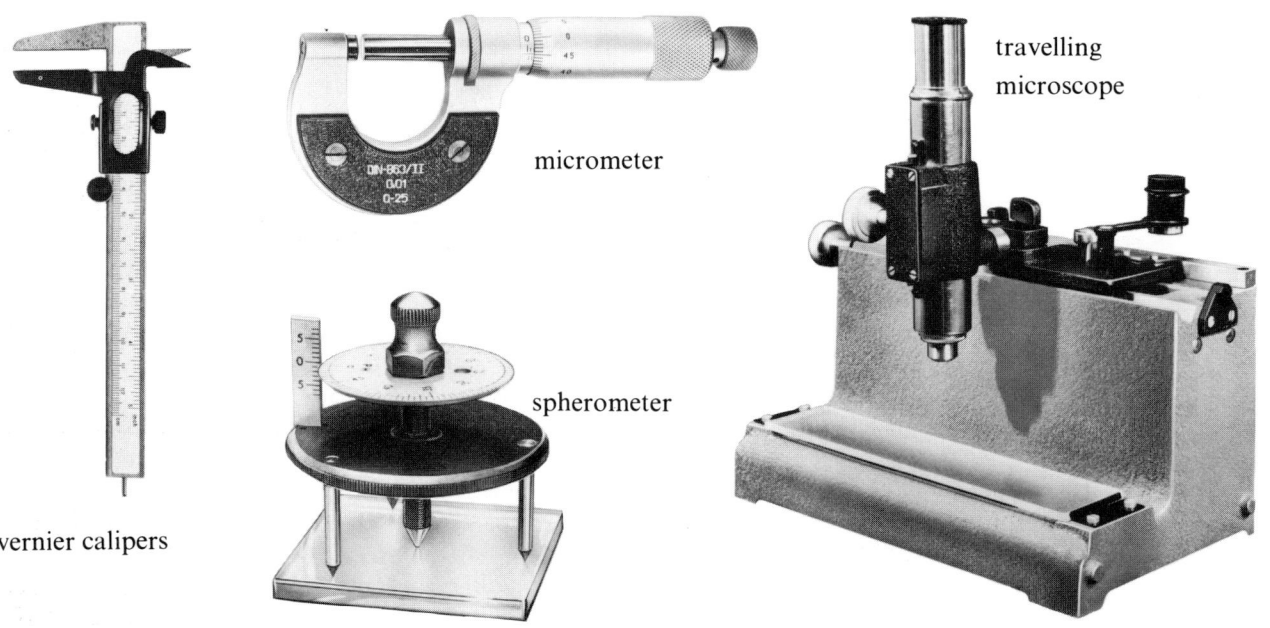

travelling microscope

micrometer

spherometer

vernier calipers

Force and mass

Time

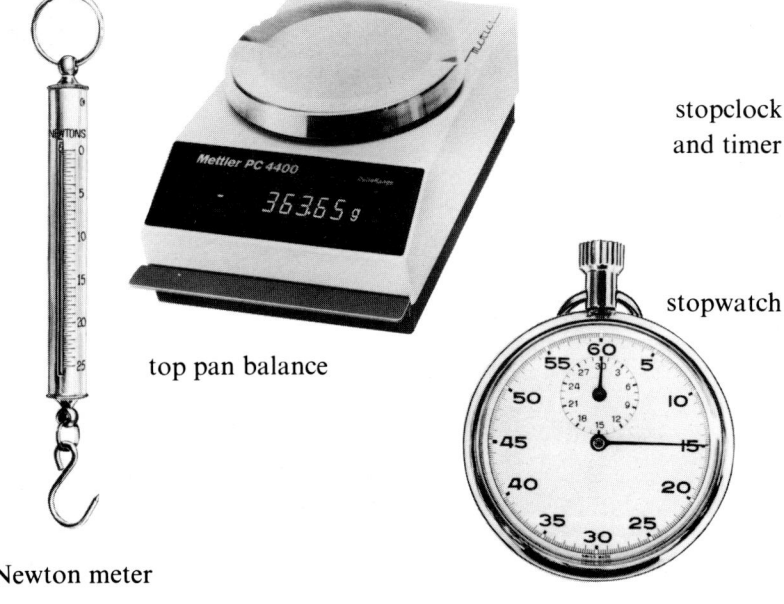

top pan balance

stopwatch

Newton meter

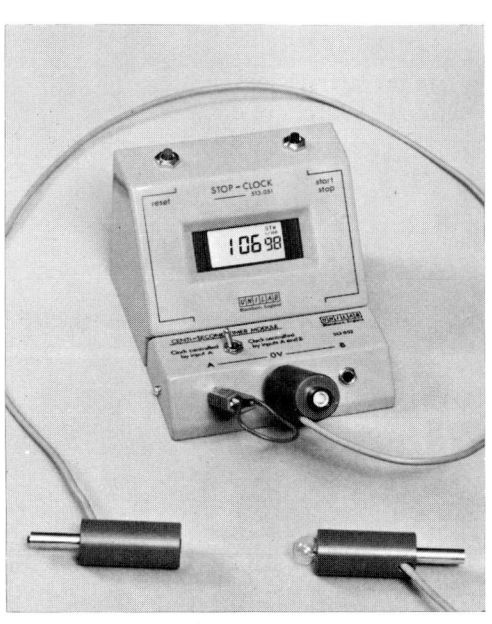

stopclock and timer

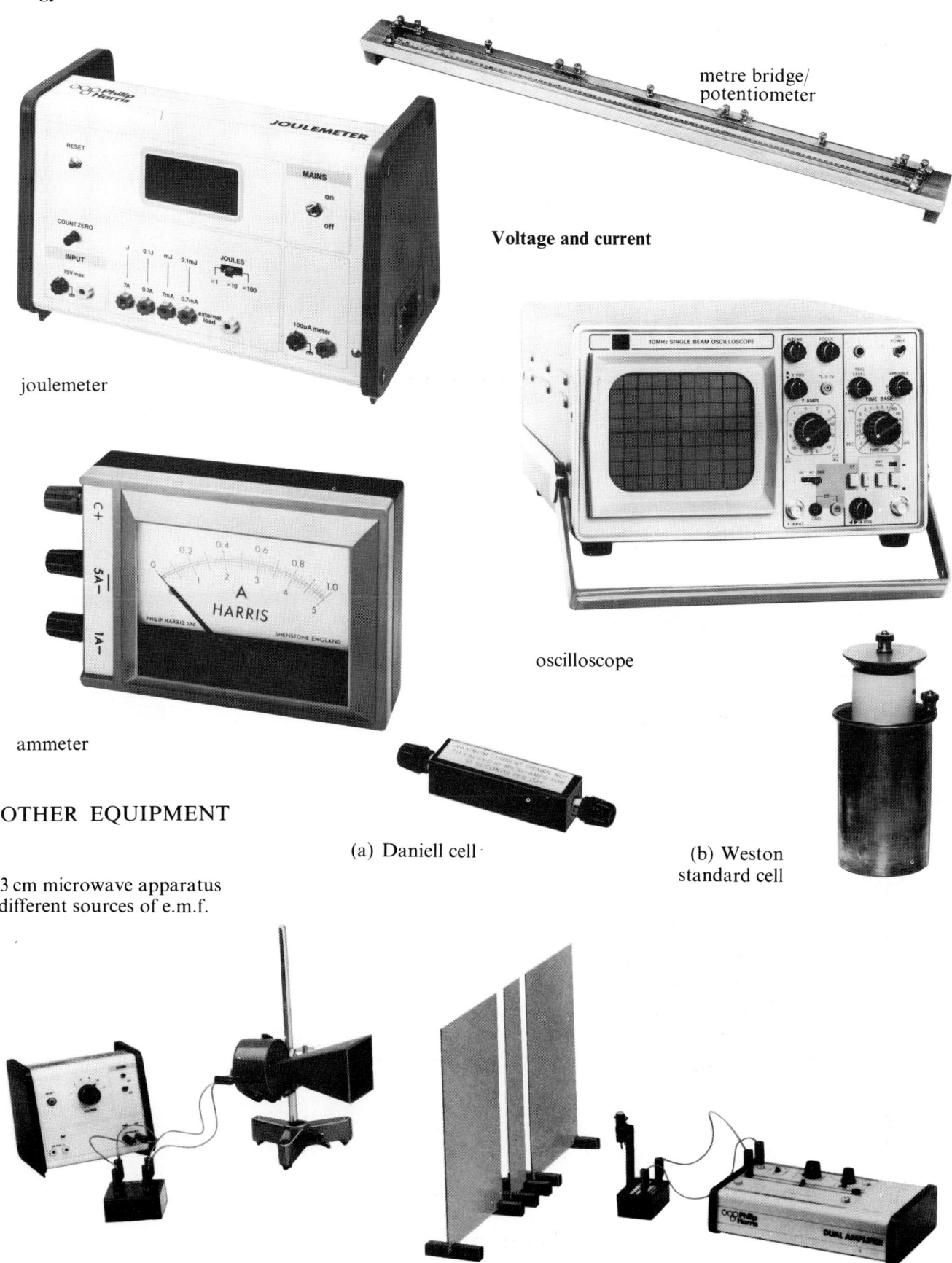

xiv   TYPICAL EQUIPMENT IN AN A LEVEL PHYSICS-LABORATORY

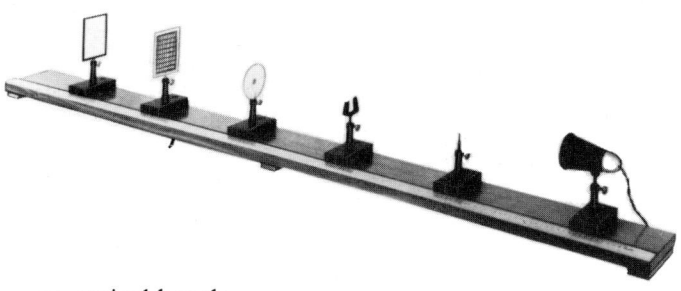

an optical bench

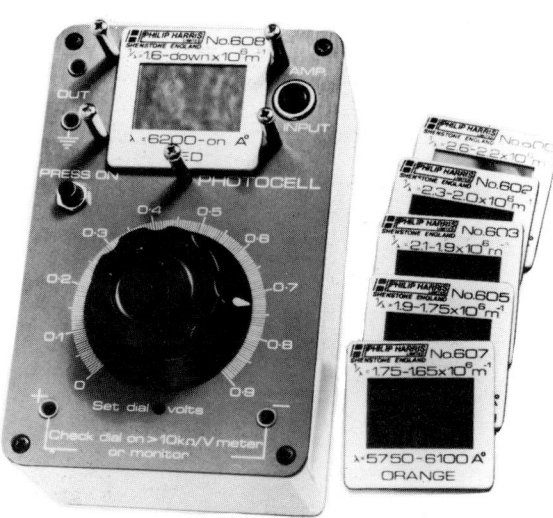

photoelectric effect

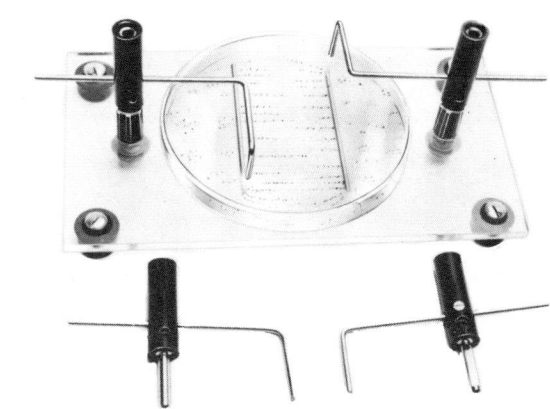

electric field patterns

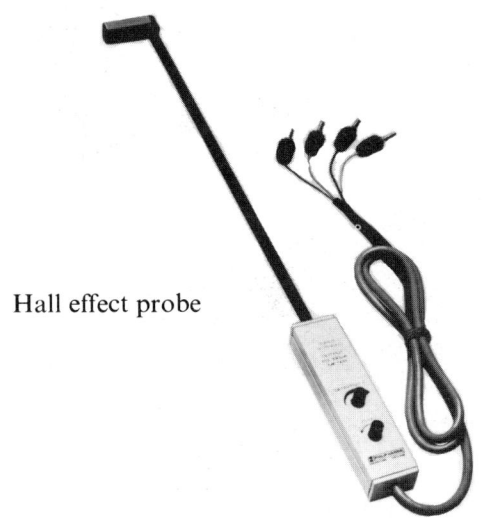

Hall effect probe

measuring the electronic charge on oil drops

measuring small currents and electrical charge

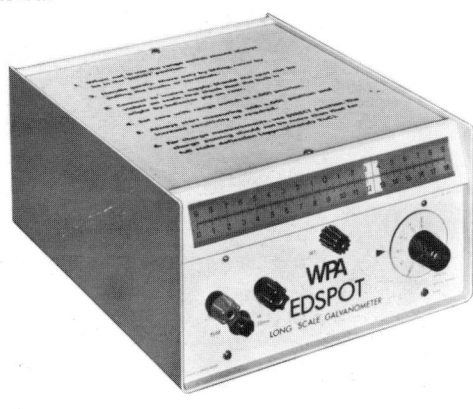

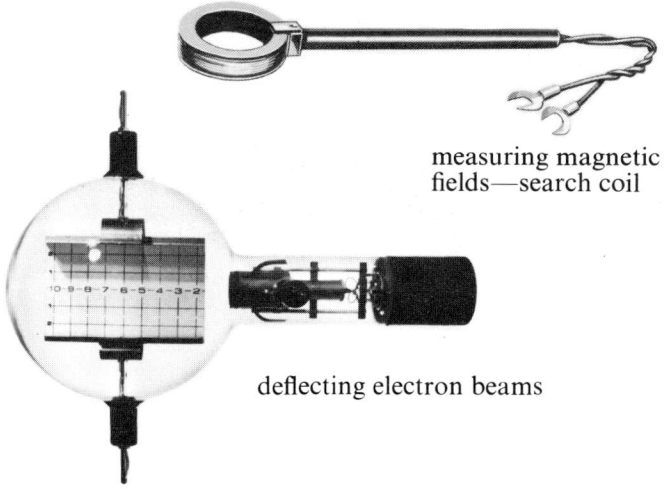

measuring magnetic fields—search coil

deflecting electron beams

TYPICAL EQUIPMENT IN AN A LEVEL PHYSICS LABORATORY

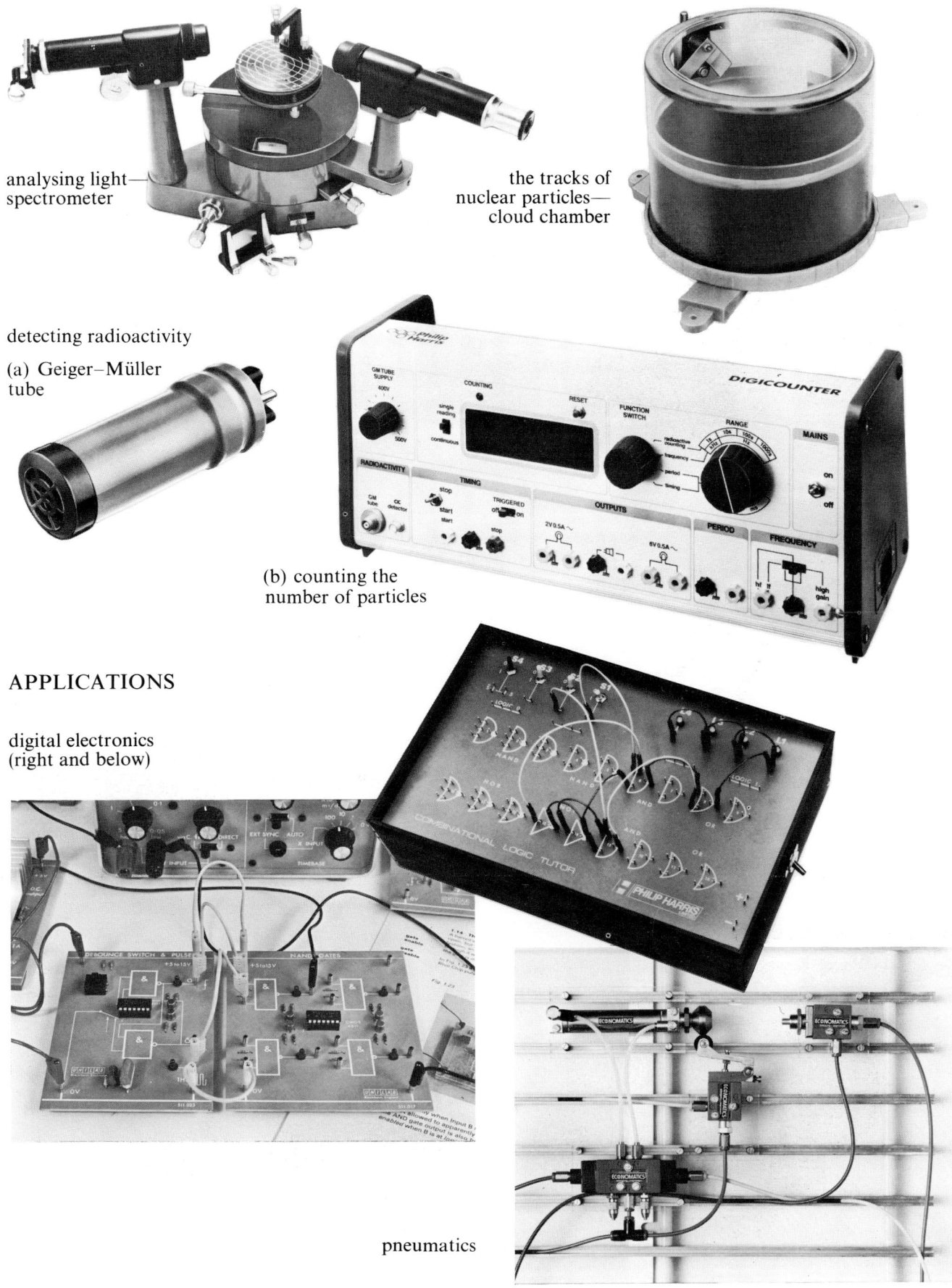

analysing light—spectrometer

the tracks of nuclear particles—cloud chamber

detecting radioactivity

(a) Geiger–Müller tube

(b) counting the number of particles

APPLICATIONS

digital electronics (right and below)

pneumatics

COLLECTING DATA—DATA LOGGING

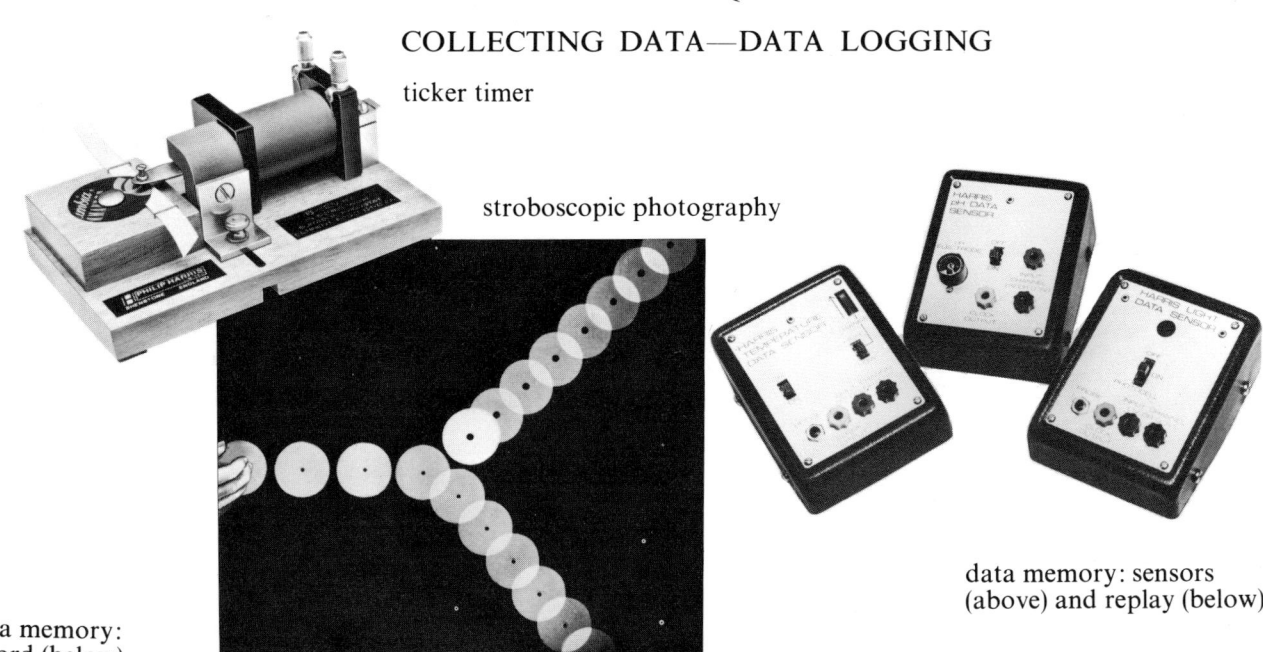

ticker timer

stroboscopic photography

data memory: sensors (above) and replay (below)

data memory: record (below)

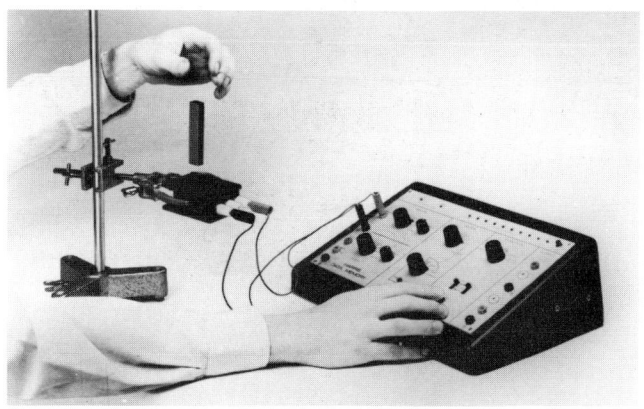

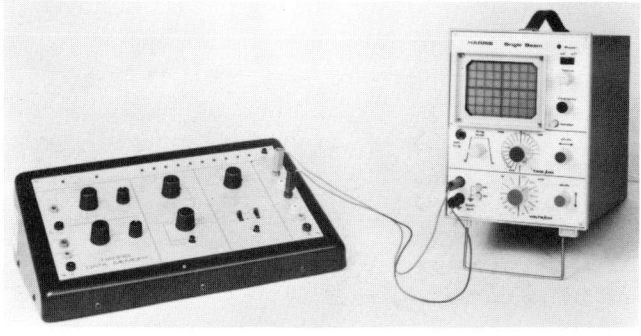

recording a series of measurements

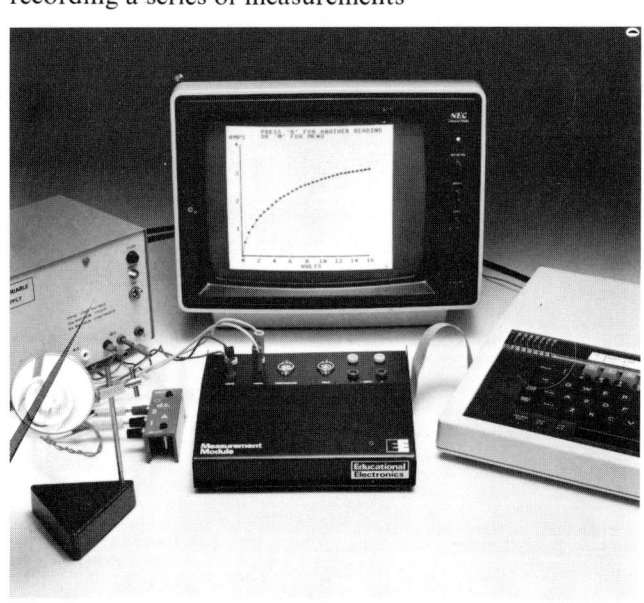

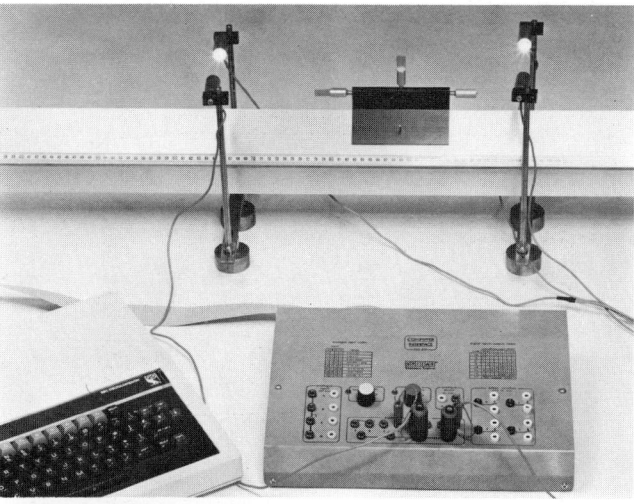

measuring speed (above)

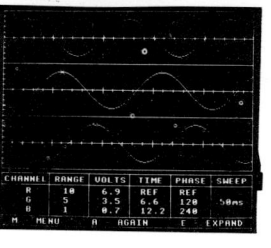

a 3-channel oscilloscope

TYPICAL EQUIPMENT IN AN A LEVEL PHYSICS LABORATORY xvii

SIMULATIONS

Analogue computing

Digital computing

two makes of computer commonly used in schools

Simulations are available to help you understand complex processes more easily (especially ones difficult to visualise) or enable you to investigate experiments which would be dangerous or totally impractical in a laboratory.

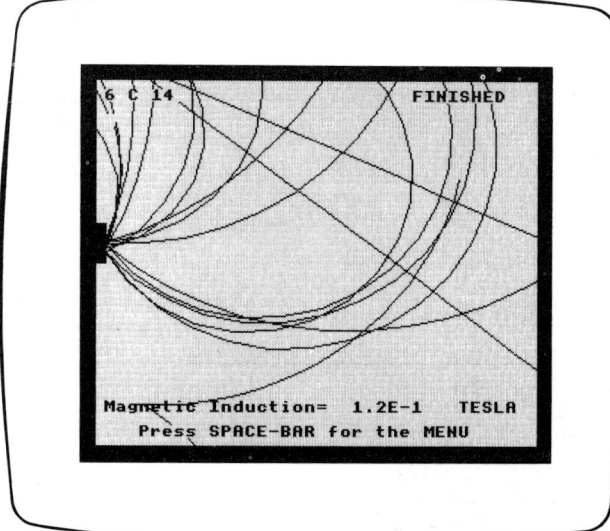

nuclear physics—tracks of particles (available from Great Sankey Nuclear Physics Project, © CET)

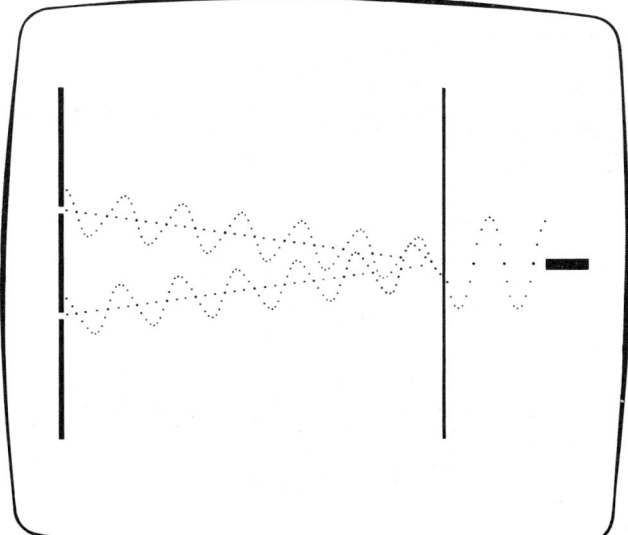

Young's slits (published by Heinemann)

TAKING MEASUREMENTS AND FINDING PROBABLE ERRORS

TAKING MEASUREMENTS

Instruments are used for measuring and recording most physical quantities, such as:

Quantity	Instrument
length	rule, micrometer, vernier calipers, travelling microscope
time	stopwatch, centisecond timer (electronic)
mass	top-pan balance
weight	spring balance (newton meter)
electric current	galvanometer, ammeter
potential difference (voltage)	voltmeter
angle	protractor
electromagnetic radiation	radio receiver, photodiode, spectrometer, photographic film, Geiger counter

You have probably come across many of these already in your practical work. They are used to take individual readings which you record on paper. As such, there is a maximum rate at which you can take readings. One reading every two seconds would be very fast and difficult to maintain accurately. There is also a maximum length of time during which you could continue to take accurate readings. Half an hour would be quite long enough. It is difficult to take readings from more than one instrument at a time, and even from only one instrument if the quantity being measured changes quickly.

To overcome these problems, more complex measuring instruments must be used. One you have probably used already is a *ticker-timer*. This marks dots at fixed time intervals, usually 50 per second, on a piece of paper tape. This process is called *data logging*. Other forms of data logging are:

(a) photographic methods;
(b) data memory;
(c) microcomputer with an analogue-to-digital converter (this converts the voltage input into digital numbers which can be stored);
(d) speed–time computer;
(e) microprocessor based recording instruments.

1. STROBOSCOPIC AND PHOTOGRAPHIC METHODS OF MEASURING CHANGING POSITION WITH TIME

By illuminating a moving object with short flashes of light at regular intervals, a photograph showing the position of the object at regular time intervals can be taken. An alternative way is to illuminate the object with a light source and have a rotating shutter which lets glimpses into the camera at regular intervals, as in the following experiment.

Example: Trolley rolling down a slope

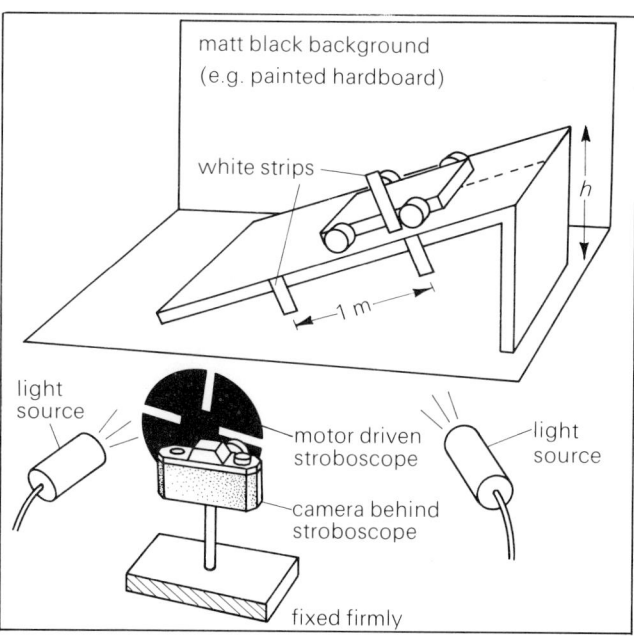

Figure 1 Equipment

The apparatus is set up as in figure 1.

First the stroboscope and lights are switched on. The camera shutter is opened and then the trolley released from the top of the slope. The camera shutter is closed when the trolley has reached the bottom of the slope.

The stroboscope must be driven at a constant known speed. The time for one revolution of the strobe disc

$$= \frac{1}{\text{number of revolutions/second}}$$

There are four slits, so four glimpses are seen in one revolution.

Time between images = time between glimpses

$$= \frac{1}{4} \times \frac{1}{\text{number of revolutions/second}}$$

A photograph should be obtained similar to that in figure 2.

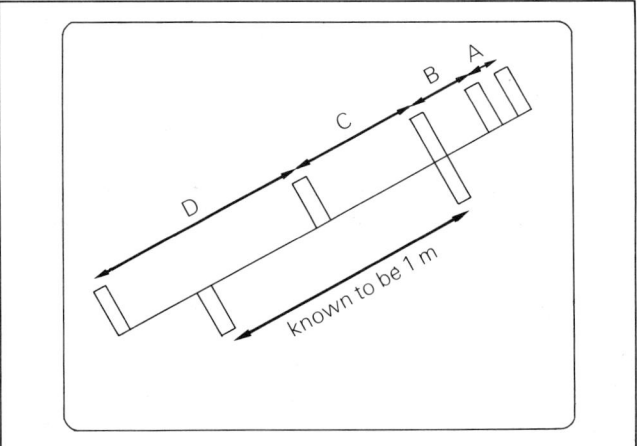

Figure 2 Example results

Work out the average velocities for each of the sections, A, B, C and D:

$$\text{average velocity} = \frac{\text{distance}}{\text{time}}$$

2. DATA MEMORY

With this method, voltages are measured by being converted into a digital form and successive measurements are stored in successive stores (figure 3).

Transducers can be used to convert light, temperature, etc. into a voltage. Measurements can be taken at intervals of between one hundredth of a second and several hours. The measurements recorded can be played back on an oscilloscope or chart recorder.

3. MICROCOMPUTER

A microcomputer system contains: a store, a screen to display information, and often a printer or plotter to produce a 'hard copy' of the results. The addition of an analogue to digital converter and a suitable program can make the microcomputer operate as a data memory. The results can be stored on magnetic tape or floppy disk for future use, calculations can be done on the data and graphs displayed in colour on the screen. The facilities available depend on the *software* used.

Computers all have an internal clock which produces timing pulses at regular intervals to control its operation. These pulses can be counted to make the microcomputer act as a timer, but with the added facility that a series of times can be measured and stored. Computers can store data very quickly; a thousand readings per second would be quite possible. Thus, experiments where a physical quantity changes rapidly can be investigated.

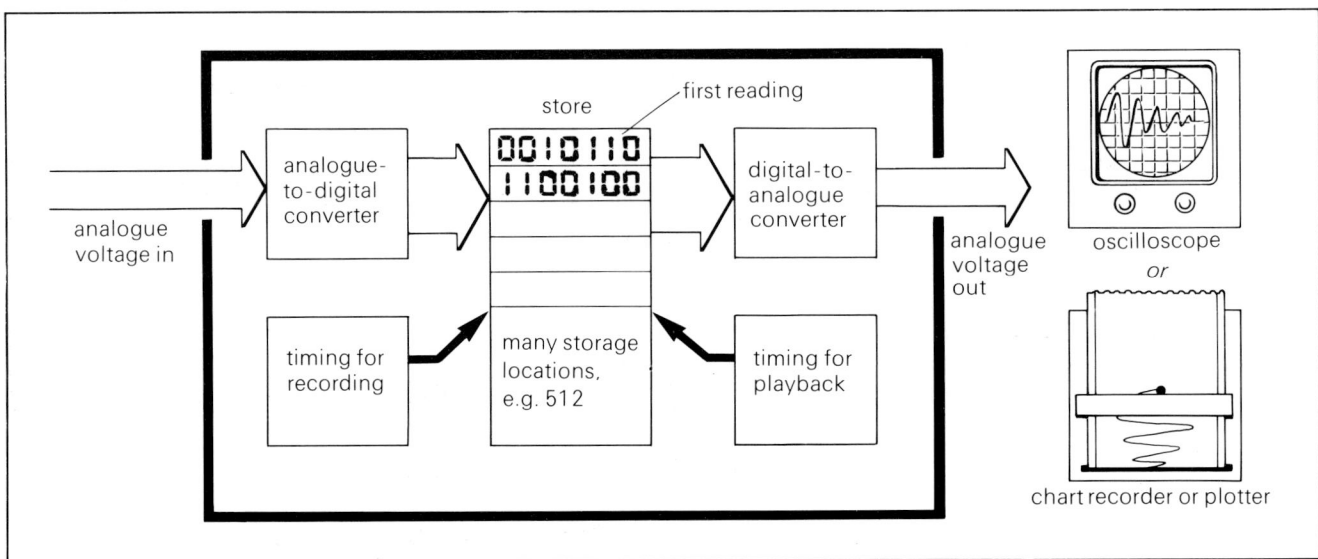

Figure 3 Block diagram of a data memory

TAKING MEASUREMENTS AND FINDING PROBABLE ERRORS

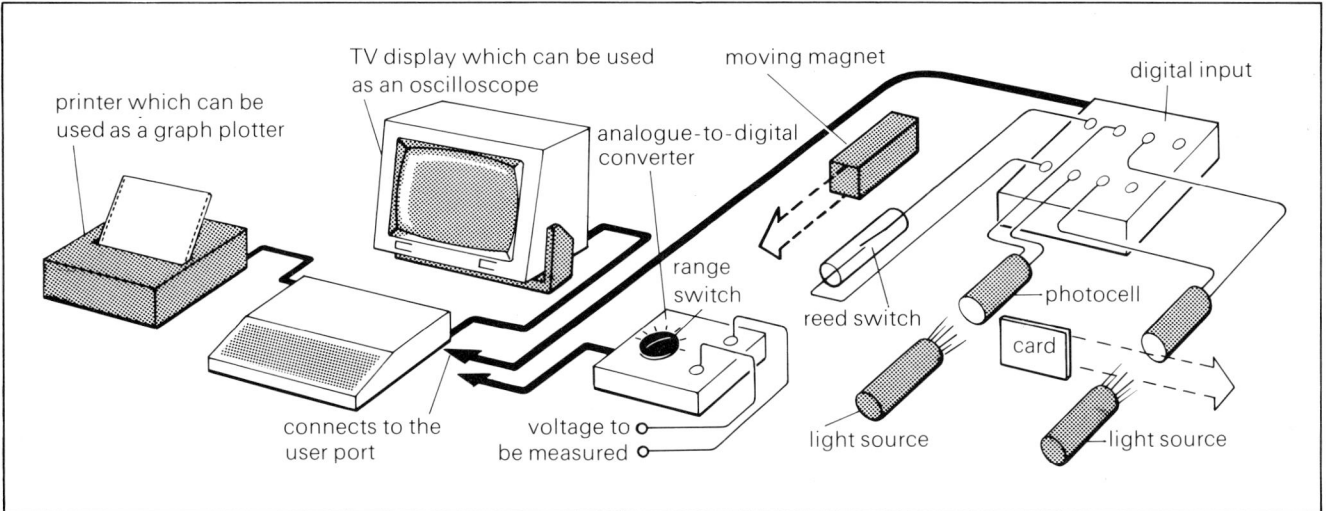

Figure 4 Using a microcomputer.

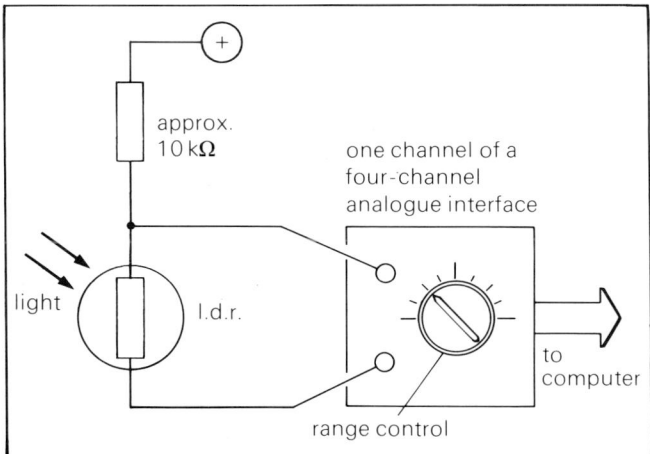

Figure 5

Programs are available which allow the computer to:

(a) record and display voltages from several different sources;
(b) operate as a flexible timing device which will also calculate velocities and accelerations;
(c) operate as a multibeam oscilloscope;
(d) produce a printed copy of the screen display;
(e) record a large number of readings in a given time interval.

Example

Figures 5–10 show how a computer can be used to record and display the change in light intensity as the light beam from a torch passes over a light-dependent resistor (l.d.r.).

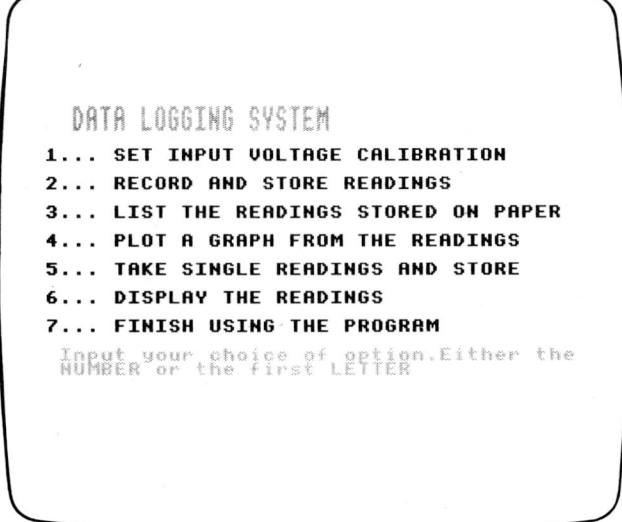

Figure 6 Menu of options available

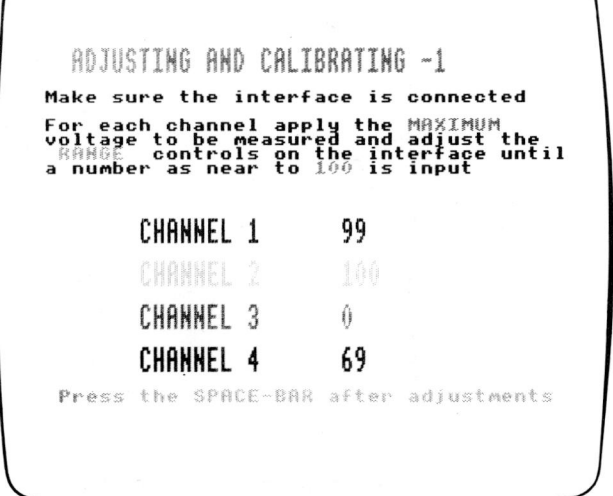

Figure 7 Calibration

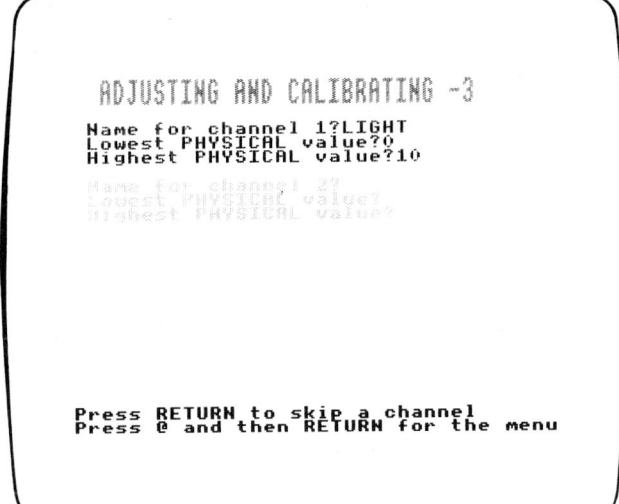

Figure 8 Initial information

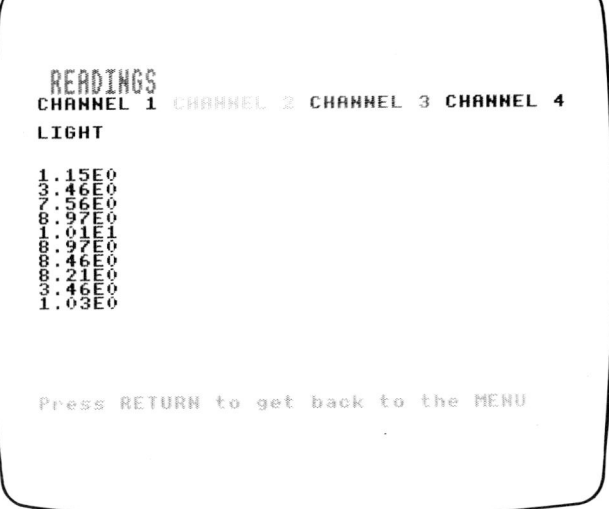

Figure 9 Readings taken

4. SPEED–TIME COMPUTERS

These are dedicated microprocessors which are pre-programmed to act as timers and then used to calculate the velocity and accelerations from a series of measurements.

5. MICROPROCESSOR BASED RECORDING INSTRUMENTS

These operate in a similar way to the methods described for a microcomputer but are generally faster and use pre-programmed ROMs containing programs to turn the unit into a variety of instruments. Such a unit is the VELA (Versatile Laboratory Aid) developed by the

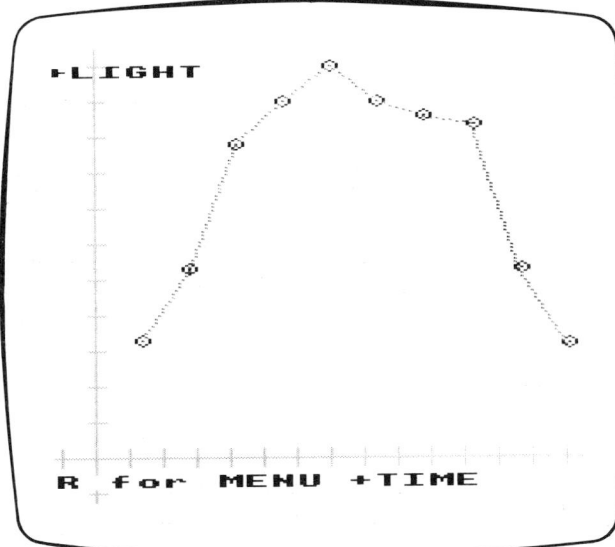

Figure 10 Graph plotted

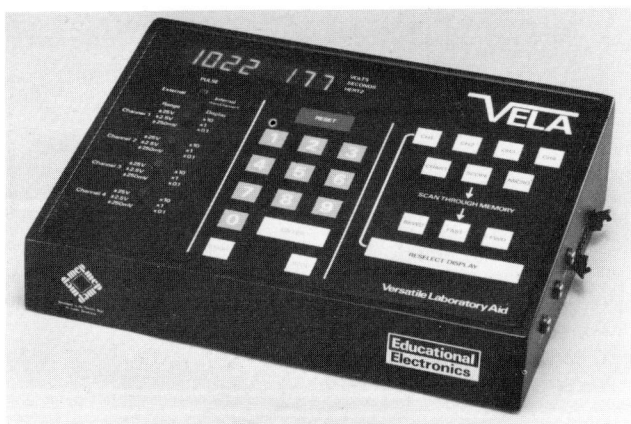

Figure 11 The Versatile Laboratory Aid (VELA)

00	Four channel digital voltmeter	1 to 4 (channel no.)
01	Fast transient recorder	0 to 999 (×50 µs)
02	Analogue (transient) recorder	1 to 999 (ms)
03	Analogue (transient) recorder, slow	1 to 999 (s)
04	Frequency meter	
05	Event timer	1 to 4 (pulse type)
06	Multichannel timer	
07	Pulse counter	1 to 999 (s)
08	Statistics of interpulse times	1 to 999 (×10 ms)
09	Statistics of random events	1 to 999 (s)
10	Versatile waveform generator	0 to 999 (ms)
11	Control sequence generator	1 to 999 (s)
12	Ramp generator	0 to 999 (s)
13	Decimal to binary conversion	
14	Dual beam oscilloscope	
15	Transfer data, VELA to microcomputer	
16	User program creation	

Figure 12 Menu of options

TAKING MEASUREMENTS AND FINDING PROBABLE ERRORS

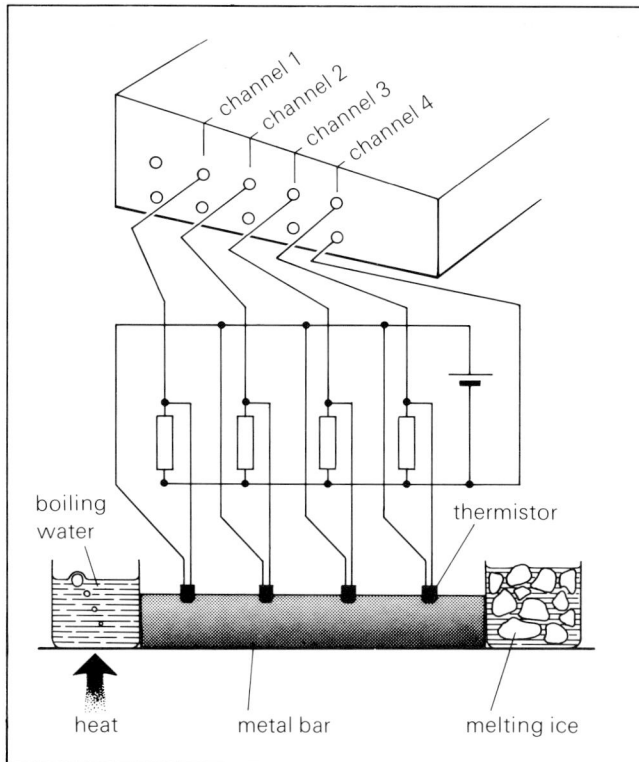

Figure 13 To investigate how the temperature distribution along a bar varies with time.

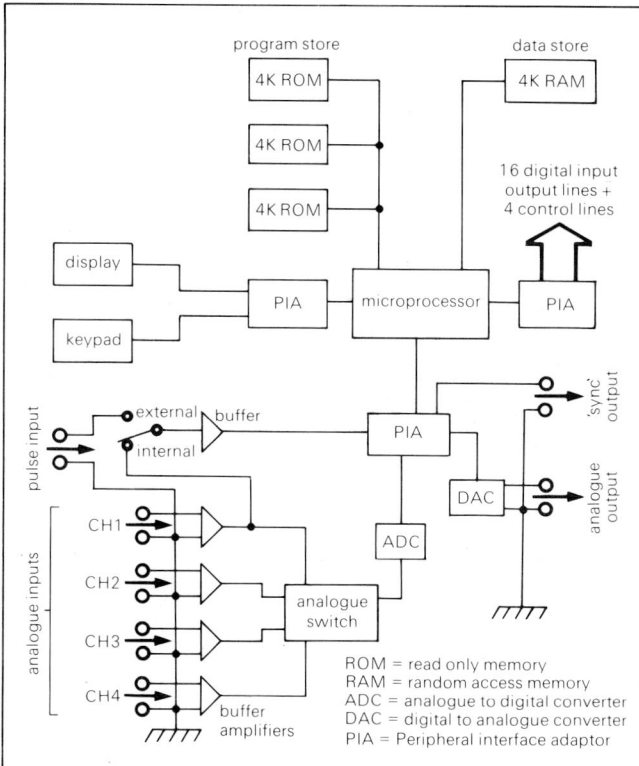

Figure 14 Block diagram of the inside of the VELA

Figures 11 to 14 are all taken from the VELA manual; © 1983, The Council for Educational Technology.

University of Leeds, JMB and MEP. It has four analogue inputs and the readings recorded can be displayed either on an oscilloscope or a chart recorder, or they can be 'downloaded' into a normal micrcomputer. There are 16 built in programs. (See figures 11–14.)

6. EXERCISES IN TAKING MEASUREMENTS

Here are three examples of data collected by photographic and data logging methods. Make a table of results in each case.

1. Wave form on an oscilloscope

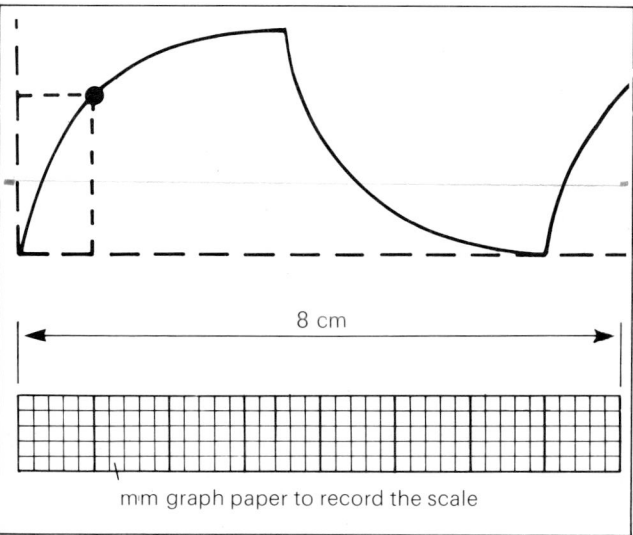

Figure 15 Diagram based on an osiclloscope waveform.

In figure 15, the oscilloscope time-base sensitivity = 1 ms cm^{-1} and Y-axis sensitivity = 2 V cm^{-1}.

From photograph		Real values	
Time/mm	Voltage/cm	Time $(t)/\text{s} \times 10^{-3}$	Voltage/V

Question

For what period of time is the voltage less than 2 V?

2. Stroboscope photograph of a pendulum swinging

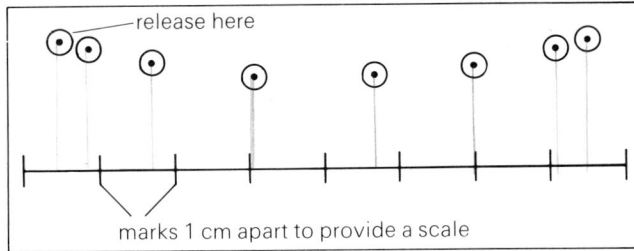

Figure 16 Diagram based on a stroboscope photograph of a pendulum swinging. The stroboscope was set to 25 flashes per second.

From photograph		Real values	
Position	x/mm	Time/s	x/mm
1		0	
2			
3			

Question
Is the shape of a graph of *x* against time the same as a sine function?

3. Temperature change as a hot liquid is poured into a cold liquid

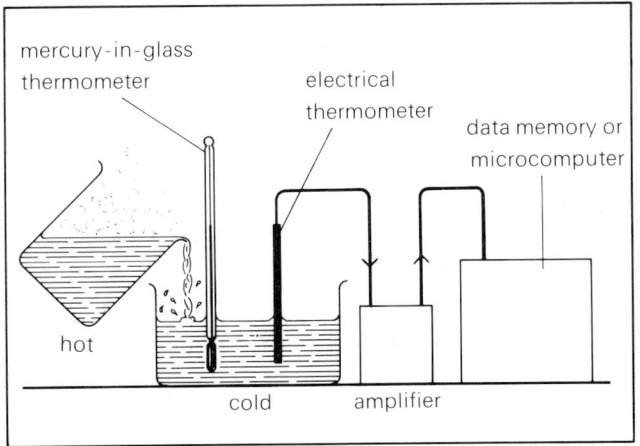

Figure 17 Equipment: the electrical thermometer produces a voltage dependent on the temperature.

The mercury thermometer is for *calibration* measurements, which use the fixed points of (i) melting ice and (ii) steam above boiling water, both at 760 mmHg pressure.

Temperature	Number
0°C	4 096 (a)
100°C	52 096 (b)

A numerical change of ... is produced by 100°C. Therefore a change of 1°C produces a numerical change of $\frac{[b-a]}{100} = \ldots\ldots$

Numerical reading	time/s
10992	0
22992	0.2
32016	0.4
36976	0.6
41504	0.8
43008	1.0
43472	1.2
43024	1.4
42512	1.6
41792	1.8
41008	2.0
40192	2.2
39712	2.4
39024	2.6
38800	2.8
37504	3.0

Figure 18 Example readings

Use this value to work out the real temperatures associated with each numerical reading, or use the following.

The real temperature, θ°C, is defined by the equation:

$$\theta°C = \frac{\text{number at } \theta°C - \text{number at } 0°C}{\text{number at } 100°C - \text{number at } 0°C} \times 100$$

Number recorded	Real temperature (θ)/°C	Time/s

Question
What do the results tell you about the mixing of hot and cold water?

ACCURACY AND ERRORS

The *true* value of a reading that you take may not be *exactly* the value you record. There are several reasons for this, and in A-level practical work you must learn to make these errors as small as possible and give the probable error in the results recorded.

For example:
a length 56.3 ± 0.5 mm
a time   3.0 ± 0.5 s

Deciding on a degree of accuracy for an individual reading involves a certain amount of subjective judgement, coupled with observation of the equipment used and common sense. Errors can be a result of the design of the apparatus or instrument. Others are of human origin and some are of a statistical nature.

Look at this experiment which measures the time of fall of a model parachute (figure 19). There are several sources of error indicated.

(a) Lining up the parachute with the marker each time could be difficult and could result in an error of ±2 mm.
(b) The stopwatch must be checked to see if it is measuring time accurately and consistently.
(c) Your own reaction time in starting and stopping the stopwatch has an error of approximately ±0.5 s.
(d) Measurement of height h with a metre rule has an accuracy of ±0.5 mm; not a large error.
(e) Random variation in the effect of air-resistance forces; completely outside your control, but could produce a large spread of results, much larger than the effects of other errors, e.g. 4.5 s, 4.2 s, 4.9 s.
(f) Deciding exactly when the parachute has hit the ground: take several readings and calculate an average.

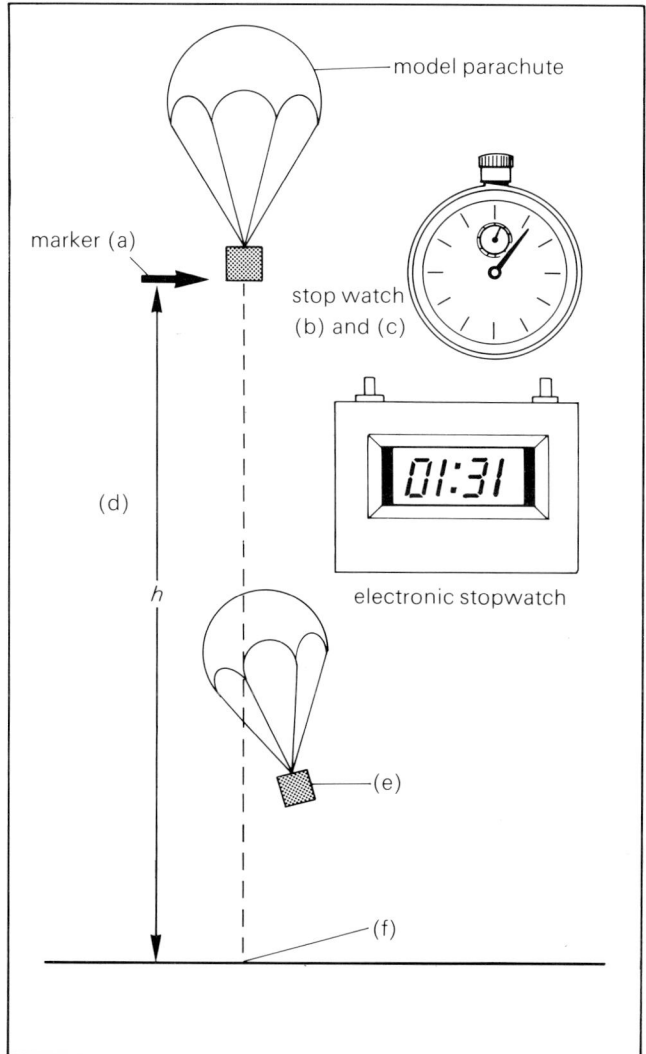

Figure 19 Sources of error in the model parachute experiment

TYPES OF ERRORS

1. **Your own error** in reading the scale incorrectly. One error is parallax, and a mirror can be used to make sure you are looking at right angles to the scale. Another common mistake is to assume the scale is marked in 0.1 of a major division when it is 0.2 or 0.05 of the major divisions. The thickness of the pointer in relation to the division size is also a large source of error.

Only experience and good experimental technique can reduce these errors.

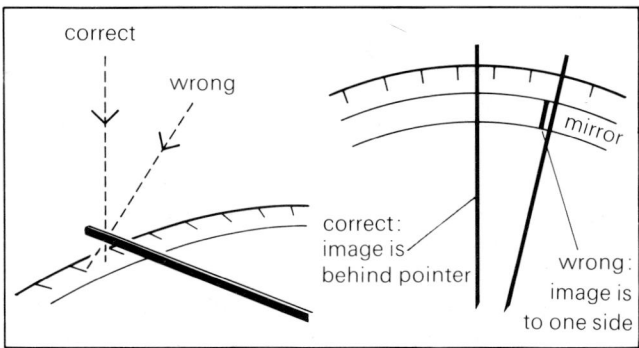

Figure 20 Use of a mirror to avoid parallax when taking a reading.

2. There may be **a zero error** caused by the instrument not being set on zero accurately (figure 21). This causes a constant error in all readings. It could eventually show up in a graph, which perhaps should go through the origin but does not do so. If discovered at the end of an experiment, the error can be added or subtracted from the measured reading to give the true value.

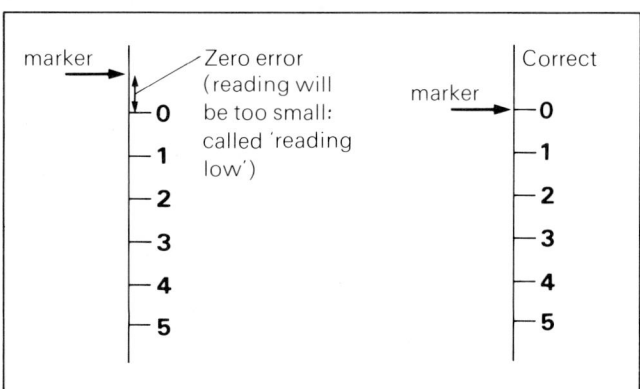

Figure 21 Zero error

3. Another effect which influences the accuracy is the **linearity of the instrument**. For example, up to now you have probably assumed that the number taken from the scale of an instrument is true, but an accurate *calibration* of the instrument against a known standard may reveal fluctuations. The *true* voltage and voltage *reading* on a voltmeter may show this relationship when the instrument is calibrated.

Looking at figure 22, the true voltage for a scale reading of 3.0 V is 3.0 − 0.07 = 2.93 V. A probable error should be given, and this will depend on the accuracy of the meter. If this was ±1 per cent, the voltage would be written 2.93 ± 0.02 V.

4. **Some other factor** may affect the reading:

(a) The zero may drift as the instrument heats up with use.

(b) The instrument may not show the true reading, because its presence affects the reading being measured. For example, a voltmeter may read 'low' because the effect of its own resistance on the circuit will alter the total current flow and so alter the voltages across the resistors. The voltmeter will be measuring the voltage correctly, but it will measure the wrong voltage. (See figure 23.)

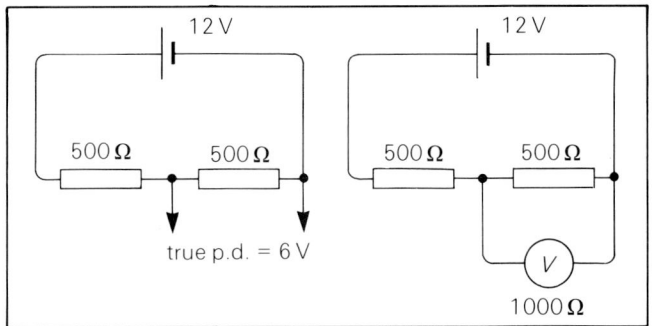

Figure 23 Although the true p.d. = 6 V, the measured p.d. = 4.8 ± 0.1 V, which is low.

5. **The effect of sensitivity** is a measurement of the movement or change in the position of a pointer, level, etc., as the input to the instrument changes. It is the deflection on the scale per unit input:

$$\text{sensitivity} = \frac{\text{change in scale movement}}{\text{change in 'input'}}$$

For example, an oscilloscope may have a sensitivity of $2\,\text{V cm}^{-1}$; a ballistic galvanometer may have a sensitivity of $3.7\,\mu\text{C mm}^{-1}$; a meter might deflect 0.1 radian per µA. If the scale covers 1 radian, this would be given as a full-scale deflection (f.s.d.) of 10 µA.

Many instruments have a minimum change of input which will cause a change on the scale reading. This is often more important than the inherent sensitivity in the

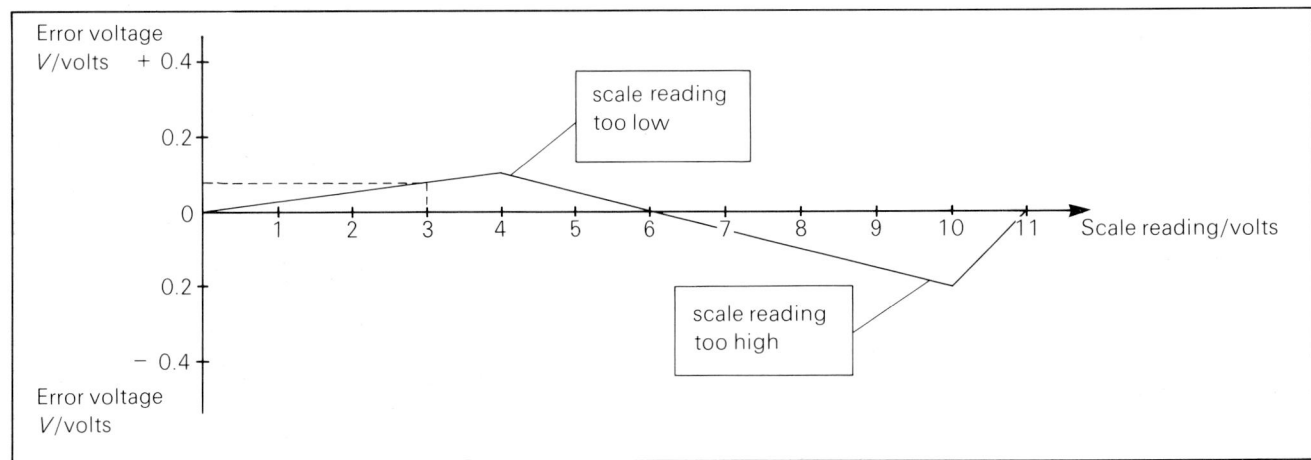

Figure 22 Graph for the calibration of a voltmeter.

design, since it also affects the accuracy of the instrument. For example, friction between the tube and the sliding part in a spring balance designed to measure 0–10 N may mean that the force has to be changed by 0.05 N before any movement occurs. To mark the scale every 0.01 N would therefore be pointless.

You may find the need to change an instrument for one which has a different sensitivity. For example, to measure a small temperature change use either (a) a thermometer with a smaller bore tube, or (b) a thermometer with a larger volume of liquid in the bulb so that a given temperature change produces a larger physical change and a larger deflection on the scale, or (c) a different type of thermometer based on a thermocouple or thermistor, for example.

6. There are always **random errors** associated with the way any instrument behaves, and the same measurement taken several times will give different values. It is difficult to explain why this happens, but one reason applicable to instruments with moving parts is that, as the new reading is approached, the instrument moves more slowly and at some stage frictional forces will balance the force making the instrument move and it will stop. This may not be at exactly the 'true' position and so a random error has been caused. There is little which can be done to eliminate this error, but it can be kept to a minimum. One method is to record the reading when the quantity is being increased and again when the quantity is being decreased. Calculate the average and take this as the true reading. Electronic instruments have the advantage that this type of error does not occur, but they are usually so sensitive that the reading is continually changing, for example, a balance might show 42.35 g, 42.36 g, 42.37 g, 42.35 g in quick succession and in this case a 'central' value should be chosen and the spread of values used to estimate the error, e.g. 42.35 ± 0.02 g.

Dealing with random errors
A more accurate value can be found by taking more readings and finding the average (or more correctly the *mean average*), but some method must be used to find a measurement of accuracy or error. For example, if x_1, x_2, x_3, etc. are the readings, then

$$\text{mean average} = \frac{x_1 + x_2 + x_3 + \cdots + x_n}{n} \quad \text{or} \quad \frac{\Sigma x_i}{n}$$

The usual symbol for the mean is $\bar{x}$.

The spread of readings due to random errors can be treated statistically because the readings follow what is called a *normal distribution*, and we can use the *standard deviation* as a guide to the *probable error*.

$$\text{standard deviation} = \sqrt{\left\{\frac{\Sigma(x - \bar{x})^2}{n - 1}\right\}}$$

A normal distribution has the type of shape shown in figure 24.

The dark shading shows all results within one standard deviation of the mean and this is 66 per cent of all possible results. Because of this, it is reasonable to take the standard deviation as a way of calculating a *probable error*. It is very unlikely to get a reading more than two standard deviations away (light shading).

The minimum number of readings needed to use the standard deviation meaningfully is about 30, which is more than are usually taken in an experiment. However, it is still a useful guide even if fewer readings are available.

For example, suppose four spring balance readings are 8.6 N, 8.2 N, 8.8 N, 8.5 N. The mean average is $\frac{34.1}{4} = 8.53$ N, and the spread +0.27 N and −0.33 N.

The probable error is less than this, because one or more of the results might be outside two standard deviations. We might estimate the error as ±0.2 N and give the average as 8.5 ± 0.2 N.

Assuming that the readings would follow a normal distribution, the standard deviation could be worked out:

the mean $\bar{x} = 8.5$

$$\text{the standard deviation} = \sqrt{\left(\frac{\Sigma(x - \bar{x})^2}{n - 1}\right)}$$

$$= \sqrt{\frac{(8.6 - 8.5)^2 + (8.2 - 8.5)^2 + (8.8 - 8.5)^2 + (8.5 - 8.5)}{3}}$$

$$= \sqrt{\frac{(0.1)^2 + (-0.3)^2 + (0.3)^2 + (0)^2}{3}}$$

$$= \sqrt{\frac{0.01 + 0.09 + 0.09}{3}}$$

$$= \sqrt{\frac{0.19}{3}}$$

standard deviation $= \sqrt{0.0633} = 0.25$ N.

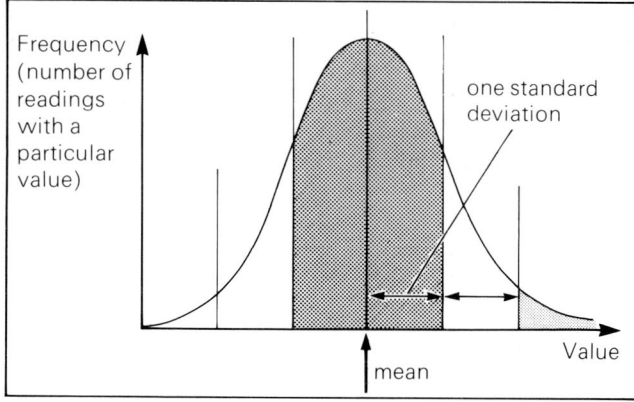

Figure 24 Normal distribution curve

Any readings more than three standard deviations from the mean are extremely unlikely and therefore indicate a misreading and should be rechecked.

7. In experiments involving completely random processes, such as radioactive decay, **the error in a value N is $\pm\sqrt{N}$**; for example, for a background count:

if 100 counts are recorded the value should be given as $100 \pm \sqrt{100} = 100 \pm 10$;

if 500 counts are recorded the value should be given as $500 \pm \sqrt{500} = 500 \pm 22$.

The percentage errors would be $\dfrac{\sqrt{N}}{N} \times 100$, and are 10 per cent and 4.4 per cent respectively. Thus a *larger number* of readings gives a more *accurate* value.

Reducing errors

1. Always use an instrument so that the reading is as near to the full-scale deflection as possible—for example, if a current of 7 mA is to be measured, a 0–10 mA meter should be used rather than a 0–100 mA meter.

2. Try and make sure that, when a variable changes, the largest *numerical change* in reading occurs. This involves using an instrument of the correct *sensitivity*.

3. If you can measure the value of the sum of several 'events' together and then divide by the number of events, then the error is reduced. For example, when timing a pendulum: a stopwatch has a probable error of 0.2 s. Suppose the periodic time was 0.8 s. Then, timing one oscillation, the periodic time would have to be given as 0.8 ± 0.2 s but if, let us say, ten oscillations are timed, the error is divided by ten, because the error only occurs at the 'ends' when the stopwatch is started and stopped. If ten oscillations are timed as 79.0 s, the average value for the periodic time would be $\dfrac{79.0 \pm 0.2}{10} = 7.90 \pm 0.02$ s.

The same idea would apply to measuring the mass of a number of small mass objects such as pins or ball bearings. Find the mass of a large number and then divide by the number of items to find the mass of one of them.

4. Always take several readings and work out the *mean average* ($\bar{x}$) by adding the readings together and dividing by the number of readings.

$$\bar{x} = \frac{\Sigma x_i}{n}$$

Estimating the total error in a result

1. Estimate the error in each instrument you are using and find the probable error
Sometimes the standard deviation can be worked out, but in many cases you will have to use your own judgement.

For example, in finding the position of a sharp image in an optics experiment, the image may seem equally sharp to you between, say, 36.4 cm and 37.2 cm. The average value is 36.8 cm. The probable error here would be ± 0.4 cm rather than the inherent accuracy of a metre rule of ± 0.05 cm. The reading would be given as 36.8 ± 0.4 cm.

For example, using a spring balance or force meter, find out if the reading produced is the same if the weight is lowered slowly or fast. Does moving the weight down from the top give the same reading as moving up from the bottom? Once the reading is steady, 'nudge' the weight up and down to see if an error is caused by the balance sticking. From this information decide on an error for the balance. You may decide that the balance is accurate or consistent to say $5\,N \pm 0.3\,N$, i.e. 6 per cent.

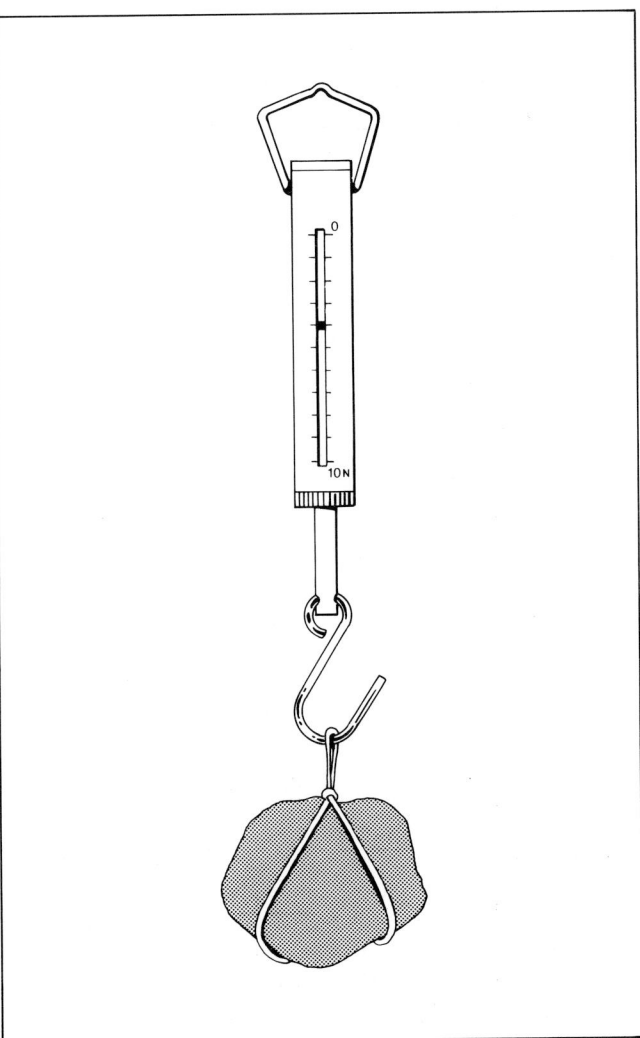

Figure 25 A spring balance

2. Combine the errors into a final error
The readings you have taken will almost certainly be used either (a) directly in an equation, or (b) to draw a graph.

TAKING MEASUREMENTS AND FINDING PROBABLE ERRORS

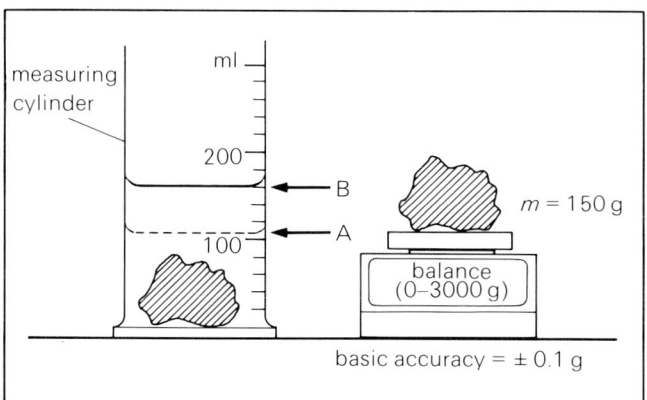

Figure 26 To measure the density of an irregular object.

Look at the simple experiment to measure the density of an irregular object shown in figure 26. The accuracy of the volume measurement is affected by:

(a) the size of the divisions of scale which is determined by the cross-sectional area of the cylinder; and
(b) the estimation of the bottom of the meniscus; if the scale is in 20 ml divisions, then a possible error of 5 ml could be expected.

Including estimates of accuracy, the measurements are:

$$A = 105 \pm 5 \text{ ml}$$
$$B = 160 \pm 5 \text{ ml}$$
$$M = 150 \pm 0.1 \text{ g}$$

The volume displaced is 55 ml, but it could be as low as 45 ml (155 − 110) or as high as 65 ml (165 − 100).

Three values for density can be calculated from

$$D = \frac{M}{V}$$

(a) 'Best' answer $\frac{150}{55} = 2.7(\text{27272}) \text{ g cm}^{-3}$

(b) Lowest answer $\frac{149.9}{65} = 2.3(\text{06153}) \text{ g cm}^{-3}$

(c) Highest answer $\frac{150.1}{45} = 3.3(\text{35555}) \text{ g cm}^{-3}$

Some students will insist on giving all figures given by a calculator, *without thinking*. Since the answer could be between 2.3 and 3.3, any further figures are meaningless. You should only give figures if you are certain they are accurate, i.e., quoting 2.7272 means that you are saying your experiment is accurate to 1 part in nearly 2000!!!

The density example answer would be given as $2.7 \pm 0.5 \text{ g cm}^{-3}$.

One equation which can be used to calculate the probable error is:

probable error
$$= \pm \sqrt{\{(\text{error 1})^2 + (\text{error 2})^2 + \cdots + (\text{error } n)^2\}}$$

If the value is taken to a power in an equation, then the *error* for that reading is multiplied by the power. For example:

1. If the radius of a liquid drop was 3.0 ± 0.5 mm and it was used to calculate the *volume* of the drop, $\frac{4\pi a^3}{3}$, the volume would be $113.1 \pm 1.5 \text{ mm}^3$. Note that there is *no point* in quoting any more significant figures, because they would be smaller than the range of accuracy.

2. The potential difference across a resistance is measured and found to be 10.0 ± 0.3 V, and the current flowing through is measured and found to be 1.3 ± 0.2 A. The errors of ± 0.2 and ± 0.3 are of comparable size, but the readings of 10 and 1.3 are not, so it is necessary to work with fractional or percentage errors, i.e. $\frac{0.3}{10}$ and $\frac{0.2}{1.3}$, which gives 0.03 and 0.15.

Using the equation above:

$$\text{fractional probable error} = \pm \sqrt{(0.03)^2 + (0.15)^2}$$
$$= \pm \sqrt{0.0234}$$
$$= \pm 0.15$$

$$\text{resistance} = \frac{10}{1.3}$$
$$= 7.6 \,\Omega \pm (0.15 \times 7.6)$$
$$= 7.6 \pm 1.2 \,\Omega$$

Showing the range of error on a graph

The conventional way of 'plotting' a point is a dot inside a circle, ⊙. It is not good practice to use either a single dot or a cross, +.

When *one* reading has an error, the marker used is I, an error bar. When *both* readings have errors, the marker used is ○ or ∎, an error box. These can be of use in deciding the range of lines which will fit a set of points.

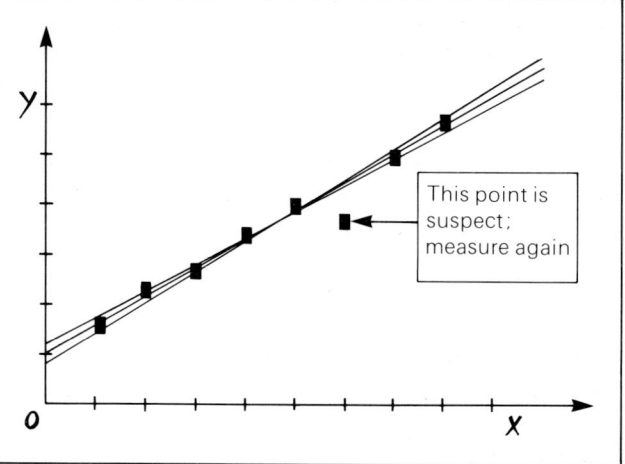

Figure 27 A graph with errors in both *x* and *y* values, showing error boxes.

RECORDING, DISPLAYING AND ANALYSING THE RESULTS

PLANNING BEFORE YOU START

One of the main differences between practical work you have done before and practical work at A-level is that you will have to do much more planning yourself. You will often have to plan the range of readings, the number of readings to be taken and the interval between readings, and you will have to decide which variable is more easily altered in convenient steps. You may also have to choose the most suitable instrument from a range of instruments.

Remember:
1. To plot a graph of reasonable accuracy, at least ten readings are needed. Five would be a minimum for a straight-line graph.
2. Readings should be evenly spaced over the range required.
3. Extra readings should be taken where the graph shows a curve rather than a straight line.
4. Always be prepared to take extra readings *after* you have plotted a graph to determine the shape of the graph more accurately.

Questions
The graph in figure 28 was drawn by a pupil who had not planned his experiment very well. Think about these questions.

1. Have enough points been plotted?
2. Where should more readings be taken?
3. Has he been correct in drawing two straight line sections?
4. What defects could only be found out *after* plotting the graph?
5. Why should you always plot a graph before taking the apparatus apart?

RECORDING THE INFORMATION

In nearly every experiment results are recorded and/or qualitative observations made. Recording these results in an orderly way is important. For example, here are pages from two students' rough observations. You will notice the difference!

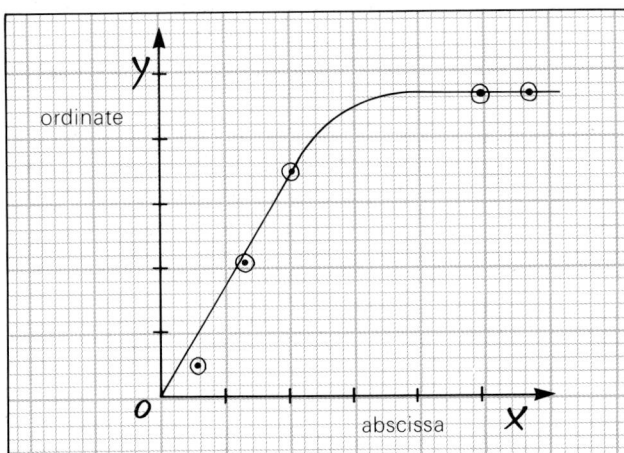

Figure 28 The abscissa is the value which has been varied in steps of a known size, or is the second value mentioned, i.e. if you plot a graph of (A) against (B), (B) is the abscissa.

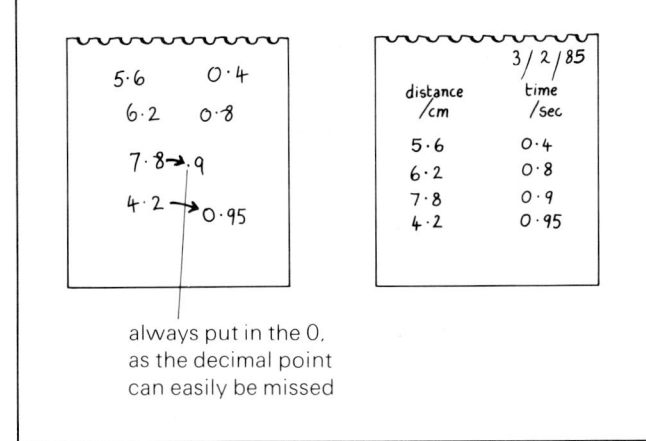

Figure 29 Recording of results

RECORDING, DISPLAYING AND ANALYSING THE RESULTS

Types of results

Results can be divided into two types:

(a) recorded—those that you measure and record during the experiment;
(b) calculated—values calculated or derived from the recorded results.

Information taken from tables, books or marked on the apparatus also needs to be recorded, together with general observations and comments. Having decided on a likely range of readings to be taken, the axes of a graph can be labelled. A rough graph should then be drawn as the experiment progresses. Any information which has not been recorded should then be evident. In the same way, the apparatus should not be dismantled until you are satisfied with the results and have checked any which do not seem to fit in with the rest.

Imagine an experiment in which a connection between the surface area of a model parachute and its terminal velocity is being investigated. Measurements taken could be:

(a) weight of parachute;
(b) surface area of parachute;
(c) distance fallen and time taken;
(d) air pressure and temperature (may be relevant).

From these the average terminal speed can be calculated, and a graph drawn of average terminal speed against surface area. The weight of the parachute is not actually needed, but you might decide to extend the experiment in the future using parachutes of different weights.

The results might be displayed as follows.

Recorded results

Weight of parachute/N	0.1	0.22	0.1	0.22
Area of parachute/cm²	50	50	100	100
Distance fallen/cm	100	100		
Time taken/s (several tries)	2.7, 2.6, 2.7, 2.1*, 2.5			

* rather low—check again

$$\text{average speed} = \frac{\text{distance}}{\text{time}}$$

Calculated values

The terminal speed seems to depend on the area as well as the weight, because the times for a larger surface area are longer. The frictional force equals weight when the parachute is falling at its terminal velocity. The frictional force per unit area might therefore be more important than just the weight or area alone.

In the table below, * is an approximate error which can be found by taking the highest and lowest values for time and distance and working out the extreme values of velocity, i.e. the distance could be in error by approximately ±1 mm if a metre rule is used. Therefore:

$$\text{lowest velocity} = \frac{99.9}{2.7} = 37 \text{ cm s}^{-1}$$

$$\text{highest velocity} = \frac{100.1}{2.5} = 40.0 \text{ cm s}^{-1}$$

This indicates about $\pm 2 \text{ cm s}^{-1}$ error.

It is as well to remember not to quote calculated values to a larger number of figures than is justified if you have used a calculator, e.g. 45.67231. If you give a value of, say, 45.67 you are saying that it is accurate to one part in 4500, i.e. it is *not* 45.66 or 45.68. This really is beyond the accuracy of any experiment, except possibly where vernier scales are being used. A more realistic value would be 45.6 or 45.7.

Plotting the graph

Graphs are plotted:

(a) to show any general connection between the two quantities plotted;
(b) to produce a way of finding the best estimate of a 'true connection';
(c) as a means of 'averaging' the results.

The variable over which you have direct control and can change is usually plotted as the abscissa (x) and is often altered in regular steps, whereas the variable which has values that are dependent on other variables is usually plotted as the ordinate (y).

One main aim is to plot a straight-line graph, because then the mathematical connection between the two quantities is known. A straight-line graph has the general equation $y = mx + c$, where m = gradient and c = intercept on the y axis, i.e. when $x = 0$.

Frictional force per unit area/N cm⁻²	Average time/s	Average speed/cm s⁻¹	Error/cm s⁻¹
0.1/50 = 2 × 10⁻³	2.63	38	*±2

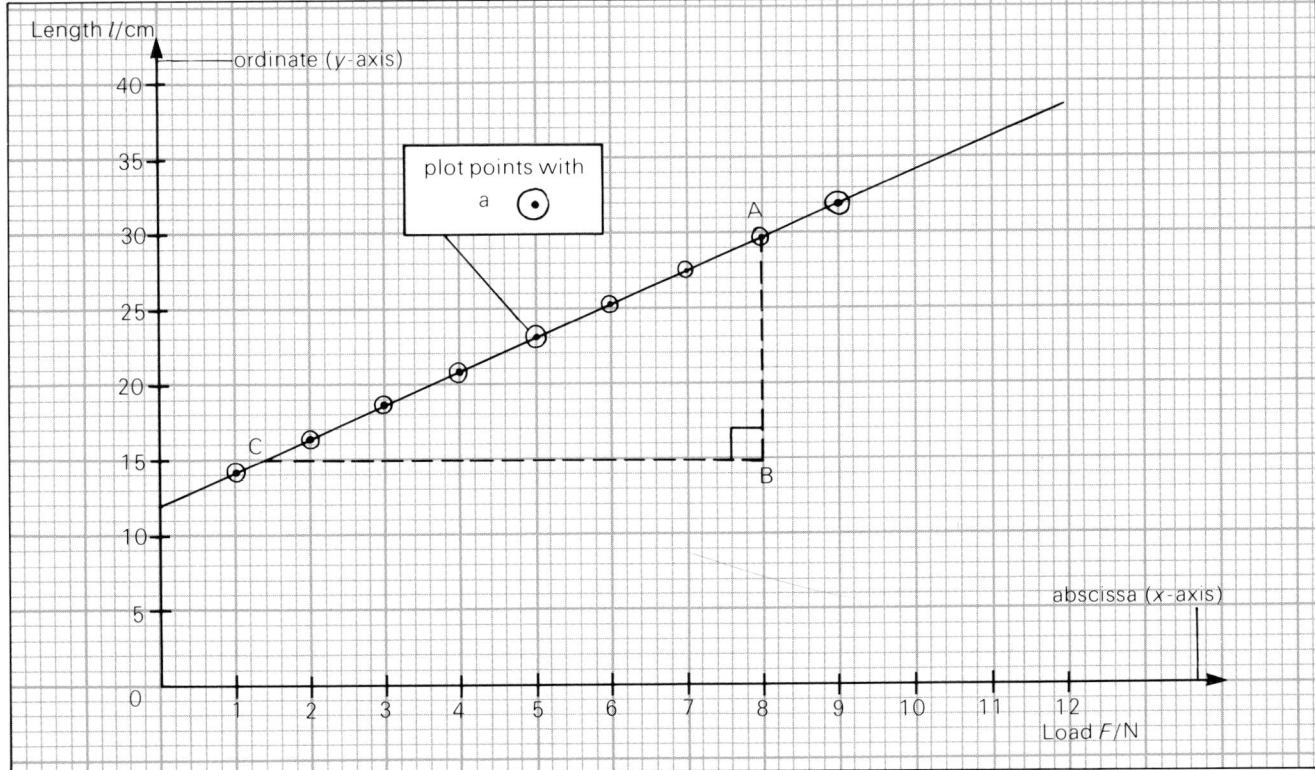

Figure 30 Graph showing the change in extension of a spring with a load.

For example, in an experiment on the extension of a spring the graph in figure 30 might be plotted. This is a straight line graph of $y = mx + c$, where $y = $ length (l) and $x = $ load (F). The intercept is the length of the spring with *no* load, i.e. the natural length of the spring, therefore $c = 12$ cm.

Thus, $\qquad l = mF + 12$

$$m = \frac{AB}{BC} = \frac{32-15}{8-1.2} = \frac{17}{6.8} = 2.5 \text{ cm N}^{-1}$$

Therefore, $l = 2.5F + 12$ is the relation between length (l) and force (F).

The graph for the parachute experiment (p. 13) might be drawn as in figure 31. It is clearly not a straight line.

It is usual to find some method by which a straight-line graph can be plotted. Often a curve has an equation of the form:

$$y = kx^n$$

where one variable is raised to a power. The usual method is to take logs:

$$\log_e y = \log_e k + n \log_e x$$

Comparing this with the equation of a straight line $y = mx + c$, it is seen that a graph of $\log_e y$ against $\log_e x$ should be a straight line with gradient n and intercept on the $\log_e y$ axis of $\log_e k$.

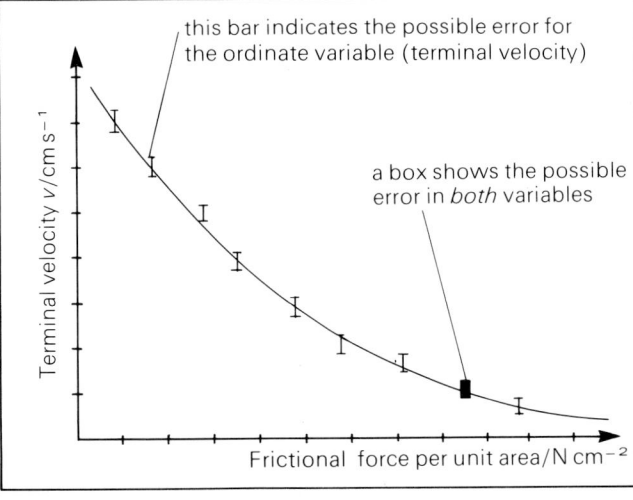

Figure 31 Graph for the model parachute experiment

Example
A gas in a cylinder is allowed to change adiabatically. This means that no energy is absorbed by or removed from the gas. It is the type of change produced in a bicycle pump. As you will probably know, the temperature is not constant since the pump gets hot. The equation for the process for a fixed mass of gas is:

$$\text{constant} = PV^\gamma$$

where $P = $ pressure, $V = $ volume and γ is a constant called the 'ratio of the principal specific heat capacities'. For air, $\gamma = 1.4$, which is a value found by experiment.

RECORDING, DISPLAYING AND ANALYSING THE RESULTS

The following set of results has been taken for pressure and volume during the adiabatic change. The object is to plot a straight-line graph and find a value for γ.

Pressure $(P \pm 0.03)/\times 10^4$ Pa	Volume $(V \pm 0.02)/\text{m}^3$
6.5	0.05
2.5	0.1
1.4	0.15
0.94	0.2
0.69	0.25
0.53	0.3

If constant $= PV^\gamma$, then $\dfrac{1}{P} = \dfrac{V^\gamma}{\text{constant}}$

and $\log_e\left(\dfrac{1}{P}\right) = -\log_e(\text{constant}) + \gamma \log_e V$.

Make a table of values for $\log_e\left(\dfrac{1}{P}\right)$ and $\log_e V$ and plot a graph. Remember that the $\log_e$ of fractions are *negative*.

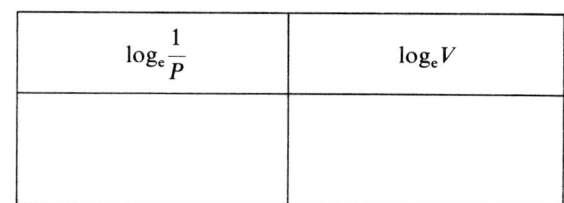

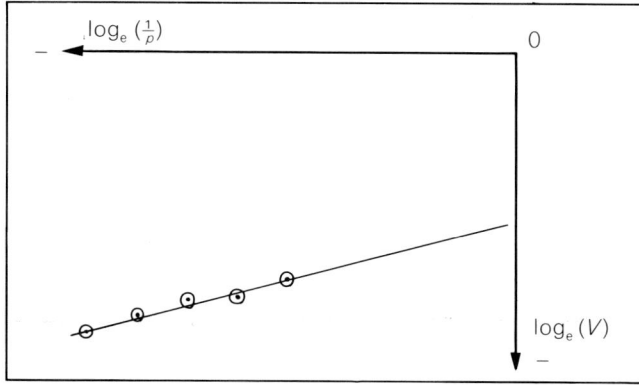

Figure 32

The graph should be of the form shown in figure 32. Find the gradient which is γ. Compare your answer with 1.4 and decide if the gas used is *air* (within the limits of experimental error).

Shapes of graphs

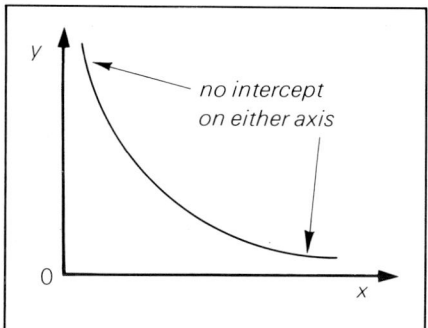

Figure 33 $y = \dfrac{k}{x}$; y against $\dfrac{1}{x}$ would be a straight line.

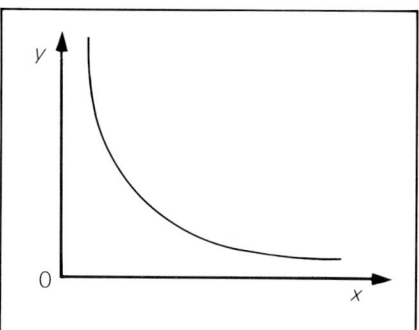

Figure 34 $y = \dfrac{k}{x^2}$; y against $\dfrac{1}{x^2}$ would be a straight line.

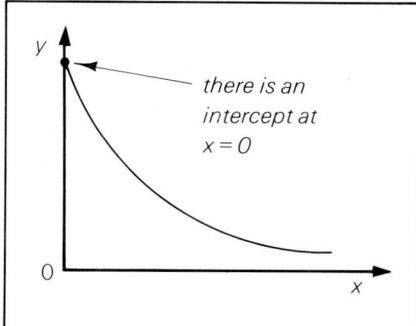

Figure 35 $y = e^{-kx}$; $x = \log_e y$ would be a straight line.

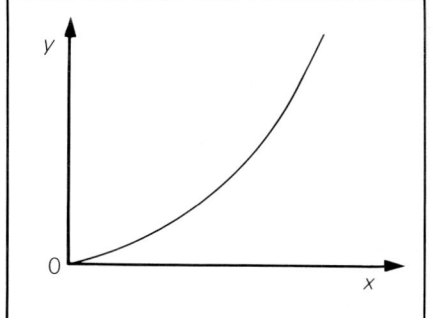

Figure 36 $y = kx^2$

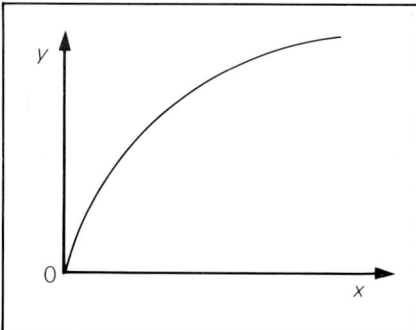

Figure 37 $y = k\sqrt{x}$ and $y = 1 - e^{-kx}$ have this type of shape.

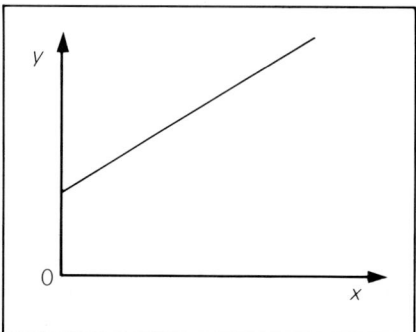

Figure 38 A straight line ($y = mx + c$). If $c = 0$, the graph passes through the origin.

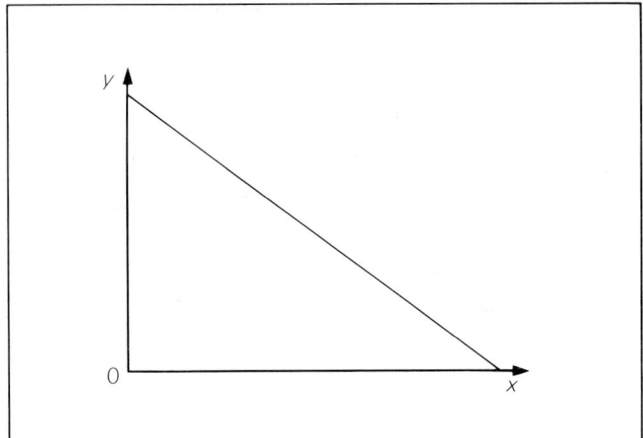

Figure 39 A straight line with a negative gradient, $y = -mx + c$.

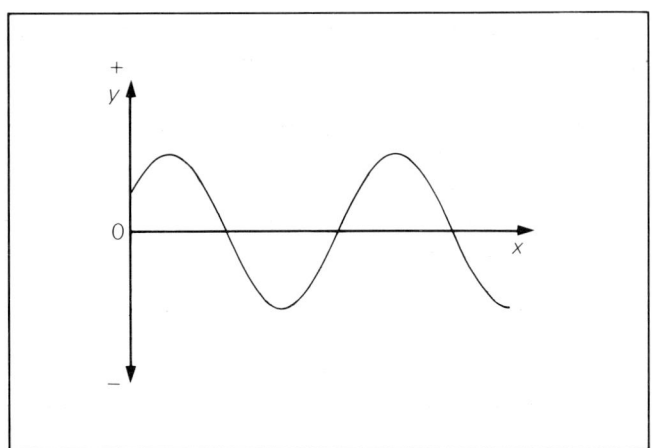

Figure 40 $y = A \sin(kx + \delta)$, the initial value on the y axis when $x = 0$ is determined by the values of δ and A.

Positive and negative values:

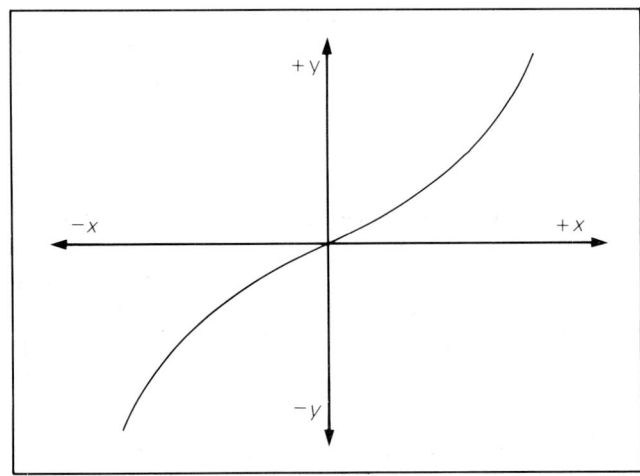

Figure 41

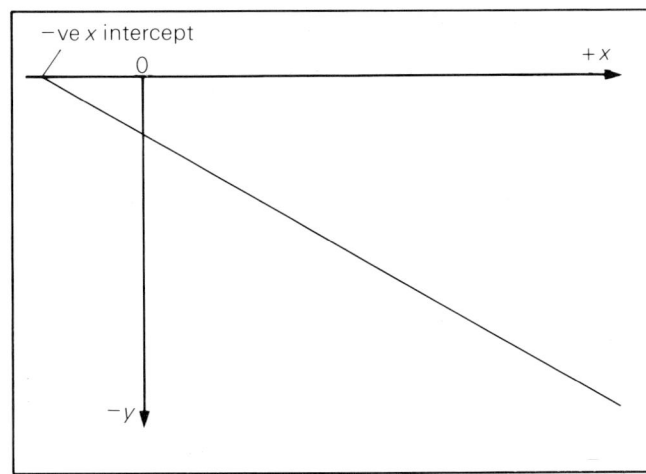

Figure 42

No point in trying to find a straight line:

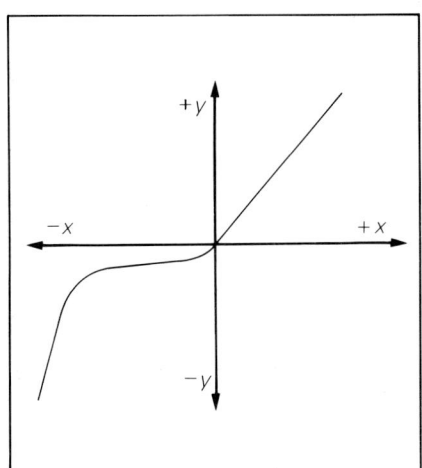

Figure 43

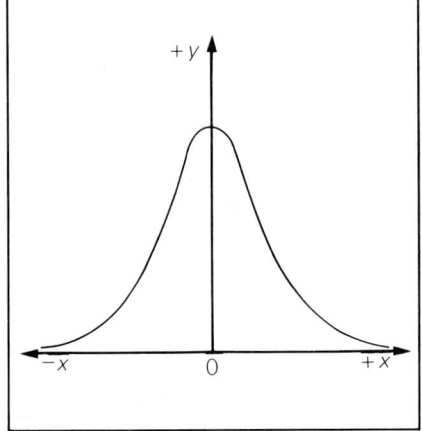

Figure 44

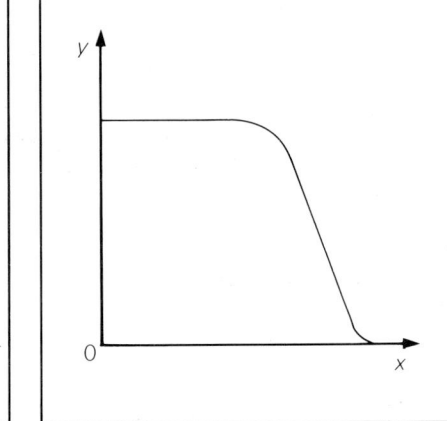

Figure 45

RECORDING, DISPLAYING AND ANALYSING THE RESULTS

Graphs of the type shown in figures 43–45 are described qualitatively and are used to try and deduce the *reasons* for the shape of the graph.

Often when investigating an unknown relationship, you do not know the form of the mathematical relationship. A log–log graph can be plotted, but an alternative method is to manipulate the results by computer. The program PROCESS enables you to enter a set of raw results. Then you can try to produce a straight line through the origin by trying different powers of the variables, taking logs and altering constants until a straight-line graph is produced (figures 47–52). The data can then be printed out so that you can plot the graph yourself, and a copy of the graph can be produced if you have a suitable printer.

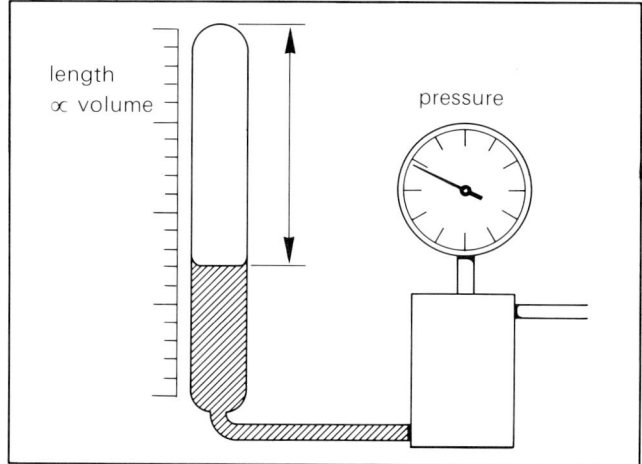

Figure 46 Apparatus for investigating Boyle's Law.

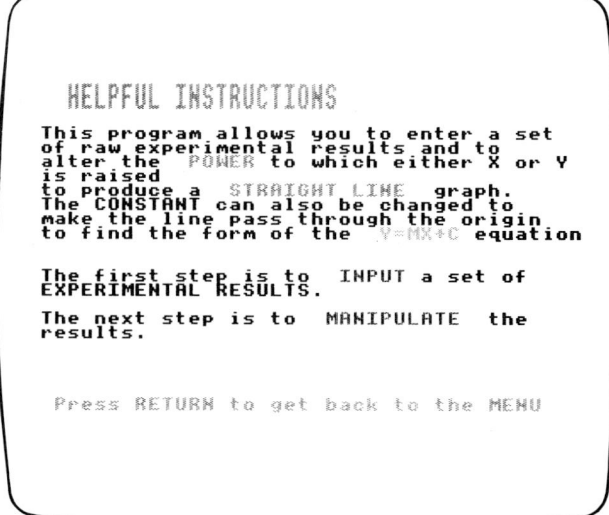

Figure 47 Helpful instructions

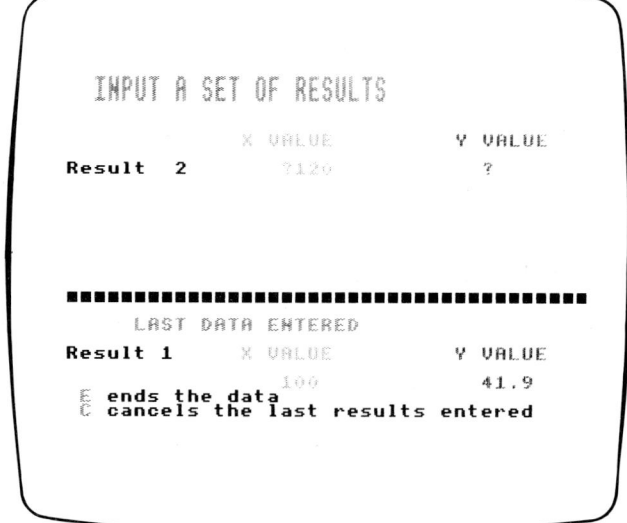

Figure 48 Data entry

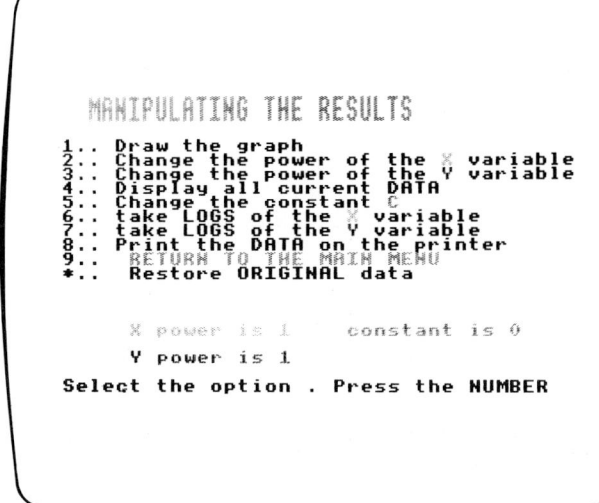

Figure 49 Manipulating the results

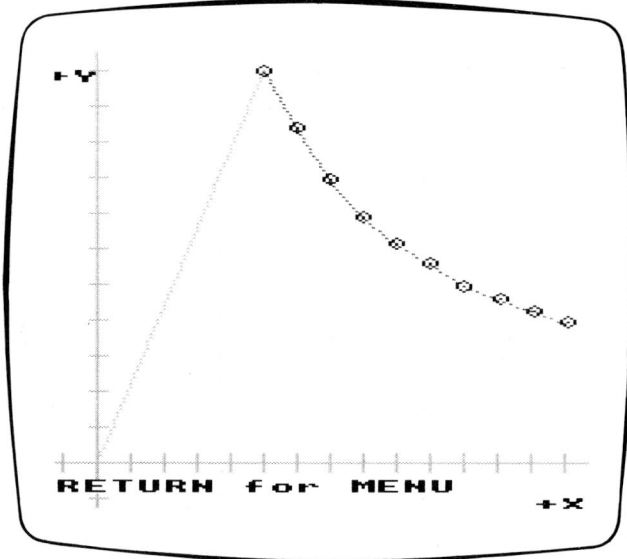

Figure 50 Graph from the raw data *p* against *V*

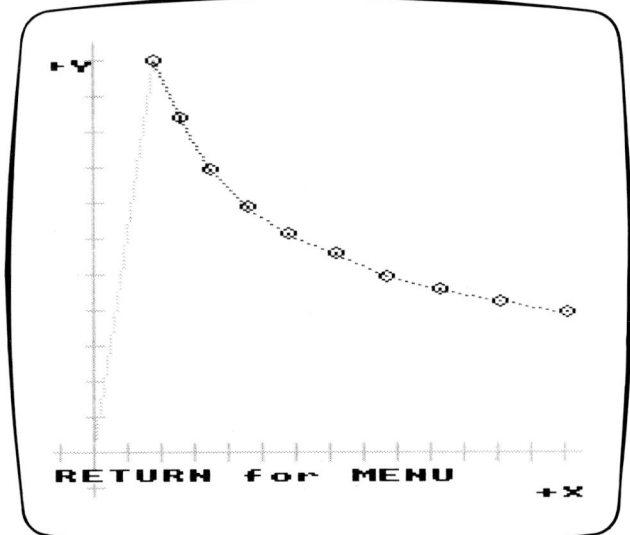
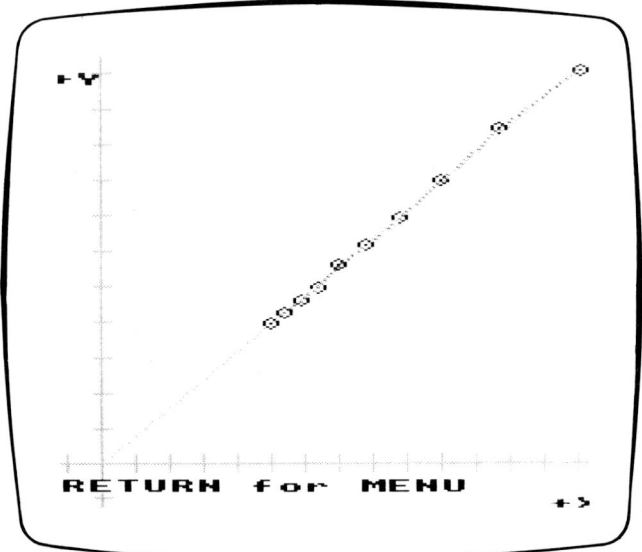

Figure 51 First try: p^2 against V

Figure 52 Second try: $1/p$ against V. Therefore pV is constant.

The example given in figures 47–52 is from an experiment investigating Boyle's law; you probably already know that the relationship is $P \propto \dfrac{1}{V}$.

Length of column ($\propto$ volume)/cm	Pressure/$\times 10^5$ Pa
41.9	100
35.8	120
30.2	140
26.25	160
23.3	180
21.2	200
18.9	220
17.5	240
16.2	260
15.0	280

The relationship between pressure (P) and volume (V) is

$$\text{pressure} = \frac{\text{constant}}{\text{volume}}$$

because the graph is a straight line and it passes through the origin.

Exercise

Here are two tables of results. A straight-line graph passing through the origin is required. Use the computer program, or plot a log–log graph, or just try plotting what you think might be a suitable graph, to find the relationship between the x and y variables.

Expansion of a gas

x Temperature/°C	y Volume/cm^3
0	40.1
25	43.6
50	45.3
75	50.2
100	55.6

A conducting metal

x Current I/A	y Resistance/Ω
0.1	3.1
0.2	13.2
0.3	28.7
0.4	51.3
0.5	77.2
0.6	115.1
0.7	151.6

Hints for plotting graphs

1. Simple scale divisions should always be used, using two, five or ten divisions on the scale for each physical unit.

   For example:

   2 mm represents 10 g
   5 mm represents 1 V
   1 cm represents 0.1 A

2. Mark the axis and scales in ink. Plot the points in pencil using ⊙, I or ▮ to mark on the position of the points.

3. The convention for showing the variable and units is:

$$\text{force} \qquad F/N \quad \times \quad 10^{-2}$$

variable name, symbol, unit, any power

The numbers marked on the axis should be ≥ 1.0 and <10 as a general guideline, rather than 0.001, 0.002 etc. A scale of 0.1, 0.2, 0.3, etc., should be shown as 1, 2, 3 and the power 10^{-1} shown in the labelling.

4. When drawing a smooth curve freehand, always have your hand in the *concave* side of the curve (figure 53).
5. A plane mirror can be used to find the perpendicular to a curve at a point. Using this perpendicular, a tangent can be drawn. This operation is needed to find the gradient at a point.

    (a) Place the mirror across the line with the *back* of the mirror (the reflecting surface) in line with the point (figure 54).
    (b) Look into the mirror and adjust the position of your eye until a reflection of the curve nearest your eye (AB) can be seen.
    (c) Rotate the mirror until the curve AB appears *smoothly* joined to its reflection (figure 55).
    (d) Draw a line along the back of the mirror. This is perpendicular to the curve. Use a protractor to draw the line at 90° to this perpendicular line. This is the tangent to the curve.

6. Graphs should always use an absolute origin, i.e. both variables plotted should start from zero.
7. Plot the independent variable (the one changed by known or set steps) as abscissa → and the variable changed as a result, the dependent variable, as the ordinate ↑.

ANALYSIS OF INFORMATION

When the data have been gathered by one of the following methods

(a) direct measurement of individual readings,
(b) taking a photograph,
(c) data logging by data memory, computer, ticker-timer, etc.,

deductions and conclusions must be made from them. A usual first step is to plot a graph, because the relationship between two variables can be seen visually, whereas from a table of figures any pattern would be difficult to see. Alternatively, you may be asked to evaluate an equation containing several variables. You may also have recorded some descriptive information during the experiments.

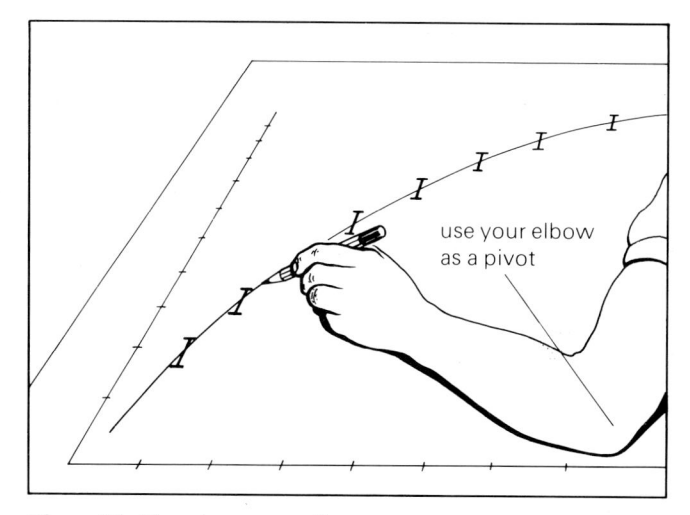

Figure 53. Drawing a smooth curve.

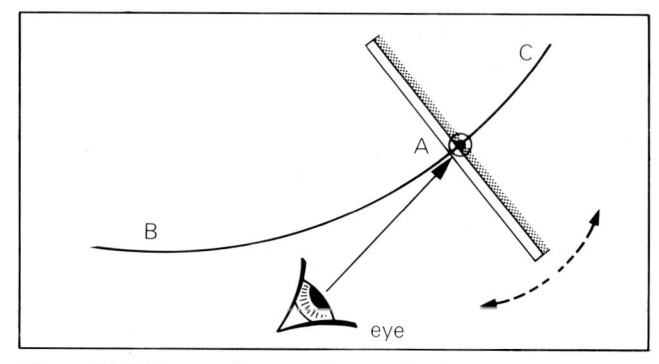

Figure 54 Using a mirror to draw a perpendicular to a curve.

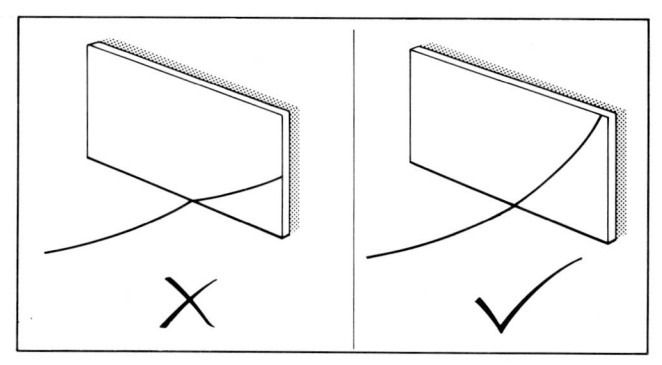

Figure 55 Turn the mirror until the curve appears continuous.

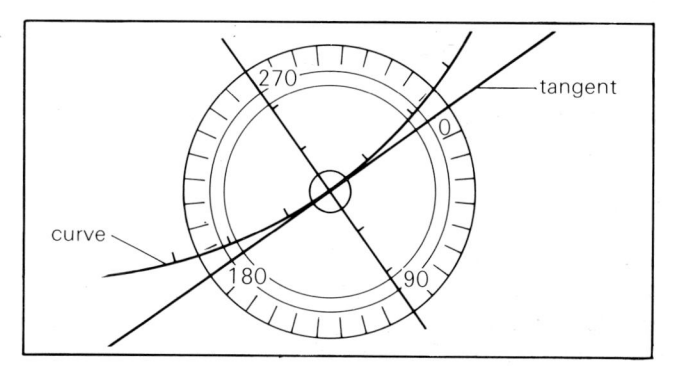

Figure 56 The tangent is at 90° to the perpendicular line.

Deductions can be:

(a) *qualitative*, which involves the general pattern followed by the results and interesting aspects that are shown, but without any strict numerical connections;
(b) *quantitative*, which involves finding numerical values, the equation of the graph and rules connecting the variables.

An example to make you think

An object rests on a table and an external force is applied.

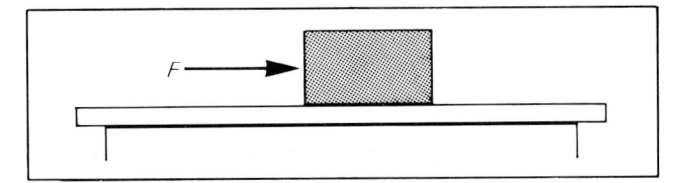

Figure 57

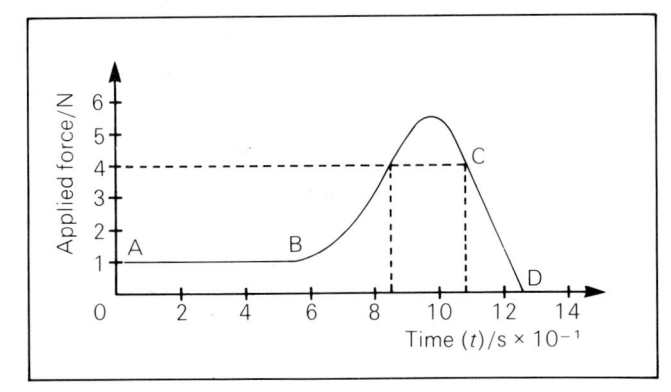

Figure 58

The effect of the force on any subsequent movement of the object could depend on the amount of frictional force between the object and the table. In answering the questions, think about the effect of having (a) no friction, and (b) friction.
1. What is the intercept A and the physical significance of the part AB?
2. What is the change of momentum of the object from the 'area' under the curve if there is no frictional force?
3. What is the time at which maximum force occurs?
4. Describe the resulting movement of the object.
5. What are the times when the applied force is 4 N?
6. What will happen to the object if the frictional force is greater than 5.5 N?

Gradient

The gradient shows the way in which one variable changes relative to the other:

$$\text{gradient} = \frac{\text{change in } y \text{ variable}}{\text{change in } x \text{ variable}}$$

Remember to use the correct numbers from the scale and to give the units of the gradient. The gradient often has a physical significance, e.g. for a graph of velocity against time, the physical significance of the gradient is that it is the *acceleration*.

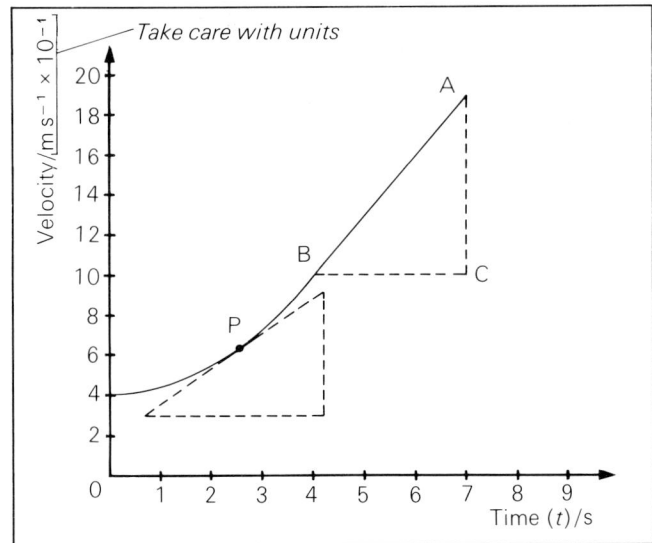

Figure 59 Finding gradients.

In figure 59, AB is a straight line, which shows that the acceleration is constant.

$$\text{gradient} = \frac{AC}{BC} = \frac{(19 - 10) \times 10^{-1}}{7 - 4} = 0.3 \, \text{m s}^{-2}$$

Always use the largest convenient length of straight line that you can, so that the percentage error is reduced to as small a value as possible.

The curved section shows a changing acceleration. At point P draw a tangent (using a plane mirror will help), complete the triangle and work out the gradient. Remember that a gradient can be negative.

Intercept

The intercept is the value at which a curve cuts an axis. Often *extrapolation* needs to be done to project the line of the curve until it cuts the axis. If the graph is *known* to be a straight line through the origin, an intercept could indicate a *zero error* in one of the instruments used. The intercept often has a physical significance, and remember that intercepts could be on any axis, including the negative ones. For example:

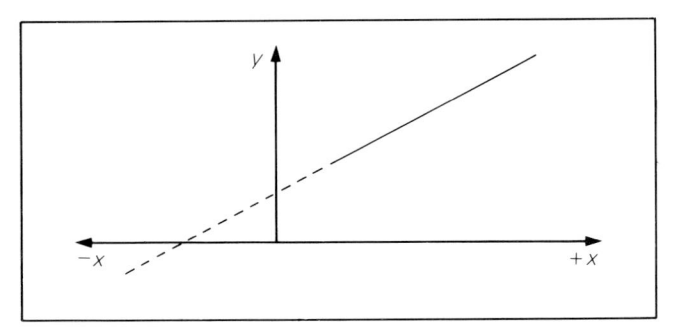

Figure 60

RECORDING, DISPLAYING AND ANALYSING THE RESULTS

In an experiment to find the focal length of a lens, the equation connecting the object distance (u), the image distance (v) and the focal length (f) is known to be

$$\frac{1}{v} + \frac{1}{u} = \frac{1}{f} \quad \text{or} \quad \frac{1}{v} = -\frac{1}{u} + \frac{1}{f}$$

If a graph of $\frac{1}{v}$ as ordinate and $\frac{1}{u}$ as abscissa is plotted, the intercept on the $\frac{1}{u}$ axis will be $\frac{1}{f}$. Also the intercept on the $\frac{1}{v}$ axis will be $\frac{1}{f}$.

Extrapolation

Sometimes an experiment can only be carried out with a certain range of values. For example, the way the pressure of a gas varies with temperature can only realistically be investigated over a temperature range of 0°C to 100°C with a possible extension to lower temperatures if some solid carbon dioxide is available. The graph plotted might be:

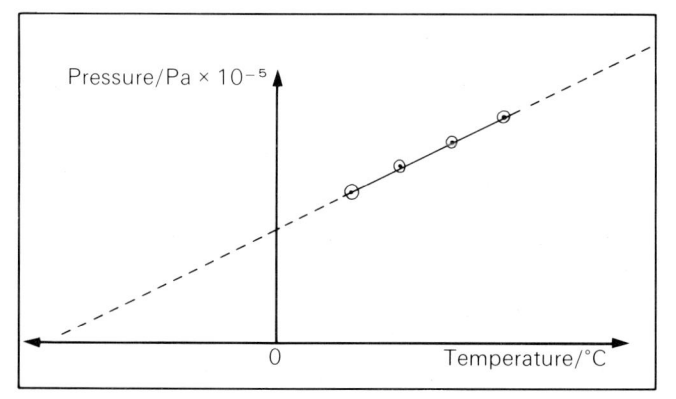

Figure 61 Extrapolation of a straight line using a ruler.

Extrapolation is the projection of the graph to lower and higher values. With a straight-line graph it is easy, as shown above. With a curve, practice and care are needed. Follow the arc of the curve with your hand. This practice is also useful if points on a curved graph are to be joined with a smooth curve, particularly where maxima or minima are involved.

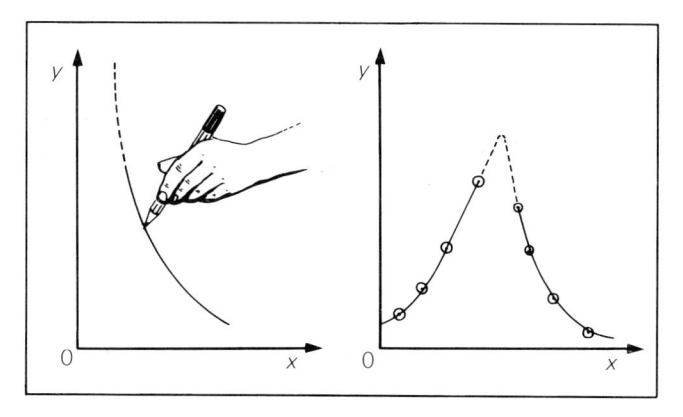

Figure 62 Extrapolation of a curve by free-hand sketching.

Area under the curve

The 'area' under the curve often has a physical significance, for example, in a velocity–time graph it represents the distance travelled.

To find the 'area' count the squares, but remember to use the *scale values* to produce the correct numerical answer and units. For example, a capacitor discharging has the graph of current against time shown in figure 63. The 'area' under the curve $= \int I\,dt$, which equals the total charge, in coulomb, which has flowed. Each square centimetre has a 'charge' value of $10^{-6} \times 60$ C (10^{-6} from current axis; 60 to get the time-scale to seconds).

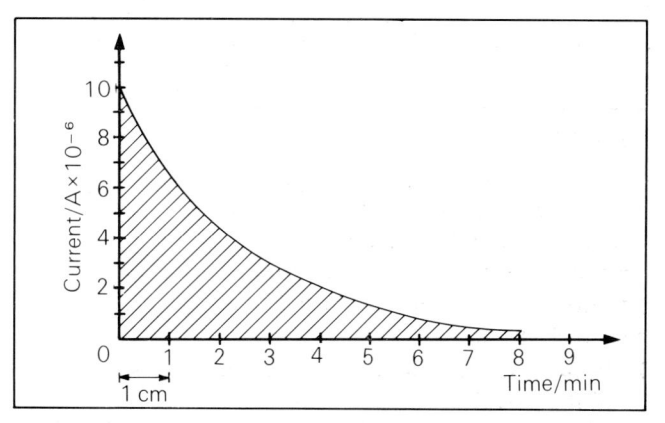

Figure 63

WRITING EXPERIMENTAL REPORTS

Up to now you have probably written up practicals in the form diagram, method, results, conclusion. As practicals become more involved and more varied at A-level, and often with less precise conclusions, this simple structure evolves into a more readable report. Much more emphasis is placed on explanation of what you are doing and why, and about how your results and observations lead to the conclusions made. The report should flow in a logical and clear sequence from beginning to end. The form of the report will depend on the experiment done, but a basic outline could be as follows.

1. *Outline of the problem*
A brief description of the purpose of the experiment, the problem or question to be solved, and the general method behind the experiment.

2. *Mathematical theory*
This section includes any mathematical theory associated with the experiment, if known, as this often leads to the factors to be measured and any graphs which will be drawn.

3. *Diagrams of equipment*
This section contains fully-labelled diagrams showing the apparatus used and possibly diagrams on a larger scale showing any particular methods of taking results. Remember that diagrams can often convey ideas better and more clearly than writing.

4. *Experimental details or procedure*
Apart from a clear set of experimental instructions, this will include points which you found difficult, and the best way of taking measurements, arranged in a clear, logical order. Precautions to ensure accurate and consistent results should also be recorded.

5. *Recorded results*
These are the measurements taken during the experiment. Results should be given in the order in which they were taken. If any readings have been re-checked or appear unusual, mention should be made here.

6. *Calculated values or graphs*
This section contains tables calculated from the recorded results in order to plot graphs, or re-arranged tables which show more easily how the results lead to the conclusions. The graphs and any gradients and intercepts worked out are given, together with discussion on what the graphs show. Explanation of how this information *leads* to the final result or conclusions must be given. This is one of the most important parts of any practical write-up.

7. *Accuracy and errors*
This would contain a summary about the overall accuracy of the experiment, with a numerical range of accuracy if you have been able to calculate it. If there are large errors, try to suggest where they might have come from, but make the suggestions sensible and realistic. Do *not* do what one student did to try and explain why the periodic time of a pendulum varied by 20 per cent from the expected answer. Instead of suggesting that it was his measurement of time which was at fault, he wrote that it was due to 'an error in measuring the length of the pendulum'. What he said in effect was that he couldn't measure a 1m pendulum with a metre rule to within *20 cm!!*

8. *Ideas, suggestions and discussion*
This might contain ideas about alterations to the apparatus to make it easier to use or to get more accurate results, and suggestions about further experiments which might be done.

9. *Final conclusion*
A concise summary of your conclusions, including:

(a) final numerical results, with approximate errors;
(b) any mathematical rule by graphs or results;
(c) any less quantifiable trends and relationships which have become apparent or which are indicated by the results;
(d) any disagreement between your conclusions and what might be expected from theory;

(e) answers to questions set in the practical notes;
(f) any intuitive ideas gained during the experiment.

You can see that a report at A-level may be several pages long, even for what might seem a simple experiment.

Sample reports written by an A-level student

The reports are unmarked and you are asked to read them critically and decide how well each matches up with the following criteria. Points to pay particular attention to are marked with an *. Mark each point out of three.

1. Is the aim properly described?
2. Are there any mistakes in the diagram?
3. Is the diagram clear and large enough to see all detail clearly?
4. Is the diagram fully labelled?
5. Is the procedure clear—can you follow what to do, even though you may not have done the experiment?
6. Has the student stated what quantities are to be measured and what instruments will be used?
7. Are the results clearly recorded, with correct units and the correct number of significant figures?
8. Are probable errors given for each result, and are they correct values?
9. Is any theory shown correct and are any equations derived correctly?
10. Has a calculator been used correctly?
11. Are the axes of any graphs drawn and labelled correctly?
12. Have the points been plotted correctly?
13. Are any curves or straight lines drawn correctly?
14. Have any gradients and/or intercepts been found correctly and given with correct units?
15. Has the correct physical significance been given to gradients and intercepts?
16. Is there a discussion of errors and of the experiment in general?
17. Are errors explained with proper reasons and not just vague terms?
18. Has the relative numerical size of different errors been given?
19. Are key results highlighted and do the conclusions follow logically from the results?
20. Are the conclusions correct or as expected, and if not, is there any discussion as to the reason for the discrepancy?

Before each report is a summary of what the student was asked to do in the experiment so that you can assess how successful she was.

Afterwards, assess your own experimental reports in the same way.

Experiment 1: Measurement of the wavelength of sodium light using a diffraction grating

The student has to use a spectrometer accurately and take sufficient measurements to calculate the wavelength of yellow light from a sodium discharge lamp.

Measurement of the Wavelength of sodium Light by Diffraction Grating

Aim: To use a spectroscope in addition to a diffraction grating to find the wavelength of a source of sodium light using:

$$n\lambda = d \sin \theta$$

Procedure: The spectrometer was finely adjusted with a diffraction grating of 80 lines per mm. on the turntable, once the diffraction grating had been set at 90° to the collimator, a source of sodium light was examined.

The angles of diffraction for the different orders of diffraction were noted.

λ was calculated from each result and an average value found, which was compared to accepted values.

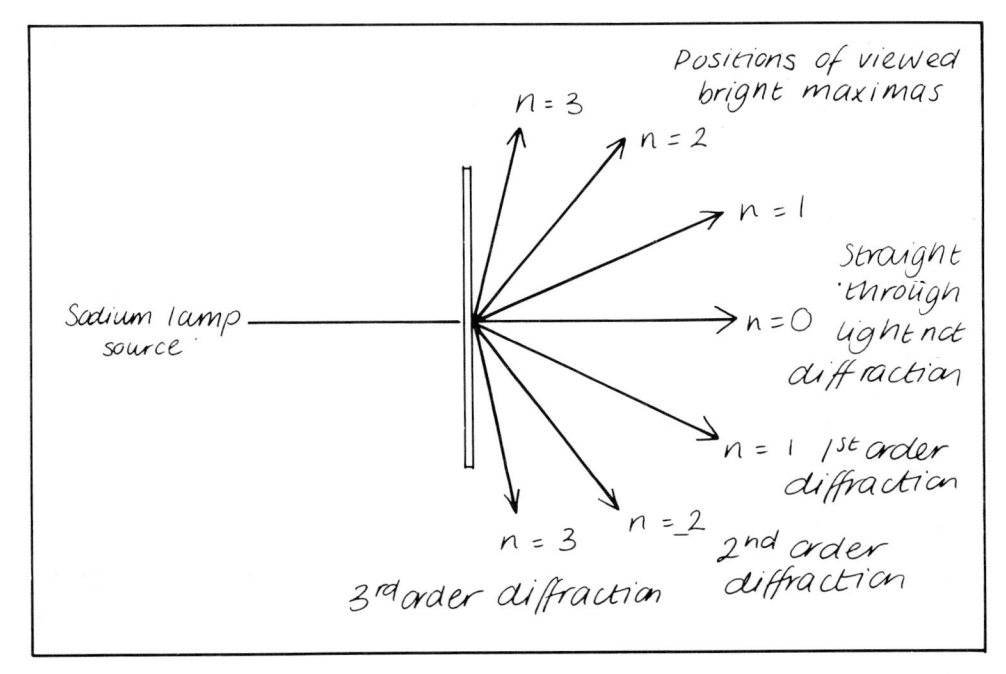

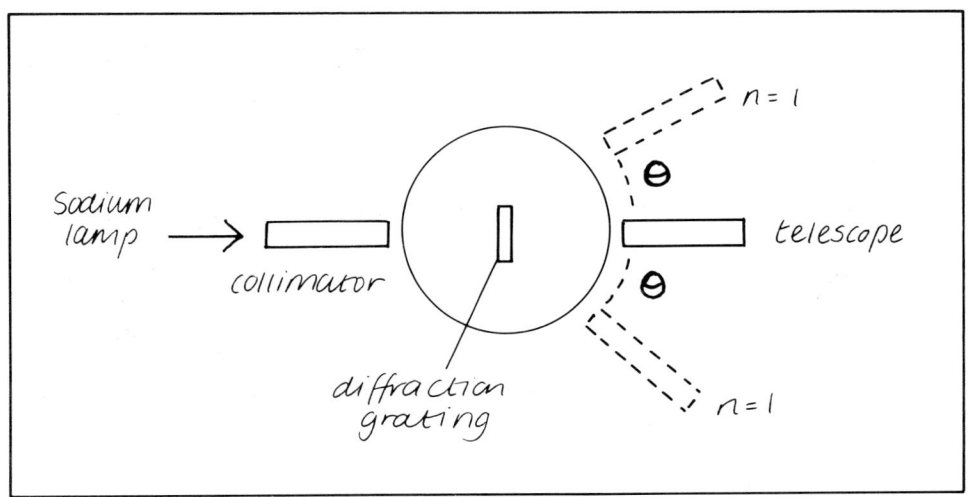

[Diagram: Sodium lamp source shines through a diffraction grating, producing viewed bright maximas labelled n=3, n=2, n=1 (upper), n=0 straight through light no diffraction, n=1 1st order diffraction, n=2 2nd order diffraction, n=3 3rd order diffraction.]

[Diagram: Sodium lamp → collimator → diffraction grating (on rotating table) → telescope, with n=1 maxima at angle θ on either side.]

Results:

n	left θ	right θ	$\bar{x}$ θ°	sin θ	Wavelength ×10⁻⁶ m	λ × 10⁻⁶
1	2.6	2.8	2.7	0.0471	λ = 0.5875	0.5875
2	5.3	5.5	5.4	0.09411	2λ = 1.1764	0.5882
3	8	8.2	8.1	0.141	3λ = 1.7625	0.5875
4	10.7	10.9	10.8	0.1874	4λ = 2.3425	0.5856
5	13.5	13.7	13.6	0.235	5λ = 2.9375	0.5875

$\bar{x}\lambda = 0.587$

Wavelength sodium light 0.58725×10^{-6} m.

Sample Calculation:

$$n\lambda = d \sin \theta$$
$$1 \times \lambda = d \underset{\text{(in mm)}}{\quad} \times \underset{\text{(in mm)}}{(0.0471)} \rightarrow \sin 2.7°$$

$$d = \left(\tfrac{1}{80} \div 1000\right)$$
$$\lambda = \left(\tfrac{1}{80} \div 1000\right) \times 0.0471$$
$$\underline{\lambda = 0.5875 \times 10^{-6} \, m}$$
※

Accuracy of Errors

The spectrometer is a very accurate instrument, with angles measured to $\pm 0.06°$.

The width d on the diffraction grating is also very accurately measured, with 80 lines per mm ※

Inaccuracies may be due to the diffraction grating not being perpendicular to the colimator but if the procedure for ensuring lining the diffraction grating is carefully followed this should not occur.
(see note 6 on spectrometer.)

Conclusion:

The value of λ, the wavelength of sodium light is 0.5875×10^{-6} m, which compares very well to the normally accepted values of 0.5896×10^{-6} m to 0.5890×10^{-6} m. The sodium lamp gives 7 visible maximas on each side of the $n = 0$ position. This angle must be measured in order that the values of θ can be measured from this position.

If the diffraction grating is not perpendic--ular to the colimator then variations in the values for θ for the maximas n=1, n=2 etc., occur, these variations cause the final value of λ to be inaccurate. It is therefore important to ensure that the diffraction grating is exactly perpendicular to the parallel rays from the light source.

When a white filament lamp is observed through a diffraction grating, at the 1st order of diffraction, n=1, a spectrum is formed. With blue which has the shortest wavelength being diffracted the least and red which has the longest wavelength diffracted most.   *

Theory:

When monochromatic light of wavelength λ falls on a grating of spacing d (width of slit and spacing) maxima are formed due to constructive interference of wavelets from A and B. Maxima are found at Card B at the same time.

The path difference between waves diffracted from A and B must be = $d \sin \theta$. A number of maxima

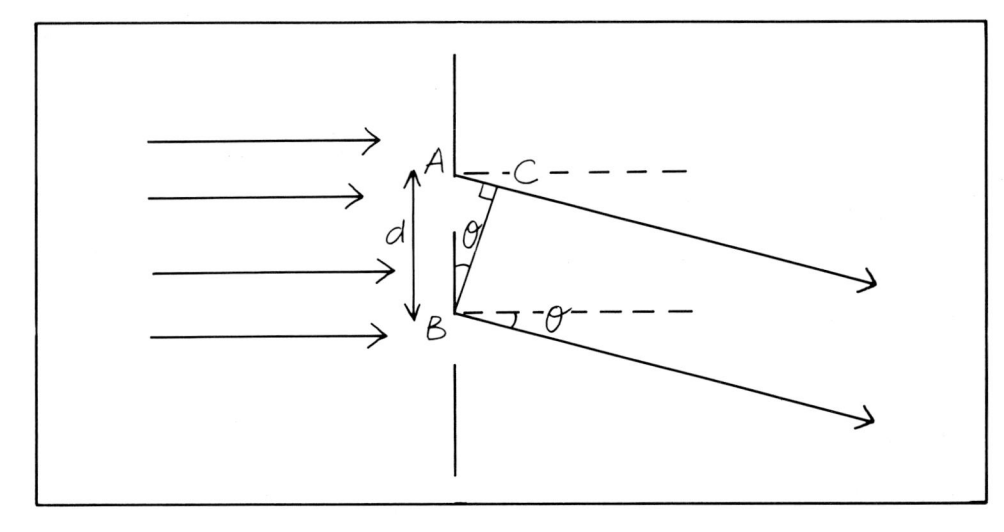

are observed on either side of the bright central band. For the 1st order maximum
$$d \sin \theta = \lambda$$

For the 2nd order
$$d \sin \theta = 2\lambda . \text{ etc}$$

Hence :-
$$\boxed{d \sin \theta = n\lambda}$$

Experiment 2: Measurement of the elastic constant of a spiral spring and the acceleration due to gravity

The student has been asked to take measurements of the length of a spring as the load is increased and to find the period of oscillation of the spring with different loads on it. All theory needed must be derived. Graphs are to be drawn and values of the elastic constant and acceleration due to gravity found from the gradients. A conclusion is to be made as to whether the results verify Hooke's Law.

Measurement of 1. The Elastic Constant of a Spiral Spring.
2. The Acceleration Due to Gravity

Aim

1. To determine the elastic constant λ of a spiral spring by
$$\lambda = \frac{\text{load}}{\text{extension}},$$
and thus to prove Hooke's Law — load is proportional to extension.

2. To determine g, the acceleration due to gravity.

Mathematical Theory

A loaded spring oscillates with S.H.M. and time period T according to
$$T = 2\pi \sqrt{\frac{M+m}{\lambda}}$$

where M is the load and m is a constant depending on the mass of the spring.

By rearrangement

$$\frac{\lambda}{4\pi^2} T^2 = M + m \quad *$$

a graph of T^2 vs. e has its gradient $\frac{g}{4\pi^2}$ and

negative intercept on $y = \frac{gms}{\lambda}$

$\therefore g = \text{grad} \times 4\pi^2$

Procedure

A spiral spring was loaded with increasing weights, the extension was noted. The time for 20 oscillations was found for each load.

Graphs were drawn of M against e to find λ and T^2 against M to calculate g.

Results

Load (g)	Load (N) M	Extension (m) e	Time for 20 oscillations	Period T = Time for 1 oscillation	T^2 secs^2
50	0.5	0.012	6	0.3	0.09
100	1.0	0.032	7.7	0.385	0.15
150	1.5	0.052	10.1	0.505	0.255
200	2.0	0.072	11.6	0.58	0.336
250	2.5	0.092	13.0	0.65	0.423
300	3.0	0.112	14.5	0.725	0.526
350	3.5	0.132	15.4	0.77	0.593
400	4.0	0.158	16.4	0.82	0.672

$\lambda = \frac{\text{load}}{\text{extension}} \times \text{original length of spring}$

$2/0.08 \times 0.02$

$= 0.5 \quad *$

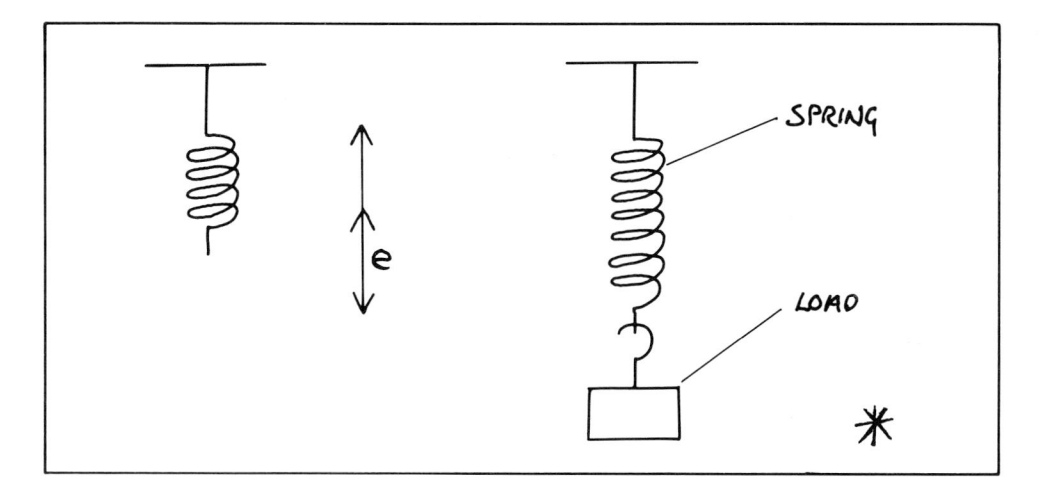

[Diagram: spring at natural length with extension e marked, and spring with load attached]

Grad of graph T^2 against e

$$\frac{0.128}{0.52} = \frac{g}{4\pi^2}$$

$$0.25 = \frac{g}{4\pi^2}$$

$$0.246 \times 4\pi^2 = g$$

$$g = 9.72 \text{ ms}^{-2}$$

Accuracy of Errors

1. Inaccuracies exist due to air resistance on the oscillating spring.
2. Inaccuracies in timing also exist due to human error in the stopping of the stop watch.

Estimated Accuracy

In timing
  ± 0.5 seconds.

Measurement of e
  ± 0.0005 m.

These are very small inaccuracies, but the largest and immeasurable one is the human error in stopping the watch.

Graph to show T^2 against e of a spiral spring

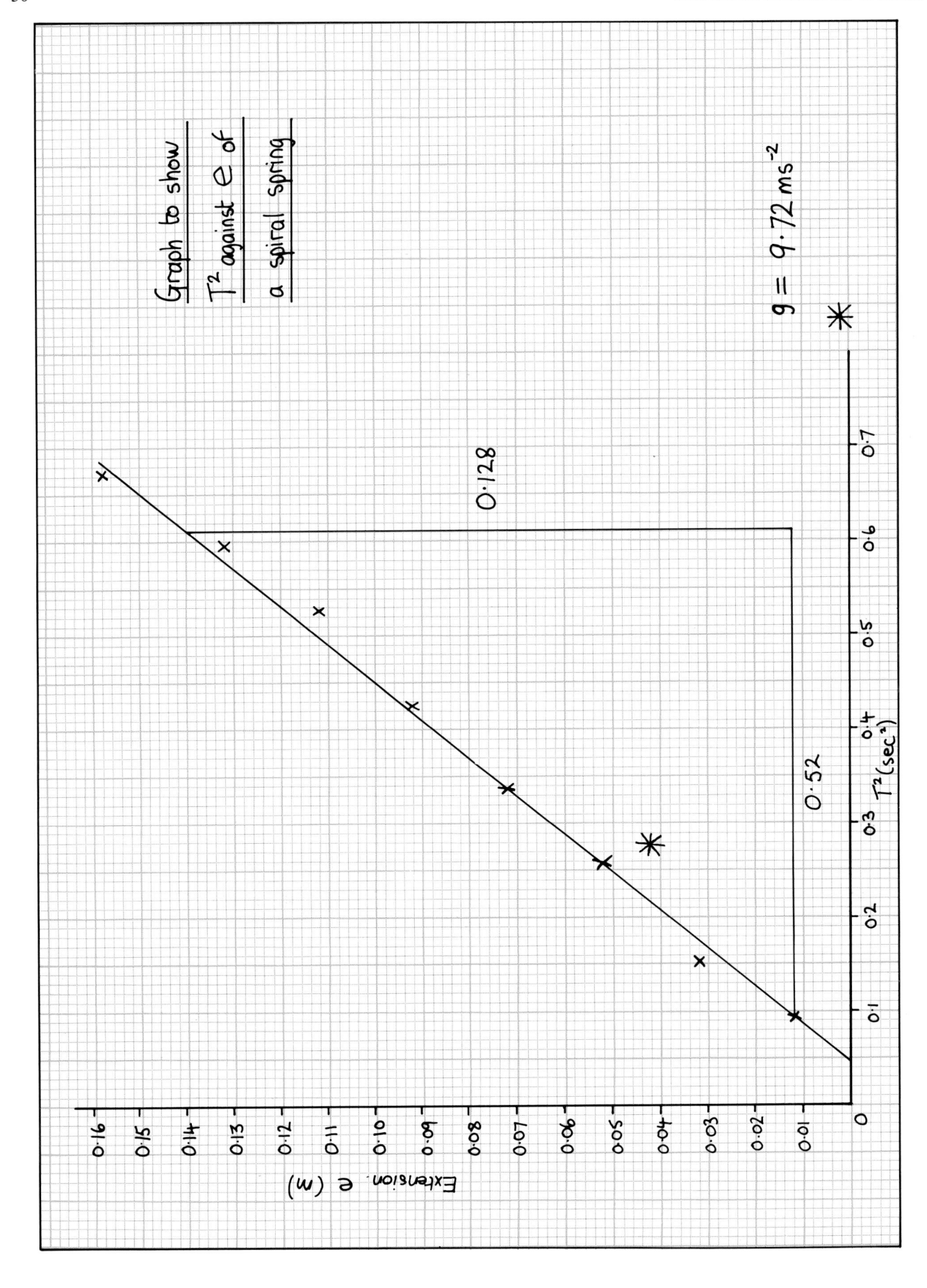

$g = 9.72\,ms^{-2}$

Discussion

The experiment verifies Hooke's Law within experimental error, and it can be said that extension is directly proportional to load applied. The experimental value of g, 9.72 ms^{-2} compares very well to the normally accepted value of 9.81 ms^{-2}, and the error can be accounted for by experimental inaccuracies as described above.

The elastic constant of the spring λ was found to be 0.5. *

The value of m was found from the negative intercept of the y axis to be -0.011 m, which relates to the mass of the spring 4.5g.

Experiment 3: Charge and discharge of a capacitor

The student was asked to:
1. take a set of readings of current and potential difference at regular time intervals as the capacitor is first charged and then discharged;
2. use a computer program which calculates the current and potential difference by an iterative method closely following the exact physical process;
3. calculate expected results using equations derived using calculus methods;
4. draw a set of graphs so that the three sets of values can be compared;
5. work out a value for the quantity of charge stored from the area under the curves;
6. write down a set of findings and conclusions.

Charge and Discharge of a Capacitor.

Aim

To determine what effect, resistance, supply voltage and capacitance have on time taken for a capacitor to charge and to discharge. The practical investigates this by plotting theoretical charge curves for the limits of experimental accuracy, and then seeing if practical results are in agreement.

The experiment also shows if the theoretical equation

$$V = V_s(1 - e^{-t/RC})$$

stands up to practical use.

V_s = supply voltage
R = resistance
C = capacitance
V = p.d. on capacitor.

Procedure

A computer programme was used to work out maximum and minimum charge curves to allow for component tolerance. The values of the capacitor and resistor were entered and by iteration and equation, theoretical curves were obtained and plotted as V against t.

The previous circuit was then set up, the capacitor was then charged and values of current and voltage were taken every 60 seconds until charging had occured.

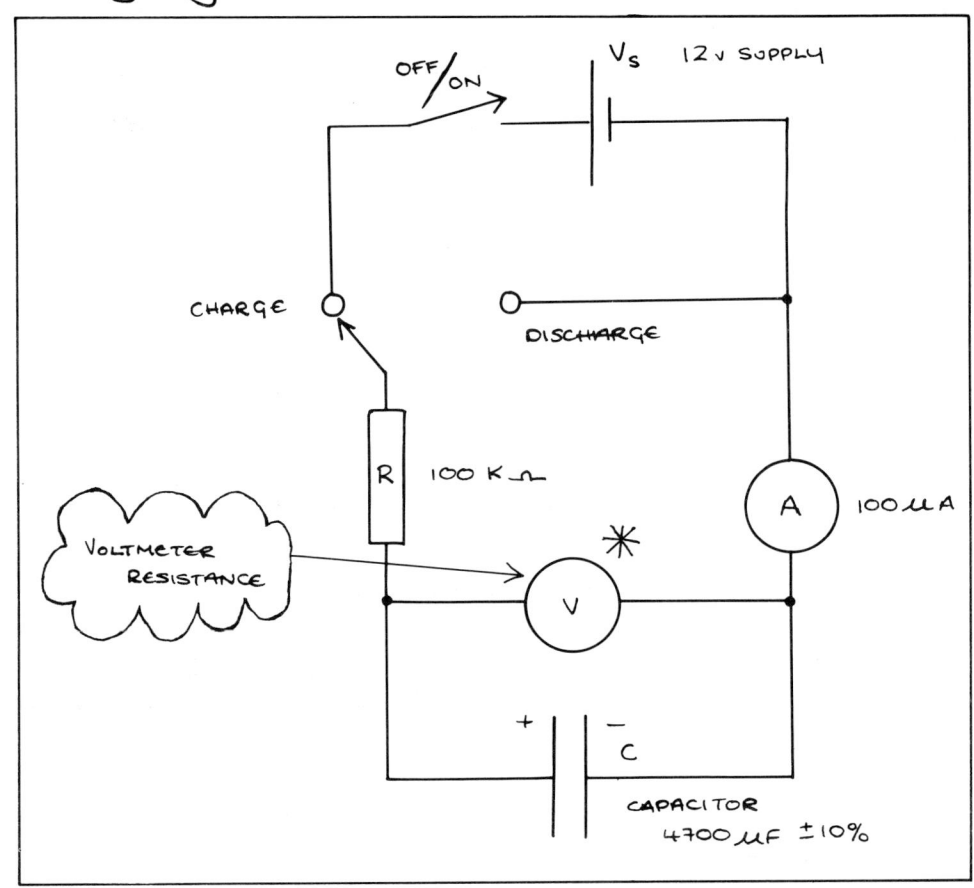

The capacitor was then discharged and similar readings taken until discharge was complete.

Results

Charging a capacitor

Time (secs)	V (Volts)	A (μA)
60	1.11	102
120	2.00	91
180	2.9	85
240	3.66	78
300	4.34	71.5
360	4.96	65.5
420	5.52	60.5
480	6.02	55.5
540	6.5	51
600	6.91	47
660	7.29	43.5
720	7.64	40.5
780	7.93	37.5
840	8.23	35
900	8.48	32.5
960	8.72	30
1020	8.93	28
1080	9.11	26

Discharging a capacitor

Time (secs)	Voltage (Volts)
0	11.17
60	10.14
120	9.5

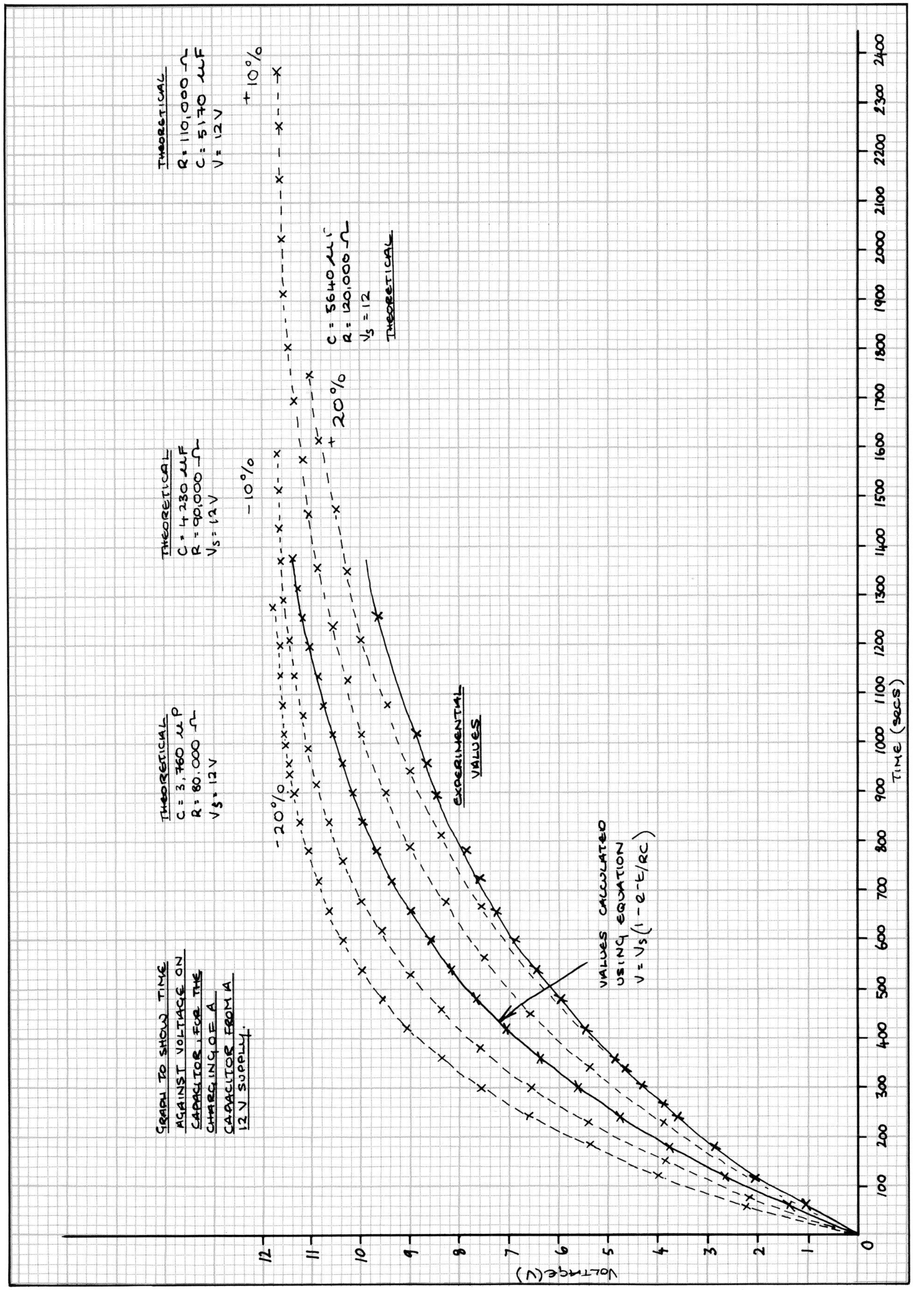
GRAPH TO SHOW TIME AGAINST VOLTAGE ON CAPACITOR, FOR THE CHARGING OF A CAPACITOR FROM A 12 V SUPPLY.
THEORETICAL
C = 3,760 μF
R = 80,000 Ω
V_S = 12 V
THEORETICAL
C = 4 230 μF
R = 90,000 Ω
V_S = 12 V
THEORETICAL
R = 110,000 Ω
C = 5170 μF
V = 12 V
C = 5640 μF
R = 120,000 Ω
V_S = 12
THEORETICAL
-20%
-10%
+10%
+20%
EXPERIMENTAL VALUES
VALUES CALCULATED USING EQUATION $V = V_S(1 - e^{-t/RC})$
TIME (SECS)
VOLTAGE (V)
0
100
200
300
400
500
600
700
800
900
1000
1100
1200
1300
1400
1500
1600
1700
1800
1900
2000
2100
2200
2300
2400
1
2
3
4
5
6
7
8
9
10
11
12

Discharging a capacitor (cont)

TIME (secs)	VOLTAGE (V)
190	8.71
240	8.09
300	7.41
360	6.8
420	6.23
480	5.74
540	5.25
600	4.83
660	4.45
720	4.07
780	3.75
840	3.44
900	3.16
960	2.91
1020	2.67
1080	2.46
1140	2.26
1200	2.08
1260	1.92
1320	1.77
1380	1.63
1440	1.5
1500	1.38
1560	1.26
1620	1.18
1680	1.09
1740	1.00
1800	0.93

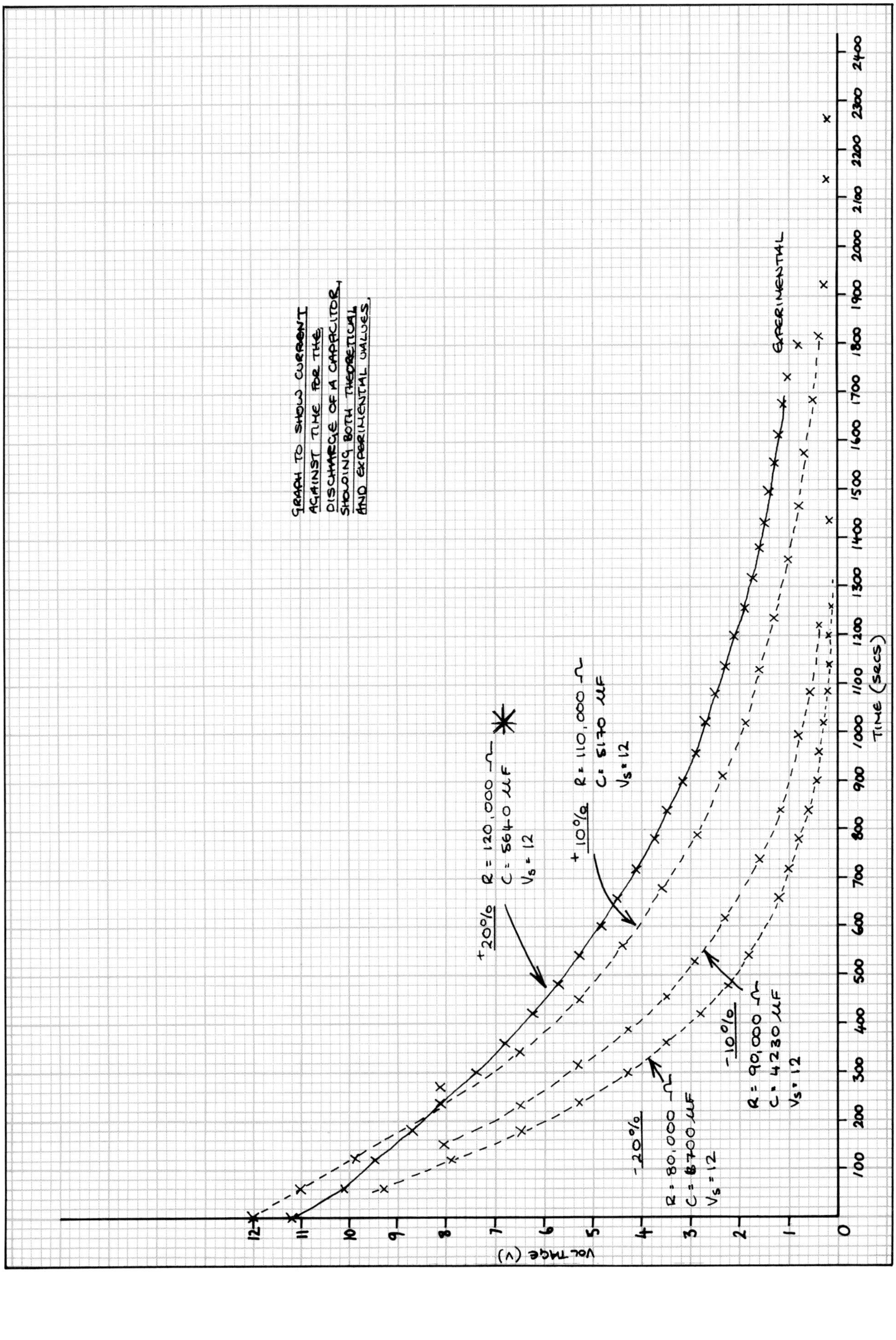
GRAPH TO SHOW CURRENT AGAINST TIME FOR THE DISCHARGE OF A CAPACITOR, SHOWING BOTH THEORETICAL AND EXPERIMENTAL VALUES.
+20% R = 120,000 Ω C = 5640 μF Vs = 12
+10% R = 110,000 Ω C = 5170 μF Vs = 12
-10% R = 90,000 Ω C = 4230 μF Vs = 12
-20% R = 80,000 Ω C = 3700 μF Vs = 12
EXPERIMENTAL
TIME (secs)
VOLTAGE (V)

Discussion

It would seem that the accuracy of a capacitor is not great, however as both curves are out from acceptable values by ±20% it is possible to deduce that the inaccuracies are due to the tolerance of the components.

The method of iteration gives graphs which are similar to experimental graphs, and ✱ thus the method works, and the relationship below gives exact values not differing greatly from experimental ones. $V = V_s(1 - e^{-t/RC})$ is experimentally plausible. Iteration and experimental curves follow the same path as those for which the equation was used. The time taken for the current to fall to 0.37 of its initial value on the 'discharge' curve has a relationship with RC.

At t = 720 secs the current is 0.37 of its initial value and RC = 6.77.

In the equation shown above the relationship between t and RC is that at the point where the current is 0.37 of its initial value t is equal to RC.

EXPERIMENTAL TECHNIQUES

1. MEASUREMENT OF LENGTH AND MASS

You have probably used the vernier slide gauge (often called just a vernier, or vernier calipers) and the micrometer before, as well as a top-pan balance; the following should remind you.

1. Vernier calipers

Vernier calipers (figure 64) are used for measuring the inside and outside diameters of pipes and distances up to about 10 cm. Always make sure that the object is square in the jaws.

Figure 64 Vernier callipers have an accuracy to 0.1 mm, but a limited accuracy at distances under 1 cm.

The pointer gives the whole number of millimetres. Then look along the vernier scale and find the line which is most closely aligned with a line on the main scale. If the line were the sixth from the pointer then the value would be 0.6 mm. Note that ten divisions on the sliding vernier scale cover only nine divisions on the main scale.

Just to remind you about reading vernier scales, what are the readings shown in figure 65?

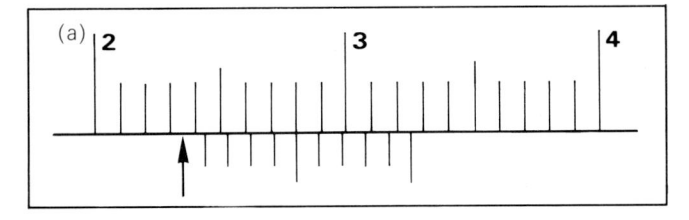

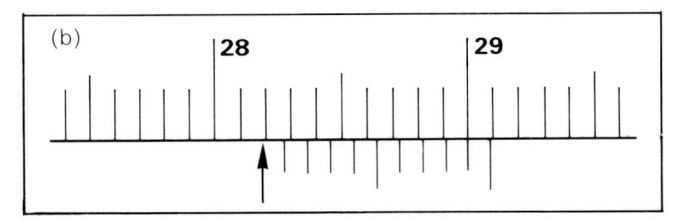

Figure 65

2. Micrometer

The micrometer (figure 66) is the most accurate gauge you will use. It has a range of 0–2.5 cm, and is used for outside measurements only. It has an accuracy of 0.01 mm.

The knob, X, is used to rotate the barrel fowards. Some barrels start to 'click' when there is enough pressure on the object being measured; others have a slipping clutch at a certain pressure. Each complete turn of the barrel is 0.5 mm, *not* 1 mm, but check this for yourself.

EXPERIMENTAL TECHNIQUES

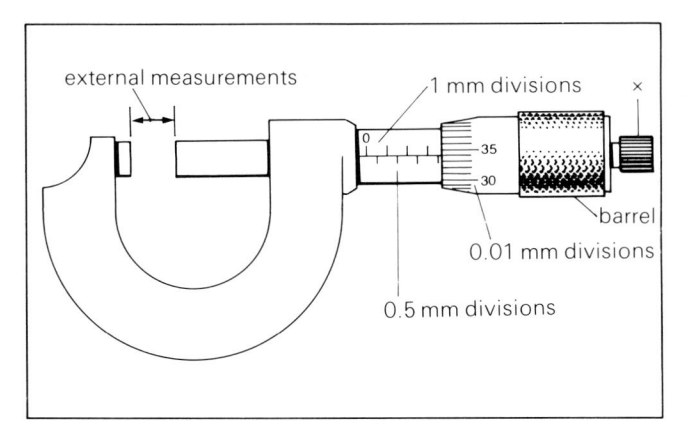

Figure 66 Micrometer showing a reading of $3 + 0.5 + 0.34 = 3.84$ mm.

3. Spherometer

The spherometer (figure 67) is used to find the radius of curvature of spherical surfaces and heights above or below flat surfaces.

Use the spherometer as follows.

1. Check the zero by using an optically flat surface, e.g. a glass block, and make corrections to the readings if it is not zero.
2. Measure the distance (x) from each of the radial points to the moving central point.
3. The spherometer will always be stable on three legs. To take a measurement, move the centre leg until the spherometer *just* rocks, and then move it back slightly. The movement can be recorded by reading the scale and correcting for any zero error. The accuracy is 0.01 mm, but less in practice because of the subjective judgement of when it 'just' stops rocking.

Working out a radius of curvature

Looking at figure 68:

$AC = CD = r =$ radius of curvature

AB is known $= h$
BD is known $= x$

$$AC = AB + BC$$
$$r = h + BC$$
$$BC = r - h$$

For $\triangle BDC$ by Pythagoras

$$BC^2 + BD^2 = CD^2$$
$$(r - h)^2 + x^2 = r^2$$
$$r^2 - 2hr + h^2 + x^2 = r^2$$
$$r = \frac{h^2 + x^2}{2h}$$

$$\boxed{\text{radius} = \frac{h^2 + x^2}{2h}}$$

If $h \ll x$, will a calculator be accurate enough with six significant figures or should you do it by long division? If $h \ll x$, then $r = \dfrac{x^2}{2h}$.

General points

1. *Always* move the centre leg *down* on to the surface until it 'just' rocks. Then readjust until it stops rocking.
2. *Always* take several readings in different places and then work out a mean value.

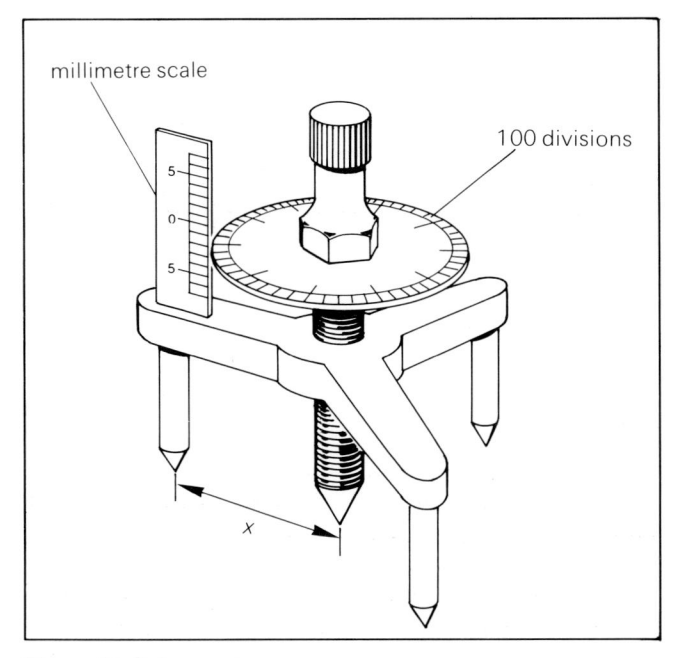

Figure 67 Spherometer

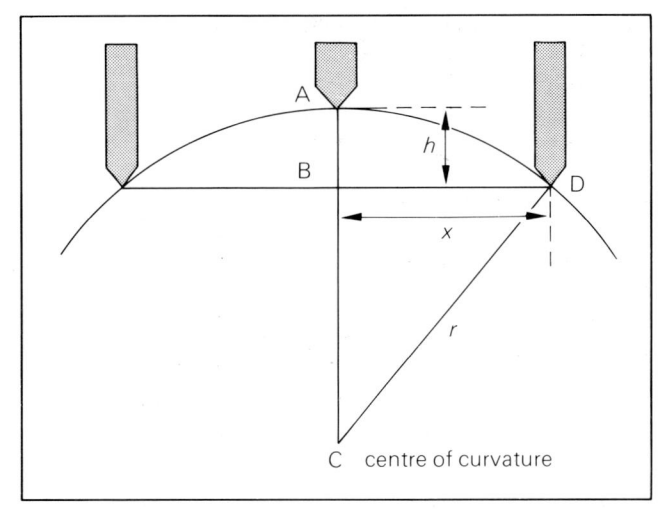

Figure 68 Working out a radius of curvature using a spherometer.

4. Balances—mass and force

Measuring mass

Most balances for measuring mass use one of three principles of operation:

1. Balancing the mass to be measured against a set of known accurate masses. This is a true measurement of mass and is used in many top-pan balances. Care must be taken when moving these balances around, and the masses should be 'locked' before doing so.
2. By using the force of gravity on the mass to extend a spring, which moves a pointer on a scale. This actually measures force, but since the earth's gravitational field strength is known and $F = mg$, then mass is proportional to force and so the balance can be calibrated in grams or kilograms.
3. By using the force of gravity on the mass to deform a substance slightly and then to use a strain gauge to produce a change of electrical current or resistance proportional to the force. Most electronic digital balances are of this type and have the advantage that the scale pan moves very little.

Many balances are now designed so that they can be connected to a computer for data logging. Make yourself familiar with the types of balance available to you.

Measuring force

Spring balance or newton meter
You have probably used one of these many times before. Remember three points:

1. Always check the zero. There is usually a ring or screw either to adjust the mark on the scale or the vertical position of the upper end of the spring.
2. Always use this balance in a vertical position.
3. If you use it to measure the pull of an object, e.g. a rope, then the weight of the *balance* itself must be added to the reading, because the weight of the balance will be producing a force as well.

The sensitivity of a spring balance is limited by the friction between the barrel and the sliding part. The minimum change of force is usually about 1 per cent of the full scale reading.

Top-pan balance
The weight of an object due to gravity is proportional to the mass, and weight is a force, so a top-pan balance can be used to 'measure' force if the mass reading is multiplied by the earth's gravitational field constant g, usually taken as 9.81 N kg^{-1}. With an electronic balance this method can be used to measure force in situations where little or no movement occurs, e.g. a bar expanding as the temperature rises, or the effects of electrical and magnetic forces.

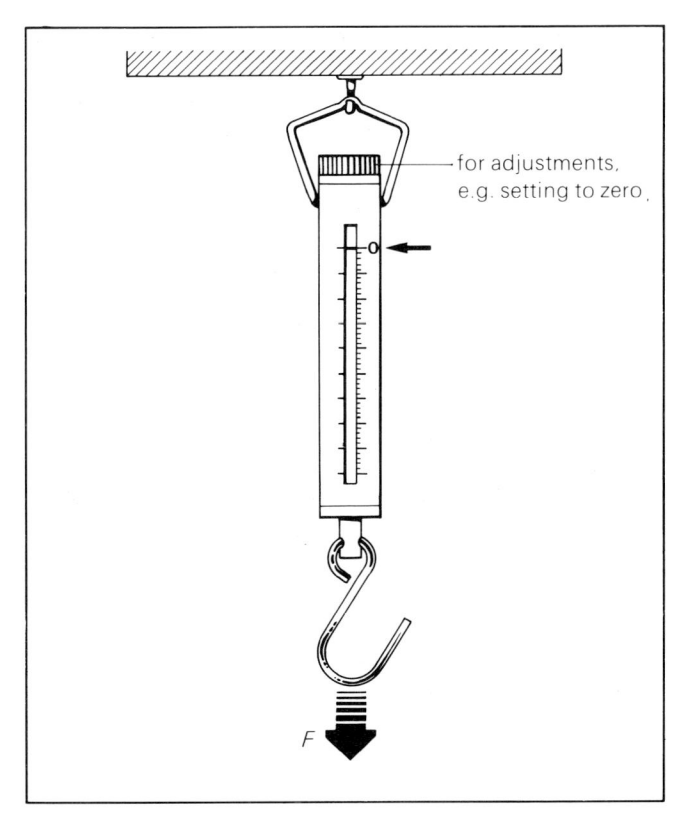

Figure 69 Spring balance

5. A series of short experiments

A. *Use the vernier calipers, micrometer and balance* to find the density of a glass microscope slide. Remember to take several evenly spaced readings (see figure 70a) and work out a mean average.

Which is the more accurate instrument for measuring the thickness? Will your balance weigh just *one* microscope slide accurately?

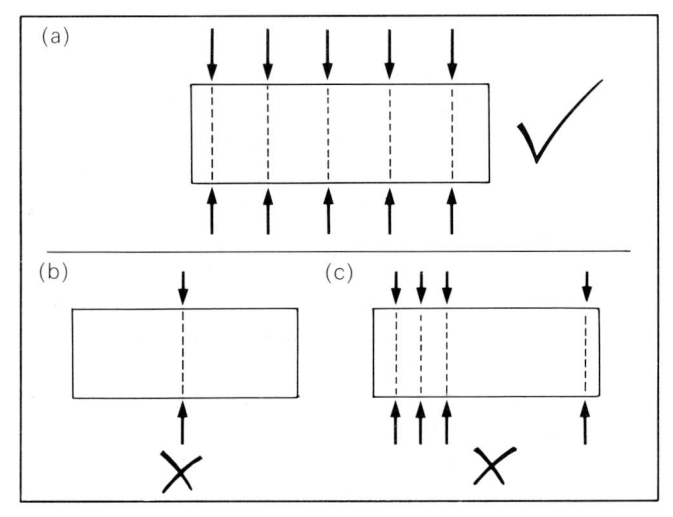

Figure 70 The arrows show the positions at which width measurements of a slide might be taken.

B. *Use the micrometer and balance* to measure the diameters and masses of each of the ball bearings given you. Plot a graph of mass against r^3 and use the gradient to find the *density* of the material from which the ball bearings are made.

$$\text{volume} = \tfrac{4}{3}\pi r^3$$
$$\text{density} = \frac{\text{mass}}{\text{volume}}$$

Do your results show that all the ball bearings are made from the same material?

C. *Use the spherometer* to find the radius of curvature of a convex lens and a concave mirror.

D. *Use the appropriate instruments and methods* to investigate the materials you have been given, as follows:
   (a) find the average diameter of the piece of wire;
   (b) find the internal diameter of the piece of pipe and decide if it is circular or not;
   (c) decide if $\tfrac{1}{2}$p, 1p and 2p coins are made from the same material;
   (d) find the average thickness, internal and external diameters and mass of washers from the batch given you;
   (e) find the density of aluminium from the pieces of aluminium foil;
   (f) measure the diameter of a stud on a Lego(TM) block.
Explain the reasons for your choice of instruments in each case.

E. *Use an electronic balance* to investigate how the force of expansion produced by a metal bar when it is heated changes with temperature (figure 71).

   1. Record the initial zero reading on the balance, and record the initial temperature; we assume that the bar has the same temperature all along its length.
   2. Switch on the heater until the temperature has risen by about 10 K and then switch it off. Wait until the temperature stops rising (the temperature can rise by a few degrees because of the heat contained in the coil itself being conducted to the bar) and then record the reading on the balance.
   3. Repeat, increasing the temperature by about 10 K each time, until either the maximum range of the thermometer is reached or the heater is switched on continuously.
   4. Calculate the force produced at each temperature by subtracting the initial balance reading from the recorded readings for each temperature. Plot a graph of balance reading against temperature and find a value for the *force* per degree K from the gradient.

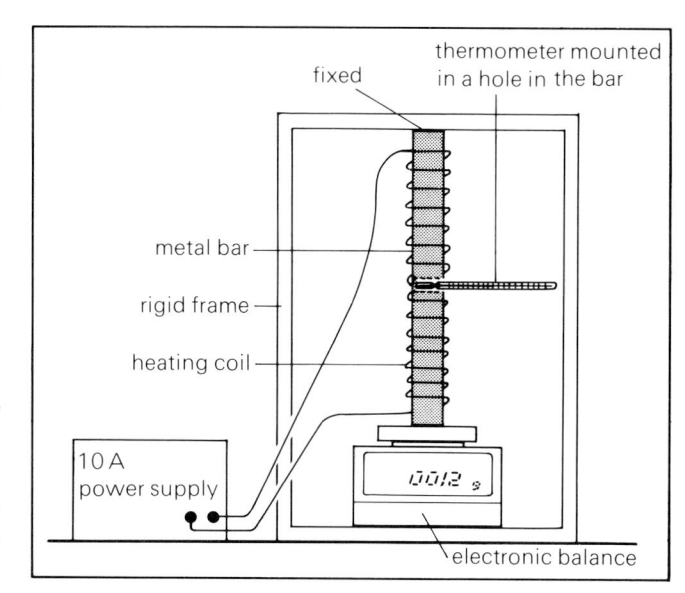

Figure 71 Apparatus for measuring the force of expansion produced by a heated metal bar.

6. Measuring the permeability of air

Outline

The ampère is defined as follows: if 1 A is flowing in two infinitely long parallel wires of negligible cross-section placed 1 m apart in a vacuum, then the force between the wires will be 2×10^{-7} N m^{-1}.

The magnetic flux density (B) due to an infinitely long straight wire, at a distance x from the wire, is:

$$B = \frac{\mu I}{2\pi x}$$

where μ is the permeability of the medium round the wire and I is the current flowing through it.

The force on the other wire is given by:

$$F = BIl$$

where l is the length of the wire.
Therefore the force is

$$F = \frac{\mu I^2 l}{2\pi x}$$

However, real wires are not infinitely long, but if the wires are longer than 100 times their distance apart, the deviation is less than one per cent, mainly due to end effects.

The value of μ for air is very nearly the same as the value for a vacuum μ_0, which is $4\pi \times 10^{-7}$ H m^{-1}. So, for wires 1 m long, approximately 2 cm apart and with a current of 10 A, the force is approximately:

$$F = \frac{4\pi \times 10^{-7} \times 10^2 \times 1}{2\pi \times 2 \times 10^{-2}} \sim 10^{-3} \text{ N}$$

This can be measured using a top-pan balance.

Equipment

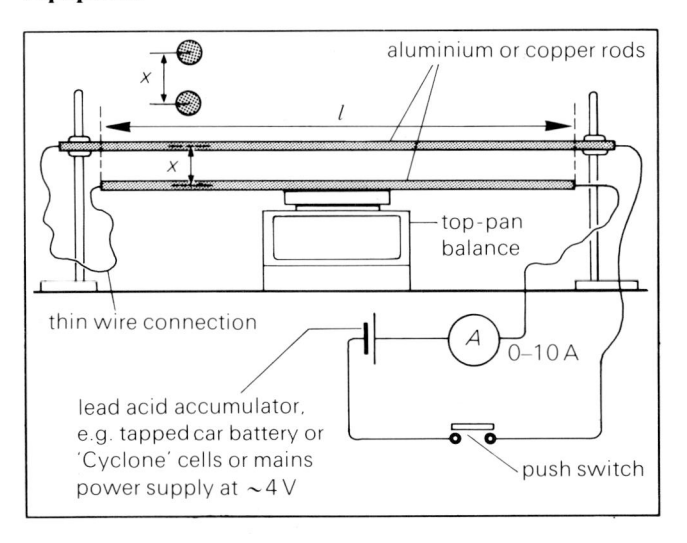

Figure 72 Apparatus for measuring the permeability of air.

Experimental details

Large currents flow in this experiment, and the circuit should only be switched on long enough to take a reading from the balance. Set the apparatus up as in figure 72, with the rods as close together as possible. The upper rod is in a fixed position, while the lower rod rests on the balance. Measure the separation x, length of overlap l and reading on the balance, M_1. Switch on and record the new reading on the balance, M_2. Convert $(M_2 - M_1)$ into kilograms.

The force $= (M_2 - M_1) \times 9.81$ N. Work out μ from:

$$F = \frac{\mu I^2 l}{2\pi x}$$

The value of μ is the permeability of the air. The permeability of a vacuum μ_0 is very nearly the same, with a value of $4\pi \times 10^{-7}$ H m^{-1}.

2. USING THE TRAVELLING MICROSCOPE

Outline

This experiment gives you practice in using the travelling microscope (figure 73). Its function is not primarily to magnify but to provide a method of measuring small distances accurately. The microscope is moved by a screw thread and, however accurately machined it is, there is always some slack in the thread, so the screw can often be moved back slightly without moving the microscope.

The main scale is fixed to the body of the instrument and divided into 1 mm divisions. The movable carriage carrying the microscope has a vernier and enables measurements to be made to 0.01 mm.

Cross-wires (figure 74) can be used to line up on an edge. These can be brought into focus for your eye by adjusting the position of the eyepiece.

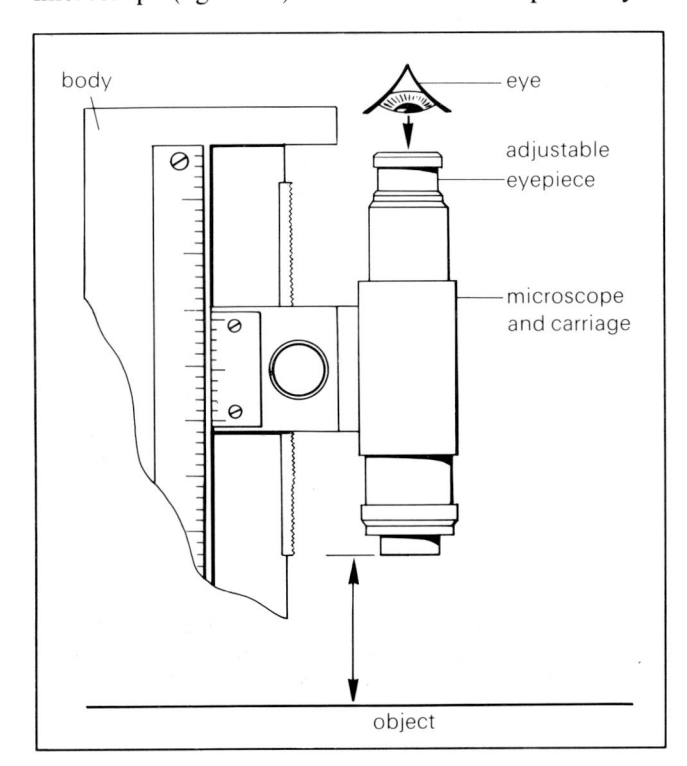

Figure 73 Travelling microscope

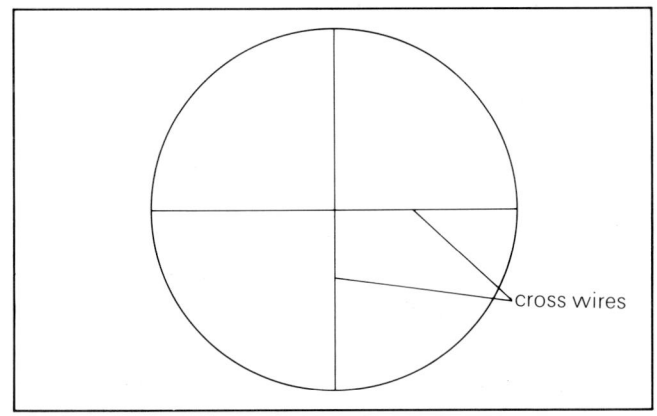

Figure 74 What you see when looking through the eyepiece.

EXPERIMENTAL TECHNIQUES

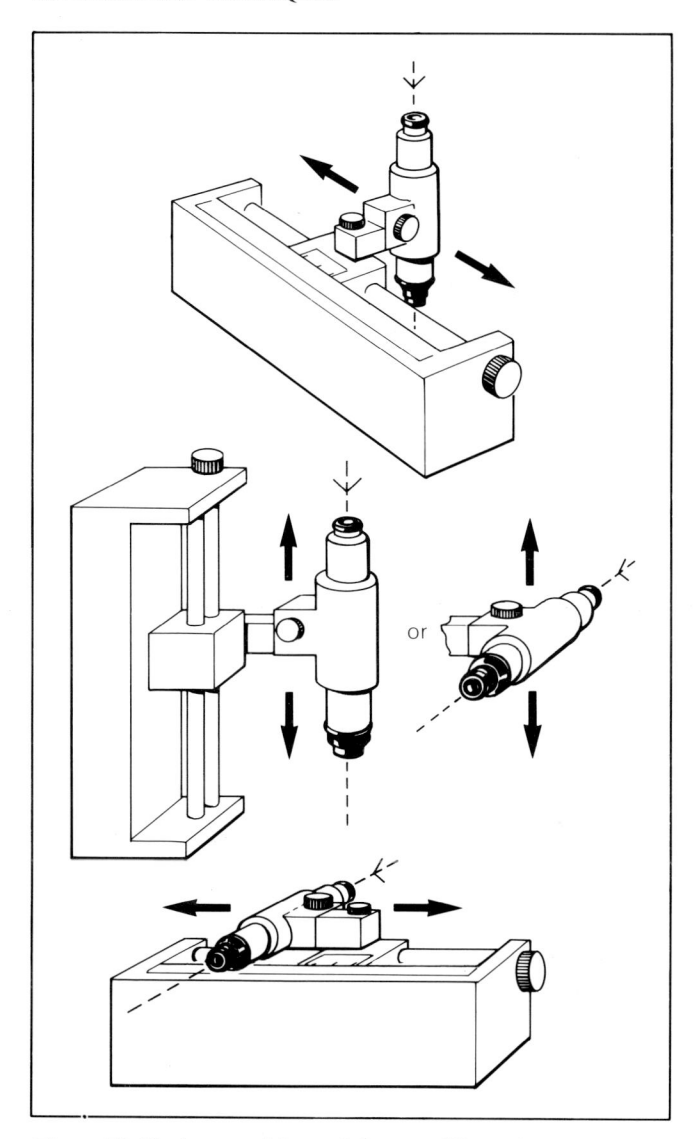

Figure 75 Various positions of the travelling microscope.

The object viewed must always be a *fixed* distance from the objective lens. The position of the microscope can usually be adjusted until the object gives a sharp image.

The microscope can usually be turned so that it can be tracked horizontally or vertically (see figure 75).

Experimental details

Use the travelling microscope to investigate the materials you have been supplied with, as follows.

A. Find the pitch of the thread of the screw (see figure 76). Remember that error can be reduced by measuring the total distance for a number of threads and dividing to find the length of one pitch.

B. Measure the spacing of the lines on the course diffraction grating (see figure 77). Find the number of lines per centimetre.

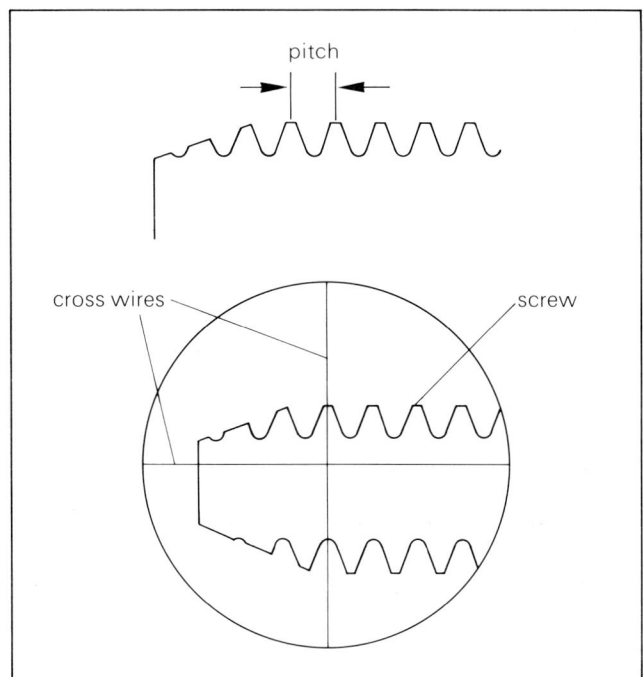

Figure 76 Screw as seen through the microscope.

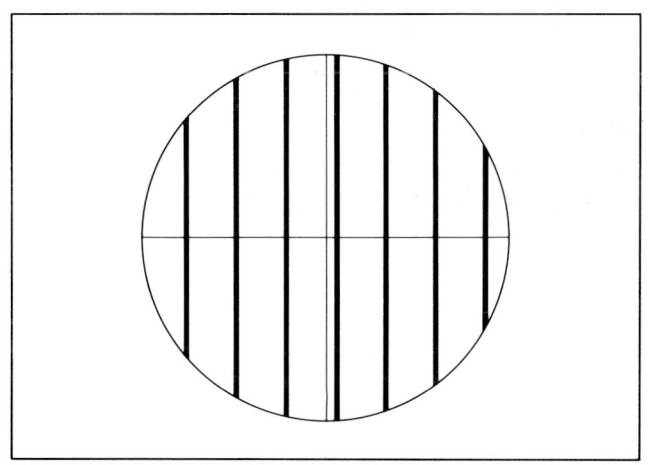

Figure 77 Diffraction grating as seen through the microscope.

C. Not everything has sharp edges, and a central position may be easier to judge than an edge. Measure the distances between the first six minima or maxima of the interference pattern (see figure 78). Is it easier to judge a minimum or a maximum?

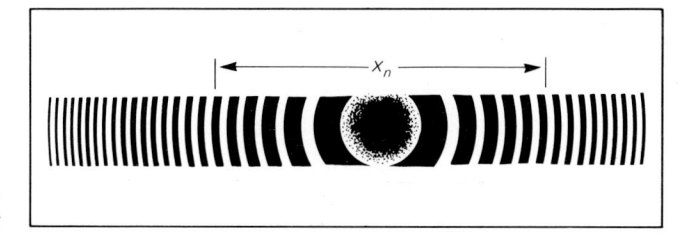

Figure 78 Interference pattern

Work out the wavelength of the light from the equation $n\lambda = 725 \times 10^{-6} x_n$ for three evenly spaced values of x_n; x_n is the distance between the nth maximum on each side. Do you think this equation is correct?

You will have to find the distance of each maximum from the central maximum, which is so diffuse that no accurate central point can be located. How can this be done? Remember that the pattern is symmetrical.

D. Measure the thickness of one of the 'tracks' or wires on the microchip circuit you are given. Try and draw an accurate diagram of part of the circuit.

E. Find the refractive index of a liquid by measuring the real depth and apparent depth (see figure 79). When an image is viewed normally:

the refractive index $n = \dfrac{\text{real depth}}{\text{apparent depth}}$

Set up the travelling microscope to view vertically and to *move* vertically.
1. Use a mark on the bottom of the beaker as an object (inside or outside?). Focus the microscope on the mark and record the reading.
2. Put the liquid in (does it matter to what depth?). The microscope will have to be moved up to see the mark in focus again. Record this reading.

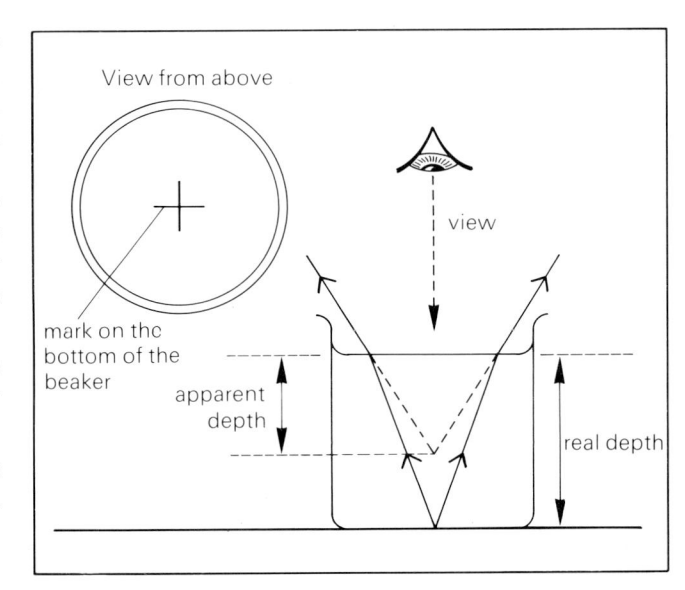

Figure 79 Distorted diagram to show the principle of the experiment.

3. Put some powder on top of the liquid; it will be supported by surface tension and the microscope can be moved to get a reading for the top of the liquid.
4. From these three readings work out the real depth, apparent depth and then the refractive index.

3. MEASURING TIMES

1. USING A STOPWATCH

There is a time delay of about 0.2 seconds between visual signals being detected by the eye, the brain making a decision and then the muscles moving into action. In theory, we should expect similar delays in starting and stopping a watch, but an overall error of about 0.1 seconds is to be expected. Stopping the watch too early through anticipation must be avoided. To make it easier for the eye and brain to decide when timing is to start and stop, a reference mark, sometimes called a fiducial mark, is used.

Example: The periodic time of a pendulum

Release the pendulum from A (see figure 80 on p. 45) and time one period several separate times, first starting and stopping as the pendulum passes through the centre and then as it passes through the maximum displacement B.

Questions
1. Which method gives the most consistent results?
2. Is there any difference in consistency between the period of a long pendulum and a short one?
3. Which method gives a time most closely agreeing with the calculated period:

$$T = 2\pi \sqrt{\dfrac{l}{g}}$$

4. How could you redesign the method of timing to reduce the starting and stopping errors?
5. Is it better to start and stop when the object is moving quickly or slowly?
6. Does the amplitude of the swing have any effect on the period measured?

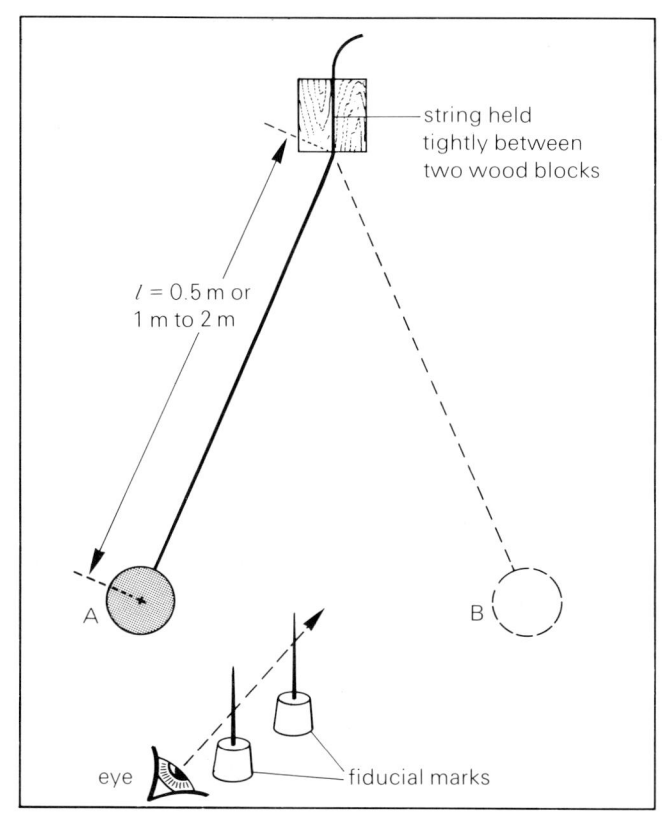

EXPERIMENTAL TECHNIQUES

Figure 80 Measuring the periodic time of a pendulum. Fiducial marks, two pins placed a distance apart so the eye can line up on them and always view the apparatus from the same angle, are used.

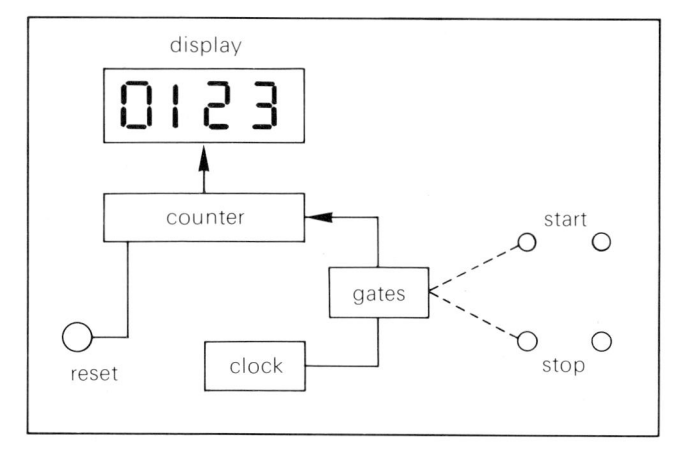

Figure 81 Digital counter

2. ELECTRONIC TIMERS

Electronic timers use a digital counter which can be started and stopped by making electrical connections to the unit. The accuracy depends on how many pulses per second are produced by the internal 'clock. One thousand counts per second would give an accuracy to ± 0.001 s and 100 counts per second to ± 0.01 s. The 'start' and 'stop' sockets control the circuitry which allows the clock pulses to pass through to the counter.

Three options are usually available, as shown in figures 82–84. Try each method out and produce solutions to the questions.

Questions

1. How would you arrange a circuit so that timing starts when a switch is closed and stops when a second switch is opened?
2. How would you arrange a circuit so that timing occurs when a piece of card breaks the light beam?
3. Find the furthest distance away from the l.d.r. that the light source you are using can be and still start/stop the timing.
4. How can the arrangement in figure 85 be used to start and stop the timing?
5. Design a suitable arrangement to measure the time taken for a trolley to roll a given distance down a slope.

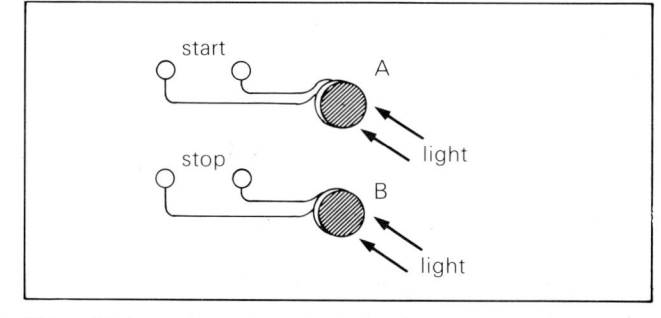

Figure 85

1. Make to start/break to stop

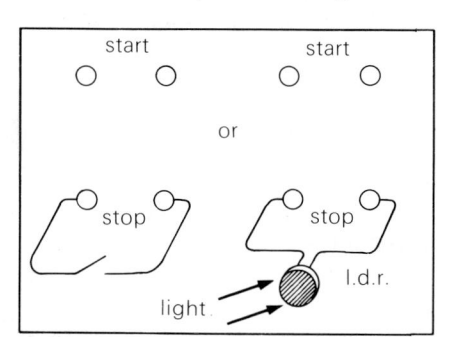

2. Break to start/make to stop

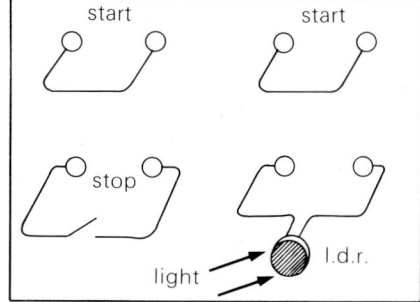

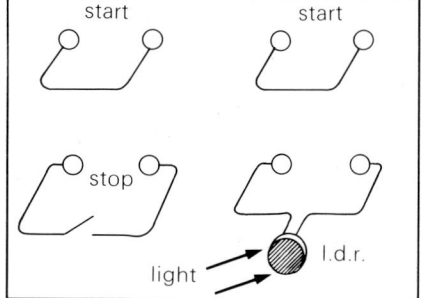

3. Pulse to start/pulse to stop

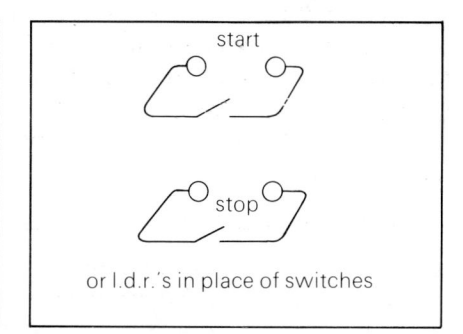

Figure 82

Figure 83

Figure 84

3. USING MICROPROCESSOR BASED METHODS

1. A multipurpose unit such as the VELA (VErsatile Laboratory Aid)

This has 16 built in programs, one of which (05) is an event timer. An 'event' is a change on an input, equivalent to the make to start/break to stop inputs on an electronic timer. Four different types of input 'change' can be selected. Read the instructions in section 2.5.1 of the booklet with the VELA and find out how to use the program to record times as in questions 1 to 4 above. Alternatively use it to measure the periodic time of a pendulum by making the pendulum bob break a light beam as it passes through its central position.

2. Using a computer

It is possible to use a computer to make a flexible timer if you have an 'interface unit' and suitable software (the program). Options are often available to store a sequence of times, to record timings from several 'channels' concurrently and to set the inputs so that timing starts for a 'make' or a 'break'. The program 'TIMER' (package PHYS2 option 7) for a BBC computer could be used with an interface connected to the user port of the computer. If you have the equipment available try it out and get used to using it by producing solutions to questions 1 to 5 (p. 45), as before.

Here is a short program which you could use to show the principle of a simple make to start/break to stop timer. It uses the analogue input to the BBC computer (figure 86a) but could be used with one of the various commercially available units (figure 86b) connected to the user port.

```
10 L=30000
15 PRINT " "
20 PRINT "PRESS SPACEBAR TO 'START"
30 IF INKEY$(0)<>" " THEN 30
40 PRINT "WAITING":F=0
50 A=ADVAL(1)
60 IF A<L AND F=0 THEN PRINT "TIMING":F=1:TIME=0
70 A=ADVAL(1)
80 IF A>L AND F=1 THEN PRINT TIME/100;" S":GOTO 15
90 GOTO 50
```

The number produced by the analogue input is between 0 and 65535. With no connection between A and B the number is large and when a connection is made it is small. A number 'halfway' is chosen, L. Lines 60 and 80 compare L with the input value, A, to decide if the contact has been 'made' or 'broken'. If you wanted to make the circuit time for other conditions, e.g. break to start/make to stop, then it is the conditions in these lines which would need to be altered.

If the *timer* box is used, then some lines need to be altered and an extra line added, as shown below.

```
5 ?65122=0

50 IF (?65120 AND 1)=1 THEN A=0 ELSE A=65000

70 IF (?65120 AND 1)=1 THEN A=0 ELSE A=65000
```

Try the program out and then alter it for the following:

(a) To reset the *time* to 0 after each timing;
(b) Break to start/make to stop;
(c) Pulse make to start/pulse make to stop;
(d) Pulse break to start/pulse break to stop;
(e) To time when a card breaks a light beam.

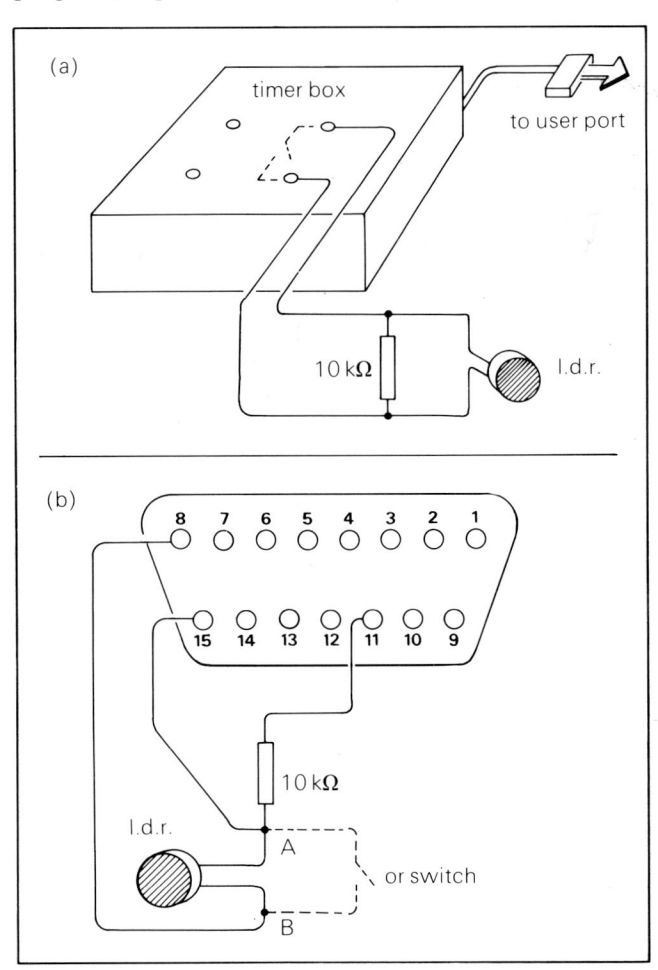

Figure 86 Timing interfaces; the timer box is available from EARO, Cambridge.

4. TIMING OSCILLATIONS

The use of a fiducial mark and the timing of several oscillations (instead of just one), thus reducing errors in starting and stopping the stopwatch, are common to all timing experiments. Here is a series of experiments which apply these techniques. Remember to start and stop timing when the object is moving at its fastest speed through its central position.

1. SPRING

Outline

According to Hooke's law, the extension of a spring (x) is directly proportional to the load (F). Therefore $F = kx$ where k is the elastic constant.

The periodic time for a spring which oscillates with simple harmonic motion is

$$T = 2\pi \sqrt{\frac{M+m}{k}}$$

where M is the mass on the spring and m is a term which is related to the mass of the spring.

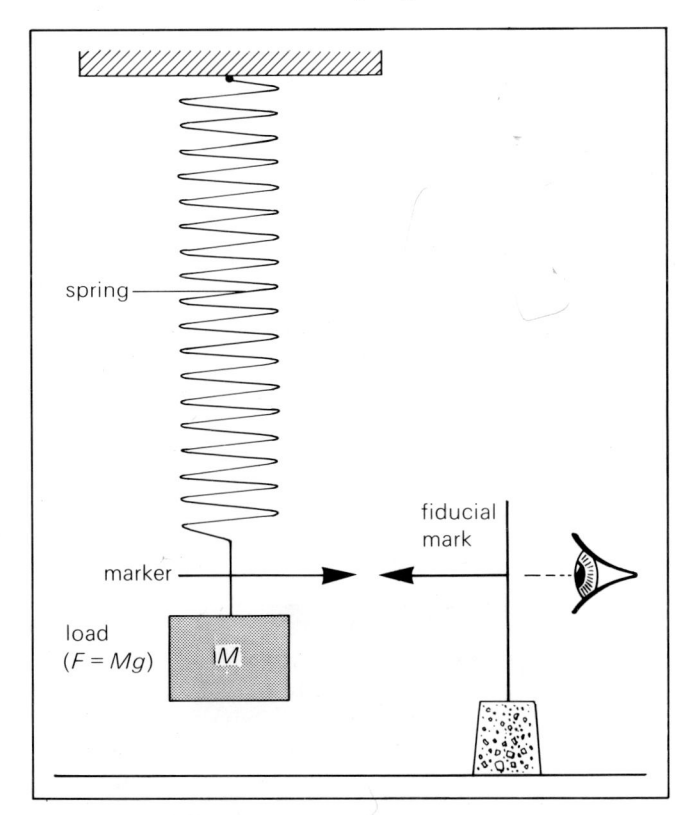

Figure 87 Equipment

Thus,

$$T^2 = 4\pi^2 \frac{(M+m)}{k}$$

rearranging gives

$$M = \frac{T^2 k}{4\pi^2} - m$$

Comparing with the equation for a straight-line graph $y = mx + c$, it follows that a graph of M as ordinate and T^2 as abscissa would have a gradient of $\frac{k}{4\pi^2}$ and a negative intercept on the M axis (i.e. m). (Usually the independent variable is plotted as abscissa, but here it is not.) Once k is known and a measurement of the extension of the spring is made, the gravitational force constant g (numerically equal to the free-fall acceleration under gravity) can be found: $Mg = kx$.

Experimental details

Using the apparatus shown in figure 87, measure the periodic times for as wide a range of values of M as is possible without exceeding the elastic limit of the spring. Remember that during the oscillation the mass will move to a lower position than the equilibrium position. Also, measure the extension produced by a mass in the middle of the range used.

From the results
(a) Plot a graph of M against T^2.
(b) Work out k and m from the graph.
(c) Estimate the error in k and m by drawing lines of maximum and minimum gradient.
(d) Work out a value for g and remember to give an error for this as well. How does your value compare with the accepted result?

2. COMPOUND PENDULUM

Outline

The compound pendulum is a bar whose centre of gravity is not at the end as in a simple pendulum. It will be in the middle if the bar is uniform. This experiment investigates any relationship between the periodic time and the distance of the centre of gravity from the pivot.

Experimental details

Using the apparatus shown in figure 88, measure the periodic times with the pivot in each hole and record the distance l between the centre of gravity and the pivot.

Results

Time for n oscillations/s	Periodic time/s	l/cm

From the results

Try to plot a straight-line graph. For a simple pendulum

$$T = 2\pi\sqrt{\frac{l}{g}}$$

so plotting T^2 against l would be your first choice. If you succeed, repeat the experiment for a second bar of the same length but a different mass and compare the results. Do the gradients and intercepts have any physical significance (i.e. connection with the mass)?

3. SWINGING CHAIN

Outline and experimental details

A friend suggests that there is a connection between the length and mass of a piece of chain and its periodic time, and that this is:

$$\text{periodic time} = 4 \times \text{mass} \times \sqrt{\text{length}}$$

You are sceptical, but want to test if the idea is correct or not. For as many pieces of chain as are available, measure the periodic times for a variety of lengths (see figure 89). Work out the periodic times from the equation. If the results agree with the theory to within 20 per cent, you can deduce that she is correct. Is she?

4. CLAMPED BEAM

Outline

The period of oscillation of a loaded beam probably depends on the mass hung on the end, the length oscillating, and the cross-sectional area, because a thicker and wider beam is stiffer.

Simple experiments show:

(a) a stiffer beam has a longer period;
(b) a longer beam has a longer period;
(c) a larger mass gives a longer period.

An equation which would satisfy these conditions might be:

$$T = \text{constant} \times A^\alpha \times M^\beta \times l^\gamma$$

This experiment attempts to find values for the powers α, β and γ.

Experimental details

Use the equipment shown in figure 90.

A. Keeping A and l constant, find the periodic times for a range of values of M. Plot a graph of T^2 against M, because this seems to be the form in an oscillating spring. If this is not a straight line, plot a graph of $\log_e T$ against $\log_e M$ and find the power from the gradient.

B. Keeping A and M constant, find the periodic times for a range of oscillating lengths. Plot a graph of T^2 against l, because this is the form in a pendulum and is as good a starting point as any. If this is not a straight line, either plot a graph of $\log_e T$ against $\log_e l$ and find the power from the gradient, or choose a power, calculate values and replot the graph.

You may find the computer program 'PROCESS' useful here (package PHYS2 option 6). This enables you to select various powers and to plot graphs to try and find a straight line.

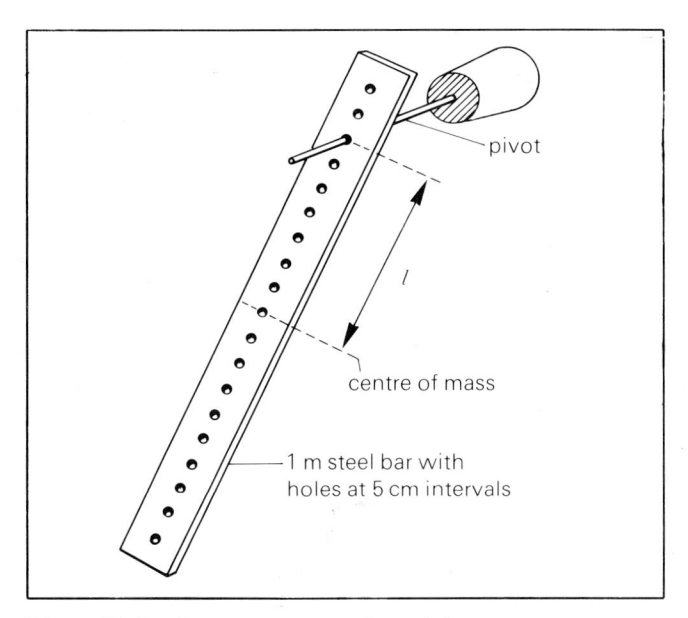

Figure 88 Equipment, compound pendulum

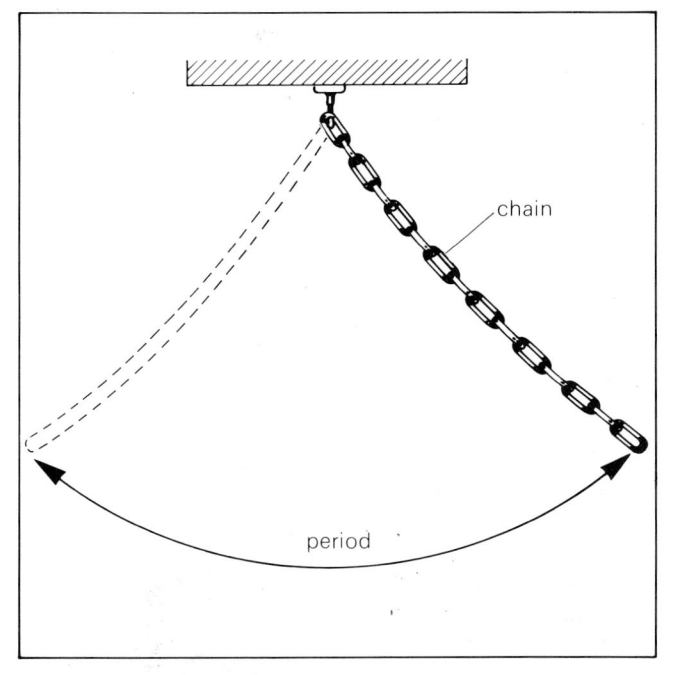

Figure 89

EXPERIMENTAL TECHNIQUES   49

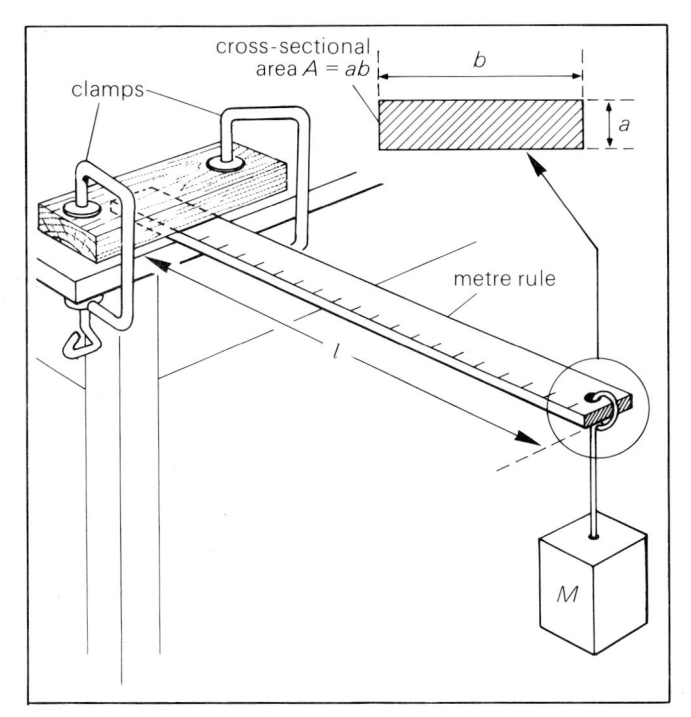

Figure 90 Equipment, clamped beam

5. Y-SHAPED PENDULUM

Experimental details

Using the apparatus shown in figure 91, measure the period time (T) for small oscillations (what does that mean?), in a line at right angles to the ruler, over as wide a range of angles θ as the apparatus will allow. Plot a graph of T against θ.

From the graph
Extrapolate to find the angle which gives a time of 0.2 s.

6. SUSPENDED BEAM

Outline

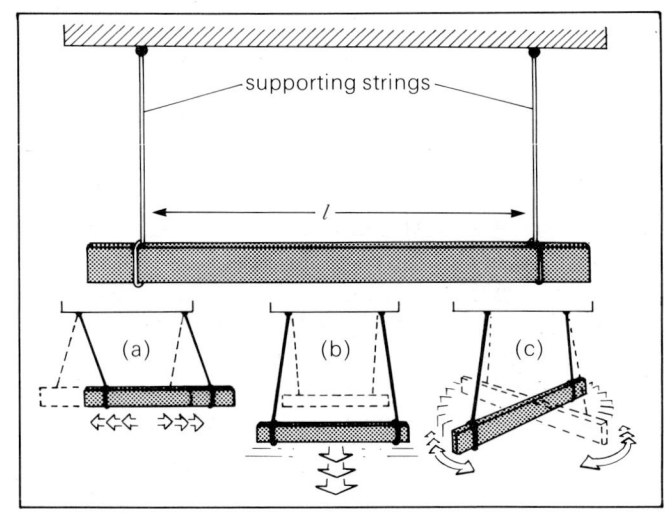

Figure 92

The suspended beam can oscillate in three different modes (as shown in figure 92):

(a) bodily in the plane of the supporting strings;
(b) bodily perpendicular to the plane of the strings;
(c) with torsional oscillations about its mid-point.

Experimental details

For each of the three modes of vibration, suspend the beam symmetrically and measure the periodic times for at least five values of l over as wide a range of l as possible.

Results

Separation l/cm	Time/s	No. of oscillations	Periodic time/s

What conclusions can you make about the effect the value of l has on the periodic time?

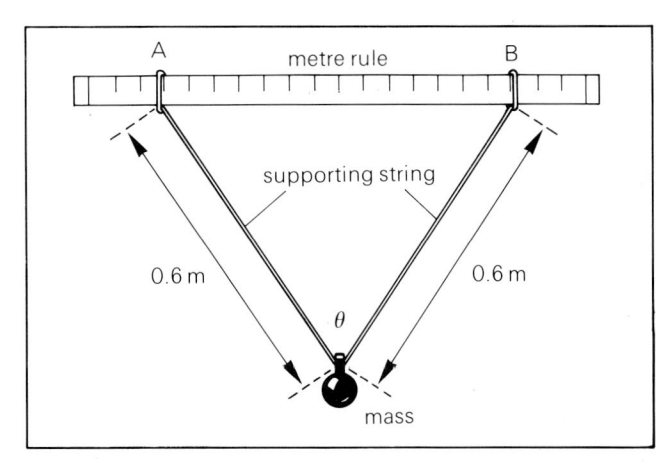

Figure 91 Equipment, Y-shaped pendulum

7. BEAM ON A CURVED SURFACE

Equipment

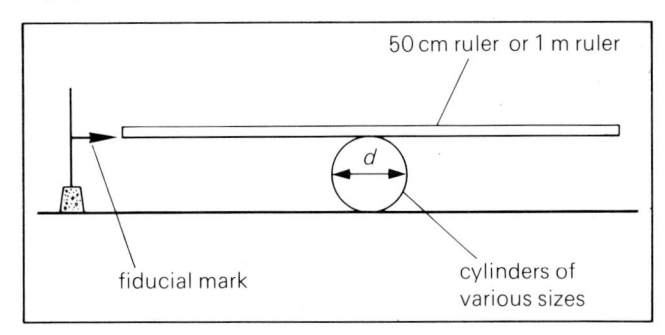

Figure 93 Equipment; the cylinders have a variety of diameters larger than about 4 cm, labelled A, B, C, D, E, etc.

Experimental details

Measure the diameter of each cylinder. Find the periodic time for small oscillations of each ruler on each cylinder. If the amplitude is too large, the ruler will slide on the cylinder. Measure the length (l) and thickness (b) of each rule. Plot a graph of T^2 against $\dfrac{l^2}{d-b}$. Find the gradient.

Results

Periodic time/s	Cylinder				
	A	B	C	D	E
50 cm rule					
100 cm rule					

Diameter of cylinders/cm				
A	B	C	D	E

Take at least three values for each cylinder and work out an average.

Explain how you used a fiducial mark and show its position on the diagram.

8. COUPLED OSCILLATORS

Outline and experimental details

The mathematical theory for coupled oscillators is quite complex, and so this experiment asks you to describe qualitatively the motions of the oscillators and to draw sketch graphs of how the displacement of points X and Y varies with time.

Looking at figures 94 and 95, is there any difference in the motions produced when the strings are (a) of nearly equal length, (b) of widely different lengths, and (c) the same length?

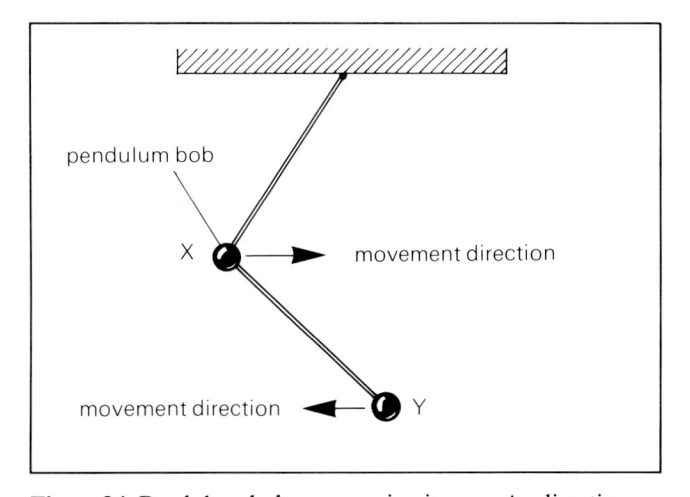

Figure 94 Pendulum bobs are moving in *opposite* directions.

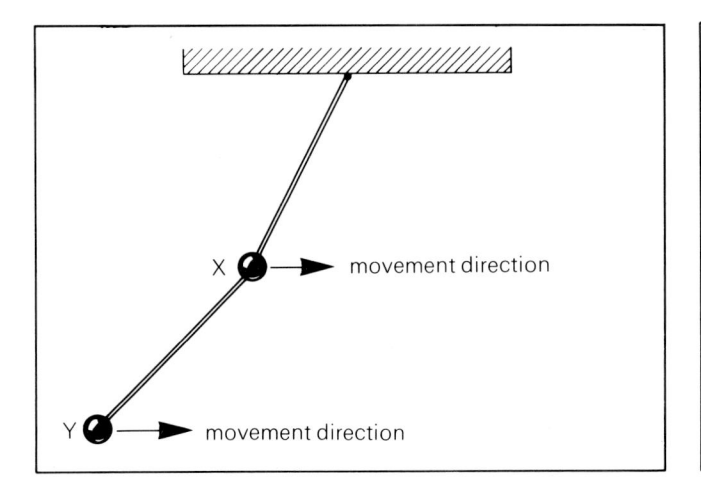

Figure 95 Pendulum bobs are moving in the *same* direction.

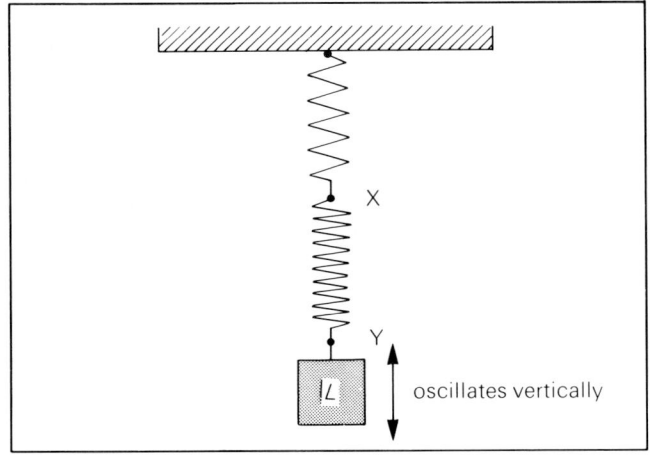

Figure 96 Two springs of equal length but with the lower spring stiffer in construction.

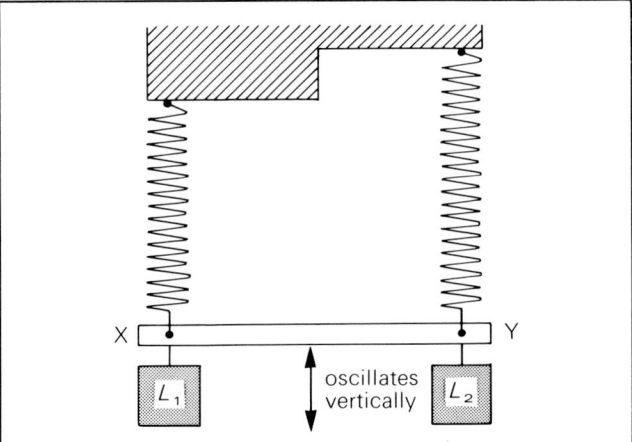

Figure 97 Two springs of similar construction, but different lengths, oscillating vertically.

EXPERIMENTAL TECHNIQUES

5. SOME EXPERIMENTS INVOLVING DENSITY

1. DEDUCTION OF DENSITIES

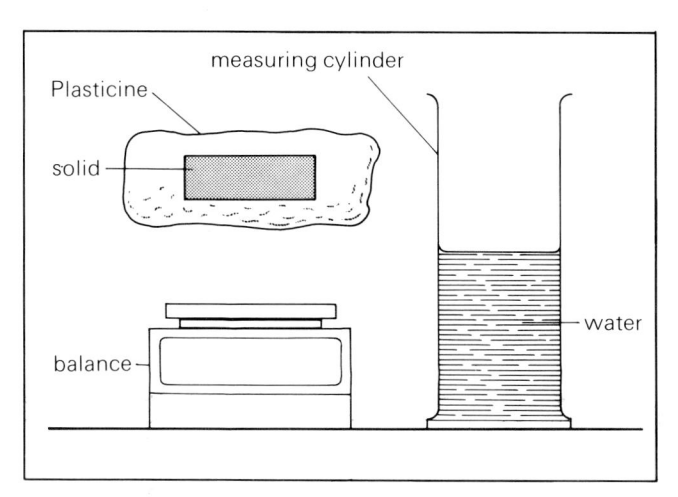

Figure 98 Equipment available

Information

Substance	Density
aluminium	2710 kg m^{-3}
brass	8500 kg m^{-3}
copper	8900 kg m^{-3}
pure iron	7870 kg m^{-3}
lead	11340 kg m^{-3}
magnesium	1740 kg m^{-3}
silver	10500 kg m^{-3}
zinc	7140 kg m^{-3}
cork	240 kg m^{-3}
marble	2600 kg m^{-3}
Perspex	1190 kg m^{-3}
wood	600–650 kg m^{-3}
wax	900 kg m^{-3}
concrete	2400 kg m^{-3}

You are given a lump of Plasticine and several other lumps of Plasticine in which are hidden different solid materials (do not take the Plasticine off the solid materials). There is 60 g of Plasticine in each lump. Take measurements of mass and volume for each lump and then work out the density of the solid material inside. Use the table to deduce the material from its density.

Logical plan

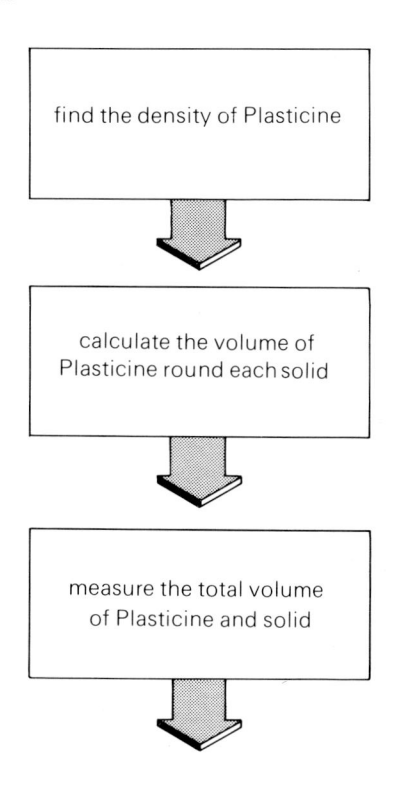

find the density of Plasticine

↓

calculate the volume of Plasticine round each solid

↓

measure the total volume of Plasticine and solid

↓

2. PRESSURE DUE TO A COLUMN OF LIQUID

Outline

The pressure due to a column of liquid is given by the equation:

pressure = vertical height × density × g

In the apparatus shown in figure 99, often called Hare's apparatus, the densities of the two liquids can be compared. Some air is drawn out of S to reduce the pressure above the liquids to a value P lower than the atmospheric pressure A.

At level 1: $\quad A = h_1 d_1 g + P$
At level 2: $\quad A = h_2 d_2 g + P$
Subtracting these gives $\quad h_1 d_1 g = h_2 d_2 g$
and cancelling g gives $\quad h_1 d_1 = h_2 d_2$

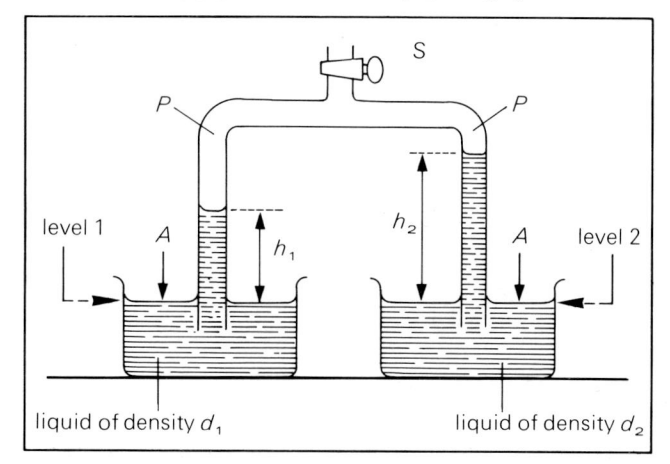

Figure 99 Hare's apparatus

This means that by measuring the two heights and knowing the density of one liquid the density of the other can be found.

Experimental details

Take measurements of h_1 and h_2 and calculate the density of the liquid.

1. Water is the liquid of known density.
2. For maximum accuracy in the measurement of length the liquids must rise as high as possible. The liquid which rises the higher has the lower density.
3. Some care is needed to measure the height as accurately as possible.
4. Remember to give an error range to your result. What liquid could it be?

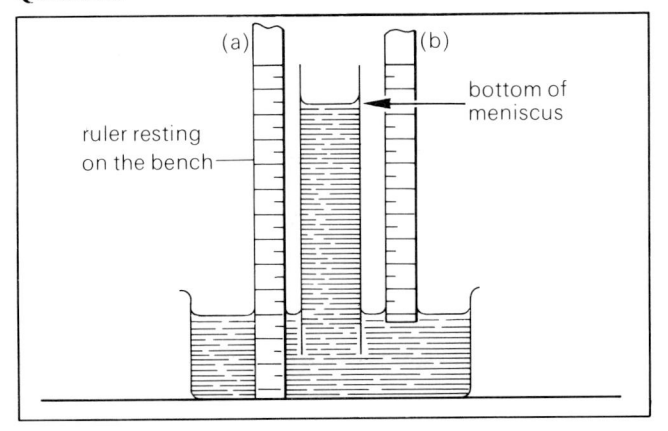

Questions

Figure 100 Measuring the height of a column of liquid.

1. Look at ruler (a). Is it better to take two readings on the scale and then subtract?
2. Look at ruler (b). Is a ruler used like this accurate enough? What happens when it touches the liquid?

3. HYDROMETER

Outline

When a hydrometer floats, its weight is equal to the upthrust produced by the liquid. This is equal to the weight of liquid displaced, or to the volume displaced × density of liquid × g. In liquids of different densities, the volume displaced must change because the upthrust must remain the same. If the volume displaced is to remain the same, then the weight of the hydrometer must change.

Experimental details

You are to make a simple hydrometer from a test tube and sand or lead shot. Put a mark on the test tube *inside* the tube. This can be positioned in line with the liquid surface by altering the mass of sand or lead shot. Think about the question of stability, and the position of the centre of buoyancy in relation to the centre of gravity. (See figure 101.)

1. Float the hydrometer in water and alter the amount of sand or lead shot until the mark is in line with the water surface. Measure the mass of the hydrometer.
2. Now float the hydrometer in the liquid of unknown density. When putting the mark on the test tube, did you allow for the density to get either larger or smaller? If your hydrometer has now sunk, go back to the beginning. Alter the amount of sand or lead shot until the mark is again in line with the liquid surface. Measure the new mass of the hydrometer.
3. From your results work out the density of the liquid, taking the density of water to be $1000\,\text{kg m}^{-3}$. (Remember that the volume of liquid displaced in both cases is the same.)

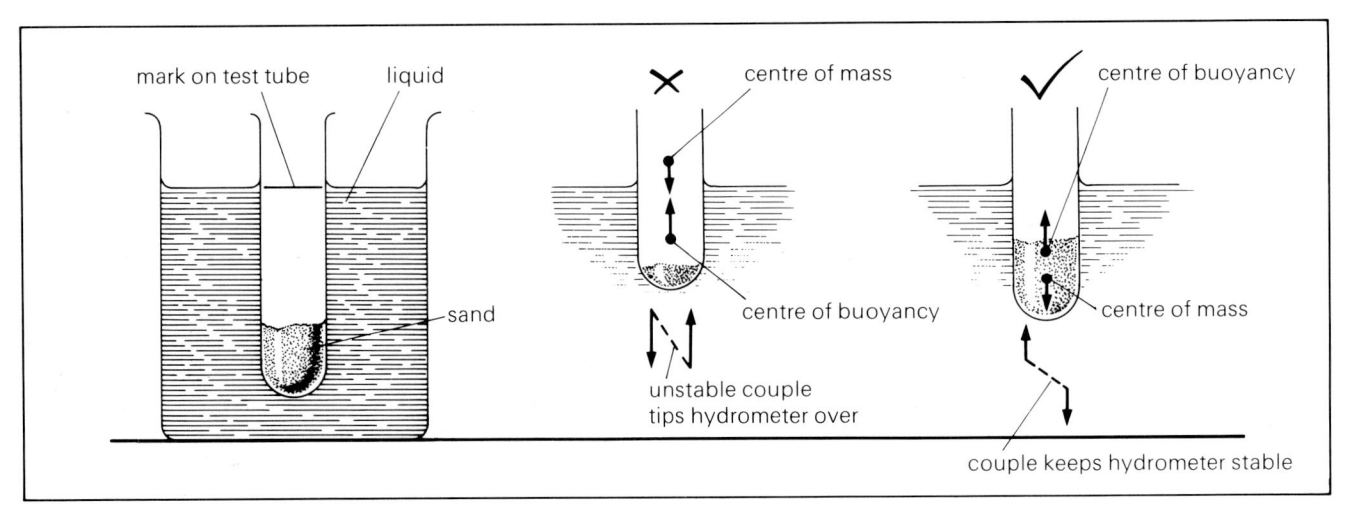

Figure 101 Hydrometer

EXPERIMENTAL TECHNIQUES

6. USING THE PRINCIPLE OF MOMENTS

1. BALANCING A BEAM

1. Using only the equipment shown in figure 102, find the weight of the ruler. The metal block has a mass of 100 g. The gravitational field strength is 10 N kg^{-1}. You can assume the ruler is uniform.

2. Arrange the apparatus as in figure 103. The aim of the experiment is to decide if the clear liquid is alcohol, water or salt solution. The mass of the stopper is given to you. You may balance the ruler on the knife-edge with the glass stopper hung at any position you choose and either submerged or not. You are not given the mass of the ruler, but may use the apparatus to find it if you need to.

Information
1. Centre of gravity of a uniform rule is at its mid-point.
2. Density of: alcohol is 0.8 g cm^{-3};
   water is 1.0 g cm^{-3};
   brine is 1.1 g cm^{-3};
   glass is 2.6 g cm^{-3}.
3. In equilibrium $Fx = Wy$.
4. Density = mass/volume.
5. Upthrust = weight of fluid displaced.
6. $g = 10$ N kg^{-1}.

Logical plan

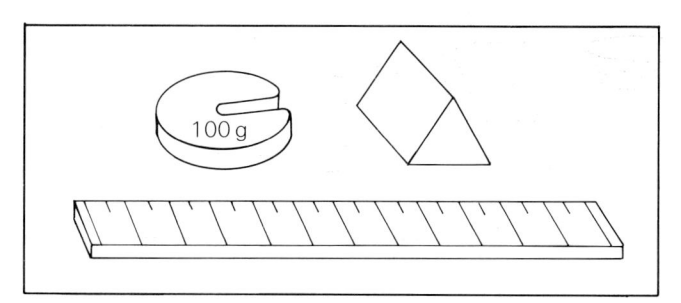

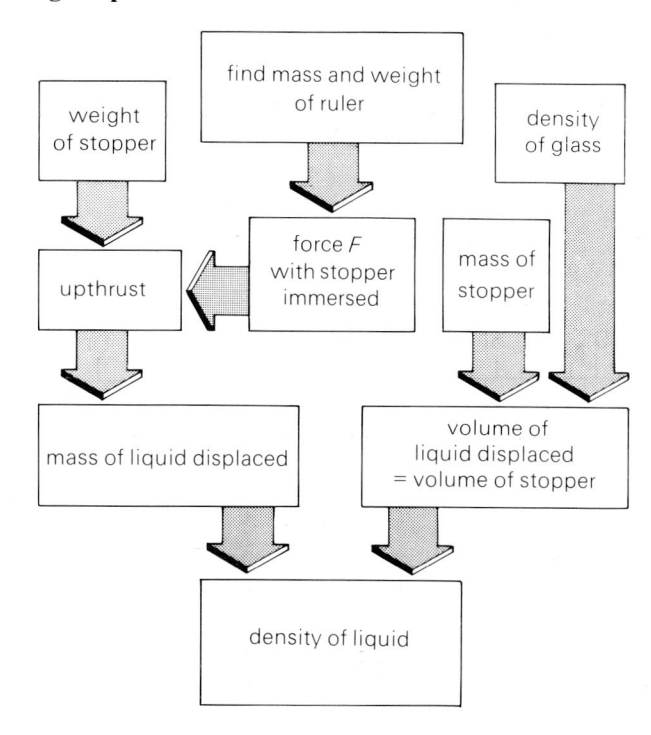

[Flow chart: weight of stopper → upthrust → mass of liquid displaced; find mass and weight of ruler → force F with stopper immersed; density of glass, mass of stopper → volume of liquid displaced = volume of stopper; → density of liquid]

Figure 102

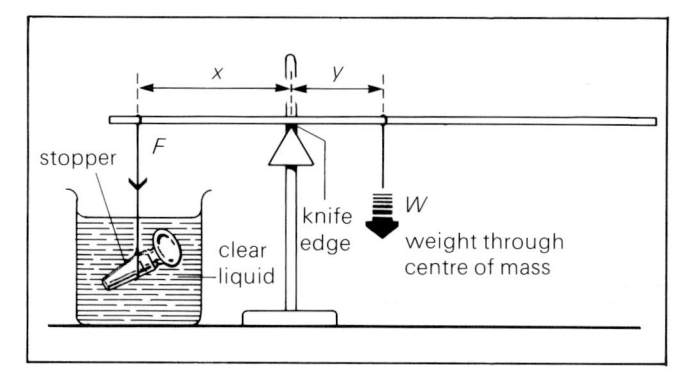

Figure 103 Equipment

2. SIMPLE CURRENT BALANCE

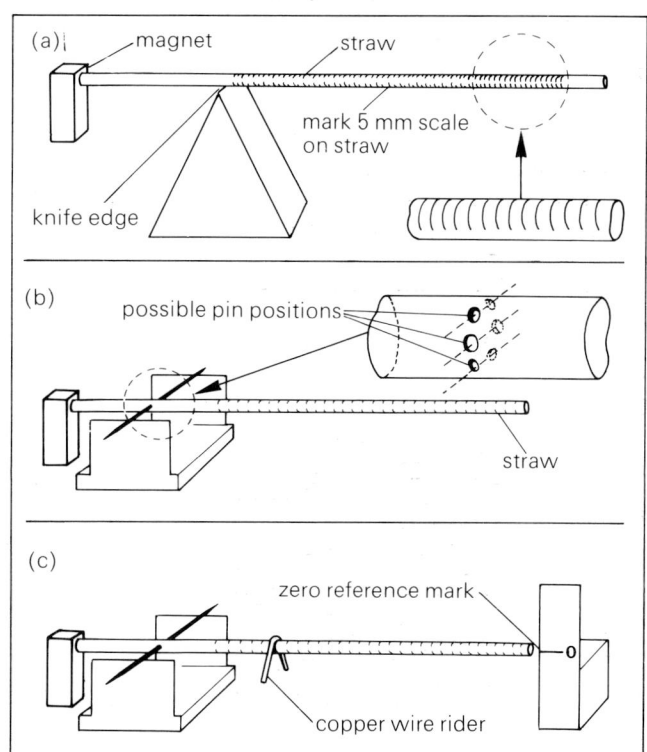

Figure 104 Simple current balance

The simple current balance is based on the Worcester current balance kit from *Nuffield Physics Year 2* and the aim is to produce a calibration graph for the current balance.

Experimental details

Arrange the apparatus (figure 104) so that the straw is balanced as horizontally as possible. This is done by finding the approximate centre of gravity, by balancing the straw on an edge (a), and then moving the position of the pin (b) and then the rider (c) until the straw is horizontal. Then, mark a zero reference line, and note the position of the rider on the 0.5 mm scale marked on the straw.

Which of the positions (see figure 104b) should the pin be in and why? Will it be unstable in one position?

Connect the balance as in circuit (a) in figure 105. Why is it a more suitable circuit than (b)?

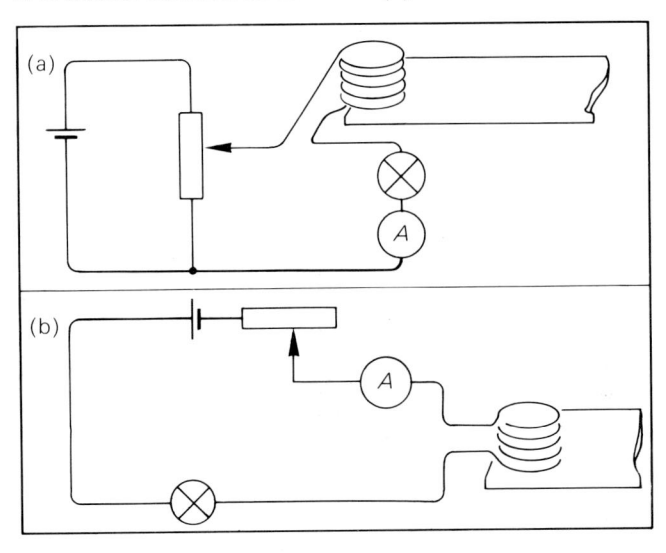

Figure 105

For at least ten values of current in the range 0–1 A, move the rider until the straw returns to the zero reference position. Note the position of the rider.

From the results
Plot a calibration graph of rider position against current (figure 106). From the graph find the sensivity of the instrument, i.e. amount of movement of rider per milliampère. Does it alter with the size of current being measured?

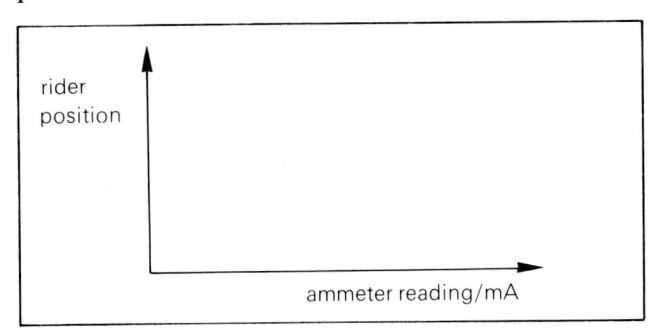

Figure 106

3. ANGLE OF A FORCE NEEDED TO SUPPORT A BEAM

This is based on the definition of the moment of a force:

moment = force × perpendicular distance from the pivot to the line of action of the force

Experimental details

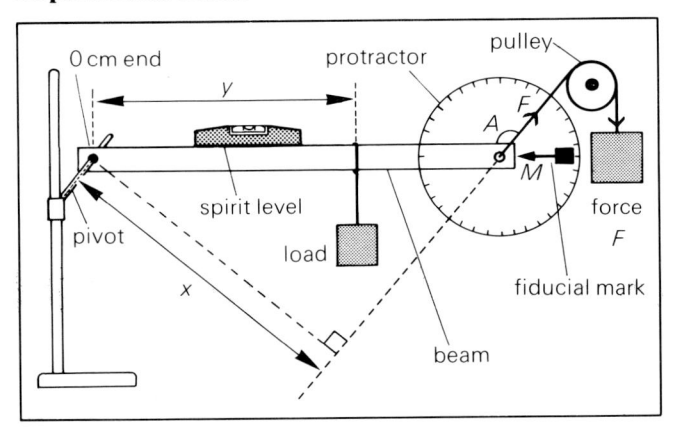

Figure 107 Equipment

Arrange the apparatus as in figure 107. The beam should be adjusted to be horizontal before any readings are taken. This is done by altering the vertical height of the pivot and the horizontal position of the pivot stand.

Place the 2 N load so that $y = 20$ cm. Find the value of the force F which will keep the beam horizontal at an angle A of approximately 130°. Record the angle A and the force F. Repeat for eight other values of A, evenly spread over a range of 0–180°.

Repeat for $y = 50$ cm and $y = 80$ cm.

From the results
Plot three graphs of force F against angle A. From the graphs find (a) the angle A for which the smallest force is needed, and (b) the weight of the ruler.

Problem
A canopy is to be suspended by a wire rope. Where should the wire be fastened on the beam to produce minimum stress in the wire?

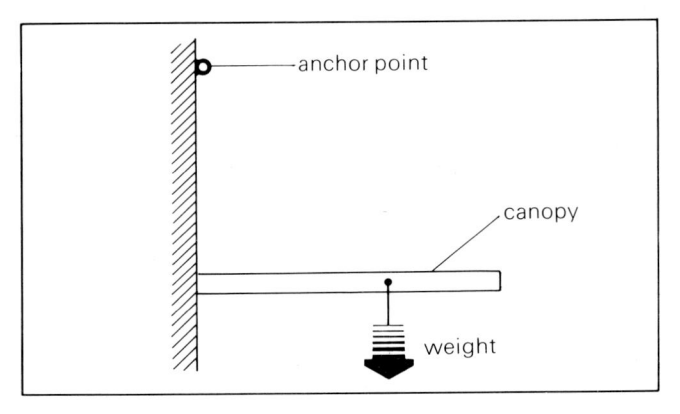

Figure 108

EXPERIMENTAL TECHNIQUES

7. DETECTING ELECTROMAGNETIC RADIATION

The electromagnetic spectrum contains *six* main regions:

radio frequencies;	ultraviolet radiation;
infrared radiation;	X-rays;
light radiation;	gamma radiation.

The only physical difference between them is *frequency*. The names are purely arbitrary divisions. The methods used for detection differ.

1. Radio frequencies

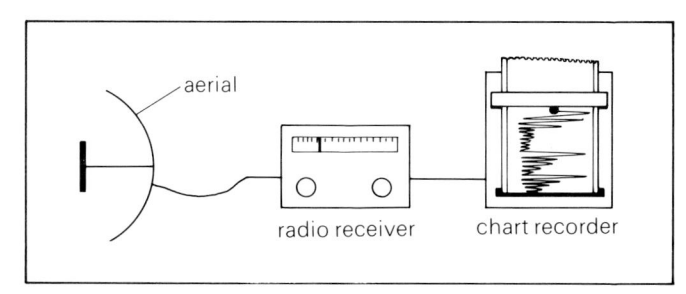

Figure 109 Measurement of radio frequencies

When detecting radio frequencies (figure 109) the length of the aerial is important. For maximum induction of an e.m.f. the simplest aerial is a half-wave dipole. A standing wave is induced, producing a maximum (antinode) in the centre where the wires to the receiver are connected. The length l is $\frac{1}{2}\lambda$. (See figure 110.)

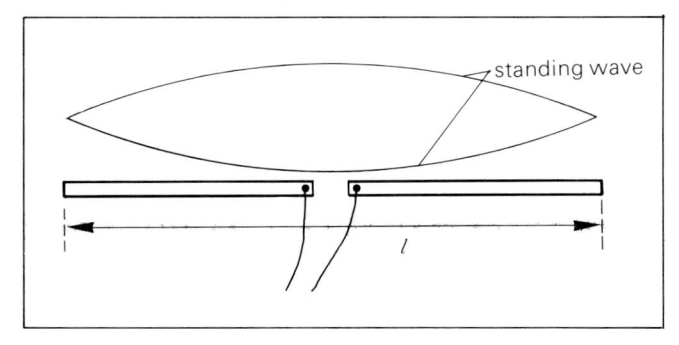

Figure 110 A simple aerial

A simple experiment to illustrate the principle is to plot out the strength of radio signals across the frequency range of an ordinary radio. This actually measures the sound content, but is also an indication of the carrier amplitude. Using the apparatus in figure 111, take voltage readings for a range of frequencies across one of the wavebands available on your receiver. The voltage on your radio receiver should be set to maximum. For each reading, first discharge the capacitor, then select the new frequency, move the switch to charge the capacitor and record the reading on the voltmeter. Plot a graph of voltage against frequency.

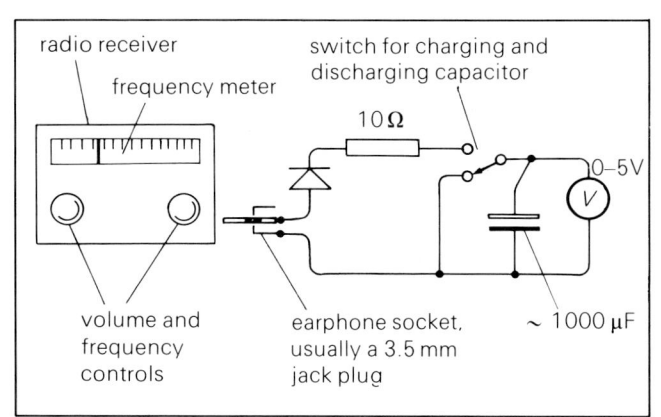

Figure 111 Equipment

2. Infrared radiation

Thermopile
A thermopile is a series of thermocouples connected in series to increase the e.m.f. produced when one set of junctions is heated.

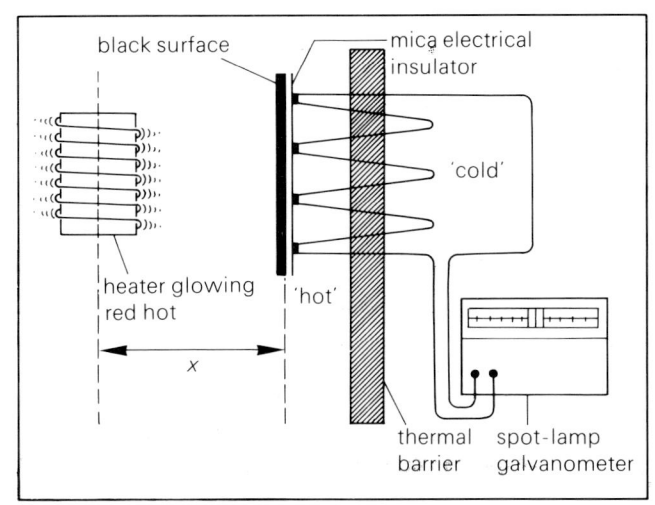

Figure 112 Detecting infrared radiation.

Using the apparatus shown in figure 112, take a series of readings of e.m.f. produced by the heater at different distances x. Ensure that you:

(a) allow the thermopile to cool between each reading;
(b) allow the thermopile to heat up for the *same* time for each reading: 10–20 seconds.

Infrared radiation should obey the same inverse square law as all electromagnetic radiation. Plot a graph of e.m.f. against $\frac{1}{x^2}$. It should be a straight line, but may not pass through the origin because of the uncertainty that the effective distance x will not be exactly the same as the distance measured.

Phototransistor

A phototransistor allows a current to flow depending on the intensity of the radiation. The presence of radiation at frequencies lower than red light can be investigated using a glass prism to disperse the radiation, although it does absorb a larger proportion of infrared radiation than light.

Using the apparatus shown in figure 113, move the phototransistor along the line XY and take a series of readings of current. Note where the visible spectrum starts and finishes. From the results, plot a graph of current against position (*x*).

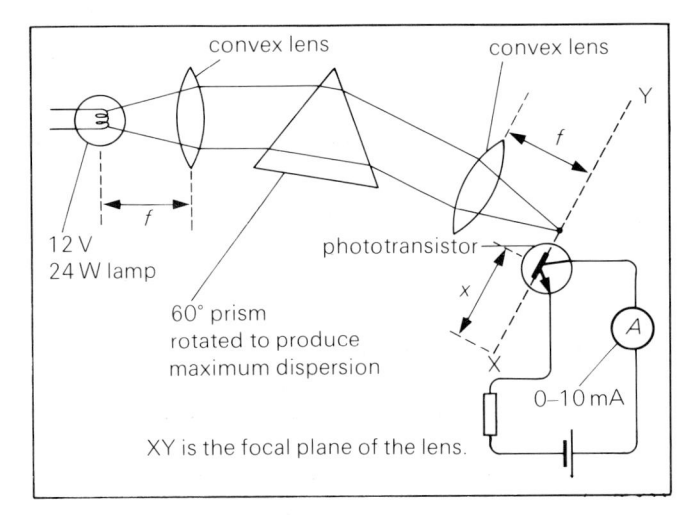

Figure 113 Measuring the intensity of radiation across a spectrum.

Figure 114 Photograph of a line spectrum as might be produced by a spectrometer; each line shows a single frequency of light.

A photograph can give a rough guide to intensity, although it does vary with the colour.

A photocell will produce an e.m.f. dependent on the intensity, but is not always linear.

A photodiode or photoresistor can enable a numerical current reading of intensity to be produced.

4. Ultraviolet radiation

Various materials fluoresce when ultraviolet radiation falls on them. Ultraviolet (u.v.) radiation can be dangerous to the eyes, and direct or reflected viewing of an ultraviolet lamp should be avoided. Fluorescent lamps are coated with a material which absorbs u.v. radiation and re-emits the energy as light. Some photographic films are also sensitive to u.v. radiation.

5. X-rays

X-rays have an ionising effect on particles in a gas. Detectors can be made in which the current produced depends on the intensity of the X-ray radiation. One use is in gauges to measure the thickness of aluminium sheets in a rolling mill. X-rays also affect photographic plates and produce an exposure dependent on the intensity of the X-rays. The ionising effect can also be used to release electrons in semiconductors so that the current flowing in a circuit will change.

3. Light (visible) radiation

A spectrometer (see p. 69) is used to measure the wavelength of light. The frequency can be calculated from the wavelength using the equation:

velocity of light = frequency × wavelength.

6. Gamma radiation

A Geiger–Müller tube is the most common method of detection used at A-level (see p. 98).

8. PLOTTING RAYS AND IMAGE POSITIONS WITH PINS

Outline

Optical pins (about 4 cm long) can be used to trace the paths of rays through transparent blocks and also to locate the images produced by mirrors and lenses. This practical gives you practice in the techniques involved. The basic principle is that when the pin and the image coincide they appear to move in line with each other when the eye is moved from side to side (no parallax). If they do not coincide, then they will appear to be in line for one position of the eye but will separate if the eye is moved (parallax). This is one application of the method of no parallax.

EXPERIMENTAL TECHNIQUES

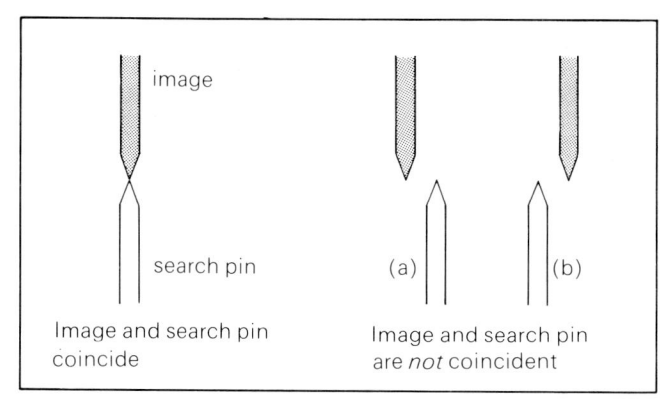

Figure 115

Looking at figure 115, if the eye is moved right, then (a) means that the image is nearer to the eye than the pin, and (b) means that the image is further from the eye than the pin.

Experimental details

A. Virtual image in a plane mirror

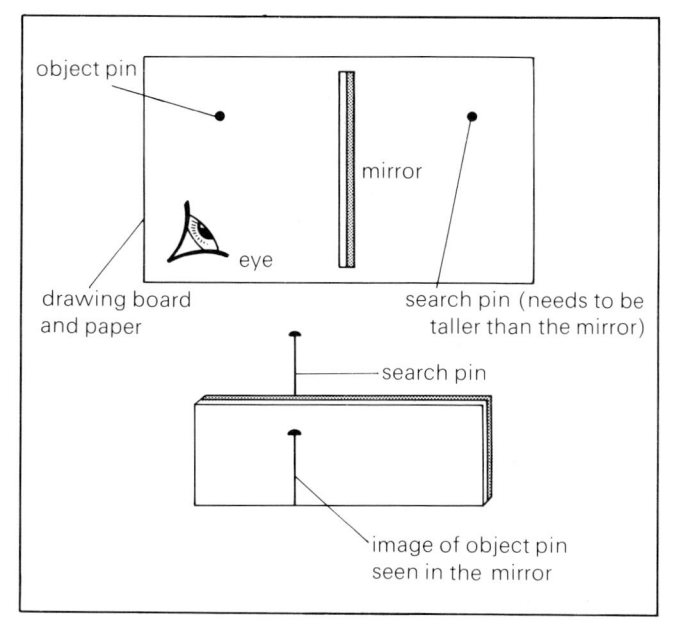

Figure 116

Using the apparatus shown in figure 116, locate the image. The search pin is coincident with the image when it remains aligned with the image in the mirror, wherever the eye is positioned in front of the mirror. Measure the distance of the object pin in front of the mirror and the distance of the image behind the mirror.

Repeat for different object positions. Record the object and image distances. What rules can you deduce about the object and image positions in relation to the mirror?

B. Path of a ray through a glass block (or Perspex block)

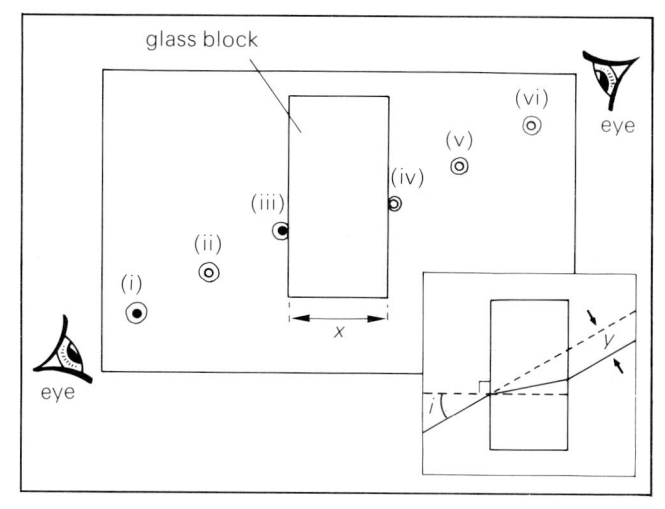

Figure 117 Plan view

Use the equipment shown in figure 117.
1. Place pin (ii) in line with the other two (i) and (iii). Draw a small circle on the paper round each pin.
2. Place pins (iv), (v) and (vi) so that they appear in line with the three pins on the left-hand side. Draw a small circle on the paper round each pin.
3. Draw round the block, remove the pins and draw in the rays, including the ray across the block.

    Measure the lateral displacement (y) and the width of the block (x). Evaluate $\dfrac{x}{y}$ and measure i. Extend the experiment to investigate the way the lateral displacement (y) varies with the angle of incidence.

C. Focal length of a convex lens

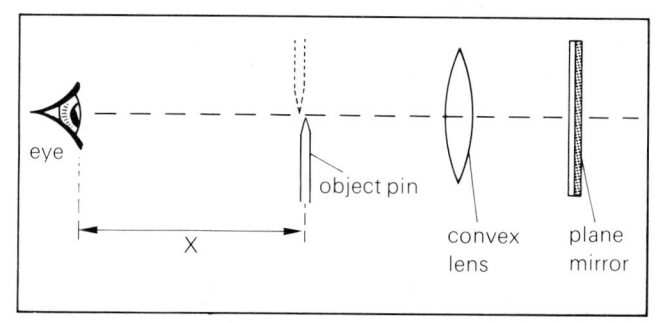

Figure 118 The top of the object pin should be near the centre line and the eye should be a minimum of 25 cm from the pin, otherwise it cannot be seen in focus.

Using the apparatus shown in figure 118, move the object pin until it coincides with its own image. The distance between the pin and the lens is the focal length. Make sure that you are looking at the correct image, because it is possible to see an image caused by surface of the convex lens acting as a concave mirror. How can you make sure that the rays producing the image have been reflected off the plane mirror?

D. *Real image in a convex lens*

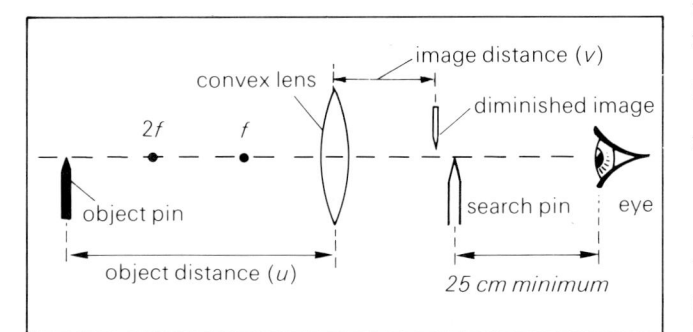

Figure 119 Side view

Using the apparatus shown in figure 119, locate the image using the 'no parallax' method. This can be slightly more confusing and difficult to adjust, because the image of the object pin appears smaller than the search pin (figure 120). This can be seen, even though the search pin is only a few millimetres from the image.

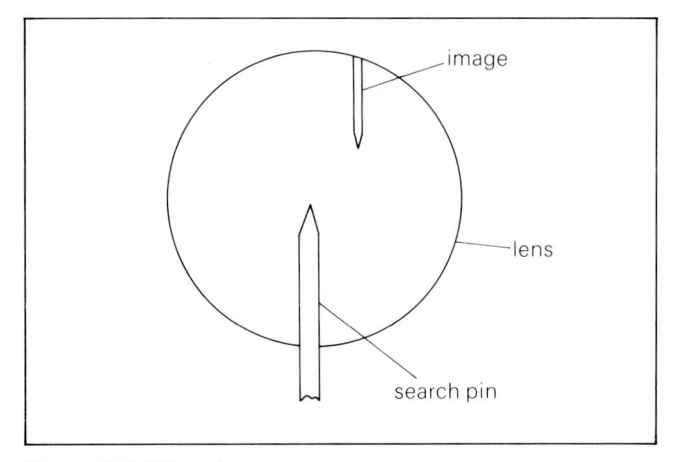

Figure 120 What the eye sees.

Move the search pin until it and the image are tip to tip. When you have found the image position, measure the object distance (u) and the image distance (v). Evaluate $\dfrac{uv}{u+v}$. What is the physical significance of this number? What are its units?

E. *Maxima seen through a diffraction grating*

Using the apparatus shown in figure 121, move pins until they are in line with a bright maximum. Mark the paper. Measure the angle θ.

Evaluate $\dfrac{\sin \theta}{N}$ for each maximum. What do you notice about the values?

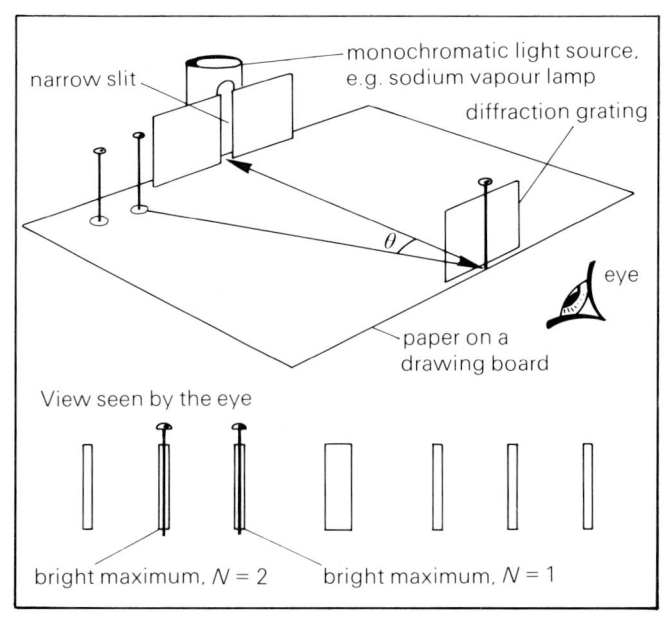

Figure 121 Plotting the positions of maxima.

9. USING AN ILLUMINATED OBJECT WITH LENSES AND MIRRORS

Outline

Unlike methods using search pins, an illuminated object can only be used when a *real* image is produced, because a screen is used to locate the image. The illuminated object is usually a triangular shape with a fine gauze or a circular hole with cross-wires, for example:

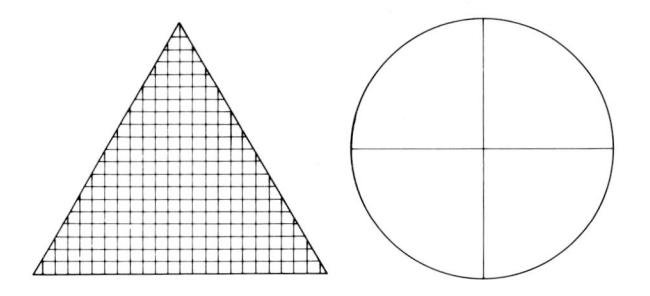

EXPERIMENTAL TECHNIQUES

Experimental details

A. *Finding sharp images*

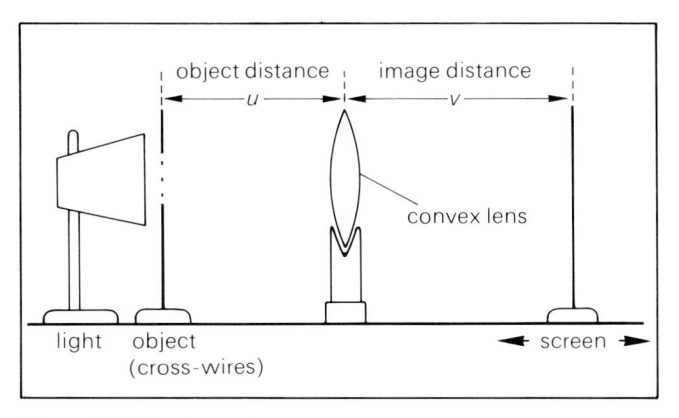

Figure 122 Equipment

Finding a sharp image is very much a process of narrowing down and then finally deciding on the best point. An estimate of the accuracy of the reading can be made by finding the range of readings for which you think the image is sharp.

A real image is required, so the object distance must be larger than the focal length. Using the apparatus shown in figure 122, move the screen out from the lens until an image appears and move slowly past the sharp image, then back and forward until you are satisfied and have three readings:

(a) the nearest position to the screen at which you think the image is sharp;
(b) the sharpest position (this could be difficult to judge with any accuracy);
(c) the furthest position from the screen at which you think the image is sharp.

This gives a measurement of the amount the reading could be in error.

Measure the object distance accurately with a ruler. The accuracy of this measurement is ± 1 mm.

The focal length of the lens can be found from the equation:

$$\frac{1}{f} = \frac{1}{u} + \frac{1}{v} \quad \text{(all values being positive)}$$

First work out f from your 'best' results.

From the extreme results you can calculate the amount the focal length might be in error. For example, suppose these results were taken:

object distance = 15 cm $\pm$ 1 mm
best sharp image = 30.1 cm
sharp image range = 29.5 cm to 30.5 cm

Results which are your 'best' estimate:

$$\frac{1}{f} = \frac{1}{15} + \frac{1}{30.1}$$
$$f = 10.01 \text{ cm}$$

Using values at the extremes of the range of results:

largest $\quad \dfrac{1}{f} = \dfrac{1}{15.1} + \dfrac{1}{30.5}$

$\qquad f = 10.09$ cm

smallest $\quad \dfrac{1}{f} = \dfrac{1}{14.9} + \dfrac{1}{29.5}$

$\qquad f = 9.89$ cm

Now, a metre rule can only measure to 1 mm in 1000 mm, so only three figures are reliable, i.e. 846 mm, but you could not say 846.2 mm, so we can only give the result to three figures of accuracy, even though the calculator you have used will give more. Thus the focal length is 10.0 cm, but could be between 10.1 cm and 9.89 cm. We can thus give the result as 10.0 cm $\pm$ 0.1 cm.

Use your own results to work out the focal length in the same way.

Extensions
1. Taking only one set of readings is not good experimental practice. How could you plot the results of several measurements graphically and find f?
2. If you have time, use lenses of a longer and then a shorter focal length to investigate any effect the focal length has on the accuracy.
3. Does the accuracy of readings increase as the object distance gets larger?

B. *Focal length of a concave mirror*

Using the apparatus shown in figure 123, alter the distance between the object and the mirror until a sharp

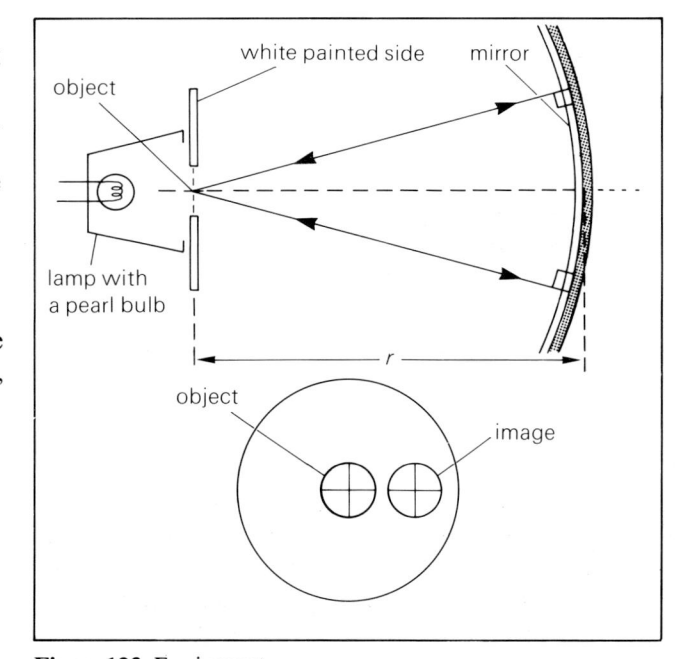

Figure 123 Equipment

image is produced next to the object. The distance between the object and the mirror is the *radius of curvature* (r) and the focal length is ½r.

C. *Focal length of a concave lens*

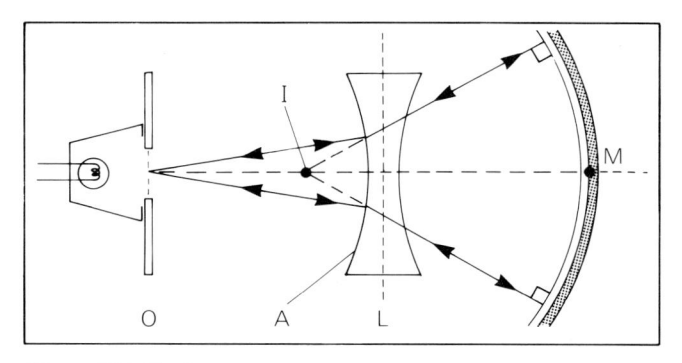

Figure 124 Equipment

Find the focal length of a concave lens using the same concave mirror as in experiment 1. Set up the arrangement (figure 124) so that an image appears beside the object. Measure the distances OL, OM and LM. Now you already know the distance IM from experiment 1, so the virtual image distance IL can be found. OL is the real object distance. Work out the focal length by scale drawing or by calculation. **(Beware of the image from face A.)**

D. *Finding the position of a hidden convex lens*
Inside the tube (figure 125) is a convex lens. You have to find out how far it is from end A.

Hint:

$$\text{the magnification} = \frac{\text{image distance } (v)}{\text{object distance } (u)}$$

distance between object and image $= v + u$

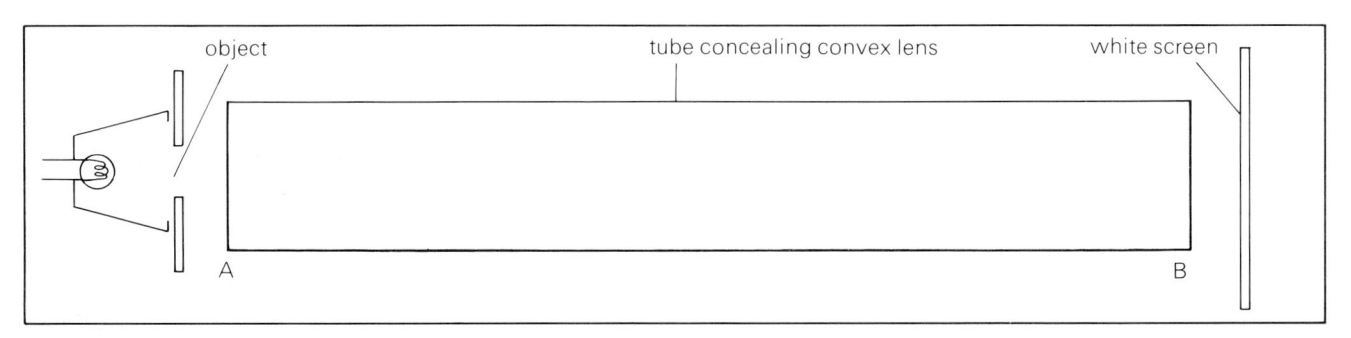

Figure 125 Equipment

10. THE PATHS OF RAYS THROUGH A PRISM

Outline

As a wave of light moves from one medium to another its speed changes, and this can cause a bending of the ray, called refraction. Except in a vacuum, different colours of light travel at different speeds. For different colours the change of speed and the angle through which the ray is bent will be different. In this way white light can be *dispersed* into its component colours to form a *spectrum*. We shall therefore not use white light, but a narrow band of red frequencies produced by a filter. The aim of the experiment is to plot the paths of the rays for a range of angles of incidence and to investigate the connection between the angle of incidence and the overall angle between the incident and emergent beams, the angle of deviation (figure 126).

The refractive index could be calculated and also the speed of red light in glass by using the value for the velocity of light in air.

Experimental details

Using the apparatus and method illustrated in figure 127, plot a series of rays through the prism for a range of angles of incidence (*i*) from 0° to 90°. About eight will be sufficient. Remember that at some stage the ray will be totally internally reflected at the face AB and this gives a

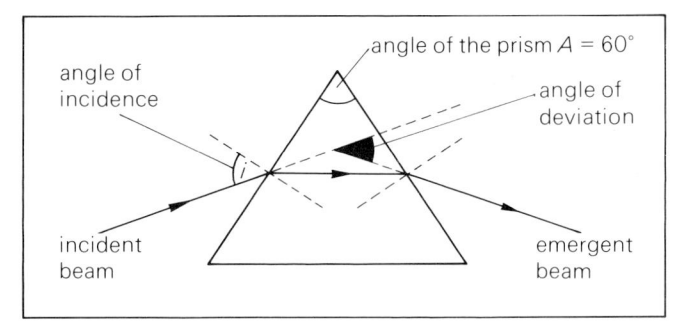

Figure 126

EXPERIMENTAL TECHNIQUES

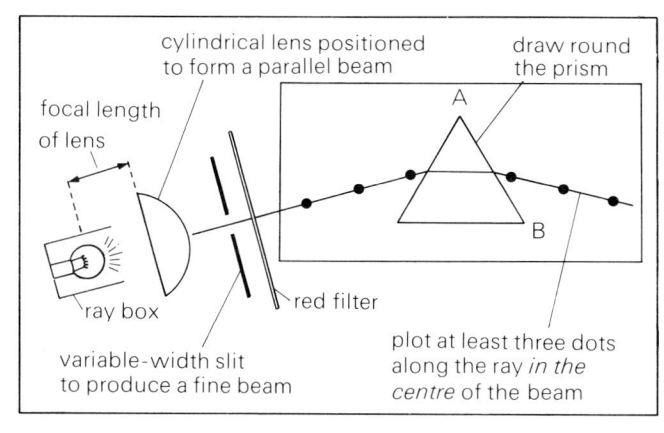

Figure 127 Plan view of equipment

lower limit to the angle of incidence. It might be a good idea to find this angle of incidence first. Then you can work out the range of possible angles of incidence and decide on about eight equally-spaced values for the experiment.

Results

From your ray diagrams measure the angle of incidence, the angle of deviation and the angle of refraction from the second face.

Plot graphs of:

(a) angle of incidence against angle of deviation;
(b) angle of incidence against final angle of refraction.

Angle of incidence on first face/°	Angle of refraction from second face/°	Angle of deviation/°

Questions
1. What is the minimum angle of deviation (D)?
2. What is the connection between the angle of incidence and angle of refraction when minimum deviation occurs?
3. Test the equation that at minimum deviation:

$$i = \frac{A + D}{2}$$

If you have time, experiment with a 30° and a 45° prism and see if your conclusions apply to these prisms as well.

11. STROBOSCOPIC AND PHOTOGRAPHIC METHODS OF MEASURING CHANGING POSITION WITH TIME

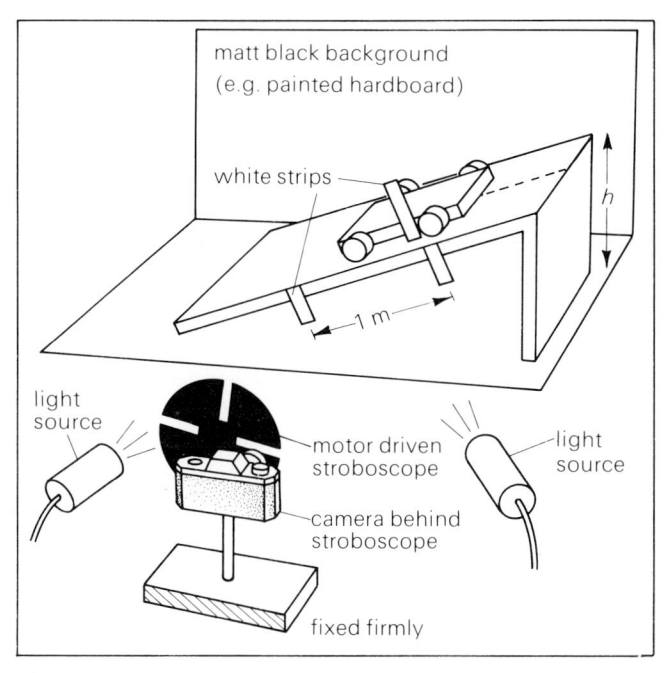

Figure 128 Equipment

Outline

By illuminating a moving object with short flashes of light at regular intervals, a photograph showing the position of the object at regular time intervals can be taken. An alternative way is to illuminate the object with a light source and have a rotating shutter which lets glimpses into the camera at regular intervals. For example, for a trolley rolling down a slope, the equipment would be set up as shown in figure 128.

Time for one revolution of strobe disc =

$$\frac{1}{\text{number of revs/second}}$$

There are four slits, so four glimpses are seen in one revolution.

Time between images = time between glimpses

$$= \frac{1}{4} \times \frac{1}{\text{number of revs/second}}$$

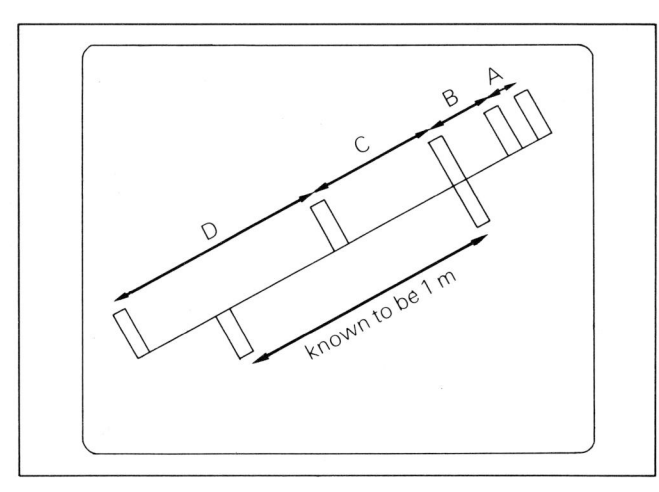

Figure 129 Example results

A photograph would be obtained similar to that shown in figure 129, from which one could work out the average velocities for each of the sections, A, B, C and D:

$$\text{average velocity} = \frac{\text{distance}}{\text{time}}$$

Experimental details

1. Set up the apparatus as shown in figure 128. Using four 100 W bulbs to illuminate the trolley and a black and white film of speed 100 ASA, e.g. Ilford FP4, an aperture of $f5.6$ should be suitable. However, since you will have a film of at least 12 exposures, it is a good idea to take exposures of successive runs at $f2.8$, $f4.5$, $f5.6$, $f8$, $f11$. The stroboscope must be driven at a constant known speed. Most motor-driven stroboscopes are driven by a synchronous motor from the a.c. mains, in which case the stroboscope will rotate at exactly 50 times each second. The time interval between exposures will depend on how many slits there are on the stroboscope disc.

2. Take a series of exposures for five runs of the trolley for heights (h) of about 20 cm, 30 cm, 40 cm. For each run, first switch on the lights and stroboscope, open the camera shutter and then release the trolley from the top of the slope. Close the camera shutter when the trolley reaches the bottom of the slope.

3. Develop the film and either make a set of prints from the 'best' negatives or project the negative on to a piece of paper and copy the positions of the white marks (black on the negative). Measure the distances A, B, C, D, etc. and convert to real distances. Work out the average velocity over each distance:

$$\text{velocity} = \frac{\text{distance}}{\text{time}}$$

Results

	Photograph distance/cm	Real distance/m	Velocity/m s^{-1}
A			
B			
C			

1 m real = ... cm on photograph

time between exposures = ... s

From the results

Plot a series of velocity–time graphs. Comment on the shapes of the graphs. Can you work out the acceleration from each graph?

$$\text{acceleration} = \frac{\text{velocity change}}{\text{time}}$$

12. BENDING BEAMS

1. BEAM LOADED CENTRALLY

Outline

When a beam is loaded in the centre, it bends. This experiment measures the depression produced by different loads and beams of different widths and thicknesses.

Experimental details

Using the equipment shown in figure 130, record the reading on the millimetre scale with no load on. Use the method of no parallax to make sure that the scale, your eye and the top of the rule are exactly in line. Record the scale readings for loads of 1, 2, 3, 4 and 5 N and work out the depressions. Measure the width and depth of the beam. Repeat for the other beams you have been given.

EXPERIMENTAL TECHNIQUES

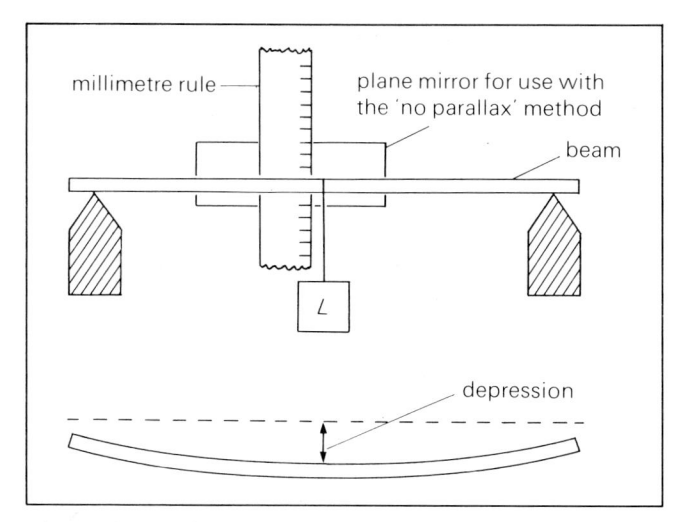

Figure 130 Equipment

Results

Beam width = ... mm
      depth = ... mm
No load scale reading = ... mm

Load/N	Scale reading/mm	Depression/mm

Questions

1. Is the depression roughly proportional to the load?
2. If the thickness of the beam is doubled, by what factor is the load which produces a depression of 10 mm increased?
3. If the width of the beam is doubled, does the load needed to produce a given depression also double?
4. Evaluate $\dfrac{\text{load}}{\text{cross-sectional area}}$ for a depression of 10 mm for each beam. Make sure you give the correct units.

2. CANTILEVER

Outline

Theory predicts that the depression of a cantilever is given by the equation $x = kl^n$ (see figure 131). This experiment attempts to find the values of n and k for the beam you have been given.

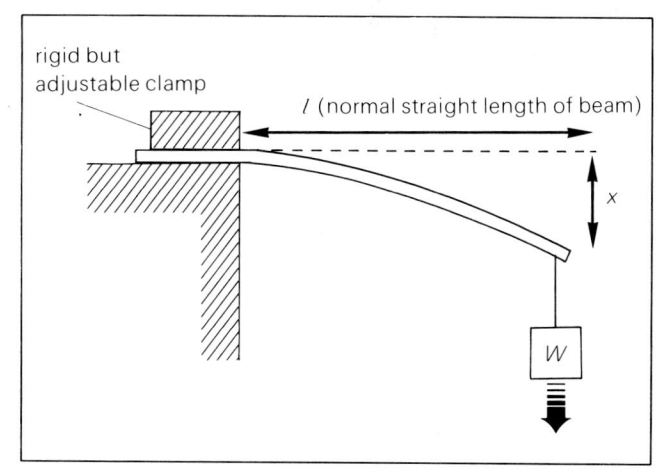

Figure 131 A cantilever

Experimental details

Find a load W which will give a depression of approximately 20 cm for the maximum practical length of beam. Measure l and x. Shorten the beam and repeat the measurement of l and x until you have taken about ten sets of readings. If you have time, repeat for other values of load W.

Results

load = ... N

Length l/cm	Depression x/cm

From the results

Experiment with values of n between 0 and 3 until a power n is found so that values of $\dfrac{l}{x^n}$ equal the same constant. Use the computer program 'PROCESS'. This enables the values of l and x to be entered and the value of the power n to be changed until the best straight line is found. Alternatively, a graph of $\log_e l$ against $\log_e x$ could be plotted and values of n and k found from the gradient and appropriate intercept. If $\dfrac{l}{x^n} = k$, then $l = kx^n$ and

$$\log_e l = n \log_e x + \log_e k.$$

Give the values of k and n. If you have used different loads, describe any conclusions you have made on the effect the load has on values of k and n.

13. MEASURING FREQUENCY

Outline

Frequency is the number of complete oscillations or vibrations made per second. It is measured in hertz (Hz) and is a measurement made on sound waves, electromagnetic waves and mechanical vibrations (most of which produce sound waves as well). This practical deals with the measurement of sound, or mechanical vibrations in the frequency range 0 to 25 Hz. For electromagnetic waves it is more usual to measure the wavelength, although frequency is the correct physical measurement. This is partly due to historical reasons and partly because simple laboratory apparatus measures the wavelength rather than the frequency. This is covered in other experiments. The methods used are outlined below.

1. Beats

Beats with a very similar frequency to the unknown are produced. When the two frequencies are produced at the same time with similar amplitudes, a periodic rise and fall in amplitude is heard. The number of these heard per second is called the beat frequency and is the difference between the two frequencies. It can be applied to sound or electrical vibrations and is actually used in radio receivers to separate out the sound frequencies from the carrier when sending signals in Morse code.

2. Using the time-scale on an oscilloscope

The waveform can be displayed on an oscilloscope and the time-scale on the timebase used. This is only an approximate method on all but the highest-quality oscilloscopes, because the variable control is not usually calibrated. For the example shown (figure 132), the actual time sensitivity would be between 1 and 0.1 ms mm^{-1} and would be approximately 0.5 ms mm^{-1}.

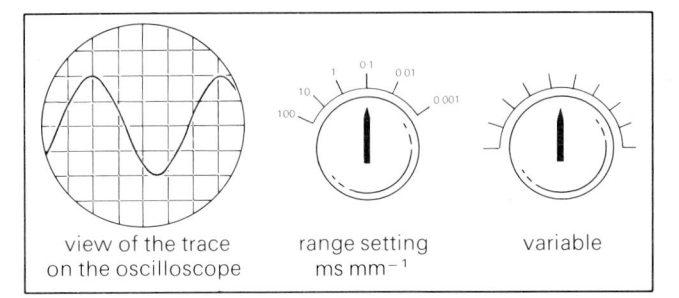

Figure 132

Calculate the approximate frequency as follows. Assume a time-scale of 8 cm ≡ 0.1 ms. If one complete wavelength covers 5.5 cm, then the periodic time is:

$$\frac{5.5 \times 0.1 \text{ ms}}{8}$$

$$\text{frequency} = \frac{1}{\text{periodic time}} = \frac{8 \times 10^3}{5.5 \times 0.1} = 1454 \text{ Hz}$$

3. Lissajous' figures

The Lissajous' figures method uses an oscilloscope. The unknown frequency is applied to the y input and the input from a calibrated signal generator is applied to the x input. (The time-base must of course be turned off.) Connect each input separately and alter the amplitudes until the size of each line trace is approximately the same. The two are then applied together and the frequency of the signal generator altered until an ellipse or circle is seen. When the trace is stationary, the two frequencies are exactly the same.

If the trace rotates clockwise, the unknown frequency is the higher of the two. If the trace rotates anti-clockwise, the unknown frequency is the lower of the

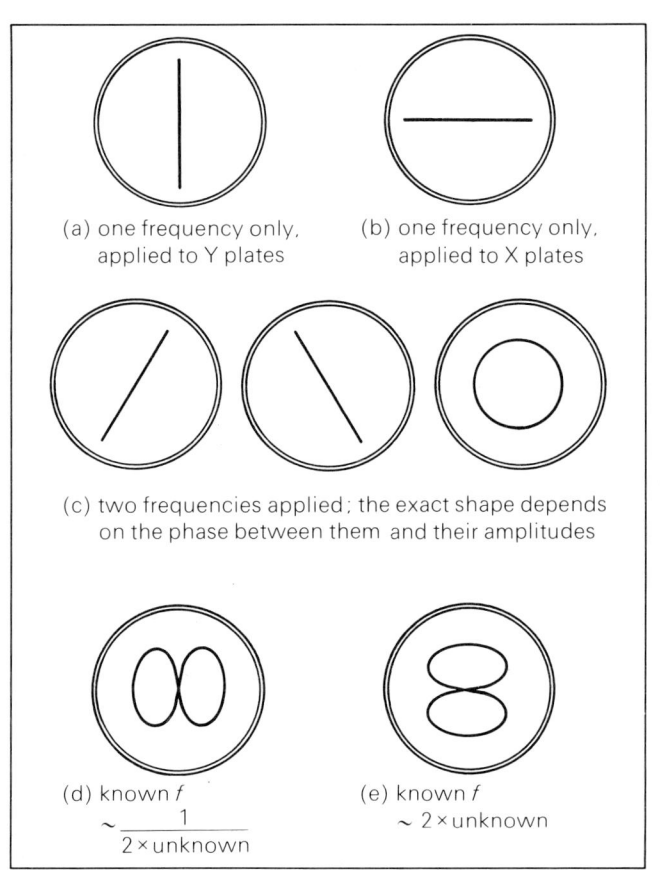

(a) one frequency only, applied to Y plates

(b) one frequency only, applied to X plates

(c) two frequencies applied; the exact shape depends on the phase between them and their amplitudes

(d) known f ~ $\frac{1}{2 \times \text{unknown}}$

(e) known f ~ 2 × unknown

Figure 133

EXPERIMENTAL TECHNIQUES

two. The number of revolutions per second is the difference between the two frequencies.

You will find this a sensitive method. However, the accuracy depends on the accuracy of the calibration of the signal generator.

If the unknown frequency is $50\,\text{Hz} \pm 5$ or integral multiples thereof up to about $10\times$, then a *low voltage* at mains frequency can be used instead of the signal generator. Traces seen will be similar to figure 133d. The number of 'peaks' is the integral multiple. In this trace:

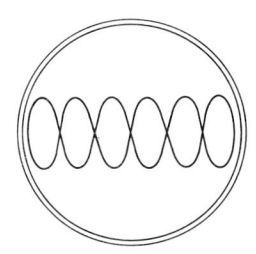

the number of peaks is 6. If this is seen rotating anticlockwise 0.5 times a second, the unknown frequency would be $(6 \times 50) - 0.5 = 299.5\,\text{Hz}$.

4. The stroboscope

The stroboscope can be used on mechanical vibrating systems, e.g. vibrating wires and rotating shafts. The stroboscope produces a short-duration flash of light at regular intervals. This is reflected from the object, and a variety of patterns can be seen, which may be rotating clockwise or anticlockwise. The flashing rate of the stroboscope is altered until the pattern is stationary. (See figure 134.)

Most mechanical vibrators do not have as constant a frequency as electrical vibrators and it will probably be impossible to make the pattern appear exactly still.

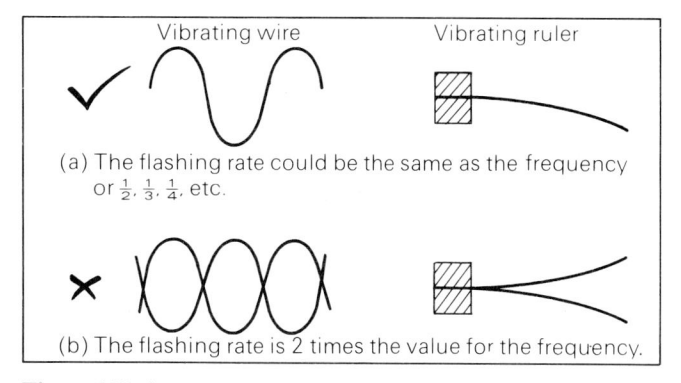

Figure 135 Appearance when using a stroboscope.

5. Direct counting (as in a digital frequency meter)

The electrical wave could be turned into a series of pulses and these could be counted on a digital counter. An accurate method of measuring the time for which counting has taken is needed.

Here is a relatively simple circuit (figure 136) which you could make up to illustrate the principle. It is best left until you have done some work on digital electronics.

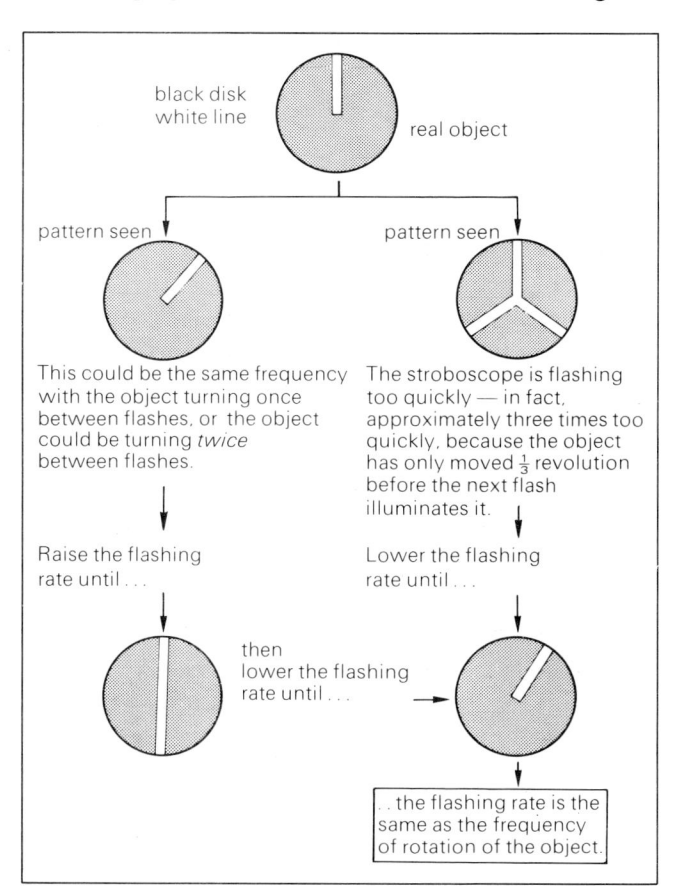

Figure 134

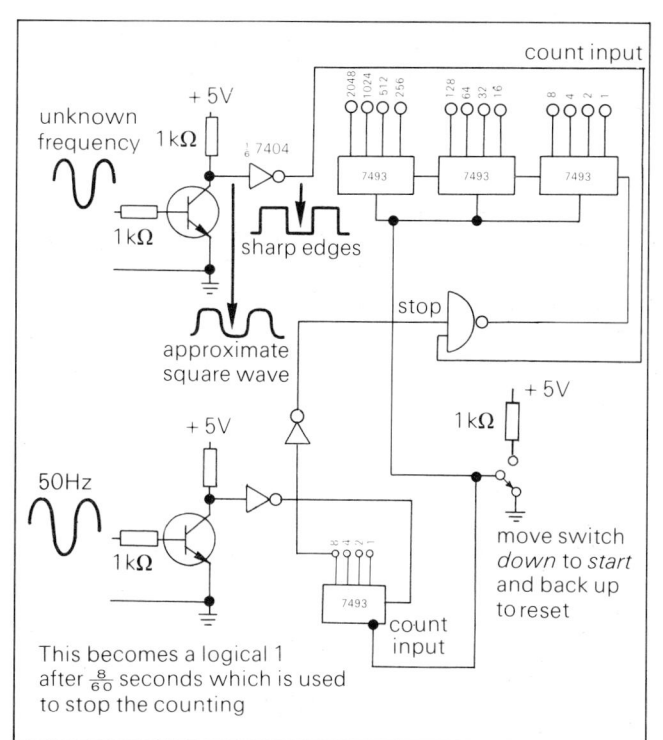

Figure 136

Work out the number counted from the output in binary, equals N.

$$\text{frequency} = \frac{N}{16/50} \text{Hz}$$

(This circuit uses only items which are in the JMB electronics option.)

6. Resonance

Any system which can be made to oscillate will produce only certain frequencies. If one or more of these frequencies is produced by *another* source in the vicinity of the first system, then stimulated vibration or resonance occurs. If the frequency of vibration of the second source is known, this gives one of the resonant frequencies of the first source. At resonance a marked increase in amplitude (or volume) is heard. An example is provided by changing the frequency of a vibrating air column (figure 137).

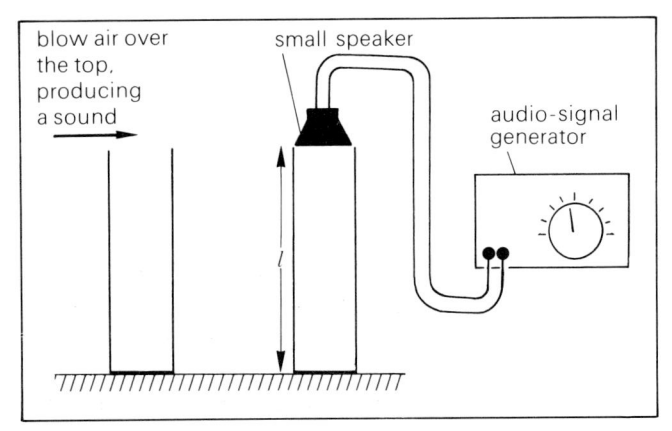

Figure 137 Resonance of an air column.

Start with a frequency of about 25 Hz and slowly increase the frequency, listening carefully. Record the frequency when the loudness shows a marked increase. It is sometimes difficult for an untrained ear to detect the difference between an increase in loudness and an increase in frequency (pitch), but practice helps. The volume of the sound produced by the speaker does not have to be very loud.

Experimental details

A. Take a gas jar and use the method described in (6) to find the frequencies at which it resonates. Simple theory predicts that the frequencies produced by a tube closed at one end are given by the equations:

$$f_1 = \frac{V}{4l}, \quad f_2 = \frac{3V}{4l}, \quad f_3 = \frac{5V}{4l}, \quad \text{etc.}$$

The velocity of sound is 331.3 m s^{-1} at 0°C and $V \propto \sqrt{\text{absolute temperature}}$. Measure the room temperature and find the velocity of sound at the frequencies.

Is there any difference between the predicted frequencies and the measured frequencies? If there is then (a) the measured frequency, or (b) the velocity, or (c) the vibrating length of the tube *l* must in some way be different to the one you have measured.

B. This involves using resonance with a sonometer wire.

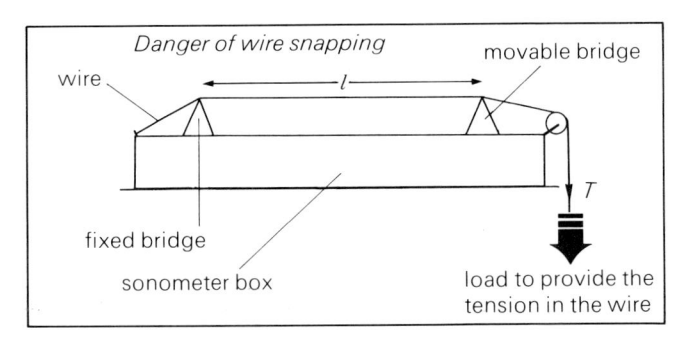

Figure 138 Resonance of a wire.

Set up the sonometer as shown in figure 138. Adjust the tension (*T*) and vibrating length (*l*) so that a frequency (*f*) of about 500 Hz is produced. Typical tensions needed are in the range 20–30 N. This can be assisted in two ways.

(a) By calculating suitable values for *T* and *l* using the equation

$$f = \frac{1}{2l}\sqrt{\frac{T}{m}}$$

where *m* is the mass per unit length of the wire.

(b) By using the arrangement below to display the frequency produced when the wire is plucked on an oscilloscope. An alternating e.m.f. is produced across the wire by electromagnetic induction. Find the time for one oscillation from the trace on the oscilloscope and calculate the frequency.

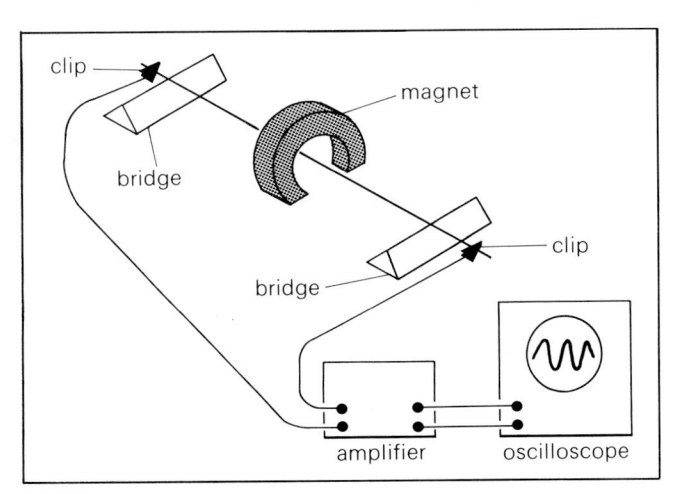

Figure 139

Now sound a 512 Hz tuning fork and place on the sonometer box. Pluck the wire and listen to the two sounds together. Alter the vibrating length (l) until beats are heard, and then continue until no beats are heard. The tuning fork and wire now have the same frequency. Test the precision of this by using resonance.

Place a small ∧-shaped paper rider on the middle of the wire (why the middle?). Sound the tuning fork and place on one of the bridges. The paper rider will fall off if the resonant frequency of the wire is the same as the tuning fork frequency.

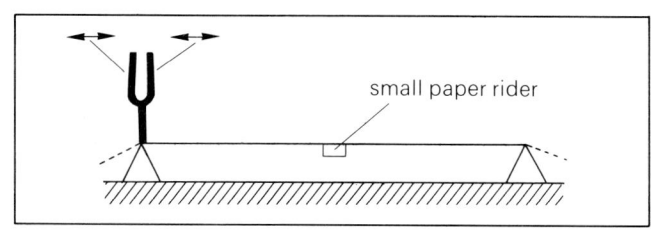

Figure 140

C. Use the 50 Hz *low voltage* supply from a power supply and use the Lissajous' figures method to find the frequency that the signal generator has been set to (figure 141). It is between 25 and 500 Hz. It would be sensible to display the frequency and use the time-base scale to work out an approximate value first.

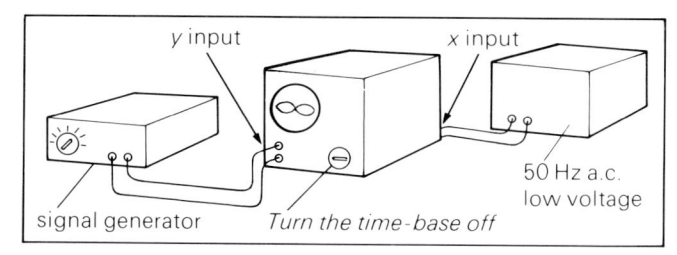

Figure 141

D. Use a stroboscope and the apparatus shown in figure 142. First (a) alter the frequency of rotation of the motor to exactly 32 Hz and then (b) calibrate the variable resistor used in the voltage divider with a speed scale in revolutions per minute.

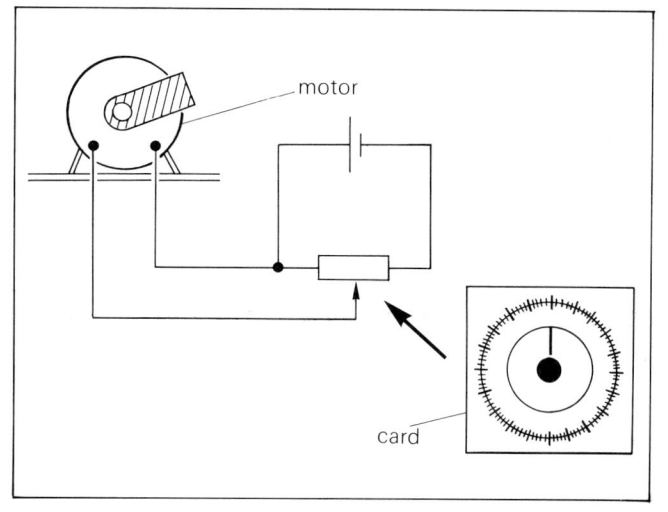

Figure 142

Proceed for (b) as follows.

1. Draw a circle on the piece of card and divide it into about 20 equal main divisions. Number them 0–20. Subdivide each into five parts (0.2 of a main division).
2. Find the frequency of rotation with the variable resistor set on each *main* mark.
3. Plot a graph of scale reading against frequency.
4. Now take a new piece of card. Using the graph, redraw the scale in equal frequency intervals. The scale will probably be non-linear.

14. THE FORCED VIBRATION OF A WIRE

Outline

A wire under tension will resonate and produce a maximum amplitude of vibration when forced to vibrate at certain frequencies. The amplitude of vibration at other frequencies is less. This experiment investigates how the amplitude of vibration changes with frequency and also uses the apparatus to measure the frequency of *low voltage* a.c. transformed down from the mains supply.

Experimental details

Use either apparatus (a) or (b) in figure 143.

1. Put a load of 5 N on the wire and adjust the voltage output of the a.c. source until it is about 5 V peak to peak.

Danger—do not use mains voltage a.c. or any other supply greater than 50 V.

Equipment

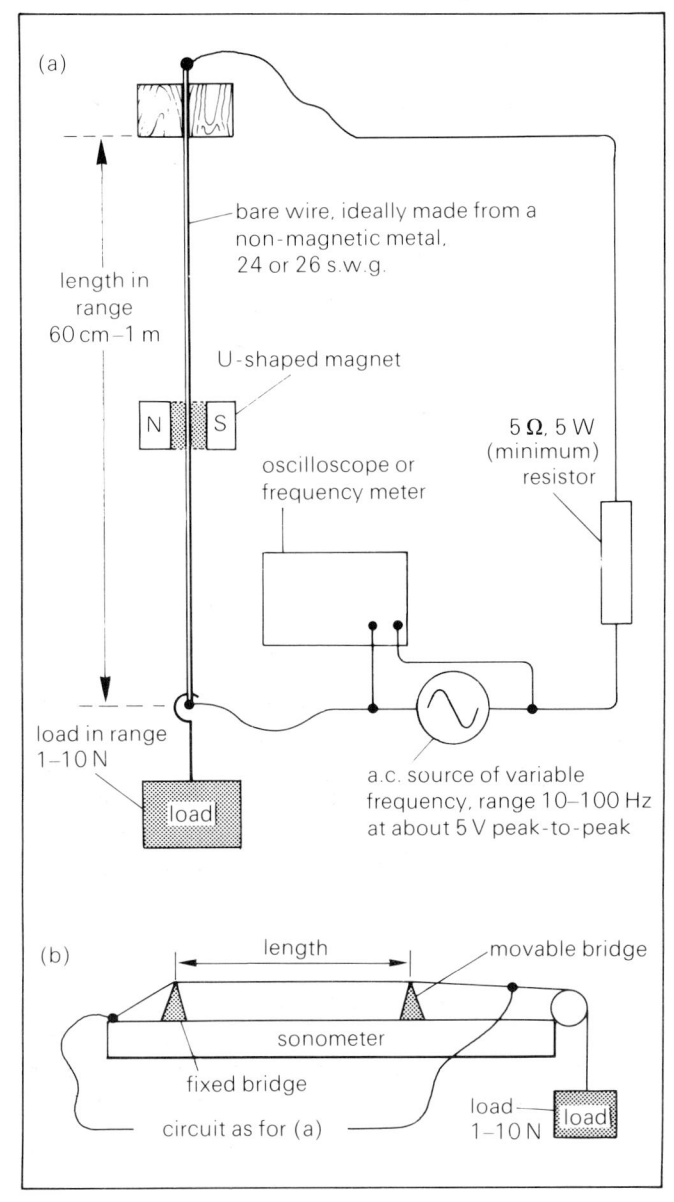

Figure 143 Apparatus

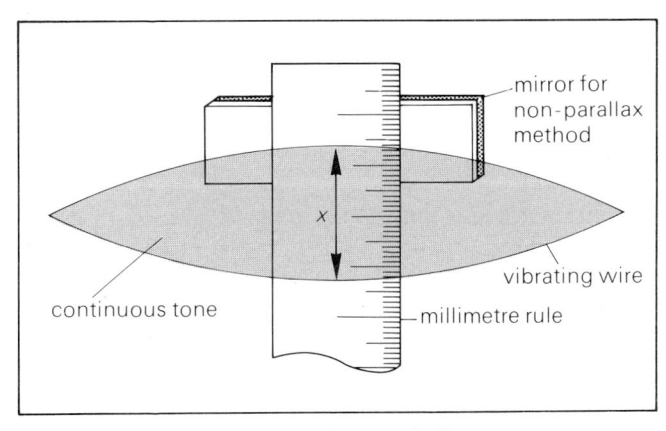

(a) bare wire, ideally made from a non-magnetic metal, 24 or 26 s.w.g.; length in range 60 cm – 1 m; U-shaped magnet; oscilloscope or frequency meter; 5 Ω, 5 W (minimum) resistor; load in range 1–10 N; a.c. source of variable frequency, range 10–100 Hz at about 5 V peak-to-peak.

(b) sonometer with length, movable bridge, fixed bridge, circuit as for (a), load 1–10 N.

Figure 144 Measuring the peak-to-peak distance.

mirror for non-parallax method; vibrating wire; millimetre rule; continuous tone; distance x.

2. Set the frequency on 10 Hz and slowly increase to find the frequency at which the wire resonates with maximum amplitude. Record this frequency and measure the peak-to-peak distance (x). See figure 144.

3. Measure the distance (x) produced at other frequencies. Make the frequency range larger and smaller than the resonant frequency until the distance (x) is about one tenth of the maximum value. Is it necessary to keep the supply voltage constant? Plot a graph of distance (x) against frequency.

4. It is suggested by your partner that the graph is part of a sine curve. Draw a sine curve (e.g. figure 145) in a different colour on the same sheet of graph paper and using the same maximum amplitude. Is she correct?

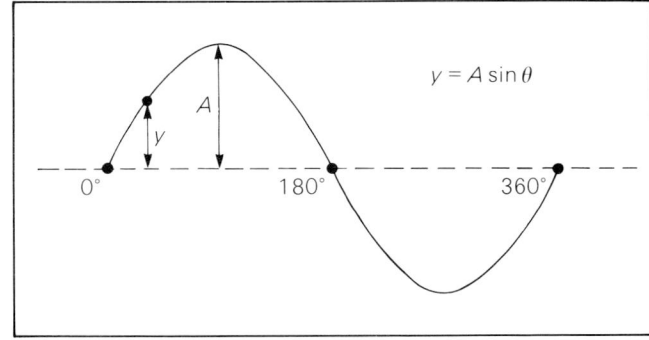

Figure 145 A sine wave $y = A \sin \theta$

5. Change the source of a.c. to a low voltage supply from a lab power supply transformed from the a.c. mains.

Never use the mains voltage directly.

Any r.m.s. voltage between 2 and 6 V would be suitable. Alter the load and/or the length until resonance occurs. Which will enable fine adjustment to be made more easily?

Work out the frequency from

$$f = \frac{1}{2l}\sqrt{\frac{T}{m}}$$

where

l = length of wire (m)
T = tension (load) in newtons
m = mass per unit length (kg m^{-1})

You will have to measure the mass per unit length.

Questions

1. Is the frequency the value you expected?
2. Give reasons as to whether the apparatus can be used to find the frequency to ±5% or not.

EXPERIMENTAL TECHNIQUES

15. THE SPECTROMETER

Outline

The spectrometer is used with a diffraction grating to resolve the light from a source into its component frequencies (figure 146). This is because a separate diffraction pattern is produced for each frequency present.

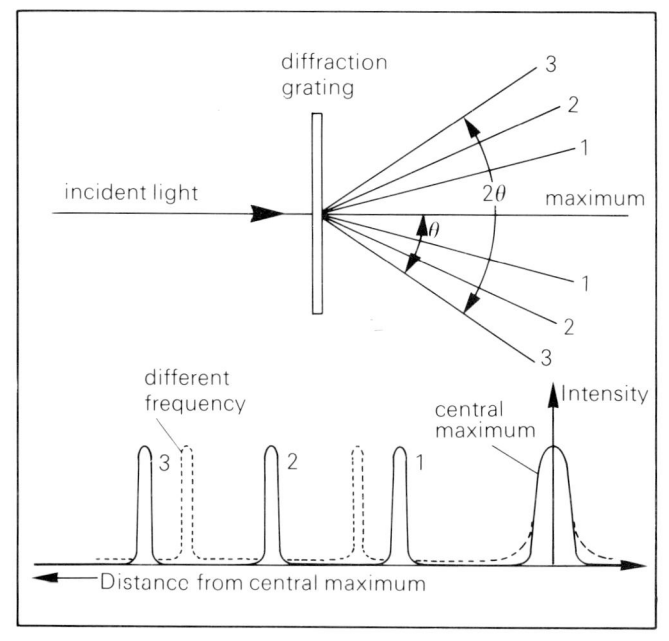

Figure 146

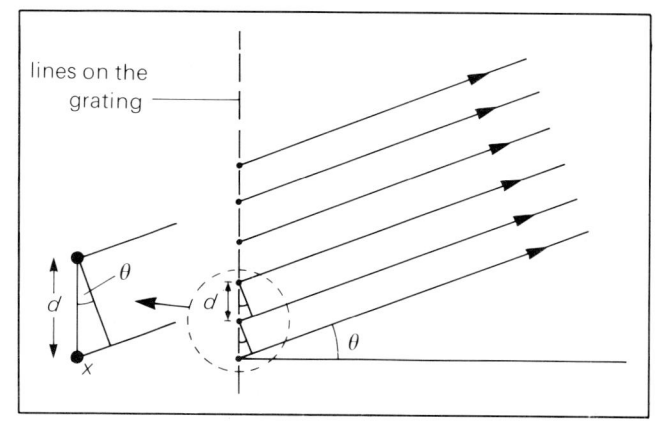

Figure 147

The lines are very sharp and different frequencies can be resolved. Each group of lines is called an *order* of diffraction. The equation is:

$$n\lambda = d \sin \theta$$

where
- n is the order of diffraction
- λ is the wavelength of the light
- θ is the angle from central line to a maximum
- d is the distance between two lines on the grating (remember this must be in metres)

The central maximum is fairly broad and flat-topped, so it is difficult to find the exact centre line. For this reason the angle (2θ) between the order on one side and the same order on the other side is measured. The vernier enables accurate readings to be taken. Using second- and third-order maxima enables several values of λ to be calculated and averaged.

Theory

Each line on the diffraction grating acts as a source of waves. A maximum occurs at angles θ (figure 147) where the light from each 'line' on the grating reaches the observer *in phase*. If the pattern is viewed from a distance (about $10 \times$ the width of the grating) and care is taken to view parallel light which would occur a very long way away (hence the use of a telescope), the path difference between any two adjacent sources is $d \sin \theta$ and this equals an integral number of wavelengths for a maximum. Hence $n\lambda = d \sin \theta$. If the rays are not viewed parallel, an interference pattern is still produced, but the angles at which maxima are viewed will not fit the equation $n\lambda = d \sin \theta$.

Experimental details

The diffraction grating should be perpendicular to the ray and at right angles to the plane of movement of the telescope (figure 148). Otherwise the image will shift up or down as the telescope is rotated and can go out of vision.

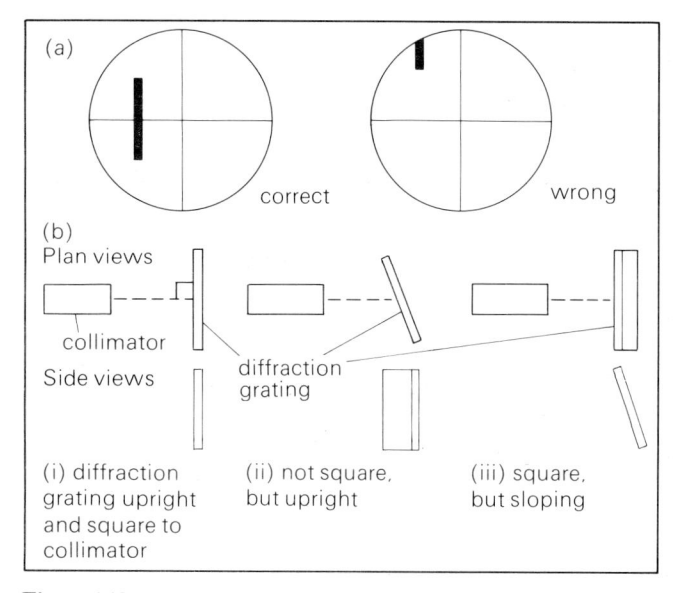

Figure 148

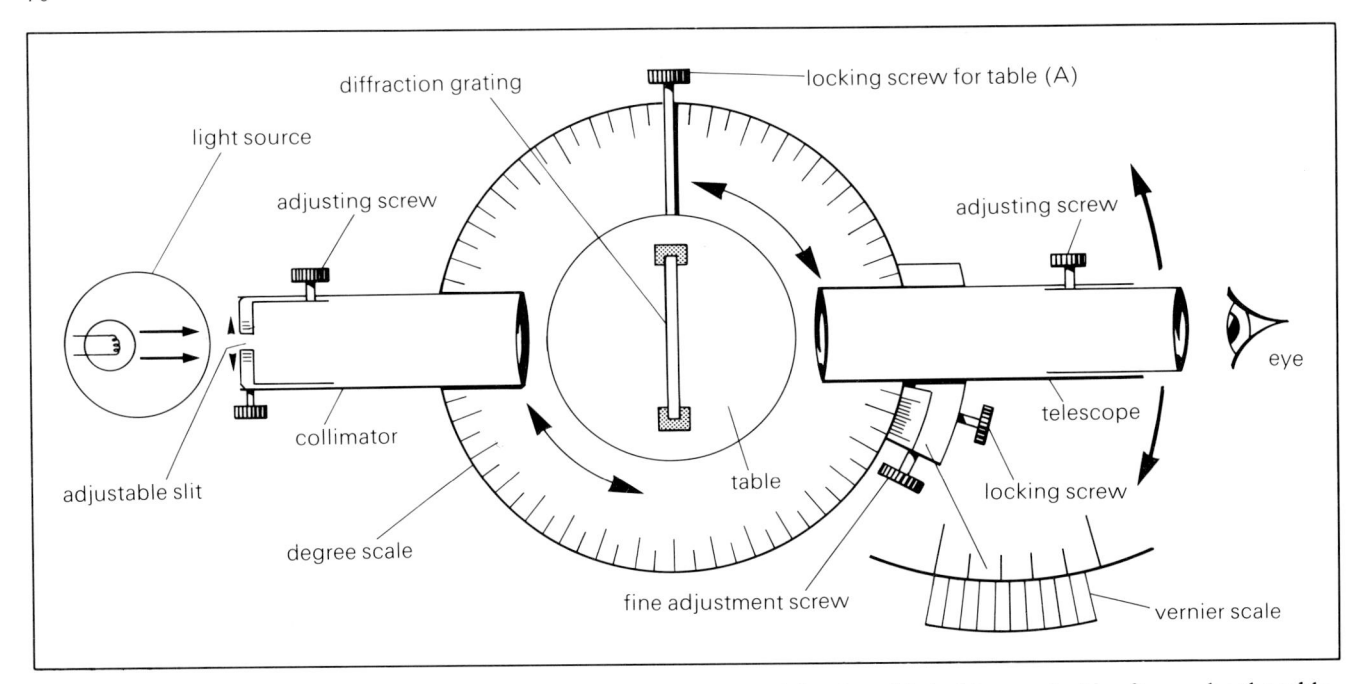

Figure 149 Plan view. On some spectrometers (A) only locks the table height; the table-locking control is often under the table.

A. Set up the spectrometer (figure 149) to view a monochromatic light, e.g. from sodium vapour. Move the telescope to each side of the central maximum and check that several orders of *diffraction* can be seen. If not, the plane of the surface of the grating is not perpendicular to the plane in which the telescope moves and the tilt of the table needs to be altered.

View the first-order maximum on one side. Fasten the locking screw and use the fine adjustment screw to move the telescope so that the cross wires are in line with the centre of the maximum. Read the angle from the scale, using the vernier to find the angle to an accuracy of at least 0.1°. Release the locking screw and move the telescope back past the central maximum to view the first-order maximum on the other side. Repeat the measurement of the angle. Find the angle through which the telescope has moved. (Remember that the scale is circular and the 0°/360° mark may be in between your readings. See figure 150.)

Calculate the wavelength, λ, from $n\lambda = d \sin \theta$ and repeat for as many other orders of diffraction as you can. Find an average value for λ and give an estimated error.

Repeat for any other gas discharge lamps which are available, e.g. mercury, and find the wavelengths of the lines present.

B. White light consists of a very wide range of frequencies and is often called a continuous spectrum. Set up the filament bulb and draw a set of diagrams to show what happens to the spectrum as the supply voltage is increased slowly from zero to the working voltage. Can you explain why this happens?

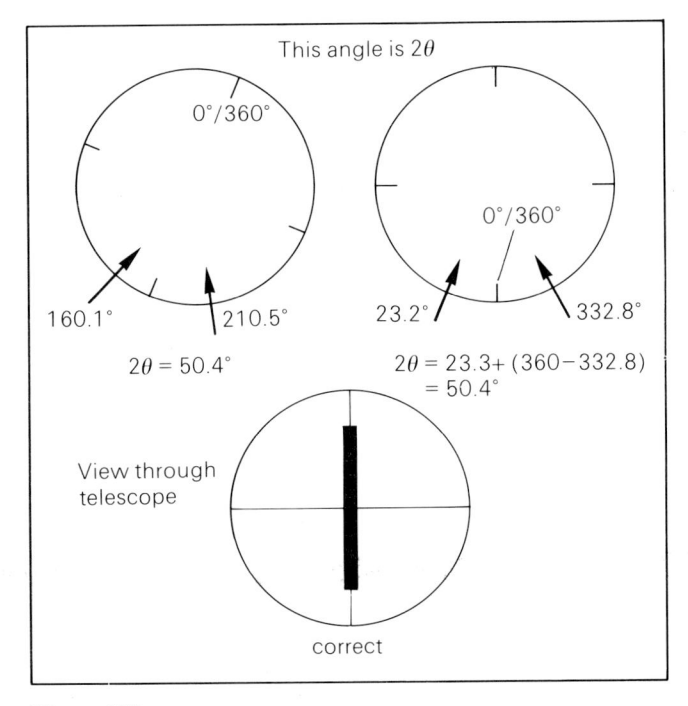

Figure 150

C. With the bulb at its normal brightness, place various coloured filters between the bulb and the slit. Take measurements and find any wavelengths you can. Draw diagrams of the spectra. Try and answer these questions:

1. Does a yellow filter let through red and green as well as yellow?
2. Can you combine filters to get as pure a green as possible?
3. What is the wavelength of the light through the blue filter?

EXPERIMENTAL TECHNIQUES

D. Some liquids absorb one or more frequencies of light so that the spectrum of white light passed through them has gaps in it. (Fraunhofer discovered gaps in the spectrum from the sun because of energy absorbed by hydrogen, helium, etc. in the sun's atmosphere.)

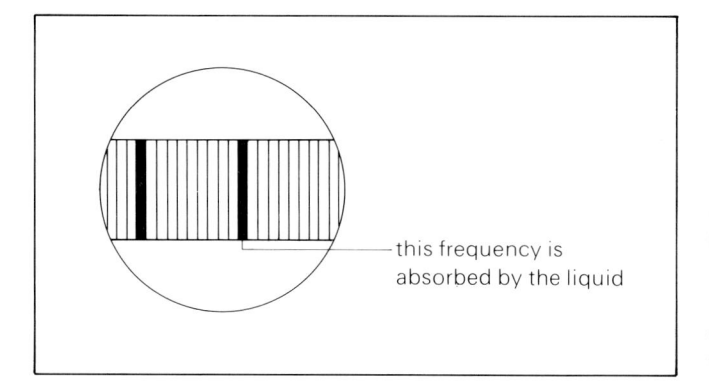

Figure 151 Absorbtion spectrum

E. Fluorescene can appear green or red. Find what colour it absorbs and estimate the wavelength.

Questions

1. Assuming the patterns are all viewed with the telescope at the same angle, work out the wavelengths of the lines in figure 152a and b.
2. A 1 cm wire mesh can be used as a diffraction grating for microwaves.
   The intensity pattern shown in figure 153 is plotted when a small aerial is moved along the line AB. Find the wavelength of the radio wave, assuming that the mesh spacing is 1 cm.

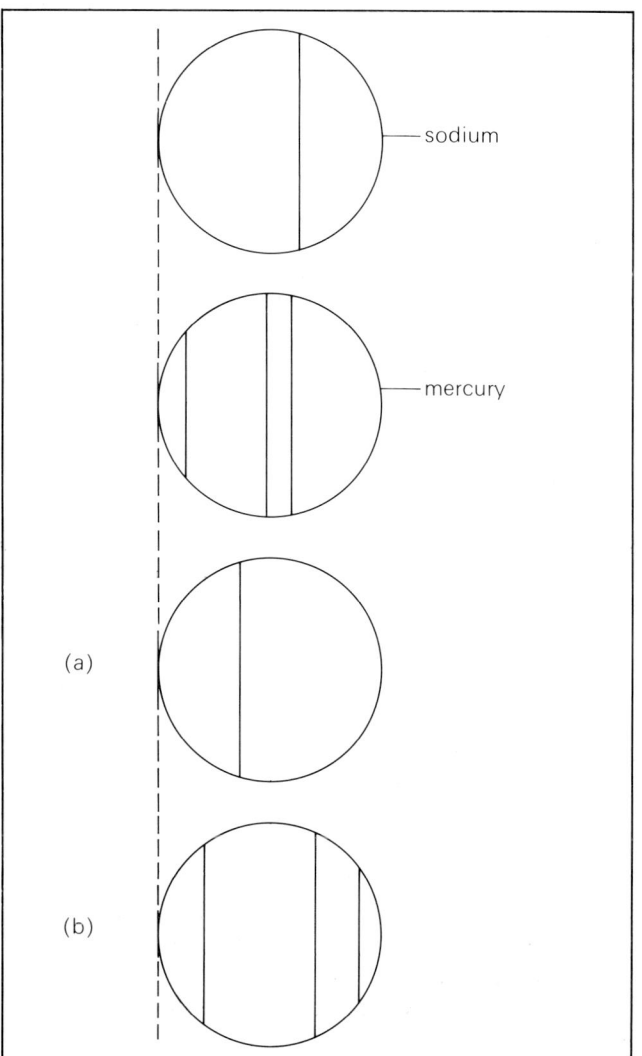

Figure 152

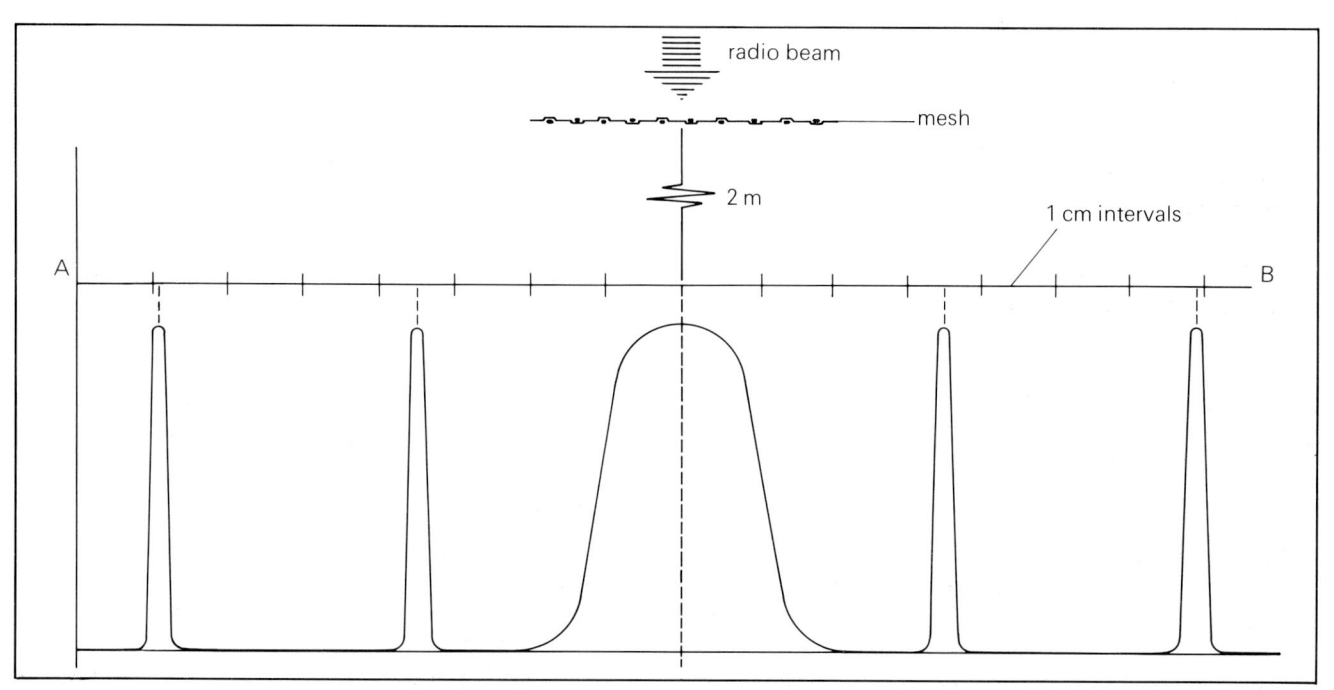

Figure 153

16. MEASURING POTENTIAL DIFFERENCE

Outline and information

So far you have probably only used a moving-coil voltmeter. This is an ammeter with a series resistance and so always draws some current from the circuit being measured. The instrument cannot follow any fluctuation in the voltage which would cause the pointer to move at a rate greater than about 0.5 Hz. If a rapidly fluctuating voltage is applied, the meter will tend to show an average value (figure 154). In the case of an a.c. (alternating current) voltage this would be zero and so the instrument is unsuitable for measuring a.c., and other methods must be found.

Voltages which are always positive or always negative are referred to as direct current (d.c.). Voltages which have both positive and negative parts are referred to as alternating current (a.c.). Zero voltage is often referred to as *ground* ('*GND*') or *earth*.

There is also a limit to how small the current needed to move the pointer can be made. This sets a limit to the sensitivity and also means that the effect of the meter on the *circuit* being measured needs to be considered. The movement of a typical moving coil meter has a full-scale deflection (f.s.d.) of 100 µA.

Calculation of the series resistor needed
Suppose the meter movement is marked f.s.d. 100 µA or 100 mV.

$$\text{resistance of the coil} = \frac{V}{I}$$
$$= \frac{100 \times 10^{-3}}{100 \times 10^{-6}}$$
$$= 1000\,\Omega$$

To measure, say, 0–5 V a 5 V p.d. must cause a current of 100 µA to flow. Using $R = \frac{V}{I}$, $R = 50\,000\,\Omega$, and so the series resistor needed is $50\,000 - 1000 = 49\,000\,\Omega$.

This is quite satisfactory for circuits where resistors of about 1 kΩ and less are used, because the current drawn is

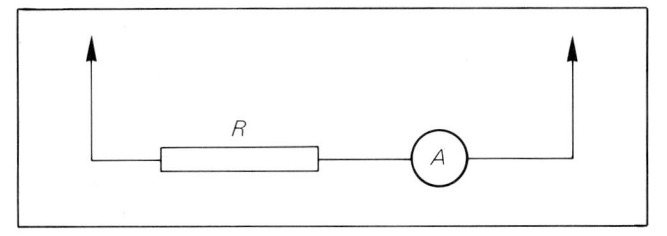

Figure 155 A voltmeter is an ammeter with a high resistance in series.

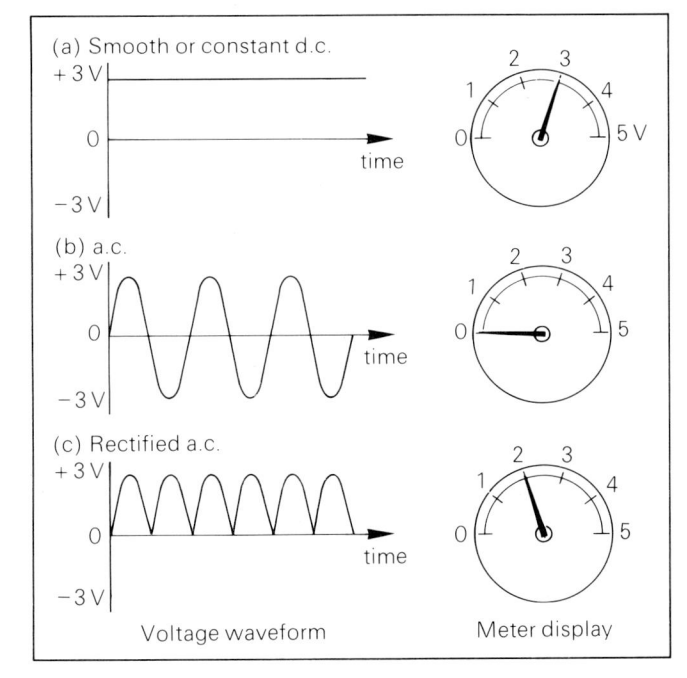

Figure 154

less than about 5% of the current flowing in the circuit and the meter is only accurate to about 5% anyway. Many electronic circuits contain resistors of 50 kΩ and larger, so that adding the meter into the circuit will significantly change the current flow. The instrument is therefore unsuitable. Some way must be found to increase the input resistance of the meter so that it draws a very small current (ideally zero). Four suitable instruments are:

(a) an operational amplifier used as a voltage follower;
(b) an oscilloscope;
(c) a potentiometer;
(d) an electronic digital voltmeter.

Alternating voltage (a.c. voltage)
A moving-coil meter cannot measure a.c. directly because at frequencies above about 2 Hz the mass of the coil and pointer prevents it moving fast enough to follow the voltage, and it remains at rest. One solution is to include a diode to rectify the a.c. into d.c. (figure 156).

One possible problem is that the average current produced depends on the frequency and the peak voltage, and the meter may need to be calibrated for each frequency.

An oscilloscope is ideal because it can display the waveform and the way the voltage changes with time as

EXPERIMENTAL TECHNIQUES

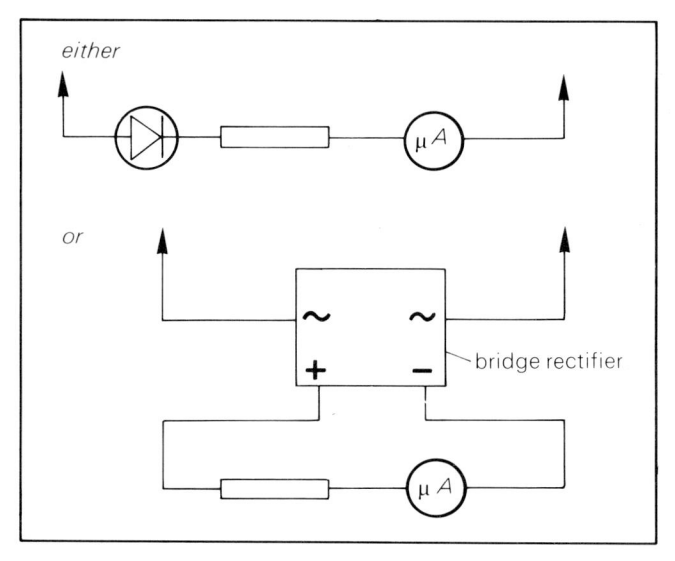

Figure 156

well. The peak-to-peak voltage is usually measured. The amplitude is half this value and the r.m.s. voltage (equivalent steady d.c. in a pure resistor) is

$$\frac{\text{amplitude}}{\sqrt{2}}$$

Another advantage is the high input resistance.

Moving-iron meter. The current produced in a coil induces a magnetic field in two pieces of soft iron which repel and move a pointer on a scale. The magnetic force produced depends on the shape of the pole pieces and on their distance apart but does not decrease *linearly* with distance. This means that the scale is usually non-linear. More current is needed to operate it than a moving coil meter, and so it generally has a *low* input resistance.

1. DIRECT VOLTAGE (D.C. VOLTAGE) EXPERIMENTS

Use each method, described in 1, 2, 3 and 4 below, that you have available and measure the potential difference AB across the resistor in the circuits shown in figure 157. Use the same source of e.m.f. each time. A 1.5 V dry cell battery is suitable.

Are the values for the voltages measured by each method as expected? Will the internal resistance of the dry battery have any effect? Comment on your results and findings in your report.

1. Moving coil voltmeter

You may be given a meter with the correct series unit to produce the range needed or a basic meter and asked to calculate the value of the resistor needed.

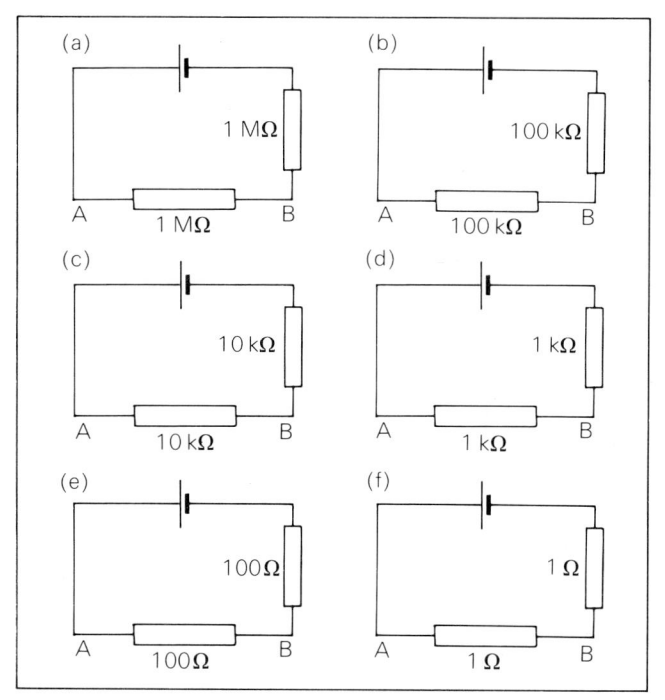

Figure 157

2. Operational amplifier as a voltage follower

The operational amplifier has an input resistance of at least 1 MΩ, and is connected in a *voltage follower* arrangement, as shown in figure 158.

A digital voltmeter uses an operational amplifier at its input and so have a very high input resistance.

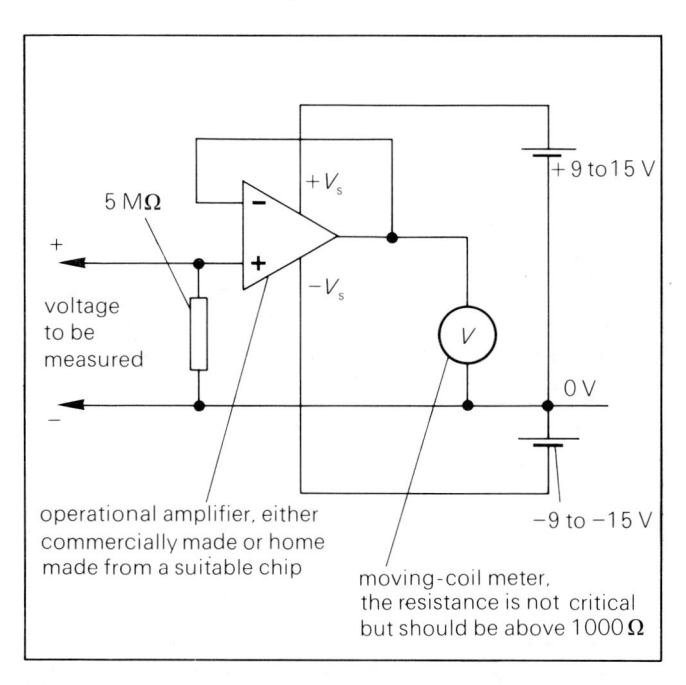

Figure 158 A voltage follower circuit

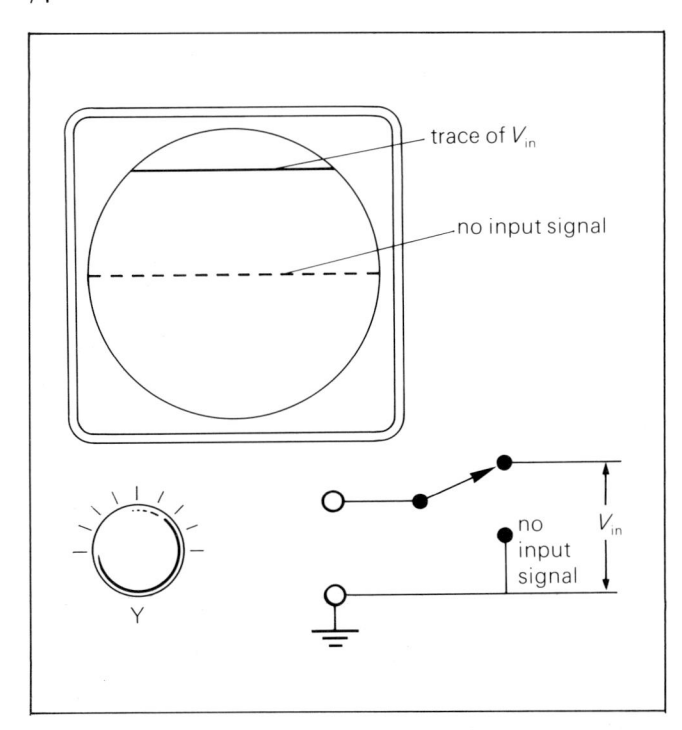

Figure 159 Ground the input to check for any movement of the origin.

3. Oscilloscope

An oscilloscope has an input resistance $>5\,\text{M}\Omega$.

1. Set the time-base to produce a steady line.
2. Set the trace to the middle of the screen with no input signal. A circuit with a two-way switch can be used to keep checking any movement of the origin during the experiment (see figure 159).
3. Always check the Y calibrator with a known voltage, e.g. Weston standard cell 1.0186 V.
4. Record the distance of movement of the trace on the screen and the Y sensitivity. Then calculate the actual voltage. The oscilloscope has the advantage of being able to show any change of potential difference with time.

Note: Some oscilloscopes have an a.c./d.c. switch (figure 160). The circuit usually contains a capacitor to block any d.c. component, so it should really be labelled a.c. only/any voltage.

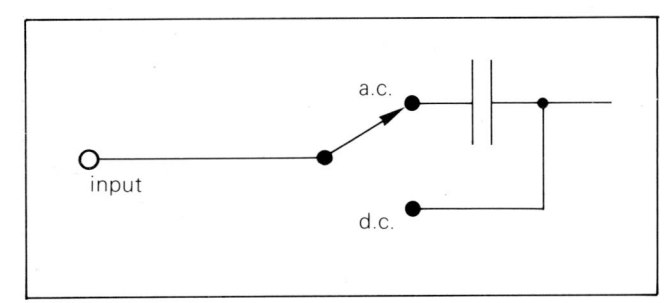

Figure 160

4. Potentiometer

When adjusted to measure a voltage, a potentiometer draws *no* current at all and so has an *infinite* input resistance. It is suitable for measuring e.m.f.s. An e.m.f. is defined as the potential difference when *no* current flows.

The instrument you will use in the laboratory needs assembling from separate parts before use!

Part 1 consists of a circuit which produces a continuous change of voltage across a wire AB (see figure 161). The total voltage drop across the wire must be larger than the voltage to be measured. The wire AB is usually 1 m or 2 m long with a millimetre scale alongside, and has a typical resistance of 10 Ω.

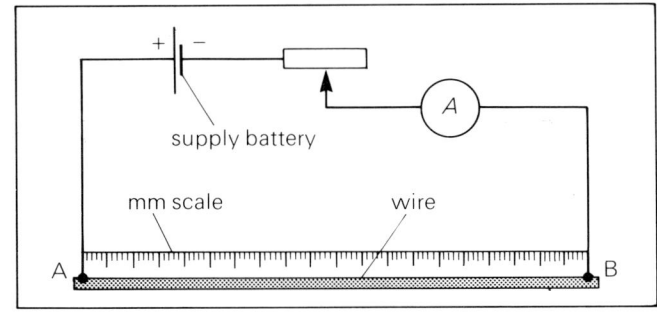

Figure 161

The current which must flow to produce a p.d. between A and B of, say, 3 V, is $\frac{3}{10}\,\text{A} = 300\,\text{mA}$. Once set to the particular value, the current must not be altered. The current should not exceed 500 mA, otherwise the heat generated will cause the potentiometer wire to expand too much.

Part 2 consists of the connections to the voltage to be measured (see figure 162).

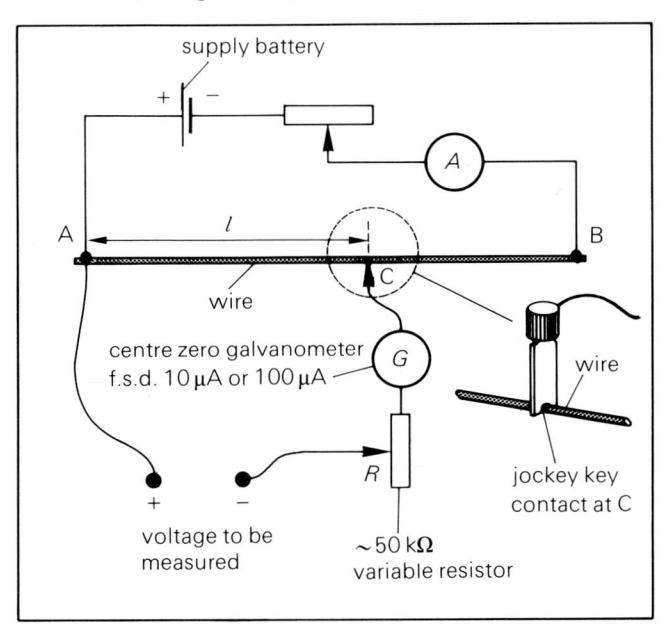

Figure 162 A full potentiometer circuit; the jockey key contact at C is accurate to 1 mm, do not *slide* it along the wire.

EXPERIMENTAL TECHNIQUES

To measure a voltage:

1. Set the variable resistor on maximum.
2. Check that the *positive* (+) of the voltage to be measured is connected to A.
3. Place the contact (C) at A and note the direction the galvanometer deflects in.
4. Place the contact at B, and if the galvanometer deflects in the opposite direction all is well. If it does not, then either
   (a) the two polarities at A are not the same sign, or
   (b) the voltage drop across the wire is *less* than the voltage being measured, so the current must be increased or a longer wire used.
5. Move the contact until a null balance position is found where no current flows through the galvanometer G. Reduce the value of the 'safety' resistor R to make the galvanometer more sensitive so that the null balance position can be found with the greatest accuracy.
6. Measure the distance (l) of the null balance position *from end A*. For maximum accuracy, l should be as large as possible. Adjust the current if necessary.
7. In order to translate this distance l into a voltage, the potentiometer must be calibrated *without altering the current* flowing through the wire. To calibrate the potentiometer, use a voltmeter to measure the p.d. across the wire. Then choose a stabilised e.m.f. less than this value, find a null balance point and measure l_{cal}. Ideally, for lowest error l_{cal} should be longer than half-way, but this is often not possible in practice. The common standard source is a Weston standard cell, e.m.f. 1.0186 V to within 0.01% at 20°C.

The voltage measured is calculated by proportion:

$$\frac{V}{l} = \frac{V_{cal}}{l_{cal}}$$

Note that because the current flowing through the wire is kept constant the wire does not have to be ohmic, only of uniform cross-sectional area and composition.

2. ALTERNATING VOLTAGE (A.C. VOLTAGE) EXPERIMENTS

1. Using an oscilloscope to measure the peak-to-peak voltage

Connect a *low voltage* 50 Hz supply of about 6 V to an oscilloscope with the time base turned off. The display will be a vertical straight line. Alter the Y-sensitivity until the trace is as large as possible without going outside the edges of the screen. If there is a vertical scale on the graticule use the X-shift control to position the trace on the scale. Otherwise fasten a piece of mm graph paper

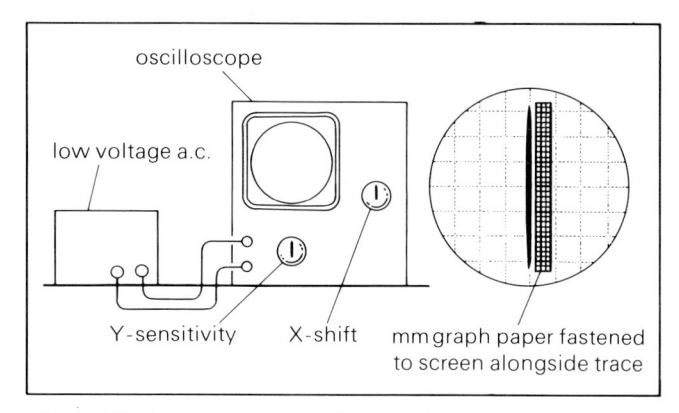

Figure 163 Measuring the peak-to-peak voltage.

vertically on the screen. Measure the length of the trace and use the Y-sensitivity to calculate the peak-to-peak voltage.

Now calculate the r.m.s. voltage. This is the value usually given for an a.c. voltage. This is because it is the value of the steady d.c. voltage which would transfer the same amount of energy as the a.c. voltage when a current flows. In the instructions for setting up this experiment the 6 V should more correctly have been given as 6 V r.m.s. (root-mean-square).

$$\text{r.m.s. voltage} = \frac{\text{(peak-to-peak)}}{2\sqrt{2}}$$

2. Calibration of a moving-coil a.c. voltmeter

Set up the apparatus as in figure 164. Adjust the voltage sensitivity of the oscilloscope so that a peak-to-peak voltage of 30 V can be measured (5 V cm^{-1} is suitable). Start at a frequency of 25 Hz. Alter the voltage produced.

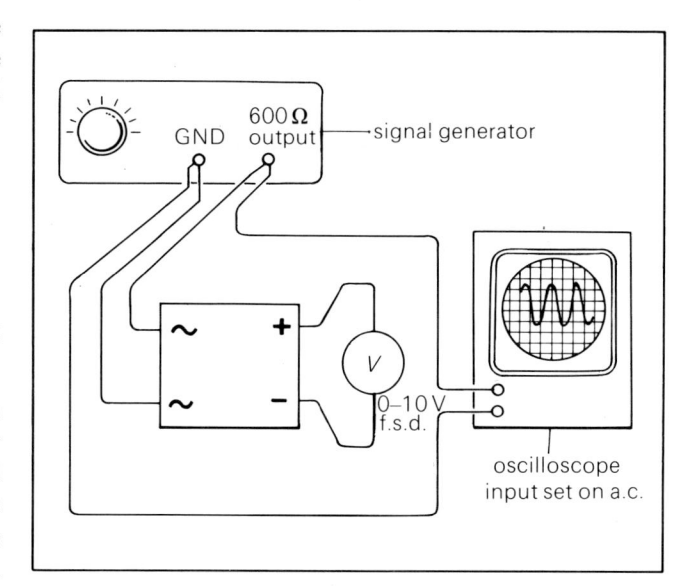

Figure 164

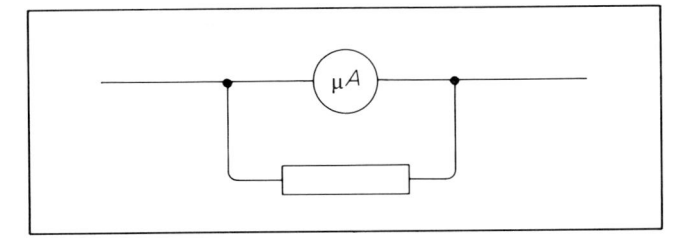

Figure 167 A shunt

To enable the instrument to measure larger currents, a resistance smaller than that of the meter is connected in *parallel* and is called a *shunt* (figure 167).

To enable the instrument to measure potential difference, a high resistance is connected in *series*, and is called a *multiplier* (figure 168).

The range used must be correctly chosen for the current or voltage being measured, i.e. full-scale deflection (f.s.d.) of 1 mA, 100 mA, 1 A, 1 V, 5 V, etc. Most scales increase by a factor of 10, so if a reading is less than ten per cent of f.s.d., use the next higher sensitivity.

Equipment

You are provided with: ammeters and voltmeters with shunts and series units for various sensitivities in the range 1 mA to 5 A and 0.1 V to 10 V; an oscilloscope; digital ammeters and voltmeter if available; resistors in the range 5 Ω to 1 MΩ; BBC computer (optional).

Experimental details

Using approximately 6 V d.c. as a supply voltage, find the resistance of each resistor you have been given. Use first circuit (a) and then circuit (b) (shown in figure 169) to investigate if each type of circuit is suited to a particular range of resistance values.

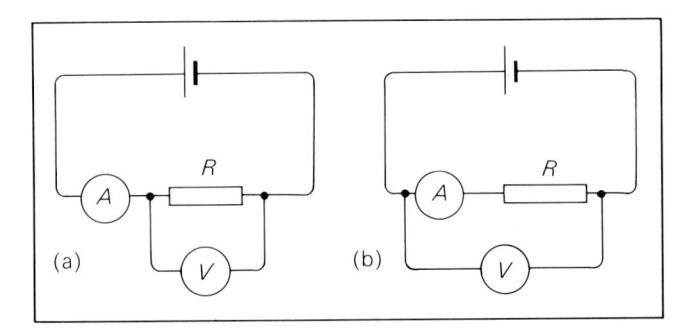

Figure 169

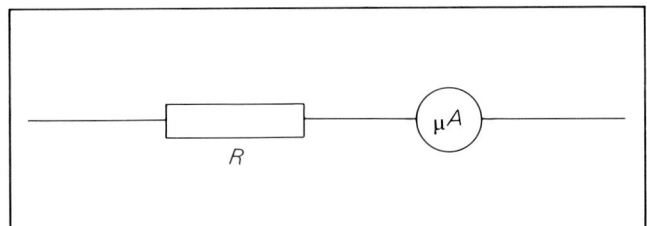

Figure 168 A multiplier

Measure the potential difference with both the moving-coil meter and with the oscilloscope or digital voltmeter.

Results

As well as measuring the resistance you can calculate the value which will be produced by each circuit for any given resistance. The calculation uses the resistances of the ammeter, the voltmeter and the marked resistance value. This can give you information on the accuracy to be expected.

The computer program 'METERS' (package PHYS1 option 6) will enable you to enter the supply voltage, the ammeter and voltmeter resistances and a range of resistances. It can display a graph of actual resistance against measured resistance or a list of the two sets of resistances so that the percentage error can be calculated if required. (See figure 170.)

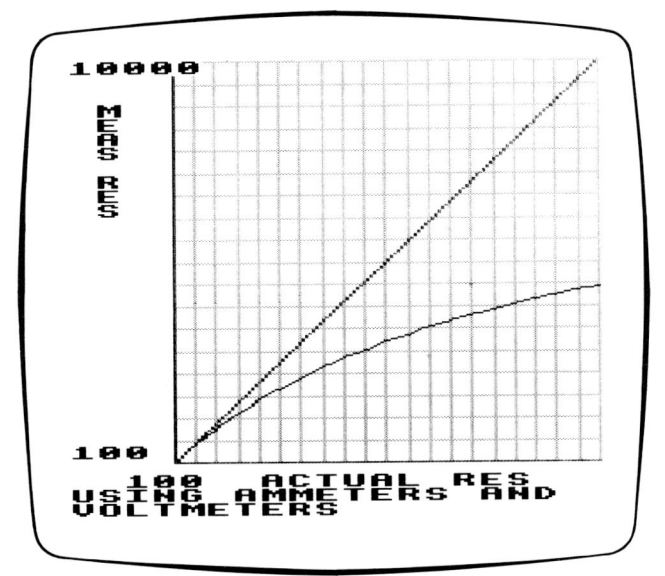

Figure 170 Example computer output

Marked resistance value/Ω	Moving coil meter			Oscilloscope		
	p.d./V	current/A	calculated resistance/Ω	p.d./V	current/A	calculated resistance/Ω

EXPERIMENTAL TECHNIQUES

Use the program with the same range of values of resistance as used in the experiment. The values produced can help you to answer the questions. Another use of the program would be to investigate the effect of using different values of ammeter and voltmeter resistance.

Further experiment

Find the resistance of the basic coil movement of the meter. You know it must be low (or do you?) and that you must choose the correct circuit (a) or (b) to use. Find the f.s.d. of the basic coil movement.

From these two, calculate the value of the series resistor needed to make a voltmeter of range 0–15 V.

Calculate also the parallel (shunt) resistor needed to make a 0–50 mA ammeter.

Connect a resistance box to your meter and set up your calculated resistance on the box. Then test them out and comment on the results.

19. WHEATSTONE BRIDGE AND METRE BRIDGE

Outline

Wheatstone bridge

The Wheatstone bridge was devised as an accurate method of measuring resistance or detecting a small change of resistance which could not be accurately detected by the normal ammeter/voltmeter method, e.g. platinum resistance thermometer. Four resistors are used in a bridge network. Two are fixed values (P and R), one is variable in known steps (Q) (e.g. decade resistance box) and one is the unknown resistor (X).

To find X, resistor Q is altered until a null balance is found, that is, when the current through the galvanometer (G) is zero. The choice of values for P and R will affect both the sharpness of the null balance point and the number of significant figures to which X can be found. At the null balance point,

$$\frac{P}{Q} = \frac{R}{X}$$

which is derived knowing that p.d.$_{AB}$ = p.d.$_{AD}$ and p.d.$_{BC}$ = p.d.$_{DC}$ because B and D must be at the same potential if no current flows through G.

Metre bridge

The metre bridge is a form of Wheatstone's bridge which is simpler to use. A length of resistance wire is used for the lower two resistors. This often has a resistance of approximately 10 Ω.

The contact on the resistance wire is altered until a null balance position is found. This is when the current through the galvanometer (G) is zero. Then, provided the resistance wire is uniform,

$$\frac{U}{x} = \frac{R}{y}.$$

For greatest accuracy, the balance point should be in the centre section of the wire and R should be adjusted until it is. If $U \gg R$ or $U \ll R$, the null balance point may be so near the end of the wire that it *seems* as if there is no null balance point. Watch out for this. The solution is to increase or decrease R.

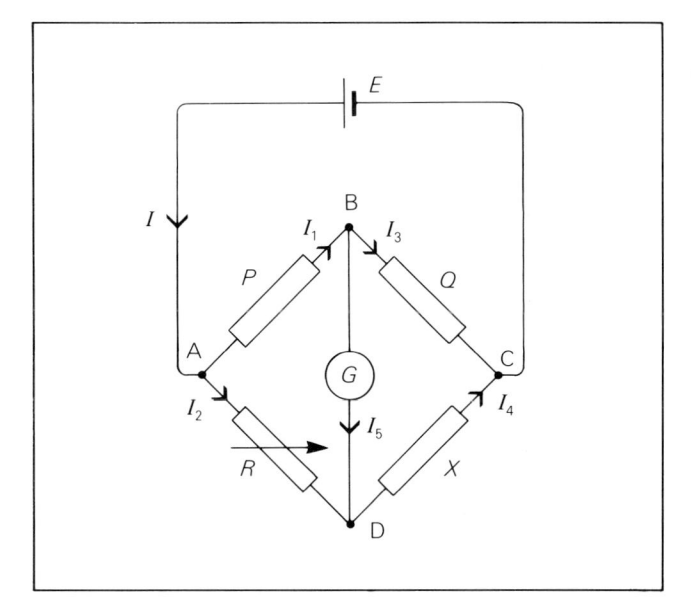

Figure 171 A Wheatstone bridge

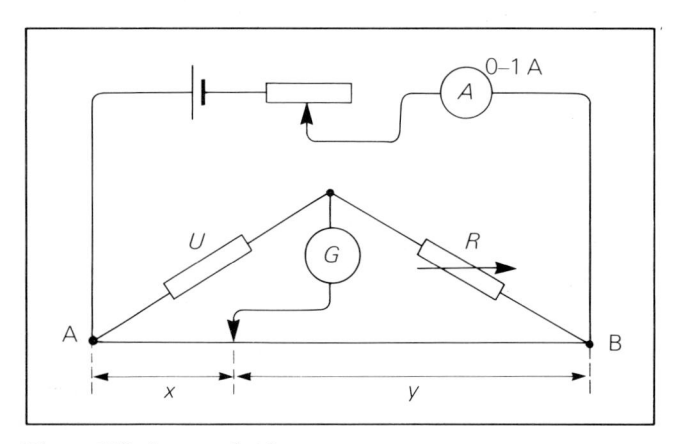

Figure 172 A metre bridge

Equipment

AB is a 1 m length of uniform resistance wire. R is a resistance box with a range of 0–10 000 Ω in 1 Ω steps. U is the unknown resistance (the maximum value of R will govern the maximum value which can be measured). G is a centre-zero galvanometer of f.s.d. 100 µA or less with a series limiting resistor if necessary. The battery is approximately 1.5 to 2 V.

Assemble the apparatus as shown in figure 172, using thick connecting wires because the resistances of the connecting wires are included in the values of U and R and need to be kept as small as possible.

Experimental details

A. Find the value of the unknown resistance U by placing it in position in the circuit. Remember to give an accuracy to which the null balance position can be found.

B. Find the resistance of the thermistor at a temperature of $45 \pm 1°C$. (The problem here is to find a way of keeping the temperature in range long enough to balance the bridge and take measurements.)

C. Is it possible to use the metre bridge to measure the resistance between two electrodes placed about 0.5 m apart (a) in dry earth and (b) in damp earth?

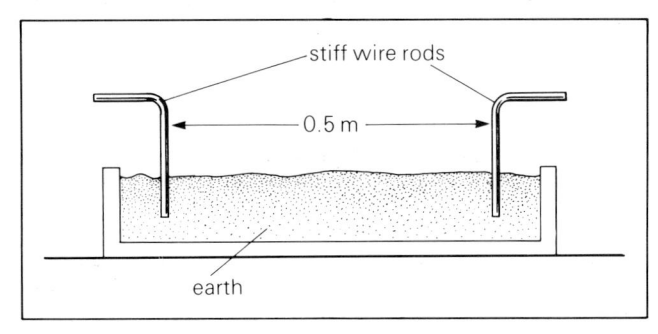

Figure 173

D. You are given two lengths of resistance wire. Measure the resistance of each. Work out the resistivity of each and decide if the wires are made from the same material.

$$\text{resistance} = \frac{\text{resistivity} \times \text{length}}{\text{cross-sectional area}}$$

In your report
1. Describe a metre bridge and explain how to use it.
2. Describe the procedure for each experiment and discuss any problems you found. Present the results taken and show how they lead to the conclusions that you made.

Further investigation

In the form of Wheatstone bridge that uses four separate resistances P, Q, R, S, the relationship between them is

$$\frac{P}{Q} = \frac{R}{X}$$

This equation is found in most A-level textbooks. It is interesting to use Kirchhoff's laws to find an equation for I_5 out of balance. The current through the galvanometer (I_5) equals:

$$\frac{E(RQ - PX)}{RPQ + RGQ + PXQ + PGQ + RPX + QGX + PGX + RXQ}$$

The sharpness of the null balance position depends on the values of P and Q used in relation to X and R. For example:

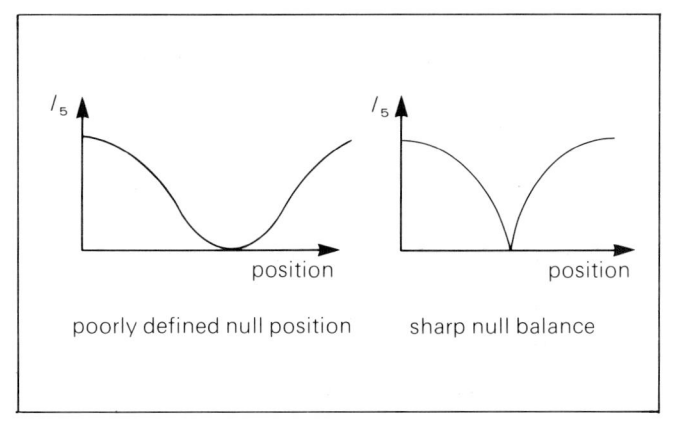

Figure 174

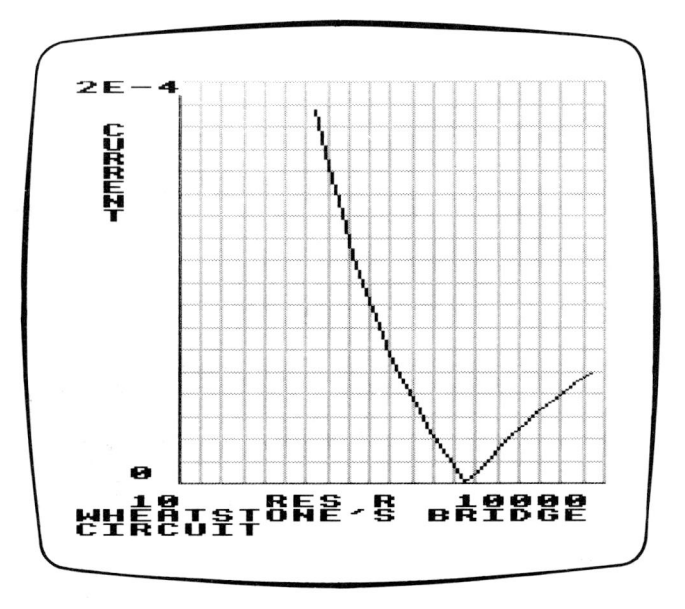

Figure 175 Sample computer output on the BBC computer

EXPERIMENTAL TECHNIQUES

Use the computer program 'WHEAT' (package PHYS1 option 8) to find the values of P and Q which produce the sharpest null balance for a given unknown resistor size (produced at random by the computer). Tabulate your findings, as shown here, and then make any conclusions that you can. Figure 175 shows a sample computer output on the BBC computer.

Resistance X/Ω	R/Ω	P/Ω	Q/Ω

20. FINDING THE RESISTIVITY OF A RESISTANCE WIRE USING A METRE BRIDGE

Outline

The usual form of metre bridge used at A-level has thick copper strips for the conductors to produce low resistance connections. Most experiments you may be required to do in a practical examination involve measuring the resistance of wires of varying lengths and diameters. From the measurements, you are often required to plot a graph and to find the resistivity of the material of the wire from it.

At a null balance position (no current through the galvanometer G):

$$\frac{\text{resistance of the wire}}{R} = \frac{x}{y}$$

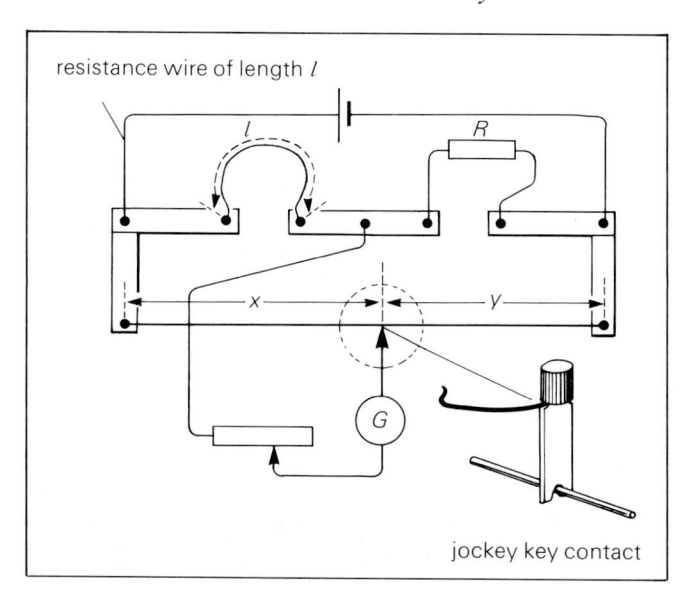

Figure 176 Equipment; R is a known standard resistor connected by short thick wires (you have a set of different values available).

Experimental details

You are given a 1 m length of resistance wire with a total resistance in the range 5–30 Ω. Use the metre bridge to measure the resistance of different lengths of the wire. You will need to choose which standard resistors(s), R, to use. Remember that for maximum accuracy the null balance position should be near the centre of the wire. Measure the diameter of the wire at several places. Calculate the average diameter and then the cross-sectional area.

$$\text{resistance} = \frac{\text{resistivity} \times \text{length}}{\text{cross-sectional area}}$$

Plot a suitable graph and find the resistivity from it.

Results

Length of wire/cm	R/Ω	x/cm	y/cm	Resistance of wire/Ω

Use the following data of resistivities to decide the type of material from which the wire is made

eureka	=	$53 \times 10^{-8}\,\Omega\text{m}$
German silver	=	$33 \times 10^{-8}\,\Omega\text{m}$
Manganin	=	$45 \times 10^{-8}\,\Omega\text{m}$
invar	=	$81 \times 10^{-8}\,\Omega\text{m}$
nichrome	=	$117 \times 10^{-8}\,\Omega\text{m}$
nickel	=	$59 \times 10^{-8}\,\Omega\text{m}$
Constantan	=	$47 \times 10^{-8}\,\Omega\text{m}$
bronze	=	$30 \times 10^{-8}\,\Omega\text{m}$

21. DISPLAYING AND DRAWING WAVEFORMS ON AN OSCILLOSCOPE

Outline

This practical shows you how to set up an oscilloscope and gives you practice at drawing accurate diagrams of the traces and explaining how their shape is caused.

An oscilloscope plots a graph of voltage against time. The maximum sensitivity is usually about 10 or 100 mV cm^{-1} vertical deflection, and so small voltages can be measured. Its advantage over a moving-coil meter is its very large input resistance and its rapid response. This means that it draws virtually no current from the circuit being measured and so will hardly affect the circuit being measured. This effect is more noticeable the smaller the currents flowing in the circuit and so the oscilloscope is widely used in measurements on electronic circuits.

All oscilloscopes have the same basic controls (see figure 177).

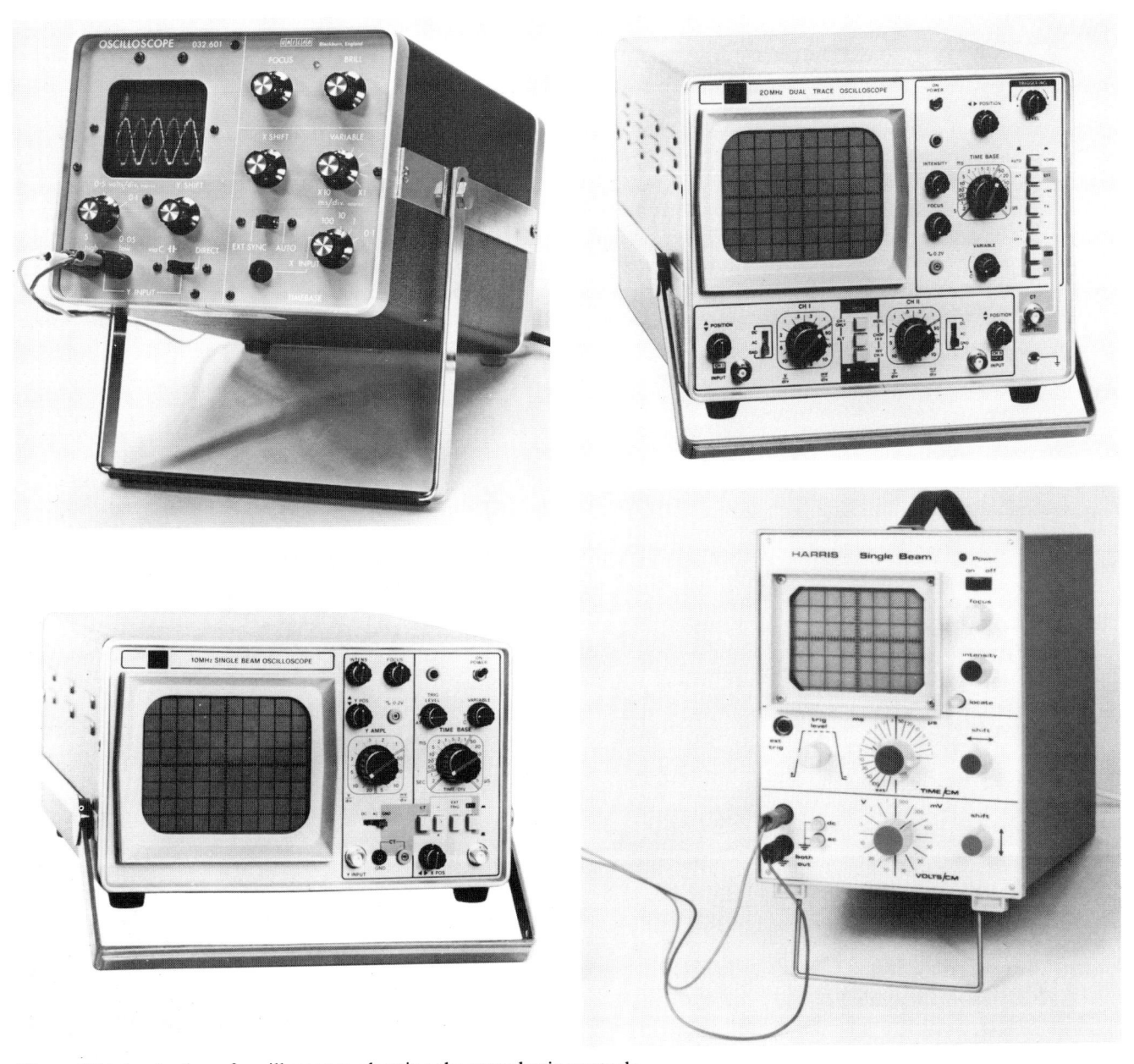

Figure 177 A selection of oscilloscopes, showing the same basic controls.

EXPERIMENTAL TECHNIQUES

1. *Setting up the oscilloscope*

The first step is to switch on and alter the controls to get a sharp line in the centre of the screen. Turn the brightness to about half. If there is no spot or line visible, make sure the *time-base* is turned on and the *stability* control is turned fully to one side. It is usually clockwise. If this does not produce the spot or line, the *trigger level* could be set too low. Look at figure 178 and then alter the controls until a sharp line is in the centre of the screen.

Connect a signal generator to the oscilloscope (figure 179). If there are *earth* symbols on the output and input, make sure these are connected together (usually a ⏚ symbol or a green or black terminal).

Choose any frequency between 500 and 5000 Hz and, using figure 180, set up the oscilloscope to display a suitable waveform.

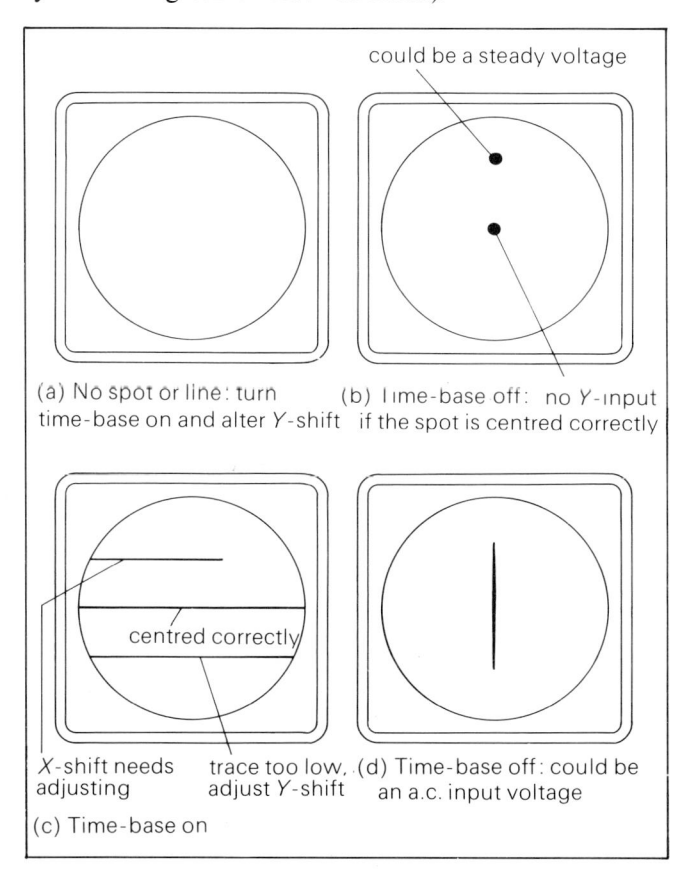

Figure 178 Setting up the oscilloscope.

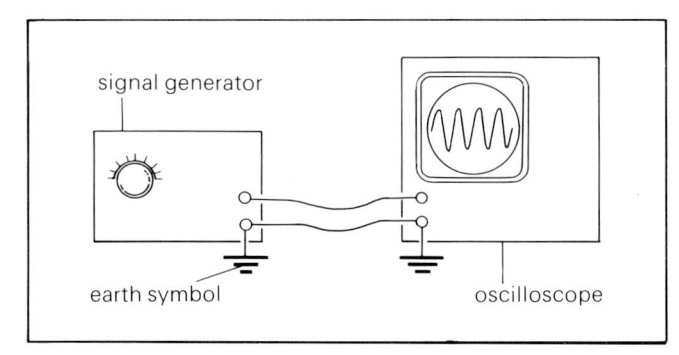

Figure 179

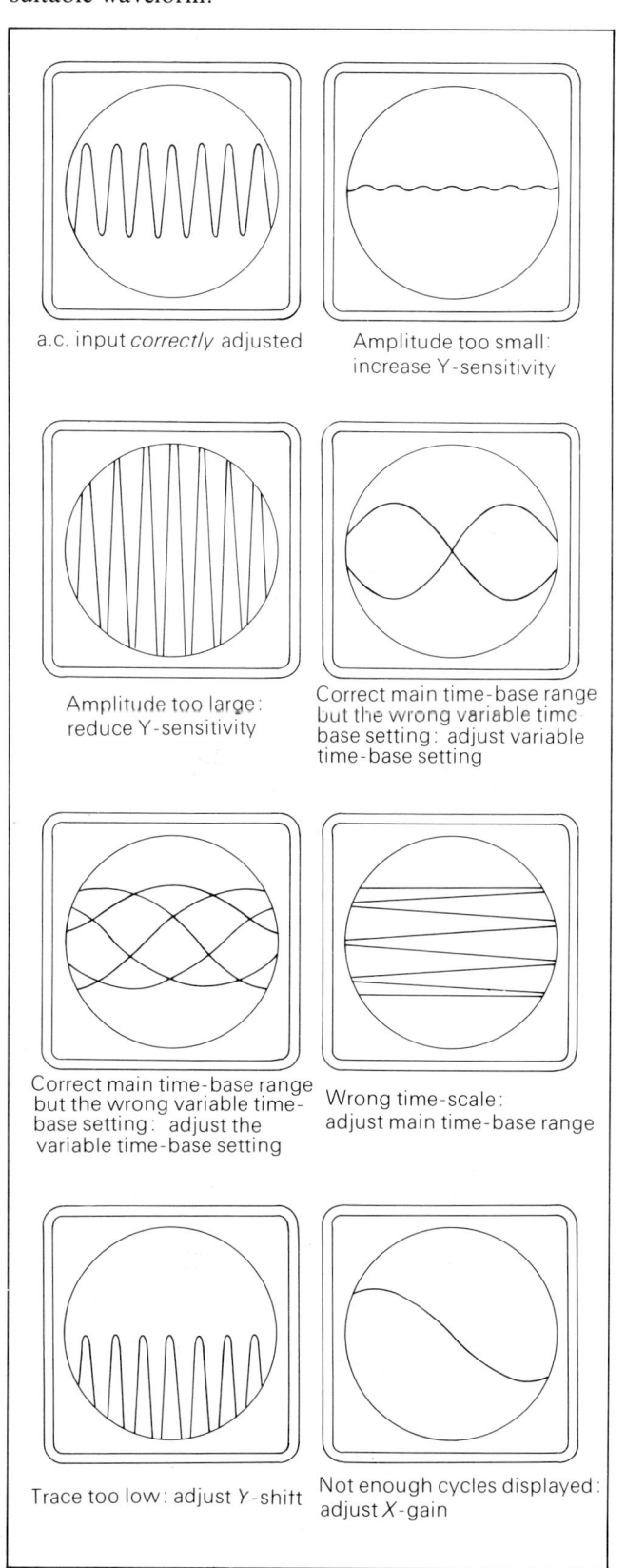

Figure 180 Setting up a suitable waveform.

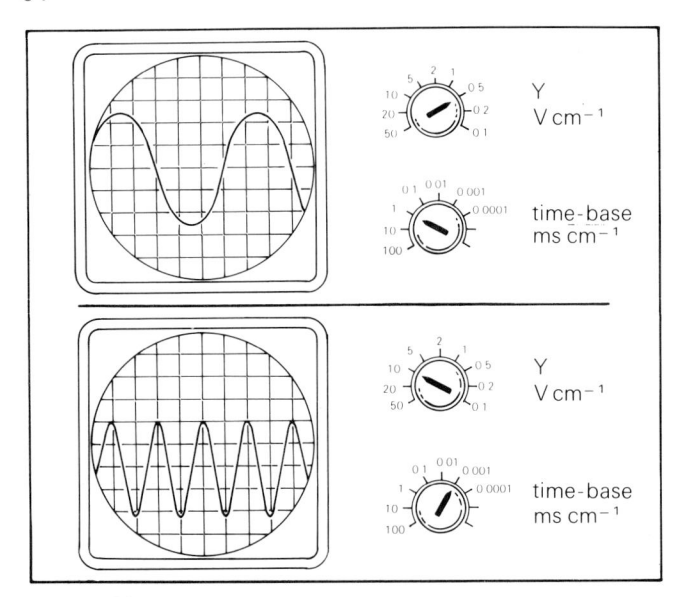

Figure 181

Work out the *amplitude* and *frequency* of the signals shown in figure 181.

2. *Hints on drawing traces*
(a) Always use graph paper.
(b) Note the Y sensitivity and time-scale used so that true scales can be used.
(c) Using the usual linear time-base, a trace can never turn back on itself, i.e must be *wrong*.

(d) Always take measurements from the zero voltage line which should be adjusted to be in the centre of the oscilloscope:

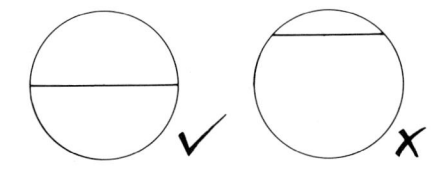

(e) Draw any changes of slope accurately. Look carefully to see if the change is continuous or sharp, i.e.

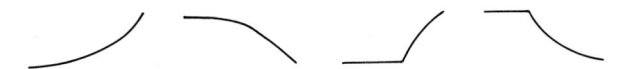

(f) Take scale measurements for important points. These can be plotted on the graph paper first and the trace drawn in sections.

3. *Typical input waveforms applied to circuits*
(a) sine

(b) square

(c) triangular or sawtooth

(d) ramp

(e) a square wave with unequal mark–space ratios

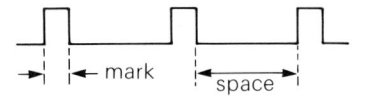

(f) a.c. with a positive or negative d.c. component as well.

Waveforms are usually affected by:

(a) rectification—use of diodes;

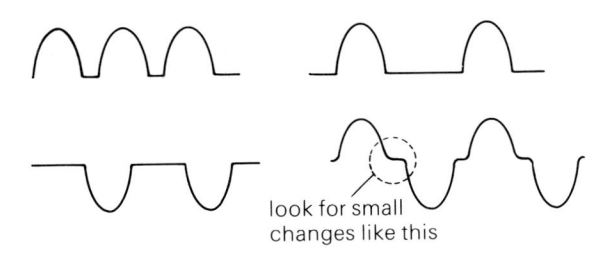

(b) capacitor–resistor charge or discharge giving characteristic shapes;

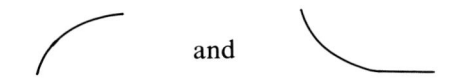

(c) output from an amplifier which may be a similar shape to the input but larger or there may be distortion, such as
(i) clipping of the top

(this may look similar to half-wave rectified but the zero voltage line will show that it is a.c.);

EXPERIMENTAL TECHNIQUES

(ii) rounding at the bottom

(look carefully at the wave shapes above and below zero voltage).

Experimental details

Use the equipment shown in figure 182.

Display and draw accurately each trace produced by the circuits given you. Explain how the circuit could cause the shape of the trace and draw a diagram of the circuit you think is inside the box.

Make sure that you connect the a.c. input to the *correct* terminals.

Equipment

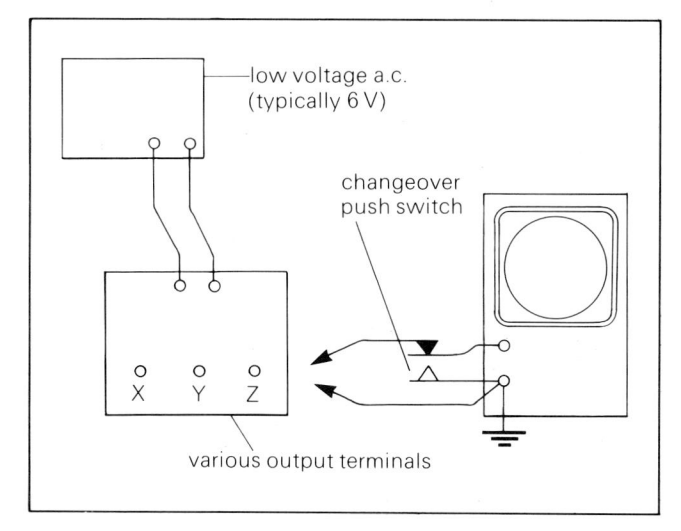

Figure 182 x, y and z represent any one of a range of circuits you may be given, which can contain resistors, capacitors, diodes and transistors. The changeover push switch enables the input terminal to be earthed to display the zero voltage line.

22. MEASURING IMPEDANCE

Outline

A circuit working from a d.c. supply is said to have a *resistance*. On an a.c. supply it is said to have an *impedance*. This practical investigates how the impedance of a capacitor and an inductance depend on the frequency of the supply.

The impedance is defined as

$$Z = \frac{\text{amplitude of voltage applied}}{\text{amplitude of current flowing}} = \frac{V_{r.m.s.}}{I_{r.m.s.}}$$

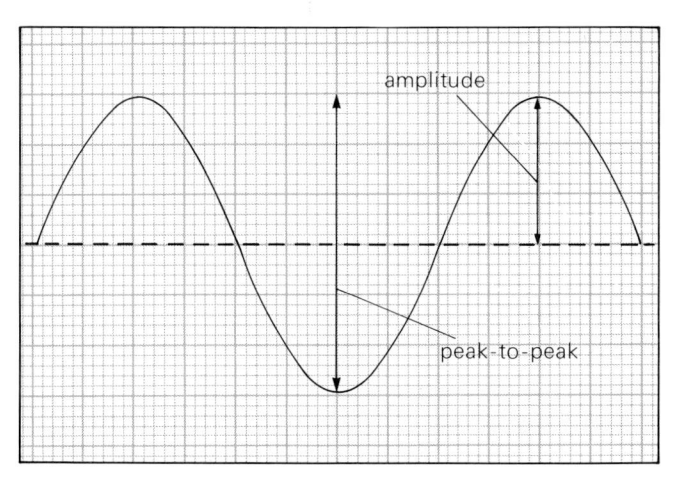

Figure 183

Since the peak-to-peak value is twice the amplitude and is the practical measurement taken from an oscilloscope,

$$Z = \frac{\text{peak-to-peak voltage}}{\text{peak-to-peak current}}$$

Measuring the voltage is straightforward; an oscilloscope is used. Measuring the current is more difficult. There are moving-iron ammeters, but these are not sensitive enough. Essentially, a voltage proportional to the current must be measured. Two possible ways of doing this are as follows.

1. Use an accurately known resistor (R) in series and measure the p.d. across it:

$$I_{\text{peak-to-peak}} = \frac{V_{\text{peak-to-peak}}}{R}$$

2. Use a transformer. The induced voltage in the secondary will be proportional to the rate of change of flux, which is proportional to the current provided the core does not saturate. This does need to be calibrated and is little used in practice.

All oscilloscopes will have a common earth and so *must* be connected to the wire between the capacitor or inductor and R, at Y. It is *very important* that the oscillator output is not earthed. Check with your teacher to make sure you have the correct apparatus.

In figure 184, oscilloscope (a) measures the peak-to-peak voltage across the capacitor or the inductor, while oscilloscope (b) measures the peak-to-peak voltage across the resistor (R) so that the peak-to-peak current can be found.

The sine wave oscillator is battery operated, so it has a floating output. Neither output is earthed.

Experimental details

The equipment is set up as shown in figure 184, with either the capacitor (C) or the inductor (L) connected into the circuit.

Start at a frequency of about 50 Hz. Record the frequency and the peak-to-peak voltages across the capacitor and the resistor. This involves measuring the trace on the oscilloscope and recording the voltage sensitivity used. Increase the frequency by 50 Hz and find the voltages again. The current flowing will change and the supply voltage should be adjusted if the current becomes too low or too high. Repeat in 100 Hz steps to about 2 kHz.

Replace the capacitor with the inductor and repeat the experiment.

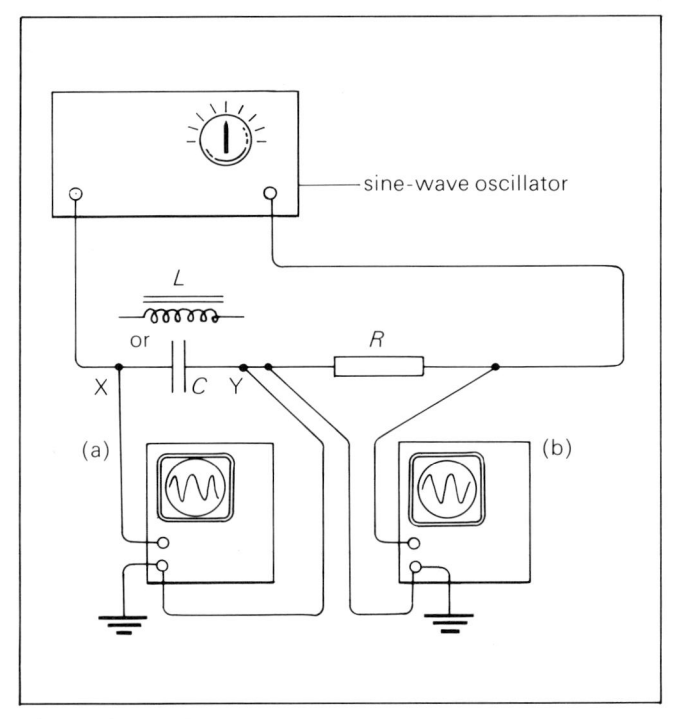

Figure 184 Equipment

Results

Capacitor

resistance $R = \cdots \Omega$ $I = \dfrac{\text{p.d. across resistor}}{R}$

Frequency/Hz	Reading across capacitor/cm	Sensitivity/V cm^{-1}	p.d. across capacitor	Reading across resistor/cm	Sensitivity/V cm^{-1}	p.d. across resistor

p.d. across capacitor/V	Current I/A	Impedance/Ω	Frequency/Hz	$\dfrac{1}{\text{frequency}}$/s

EXPERIMENTAL TECHNIQUES

From the results

Work out the impedance (Z) at each frequency (bottom table). The most likely relationship between impedance and frequency is

$$f \propto Z \quad \text{or} \quad \frac{1}{f} \propto Z$$

A straight-line graph is required. What is the physical significance of:

(a) the gradient of the graph;
(b) any intercept on the impedance axis?

Data analysis

A double-beam oscilloscope could be used to show that the voltage across the capacitor or the inductor is not in phase with the voltage across the resistor. Not in phase means that the peaks do not occur at the same time. The current and voltage are in phase for a resistor, so we must conclude that current and voltage are *not* in phase for a capacitor or inductor. Most double-beam oscilloscopes have a common input terminal and so, in effect, one of the inputs has a phase reversal. The ideal situation is where there is no phase reversal, and this is the situation taken in the following two problems.

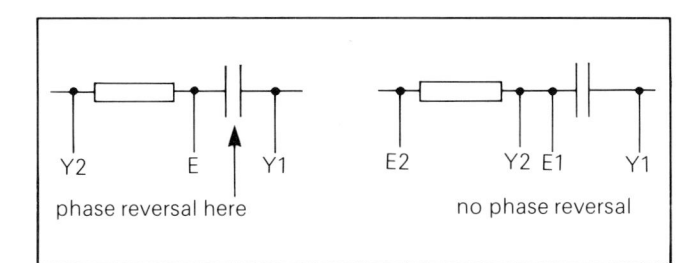

Figure 185

1. The current can be calculated from $V = IR$ for the 10 Ω resistor. For the capacitor $Q = CV$. (See figure 186.)

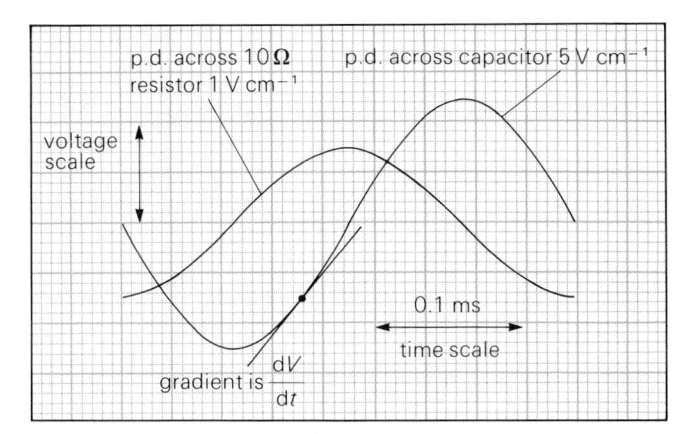

Figure 186 Example traces for a resistor and a capacitor

Now $\quad \dfrac{dQ}{dt} = I \quad \therefore \dfrac{dQ}{dt} = \dfrac{C\,dV}{dt} = I$

and $\dfrac{dV}{dt}$ is the gradient of the voltage curve at any instant. Find the value for the capacitance C by finding values of $\dfrac{dV}{dt}$ and I at various times. Use the spread of your results to quote a probable error.

$\dfrac{dV}{dt} / \text{V s}^{-1}$	I/A	C/F

2. From Faraday's laws of electromagnetic induction, the back e.m.f. $E = -\dfrac{L\,dI}{dt}$ and, assuming zero resistance in the inductance, this must also equal the applied voltage across the inductance. Otherwise a large current would flow.

Find a value for the inductance L by finding values for $\dfrac{dI}{dt}$ and V at various times. Use the spread of your results to quote a probable error. (See figure 187.)

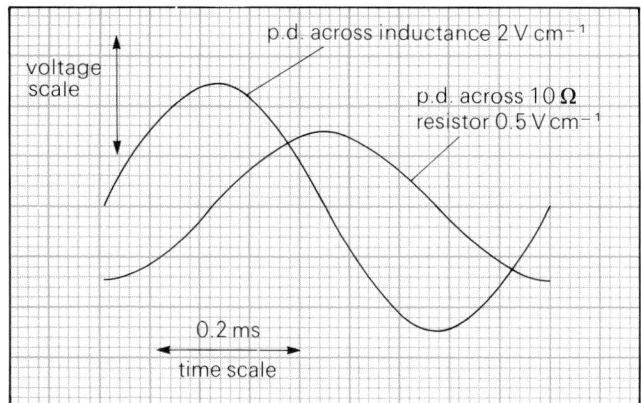

$\dfrac{dI}{dt} / \text{A s}^{-1}$	V/V	L/H

Figure 187 Example traces for a resistor and inductance

23. METHODS OF MEASURING MAGNETIC FIELDS

What in fact one measures is the magnetic induction or flux density, B.

1. Search coil and ballistic galvanometer

A coil of wire is connected to a galvanometer which has a long period of natural swing of the order of 20 seconds. When the magnetic flux through the search coil is changed, an e.m.f. is induced which causes a flow of charge through the galvanometer. This sudden flow of charge causes the spot or pointer of the galvanometer to deflect and stay stationary for long enough to enable a reading to be taken. This scale reading can be converted to a charge by using the calibration given with the galvanometer.

For example, if the sensitivity is $21.5\,\mu\text{C}\,\text{mm}^{-1}$ and the deflection is 8.4 mm, then the charge which has flowed is

$$21.5 \times 8.4 = 180.6\,\mu\text{C} \text{ or } 1.81 \times 10^{-4}\,\text{C}.$$

If an aperiodic galvanometer is used, e.g. spot-lamp galvanometer which has a period of about 2 s, the reading will need to be taken more quickly. It can be shown that

$$Q = \frac{BAN}{R}$$

if the time of change of the field is short compared to the time period of the galvanometer (Q = charge, B = magnetic flux density, A = area of the search coil, N = number of turns on the search coil, R = total resistance of the circuit).

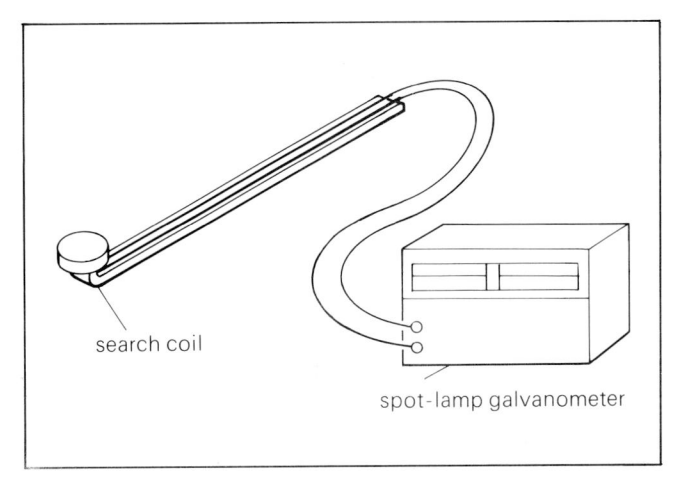

Figure 188

In practice the field is reduced to zero or brought from zero to a maximum, by:

(a) turning the search coil quickly through 90°;

(b) switching the field off or on if it is produced by an electromagnet (switching off is better—why?); or

(c) removing the coil quickly from the field.

2. Search coil and integrator

This method also uses the flux change through a coil to induce a voltage. This voltage causes a current to flow.

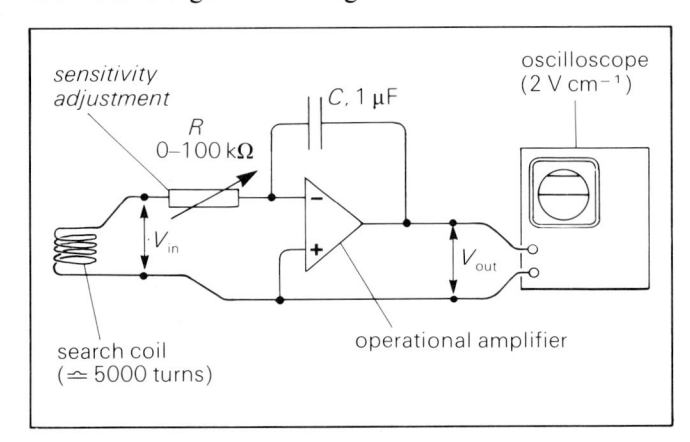

Figure 189 Using an integrator. $V_{\text{out}} = -\frac{1}{RC}\int V_{\text{in}}\,dt$.

The operational amplifier in figure 189 functions as an integrator which effectively sums the input and so does not depend on the speed at which the flux changes. The search coil can be moved slowly or quickly since the final reading will be the same.

Unfortunately, the instrument has to be calibrated using a known magnetic field.

3. Hall effect probe

The Hall probe gives a direct reading of the field at the conducting material, but still needs calibration.

The charge carriers moving in the conducting material experience a force because of the magnetic field, and tend to move at right angles to the field and current. This increases the concentration of charge carriers at one

EXPERIMENTAL TECHNIQUES

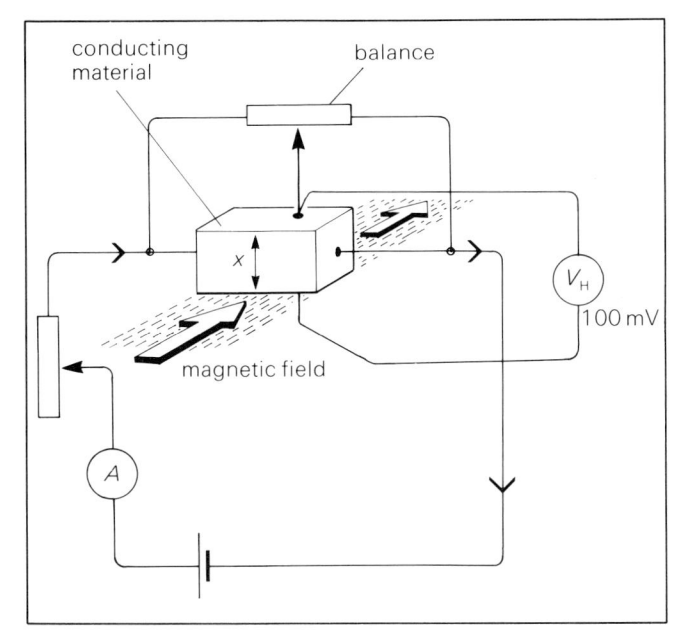

Figure 190 Circuit needed to use the Hall effect.

surface parallel to the current direction and reduces the concentration at the other. The effect is to produce a voltage called the Hall voltage (V_H) across the conductor. With semiconductor materials, such as germanium, voltages as high as 0.1 V are possible, but often a d.c. amplifier is needed. The Hall voltage is given by:

$$V_H = \frac{BI}{nQx}$$

where n is the number of charge carriers per cubic metre (determined by the type of conductor), Q is the charge on each carrier (normally the electronic charge) and x is the thickness of the conductor.

V_H is largest for thin slices, large currents and few charge carriers per unit volume. I is typically 50 mA. A small voltage may be produced if the contacts on the upper and lower surface are not exactly opposite each other. The *balance* potential divider produces a voltage to offset this, so that the meter reads 0 with zero field.

4. a.c. induction

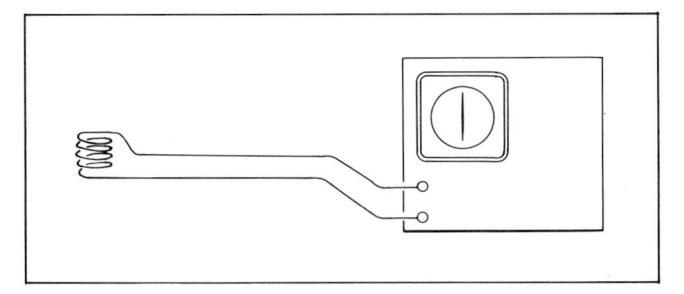

Figure 191 Using a continuously changing field to induce a voltage.

This method is suitable for measuring alternating fields. The search coil acts in the same way as a winding on a transformer, and an a.c. voltage is induced because of the changing magnetic flux. The a.c. voltage can be measured using an oscilloscope. The oscilloscope is best set up with the time-base off so that the trace is a vertical line. Measure the peak-to-peak voltage, and calibrate if necessary.

The sensitivity of the instrument increases with frequency, because the rate of change of flux is larger for higher frequencies.

The voltage is induced in the coil because the flux in the coil is changing:

$$E = -\frac{d\Phi}{dt} = -\frac{d(BAN)}{dt}$$

$$\therefore B = -\int \frac{E\,dt}{AN} \quad \text{and} \quad E \propto \frac{dB}{dt}$$

5. The current balance

This method enables the actual value of the magnetic induction, B, to be found by measuring the force produced by the field on a wire carrying an electric current.

The force on a straight wire at right angles to the field is given by

force = magnetic induction × current × length of wire

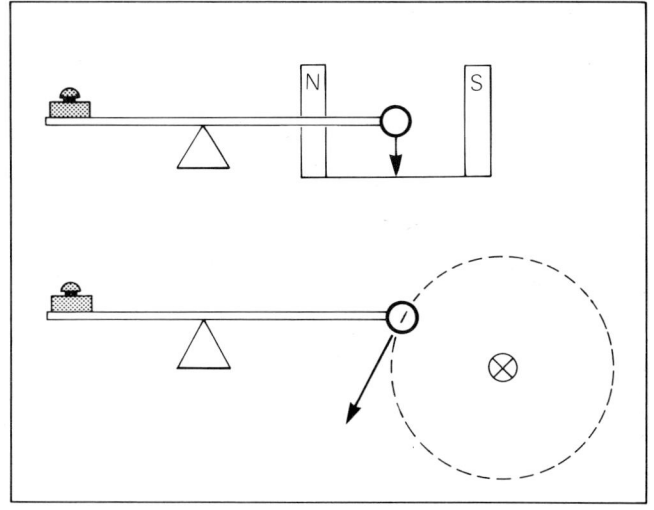

Figure 192

If the current is set to a known value and the force produced measured then the magnetic induction can be calculated if the length of the wire is measured on the apparatus.

It is usual to provide the balancing force by weights and this means that it is the size of the vertical component of the field which is being measured. This must be remembered when positioning the balance in the field. Consider the situations shown in figure 192.

There are several different designs of current balance but all involve adjusting a weight until the balance has returned to the position it was in when the field was not present. Some designs use a light beam pointer to position the balance more accurately. You may well find a damper to reduce the time taken for the balance to come to rest after changing the value of the weight (it oscillates in much the same way as a pendulum). Figure 193 shows the main features of a typical design.

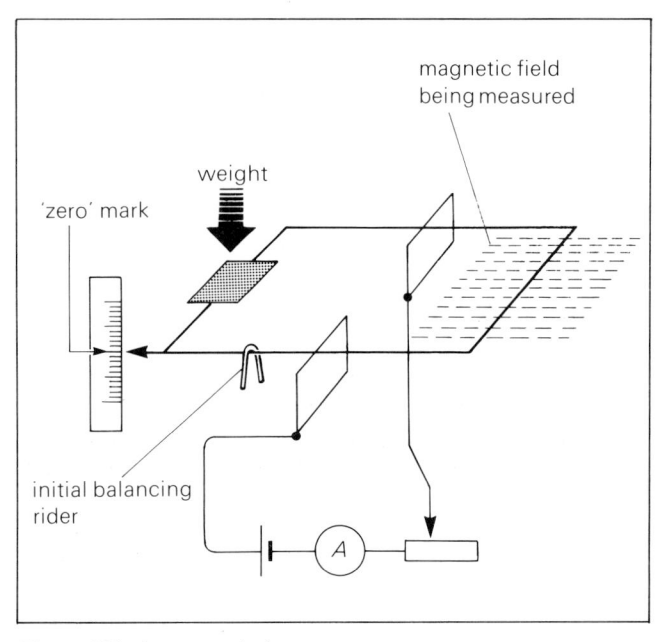

Figure 193 A current balance

Figure 194 Equipment

scale reading and the sensitivity used. Put the bar of soft iron inside the coil and repeat. Do the same for the steel bar.

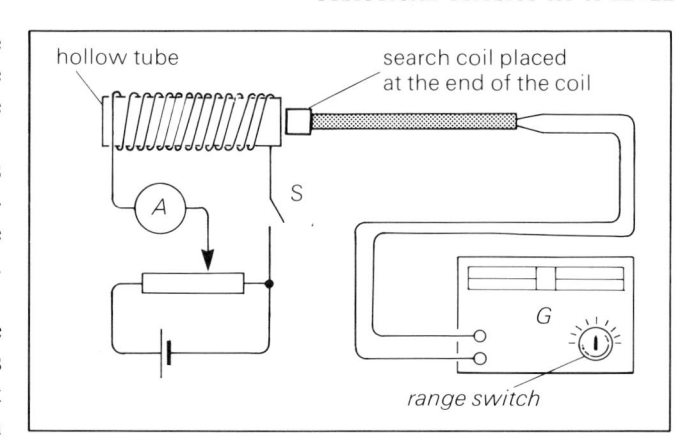

Results

Material	Scale reading/mm	Range	True reading/mm
air			
soft iron			
steel			

$$\text{relative permeability} = \frac{\text{true reading for material}}{\text{true reading for air}}$$

Further investigation

A certain minimum field is needed before the magnetic moments of atoms in the soft iron are aligned. An extension experiment investigates this and also the variation of field strength with current in the coil using a steel bar.

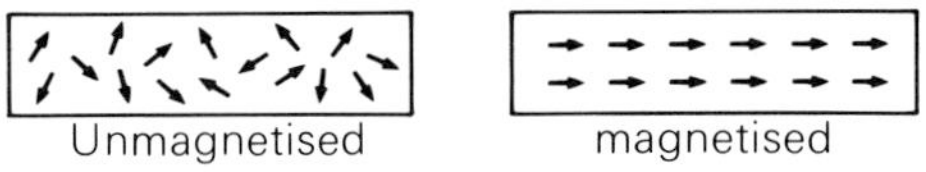

1. MEASURING THE RELATIVE PERMEABILITY OF SOFT IRON

This is done using a search coil and a ballistic galvanometer coil or solenoid (figure 194).

Close the switch and alter the current to about 80 per cent of the maximum marked on the coil. Open the switch and alter the range of the galvanometer until a reading on the scale is obtained. The switch may have to be opened and closed several times before the correct range has been found. Zero the ballistic galvanometer at one end to use as large a scale as possible. Record the

1. Demagnetise the steel bar by placing it in an alternating field and then decreasing the field to zero.
2. Starting with zero current, open switch S and record the reading on the galvanometer. Increase the current in small steps, at least 20, until the maximum current is reached, and record the reading on the galvanometer each time.
3. Plot a graph of scale reading against current. Account for the shape of the graph.

EXPERIMENTAL TECHNIQUES

2. MEASURING THE MAGNETIC FLUX DENSITY BETWEEN THE POLES OF A MAGNET

This can be done using a search coil and operational amplifier as an integrator or a current balance.

Search coil and integrator

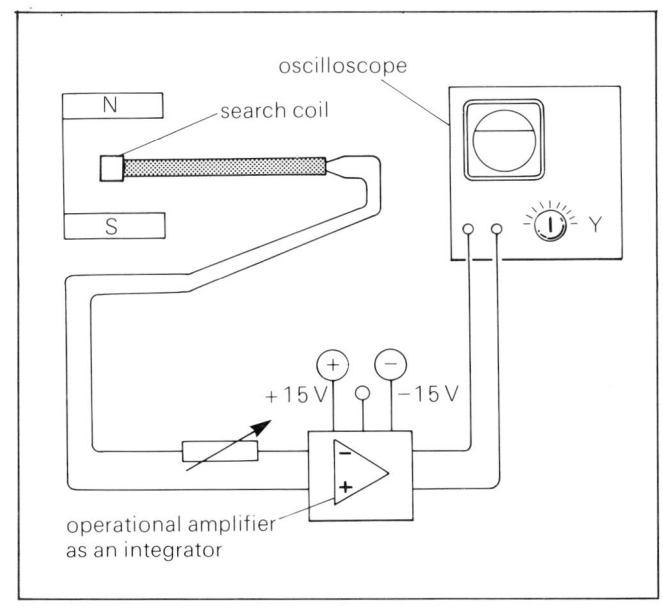

Figure 195 Equipment. Use the input resistance and oscilloscope Y sensitivity controls to adjust the vertical movement of the trace.

1. Place the search coil into the field so that its plane is perpendicular to the field.
2. Short the inputs to the integrator together and zero the oscilloscope trace.
3. Connect the search coil to the integrator.
4. Move the coil out of the field and make sure that the induced voltage does not 'saturate' the integrator. (The output voltage must always be less than the supply voltage.) Alter the sensitivity of the oscilloscope as necessary.
5. If the integrator saturates the only solution is to use a different search coil, with fewer turns, a smaller area, or a higher input resistance.
6. When you are satisfied, record the reading on the oscilloscope. (Did you check that the zero had not altered?) $= V_{\text{pole}}$.
7. The instrument must now be calibrated using a known field. Use a solenoid (figure 196). $B = \mu_0 n I$, where n is the number of turns per metre.

$$\mu_0 = 4\pi \times 10^{-7} \, \text{H m}^{-1}$$

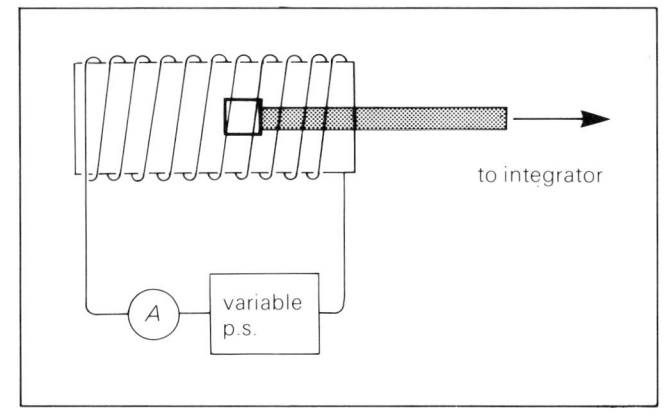

Figure 196 Make sure that the search coil is well inside with its plane perpendicular to the axis of the solenoid coil.

Alter the current to get a similar-sized reading on the oscilloscope to when the search coil is between the poles.
Work out the true value of B_{cal} and record the reading on the oscilloscope (V_{cal}).

8. Work out the true field between the poles of the magnet:

$$\frac{B_{\text{pole}}}{B_{\text{cal}}} = \frac{V_{\text{pole}}}{V_{\text{cal}}}$$

Current balance.

1. Set up the apparatus with no applied field present round the wire and adjust to the 'zero' position. There is always the Earth's magnetic field present but since the balance is to be re-adjusted to the same position it can be ignored. If there is an advised current given with the apparatus then use that, otherwise a current of 1 A is typical. Measure the length of the wire in the field. You have a problem on deciding the exact length if the wire is longer than the 'area' of the field because of the edge effects as the field does not just suddenly stop.

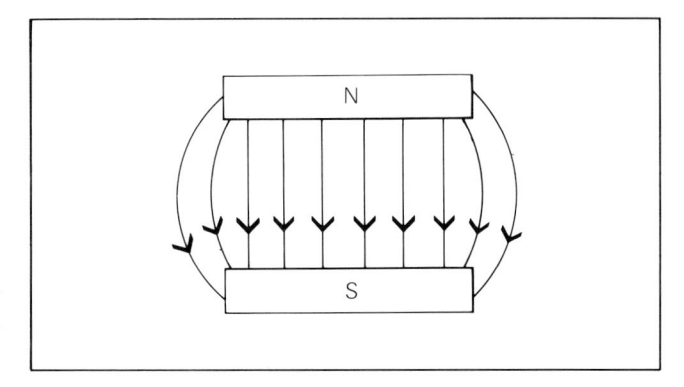

Figure 197 Magnetic field showing edge effects.

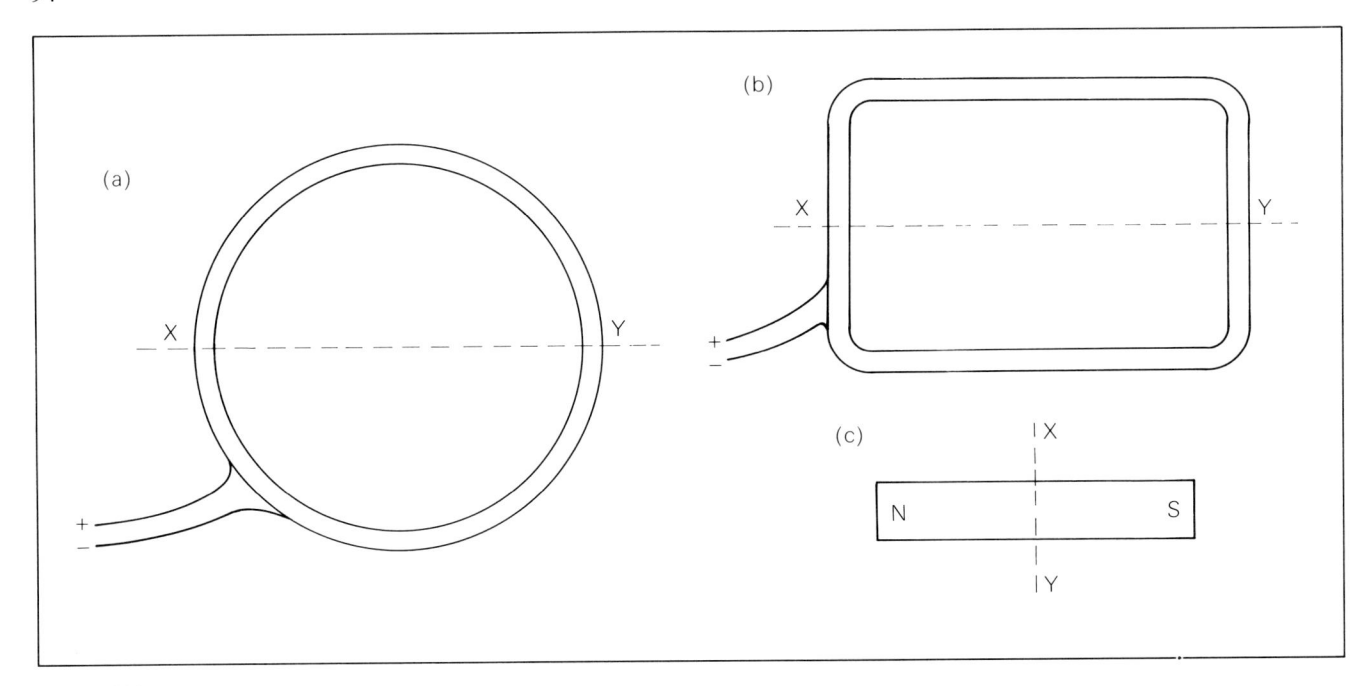

Figure 202

24. USING THE COMPUTER AND DATA MEMORIES AS MEASURING INSTRUMENTS

Outline

Many of the experiments you will do involve taking a series of readings over a period of time. It may be a few minutes, but rarely exceeds about 30 minutes. There are experiments which involve:

1. readings which change quickly and have to be taken over a short timespan;
2. readings which change slowly and have to be taken over a longer timespan which may involve inconvenient times such as at night;
3. timing operations where several readings are taken at the same time or in quick succession and it is impossible for you and your partner to do this with accuracy.

By using apparatus such as data memories, speed–time computers or by suitable programs in a microcomputer, measurements can be taken which would not be feasible otherwise. This is called *data logging*.

Data memory

Data memories measure a voltage, usually in the range 0–1 V, turn it into a digital number and store it, taking readings at a range frequency of 1000 per second to a few per hour. The data stored are converted back to a number and displayed:

(a) individually on a voltmeter;
(b) as a voltage–time graph on an oscilloscope;
(c) on a chart recorder.

Speed–time computer

These computers store the times that events happen, for example, the time a light beam is broken as a card fastened to a moving object passes in front of it. Velocity and acceleration are then calculated by the computer from these times and the values displayed on the screen.

Microcomputer

This has all the elements of a data memory and speed–time computer, a memory to store data, and the internal 'clocks' which control the operation of the computer can be used for timing. There is often the added advantage of a colour display to draw graphs, possibly showing several 'runs' on the screen at one time for comparison, and the ability to produce a printed copy of the data stored and/or the screen display.

The computer needs an *analogue* input or an analogue-to-digital converter (A to D) to convert the

EXPERIMENTAL TECHNIQUES

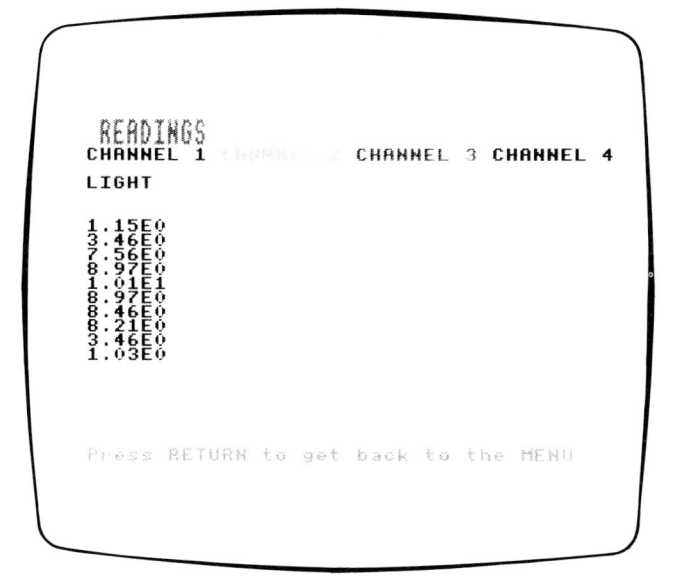

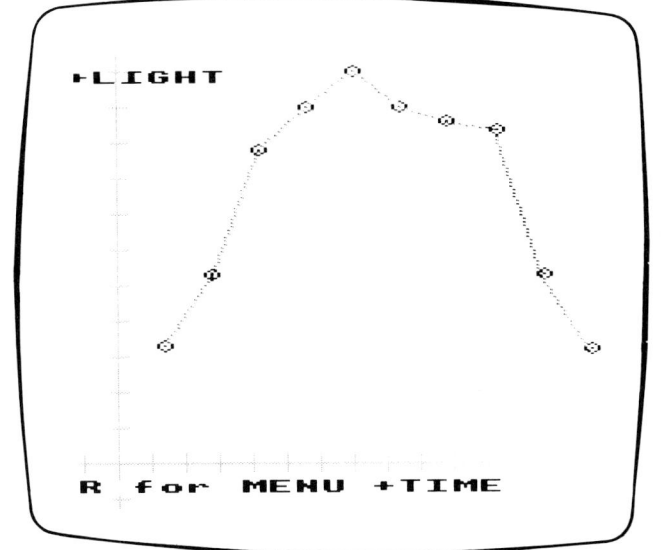

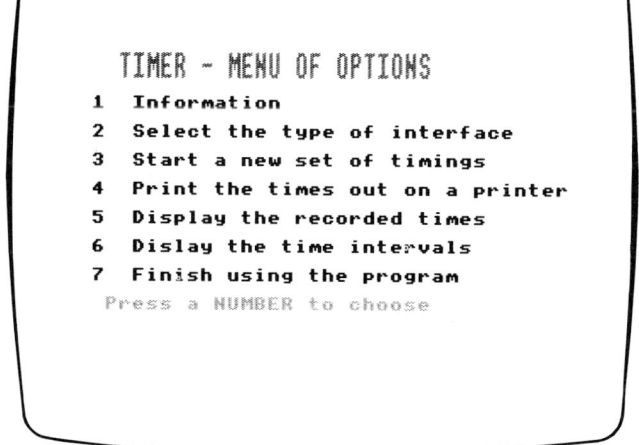

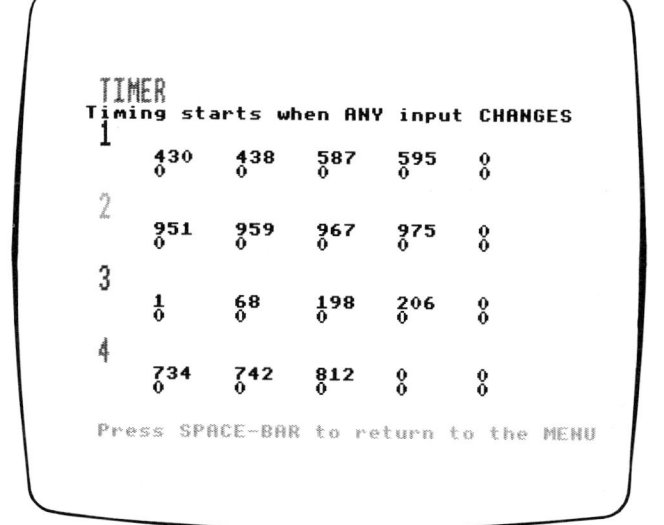

Figure 203 Typical screen displays from Datalogging and Timing packages

voltage input to a digital number so that it can be stored. But without a *program*, the 'hardware' is useless. Your teacher will give you more information about the equipment available at your school.

Figure 203 shows some examples of screen displays from programs which are available for the BBC model B computer.

VELA (VErsatile Laboratory Aid)

This is a dedicated microprocessor-controlled unit using built in programs to turn it into a variety of instruments. The program 06 is used for timing experiments and either 02 or 03 for recording a series of readings at regular time intervals. Your teacher will give you more details about using this instrument. (See pp. 4 and 5.)

1. TIMING FREE FALL

Experimental details

Use the equipment shown in figure 204.
1. Set the speed–time computer into its timing mode (or the appropriate option of the computer program).
2. Drop the card in front of the photodiode (or a larger card with several holes in it, which would give several readings).
3. Recall the times, velocities and accelerations and record them in a table. Give the value for the acceleration produced on the card by gravity. There will be very little air resistance, so this should give a value for the acceleration due to gravity in free fall.

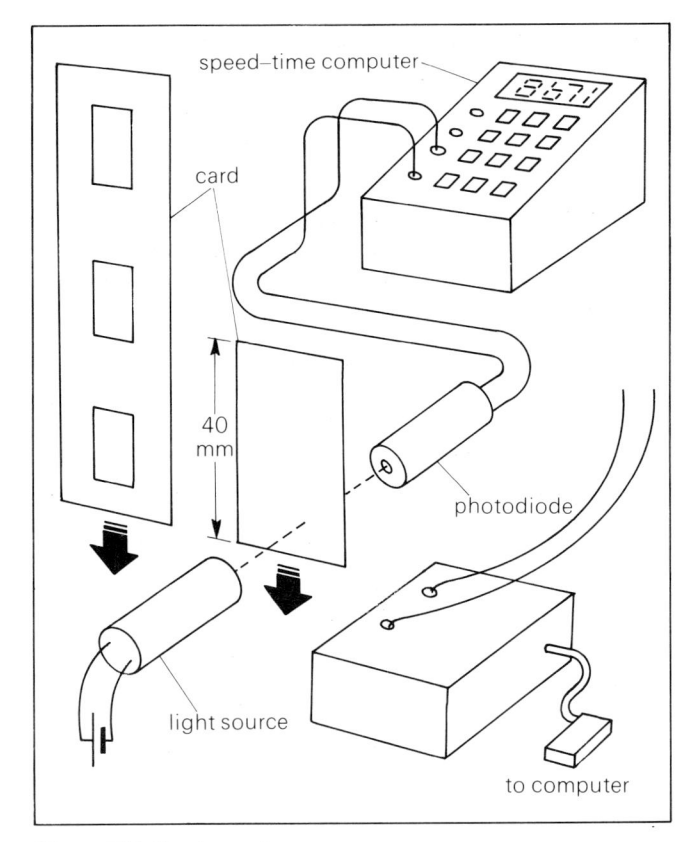

Figure 204 Equipment

2. RESISTANCE AGAINST TIME AS A LAMP HEATS UP

Outline

As soon as a lamp is switched on, the heat generated starts to raise the temperature of the filament, which increases the resistance of the filament so that the current changes and so does the rate of heating. As the filament gets hotter, it loses more energy by radiation. An equilibrium temperature is reached when the rate of energy loss equals the rate at which electrical energy is being supplied. All this happens within seconds of switching on. The experiment measures two voltages, from which the resistance can be worked out.

Experimental details

Set the apparatus up as shown in figure 205.

The $\sim 60\,\Omega$ resistor has a large surface area, so temperature will change by only a minute amount over the time readings are taken. Measure the value of R by recording the steady readings of voltage and current and then using $R = \dfrac{V}{I}$. Set the input voltage range to $\sim 12\,\text{V}$ and the frequency of reading to at least 50 per second.

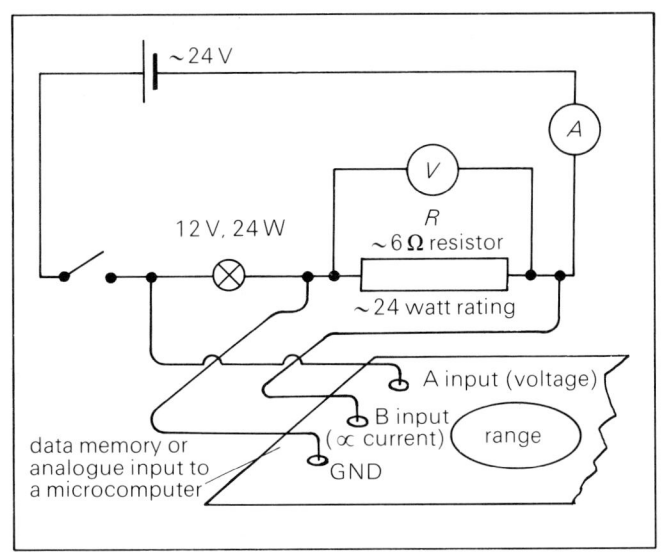

Figure 205 Connections to the interface

Set the data memory or computer recording and switch the circuit on until the ammeter reading is constant.

Displaying the 'B input' results will give an effective graph of current against time. To obtain a graph of resistance against time, select the *manual* option from the choices given and record the voltages of A and B at each time interval on a voltmeter and the current $I = \dfrac{V_B}{R}$.

Therefore:

$$\text{resistance of the lamp} = \frac{V_A}{I} = \frac{V_A}{V_B} \times R$$

3. DAMPED SIMPLE HARMONIC MOTION OF A COMPOUND PENDULUM

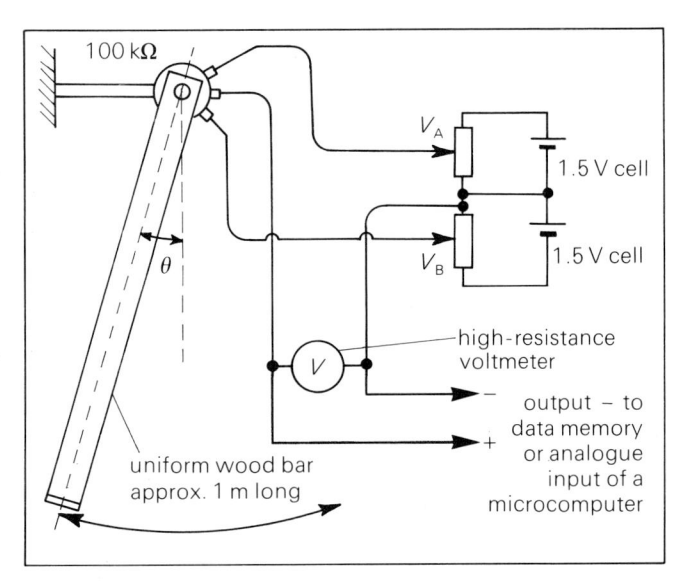

Figure 206 Equipment to investigate damped simple harmonic motion

EXPERIMENTAL TECHNIQUES

The supply voltage V_A (+) and V_B (−) must be adjusted so that the voltage produced at the *output* changes from as near zero as possible to as near the maximum required by the particular computer as possible. **Do this before connecting to the computer.**

Typical voltage ranges:
Harris data memory: 0–1 V
BBC model B microcomputer: 0–1.8 V
VELA: ±250 mV, ±5 V, ±25 V

Other typical inputs are: 0–2.5 V and 0–5 V, depending on the make of computer and analogue to digital board used.

Experimental details

1. Decide on the maximum arc of swing you wish to use and adjust the supply voltage so that when the pendulum is at its maximum amplitude, the voltage output (measured in volts) to the data memory or computer is near the maximum needed. This will produce the largest change in the digital number recorded and makes the sensitivity a maximum.
2. Using a stopwatch, find the approximate periodic time and decide how many swings you want to record. Then set the recording time interval to a value that takes at least 20 readings for each swing. For example, using the program 'DATALOG' (package PHYS2 option 5) for the BBC computer the initial screen display would offer a choice of options. The first step might be to adjust and calibrate the instrument to produce the largest possible change in the number input to the computer, followed by the association of the highest and lowest *physical* values expected. (See figure 207.)
3. Measure the maximum angle of swing θ_{max}. Set the pendulum swinging and the data memory or microcomputer recording. Make a record of the results by whatever means you have available:
   (a) printed copy of data (computer);
   (b) graph on a chart recorder (data memory);
   (c) individual voltage readings (data memory);
   (d) copying the trace from TV or oscilloscope onto an acetate sheet.

   Plot a graph of the reading against time.
4. You have actually measured the angle of the swing, and for small-amplitude oscillations the variation of angle with time should be $\theta = \theta_{max} \sin \omega t$ if the movement is simple harmonic motion (s.h.m.), where ω is the angular frequency ($r\,s^{-1}$); periodic times $T = \dfrac{2\pi}{\omega}$; $\omega = 2\pi f$, where f is measured in hertz.

   Obtain values for θ_{max} and the periodic time T, where θ_{max} is the maximum reading from the data memory or microcomputer.

   Plot a graph of $\theta = \theta_{max} \sin \omega t$ using the same timescale as in (3). Compare the experimental and the calculated graphs.

4. TEMPERATURE CHANGE AS LIQUIDS MIX

Outline

When hot and cold liquids are mixed, the temperature of the hot liquid falls and the temperature of the cold liquid rises until they come to a common final temperature. Experiments have been done for many years using this

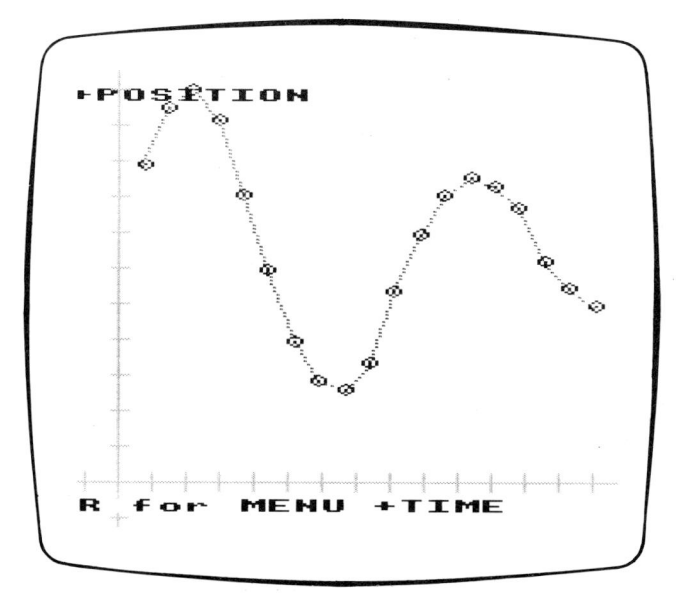

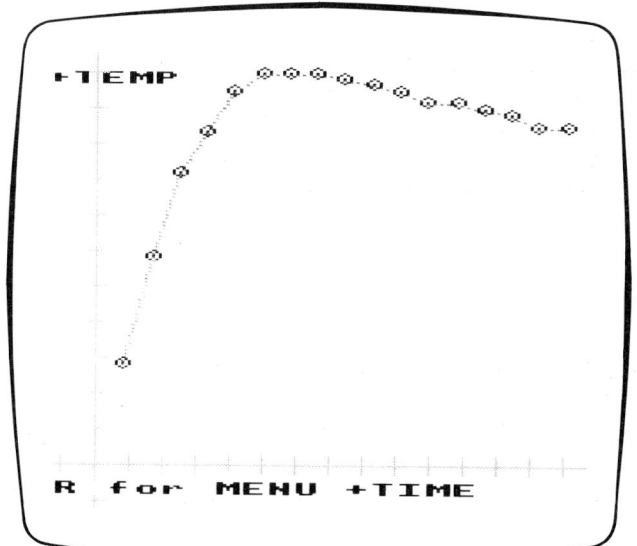

Figure 207 Example graphs produced by the 'DATALOG' program.

'method of mixtures' to find the specific heat capacity of a liquid, but this is now omitted from most A-level syllabi. A much more interesting investigation is to look at the way the temperature changes as the liquids mix. Does it, for instance, make a difference if the liquids are miscible or immiscible? Can any conclusions be made from the results about the movement of the molecules as the liquids mix?

Equipment

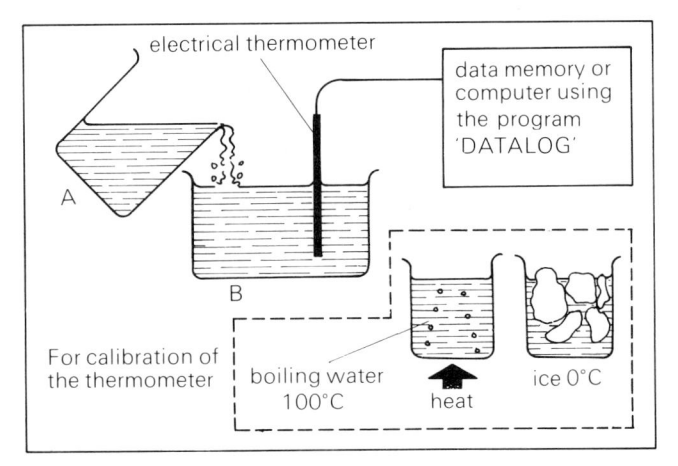

Figure 208 Suitable liquids for A and B include: water, oil and copper sulphate solution.

Experimental details

1. Set up the data memory or computer. Place the thermometer in the ice and record the reading (a) produced. Repeat for the boiling water (b). The calibration of the thermometer is:

$$1°C = \frac{(b-a)}{100}$$

because in any calibration the scale is assumed to be uniform.

2. Choose the liquids A and B. There are six combinations of the three liquids you can use. Heat liquid A to about 90°C. Pour into B and record the temperature readings on the computer or data memory.

   Repeat for other combinations of liquids. In your planning, you should consider:

   (a) Should the same volumes or masses of liquids be used or does it not matter?
   (b) Should liquids A and B be at the same initial temperatures each time?

Results

Time/s	Digital reading (number)	Real temperature/°C

From the results

Plot graphs of temperature against time and make any qualitative conclusions that you can about the similarities or differences between the results.

25. DETECTING NUCLEAR PARTICLES

Outline

'Nuclear' particles come from the following.

1. Naturally occurring radioactive materials such as compounds of uranium, thorium and potassium.
2. From purified or man-made sources, which are stronger than natural sources. The ones you will use are sealed and are called *closed* sources. They are stored in a lead-lined box.
3. Space: high-energy particles such as muons, pions, sigmas reach the earth's surface from space. All of these decay into other particles very quickly. They can also be produced artificially in particle accelerators. There are various theories that these 'fundamental' particles (including p, n, e) are made from even more fundamental particles called *quarks* with a charge of $\pm \frac{1}{3}e$. It is unlikely that you will be able to detect these in the laboratory.

Particles can be detected as follows.

1. By their ionising effect:

   (a) on a gas, as in a Geiger–Müller tube or spark counter, or
   (b) in a cloud chamber, where the vapour condenses on the track of the ions produced by the particles, or
   (c) in a bubble chamber, where the particle causes a liquid to 'boil' along its track, producing small bubbles.

EXPERIMENTAL TECHNIQUES

2. In an organic substance acting as a scintillator, in which a flash of light is produced each time a particle enters and collides with an organic molecule.
3. By photographic emulsions.

Because you cannot 'see' the particles and because they are so small, it is easy to ignore the fact that they have a large energy. The ionisation they cause when absorbed can affect the cells in your body. This experiment investigates:

(a) the correct and safe handling of radioactive sources;
(b) the background radiation present in your laboratory;
(c) the use of the Geiger–Müller tube;
(d) the use of a diffusion-type cloud chamber.

1. MEASURING THE BACKGROUND RADIATION

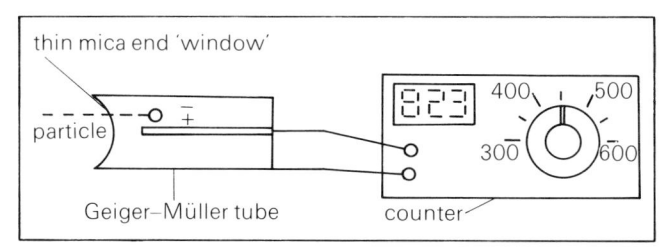

Figure 209 Equipment. Most particles detected enter through the mica end 'window'. The potential applied to the tube is set to 450 V.

Background radiation is the natural radiation produced by the earth and coming from space. Measure it by using a Geiger–Müller tube, as shown in figure 209.

When a particle enters the tube, it may collide with a gas atom and ionise it. The electron and ion produced move under the potential applied to the tube, causing further ionisations, and a pulse of current is produced which is 'counted'. One assumption you are making is that one pulse is produced by each particle. Is this true?

The particles arrive in a purely random pattern, and so the error in the measurement is given by $N \pm \sqrt{N}$.

Measure the number of particles counted in:

(a) five 1-minute periods;
(b) two 10-minute periods.

Find the average for each and give the error.

Does the background sound change as the orientation of the tube changes? What is the physical significance of the results?

2. SAFETY IN THE USE OF RADIOACTIVE SOURCES

Regulations allow a total exposure level of half the normal background radiation in any one year, and in any one experiment one tenth of this is the maximum allowed. You are also only allowed to use radioactive sources if *you are 16 or over* and *when your teacher is present*. Since the amount of radiation reaching you depends on the distance you are away from the source and on any shielding round the source, the **essential rules** are as follows.

(a) *Always* keep sources in their containers when not in use. Only take out one source at a time and only for as long as it is needed.
(b) *Always* use tongs or a holding tool to keep the source at least 10 cm from your hand or any other part of your body.
(c) *Never* look directly at the open side of a source and never point it at anyone.
(d) Wash your hands at the end of the experiment.
(e) If you have open cuts on your hands, you should wear rubber gloves.

Remember also:

1. That the other people in the room will be exposed to some radiation, so do *not* work close to other groups.
2. If you are in any doubt, *ask* your teacher.
3. The activities of the sources are chosen so that *if these are handled properly* the maximum exposure during a two-hour practical is about $\frac{1}{50}$ of the permitted limit on any one occasion. If the sources are not handled properly, you could receive as much as 100 times the permitted limit, so *always use the correct procedure*.

3. USING THE GEIGER–MÜLLER TUBE

The α, β and γ sources you will use are sealed and shielded except on one face. The radiation is emitted through the side with the wire mesh.

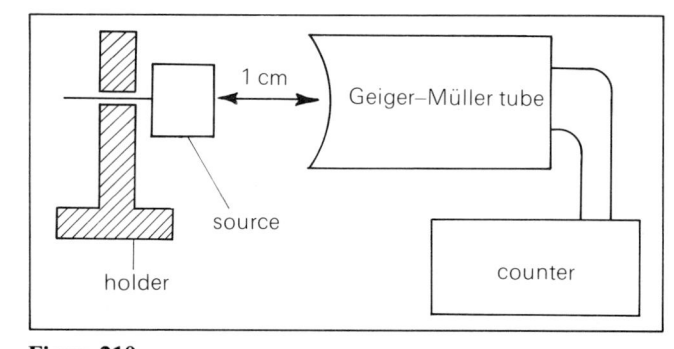

Figure 210

1. Start with the α source and place it about 1 cm from the window of the tube (figure 210).
2. Find the count rate (number per second) for different voltages over the range available (usually 250 V to 600 V). About ten readings are needed initially to draw the graph of count rate against voltage, but remember that other readings may become necessary after the graph has been plotted to find the exact line of certain sections of the graph.

3. Repeat for the β^- source and the γ source.

From the results and graphs
1. Why do you think 450 V is chosen as an operating potential?
2. Compare the *activities* of three sources. (This is nothing to do with their penetrating power, just the number produced per second.)

4. USING A CLOUD CHAMBER

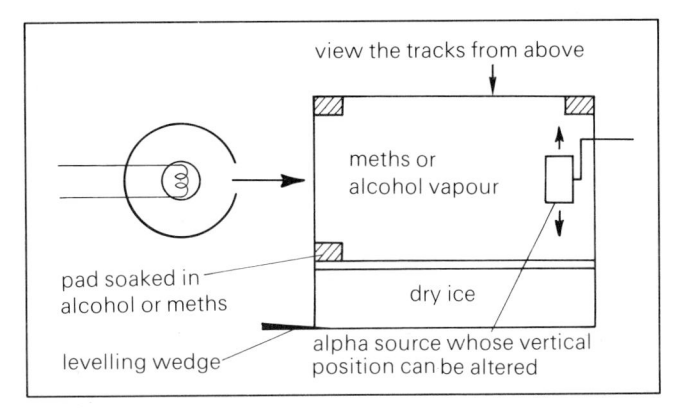

Figure 211 Side view of a diffusion cloud chamber

1. Put dry ice (solid carbon dioxide) in the base of the cloud chamber, just cover the base and soak any pads with meths or alcohol, replace the lid and leave for about 10–15 minutes for the vapour to settle down. The temperature gradient will produce regions of supersaturated vapour. For one band of temperatures the vapour will be saturated, and this is the region in which tracks can be seen.
2. Alter the vertical position of the source (usually by turning the mounting wire rod) until tracks are seen.

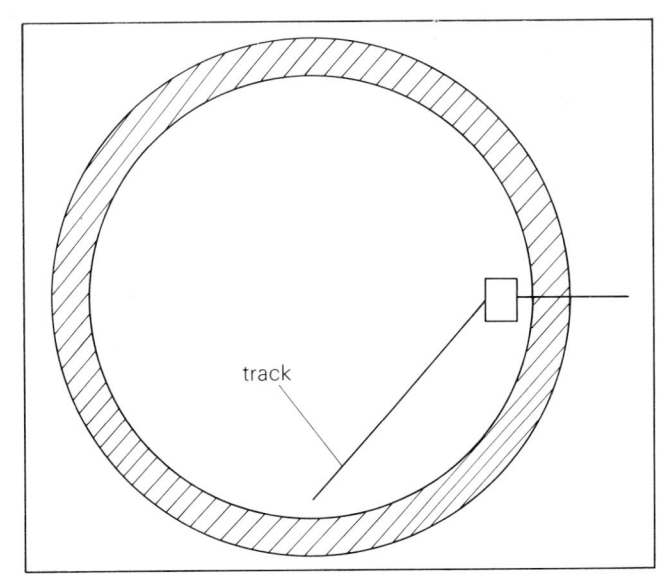

Figure 212 View seen (from top) for one track, visible for about 5 s

Draw the paths of about 20 tracks. Do they give any information about a property of all α-particles emitted?

3. Place a piece of polythene round the source (1000 gauge is suitable, i.e. it should be fairly thick). Some α particles will collide with the hydrogen nuclei in the polythene.

Draw the paths seen now and try and spot any differences between these and the tracks with the α-source alone. Can you suggest a particle which could cause the extra tracks?

5. USING PHOTOGRAPHIC PAPER

1. Place a sheet of photographic paper in a black polythene bag in the dark or under a red photographic light.
2. Place any object on the bag and hold a source of radiation about 10 cm above. You can experiment with β^- and γ, and with the time of exposure, but about 5 s is a starting time.
3. Develop the paper in the normal way.

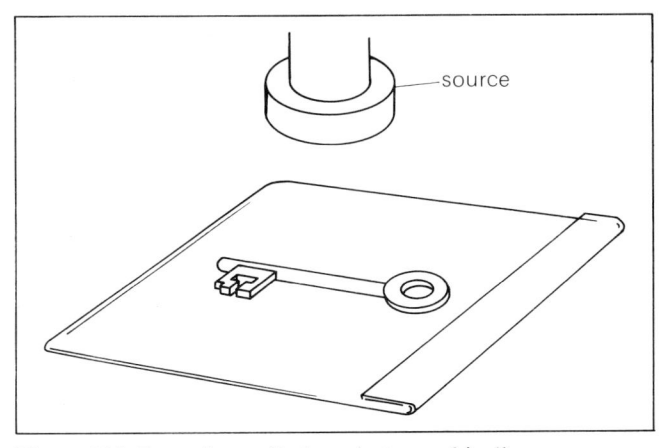

Figure 213 Detecting radiation photographically.

6. INVESTIGATING TRACKS AND COLLISIONS USING A SIMULATION

The only experiments which you can do in the laboratory involve natural radioactive decay. It is not possible for you to do experiments to look at the tracks of the large number of other sub-atomic particles or carry out investigations in which fast-moving particles produced by a particle accelerator are collided with nuclei. A computer simulation is available in the Nuclear Physics Package, Great Sankey Project (© CET) which provides you with experience of these types of investigations. You are able to record results, alter the setting of various parameters and then analyse the results and make conclusions. Full notes are available with the computer package. Figure 214 gives some idea of the experiments available.

EXPERIMENTAL TECHNIQUES

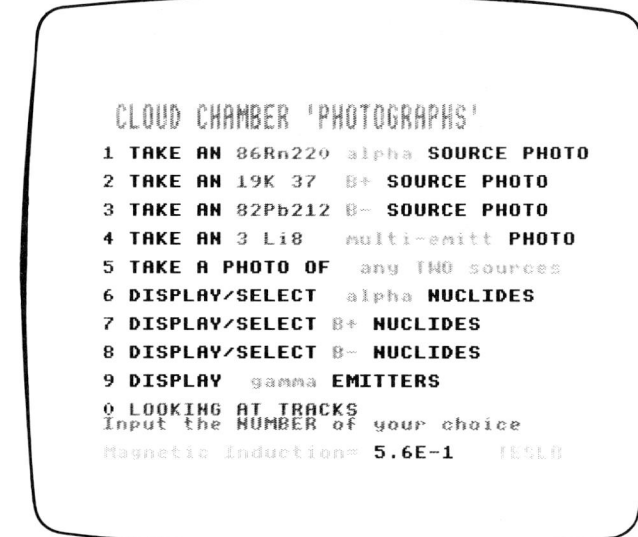

```
CLOUD CHAMBER 'PHOTOGRAPHS'
1 TAKE AN 86Rn220 alpha SOURCE PHOTO
2 TAKE AN 19K 37   B+ SOURCE PHOTO
3 TAKE AN 82Pb212  B- SOURCE PHOTO
4 TAKE AN 3 Li8    multi-emitt PHOTO
5 TAKE A PHOTO OF  any TWO sources
6 DISPLAY/SELECT   alpha NUCLIDES
7 DISPLAY/SELECT   B+ NUCLIDES
8 DISPLAY/SELECT   B- NUCLIDES
9 DISPLAY          gamma EMITTERS
0 LOOKING AT TRACKS
Input the NUMBER of your choice
Magnetic Induction= 5.6E-1     TESLA
```

```
             ALPHA EMITTERS
@ UNKNOWN SOURCE
            Mev                    Mev
A 84Po218  6.00       I 95Am241  5.50
B 86Rn220  6.28         3 Li8   13.00
C 89Ac214  7.20         5 B 8   21.60
D 90Th232  4.01         11Na22   2.14
E 91Pa226  5.86         83Bi214  1.50
F 92U 235  4.40
G 92U 238  4.19
H 93Np237  4.90
Current source 86Rn220  B
To change press WHITE 'letter'
Press SPACE-BAR to return to the MENU
```

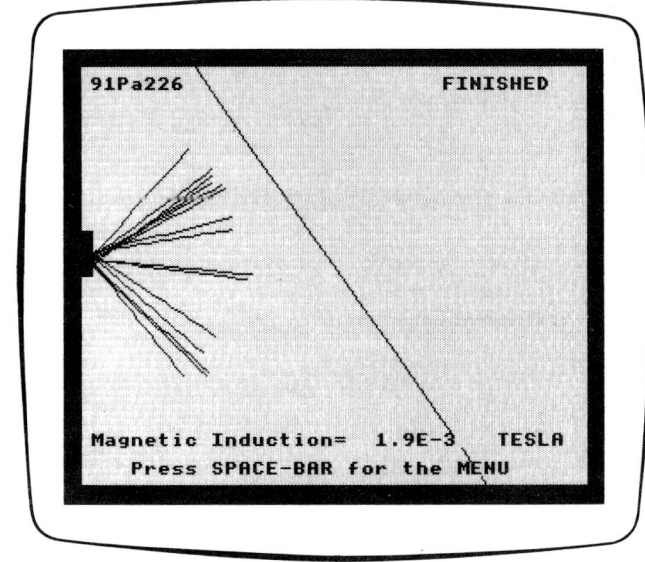

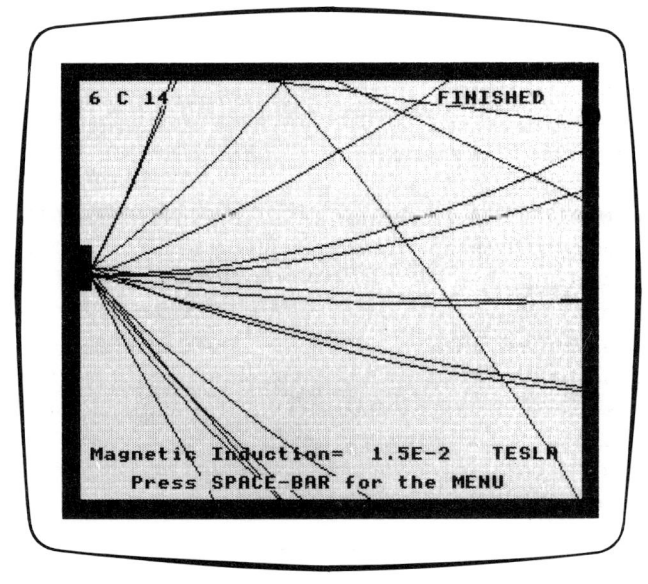

```
91Pa226                    FINISHED




Magnetic Induction=  1.9E-3   TESLA
   Press SPACE-BAR for the MENU
```

```
6 C 14                     FINISHED




Magnetic Induction=  1.5E-2   TESLA
   Press SPACE-BAR for the MENU
```

Figure 214 Investigating the range of alpha particles with energy and identifying an unknown source.

INVESTIGATING RELATIONSHIPS

26. FRICTIONAL FORCES

Outline

This experiment investigates the way in which the maximum *static* friction between two surfaces just before sliding depends on the *area of contact* and the *force* holding the surfaces together (the normal reaction). The amount of sliding friction is also measured to see if there is any truth in the statement 'a car takes longer to stop if the brakes are locked than if the wheels keep rolling until just before it stops'.

Equipment

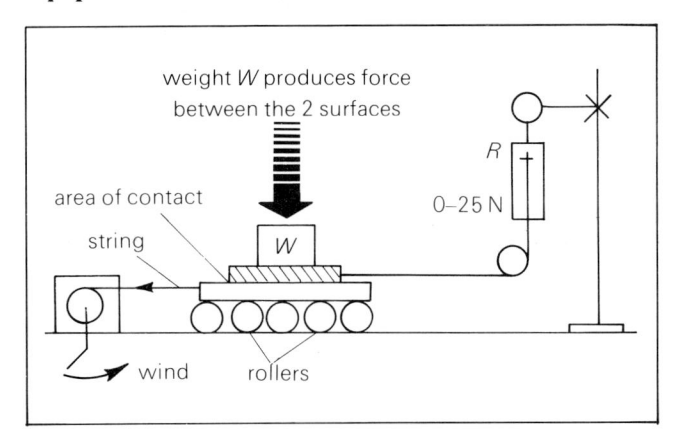

Figure 215 Equipment

Experimental details

Using the apparatus shown in figure 215, choose any pair of surfaces. Apply a weight W. Wind the handle and record the maximum reading R, on the spring balance, just before the block slips and when it is sliding at a steady speed. Repeat for a range of areas and weights in the range 1–10 N. Does the speed at which the block slides affect the value of the sliding friction? If so, ought you to try to keep the speed the same in successive experiments?

Results

Surfaces: paper and wood

Weight of block (W) = ... N
Area of block = ... cm

Load/N	Maximum force R/N	Sliding force R/N

From the results

Plot graphs of:

(a) maximum static friction against area;
(b) maximum static friction against total normal reaction (N);
(c) maximum static friction against sliding friction.

In your conclusions show how the graphs prove or disprove the following statements.

(a) The frictional forces are independent of surface area.
(b) The maximum static friction is proportional to the normal reaction ($F = \mu N$). Find a value for μ if this is possible.
(c) 'A car takes longer to stop if the brakes are locked than if the wheels keep rolling until just before it stops.'

27. FLUID FRICTION

Outline

An object moving through a liquid has a frictional force acting on it. A simple experiment such as pulling an object through water shows that the frictional force increases as the speed increases. Stokes suggested that the resistive force on a spherical object is given by the equation:

$$F = 6\pi\eta a v$$

where η = viscosity, a = radius and v = velocity. This experiment is designed to investigate the equation and, in particular, to find out if the constant 6π is correct.

When the sphere is falling under gravity vertically through a liquid, its speed will increase until the frictional force equals the weight. The resultant force is now zero and the object will have a constant velocity. This is usually called the terminal velocity.

Equipment

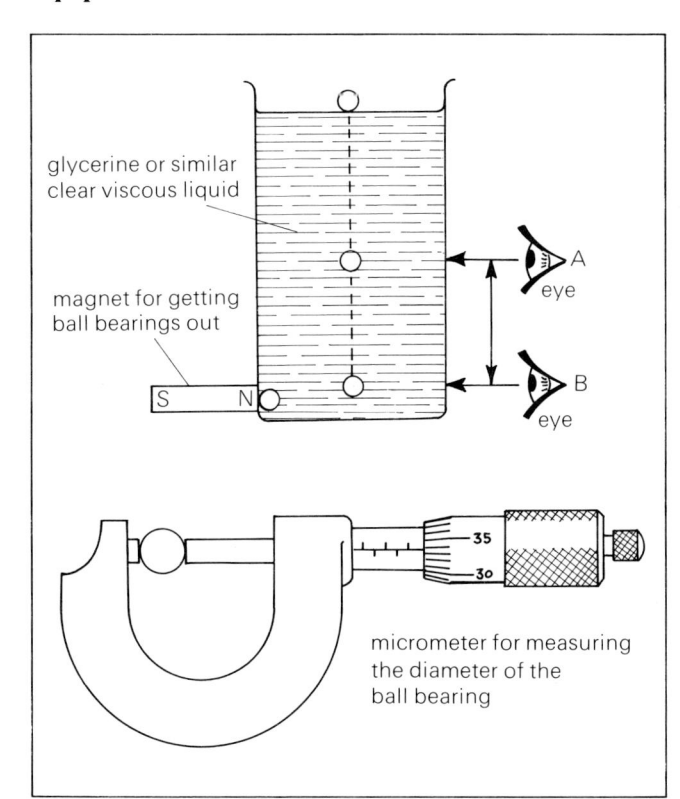

Figure 216 Equipment

Experimental details

Ball bearings of several different sizes are used; measure their diameters using the micrometer.

Hold one of the ball bearings on the surface of the liquid and then release it (see figure 216). Once the ball bearing has reached its terminal velocity, time its fall over a measured distance (A–B), with a stopwatch.

Repeat the procedure with the other sizes of ball bearing.

Plan your experiment with the following points in mind.

1. You will need to make sure that the ball bearing is in line with the marks A and B when timing is started and finished. The marks A and B should be circles, so that the marks on both sides of the glass can be lined up by the eye to avoid parallax errors.
2. You will need to get as accurate and consistent a timing as possible. Several readings need to be taken for each size of ball bearing and an average value calculated.
3. By using ball bearings with different radii, a set of terminal velocities for a range of radii can be found.
4. The weight of each size of ball bearing is needed.

Recording and displaying the results

Recorded results

(a) diameters of the ball bearings;
(b) times measured;
(c) weights measured;
(d) distance fallen;
(e) viscosity of the liquid, which is found from tables (viscosity of glycerine = 1500 N s m^{-2}).

Calculated values

(a) average radius for each size of ball-bearing;
(b) average weight of each size of ball-bearing in newtons;
(c) speeds of fall, with an average for each size of ball-bearing.

Graph

The equation is: weight $(W) = 6\pi\eta a v$

rearranged: $$v = \frac{W}{6\pi\eta a}$$

Comparing with the equation for a straight line $(y = mx + c)$, the graph should be a straight line through the origin if:

(a) velocity, v, is plotted as ordinate (y);
(b) weight/radius, W/a, is plotted as abscissa (x).

The gradient should be $\dfrac{1}{6\pi\eta}$.

Conclusions

Comment on the nearness of the graph to a straight line, the consistency and spread of the times and the agreement of the gradient to $\dfrac{1}{6\pi\eta}$.

28. SPRINGS AND DAMPING

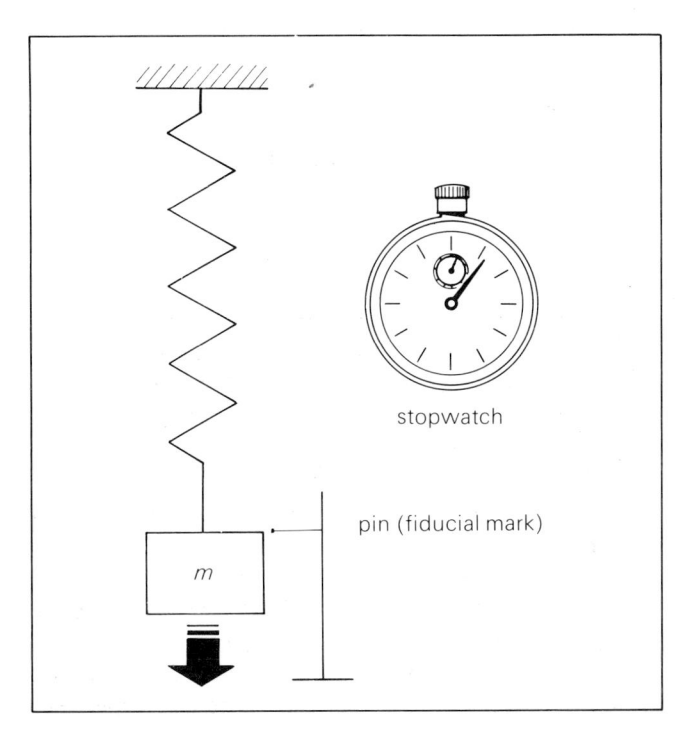

Figure 217 Apparatus for part 1.

Outline

If a mass is put on the end of a spring and then pulled down and released, the spring oscillates up and down. The energy stored in the spring when the weight is pulled down is gradually converted to heat. Work is done to overcome the slight air resistance and to stretch the spring, causing the amplitude of the oscillation gradually to get less. This practical (a) investigates the effect of altering the mass on the periodic time of the oscillation and (b) uses an electronic data memory to record the position of the weight, so that the changes in amplitude can be investigated. The experiment can be extended by using (a) different liquids as 'dampers' and (b) different surface areas.

Experimental details

1. Using the apparatus in figure 217, alter the mass over as wide a range as possible with the spring you are given and measure the periodic time for each mass. Remember to use the fiducial mark and to start and stop timings when the mass is passing through its equilibrium position. Does it matter what amplitude the displacement has? Plot a suitable straight-line graph and produce a final equation for the periodic time. (*Hint:* try m^2 and $\sqrt{m}$.)

2. In figure 218 the motion is being *damped*. First find the approximate time for the mass to stop. This will tell you what time-scale to set on the data memory. Displace the mass and take a set of position readings. Play them back onto an oscilloscope and you will see a graph of position against time. A piece of acetate sheet can be placed over the screen and a felt-tipped pen used to trace over the pattern. Investigate the effect of altering the area of the aluminium plate and the liquid used.

Results

From the traces of the oscilloscope patterns, you could measure successive amplitudes, and then use these figures

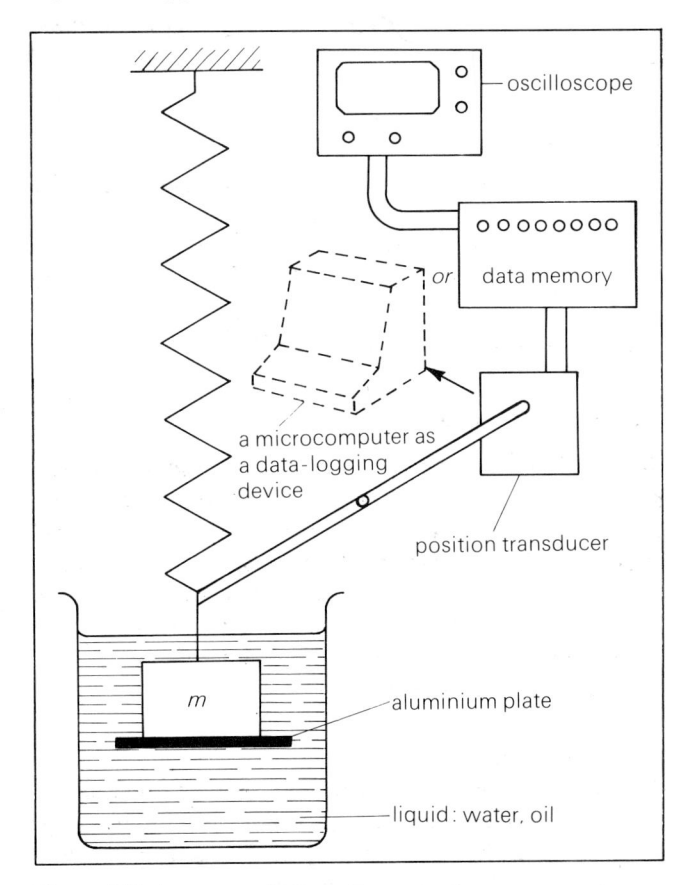

Figure 218 Apparatus for part 2.

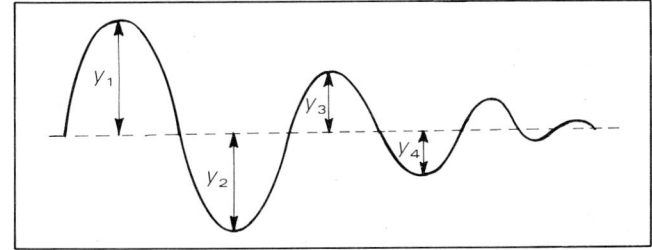

Figure 219 A damped oscillation

to test theories or to see if any pattern emerges. For example, you can test whether the amplitude gets smaller exponentially with time, i.e. if

$$y = y_0 e^{-kt}$$

where y_0 is the initial amplitude and k a constant. Taking logs,

$$\log_e\left(\frac{y}{y_0}\right) = -kt.$$

Since the time between successive maxima in the same direction is one periodic time, it follows that:

$$\log_e\left(\frac{y_2}{y_1}\right) = -kt = \log_e\left(\frac{y_3}{y_2}\right) = \log_e\left(\frac{y_4}{y_3}\right) \text{ and so on.}$$

Conclusions

Write a general report of your findings.

29. ENERGY ABSORBED BY A BOUNCING BALL

Outline

When a ball is dropped, its potential energy (PE) is converted into kinetic energy (KE). When it collides with a surface, some energy is used to deform the ball and is eventually converted into heat. The ball rebounds with less kinetic energy and so rises to a lower height than before.

The initial PE equals mgh, therefore, if no energy is lost as the ball falls, the KE before impact ($\frac{1}{2}mv_1^2$) equals the loss of PE (equals mgh_1). The PE at maximum height after the first bounce equals mgh_2, therefore, the initial KE after the bounce equals $\frac{1}{2}mv_2^2$, equals PE gain, equals mgh_2. The fraction of energy lost at bounce

$$= \frac{\text{KE before collision} - \text{KE after collision}}{\text{KE before collision}}$$

$$= \frac{h_1 - h_2}{h_1}$$

Measurements of h_1 and h_2 will enable the fraction of energy absorbed to be worked out.

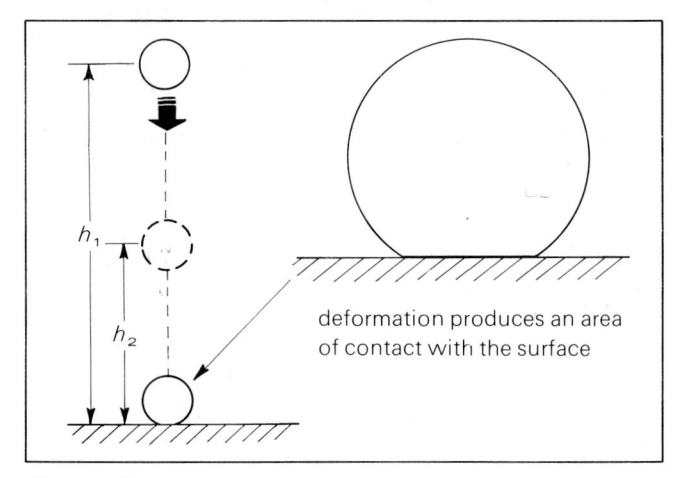

Figure 220

Three questions come to mind:

1. Is the fraction of energy absorbed the same for each successive bounce?
2. Does the fraction of energy absorbed depend on the initial height and, if so, is there any simple connection?
3. Is there any connection between the energy absorbed and the surface area of contact, or is this dependent on the initial KE?

This experiment attempts to find answers to these questions.

Equipment

You will need: a hard surface, a table-tennis ball and a tennis ball, or other type of 'hard ball'.

You will have to devise a reliable method for (a) measuring the heights of successive bounces, and (b) to measure the surface area of contact. Make sure that in your report you explain the methods used.

Experimental details

Start with the ball at a height of 1 m. Release the ball and measure the heights of as many successive bounces as are practical (or could you just measure the first bounce and choose this height as the next initial height). Measure the area of contact. Work out the fraction of energy absorbed.

Repeat for as wide a range of initial heights as is practical in your laboratory and record your results in a table, as shown on the next page.

From your results
Plot graphs from which you can make deductions in order to find answers to the questions posed in the outline. Explain clearly how you arrive at your conclusions from the results and graphs.

Initial height/m	Rebound height/m	k	Fraction of energy absorbed (1 − k)	Energy absorbed/J	Diameter of contact circle/m	Area of contact/m²

30. AIR RESISTANCE ON A FALLING OBJECT

Outline

In free fall there is no air resistance at all, and the only force acting is gravity. The resulting acceleration is uniform. The usual laboratory experiment drops a steel ball, and measurements of distance fallen and time taken are made. The equation $s = ut + \frac{1}{2}at^2$ is used; $u = 0$ because the ball starts from rest and the equation becomes $s = \frac{1}{2}at^2$. A graph of s against t^2 is drawn and the gradient is $\frac{1}{2}a$. Air resistance is neglected.

In this experiment an object is taken on which there is an appreciable air resistance. Your own experience riding a bicycle tells you that air resistance gets larger as the speed increases. The force on the falling body will not be constant and the acceleration produced will alter. The aim is to investigate how the velocity varies with time and to explain the results. You can also try to show if the air resistance force is proportional to v or v^2 or v^3.

Equipment

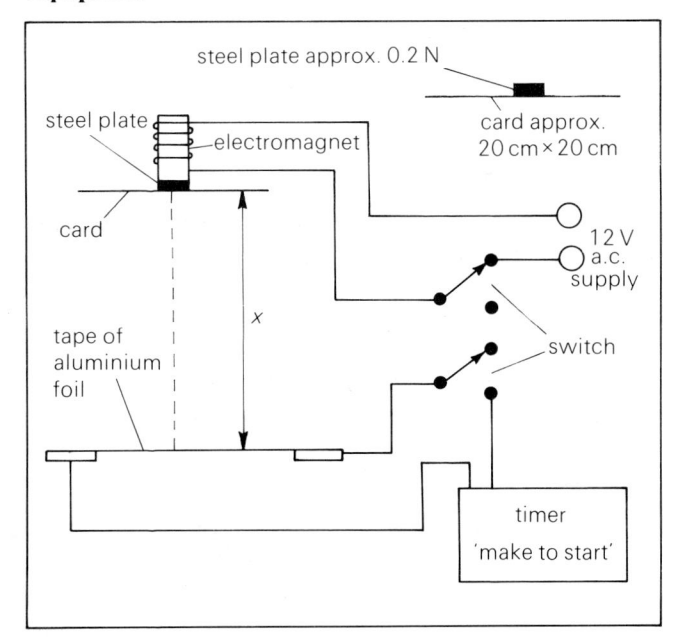

Figure 221 Equipment. Cards of different size can be used.

Experimental details

Use the apparatus shown in figure 221. To take a reading, move the switch down, which both breaks the current to the electromagnet, so the plate drops, and starts the counter. When the plate hits the aluminium foil it breaks the circuit, and so stops the counter.

Record the masses of the steel plate and each card. Take measurements of the time of fall for distances x in the range 40 cm to 200 cm. You will need at least ten results to plot a graph. Think about the need to measure several times for the same height. Plot a graph of distance against time. Since the acceleration is altering, it ought to be a curve. Draw tangents at ten points and produce a table of velocities and time. Remember the method of using a plane mirror to draw the tangent to a curve (figure 222).

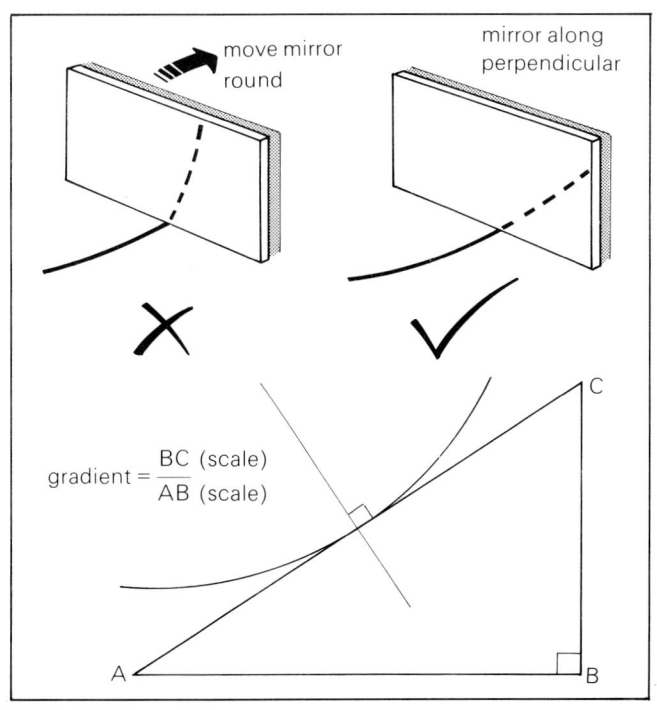

Figure 222 Drawing a tangent to a curve.

INVESTIGATING RELATIONSHIPS

From your results
1. Plot a graph of velocity against time.
2. Assuming no air resistance, the equation $v = gt$ would apply, because the acceleration is constant since the force is constant (g can be taken as 9.81 m s^{-2}). Plot this line on your velocity–time graph, and describe qualitatively how the two graphs differ.
3. When the object is falling and experiencing a resistive force A, the force equation is $mg - A = ma$, in which we believe possible expressions for A are:

$$k_1 v, \quad k_2 v^2, \quad k_3 v^3.$$

Substituting for A gives:

$$k_1 = \frac{mg - ma}{v}, \quad k_2 = \frac{mg - ma}{v^2}, \quad k_3 = \frac{mg - ma}{v^3}.$$

Draw gradients at four places on the velocity–time graph to find values for the acceleration and calculate values of k for each equation at each place. The values of k should be consistent for the dependence on v which is correct. Make a conclusion from your results if you can.

31. EFFICIENCY OF AN ELECTRIC MOTOR

Outline

In converting electrical energy to mechanical energy there is energy loss as heat in the windings, by induced currents in the armature core and by friction. You may also remember from your O-level work that the efficiency of any machine varies with load. An electric motor can be made to lift a load at different speeds, and one question to be investigated is whether the efficiency varies with the power output. These ideas are investigated by using an electric motor to raise a load vertically.

Equipment

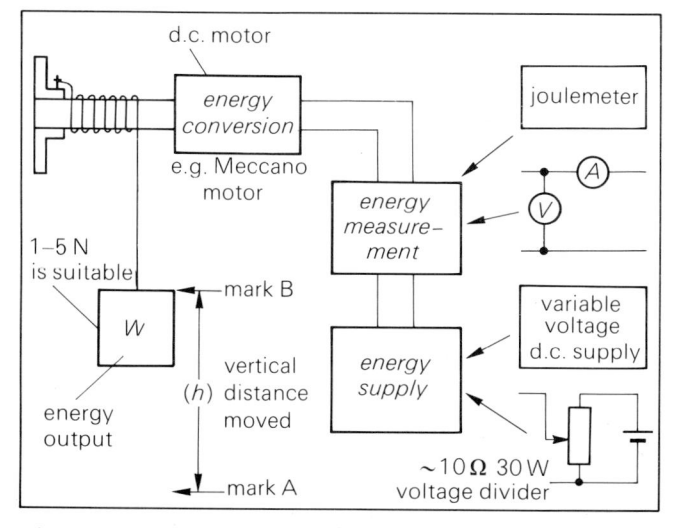

Figure 223 Equipment

Experimental details

1. The energy input can be measured either directly with a joulemeter or from $E = VIt$.
2. The first experiment involves choosing a load and a fixed, known distance to move through. Find the energy required to raise the load through the distance in a range of times. To alter the time, the speed of the motor must be changed, and so the voltage applied to the motor must be variable. Remember that this voltage will therefore be changed during the experiment. From the results the efficiency can be worked out.
3. The load can now be altered and the experiment repeated.

Useful data: energy out equals the gravitational PE gained by the load

$$\text{energy out} = W \times h = mgh.$$

$$\text{efficiency} = \frac{\text{energy out}}{\text{energy in}} \times 100\%$$

Recording and displaying results

Recorded results: height risen, weight, time, energy in (or voltage and current)

Calculated values: energy out, efficiency

Graph: a series of graphs of efficiency against time plotted on the same axes.

Questions

1. Does the motor become more efficient for higher loads?
2. Does the motor become more efficient if the load rises faster?
3. Where is energy wasted in the system?

32. ENERGY STORED IN A FLYWHEEL

Outline

The quantity of energy stored in a flywheel depends on the moment of inertia (I) and the angular velocity (ω) (equivalent to mass and velocity in linear motion):

$$\text{KE} = \tfrac{1}{2}I\omega^2$$

The moment of intertia of a solid disc equals $\tfrac{1}{2}mr^2$, where m is the mass and r is the radius.

The moment of inertia of the flywheel can be found by measuring the energy supplied to an electric motor driving the flywheel.

$\tfrac{1}{2}I\omega^2$ + energy lost as heat in the motor and by friction = total energy supplied

The problem is in finding a value for the energy losses. As soon as the motor is switched on, the flywheel begins to turn and gradually increases in speed and reaches a maximum speed when the rate of energy losses equals the rate of energy supply. Plotting a graph of total energy supplied against time will enable the rate of loss to be found and then the energy which must be stored in the flywheel to be calculated.

Equipment

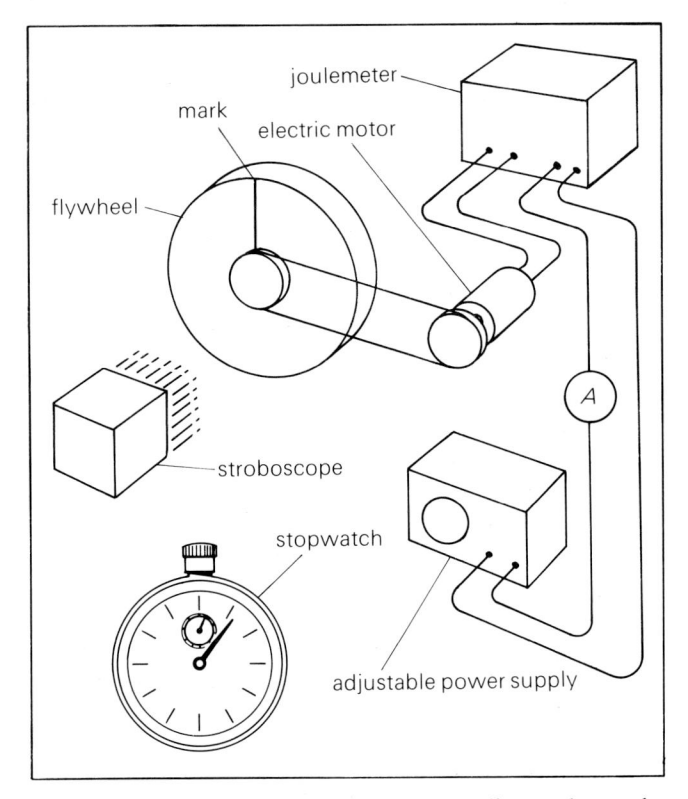

Figure 224 Equipment. Use the ammeter reading to choose the correct range on the joulemeter.

Experimental details

The range of supply voltages used will depend on the voltage required by the motor. About four or five different voltages are required. There is a lower limit to the voltage because of static friction in the bearings.

Reset the joulemeter. Switch on the supply and in the same instant start the stopwatch. Record the reading on the joulemeter every 15 s until the flywheel has been running at a constant speed for at least one minute.

Use the stroboscope to find the speed of rotation (number of rotations per second) of the flywheel. Repeat for the other voltages chosen.

From the results

1. Plot graphs of total energy against time (figure 225). From the straight-line part (when the flywheel is turning at a constant speed), work out the rate of energy supply from the gradient. This equals the rate at which energy is being lost. Assuming that this rate has been constant since the motor was switched on, use the total time to work out the total energy loss and hence the energy which must be stored in the flywheel. (Is it reasonable to assume this?) If the rate of energy loss = R, then total energy loss = Rt.

$$\text{KE stored on flywheel} = E - Rt$$

2. Calculate the angular velocity ω from the speed of rotation. Remember that 1 revolution is 2π radian. Calculate the moment of inertia for each set of results, using $\text{KE} = \tfrac{1}{2}I\omega^2$, and then work out an average value for the moment of inertia.

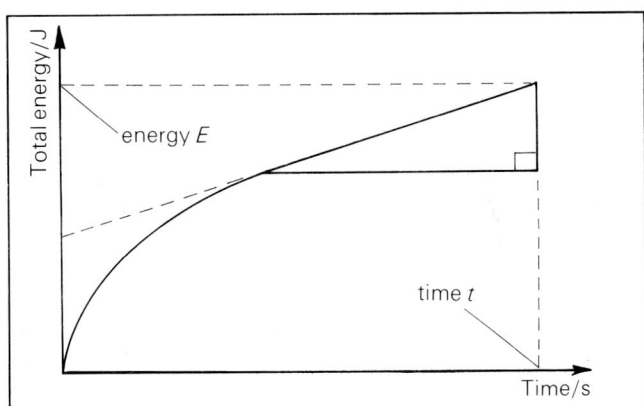

Figure 225

33. HEAT LOSSES FROM A WIRE UNDER DIFFERENT PRESSURES

Outline

A heated wire in a gas loses heat energy by radiation and by gas particles hitting it and taking energy away (convection and some conduction). The law determining the energy lost by radiation is known as Stefan's law:

$$E = \sigma T^4$$

E = total energy per second radiated
A = surface area
ε = total emissivity: a black object has a value of 1, anything else has a value of less than 1
T = temperature of wire
T_a = ambient temperature (temperature of the surroundings)
σ = Stefan's constant

The rules about the energy lost by gas particles hitting the wire are less well known, but we might expect that the energy loss should be proportional to the number of particles hitting it. The pressure is produced by particles hitting a surface, and so we might expect energy loss to be proportional to pressure. This experiment is to investigate the use of this idea and any dependence on the temperature of the wire.

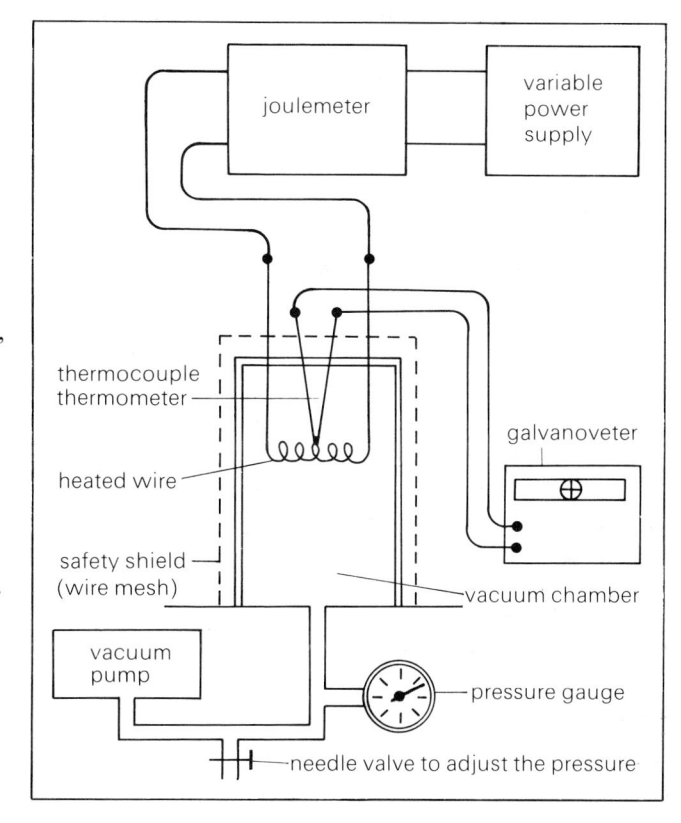

Figure 226 Equipment. The thermocouple thermometer enables the wire to be kept at a constant temperature.

Experimental details

Use the apparatus shown in figure 226.

1. With normal atmospheric pressure in the chamber, increase the voltage from zero until the wire just begins to glow.
2. Set the range on the galvanometer so that about half the scale range is used between the wire being at room temperature and the wire just glowing.
3. Since the wire will be kept at constant temperature:
   (a) the energy loss by radiation and conduction will be constant, and
   (b) the energy absorbed from outside will be constant if the ambient temperature is constant, and
   (c) the energy input will equal the net energy loss, since no energy is being absorbed to change the temperature of the wire.
4. Using the joulemeter, find the energy per second required to keep the wire at this constant temperature. This is the total energy being produced by the wire in the form of radiation, convection and conduction.
5. Change the pressure by switching on the vacuum pump and adjusting the amount of air getting in by altering the needle valve. Find the new energy per second required to keep the wire at the *same* constant temperature. Repeat this for as wide a range of pressure as possible.
6. Plot a graph of total energy loss per second (power) against pressure.
7. If you have time, use a different temperature (higher or lower) and repeat everything.

Questions

1. What physical significance does the intercept on the energy per second axis have in relation to the energy loss by radiation and/or conduction and/or convection?
2. What does the shape of the graph tell you about the connection between the heat loss by convection and the pressure?

34. VARIATION OF BOILING POINT WITH PRESSURE AND S.V.P. WITH TEMPERATURE

Outline

A liquid boils when its saturated vapour pressure (s.v.p.) equals the external pressure on it. Looking at figure 227, the force on the bubble at A is $p + hdg =$ s.v.p. When the bubble reaches the surface at S, the s.v.p. $= p$, where p is the atmospheric pressure.

Since the pressure inside the bubble depends on the speed of the vapour particles and this depends on the temperature, we should expect the s.v.p. to vary with the temperature.

Equipment

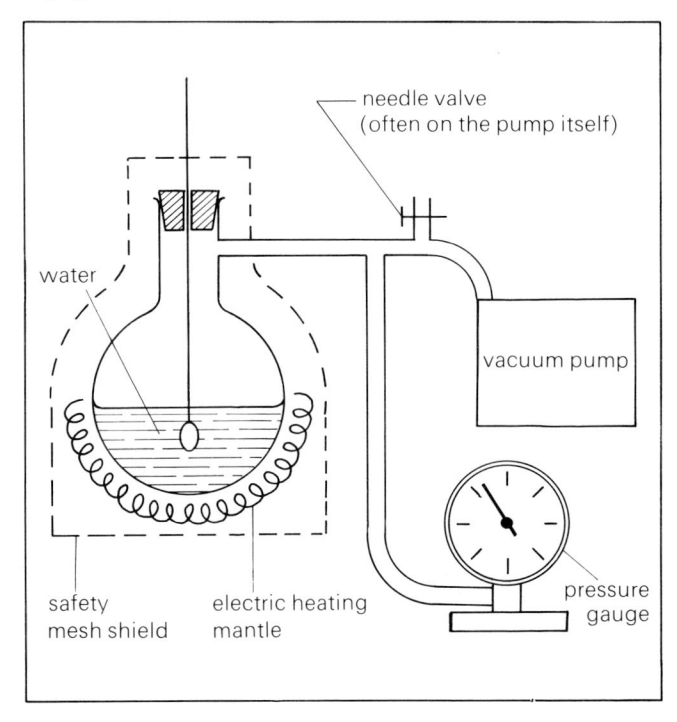

Figure 228 Equipment

Experimental details

Using the apparatus shown in figure 228, open the needle valve so that the system is at atmospheric pressure. Switch on the heating mantle until the liquid boils. Record the temperature and pressure. Allow the liquid to cool by about 5°C. Switch on the vacuum pump and adjust the pressure with the needle valve until the liquid just boils again. Record the temperature and pressure again. Repeat in about 5°C steps until the pump is producing the lowest pressure possible.

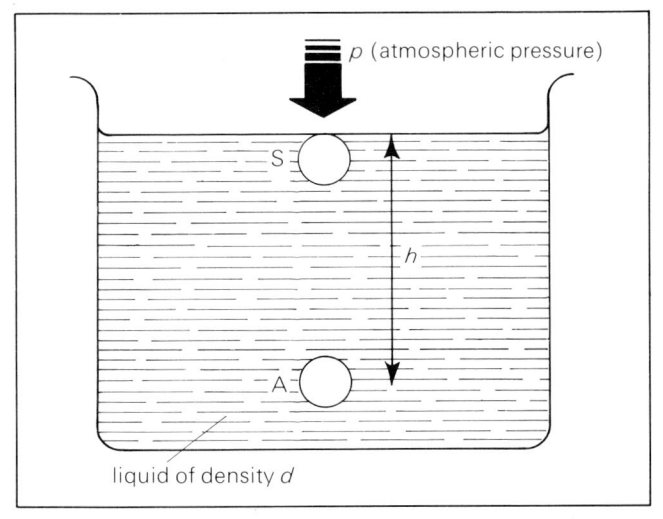

Figure 227

Results

Temperature/°C	s.v.p./N m^{-2} or Pa

From the results

Plot a graph of s.v.p. against temperature. Should the temperature be in centigrade or Kelvin, or does it not matter?

From the graph

1. Find the pressure needed to produce a temperature of 110°C.
2. Describe the general way in which the s.v.p. varies with temperature.
3. The equation connecting s.v.p. and temperature is

$$\log_e p = A - \frac{B}{T} + C \log_e T$$

where A, B and C are constants and T is in Kelvin.

Choose three points on the graph and use the values of pressure (p) and temperature (T) to form three equations. Attempt to find approximate values for the constants A, B and C.

35. THE GENERAL GAS LAW

Outline

When the pressure and/or volume and/or temperature of a gas change, it is proposed that, for a fixed mass of gas,

$$\frac{\text{pressure} \times \text{volume}}{\text{temperature (in K not °C)}}$$

is constant. The constant equals nk where n is the number of particles and k is the Boltzmann constant ($1.38 \times 10^{-23}\,\text{J K}^{-1}$). This experiment investigates this idea and attempts to find a value for the constant for the mass of gas used.

Equipment

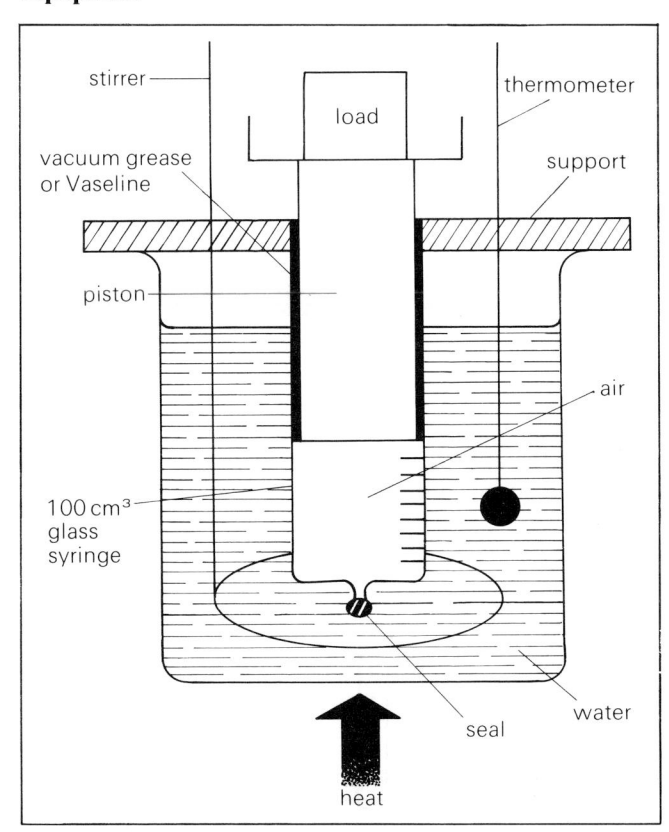

Figure 229 Equipment

Experimental details

1. Measure the weight of a syringe piston directly or measure its mass and calculate its weight using $g = 9.81\,\text{N kg}^{-1}$.
2. Coat the piston with vacuum grease or Vaseline and insert it in the syringe so that there is about $60\,\text{cm}^3$ of air in the cylinder. Seal the end.
3. Measure the atmospheric pressure in pascal (N m^{-2}).
4. Assemble the apparatus as shown in figure 229, but without a load.
5. Allow five minutes for the gas to come to the same temperature as the water. Record the temperature and the volume of the gas, which can be read from the scale on the side of the cylinder.
6. Repeat for loads of 1 N, 2 N, 3 N, 4 N, 5 N.
7. Heat the water until its temperature rises by about 10°C (or 10 K; the *interval* is the same) and repeat steps 5 and 6. Use the stirrer to produce an even distribution of heat. You will have to estimate the accuracy to which you keep the temperature steady.

Results

diameter of piston = ...mm
area of piston = ...m²

From the results

Calculate the value of $\frac{p \times V}{T}$ for each set of readings. Do they show a consistent value? This is a case where working out the mean and standard deviation can help in making the decision. If about 60–70 per cent of values lie within one standard deviation from the mean, the values can be considered consistent. The mean value of $\frac{pV}{T}$ is the gas constant for mass of gas in the cylinder.

Use the Boltzmann constant to calculate the number of particles in the gas in the cylinder.

Temperature/°C	Temperature T/K	Volume/cm³	Volume V/m³	Load/N	Load pressure/Pa	Total pressure/Pa

* Total pressure = atmospheric pressure + piston pressure + load pressure

and the effect on V of altering A, x and ε investigated as a way of finding the powers α, β, γ.

Assuming the charge remains constant,

$$\text{since } C = \frac{Q}{V} \text{ then } C \propto \frac{1}{V}$$

and changes in the value of $\frac{1}{V}$ will accurately show changes of C. A value for C can only be found if the charge Q is known.

Equipment

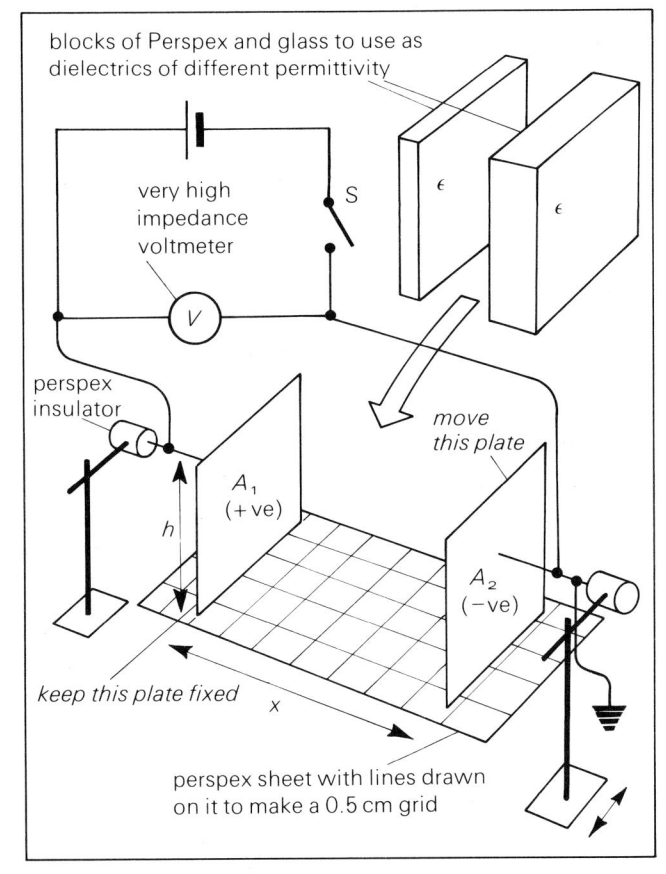

Figure 234 Equipment. The negative plate (A_2) can move forwards, backwards and sideways and is earthed to avoid charge loss by leakage through the body if the plate is touched.

Experimental details

Using the apparatus shown in figure 234, set the supply voltage at about half the range of the meter you are using and *no* more than 25 V, e.g. for a 10 V f.s.d. meter set to 5 V. Measure the height of the plates, h, so that the area of overlap of the plates can be calculated later. Connect the capacitor and allow it to charge. Disconnect the battery or source of e.m.f. by opening switch S.

Moving the plates relative to each other will alter the capacitance and alter the potential difference.

If the p.d. changes, then the energy stored must change. Why is this so?

Do a series of experiments in which the potential difference across the capacitor is measured, changing only one variable in the equation $C = kA^\alpha x^\beta \varepsilon^\gamma$ at a time. Measure the potential difference each time. The lines drawn on the Perspex base will help you to keep the plates parallel. Using the 0.5 cm grid, measure the distance (x) between the plates. Find the area of overlap between the two plates. Use as wide a range of values as the apparatus will allow. About ten results are needed for each to plot accurate graphs. Work as quickly as you can. (Why?)

The following table gives relative permittivities of dielectrics you may be able to use.

Dielectric	Relative permittivity
ebonite	2.8
glass	5–10 (not very useful)
ice	75 (good one to try)
marble	8.5
paraffin wax	2.2
Perspex	3.5
polystyrene	2.6
sulphur	4
ethyl alcohol	26 ⎫ In a set of suitable containers
glycerine	43 ⎬ the effect of thickness of dielectric
water	80 ⎭ can be investigated.

Results

1. A and ε constant

Potential difference/V	x/cm

2. x and ε constant

Potential difference/V	A/cm^2

3. A and x constant

Potential difference/V	Material

INVESTIGATING RELATIONSHIPS

Thickness of dielectric

4. A and x, ε constant

Potential difference/V	Thickness/cm

From the results

Remember that $C \propto \dfrac{1}{V}$. Therefore use values of $\dfrac{1}{V}$ in place of C. For the first experiment where the separation x was varied but A and ε were kept constant, the equation can be simplified to $C = k_1 x^\beta$. Taking logs gives $\log_e C = \beta \log_e x + \log_e k_1$.

Plotting a graph of $\log_e C$ against $\log_e x$ should be a straight line with β as the gradient.

The same idea will apply to the other experiments and in this way the powers α, β and γ can be found.

Alternatively, you could use the computer program 'PROCESS' (package PHYS2 option 6) which allows you to enter the raw data values, to manipulate the powers and to plot the resulting graphs so that the power which gives a straight-line graph can be found. Try the simplest powers of 1, −1 and 2 first. Plot the final graphs on paper and include them in your report.

Conclusion

Give the final equation you have derived for the capacitance in terms of area, permittivity and separation of the plates.

38. ENERGY STORED IN A CAPACITOR

Outline

As electrons flow onto one plate of a capacitor and off the other plate, work is done to separate the charge, and potential energy is stored.

Potential difference is measured in volts and is the number of joules per coulomb of charge. Current is the number of coulombs flowing per second. However, the potential difference and current change with time as the capacitor charges (or discharges), and so:

$$\text{energy} = \int VI\, dt$$

Now, $V = \dfrac{Q}{C}$ (from the definition of C) and $I = \dfrac{dQ}{dt}$.

Thus
$$E = \int \frac{Q}{C}\frac{dQ}{dt}\,dt = \int \frac{Q\,dQ}{C}$$

$$E = \frac{1}{2}\frac{Q^2}{C} + \text{constant}$$

If the capacitor is uncharged at $t = 0$, then

$$E = \frac{1}{2}\frac{Q^2}{C} = \tfrac{1}{2}CV^2$$

This experiment uses a joulemeter to measure the energy stored by various charging voltages and so find a value for the capacitance used.

Equipment

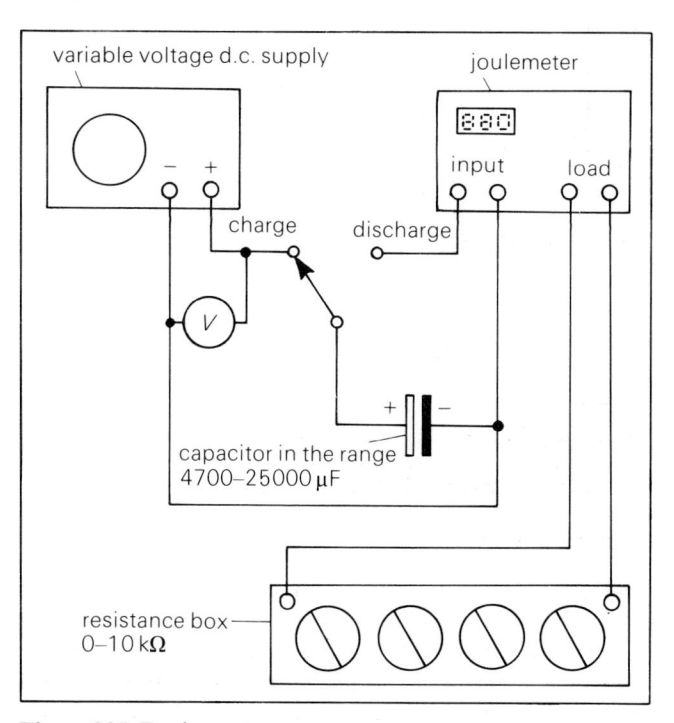

Figure 235 Equipment

Experimental details

Set up the apparatus as shown in figure 235, making sure that the electrolytic capacitor is connected the right way round.

A supply voltage is chosen and the capacitor charged. The capacitor is then discharged through the resistor and the joulemeter measures the energy flowing. The charging voltage is altered and the process repeated until there are enough readings to plot a graph. Make sure they are spaced evenly over the range of p.d. used.

The equation is $E = \frac{1}{2}CV^2$ and a straight-line graph through the origin is needed from which C can be found from the gradient. However, unless some planning is done, the reading on the joulemeter may not give a true value for the energy.

1. The range used may specify a maximum current. A larger current will cause error. From the value of charging potential used, the minimum resistance which should be used can be calculated using $V = IR$. If $V = 4.7$ V, and $I_{max} = 1$ mA, then $R_{min} = 4700\,\Omega$.
2. How long should be allowed for the capacitor to become sufficiently discharged so that it has a negligible energy left? What criteria do you use and how are they related to the values of R and C used?

Results

Charging voltage/V	Energy/mJ

Comparing $E = \frac{1}{2}CV^2$ with the equation of a straight line $y = mx + c$, a graph of E as ordinate and V^2 as abscissa should be a straight line through the origin with a gradient of $\frac{1}{2}C$.

Conclusion

State the value of C which you have calculated and use the graph to estimate the accuracy of your result. Explain how you used the graph to find this estimate of accuracy.

39. CHARGE AND DISCHARGE OF A CAPACITOR

Outline

The time taken for a capacitor to charge and discharge may depend on the values of capacitance (C), resistance (R) and initial charging (or charged potential) V_s.

This practical plots charge and discharge curves produced by:

(a) experimental measurements on an RC circuit;
(b) a mathematical iteration process which follows the physical changes taking place;
(c) the equation derived (by calculus)

for charging

$$V = V_s(1 - e^{-t/RC})$$

and for discharging

$$V = V_s e^{-t/RC}$$

In this way the agreement between theoretical calculations and practical results can be investigated. You will have to take into account that most resistors have tolerances of ± 10 per cent and capacitors ± 20 per cent and it may be a good idea to measure the actual value of the resistance first.

1. CHARGE AND DISCHARGE

Equipment

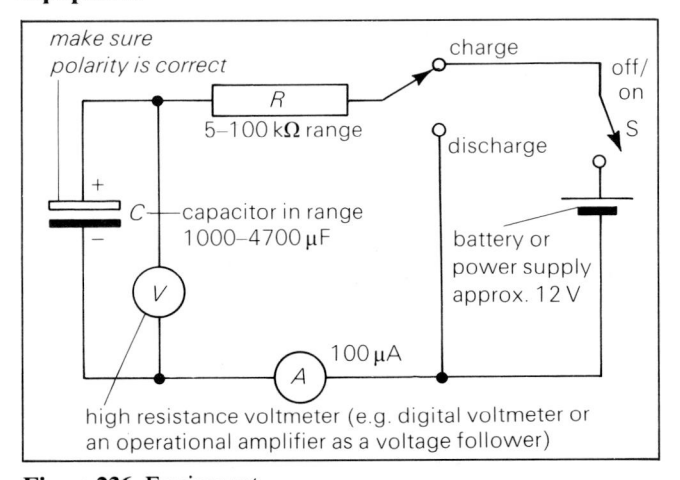

Figure 236 Equipment

Experimental details

1. Choose a value for R, C and the supply voltage, and assemble the circuit (see figure 236). Make sure the positive side of the capacitor is connected via the resistor and switch to the positive side of the power supply, otherwise there is a risk that the capacitor might *explode*.

INVESTIGATING RELATIONSHIPS

2. Discharge the capacitor. Move the switch to 'charge' and turn switch S *on*. Find the approximate time the capacitor takes to 'charge'. It never actually stops charging and you will have to decide the point at which you cannot detect any further change of voltage. Use this time to work out how often readings must be taken to produce about 20 sets of results.
3. Measure the supply voltage from the battery.
4. Discharge the capacitor again and make sure it is completely discharged by shorting across it momentarily with a wire.
5. Set the switch to 'charge' and take readings of voltage and current at your decided time interval.
6. When 'charged' move the switch to 'discharge' and repeat the measurements of voltage and current, again at your decided time interval.

An alternative method of measuring the current, potential and time is to use a computer (see figure 237). The program 'DATALOG' (package PHYS2 option 5) will allow you to record readings at time intervals, plot graphs and integrate to find the charge by calculating the 'area' under the curve.

Your teacher will give you more details of any data logging equipment which is available for you to use.

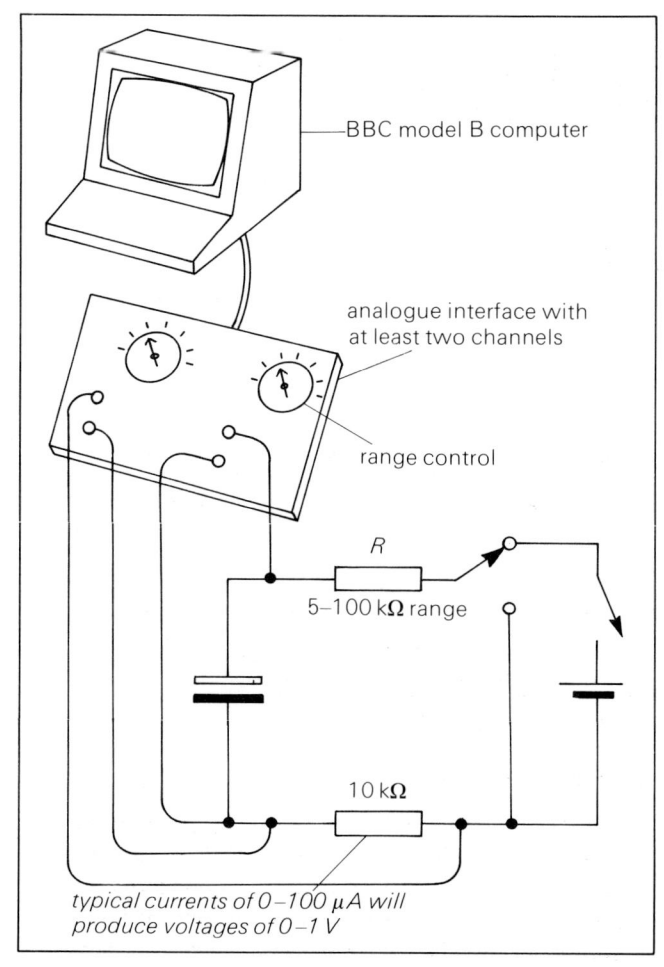

Figure 237 Datalogging using a computer

Results

Charging

Time/s	Voltage/V	Current/µA

Discharging

Time/s	Voltage/V	Current/µA

From the results
1. Plot graphs of voltage against time and current against time for both charging and discharging.
2. The total charge stored is $\int I \, dt$ and this equals the 'area' under the current against time graphs. Work out the total charge under each of the two curves.
   (a) Are the two values equal?
   (b) Do the values for the charge agree with $Q = CV$? If not, can you suggest any reasons?
3. Some connection between the product RC and the graphs is needed. You will notice from the graphs that there is no clearly defined time at which the capacitor is 'charged' or 'discharged'. A time must be defined; define it as the time taken for the current to fall to 0.37 of its initial value. Work out this time from the graphs. What is the connection with RC?

2. THEORETICAL CALCULATIONS FOR THE POTENTIAL DIFFERENCE (V) ACROSS THE CAPACITOR

Charging

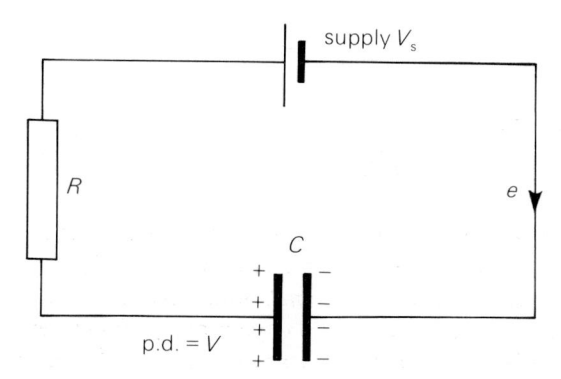

Figure 238

Initially the capacitor is uncharged and has zero potential.

$$\text{initial current} = \frac{\text{supply voltage}}{\text{resistance}}$$

In a small time t the charge which flows, x, is It. This will increase the potential on the capacitor, since $V = \frac{Q}{C}$, and the effective potential difference causing current to flow will get less:

effective p.d. = supply p.d. − p.d. across capacitor.

This in turn alters the current

$$I = \frac{(V_s - V)}{R}$$

which in turn alters the charge flowing, and so on.

A. By using a process of iteration with a small time interval, a prediction can be made for the variation of potential with time. Use one of the following methods:

(a) work through the flowchart below using a calculator, or
(b) use the computer program 'CAPDIS' from the Schools Council *Computers in the Curriculum* series (© Longman), or
(c) use the computer program 'CHADIS' (package PHYS1 option 7).

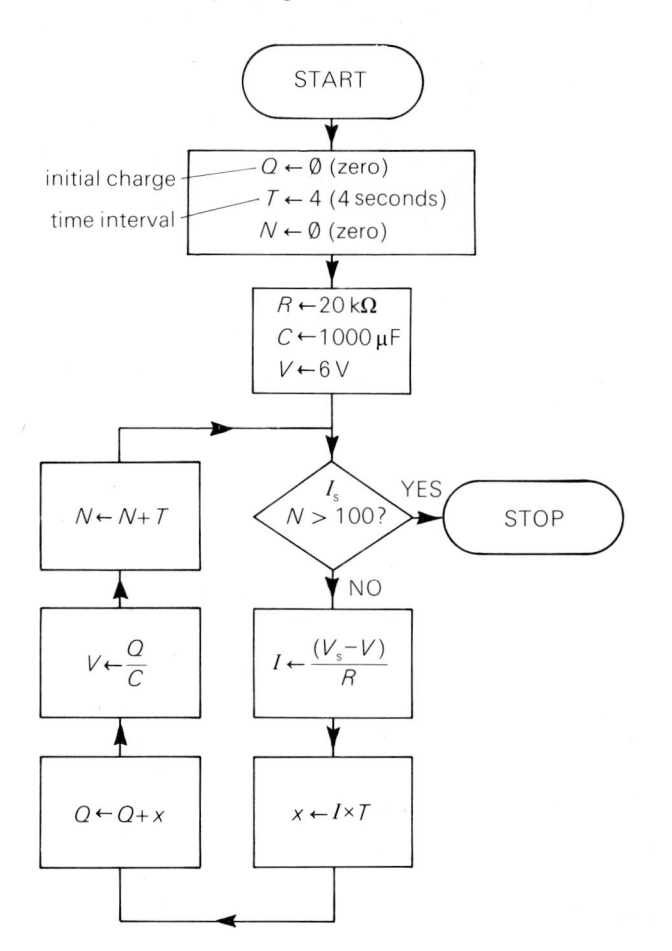

Investigate the effect of using a large time interval T and a small interval t. Which time interval would produce the most accurate prediction?

N	I	x	Q	V
	0	0	0	0
4				
8				
12				
16				
20				
24				

B. The p.d. of the capacitor V is given by the equation:

$$V = V_s(1 - e^{-t/RC})$$

This can be derived by calculus. Does the *final* charged potential depend on the time?

For the same values of R, C and V_s as you used in the iteration, work out about 20 values of V at evenly spaced times, over the time of 'charge'. Remember the time must be in seconds.

Time/s	V/volts

$V_s = \ldots$ Volts
$R = \ldots \Omega$
$C = \ldots$ F

Discharging

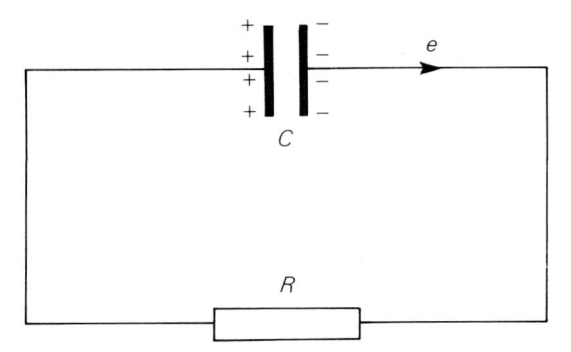

Figure 239

INVESTIGATING RELATIONSHIPS

As electrons flow from the capacitor, the potential across the capacitor falls because the amount of charge on the capacitor falls. In the same manner as for charging, predict values by iteration and by the equation from calculus: $V = V_s e^{-t/RC}$.

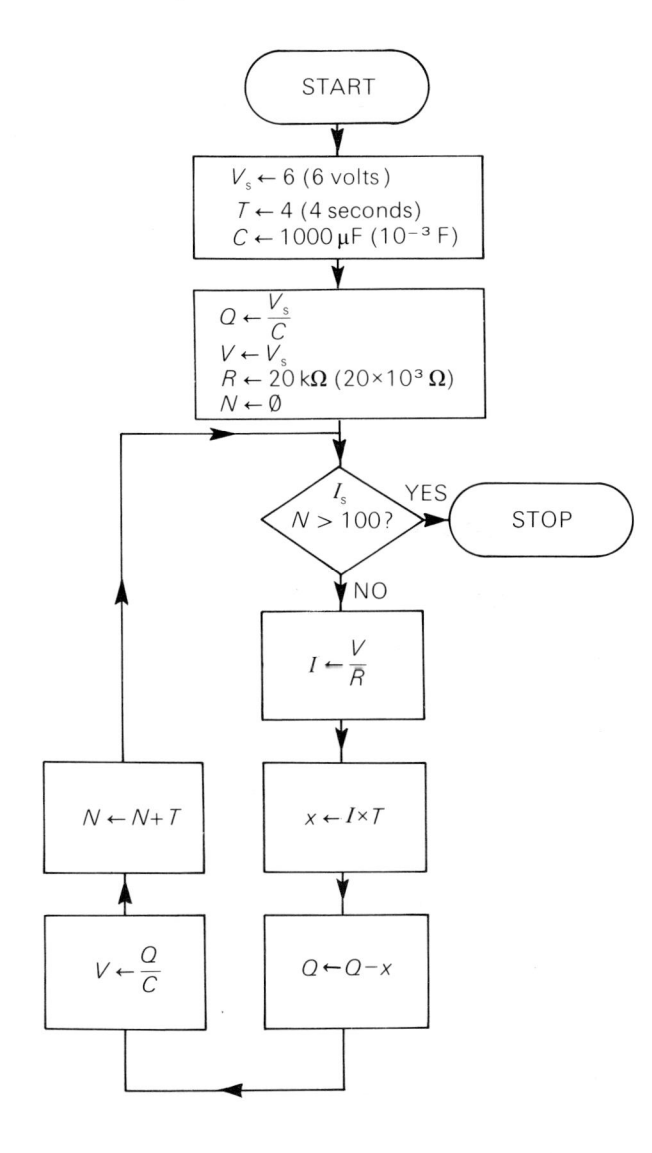

Iteration

N	V	I	x	Q
0				
4				
8				
12				
16				
20				
24				

Calculus

Time/s	V/volts

Flow chart:
START
$V_s \leftarrow 6$ (6 volts)
$T \leftarrow 4$ (4 seconds)
$C \leftarrow 1000\,\mu F$ (10^{-3} F)

$Q \leftarrow \dfrac{V_s}{C}$
$V \leftarrow V_s$
$R \leftarrow 20\,k\Omega$ ($20 \times 10^3\,\Omega$)
$N \leftarrow 0$

I_s : $N > 100?$ — YES → STOP
NO ↓
$I \leftarrow \dfrac{V}{R}$
$x \leftarrow I \times T$
$Q \leftarrow Q - x$
$V \leftarrow \dfrac{Q}{C}$
$N \leftarrow N + T$

From the calculations

Plot the values on the graphs made from the experimental results. Compare the graphs and comment on the agreement between the graphs.

Remember that the marked values on the resistor and capacitor may not actually have the values marked. For example, if R is marked as $22\,k\Omega$ and C as $4700\,\mu F$, then $RC = 103.4\,s$. The maximum value if R is $+10$ per cent and C is $+20$ per cent would be:

$$(22k + 10\%) \times (4700\,\mu F + 20\%) = 24\,200 \times 5.64 \times 10^{-3}$$
$$= 136.4\,s$$

The minimum value would be if R is -10 per cent and C is -20 per cent.

40. ELECTRICAL RESISTIVITY AND CONDUCTIVITY

Outline

Electrical resistance (see figure 240) is defined:

$$R = \frac{\text{potential difference applied}}{\text{current flowing}} = \frac{V}{I}$$

This is similar to thermal conduction (see figure 241).

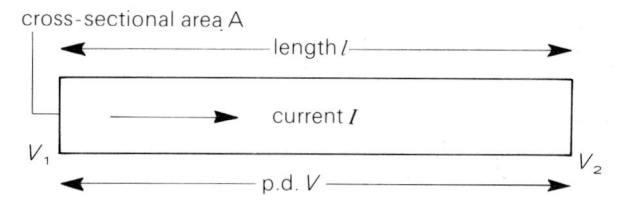

cross-sectional area A, length l, current I, p.d. V, V_1, V_2

Figure 240

For thermal conduction, heat energy flows and the equation is

$$\frac{dE}{dt} = \frac{kA(T_1 - T_2)}{x} = kA\frac{dT}{dx}$$

where $\frac{dT}{dx}$ is the temperature gradient.

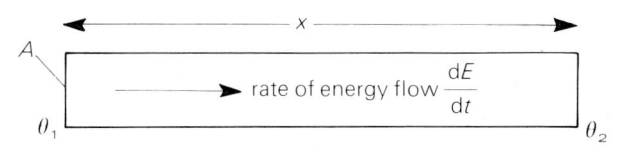

Figure 241

For electrical conduction, charge Q flows and the current $I = \frac{dQ}{dt}$ so comparing the two situations suggests an equation

$$\frac{dQ}{dt} = \text{constant} \times A \times \frac{dV}{dl}$$

$$= \text{constant} \times \text{area} \times \text{potential gradient}$$

where the constant is the electrical conductivity.

Conversely, the thermal conductivity equation can be thought of as:

$$\text{rate of flow of energy} = \frac{\text{temperature difference}}{\text{thermal resistance}}$$

in comparison to

$$\text{rate of flow of charge} = \frac{\text{voltage difference}}{\text{electrical resistance}}$$

where

$$\boxed{\text{electrical resistance} = \frac{\text{length}}{\text{constant} \times \text{area}}}$$

provided the material is of uniform thickness, with the constant being a coefficient of electrical conductivity in comparison with thermal conductivity.

This experiment investigates this relationship using:

(a) resistance wires of various lengths and diameters;
(b) resistive putty which can be formed into any shape or length;
(c) carbon films which you will make yourselves.

Experimental details

A. Using the equipment shown in figure 242a, you should be able to set up wires of different length and thicknesses but of the same material and plan an experiment to verify or otherwise the equation:

$$\text{resistance} = \frac{\text{length}}{\text{conductivity} \times \text{area}}$$

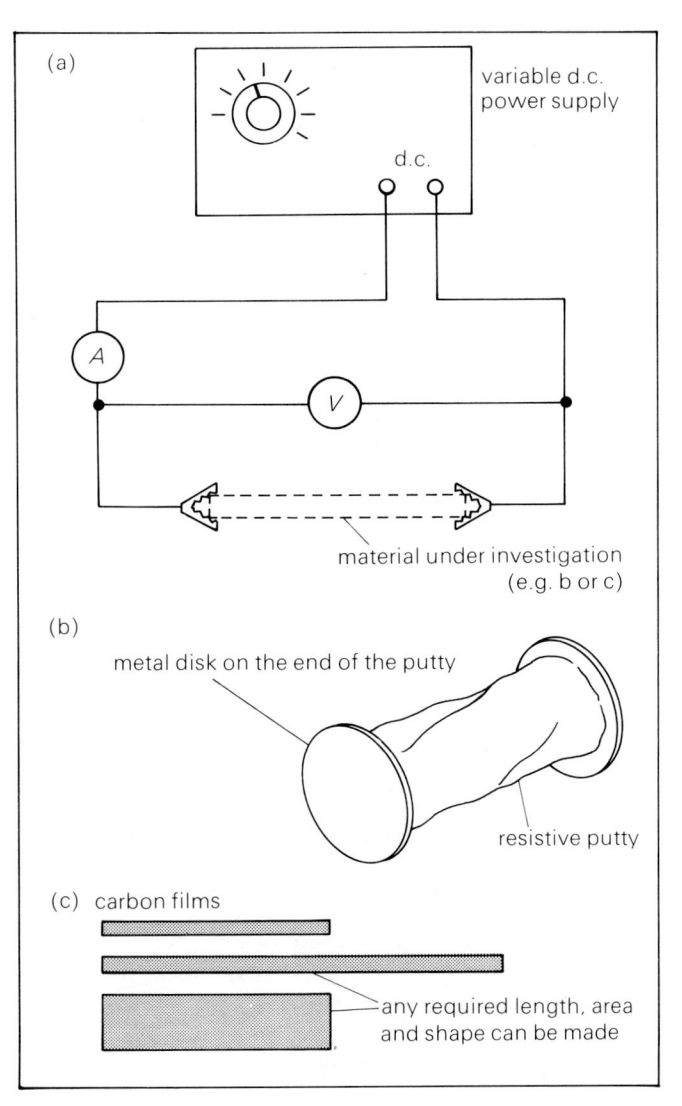

Figure 242 Equipment. Shunts and multipliers will be needed for the meters, because you have no idea what size of current you will need to measure.

If the equation is shown to be valid, you should be able to find a value for the conductivity of the material.

Will showing resistance to be proportional to (a) length and (b) $\frac{1}{\text{area}}$ be sufficient to verify the equation, or will you have to show resistance to be proportional to $\left(\frac{\text{length}}{\text{area}}\right)$?

Will the conductivity be the same for all materials?

B. Use resistive putty (figure 242b) to investigate the effect of cross-sectional *shape* (such as the shapes shown in figure 243) and length on the resistance.

Use gloves to handle the putty and roll it like pastry. Attach the crocodile clips to the metal disks, one at either end of the putty. The conductivity of the putty is approximately $40\,\text{m}\Omega^{-1}\,\text{m}^{-1}$ (e.g. Unilab).

INVESTIGATING RELATIONSHIPS

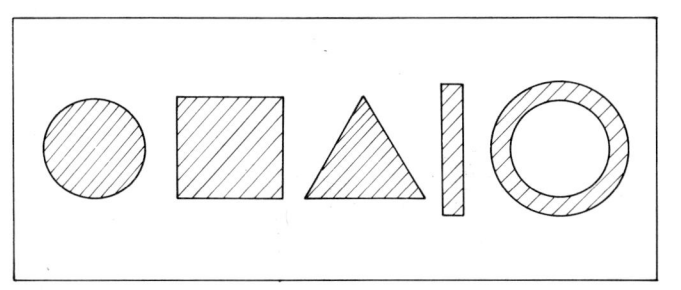

Figure 243 Different cross-sectional shapes of resistive putty

C. Make carbon films (figure 242c) of various lengths and widths, using a soft 3B pencil or carbon crayon on graph paper (making the area easy to determine). Make sure you get a uniform density of carbon. Take measurements of voltage and current so that the resistance of each can be worked out. Use your results to try to find an equation which connects resistance with the length and width.

Results and your report

For (A) give tables of results, graphs and show how the shape of the graph leads you to your conclusion about the proposed equation. Show how the conductivity was worked out from the graph. Have you shown if the conductivity differs for different materials?

For (B) write a summary of your findings.

For (C) give tables of results. Explain your attempts to use them to find an equation and give the equation if you were successful.

Find the connection between the *resistivity* of a wire (found from tables) and its *conductivity*.

41. CONDUCTION IN LIQUIDS AND GASES

Outline

Liquids and gases will conduct only when there are charged particles present which can move under the electric field produced by the supply potential. In a liquid, conduction is carried by positive and negative *ions*. Oil molecules are held together by covalent bonding and will not conduct because there are no ions. For this reason oil is used as a coolant in transformers and high-current switches on power lines. Copper sulphate molecules are held together by an ionic bond and will dissociate into separate ions when dissolved in water, which reduces the electrostatic force by 81 times so that the ions no longer stick together. In a gas, the conduction is by electrons and the positive ions left after electron(s) have been removed. Electrons can be removed from atoms or molecules by:

(a) collision with another electron (ionisation), or
(b) direct pull under a large potential difference (field emission).

This experiment investigates:

1. the variation of current with applied potential difference, surface area and separation of the electrodes for copper sulphate solution;
2. the variation of current with applied potential difference for a neon bulb;
3. a measurement of the ionisation potential for xenon and argon.

1. COPPER SULPHATE SOLUTION

Equipment

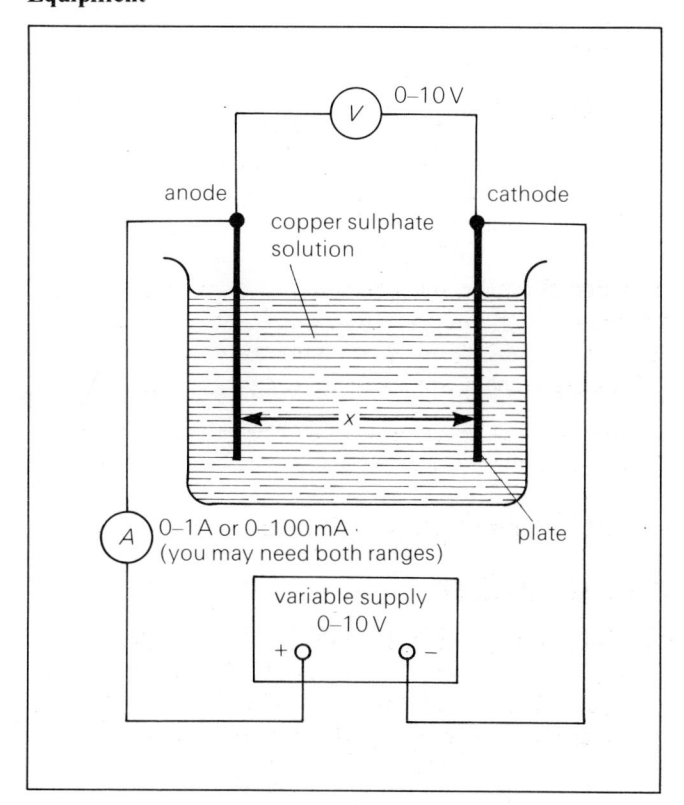

Figure 244 Equipment

Experimental details

1. Choose a pair of plates and assemble the apparatus as shown in figure 244. The *anode* is the plate connected to positive. The *cathode* is the plate connected to negative. Measure the separation of the plates (x).
2. Starting at a potential difference of zero volts take a series of readings of current and voltage. Do not exceed 10 V or 1 A. Observe and record any changes which occur on or around the plates.
3. Find the area of either plate *immersed* in the copper sulphate solution (remember it has two sides).
4. Repeat for as many other pairs of plates (of different size to the first pair) as are available, or alternatively the plates can be raised or lowered to alter the area immersed.

Results

width of plate = ...cm separation x = ...cm
height of plate = ...cm surface area A = ...cm^2

Potential difference V/V	Current I/mA

From the results

1. Plot a series of graphs of potential difference against current for different surface areas for a given separation (that is, unless you have planned badly and used a random set of separations).

   What can you conclude about:
   (a) the way a liquid conducts; and
   (b) the effect of surface area?

2. For any value of potential difference and surface area you choose, plot a graph of current against separation. Test the idea that:

$$\text{current} \propto \frac{1}{\text{separation}}$$

Which 'straight-line' graph would you plot to show this?

2. NEON LAMP

Experimental details

1. Use the circuit shown in figure 245. Starting from zero volts, increase the potential difference until conduction starts (note the approximate voltage) and continue increasing the voltage until 100 mA or 300 V is reached (note the approximate voltage). Decide on the voltage steps needed to take approximately 20 readings. Plot a graph of voltage against current.

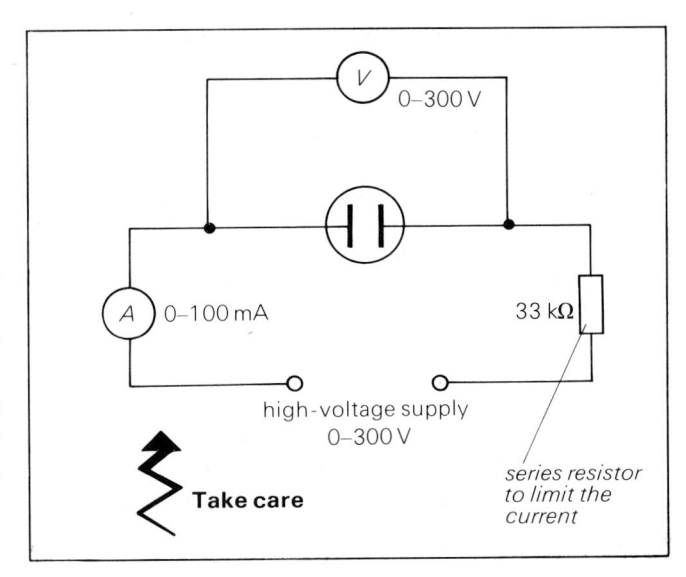

Figure 245 Discharge in a gas.

Comment on the shape of the graph and on the physical significance of any particular parts or points.

2. Reduce the voltage from the maximum value and note the currents. Can you explain the differences that occur?

3. MEASUREMENT OF THE IONISATION POTENTIAL OF A GAS

Equipment

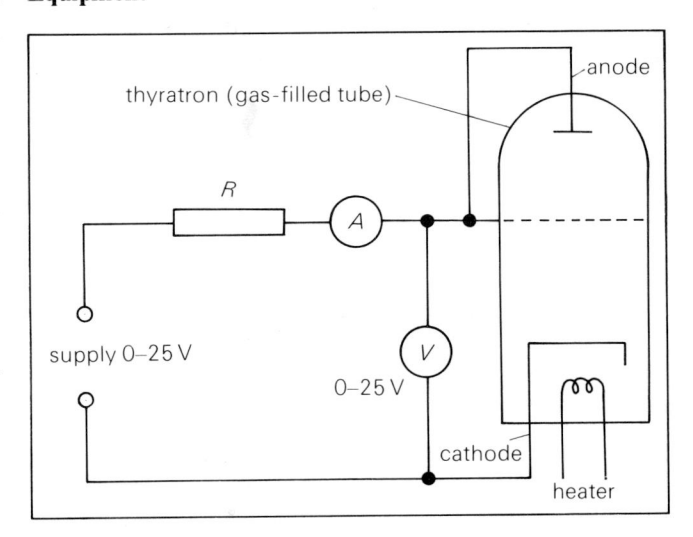

Figure 246

Experimental details

Use either:

(a) a xenon EN91 thyratron, with a 1 kΩ 1 W resistor and 0–10 mA ammeter; or
(b) an argon 884 thyratron, with a 100 Ω 5 W resistor and 0–100 mA ammeter.

INVESTIGATING RELATIONSHIPS

Electrons are produced from the heated cathode and attracted towards the positive anode, causing a small current to flow. As the supply voltage is increased, the electrons gain more energy (remember that voltage is a measurement of the number of joules per coulomb). At some stage they have enough energy to knock out an outer electron from the gas atoms. This will produce more charge carriers (electrons and ions) and so the current flowing should increase. Starting from zero volts, take a series of readings of voltage and current. Plot a graph of voltage against current. Take any extra readings if necessary to produce an accurate curve.

From the graph find the p.d. when the gas becomes ionised, and from it work out the energy needed to cause ionisation. If you have used both tubes, can you account for the difference?

42. INVESTIGATING THE OPERATION AND APPLICATIONS OF A TRANSISTOR

Outline

The transistor can be thought of as another controlling device, rather like a variable resistor, although it contains an n–p–n type semiconductor sandwich. It has three leads (see figure 247): collector (c), base (b), and emitter (e). The main current flow is from c to e. Its importance lies in the fact that the amount of conduction can be controlled by the amount of current flowing into the *base*.

This experiment investigates some of the properties of the transistor in what is called 'common emitter mode' (because the emitter is connected to the negative which is common to both input and output circuits).

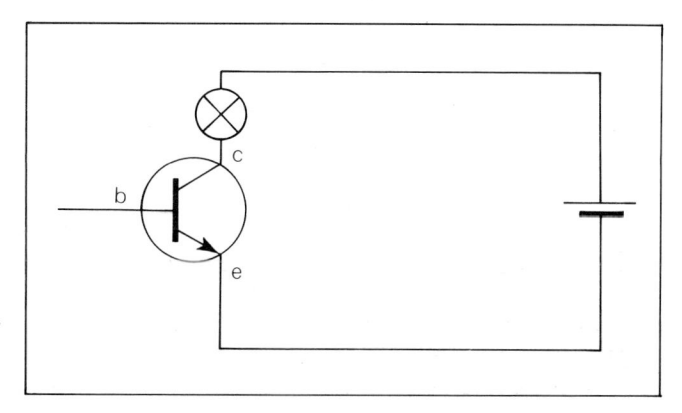

Figure 247 *n*-*p*-*n* transistor

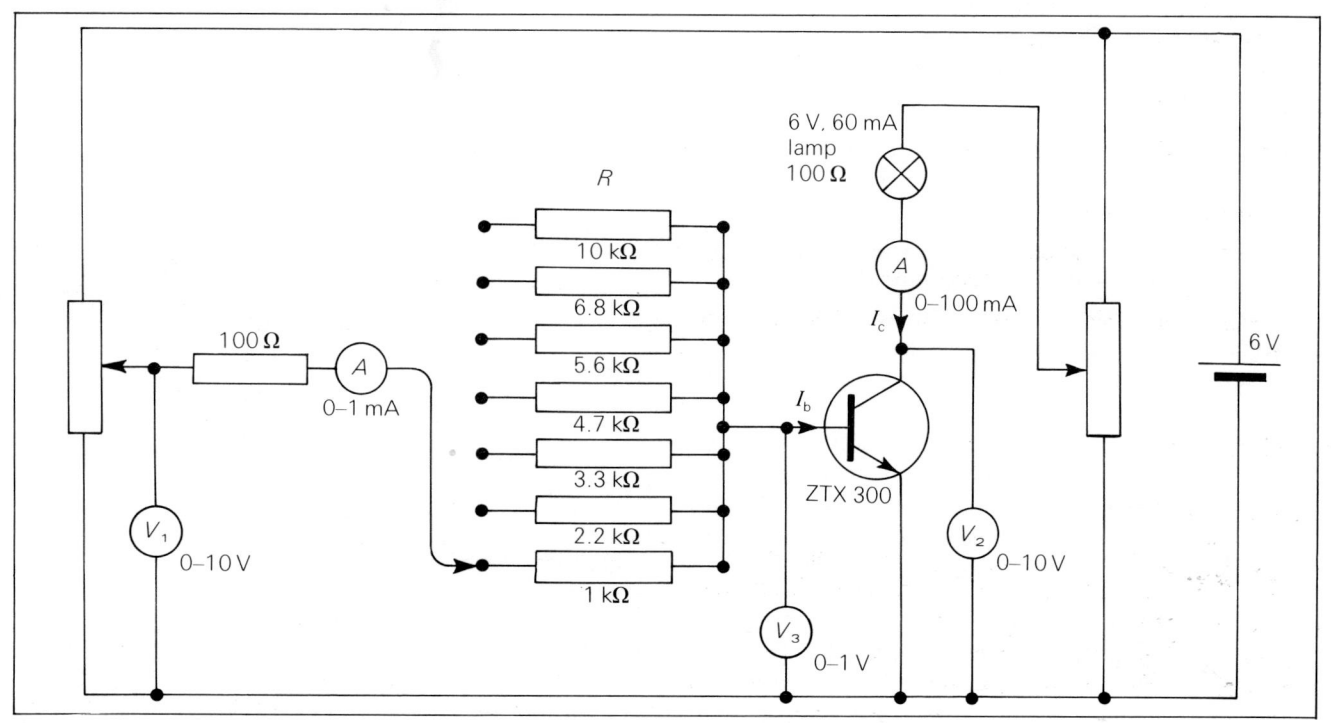

Figure 248 Circuit for experiment 1.

1. FINDING THE BASE–EMITTER RESISTANCE WHEN THE TRANSISTOR IS FULLY CONDUCTING

Experimental details

1. Using the circuit shown in figure 248, set the supply voltage to the collector to 6 V and connect the oscilloscope to measure the voltage on the collector (c) (meaning between *ground* and the collector).
2. Use a 1 kΩ resistor for the base circuit resistor, R.
3. Adjust the voltage supply to the base circuit from zero until the voltage on the collector starts to fall as the transistor conducts, and continue until the voltage stops falling. The transistor is now fully conducting. Record the *base current* (I_b), and the supply voltage to the base circuit (V, measured in volts).
4. Increase R by 1 kΩ, adjust the supply voltage to the base circuit until the same base current I_b flows, and record values of R and VI.
5. Repeat in 1 kΩ steps up to 10 kΩ.
6. Plot a graph of total resistance in the base circuit ($R + 100$) against supply voltage.
7. The base–emitter resistance will be the negative intercept on the resistance axis.
8. What is the physical significance of the intercept on the voltage axis?
9. A problem: The transistor must be made to conduct fully for a voltage on the base resistor of 4.6 V or larger. What is the maximum value of base resistor which could be used?

2. THE RELATION BETWEEN BASE CURRENT AND COLLECTOR CURRENT

Experimental details

Use the same equipment as in experiment 1, illustrated in figure 248.

1. Use a value for R of between 2 and 6 kΩ. Set the supply voltage to the collector circuit to about 6 V.
2. Start with a supply voltage to the base circuit of zero volts so that the base current is zero amps. Record the base voltage at Y, collector current (I_c) and collector voltage at C.
3. Increase the base current in steps of approximately a tenth of I_b, where I_b is the base current which just causes full conduction (from experiment 1), until about 15 readings have been taken or the supply voltage has reached maximum.
4. Plot graphs of collector current against base current, and total power dissipated in the transistor against base current.
5. On the graphs, mark the following points or sections:

   (a) region of amplification;
   (b) region of saturation;
   (c) maximum power dissipated.

6. Find an approximate value for the current *gain* produced by the circuit from the rising straight-line part of collect current against base current graph. Gain, $h_{FE} = \dfrac{I_c}{I_b}$. It is usually between 50 and 200 for small-signal transistors.
7. When a transistor is used as a 'switch', the value of base current used is sufficient to cause saturation. Two examples are:

   (a) a touch-sensitive circuit (figure 249), in which there are two stages of amplification;
   (b) a relay drive circuit (figure 250). Any voltage larger than about 6 V will cause the relay to switch on, but will draw a current of only about 1 mA.

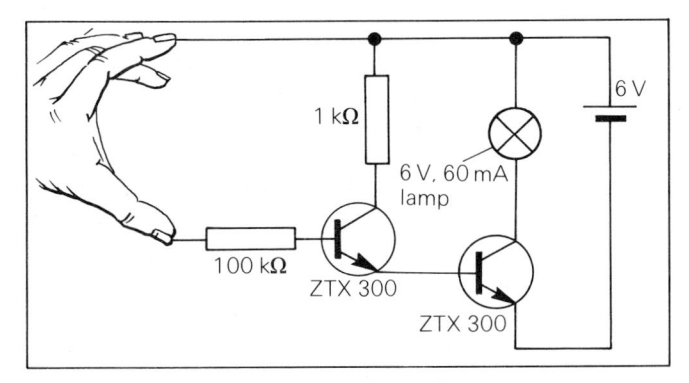

Figure 249 A touch-sensitive circuit

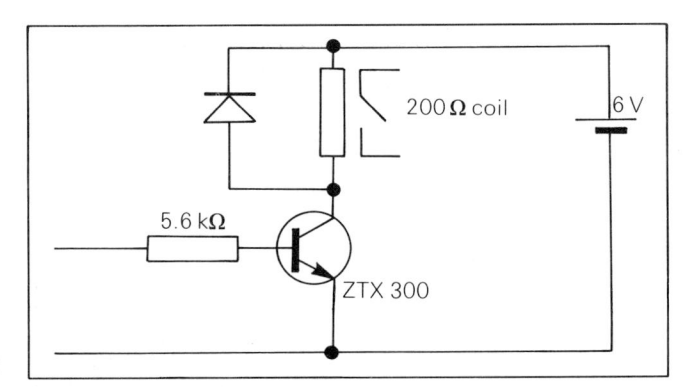

Figure 250 A relay drive circuit

Base current/mA	Base voltage V3/V	Collector current/mA	Collector voltage V2/V

INVESTIGATING RELATIONSHIPS

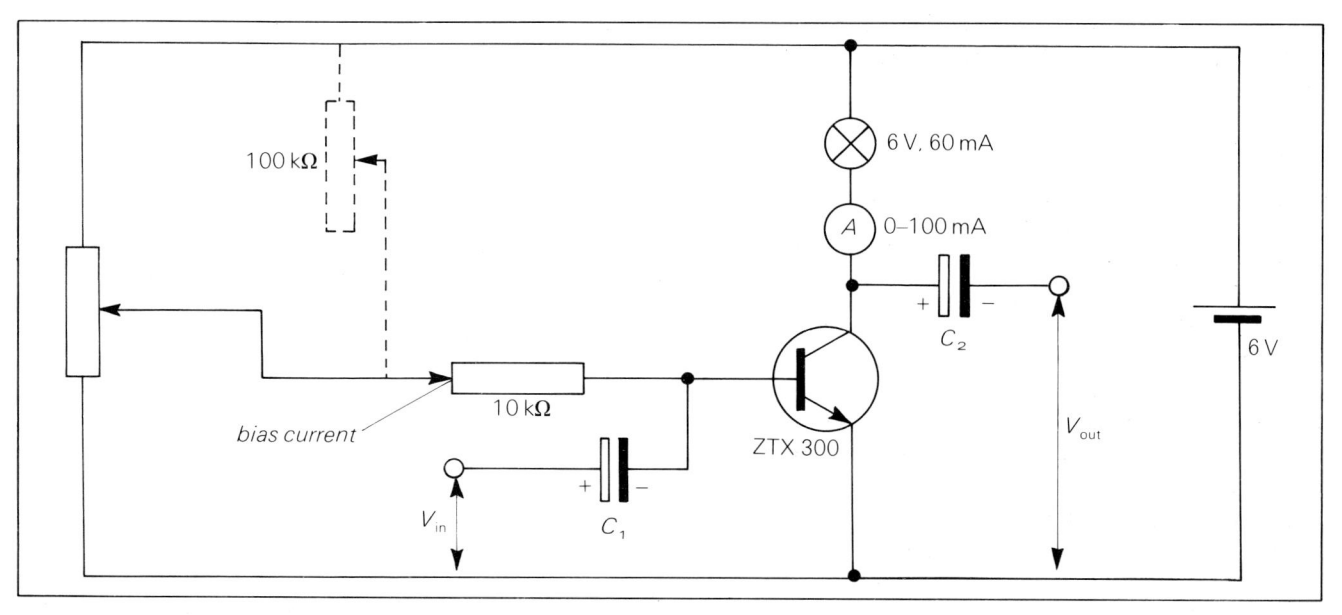

Figure 251 Simple transistor amplifier

3. TO SHOW THE TRANSISTOR OPERATING AS AN A.C. AMPLIFIER

Equipment

1. Add the capacitors as shown in figure 251. Any value between about 10 µF and 200 µF will do.
2. Adjust the base current until the collector current is about half its saturation current. The bulb will be approximately half bright. Use a collector supply voltage of 6 V. The transistor should now be *biased* in the centre of the steep part of the base current–collector current curve.
3. Any a.c. current input will now add to or reduce the base current and cause a much larger change of collector current. In this way the transistor is said to amplify, but of course all extra *energy* comes from the supply (your transistor radio battery will run down faster if the volume is kept loud). If the bias point moves too high or too low, the output waveform will become distorted (see figure 252).

Experimental details

1. Alter the *amplitude* of the input so that the output is not distorted.
2. Measure the amplitude of the input and of the output. Remember that the oscilloscopes may not have the same sensitivities. Work out the gain:

$$= \frac{\text{output amplitude}}{\text{input amplitude}}$$

3. Alter the frequency over a range of 20 Hz to 1000 Hz and find the gain for each frequency chosen. Plot a graph of gain against frequency.
4. For a frequency of ~1000 Hz, alter the bias current and observe the output 'clipping' for too much bias current, and 'bottoming' when the bias current is too small.

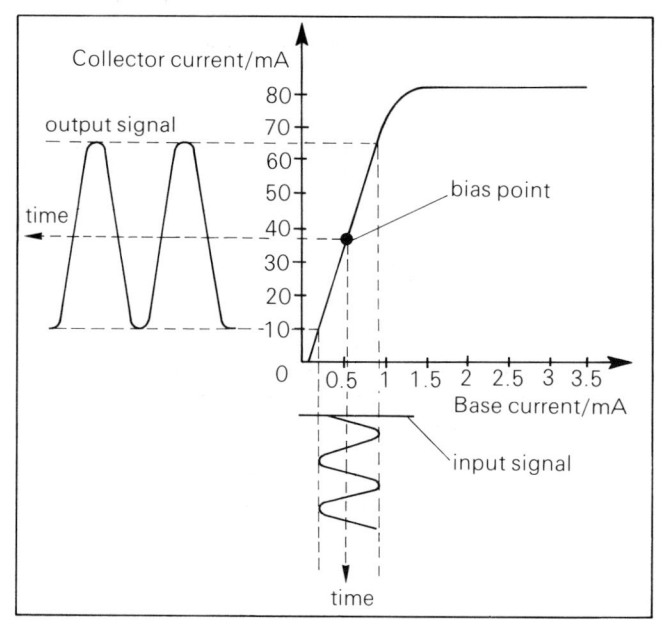

Figure 252 A small change in base current produces a large change in collector current.

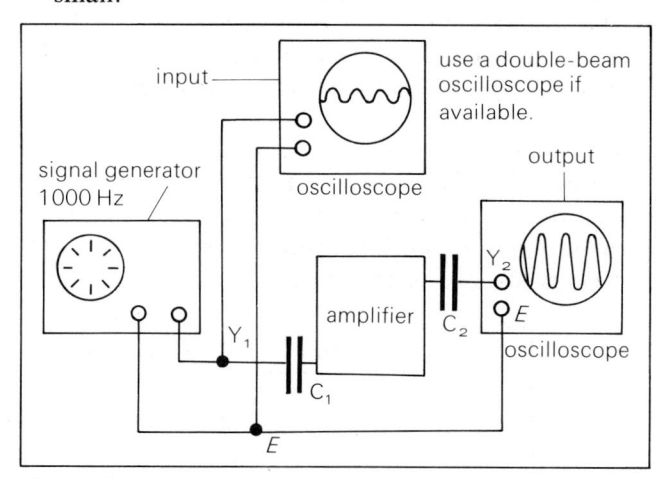

Figure 253 Apparatus

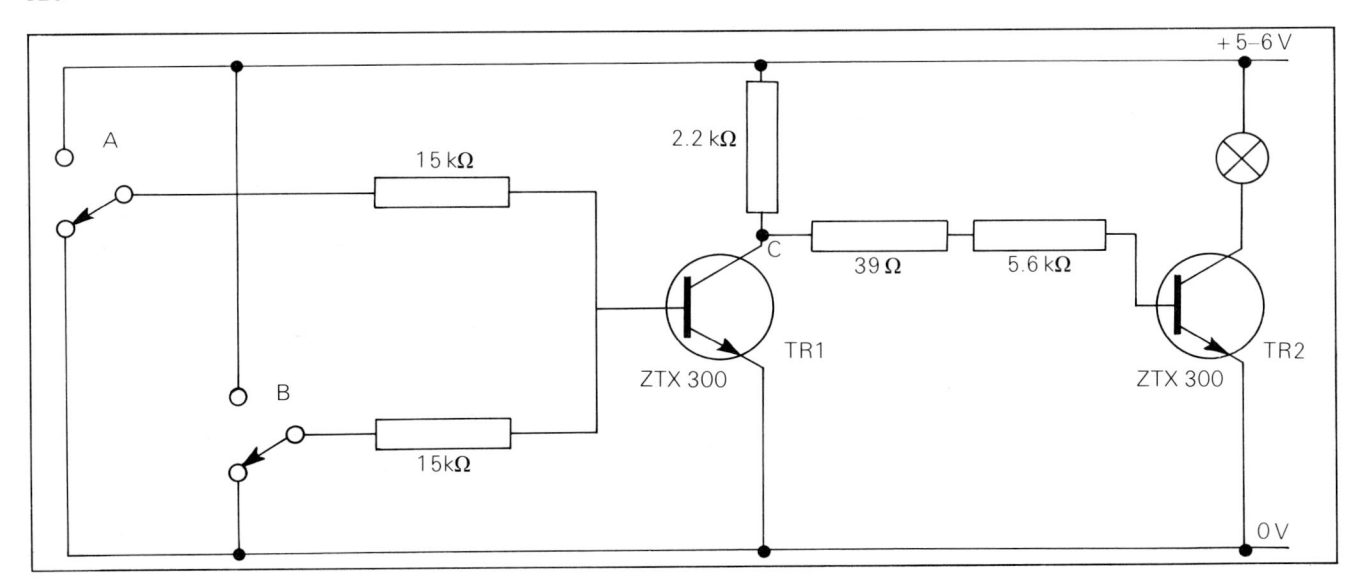

Figure 254 Circuit

4. DIGITAL ELECTRONICS

Experimental details

In digital electronics, a transistor is either fully conducting or not conducting at all. Figure 254 shows the circuit used in this experiment.

A. As shown, there is no current flowing into the base and the transistor is biased *off*. No current flows through the collector–emitter circuit, so point (C) has a 'high' potential of nearly the supply voltage. This causes enough current to flow into the second transistor TR2 to make it saturated, so that the lamp will light. Explain what happens when enough current flows into the base to saturate the transistor TR1. Using modular units, this circuit can be set up quickly (figure 255).

Copy and complete the following table:

A ON or OFF	B ON or OFF	Lamp ON or OFF	Voltage at C high or low

The circuit illustrated in figure 254 is known as a NOR gate and was a basic building block in early computers. The output is the opposite (NOT) of A OR of B. Hence NOT OR.

B. Two NOR gates can be used to 'store' a 'state', either ON or OFF (figures 257 and 258). The output of each gate is connected to one input of the other.

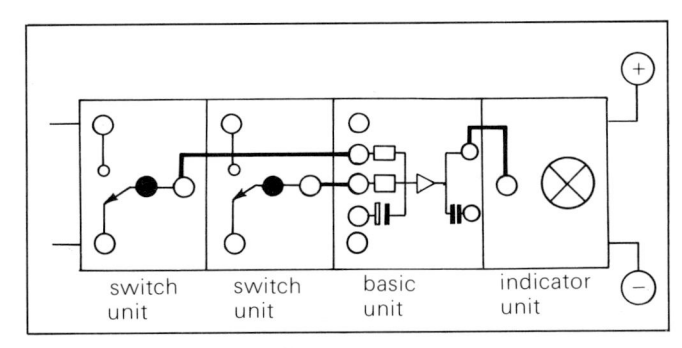

Figure 255 Circuit built from modular units

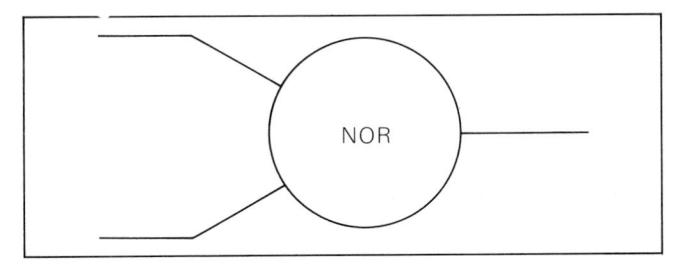

Figure 256 Symbol for a NOR gate

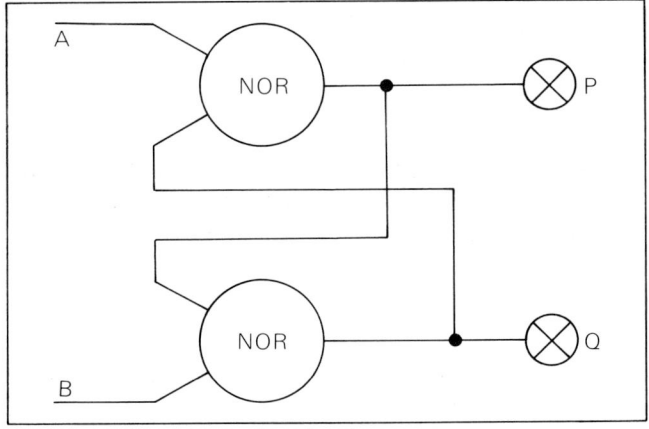

Figure 257 Two NOR gate circuit

INVESTIGATING RELATIONSHIPS

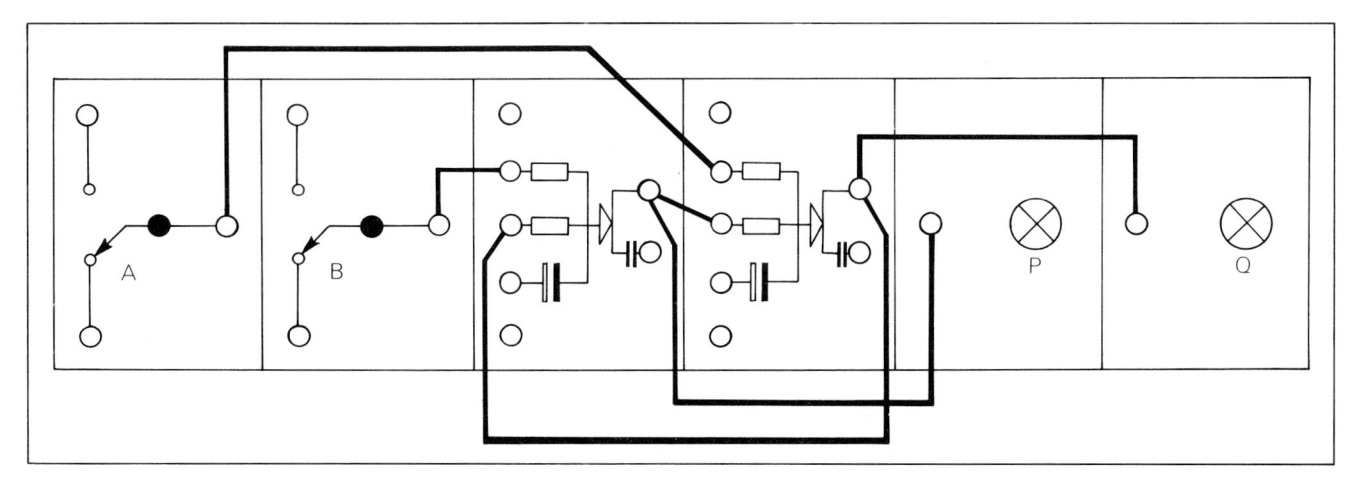

Figure 258 Two NOR gate circuit

Questions

1. What happens when A is pressed and released, then B is pressed and released, then A is pressed and released again, etc.?

2. What is the effect of connecting the 'feedback' connections to the capacitors on the input rather than the resistors?

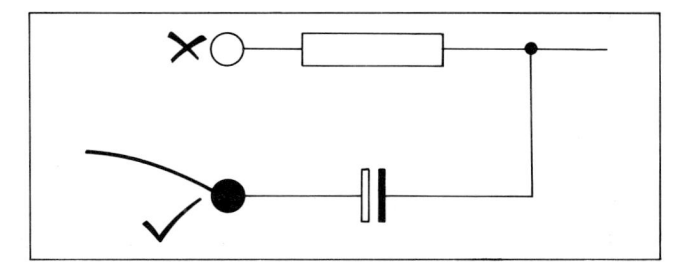

Figure 259

43. PLOTTING THE CHARACTERISTIC CURVES FOR A TRANSISTOR (COMMON-EMITTER MODE)

Outline

A transistor is a current-operated device. The size of the collector current (I_c) depends on the size of the base current (I_b) and on the voltage between collector and emitter (V_{ce}). Three families of curves can be drawn.

1. *Base characteristics* in which V_{ce} is kept constant and the relationship between I_b and the base–emitter voltage V_{be} investigated.
2. *Collector characteristics*. The base current is kept constant at a value which will not cause saturation and the relationship between I_c and V_{ce} investigated.
3. *Transfer characteristics*. The collector–emitter voltage is kept constant and the relationship between I_b and I_c investigated.

Equipment

Use either a commercially made unit, such as Unilab 'Blue Chip' range 511.008, and a separate 1 kΩ resistor or the circuit illustrated in figure 260 on the next page.

Optional

The circuit can be used with a computer and analogue interface unit with at least two channels and the program 'DATALOG' (package PHYS2 option 5).

1. BASE CHARACTERISTICS

Experimental details

1. Set the collector voltage V_{ce} to 2 V.
2. Start with a voltage of zero on the base resistor and record the base current (I_b) and base–emitter voltage (V_{be}).
3. Increase the base current and readjust the supply voltage to the collector so that the collector voltage returns to 2 V. Repeat the measurements of I_b and V_{be}. Continue increasing the base current until the voltage supply to the base resistor is at a maximum.
4. Repeat the whole process with collector voltages (V_{ce}) of 3 V and 4 V.

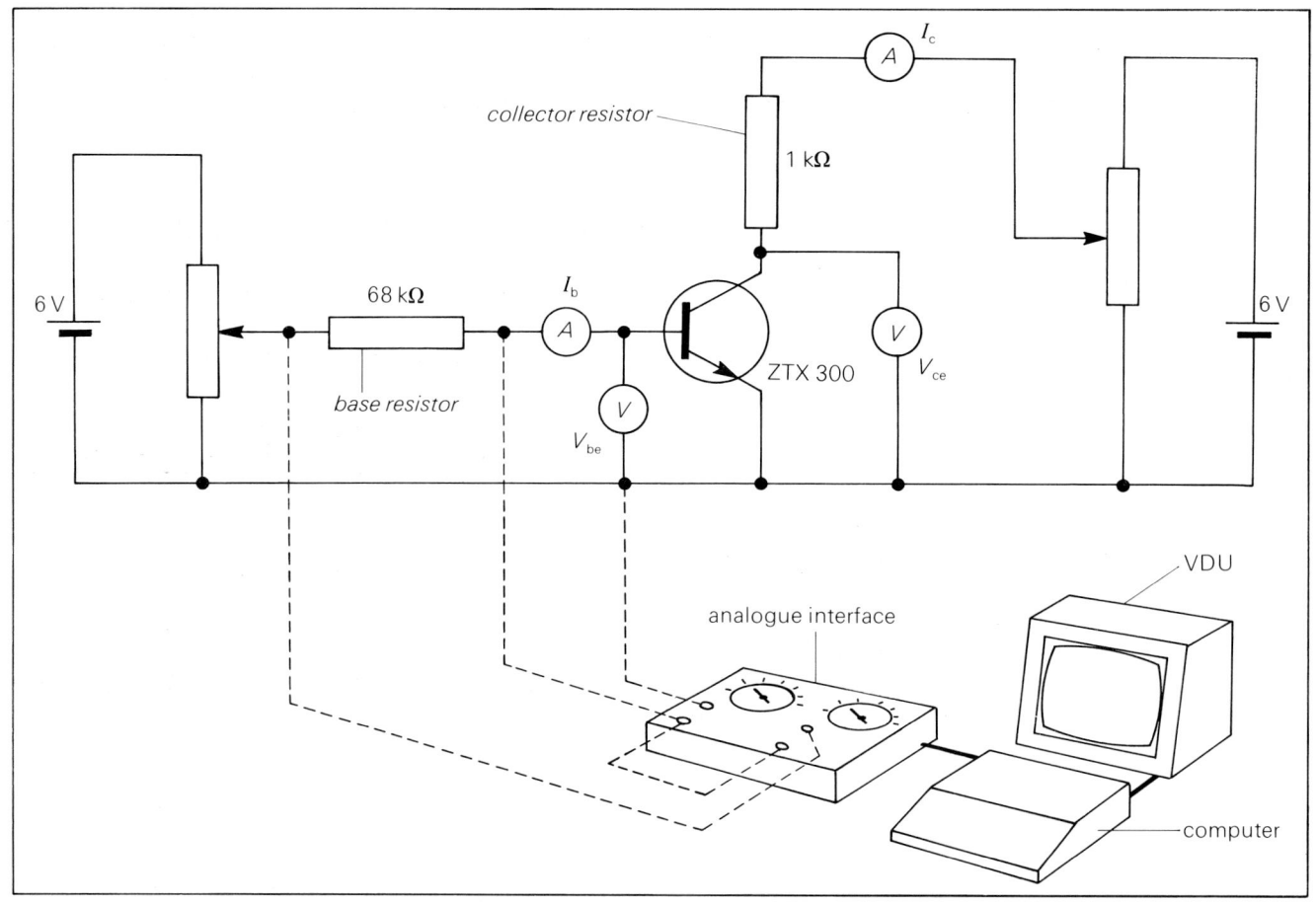

Figure 260

Results

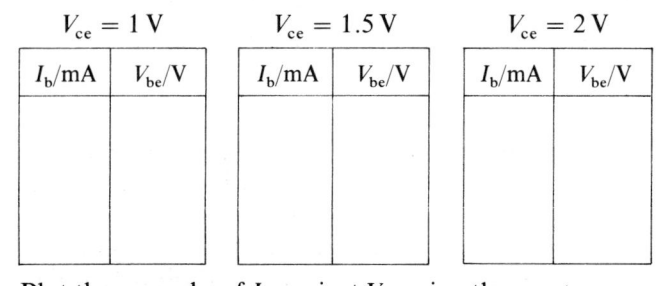

$V_{ce} = 1$ V		$V_{ce} = 1.5$ V		$V_{ce} = 2$ V	
I_b/mA	V_{be}/V	I_b/mA	V_{be}/V	I_b/mA	V_{be}/V

Plot these graphs of I_b against V_{be} using the same axes.

An alternative method is to use the computer as a measuring instrument with the program 'DATALOG' being used to record a series of single, individual sets of readings. This can reduce the time-consuming aspect of the experiment, since a large number of readings need to be taken. Note that because *both* analogue inputs have the same common connection, *one* set of readings may be shown as negative rather than positive values. In this case just use the numerical values (and not the sign). The current I_b can be found using $I = \dfrac{V}{R}$. $R = 10\,\text{k}\Omega$, therefore $I = \dfrac{V \text{ recorded}}{10\,000}$. Follow the general procedure outlined in the experimental details on p. 127.

2. COLLECTOR CHARACTERISTICS

Experimental details

1. Set the base current to about 10 µA; this has been chosen as about one tenth of the base current needed to produce saturation. You may need to calculate a suitable starting value for the apparatus you have been given. Do this as follows.

   (a) calculate the maximum collector current
   $$= \frac{\text{supply voltage}}{\text{collector resistor}}$$

   (b) calculate the minimum base current needed to produce saturation
   $$\simeq \frac{\text{maximum collector current}}{h_{FE}}$$

   (c) starting value = base current/10

2. Set the collector voltage to 0.2 V and readjust the base current to 10 µA. Record the values of collector current I_c and collector voltage V_{ce}.

3. Increase the collector voltage in 0.2 V steps up to 3 V and record the values of I_c and V_{ce}. Make sure the base current is readjusted to 10 µA each time.

INVESTIGATING RELATIONSHIPS

4. Now change the base current and repeat the whole process for base currents of 20 μA and 30 μA, but these values will depend on the apparatus you are using. Your teacher will give you the appropriate values to use.

Results

$I_b = 10\,\mu A$

I_c/mA	V_{ce}/V

$I_b = 20\,\mu A$

I_c/mA	V_{ce}/V

$I_b = 30\,\mu A$

I_c/mA	V_{ce}/V

Plot three graphs of I_c against V_{ce} using the same axes.

An alternative method is to use the computer as a measuring instrument with the program 'DATALOG' being used to take a series of sets of single, individual readings. This can reduce the time-consuming aspect of the experiment with a large number of readings to be taken. Note that because *both* analogue inputs have the same common connection, *one* set of readings may be shown as negative rather than positive values. In this case just use the numerical values and forget about the sign. Otherwise follow the general procedure outlined in the 'Experimental details'.

3. TRANSFER CHARACTERISTICS

Use the values recorded in experiments 1 and 2 to make up a table of collector current (I_c) and base current (I_b) for collector voltages of 1 V, 2 V, and 3 V.

$V_{ce} = 1\,V$

I_c/mA	I_b/mA

$V_{ce} = 2\,V$

I_c/mA	I_b/mA

$V_{ce} = 3\,V$

I_c/mA	I_b/mA

Plot a series of graphs of I_c against I_b on the same axes. The gradient of each line is the forward current transfer ratio h_{FE}.

44. CHARACTERISTICS OF LIGHT-SENSITIVE DEVICES

Outline

1. In a light-sensitive resistor (l.d.r.; figure 261) the resistance of a semiconductor material depends on the intensity of light falling on it. Resistances of 10 Ω in bright light and 2 MΩ in darkness are typical.
2. In a photovoltaic cell, light energy is converted into electrical energy and an e.m.f. is produced. A typical output in bright light is 0.5 V at 100 mA.
3. In a photocell (correctly, a photoemissive cell; figure 262) light energy releases electrons from a metal plate coated with an emissive surface such as caesium. These electrons cause conduction in a circuit when they are attracted to a positive electrode.
4. In a photodiode or phototransistor, the photons of light cause the release of electrons which reduce the potential barrier of the *p–n* junction and allow the device to conduct.

This experiment investigates the behaviour and application of these devices.

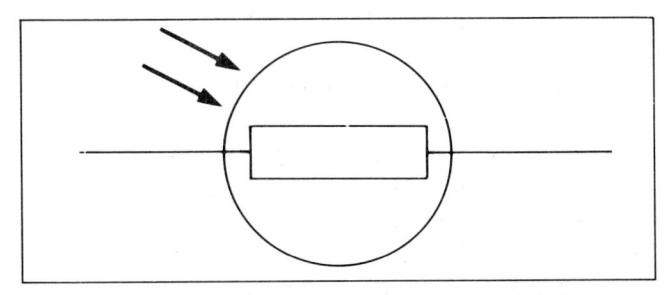

Figure 261 Symbol for a light sensitive resistor (l.d.r.)

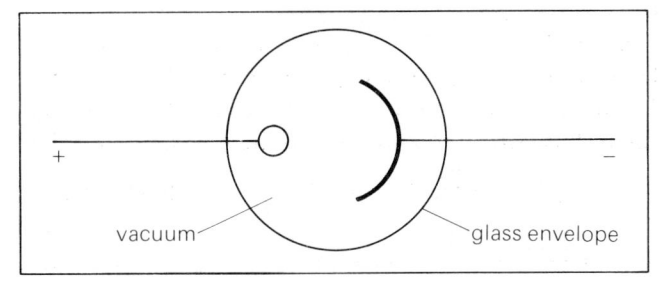

Figure 262 Symbol for a photoemissive cell

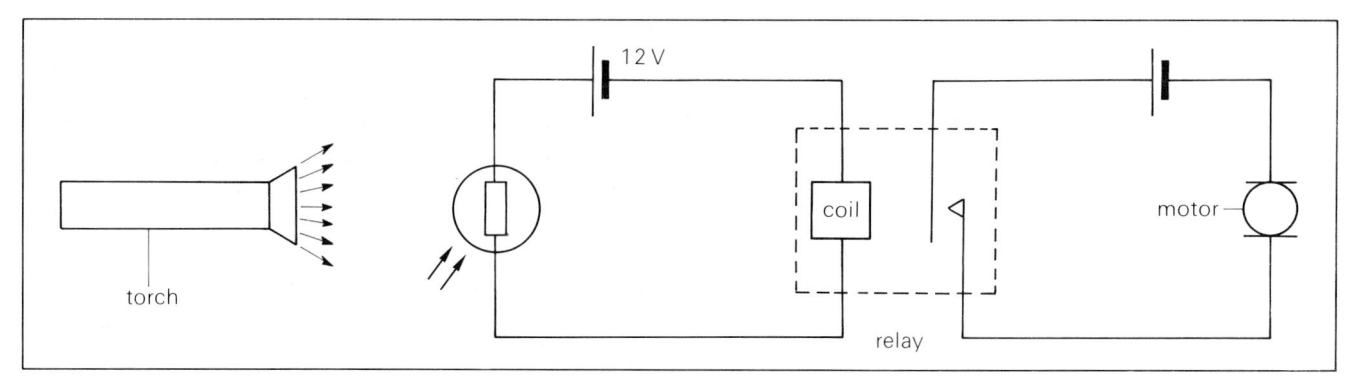

Figure 263 Apparatus

1. LIGHT-SENSITIVE RESISTOR (L.D.R.)

Experimental details

The change of resistance can be used to allow a light beam to control electrical circuits. Use the kit of parts given you (Lego, Meccano, etc.) to make a vehicle which will move when a light is shone on the l.d.r. For example, see figure 263.

How could you:

(a) alter the sensitivity of the circuit to light?
(b) make it respond to light only from a certain direction?

2. A PHOTOVOLTAIC CELL

This experiment investigates how the power output depends on the intensity and colour of the incident light. One problem is in ensuring that the intensity of each colour is the same, and this is difficult, as there is no absolute measurement. The definition of light intensity is in terms of the candela. One candela is the luminous intensity, in a perpendicular direction, of a surface of $1/600\,000\,\text{m}^2$ of a full radiator at the temperature of freezing platinum under a pressure of 101 325 Pa. This is not very helpful, and the relative brightnesses are best adjusted subjectively by eye. A white light source is used as a standard. The intensity of light varies as an inverse square law

$$I \propto \frac{1}{x^2}.$$

Equipment

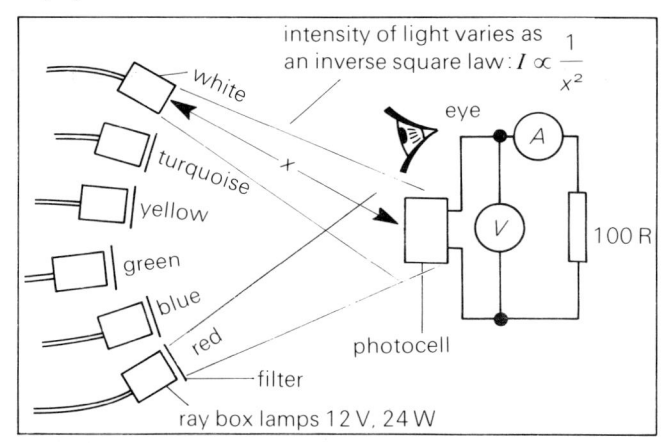

Figure 264 Apparatus

Experimental details

Set up the apparatus as shown in figure 264. Set the white light source 1 m away and alter the distances of the other colours until they all appear equally bright. This is the subjective part of the experiment. With one light only shining, record the readings on the voltmeter and ammeter so that the power generated can be found from $P = VI$. Repeat for each light in turn. Now move the white light source nearer and repeat the process.

Results

Record your results as shown in the table below. For each distance plot a graph of power against colour (figure 265). The same sheet of graph paper can be used.

Conclusion

Discuss how the power output varies with colour.

Distance of white source x (m)	$\dfrac{1}{x^2}$	Ammeter and voltmeter readings by colour											
		Red		Yellow		Green		Turquoise		Blue		White	
		I	V	I	V	I	V	I	V	I	V	I	V

INVESTIGATING RELATIONSHIPS

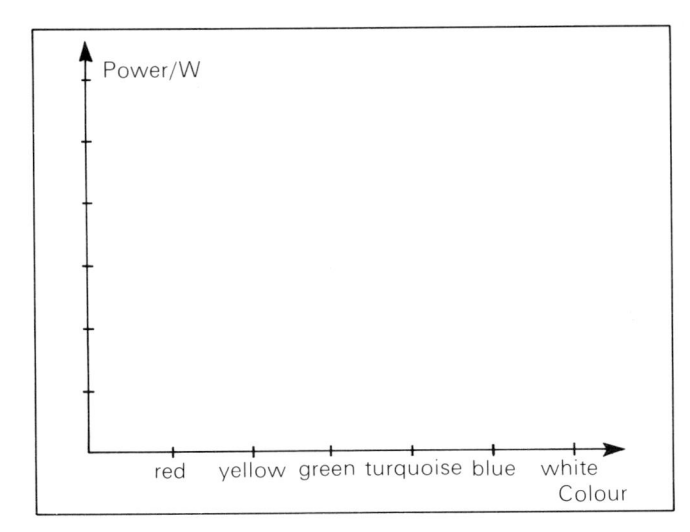

Figure 265

3. PHOTOEMISSIVE CELL

This device is investigated fully in the section on the photoelectric effect (p. 240).

4. PHOTODIODE AND PHOTOTRANSISTOR

The main use of these devices is as sensors in counting and timing equipment and as detectors when digital signals are being transmitted using fibre-optics.

Demonstrate these uses if you have the equipment available.

For example, use the apparatus shown in figure 266 to demonstrate the detection of fibre-optic transmissions by a photodiode; when the switch is closed, the voltmeter in the detector circuit should change its reading.

Can you transmit an analogue (variable) signal by replacing the switch by a variable resistor and turning the variable resistor backwards and forwards?

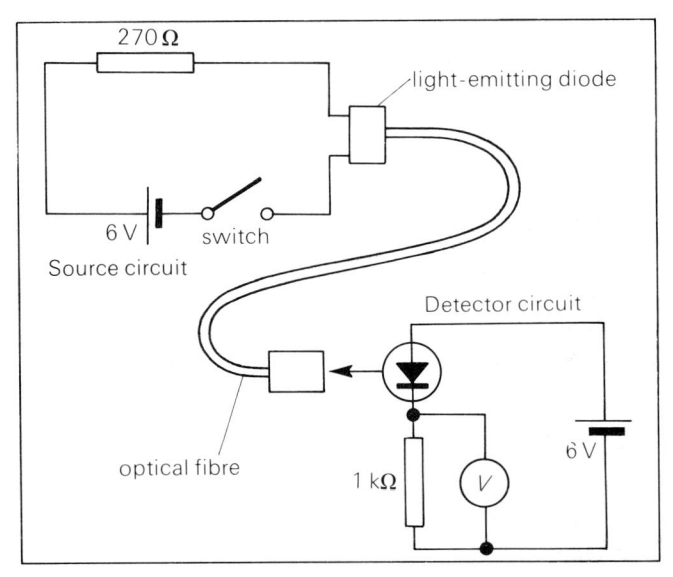

Figure 266 Use of a photodiode as a detector in fibre-optic transmission. Light is transmitted along an optical fibre by total internal reflection.

45. E.M.F. INDUCED AS A MAGNET PASSES THROUGH A COIL

Outline

When a magnet passes through a coil, an e.m.f. is produced across the ends of the coil because the magnetic flux linked with the coil changes. Faraday proposed a law:

$$E = -\frac{d\Phi}{dt}$$

where $\frac{d\Phi}{dt}$ is the rate of change of flux linked with the coil. This would predict that:

$$\text{the flux change } \Phi = -\int_0^t E \, dt$$

which can be evaluated experimentally by finding the 'area' under a graph of e.m.f. against time. This means that a large number of measurements of e.m.f. are needed in the comparatively short time the magnet takes to pass through the coil. It is also unclear what effect the speed of movement has on the size of e.m.f. at different positions in the coil.

This experiment uses a data memory or a microcomputer (with an analogue input and a suitable data logging program) as a data logging device to investigate:

1. how the e.m.f. produced depends on the speed of the magnet;
2. whether the total flux change is independent of the speed of the magnet;
3. the effect of turning the magnet round.

Equipment

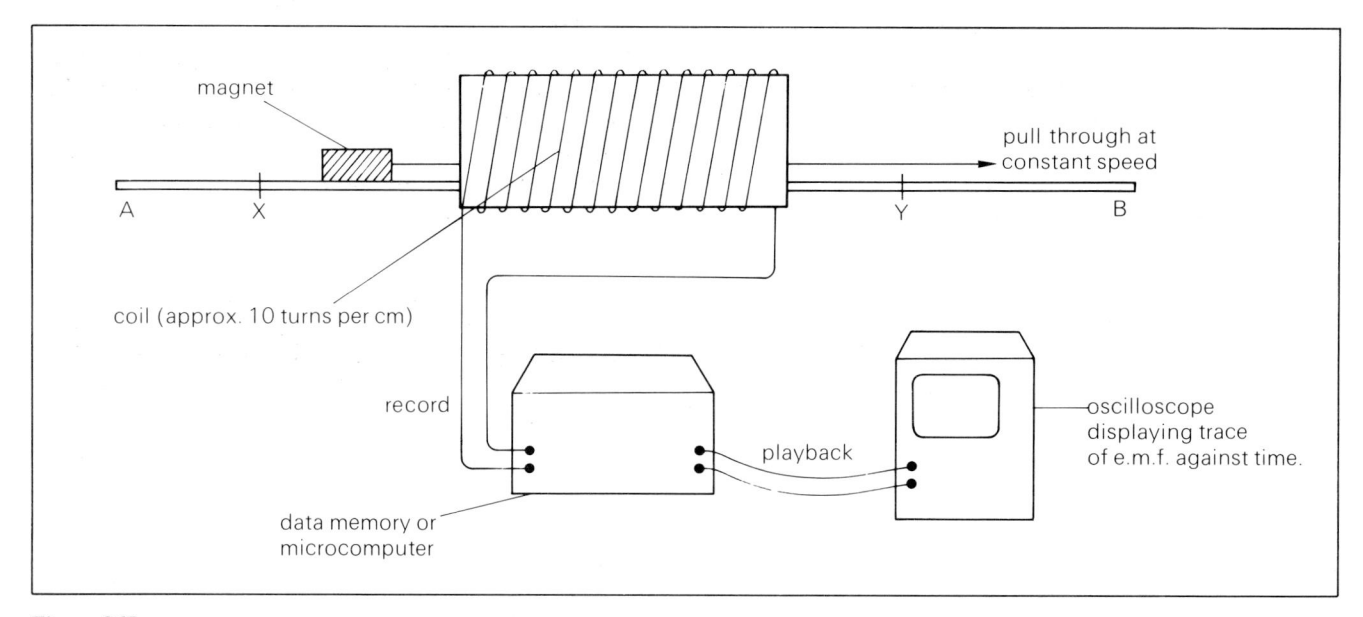

Figure 267

Experimental details

1. Make sure you are familiar with the use of the data memory, data gathering instrument (e.g. VELA) or microcomputer package. The controls which are usually available are:

   (a) input voltage sensitivity;
   (b) time interval between readings.

   The number of readings possible is usually 256, 512 or 1024.

   You will have to decide on the voltage sensitivity needed by connecting the oscilloscope directly across the coil and pulling the magnet through over a range of speeds, and also on the time interval to be used. Practise pulling the magnet at a *constant* speed.

2. Place the magnet at A. Make sure that your partner is ready to time the magnet over a measured distance XY. Start to pull the magnet at a constant speed and set the data memory recording. Stop when the magnet gets to B. Play the results back onto the oscilloscope and record the curve by placing a piece of OHP transparency over the screen and tracing the results onto it, or better still, use a chart recorder. If you are using a microcomputer, you may have the facility to display several 'runs' on the screen and then produce a printed copy on a printer.

3. Repeat for a range of speeds, with the polarity of the magnet reversed, and with coils of different cross-sectional areas, number of turns, and lengths.

Results

timing distance XY = ... cm
time = ... s
speed = ... cm s^{-1}
time-scale on oscilloscope = ... ms cm^{-1}

From the results
Work out the 'area' under each graph; this represents the total flux change. Show how the results lead you to the conclusion.

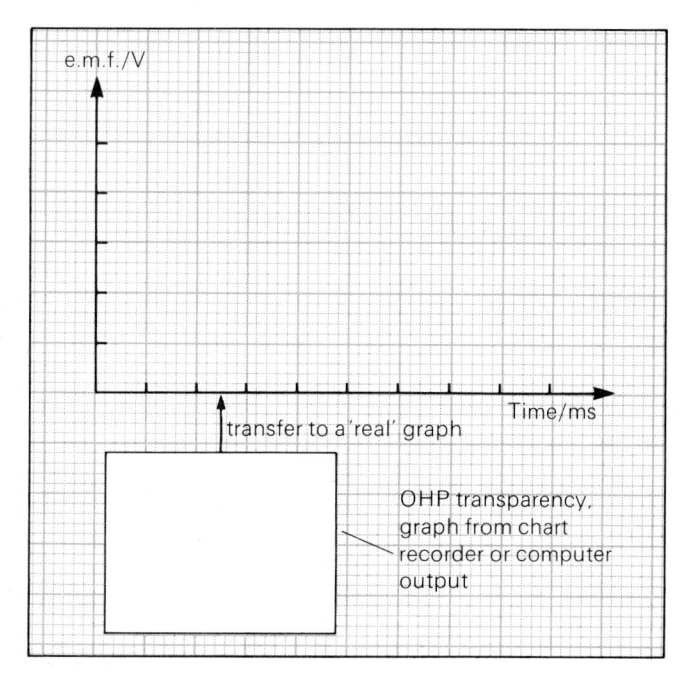

Figure 268 Suitable way of displaying each 'run'.

INVESTIGATING RELATIONSHIPS

Questions
1. Is it true that the flux change is independent of the speed?
2. Are there any particular positions of the magnet relative to the coil which produce (a) maximum e.m.f. and (b) minimum e.m.f.?
3. Is the maximum e.m.f. proportional to the speed? (You will need to draw a graph.)
4. What is the effect of reversing the polarity of the magnet?
5. What changes in the graph of e.m.f. against time are produced by a longer coil? How are these related to the cross-sectional area of the coil and the number of turns?
6. Explain the value for the e.m.f. produced when the magnet is well inside the coil.

46. MAGNETIC FIELD PRODUCED BY A PAIR OF CO-AXIAL COILS

Outline

This practical investigates how the magnetic field produced by two circular co-axial coils depends on their separation. The aim is to find a separation which will produce a uniform field between the coils. In this arrangement the coils are referred to as a pair of Helmholtz coils. Also to be investigated are how the size of the field depends on the radius of the coils, and the effect of changing the number of turns and the current. This is done either:

(a) by a series of practical investigations (if the radius of the coil is r then a series of investigations could use separations of $3r$, $2.5r$, $2r$, $1.5r$, $1r$, $0.5r$), or
(b) by using a computer to calculate the field at positions along the axis under given arrangements of the coil (figure 269) to try and evolve a hypothesis, and then to carry out a series of practical investigations to test the hypothesis.

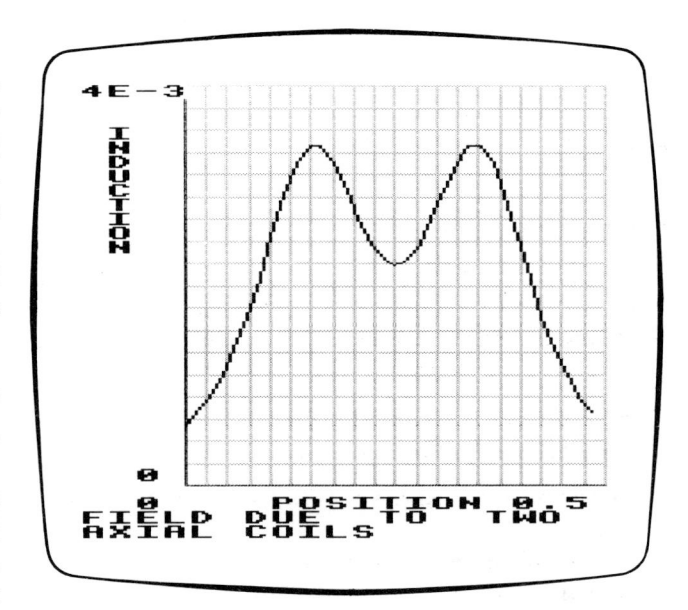

Figure 269 Example computer output

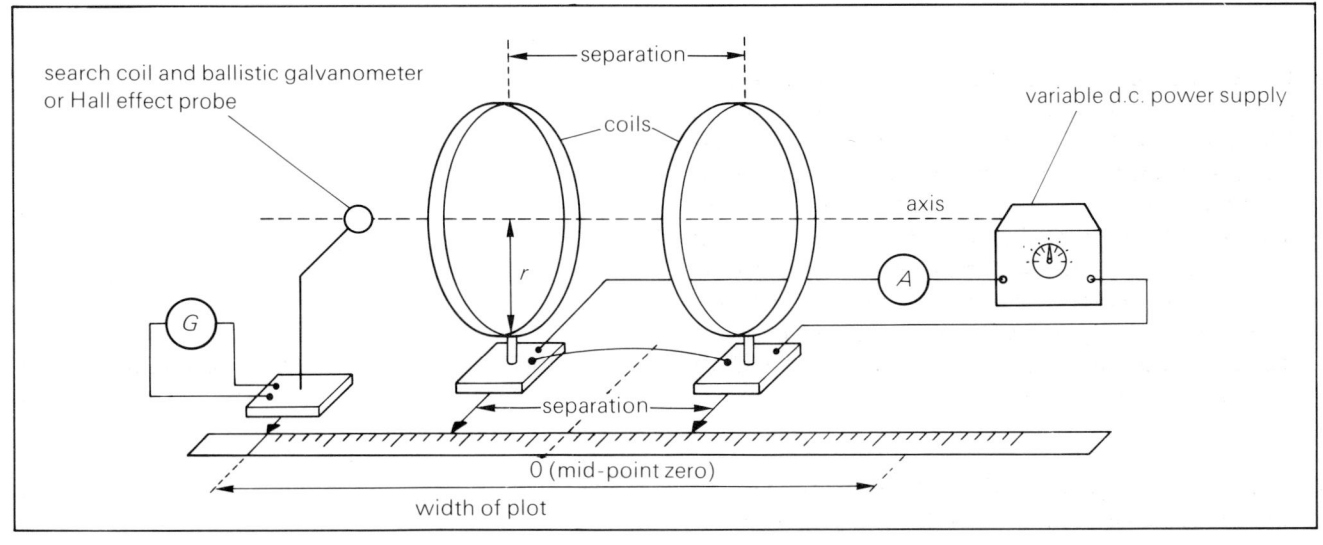

Figure 270 Equipment. The two coils are connected in series with the current flowing in the same direction round each coil.

Experimental details

Set up the apparatus as shown in figure 270. The coils are connected in series, with the current flowing in the same direction round each coil. Your teacher will tell you the maximum and minimum currents which should be used, depending on the coils used and the sensitivity of the detector.

1. If you are not using a computer, take a series of measurements of the flux density along the axis for separations of 3r, 2.5r, 2r, 1.5r, 1r, 0.5r. How many readings will you need to take? Plot graphs of flux density against distance and decide on the separation which gives the most uniform field. If you have coils of a different radius available, use these to test your conclusion. Find also the effect on the field of doubling the current flowing.
2. If you have a computer available, then use the program 'COILS' (package PHYS1 option 4) to produce a series of plots for the separations outlined in (1) above. However, you also have the ability to alter the radius of the coils, current and number of turns used in the program. When you have decided on the relation between radius and separation, set the apparatus to this separation and take a series of measurements of flux density along the axis, making sure that the width of plot is about three times the separation. Then choose a larger and then a smaller separation and repeat to show that the field is *not* uniform for other separations.

Results

radius of coils = ...cm   separation of coils = ...cm
current = ...A   number of turns = ...

Distance from centre/cm	Flux density reading (arbitrary scale)

In your report

Write a normal report of the experiment. Show your conclusions clearly and show how the investigations and results lead to these conclusions.

47. RESONANCES OF A VIBRATING WIRE

Outline

A string or wire under tension will resonate to a series of frequencies. These frequencies are the same as those which will produce standing wave patterns in the wire. Simple investigation shows that the fundamental frequency increases as the length is shortened and as the tension is increased. Displaying wave patterns on an oscilloscope shows that, when plucked, the wire produces other frequencies higher than the fundamental (see figure 271). The difference in *tone* between musical instruments depends on the relative way these frequencies are amplified by the sound box and whether the mode of vibration is longitudinal or transverse.

Theory gives equations for the velocities of transverse and longitudinal waves as:

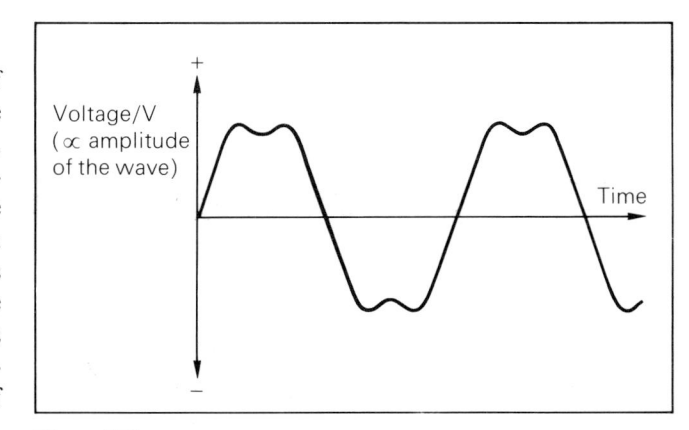

$$\sqrt{\frac{\text{tension}}{\text{mass per unit length}}} \quad \text{and} \quad \sqrt{\frac{\text{Young's modulus}}{\text{density}}}$$

Figure 271

The possible standing wave patterns should be as shown in figure 272.

If the velocity of the wave travelling along the wire is v then $f = \frac{v}{\lambda}$.

INVESTIGATING RELATIONSHIPS

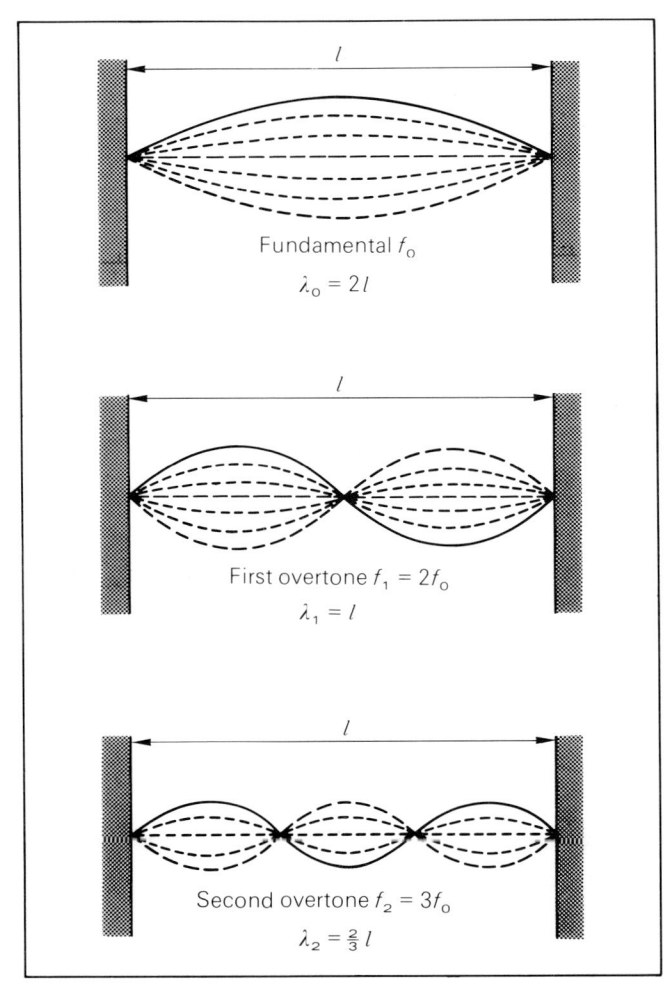

Figure 272 Standing wave patterns

- Fundamental f_0
- $\lambda_0 = 2l$
- First overtone $f_1 = 2f_0$
- $\lambda_1 = l$
- Second overtone $f_2 = 3f_0$
- $\lambda_2 = \frac{2}{3}l$

This experiment tries to answer the following questions.

1. Is the fundamental frequency inversely proportional to the length of the wire?
2. Are the overtone frequencies $2f_0$, $3f_0$, $4f_0$, etc.?
3. Are the waves in the wire transverse or longitudinal if the wire is plucked?

Equipment

1. The conventional apparatus (figure 273) uses a set of tuning forks to provide vibrations at known frequencies. A microphone and oscilloscope can be used to compare the frequencies of the tuning fork and wire, or the arrangement shown in figure 273b can be used; this measures the e.m.f. induced by the wire (non-magnetic) moving in the magnetic field.
2. An alternative apparatus (figure 274) uses an audio signal generator and frequency meter. The a.c. current flowing through the wire produces a force on it because

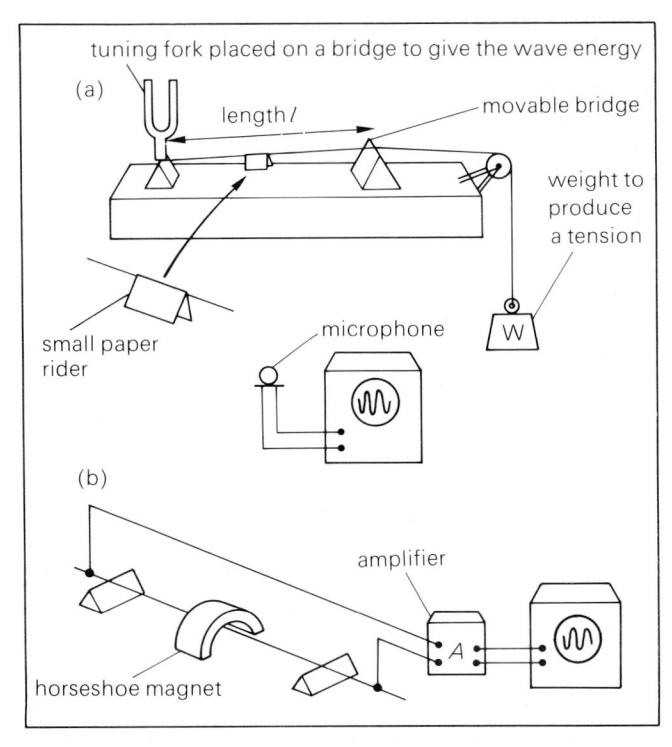

Figure 273 (a) Use a microphone and oscilloscope to compare the frequencies of the tuning fork and wire; or (b) use the induced e.m.f. produced if a non-magnetic wire moves in a magnetic field.

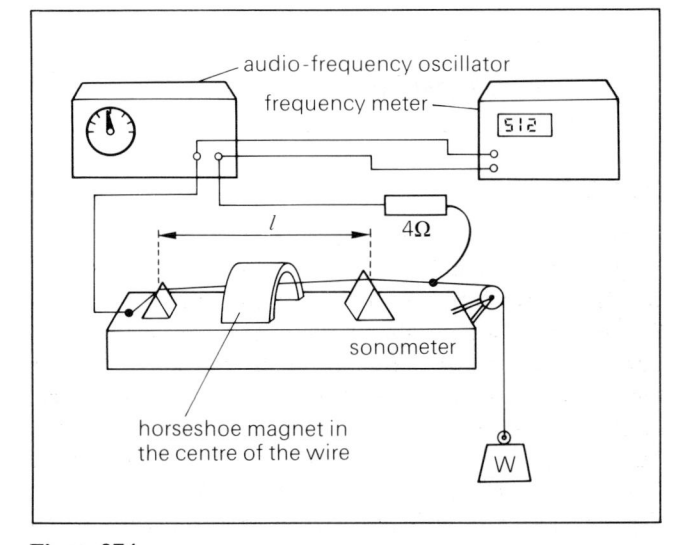

Figure 274

of the magnetic field of the horseshoe magnet. This force changes at the same frequency as the current from the signal generator and makes the wire vibrate. The amplitude of vibration is a maximum and the sound produced is largest when this frequency is the same as the natural resonant frequency of the wire.

1. TO INVESTIGATE THE RELATIONSHIP BETWEEN FREQUENCY (f) AND LENGTH (l)

Experimental details

Starting with the 256 Hz tuning fork and the full length of the wire, adjust the tension until the wire produces a frequency a little lower than the tuning fork when it is plucked. One of the difficult parts of this experiment is in deciding if the pitch of the two sounds is nearly the same. The microphone or induced e.m.f. and oscilloscope can be used to compare the two sounds, since a common error is to have the two notes an octave apart. It is best if the time-base is adjusted to produce about two complete waves across the screen.

Once this preliminary adjustment is done, you know that any frequencies above 256 Hz will need a shorter length of wire. The next stage is to find the lengths of wire which will produce resonance with the tuning forks you have available. Here are methods which can help in finding the *exact* length when the frequencies are nearly the same as adjusted using the ear, and/or microphone and oscilloscope.

(a) Use beats. Sounding the wire and the fork together will produce a noticeable periodic rise and fall of amplitude (loudness) when the frequencies differ by no more than about 10 Hz. The number of beats per second is the difference between the two frequencies. When no beats are heard, the frequencies are the same.

(b) Place a small ∧-shaped piece of paper on the wire at an expected *antinode* (a place where maximum amplitude of vibration is expected). Sound the tuning fork and place it on the wire at the bridge. At resonance, the energy from the tuning fork will make the wire vibrate with a large amplitude and the rider will fall off.

An alternative method would be as follows. Set the length (l) near to the maximum possible. Starting from about 50 Hz, alter the frequency until the wire resonates with one antinode in its fundamental mode. Record the length and the frequency. Repeat, using shorter lengths, until you have about ten sets of results.

Plot a graph of *frequency* against $\frac{1}{length}$, which you are expecting to be a straight line through the origin.

Take the wire off the sonometer and find its mass per unit length. Think: what length of wire is best taken?

Results

Frequency f/Hz	Length l/m

length of wire (l) = ... m
mass of this length = ... kg
mass/unit length (m) = ... kg m^{-1}
tension (T) = ... N
Young's modulus (E) = ... N m^{-2}
density of the wire (ρ) = ... kg m^{-3}

From the results and graph

(a) Calculate $\sqrt{\frac{T}{m}}$ and $\sqrt{\frac{E}{\rho}}$ (look up values of E and ρ for the materials of the wire you are using) to find the velocities of the transverse and longitudinal waves.

(b) If $f = \frac{V}{2l}$ for the fundamental, then the gradient of the graph of f against $\frac{1}{l}$ should be $\frac{V}{2}$. Does this value agree with the velocity for a transverse or longitudinal vibration?

2. ARE THE OVERTONE FREQUENCIES: $2f_0$, $3f_0$, ETC.?

Experimental details

Adjust the length of the wire to get as near to exact resonance with 256 Hz as is possible. Place paper riders on the wire at expected *nodes* and *antinodes* for the first overtone $2f_0$. Sound a 512 Hz fork and place it on the wire at a bridge. The paper riders at *antinodes* should vibrate off and those at *nodes* should stay on. Some slight adjustment of length may be necessary (can you suggest why?).

Repeat for a fork of 768 Hz, or use the method using the audio frequency oscillator. In the latter case, the magnet will have to be moved to an expected antinode.

Note. Any set of forks which are integer multiples will do.

Conclusions

1. What is the relationship between f and l?
2. Are the frequencies $2f_0$, $3f_0$ overtones?
3. Are the waves in the wire transverse or longitudinal vibrations?

48. INTERFERENCE PATTERN PRODUCED BY DOUBLE SLITS

Outline

This experiment involves producing a Young's slit interference pattern and taking measurements so that the wavelengths of the colours of light in different sources of light can be found.

Looking at figure 275, the parts of the wavefront incident at A and B must have a constant phase difference between them. One solution is to use wavefronts from a single source. Each slit acts as a source of spherical waves. The amplitude at any point is the sum of the amplitudes of the two separate waves. This is called supposition of waves and an interference pattern is produced. In particular there are places (the dotted lines) where the two waves are always in phase. This will occur at places where the path difference between waves from the slits A and B is an integral number of wavelengths apart, and gives rise to a maximum of intensity, called constructive interference. This appears as a bright band in the interference pattern. When the path difference is an odd number of half a wavelength, destructive interference occurs and a minimum of intensity is seen.

Looking towards the slits, a pattern of dark and light bands is seen (see figures 276 and 277).

The path difference at P between waves from A and B is $BP - AP = BC$. If $D \gg d$, then $BC \simeq d \sin \theta$. The waves will be in phase when the path difference is an integral number of wavelengths, therefore a bright band will be seen when:

$$n\lambda = d \sin \theta$$

where $n = 1, 2, 3$, etc.

Figure 275

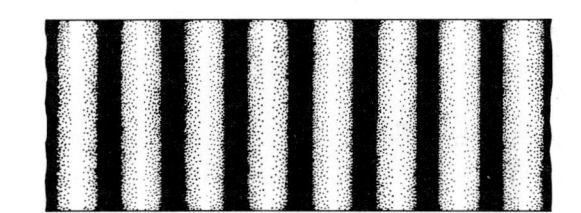

Figure 276

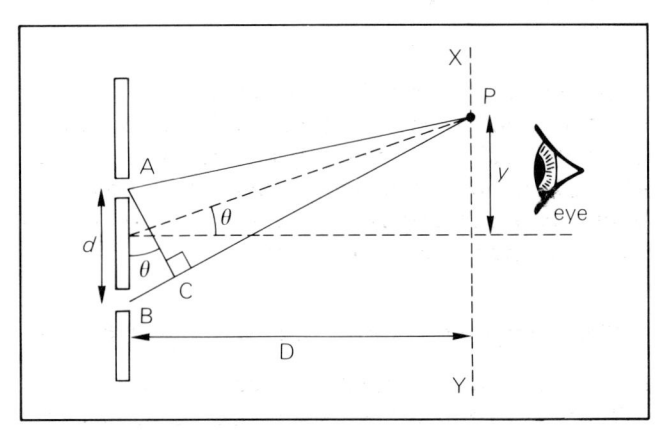

Figure 277

Unfortunately it is not usually possible to find the central maxima in the pattern seen and so θ can never be found directly. The measurement which can be taken is the distance (l) along the line XY *between* maxima (figure 278).

Using $n\lambda = d \sin \theta$ gives:

$$n\lambda = d \sin \theta_n \quad \text{and} \quad (n+1)\lambda = d \sin \theta_{n+1}$$

Now, since $D \gg d$ or y, θ is $<10°$, and the approximation $\sin \theta \simeq \tan \theta$ can be used:

$$\tan \theta_n = \frac{y_n}{D}$$

$$\tan \theta_{n+1} = \frac{y_{n+1}}{D}$$

so

$$(n+1)\lambda - n\lambda = d\left(\frac{y_{n+1}}{D} - \frac{y_n}{D}\right)$$

$$= \frac{dl}{D}$$

$$\therefore \lambda = \frac{dl}{D}$$

where l is the distance between successive maxima.

In the experiment you must:

1. measure D;
2. show that the angles θ are less than 10° so that the approximation can be used;
3. find as accurate value for l as you can;
4. measure d;
5. find a value for the wavelength.

Experimental details

1. Use the travelling microscope to measure the separation of the double slits.
2. Set up the apparatus (figure 279) and view the interference pattern. Measure the distance D between the slits and the position of the interference pattern which is forming the object for the microscope.
3. Measure the distance across a number of fringes and find the average distance l between two maxima.
4. Work out the wavelength of the source. Repeat for any other sources given.

Compare your answer with the table of wavelengths in the data section at the end of the book and determine the source.

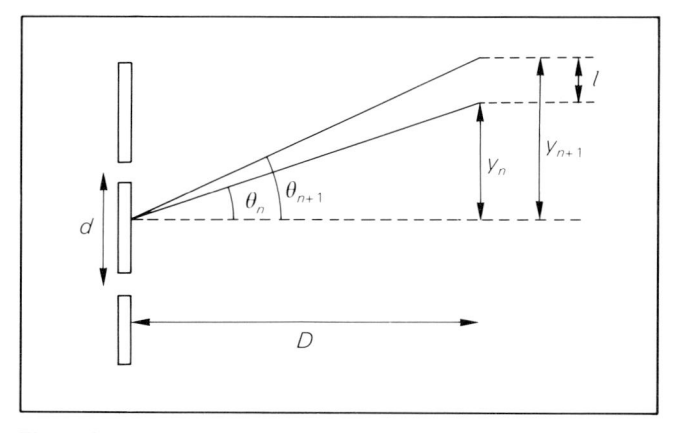

Figure 278

Questions

You have probably noticed that there is no sharp division between a bright and dark band, but rather, a continuous change. If the pattern were photographed, enlarged and a photodiode used to measure the light intensity, the situation shown in figure 280 might be found.

1. Two spectral lines are known to be present: K red and Hg violet. Identify the other sources present.

2. How could the apparatus be altered to get better *resolution* of the circled peak?

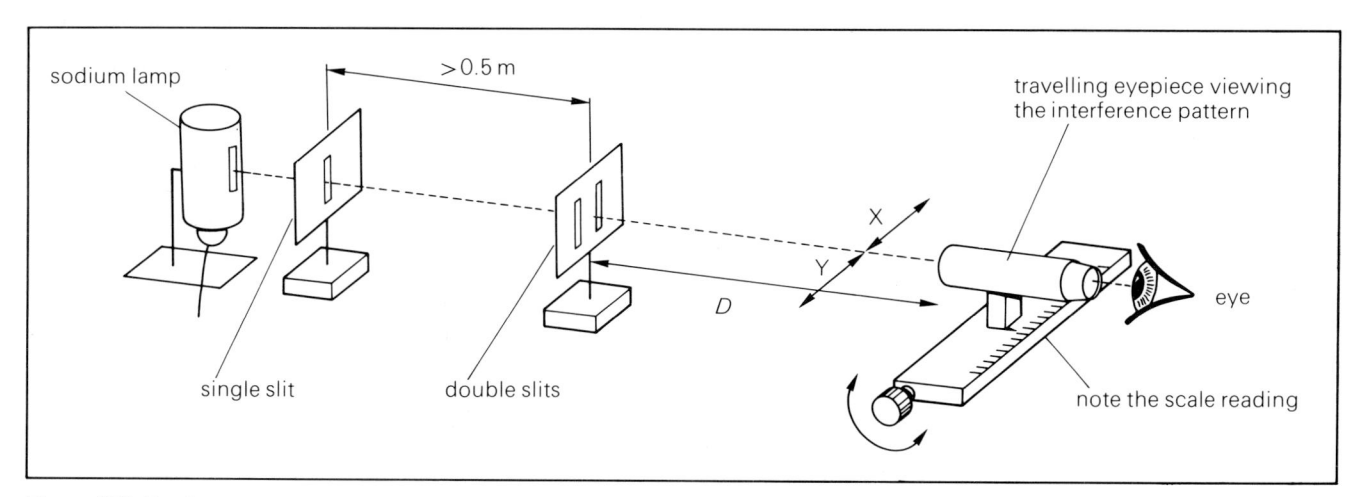

Figure 279 Equipment

INVESTIGATING RELATIONSHIPS

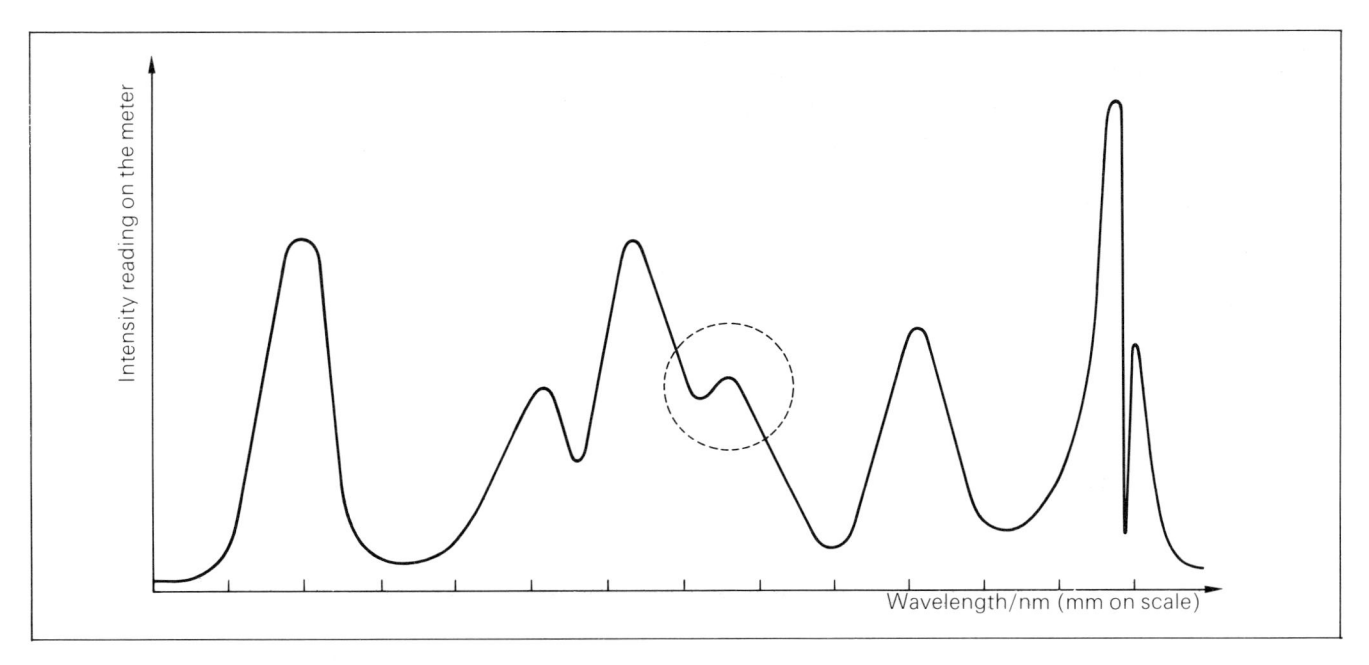

Figure 280

49. THE BEHAVIOUR OF MICROWAVES

Outline

Microwaves are electromagnetic (e.m.) waves with wavelengths of the order of centimetres. They should obey the same basic rules as other e.m. radiation such as light. For example:

1. for reflection, the angle of incidence equals the angle of reflection;
2. for refraction,

$$\frac{\sin i}{\sin r} = \frac{\text{speed in medium (1)}}{\text{speed in medium (2)}}$$

(the value depends on λ);
3. total internal reflection can occur;
4. interference can occur and for two slits should obey $n\lambda = d \sin \theta$.

The experiment sets out to investigate reflection, refraction and interference of 3 cm microwaves.

1. WIDTH OF THE BEAM

In theory the width of the beam should be the same as the width of the horn on the end of the waveguide. In practice there is some spreading of the beam and this experiment is to give you experience in using the apparatus.

If you are using the computer method, choose the option in the program which allows single readings to be taken. Move the detector along a line AB (figure 281) at 90° to the beam and approximately 30 cm away from the source (do *not* bring the detector closer because there is a risk of burning out the diode detector). Take readings of the detector current at 2 cm intervals. Repeat at approximately 60 cm away.

Now use the diode detector instead of the waveguide unit and repeat the measurements at 30 cm and 60 cm.

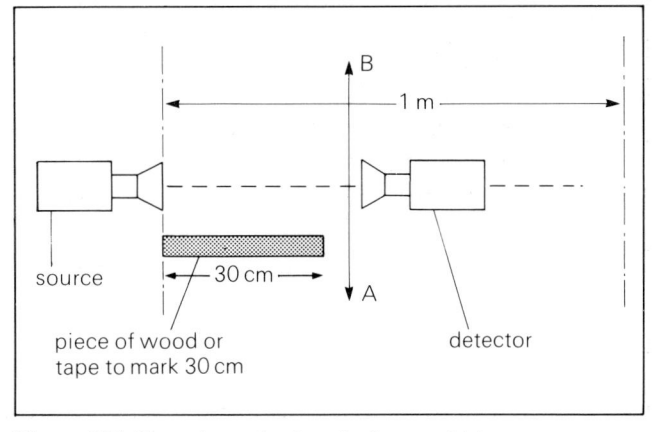

Figure 281 Plan view; plotting the beam width.

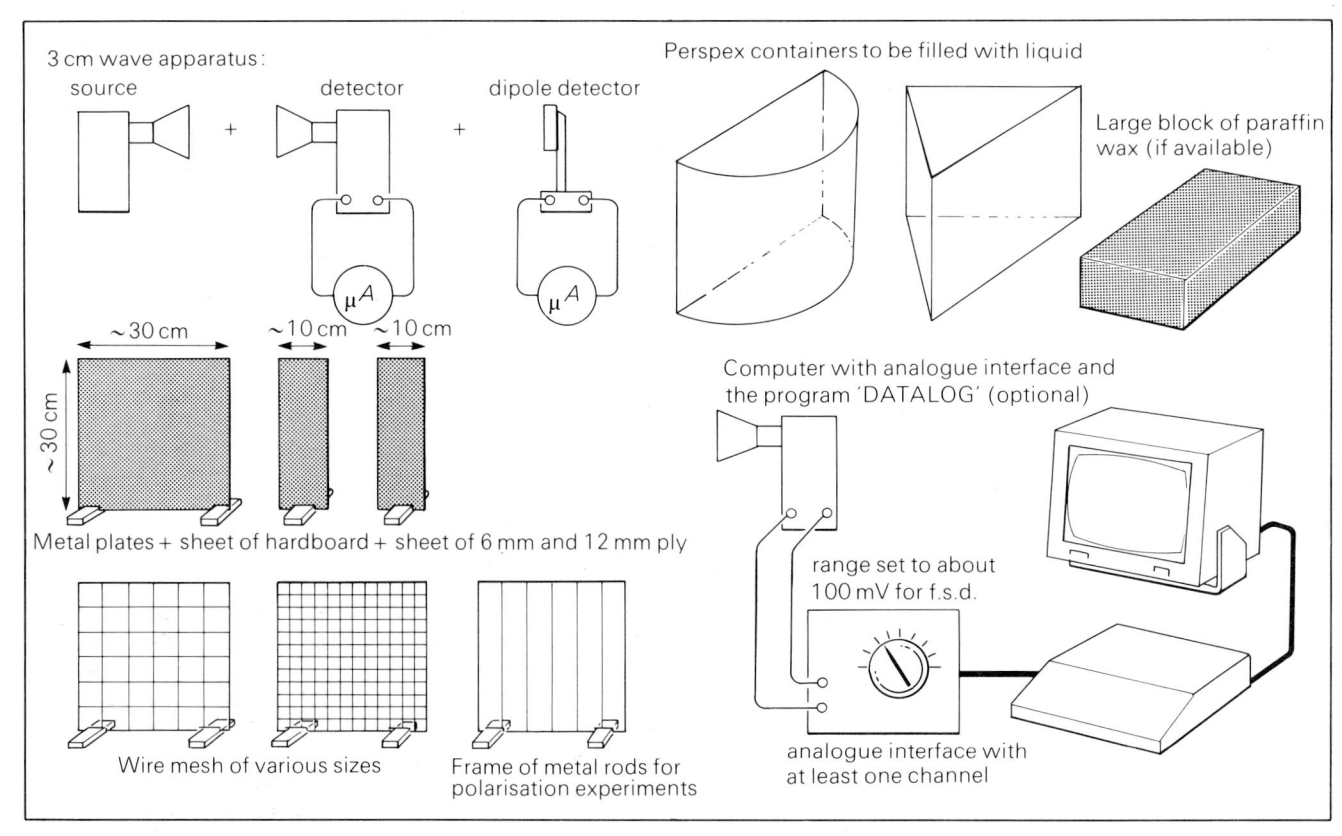

Figure 282 Equipment for microwave experiments. If a computer is used, use the option in the 'DATALOG' program which allows single readings to be recorded (see the teacher's notes for details of the program).

Results

Record your results as shown in the table below. Plot the profiles of the beam, as measured by each detector, on the same sheet of graph paper. Comment on the shape and on the accuracy to which the centre of the beam can be found.

Work out the ratio of the signals from each detector at the centre of the beam.

2. REFLECTION

Equipment

Metal plates act as reflectors because the electromagnetic wave is an alternating field having electrical and magnetic components which induce an alternating current in the surface of the metal and this re-radiates a large proportion of the energy. A dry, wooden plate is not a good reflector because the resistance of wood is much greater than that of metal. We should expect much smaller currents and so less energy reflected and more transmitted. Radiotelescopes use parabolic metal mirrors to collect radiowaves and focus them onto an aerial. However, some dishes use a wire mesh instead of a metal plate. It may well be that up to a certain size of mesh the behaviour is similar to solid metal (depending on the wavelength).

Experimental details

Move the detector along an arc until a maximum reading occurs. Mark the position of the detector on the paper. Repeat along at least two more arcs. Record the maximum current produced each time.

Complete the usual type of 'ray diagram', which you have already used in experiments on light, drawing in a *normal*, and measuring the angles of incidence and reflection. Repeat for other angles of incidence and for all the other types of reflectors you have available.

Distance along scale AB/cm	Distance from source/cm	Waveguide detector unit current/µA	Diode detector current/µA

INVESTIGATING RELATIONSHIPS

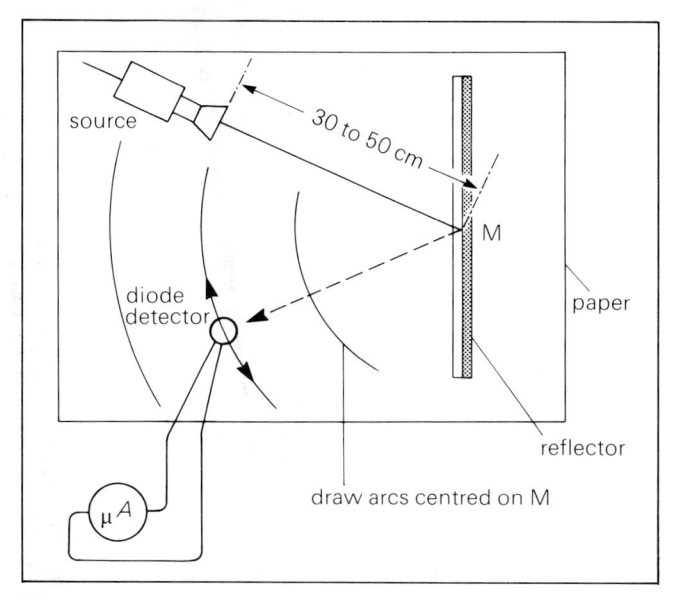

Figure 283 Plan view of equipment. Draw a line on the paper showing the direction of incident radiation and a line along which to position the reflector.

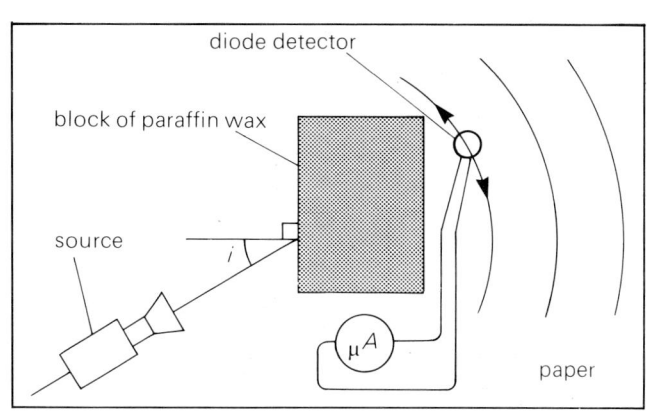

Figure 284 Equipment. Move the detector along an arc and plot the position of the maximum current on the paper.

Results

Record your results as shown in the first table below. Does the normal law of reflection apply?

To investigate the percentage of radiation reflected, the maximum currents can be compared to the maximum currents from experiment 1 (p. 140) taken at the *same* distance from the source (i.e. 30–60 cm + x). Make a second table, as shown at the bottom of the page.

Conclusions

What conclusions can you draw about:

1. the way wood and metal differ as reflectors, and
2. the effect of mesh size on reflection and transmission?

3. REFRACTION

Experimental details

In a similar manner to the method used to investigate reflection, plot the path of a wave through the wax block or container filled with paraffin (figure 284). Find the angle of incidence in air, the angle of refraction in the block or liquid and work out the speed of the 3 cm waves:

$$\text{refractive index} = \frac{\text{speed in air}}{\text{speed in material}}$$

$$= \frac{3 \times 10^8 \text{ m s}^{-1}}{\text{speed in material}}$$

By Snell's law, refractive index $= \dfrac{\sin i}{\sin r}$.

Therefore, speed in material $= \dfrac{3 \times 10^8 \times \sin r}{\sin i}$ m s^{-1}.

You can extend this experiment by using liquids in Perspex containers, in place of the wax block; see figure 285 on p. 142.

Reflector	$i_1/°$	$r_1/°$	Maximum current/μA	$i_2/°$	$r_2/°$	Maximum current/μA	$i_3/°$	$r_3/°$	Maximum current/μA
metal plate									
hard board									
mesh spacing … mm									

Reflector	Reflected current/μA	Direct current/μA	% reflection	Reflected current/μA	Direct current/μA	% reflection	Reflected current/μA	Direct current/μA	% reflection

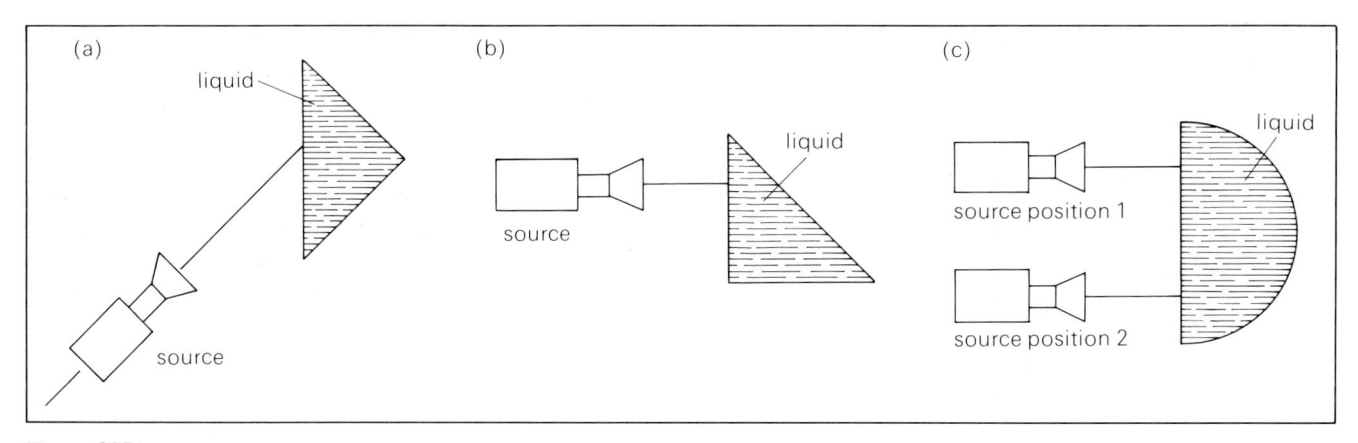

Figure 285

4. DOUBLE-SLIT INTERFERENCE PATTERN

Experimental details

Move the diode detector along the line AB (figure 286) and record the current at 2 cm intervals. Plot a graph of current against distance. Work out the angle θ for each maximum. Work out the wavelength of the microwaves from $n\lambda = d \sin \theta$ for several maxima and take an average.

Results

Position of detector/cm	Current/µA

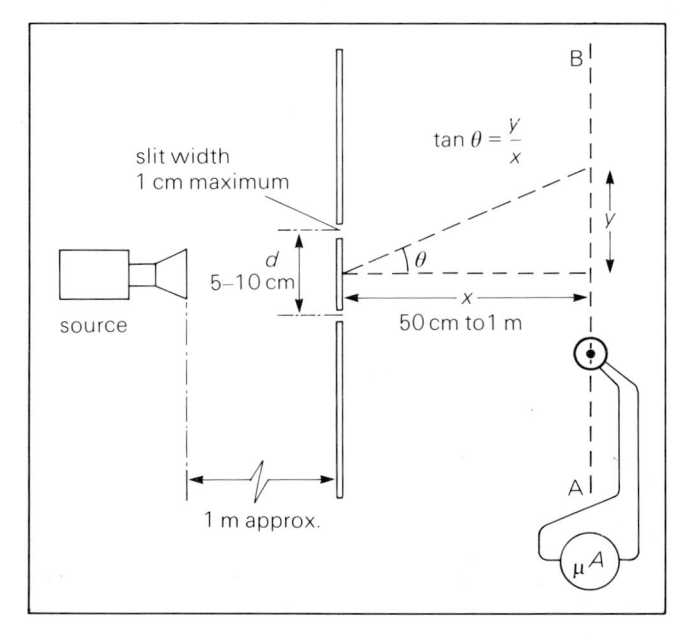

Figure 286 Equipment

50. INTERFERENCE PATTERN OF SOUND WAVES

Outline

This experiment plots the amplitude of the interference pattern produced by the waves from two speakers driven in parallel from the same signal generator. This means that the waves are in phase and a Young's slits-type pattern from two slits is to be expected.

Safety: It is a good idea to wear some form of ear protection.

Experimental details

Use the apparatus shown in figure 287. Values must first be chosen for the slit deparation d and the frequency f. Theory and Huygen's ideas indicate that the number of maxima seen from the central maxima to one side is given by an integer value of $\frac{d}{\lambda}$. λ can be worked out from $v = f\lambda$, since you know that the speed of sound is about 340 m s^{-1} at 20°C. Values of f and d should be selected to get at least six or seven maxima (figure 288).

INVESTIGATING RELATIONSHIPS

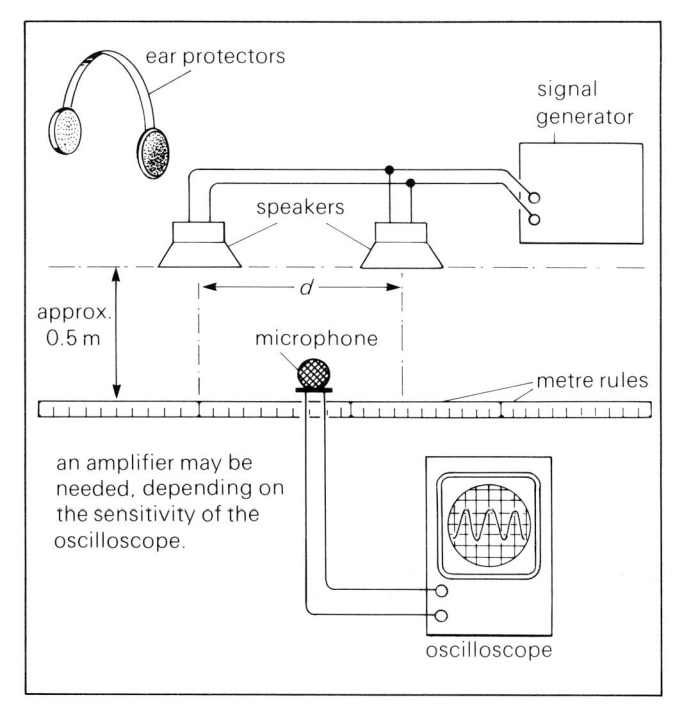

Figure 287 Equipment

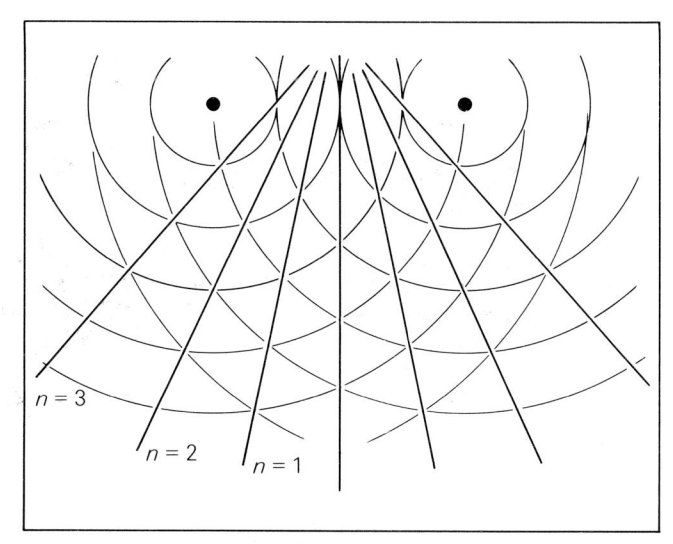

Figure 288

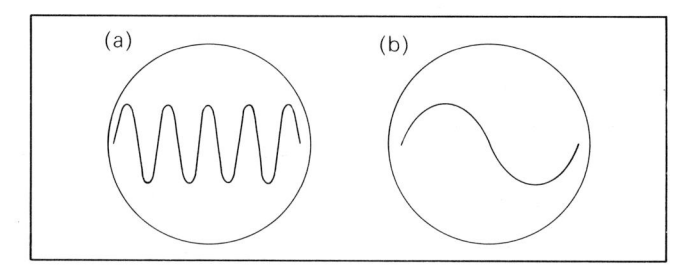

Figure 289 (a) Makes the amplitude easier to read, (b) makes it more difficult to read.

The amplitude of the signal from the microphone is measured on an oscilloscope. The time-base should be adjusted so that the peaks are close together. This makes reading the amplitude easier and leads to a more accurate measurement. (See figure 289.)

Measure the amplitude as the microphone is moved from one side of the pattern to the other. Note the position of the microphone each time. Remember that, to plot an accurate graph, readings are needed at least every 10 cm and possibly every 5 cm.

Measure the distance D between the line of the speakers and the line along which the microphone is moved.

Repeat for other frequencies and source separations (the loudspeakers) as time permits.

Displaying the results

Plot graphs of amplitude against distance for each of your sets of results. It would be sensible to use the same-sized scale for each so that they can be compared if necessary.

Questions

From your graphs try and answer the following questions.

1. What happens to the spacing of the maxima as the frequency increases?
2. What happens to the amplitude of the maxima as the order of the maxima increases?
3. Does the equation $n\lambda = d \sin \theta$ apply to your results? You will need to use the measured distance D to work out $\sin \theta$ (figure 290).

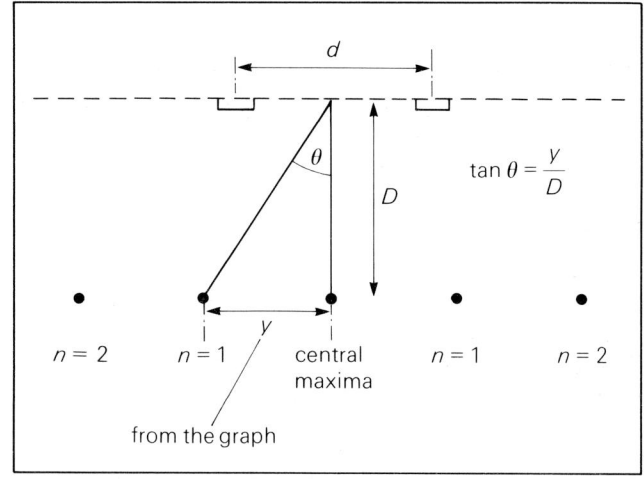

Figure 290

51. PHASE ANGLES IN A.C. CIRCUITS USING A CAPACITOR AND RESISTOR IN SERIES

Outline

In any series circuit the current flowing in each component must be in phase, but in a.c. circuits the p.d's across each component are not necessarily in phase. For a resistor, the current and potential difference (p.d.) are in phase. For a capacitor, the current leads the voltage by a phase angle of $\frac{\pi}{2}$ or 90° or $\frac{\lambda}{4}$. It follows that the p.d. of the capacitor is 90° out of phase with the p.d. of the resistor in series with it. For the complete circuit, the current flowing and supply p.d. are out of phase by an angle ϕ. This value is predicted by a phasor diagram. Suppose the current flowing at any instant is I. The impedances are:

$$Z_c = \frac{1}{\omega c} \quad \text{and} \quad Z_R = R.$$

The p.d.$_{cap} = \frac{I}{\omega c}$ and p.d.$_{res} = IR$, but they are 90° out of phase. The supply p.d. is the vector sum given by the phasor diagram shown in figure 291.

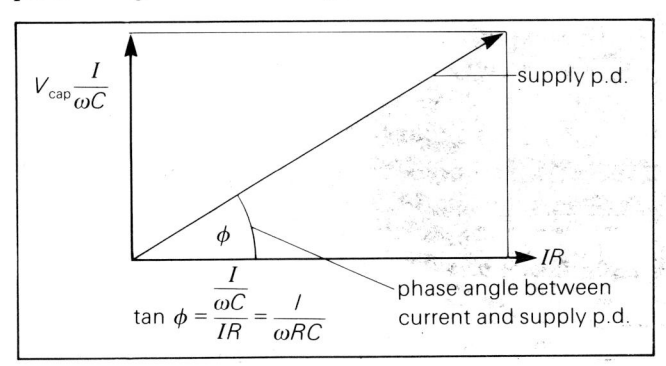

Figure 291

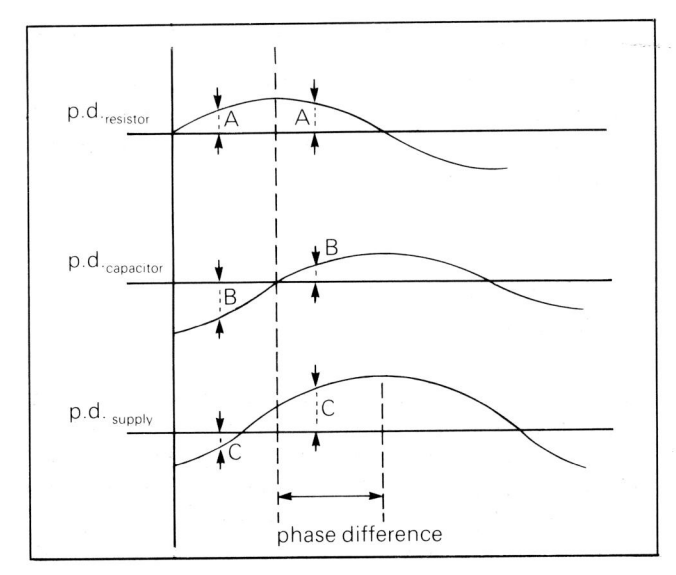

Figure 292

One condition which ought to be true at any time because of the principle of conservation of energy is:

supply p.d. = p.d.$_{capacitor}$ + p.d.$_{resistor}$

i.e. on the voltage–time diagrams any $A + B$ should always equal C at the same time instant (figure 292).

The aim of this practical is either to copy the traces from a double-beam oscilloscope or to collect enough measurements so that graphs of the curves can be drawn. The phase difference between the voltages can then be found.

Equipment

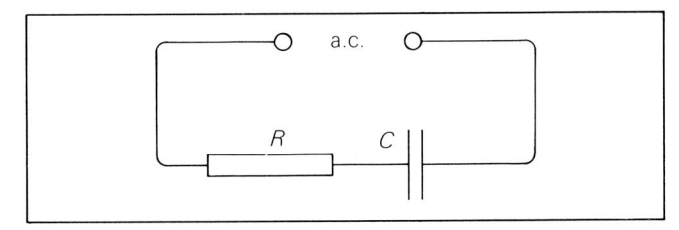

Figure 293

The obvious solution might seem to be to use an oscilloscope and to connect across the resistor (R), the capacitor (C) and the supply in turn (figure 293). However, it is not quite as simple as this, for the following reasons.

1. The oscilloscope will trigger at the same point when the input voltage rises and so the position of the trace on the screen is always the same and gives no indication of *phase*.
2. One output terminal of some a.c. generators is earthed and so is one input to the oscilloscope, for safety reasons. This means that one point is common and can have the effect of shorting out either R or C, which gives false measurements. The 50 Hz a.c. output of most low-voltage power supplies is 'floating' and this may be the only source you can use.
3. If a double-beam oscilloscope is used to display the relative phase between two inputs, one terminal is common (figure 294).

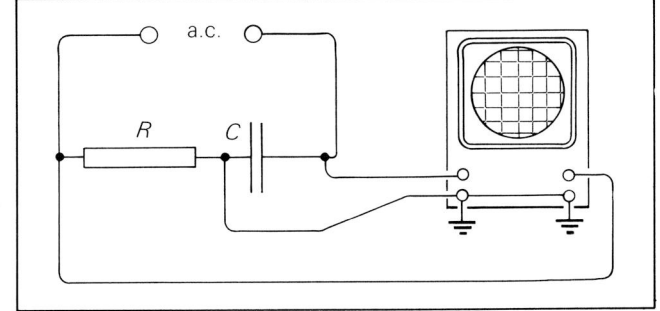

Figure 294

INVESTIGATING RELATIONSHIPS

This must be in between R and C and so a phase inversion of 180° is introduced. This could be overcome by using an inverting amplifier with a transfer function of one and a high input impedance (why?) before *one* input. Alternatively, you can just remember that when you view the traces, one of them needs a phase inversion, i.e.

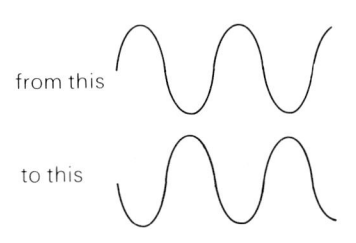

from this

to this

Another method would be to use a microcomputer with two analogue inputs and record a series of numbers which will be proportional to the voltages.

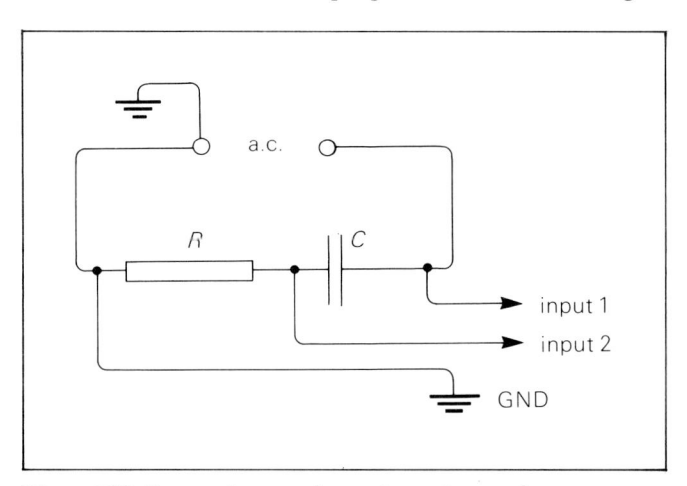

Figure 296 Connections to the analogue input of a computer

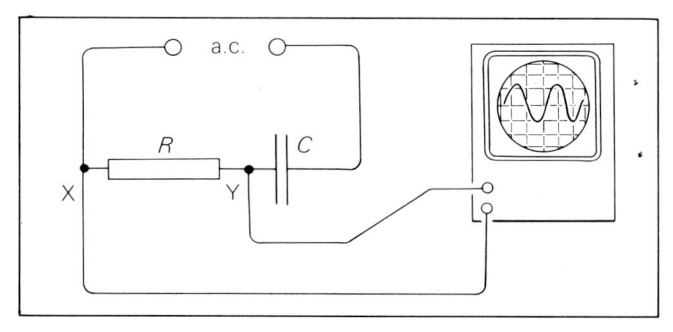

Figure 297 Equipment using a single-beam oscilloscope.

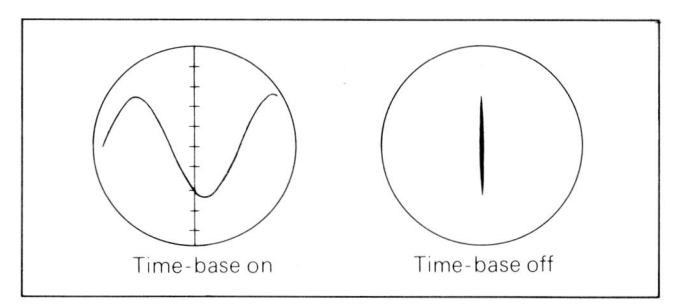

Figure 298

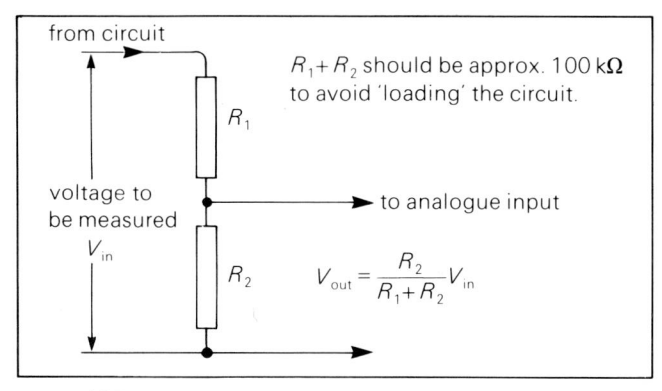

Figure 295

$R_1 + R_2$ should be approx. 100 kΩ to avoid 'loading' the circuit.

$$V_{out} = \frac{R_2}{R_1 + R_2} V_{in}$$

The BBC model 'B' has four inputs which accept voltages in the range 0–1.8 V, and so a suitable voltage divider may have to be used if voltages larger than 1.8 V need to be measured (figure 295).

There is still the problem of a common ground for each input and, if an 'earthed' a.c. supply is used, the GND output must be connected to the GND input to the computer.

The computer can 'gather' about 40 readings per second, so the frequency used can only be 1 or 2 Hz. It can also calculate the potential difference across each component from the values measured. Thus, at any instant in time (figure 296):

$\text{p.d.}_{\text{supply}} = \text{INPUT 1}$
$\text{p.d.}_{\text{cap}} = \text{INPUT 1} - \text{INPUT 2}$
$\text{p.d.}_{\text{res}} = \text{INPUT 2}$

If you have the equipment available at school, your teacher will give you more details.

Experimental details

From the resistors and capacitors given choose a pair which have similar impedances for the frequency you are using. $\left(\text{Use } Z_c = \dfrac{1}{\omega c} \text{ and } Z_L = \omega L. \right)$ If this is not done, the p.d.s will be very different in amplitude and this could cause problems of measurement, because one p.d. would be very small. The exact method will depend on the apparatus you are using.

1. USING ONLY A SINGLE-BEAM OSCILLOSCOPE

Use a *non-earthed* ('floating') a.c. supply (but with an *earthed* oscilloscope). Set up the circuit, as shown in figure 297, and measure the peak-to-peak voltage across each component R and C and across the supply. The contacts X and Y will have to be moved each time. It is probably easier to read if the time-base is turned off (figure 298).

2. A suitable range of frequency must be decided upon. Use the equation:

$$f \text{ (Hz)} = \frac{1}{2\pi\sqrt{LC}}$$

to find the expected resonant frequency and start with a range from $\frac{f}{4}$ to $4f$ (it can always be extended or more results taken on a narrower range if required).

3. Start with a resistance R of $0\,\Omega$. Take readings of V_m for at least ten frequencies in the range chosen, keeping the supply voltage V constant. Work out the value of I.

   Plot a graph, and use it to decide if any change of range for the frequency is needed (figure 303). Repeat measurements of V_m for any other frequencies used.

4. Change R to $100\,\Omega$ and repeat the measurements of V_m over your chosen frequency range. Find the value of R which gives a maximum current of about 10 per cent of that when $R = 0\,\Omega$, and then take a complete set of readings for *four* equally-spaced resistances in this range.

5. A computer program 'LCR' (package PHYS1 option 3) is available for you to produce theoretical graphs of current against frequency for any given values of L, C, R. This can be used to plan the range of frequency and R to be used.

Results

e.g. $R = 100\,\Omega$

Frequency/Hz	
V_m (peak-to-peak)	
$I_{\text{r.m.s.}} = \dfrac{V_m}{2\sqrt{2}\times 10}$	

Have you checked the value of the resistor?

From the results
On the same axes plot a series of graphs, one for each resistance, of current (I) against frequency (f).

Questions

1. Is the resonant frequency independent of resistance?
2. What is the effect of increasing the resistance?

(a) The frequency range is too large

(b) The frequency range is too small

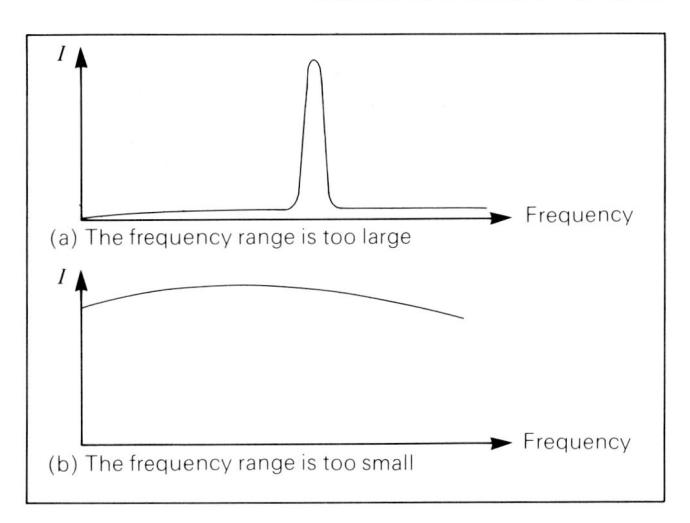

Figure 303

3. In a different colour plot a theoretical curve using the equation:

$$I = \frac{V}{\sqrt{R^2 + \left(\omega L - \dfrac{1}{\omega C}\right)^2}}$$

where $\omega = 2\pi f$ (using a programmable calculator or the computer program will save time).

(a) To what extent do the theoretical and experimental results agree?
(b) Can you estimate a value for the combined resistive parts of L and C?

4. What are the values of R and L in the circuit which produced the graph shown in figure 304 with a $1.0\,\mu\text{F}$ capacitor and a supply voltage of amplitude $6\,\text{V}$?

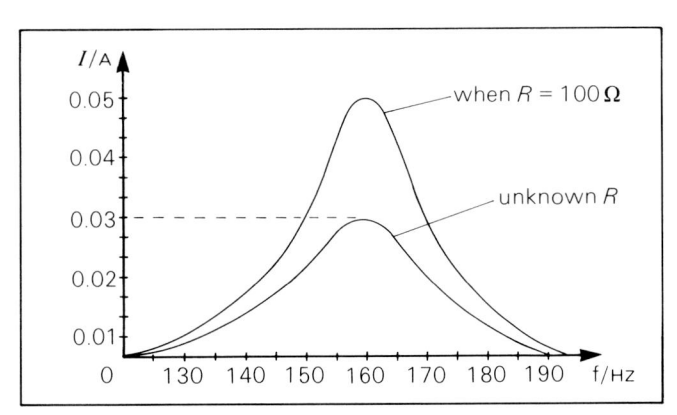

Figure 304 Graph of current against frequency

DEDUCTIONS, APPLICATIONS AND DATA ANALYSIS

53. CIRCUIT DEDUCTIONS

You are provided with a set of boxes with up to two lamps and two switches visible. The circuit is hidden. The object is to work out the circuit from the brightness of the lamps and the effect of operating the switches. You may unscrew a lamp if you wish. Since there is a maximum of two switches and two lamps, with perhaps the odd resistor, you should be able to draw out all the possible series and parallel circuits which can be made from the components before you start.

Hints
1. Are the lamps in series?
2. Is there a switch in the wire connected to the supply?
3. Are both switches in the same loop?
4. Is there more than one loop in the circuit?

In your report

When you have finished, write down logically how you decided on the circuit. Draw a flowchart if possible, for example, it might start as follows:

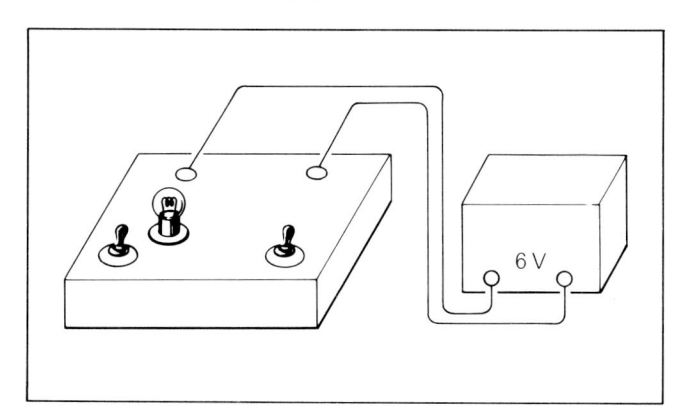

Figure 305 Equipment

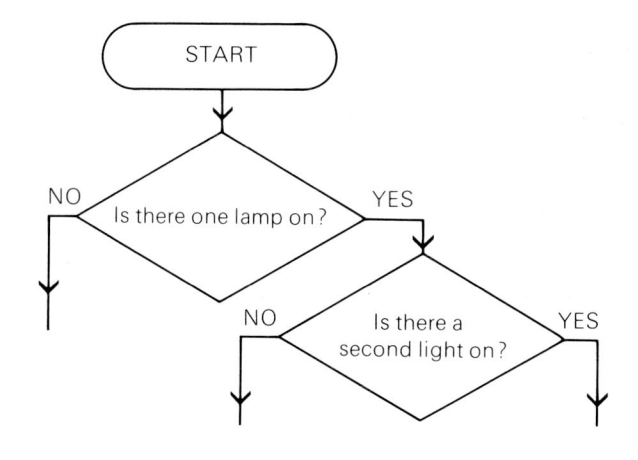

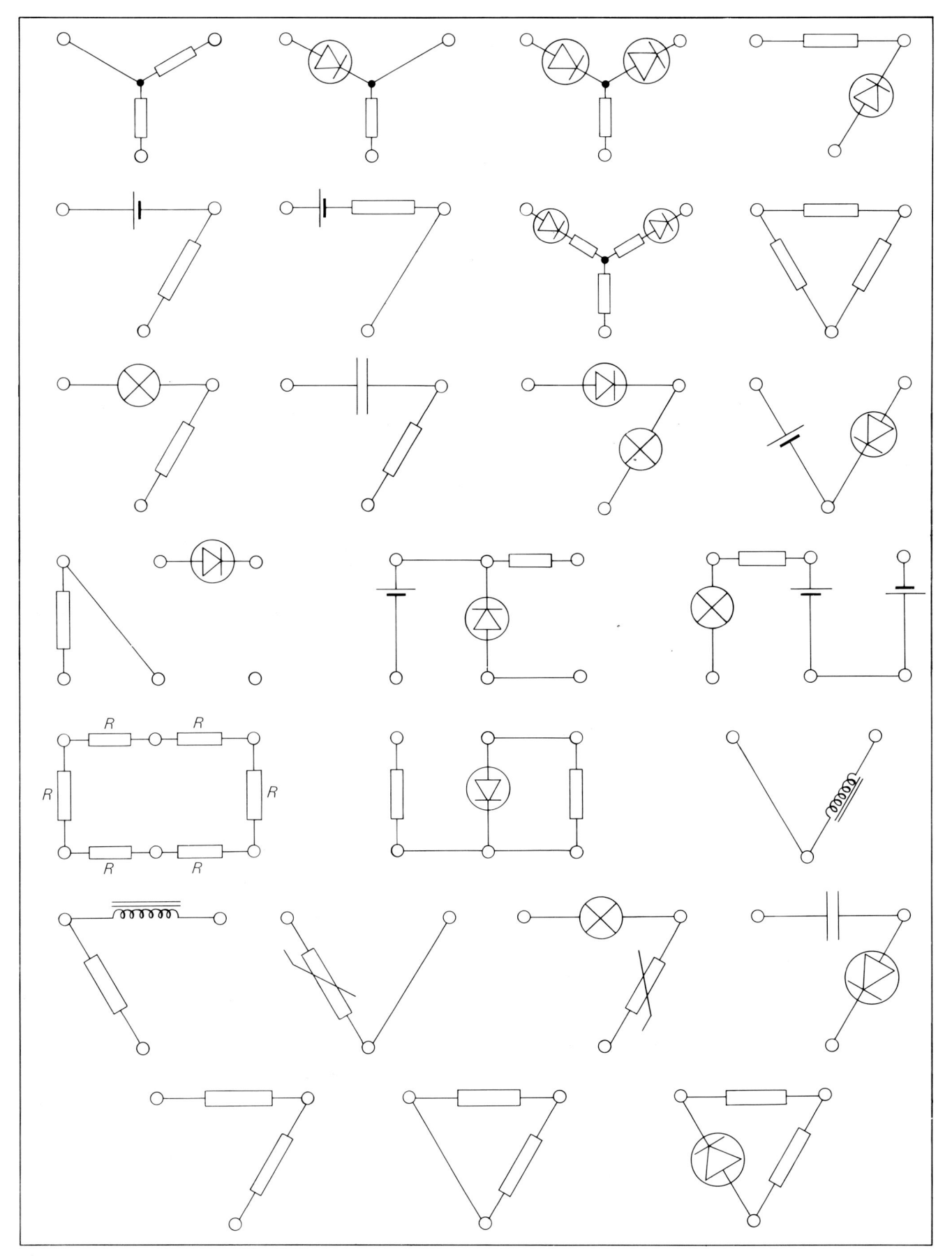

Figure 313 Possible circuits

DEDUCTIONS, APPLICATIONS AND DATA ANALYSIS

55. INVESTIGATIONS WITH A MAGNET

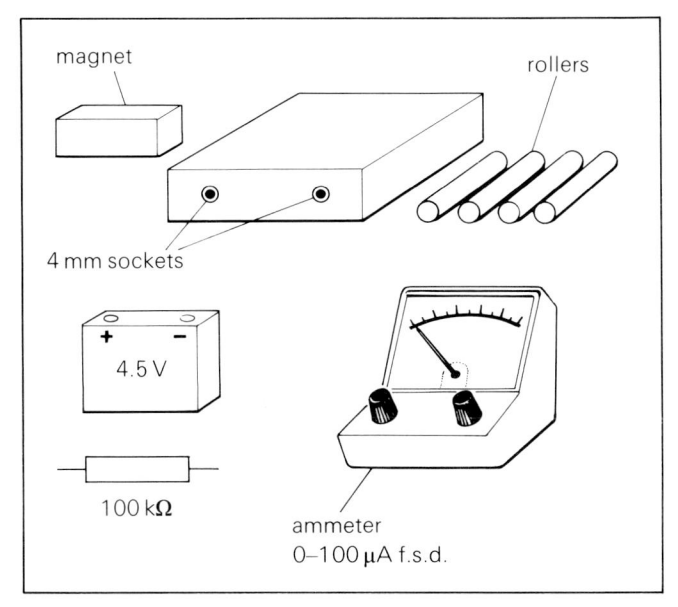

Figure 314 Equipment available

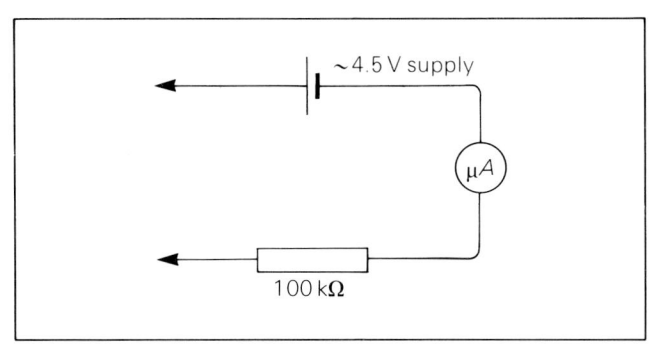

Figure 315 Circuit used

Outline

You are provided with a set of boxes containing unknowns. Find out all you can about what is inside the boxes using only a magnet, 4.5 V battery, 100 kΩ resistor, the ammeter and four rollers. Think what sort of effects are produced by magnetism or in which magnetism is used. Think about attraction, repulsion, electromagnetic induction, reed switches and coils of wire.

Experimental details

1. Try connecting the ammeter to a pair of 4 mm sockets and look for electromagnetic induction as the magnet is moved round the box.
2. Look for a reed switch by connecting the circuit in figure 315 across a pair of 4 mm sockets and moving the magnet round.
3. Put the box on rollers and test for attraction and repulsion.

56. CONTROLLING A CURRENT

Outline

A switch is the simplest component to use to control the amount of current flowing. The current either flows or is zero. Adding a variable resistor in series enables the current to be altered to lower values. It is not correct physics to say that a variable resistor can increase the current. Only an additional source of e.m.f. can do that.

A light-dependent resistor (l.d.r.) (figure 316) is a resistor whose value alters as the intensity of light falling on it changes.

A thermistor (figure 317) changes its value depending on its temperature. It has a negative temperature coefficient. This means that its resistance gets less as the temperature increases.

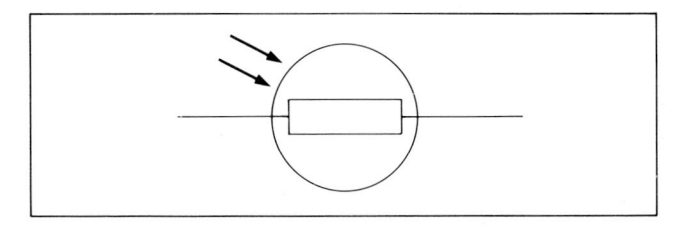

Figure 316 A light dependant resistor (l.d.r.)

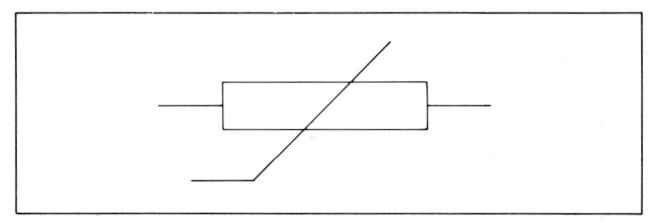

Figure 317 A thermistor

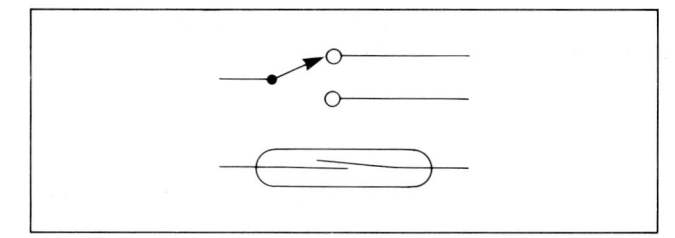

Figure 318 A microswitch and a reed switch

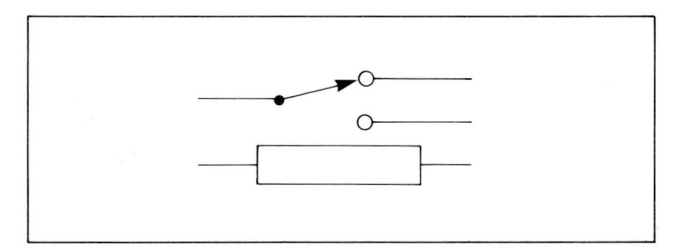

Figure 319 A relay

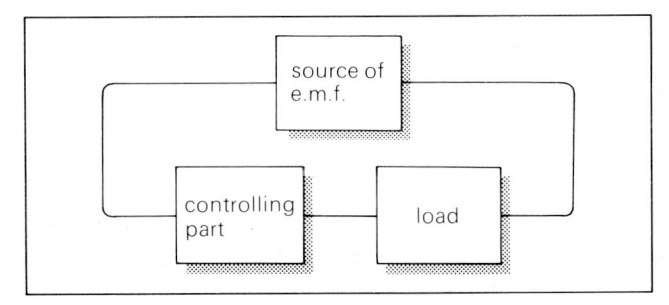

Figure 320 A circuit has three main parts.

A microswitch (figure 318) will operate with a very small force and has a momentary action. This means that it returns when the force is removed.

A reed switch is operated by a magnet close to it, and can have single pole or changeover contacts. A relay is a switch operated by an electromagnet.

This experiment finds out the approximate ranges over which the resistances of these components change and you are asked to design and test circuits which will perform given specifications. There is one overall concept of a circuit (figure 320). The control section may involve complicated wiring, but it all involves one wire in from the supply and one wire out to the load.

Equipment

Equipment you may use includes: 0–12 V variable voltage supply, 6 V, 60 mA lamp as a load, ammeter, voltmeter, switches, l.d.r., thermistor, microswitch, relay, reed switch and magnet.

Experimental details

Make up a set of series circuits using the lamp as a load. Take measurements to find out the following.

1. The approximate range over which the resistance of the l.d.r. varies.

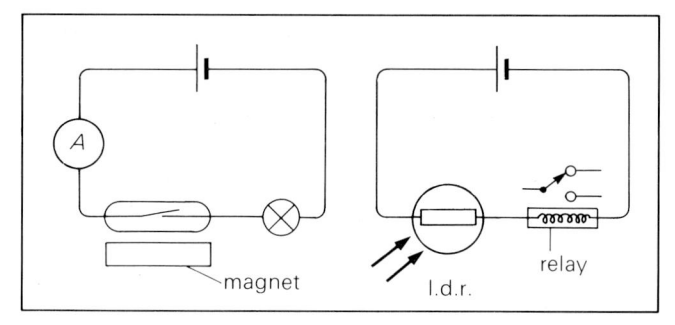

Figure 321 Two possible circuits

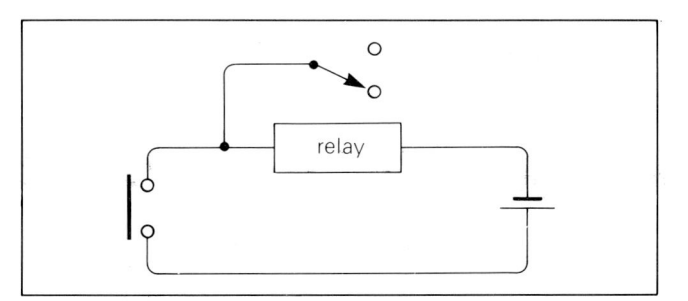

Figure 322 A partly completed latch circuit

2. The approximate range over which the resistance of the thermistor varies. Use a temperature range of −5°C to 60°C. (How can you get −5°C?)
3. The minimum current needed to operate the relay and the current at which it will switch off; explain why the two are not the same.
4. The maximum distance of the reed switch from the magnet if it is to operate when the magnet passes it (does the orientation of the magnet matter?).

Design, produce and test circuits which will meet the following specifications.

1. The lamp will come on if either of two switches is closed.
2. The lamp will come on only if both switches are closed.
3. The lamp can be switched off and on from two switch positions completely independently and independent of the position of the other switch.
4. The lamp is operated by a circuit using the switch contacts of the relay. A second circuit operates the coil of the relay. Make the lamp go off when the relay is on.
5. The lamp comes on when the magnet is brought close to a reed switch.
6. Use a reed switch and relay so that as the magnet passes the reed switch the lamp comes on and stays on. This involves making a latching circuit using the other set of contacts on the relay. Figure 322 shows a part-completed latching circuit to give you a clue.
7. Use the l.d.r. so that when light falls on the l.d.r. the lamp comes on. Add a component so that you can alter the sensitivity. This allows you to alter the level of light at which the lamp comes on.

8. Use an l.d.r. and relay to improve the above circuit so that the lamp is either fully on or off; it is never partly on.
9. Use an l.d.r. and relay so that as light falls on the l.d.r. the lamp goes off.
10. Make a circuit so that the lamp comes on if a magnet is near to the reed switch or light is on the l.d.r.
11. Make a circuit which could be used as a frost alarm. The lamp comes on when the temperature falls below 0°C.

In your report

Describe the operation of each of the components you have investigated, together with the measurements taken.

Draw each circuit diagram you have designed. Write down a comment about the operation of each.

Questions
1. Comment on the advantage or necessity (if any) of using a relay with a 12 V 185 Ω coil to switch lamps which draw:

   (a) 10 mA at 12 V;
   (b) 10 mA at 250 V;
   (c) 10 A at 12 V.

2. What series resistor would be needed if the above relay is to work from 24 V? A current of 50 mA will just cause it to operate, and a sensible design would use 10 per cent more.

57. DIODES: JUNCTION, ZENER, LED AND LAMBDA

Outline

A metal is a good conductor because it has a large number of conduction electrons, which are able to move under the electric field produced when a potential difference is applied. Semiconductor materials have only a few conduction electrons, but by replacing some atoms in silicon (a semiconductor) by atoms with one more or one less electrons than silicon a known excess or deficiency of electrons can be produced. The material is known as *n*-type or *p*-type (respectively). When these two materials are made together, electrons will move until a potential barrier has been produced at the junction. An applied potential difference can either increase the size of the barrier, giving no conduction, or it can decrease the size of the barrier, giving conduction. This is the basic *p–n* junction. The diode will conduct for one polarity of connection but not the other, a fact which, as you probably already know, has uses in rectifying a.c. into d.c.

A *zener* diode can be used in a circuit for producing a stable voltage. A light-emitting diode (LED) produces light very efficiently.

In this experiment you are going to plot current and voltage curves for the *four* types of diode (figure 323).

1. INVESTIGATING CONDUCTION

Experimental details

Using the circuit shown in figure 324, alter the voltage in suitable steps starting at zero volts, and record the voltage and current up to the maximum range of the meters given. Reverse the polarity and repeat so that a graph of

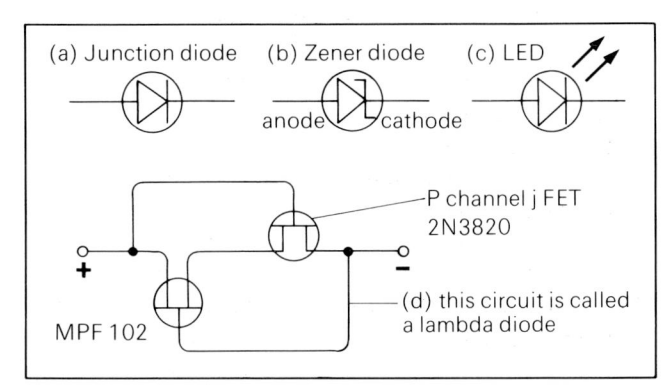

Figure 323 Different types of diode

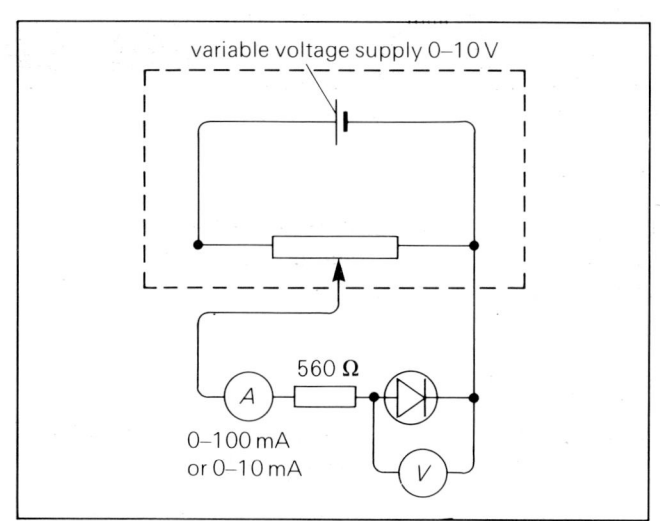

Figure 324 Circuit used

voltage against current can be drawn for positive and negative values. Remember that you will need about 20 sets of readings to plot a reliable graph. Repeat for the zener diode, the LED and the lambda diode.

Results

Junction diode	
voltage/V	current/mA

Zener diode	
voltage/V	current/mA

LED	
voltage/V	current/mA

Lambda diode	
voltage/V	current/mA

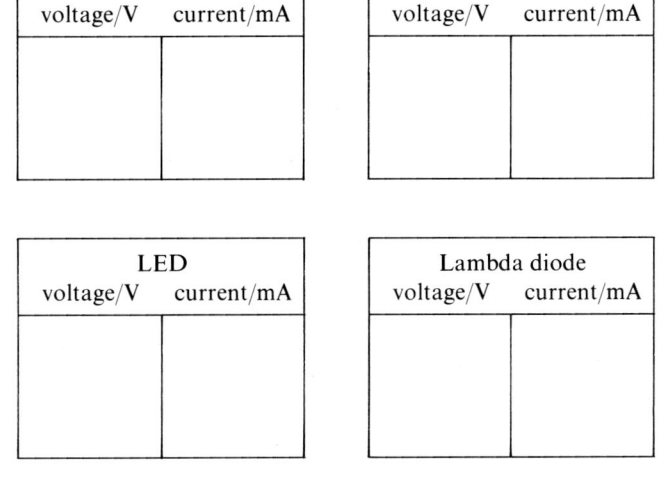

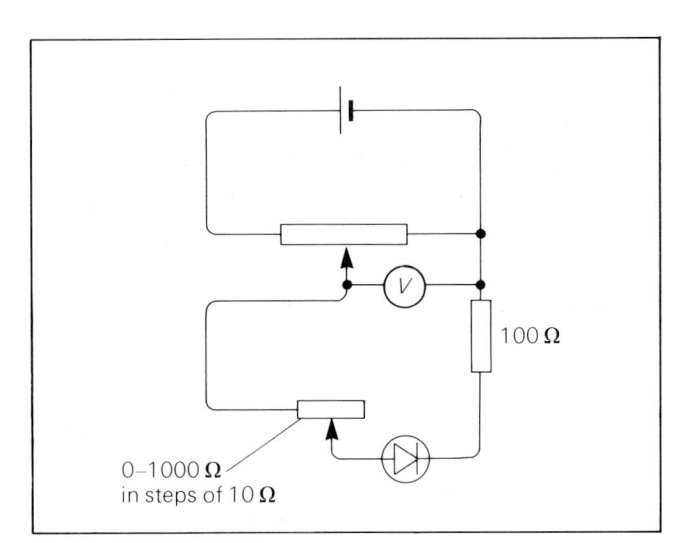

Figure 325 Circuit used

From the graphs:
(a) find the forward- and reverse-biased resistances of each diode;
(b) find the minimum potential difference needed for conduction;
(c) estimate the normal operating current for the LED;
(d) find the breakdown voltage for the zener diode;
(e) comment on the graph for the lambda diode.

2. LIGHT EMITTING DIODE

Experimental details

Using the circuit shown in figure 325, take readings so that a graph of series resistance against minimum supply potential (V_s) to light the LED can be drawn. If the equation is:

$$R = \frac{V_s - V_f}{I_f}$$

draw a suitable graph for the equation and find values for I_f and V_f. What are the physical significances of I_f and V_f?

3. APPLICATIONS

A seven-segment display can use LEDs to form the numbers. Diodes can be used in a diode matrix so that only the required segments come on for a given digit. A zener diode produces a stable operating voltage.

Set up the circuit, as shown in figure 326, so that when switch 2 is pressed

2

lights up, and when 3 is pressed

3

lights up.

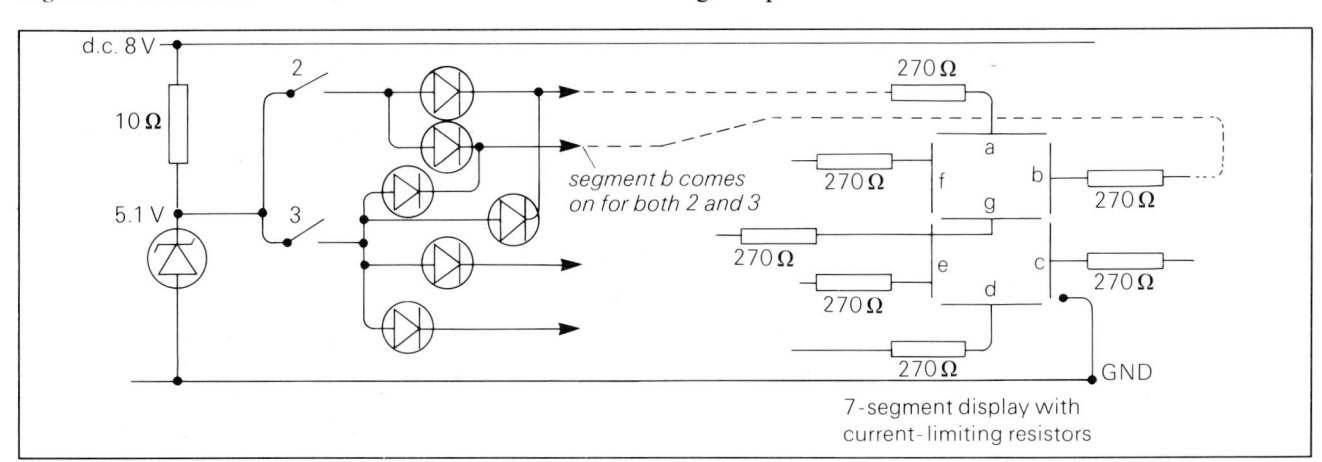

Figure 326

58. THE OPERATIONAL AMPLIFIER

Outline

An operational amplifier has a very high input resistance and a very high voltage gain; it will amplify a d.c. voltage. It has two inputs, inverting and non-inverting, and the output depends on the sum of the two inputs. However, one input inverts the voltage applied so that it is the *difference* between the two inputs that is amplified. The open loop gain is usually 10^8 or higher. The supply voltages are usually $+15\,\text{V}$ and $-15\,\text{V}$, which means that positive and negative input voltages can be used.

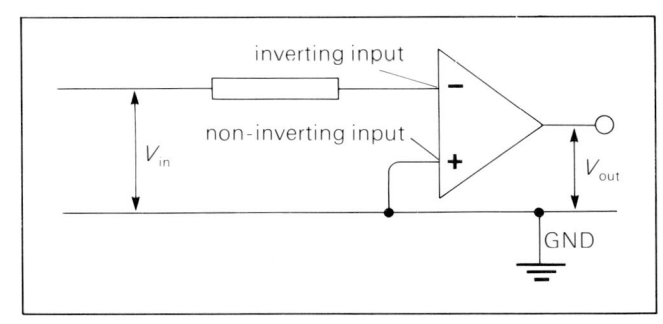

Figure 327 Operational amplifier

open loop gain $= A$
$$V_{\text{out}} = A(0 + (-V_{\text{in}})) = -AV_{\text{in}}$$

Because A is so large, this means that a minute input voltage would cause V_{out} to equal one of the supply voltages. This has an application in switching circuits, but in many applications a fraction of the output voltage is 'fed back' to the input (figure 328). This is known as *feedback*, and is an important concept.

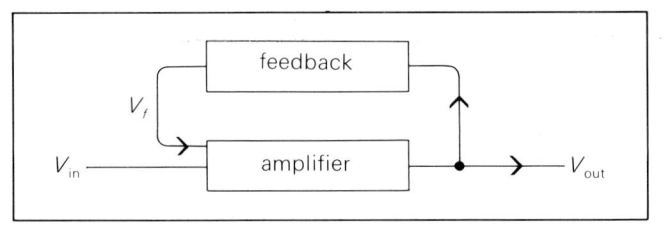

Figure 328

If the open loop gain is A, then V_f could be positive or negative.
$$V_{\text{out}} = A(V_{\text{in}} + V_f)$$

If the fraction of the output fed back is β, then $V_f = \beta V_{\text{out}}$ and so $V_{\text{out}} = A(V_{\text{in}} + \beta V_{\text{out}})$. Rearranged, this gives:
$$\frac{V_{\text{out}}}{V_{\text{in}}} = \frac{A}{1 - \beta A}$$

and is called the *transfer function*.

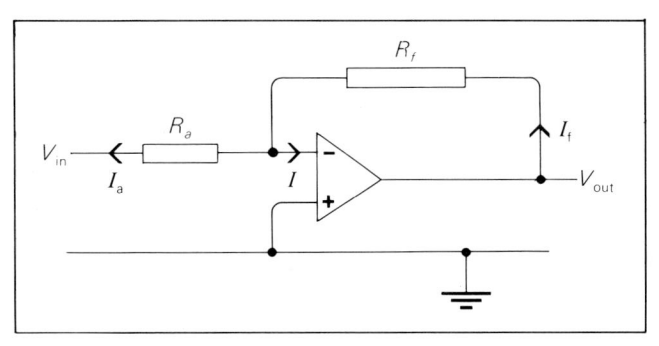

Figure 329 Inverting amplifier

Figure 329 shows a practical circuit using *negative* feedback to the inverting input.

$$V_{\text{out}} = -\frac{R_f}{R_a} V_{\text{in}}$$

Derivation
Since the current drawn by the input of the operational amplifier is very small, so as to be virtually zero, $I = 0$ and therefore $I_f = I_a$. The input to the operational amplifier is known as a *virtual earth*, since the difference between the two inputs is amplified and the positive is at zero potential; it thus follows the negative must be virtually at zero potential. In fact, $\frac{15}{10^8}$ V, therefore

$$V_{\text{in}} = -I_a R_a, \quad V_{\text{out}} = I_f R_f$$

(negative because of current through R_a.) In this case the circuit connected to the input 'sinks' a current rather than 'sources' a current.
Therefore

$$\frac{V_{\text{out}}}{V_{\text{in}}} = \frac{i_f R_f}{-i_a R_a} = \frac{-R_f}{R_a}$$

since $I_f = I_a$.

This experiment is a series of investigations on the operation and use of operational amplifiers.

Equipment

Operational amplifier.
Two variable resistors to use as voltage dividers for producing variable input voltages.
A high-impedance voltmeter.
$1\,\text{M}\Omega$, $100\,\text{k}\Omega$ and $10\,\text{k}\Omega$ resistors (three of each).
Supply ± 9 to $15\,\text{V}$, preferably stabilised.
LDR, e.g. ORP12, and light source.

1. OFFSET VOLTAGE

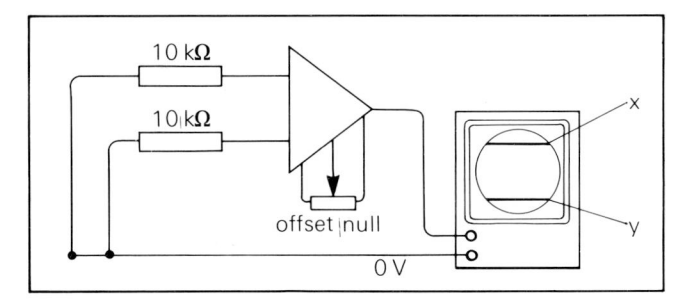

Figure 330

Because of slight differences between the internal circuits of the two inputs, in figure 330, an output voltage can be produced even with no obvious input. The variable resistor marked 'offset null' allows the output voltage to be adjusted. However, since an operational amplifier has a very high gain, the slightest difference between the two inputs will cause the output voltage to change from the positive supply voltage (X, figure 330) to the negative supply voltage (Y). The best that can be done is to adjust the 'offset null' until the output just switches state.

2. EFFECT OF INPUT VOLTAGE ON OUTPUT VOLTAGE

Set up each circuit as illustrated and answer the questions posed.

A. (i) Does the output change from being $-V_s$ to being $+V_s$ as soon as V_2 gets larger than V_1? Instead of using three separate voltmeters a VELA instrument with program 00 could be used.
   (ii) How can the output be made to change from being $+V_s$ to $-V_s$?
   (iii) Can V_2 and V_1 be arranged so that the output voltage is 0? If not, has the very high open loop gain anything to do with it?

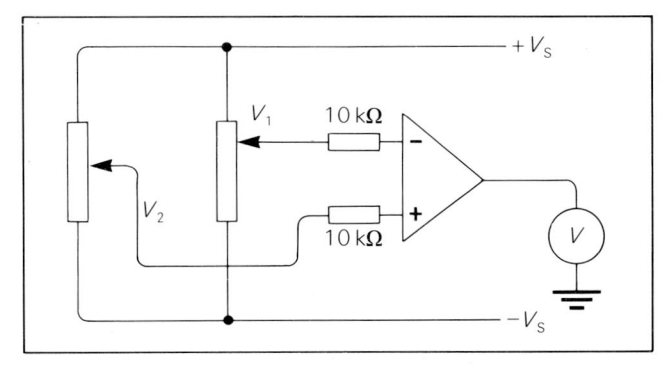

Figure 331

B.

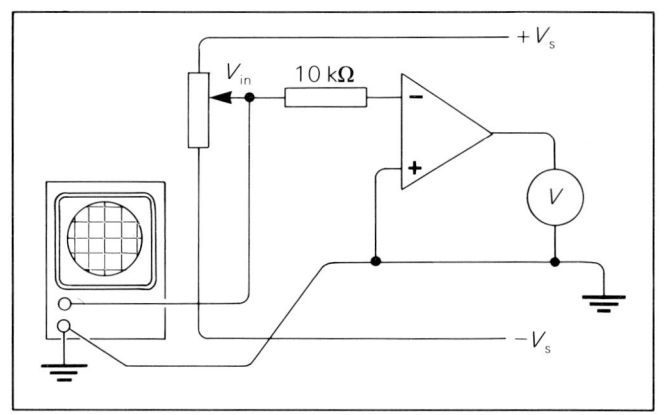

Figure 332

   (i) Find the input voltage at which the output changes.
   (ii) Does the circuit work in the same way if the positive and negative inputs are reversed?

C. Set the variable resistor at its mid-point. What is the output voltage when the l.d.r. is:

   (i) in the light?
   (ii) in the dark?

How can the sensitivity be set so that the output changes at a particular level of illumination?

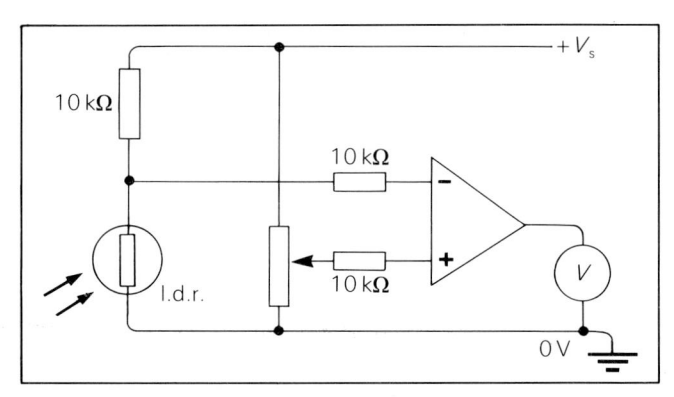

Figure 333

3. NEGATIVE FEEDBACK

This experiment investigates the use of negative feedback. You will have found out by now that the output is inverted if the negative input is used. A resistor connecting output to input would feed some of the output back, or a potential divider could be used. Remember to check that there is zero output for zero input and adjust the offset null if necessary.

DEDUCTIONS, APPLICATIONS AND DATA ANALYSIS

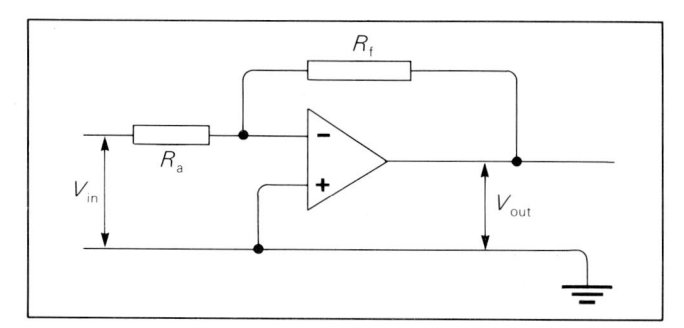

Figure 334

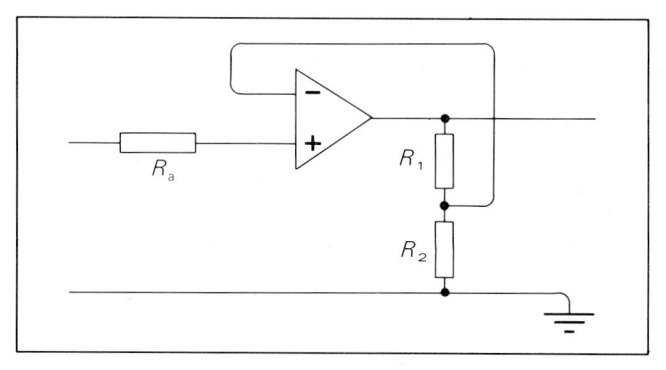

Figure 337

A. Using the circuit shown in figure 334, test the expression

$$\frac{V_{out}}{V_{in}} = -\frac{R_f}{R_a}$$

where $\frac{V_{out}}{V_{in}}$ is called the transfer function.

B. Using the circuit shown in figure 335, find an expression for the transfer function in terms of R_a, R_1 and R_2.

C. If a non-inverting amplifier is needed, the logical choice is to use the positive input with the feedback still going to the negative.

Does the circuit shown in figure 336 work? Could it not be argued that, since the input draws very little current, there is no potential difference across R_f and hence all the output voltage is fed back?

D. In the circuit shown in figure 337, a fraction $\frac{R_2}{R_1 + R_2}$ of the V_{out} is fed back. Therefore $\beta = -\frac{R_2}{(R_1 + R_2)}$.
Does the value of R_a have any effect on the transfer function?

E. *A high-impedance voltmeter.* One disadvantage of a moving-coil voltmeter is that its resistance is relatively low. Measuring 0–10 V, a value of 100 kΩ is typical but for 0–1 V values would be of about 10–20 kΩ, which is of the order of resistances used in electronic circuits. The voltmeter could affect the circuit to a marked extent.

An operational amplifier can be used as a *voltage follower* to give a high input impedance (figure 338).

If open loop gain $= A$:

$$V_{out} = (V_{in} - V_{out})$$
$$A = AV_{in} - AV_{out}$$
$$V_{out}(1 + A) = AV_{in}$$

$$V_{out} = \left(\frac{A}{1+A}\right)V_{in}$$

$$\approx V_{in}, \text{ if } A \gg 1$$

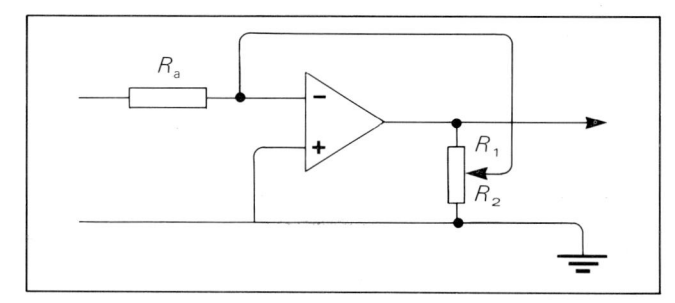

Figure 335

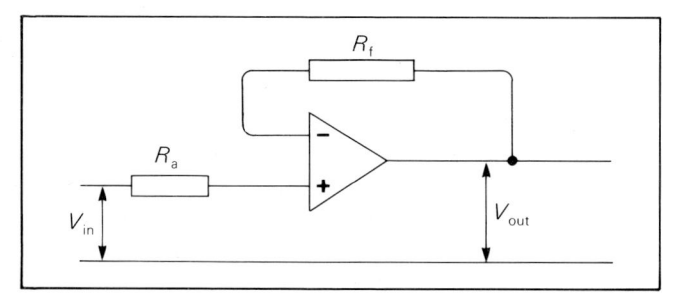

Figure 336

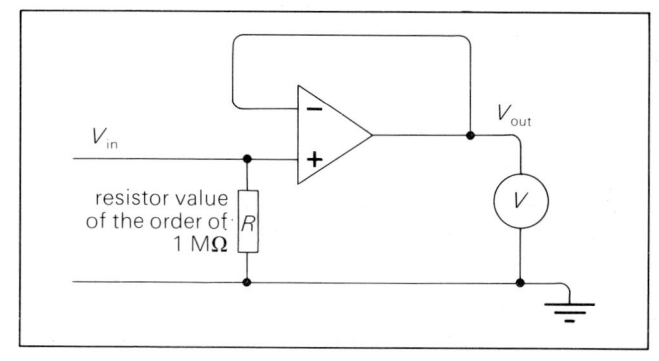

Figure 338

59. POTENTIAL DIVIDERS

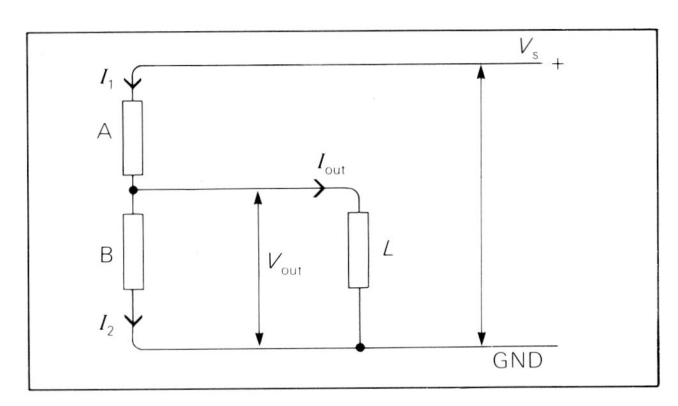

Figure 339

Outline

The potential divider is a widely used device and is important in electronics. Essentially it consists of two resistors (*A* and *B* in figure 339) connected in series between positive supply V_s and negative GND. A value for the potential V_{out} at the mid-point is needed, because this potential is used to supply current to part of the circuit, represented by the load *L*. Any change in the resistance of *A* or *B* alters the potential V_{out}.

$$V_{out} = \left(\frac{BL}{AB + AL + BL}\right)V_s$$

$$I_{out} = \frac{V_{out}}{L} = \frac{BV_s}{(AB + AL + BL)}$$

Potential dividers can use other components (see figure 340).

The experiment investigates the way in which V_{out} varies with different load resistors and for different arrangements of potential dividers.

Equipment

Resistance boxes for *A* and *B* and *L*, adjustable, 0–10 kΩ.
Smoothed d.c. power supply and voltmeter.
Oscilloscope or high-impedance voltmeter.
Computer simulation (not essential, but allows many ideas to be tried out).
Lamp
Capacitor 2200 µF, 10 V or greater.
Ammeter 0–100 mA, two diodes, 1 kΩ and 100 kΩ resistors.

Experimental details

Use $V_s = 6$ V (if you are using a variable power supply, check with a voltmeter).

A. Using the circuit shown in figure 339, make a potential divider to produce a V_{out} of 4 V which does not vary by more than 10 per cent as the load alters from 100 Ω to 1000 Ω.

   You may use the computer simulation to produce values for A and B and then try them out experimentally (see figure 341).

B. Using the circuit shown in figure 340a, design and test a circuit which gives V_{out} as zero volts when the switch is closed, and $I_{out} \approx 2$ mA with $V_{out} > 5.5$ V when the switch is open.

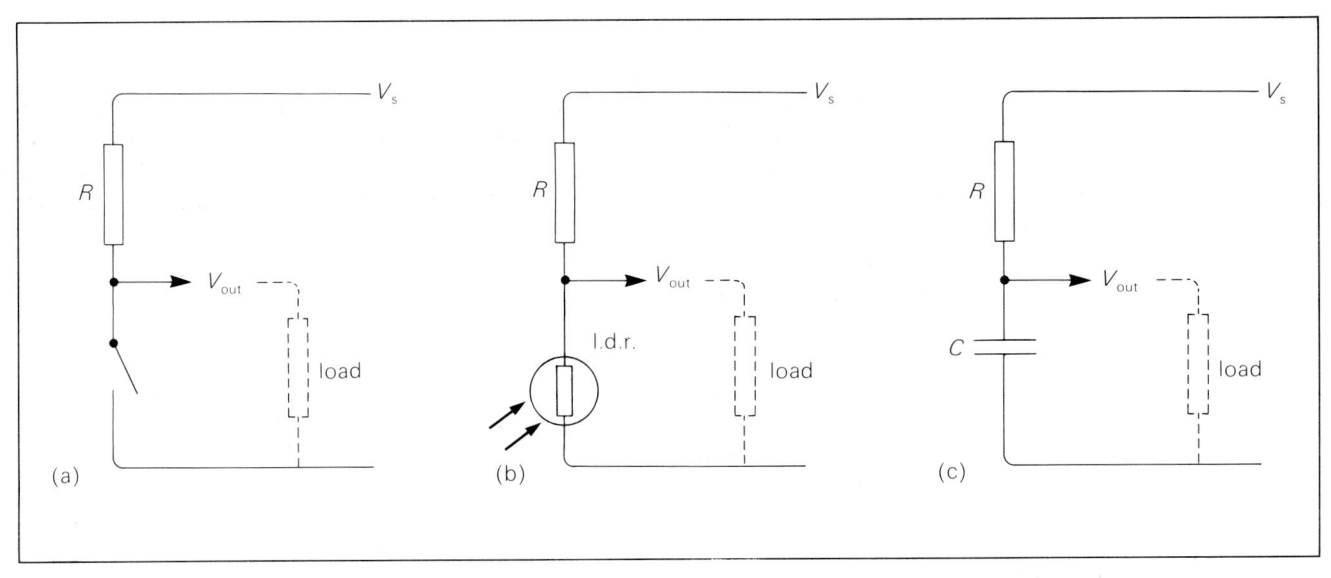

Figure 340

DEDUCTIONS, APPLICATIONS AND DATA ANALYSIS

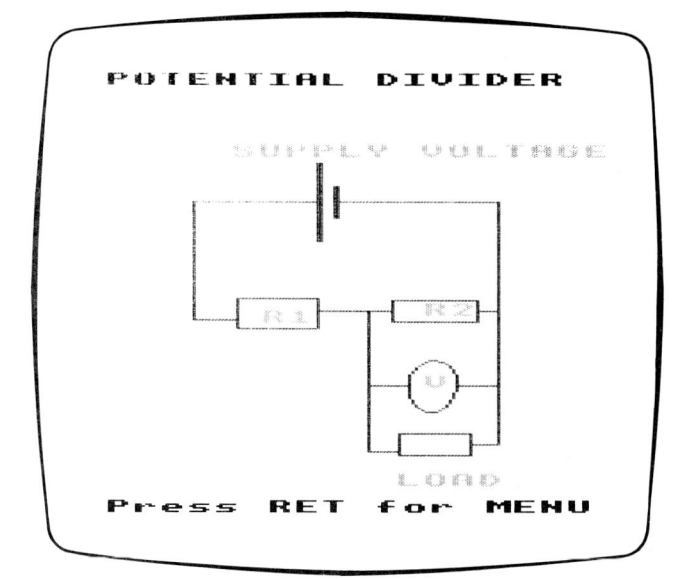

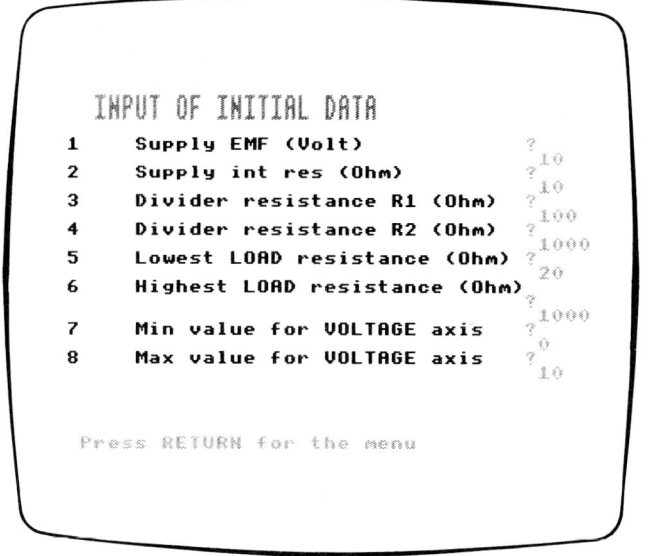

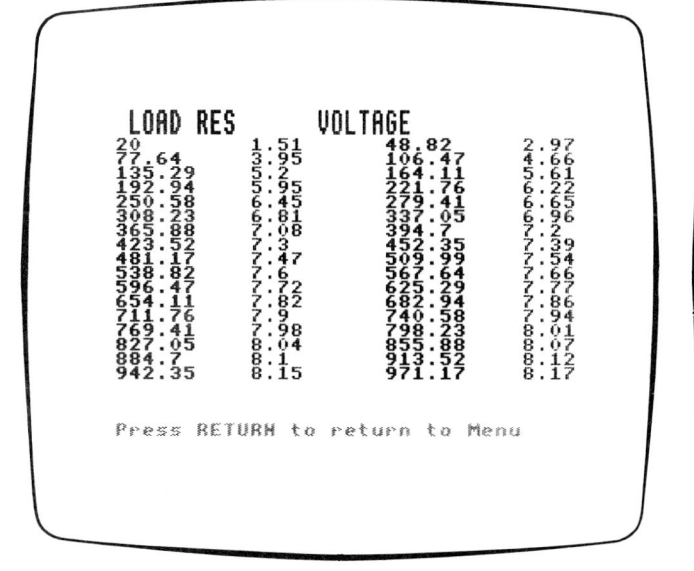

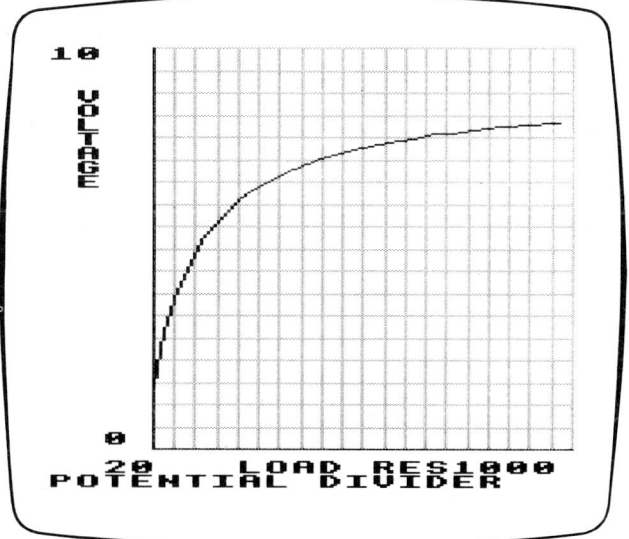

Figure 341 Four example displays from the computer simulation 'POT DIV'

C. Using the circuit shown in figure 340b, design and test a circuit which gives a V_{out} of >4 V in the dark and <0.5 V in the light, using a load resistance of $100\,k\Omega$. Remember, the maximum current through the l.d.r. is 20 mA. This should enable you to calculate the minimum value of A that is permissible.

How is the current altered if the load resistance is (i) $10\,k\Omega$, (ii) $1\,k\Omega$?

D. Using the circuit shown in figure 340c with no load on, adjust R so that it takes 10 seconds for the potential across the capacitor V_{out} to rise to 4 V. Find the times for at least ten values of load in the range $1\,k\Omega$ to $10\,k\Omega$. From your results plot a graph of the time against load resistance.

A bulb has a typical resistance of 10 to $100\,\Omega$ and operating from 12 V would draw currents of 1.2 A to 120 mA. Why do you think these timing circuits are often used in conjunction with a transistor, which only needs about 5 mA of base current to cause switching, instead of operating a load such as a lamp directly (figure 342)?

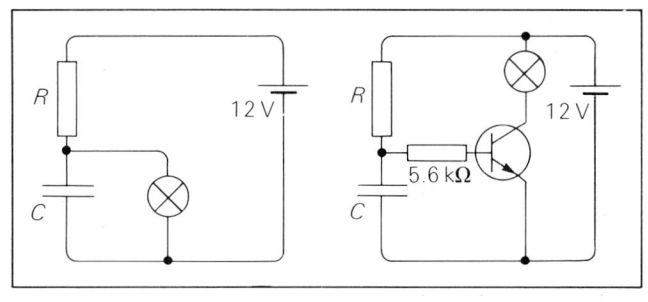

Figure 342

E. For each of the circuits illustrated in figure 343, find the output voltages produced by the voltage dividers, for A and/or B connected to zero volts or the supply voltage (either there are four or two possible combinations in each case). You may find a use for these circuits later, since they have some connection with logic gates. Try and explain the reasons for the particular output voltages in each case.

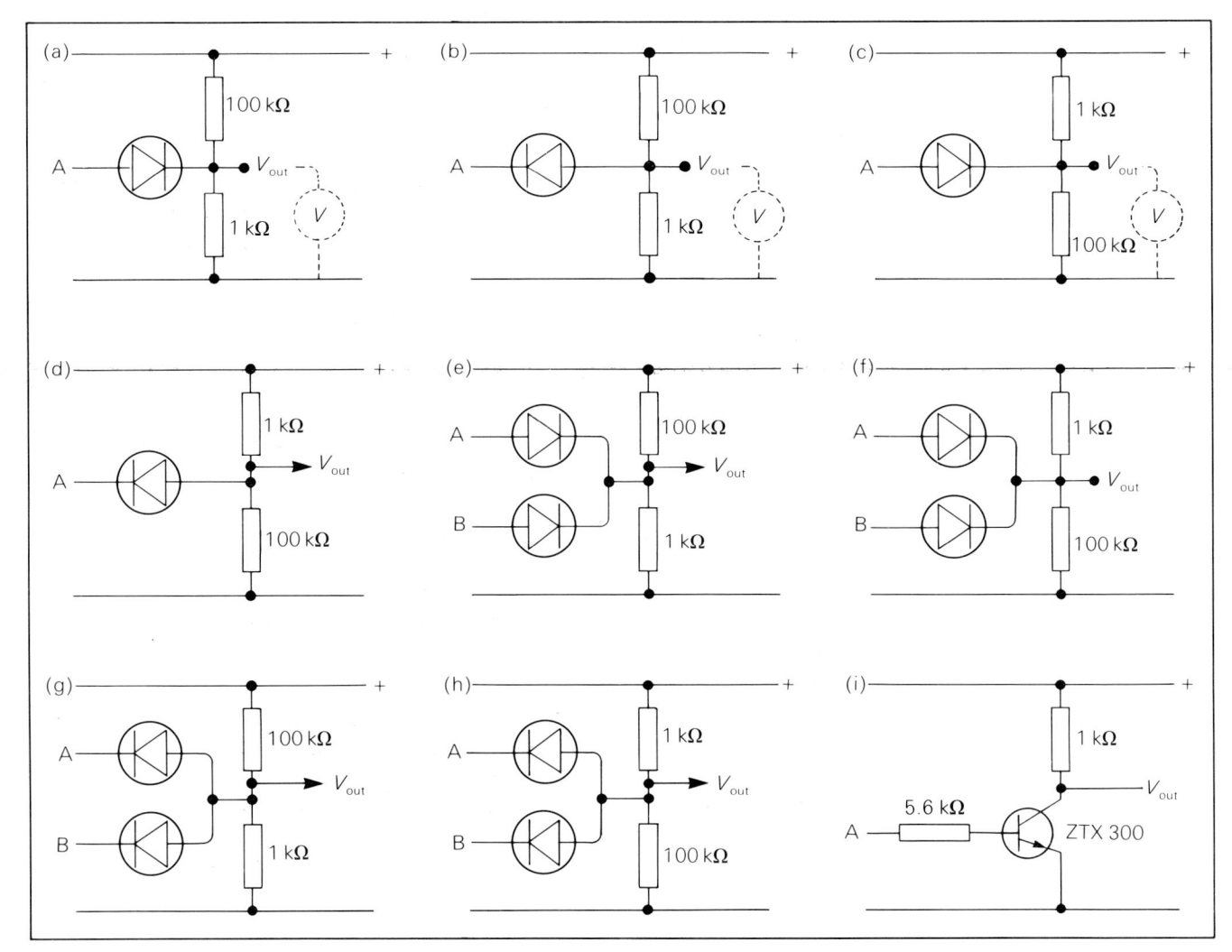

Figure 343

60. THE EFFECT OF TEMPERATURE ON RESISTANCE

Outline

Electrical conduction depends on the movement of electric charge. In metals the charge carriers are electrons. In a semiconductor they can be either electrons or positive holes, and in a liquid or molten solid they are positive and negative ions. The current which flows when a potential difference (p.d.) is applied depends on:

(a) the number of 'free' conduction charges per unit volume, and

(b) the effective drift velocity at which they move.

These factors affect the *resistance*. You have probably investigated the resistance of a resistor and bulb already.

DEDUCTIONS, APPLICATIONS AND DATA ANALYSIS

Information

1. A material which is a good conductor has a large supply of 'free' conduction electrons. These are only loosely bound to the atoms of the material, and will move easily under the electric field produced by the potential difference applied. Unless the current flow is very high, it is not limited by any shortage of conduction electrons.

2. A semiconductor contains a number of conduction electrons, but raising the temperature releases more electrons, e.g. in a thermistor.

3. Raising the temperature of a metal makes the atoms vibrate with larger amplitudes, which makes it more difficult for the electrons to travel through the metal and so the drift velocity gets less, producing an increase in resistance.

4. Current flowing through a substance produces heat (power = I^2R). If the substance has a large surface area, the temperature will not rise as much as with a small surface area.

5. A tightly-wound coil, as in a lamp, has a small effective surface area, and the temperature must be higher before the rate of heat energy loss (mainly by radiation) equals the power input.

$$I^2R = \sigma A(T^4 - T_a^4)$$

If the surface area (σA) is smaller, the filament temperature (T_a) must be higher.

6. A general equation for resistance can be expressed as $R = R_0(1 + \beta T)$, where β is a constant called the temperature coefficient of resistance. If the coefficient is positive, the resistance increases with a rise in temperature, and if negative, the resistance decreases with a rise in temperature. R_0 is the resistance at 0°C and T is the temperature in degrees centigrade.

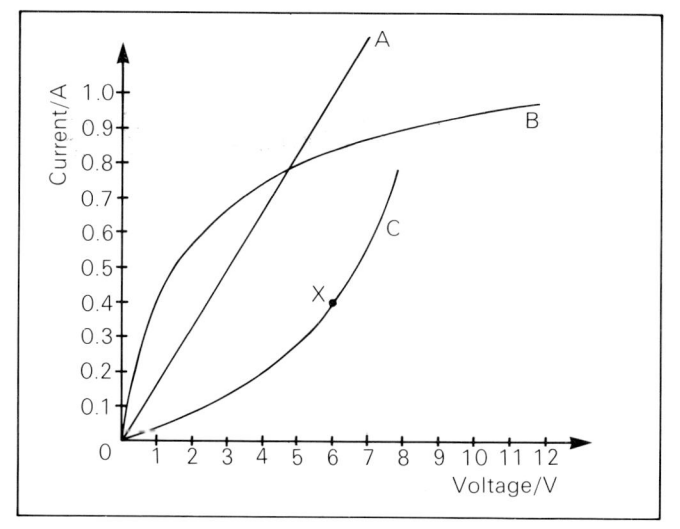

Figure 344

Questions

1. Which of the three graphs (A, B or C) in figure 344 represents a lamp and which a resistor? Explain your reasoning.
2. What is the resistance, at point X, of the component which gave graph C?
3. What sort of component could give graph C?

1. THE BEHAVIOUR OF DIFFERENT COMPONENTS

Use the circuit shown in figure 345 to plot a voltage-against-current graph for each of the 'boxes' (A–E). Use the graphs to deduce what component(s) are inside each box.

2. TEMPERATURE COEFFICIENT OF RESISTANCE

The temperature coefficient of resistance can be found from the gradient and intercept of a graph of resistance against temperature. A metre bridge is used to measure the resistance to an accuracy of approximately 2 per cent.

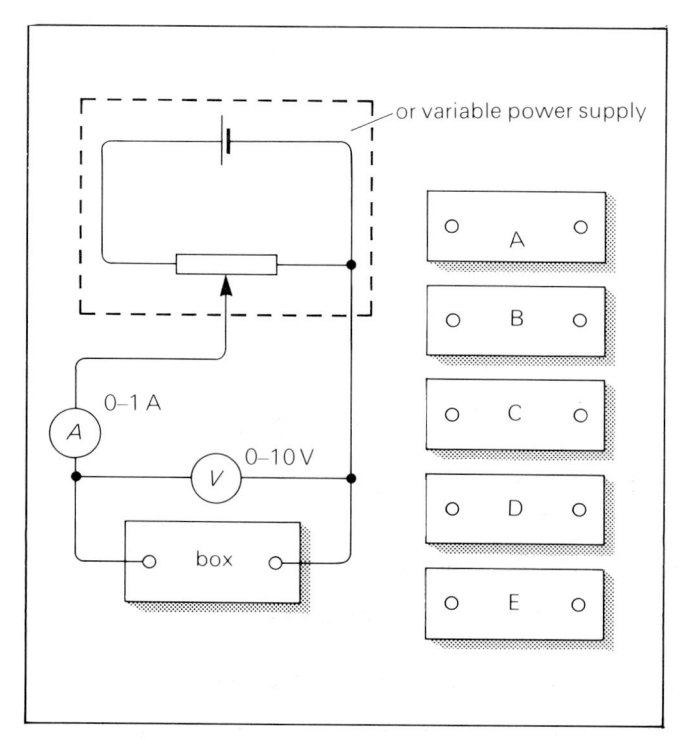

Figure 345 Circuit used

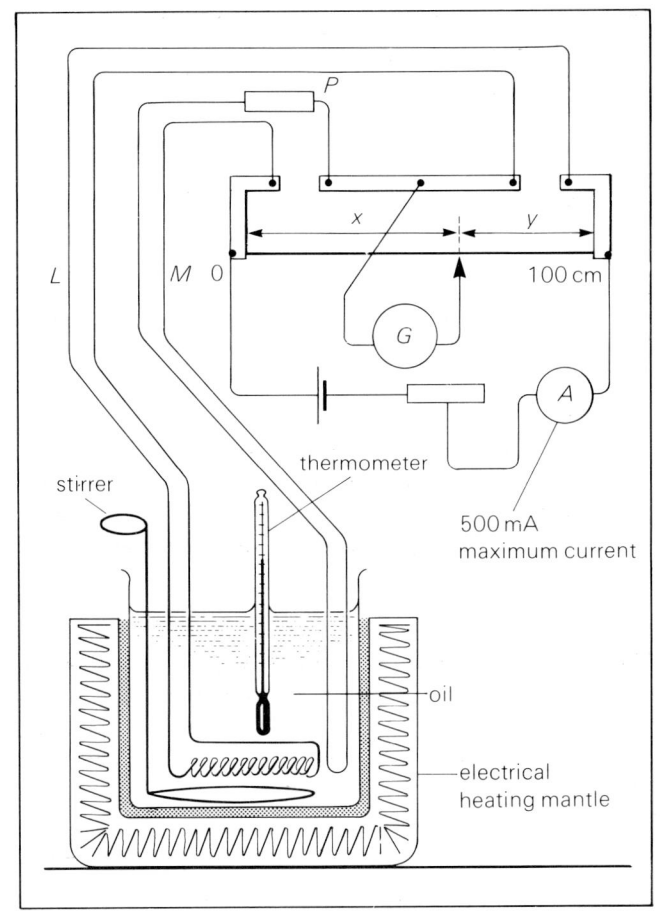

Figure 346 Equipment

1. Set the apparatus up as shown in figure 346, with the oil at room temperature. The connecting leads L and M are the same length and are to allow for any change of room temperature. The resistances of both arms of the bridge will change by exactly the same amount. Why is oil used as the liquid around the coil? Should the resistance coil ideally be non-inductively wound?

2. Choose a value for the standard resistor P so that the null balance point is near the centre of the wire. Measure distances x and y and work out the resistance of the coil R by $\dfrac{R}{P} = \dfrac{y}{x}$. Remember to give an error to the value of R.

3. Heat the oil by about 5°C and then switch off the heater. When the temperature is steady, find the null balance point and calculate the resistance and temperature.

4. Repeat in approximately 5°C steps up to about 100°C.

5. Plot a graph of resistance against temperature.

$$R = R_0(1 + \beta T) = R_0 + R_0\beta T.$$

Comparing with the equation for a straight line, $y = mx + c$, we see that the gradient is $R_0\beta$ and the intercept on the resistance axis R_0. Calculate the temperature coefficient of resistance β.

61. THERMOMETERS

1. CALIBRATION OF A THERMISTOR THERMOMETER AND ITS USE IN THE CONTROL OF TEMPERATURE

Outline

A thermistor is a component whose resistance decreases as the temperature increases. This change of resistance can be used to:

(a) change the current flow in a circuit, or
(b) the potential difference produced if the thermistor is used as part of a voltage divider.

In this experiment you will calibrate one design of thermistor thermometer against a mercury-in-glass thermometer, and from your results set up a device which will turn a lamp on when a given temperature is reached.

Experimental details

Calibration

Set up the apparatus as shown in figure 347, with the salt/ice/water solution, and record the reading on the voltmeter. Then place the thermistor in boiling water to check that the reading on the voltmeter is still on the scale. Adjust the variable resistor (v.r.) until you are satisfied with the range of reading produced between the melting ice solution and boiling water.

Place the thermistor back in the salt/ice/water solution and wait until the reading on the voltmeter is steady. (It may be interesting to find the response time for the thermistor to respond to a change of temperature and produce a new steady reading; in seconds per degree.) Record the readings on the voltmeter and the mercury thermometer. *Gently* warm the mixture, taking readings at regular intervals until it boils.

DEDUCTIONS, APPLICATIONS AND DATA ANALYSIS

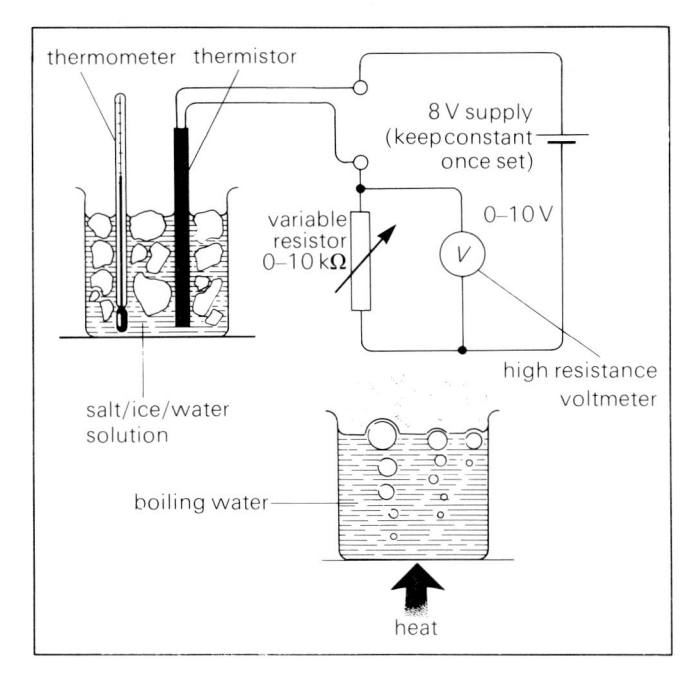

Figure 347 Equipment

Plot a graph of temperature against voltage. (*Think:* How many readings will you need? Stir to produce an even distribution of heat energy, so that the temperature in the beaker is uniform.)

Control of temperature
1. From the graph find the potential difference corresponding to a temperature of 50°C.
2. Set up the circuit shown in figure 348 with the 'black box' provided.

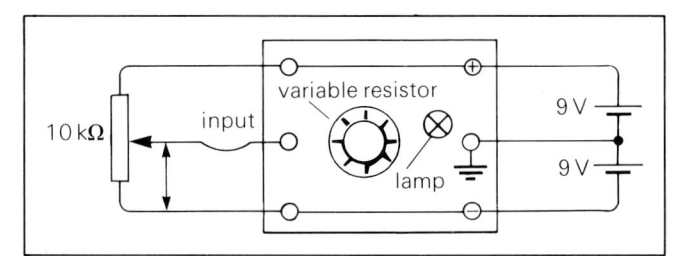

Figure 348 'Black box controller'

3. Use a high-resistance voltmeter to set the input voltage to the level that corresponds to 50°C (from the graph) by altering the 10 kΩ variable resistor.
4. Then alter the variable resistor on the box until the bulb just goes off. Any voltage that is higher should make the bulb turn on.
5. Replace the 10 kΩ variable resistor with the thermistor circuit (figure 349).
6. Place the thermistor in water and start heating. The bulb should be off and should go on when the temperature reaches about 50°C.

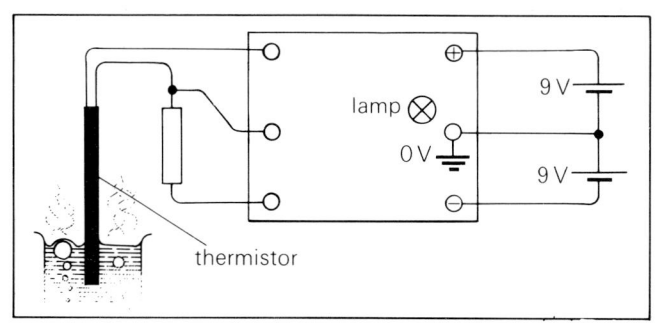

Figure 349 A thermostat

Questions
1. How accurate was your control device?
2. Did it operate at too high or too low a temperature?
3. How would you calibrate the dial of the variable resistor for a complete range of temperatures?

Information
The circuit in the box uses an operational amplifier and driver circuit. The output of the amplifier will switch from −8 V to +8 V when the voltage on input A, from the thermistor, becomes larger than the voltage from input B, set by the variable resistor.

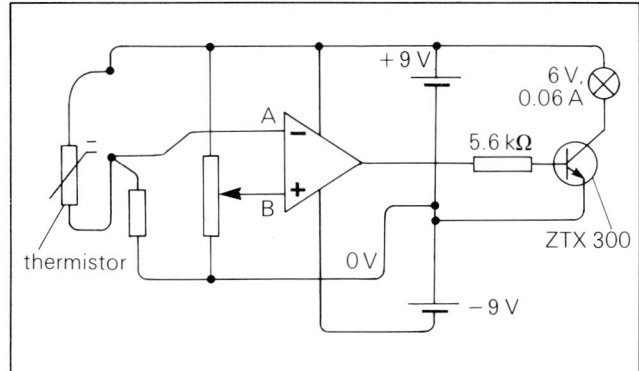

Figure 350 Circuit used in the 'black box'.

2. A THERMOMETER USING RESISTANCE WIRE

Outline

You are asked to design a resistance thermometer with a range between the temperature of solid CO_2 and boiling car-engine oil. You have no idea of the change of resistance produced by this temperature change, so some investigation is required. Once the change in resistance is known, the length and diameter of the resistance wire to be used can be chosen to give the maximum current change and the advisability of using a stabilised supply voltage decided.

Equipment

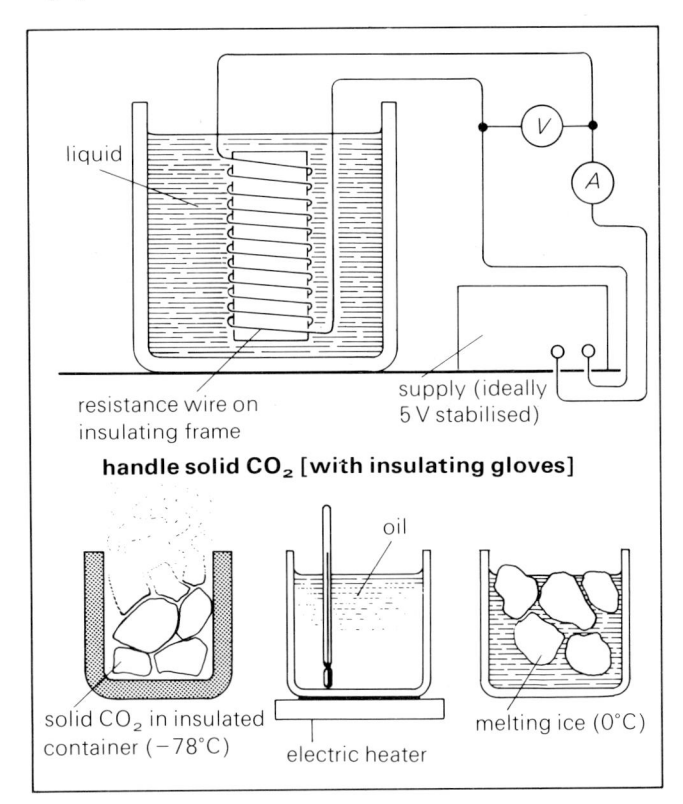

Figure 351

Experimental details

A suitable resistance wire to start with would be 34-gauge nichrome; 1 m of 34-gauge nichrome has a resistance of 25 Ω. If a 5 V supply is used, the current will be $\frac{5}{25} = 0.2$ A. A 500 mA f.s.d. ammeter would be suitable.

With your chosen type of wire repeat the experiment for a range of lengths and gauges and plot a calibration curve of current against temperature. What is the *sensitivity* in milliammeters per Kelvin of your gauge? What is your estimated accuracy ($\pm x$ mA K^{-1}) of the sensitivity?

Wind the resistance wire onto the frame. Assemble the apparatus and take measurements of voltage and current with frame immersed in:

1. solid CO_2 at an assumed temperature of $-78°C$;
2. melting ice at 0°C;
3. oil at 50°C;
4. boiling oil.

Calculate the resistance in each case. Find the resistance change, and the current change produced.

You have now to decide the length and gauge of wire to be used to produce the largest change of ammeter reading. A thinner and/or longer wire will give a larger change of resistance but lower currents, and vice versa.

Information for nichrome

Standard wire gauge	Resistance per metre/Ω m^{-1}
26	6.5
28	9.7
30	14
32	18.3
34	25.2
36	36.9
38	60

In your report

1. Give the results you recorded and the resistances calculated. Show how these lead you to the choice of wire length and size.
2. Give the range of the meter used.
3. Show results taken on your final instrument and the calibration graph.
4. State the sensitivity and accuracy of the instrument.
5. Find out and explain why practical resistance thermometers use a non-inductively wound coil and why a Wheatstone bridge circuit is used to measure the resistance.

62. LOGIC CIRCUITS AND LOGICAL CONTROL

Outline

Many control systems use logical elements or logic gates in their design. These can be electronic, using the flow of electrons, when they are called *digital electronics*. Another method, which is used industrially where electricity could be dangerous to use, is called *fluidics* and involves the flow of streams of air. Control systems have also more recently been coupled with the use of microprocessors. The three basic logic elements are the AND gate, the OR gate and the NOT or INVERT gate. All logical

DEDUCTIONS, APPLICATIONS AND DATA ANALYSIS

ideas are based on two states of input and output, 0 and 1. One (1) is circuit on, voltage present, or larger than a certain value. Zero (0) is circuit off, voltage zero or less than a certain value. In these experiments you are going to investigate each of these three logic gates and then use them together in control circuits.

Equipment

Any logic unit with AND, NOT and OR gates can be used. Ask your teacher to explain how to connect up the particular type of logic unit in your laboratory.

Experimental details

Connect up each logic circuit shown and verify their effects.

A. *The AND gate*

The AND gate gives a logical 1 output only if *all* inputs are logical 1. The combination of possible inputs and outputs can be shown in a *truth table* (below). Figure 352 illustrates a two-input AND gate.

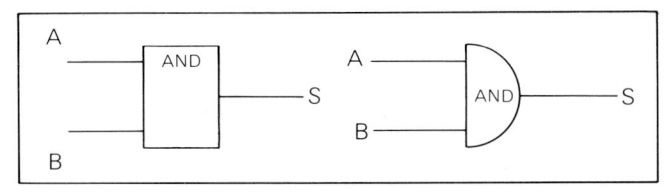

Figure 352 A two-input AND gate

A	B	S
0	0	0
0	1	0
1	0	0
1	1	1

B. *The OR gate*

The OR gate gives a logical 1 output if *any* input is logical 1 (see figure 353).

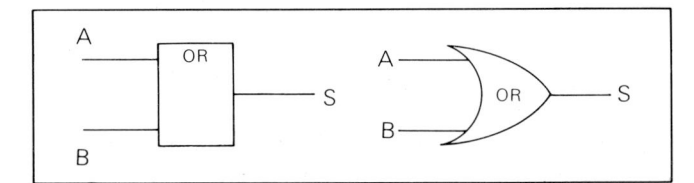

Figure 353 A two-input OR gate

A	B	S
0	0	0
0	1	1
1	0	1
1	1	1

C. *The NOT or INVERT gate*

In the NOT or INVERT gate, a logical 0 input gives a logical 1 output, while a logical 1 input gives a logical 0 output.

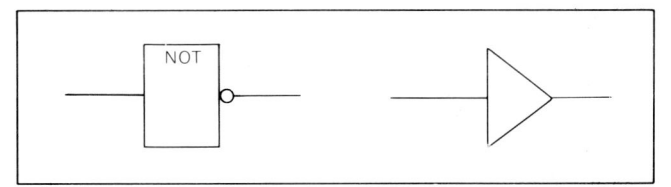

A	S
1	0
0	1

Figure 354 A NOT or INVERT gate

D. *Storing data—a latch*

A 0 or a 1 are sometimes called binary *bits*. Data which can be a binary number or some code can be represented by a series of bits. The logic circuit in figure 355 can store a two-bit code, i.e. 00 01 10 11.

Move the *reset* to 0 and then *back* to 1. This clears any previous data from the latch. Set the data to be stored on the inputs bit 1 and bit 2. Put a 1 on the *strobe* input and then put it back to 0. The data will appear on the lamps.

The inputs bit 1 and bit 2 can now be put back to 0 and the data will stay 'latched' on the lamps.

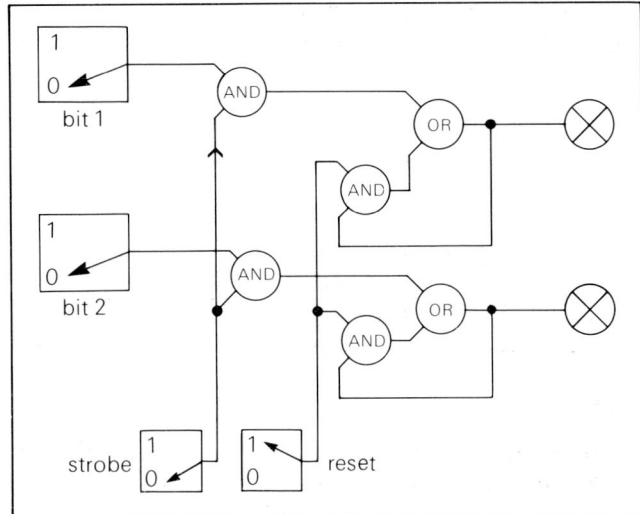

Figure 355 A latch

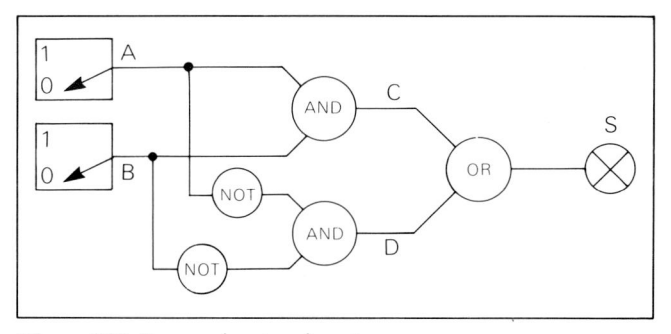

Figure 356 Comparing two inputs

E. *To compare two inputs and decide if they are the same*
Looking at figure 356, the output is a logical 1 only if A and B are the same. C will only be a logical 1 if A and B are both 1. D will only be a logical 1 if A and B are both 0, because the NOT gates will make both inputs to the AND gate logical 1. The OR gate will be logical 1 if either C or D is logical 1. Thus S will be a 1 if A and B are the same.

F. *Adding two binary bits*
Numbers (up to three) can be represented in binary, by 0 and 1, because the place values in binary are 8 4 2 1 instead of 100 10 1 as in decimal

binary	decimal
0 0	0
0 1	1
1 0	2
1 1	3

This means that:

1 and 0 input gives 0 1 output (1 + 0 = 1)
0 and 1 input gives 0 1 output (0 + 1 = 1)
0 and 0 input gives 0 0 output (0 + 0 = 0)
1 and 1 input gives 1 0 output (1 + 1 = 2)

This is called a *half-adder* circuit (figure 357).

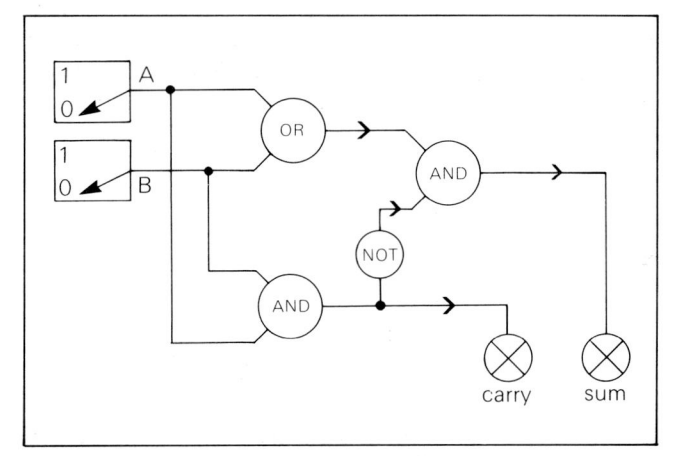

Figure 357 A half adder

G. *To operate a spin-drier only if the door is shut*
Input A: main switch on—logical 1
main switch off—logical 0
Input B: door shut—logical 1
door open—logical 0

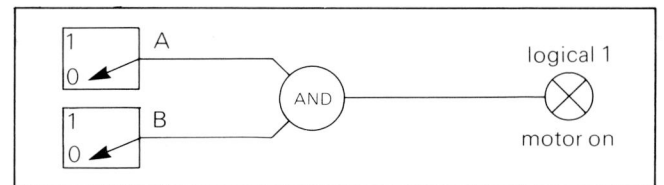

Figure 358

H. *Train signals—changing over from red to green*
Input—logical 0: output S1 logical 1 bulb on *red*
output S2 logical 0 bulb off *green*
Input—logical 1: output S1 logical 0 bulb off *red*
output S2 logical 1 bulb on *green*

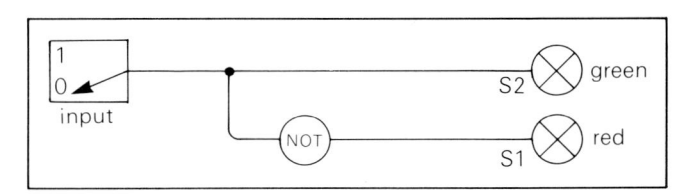

Figure 359

I. *To change a railway point automatically*
Looking at figure 360, the problem can be written as a series of conditions.

(a) If the train passes A *and* the point is to the branch, then change the point output to a 0.
(b) If the train passes B *and* the point is to the branch, then change the point output to a 0.
(c) If the train passes C *and* the point is to the main line, then change the point output to a 1 to change the point to the branch.

(See figure 361.)

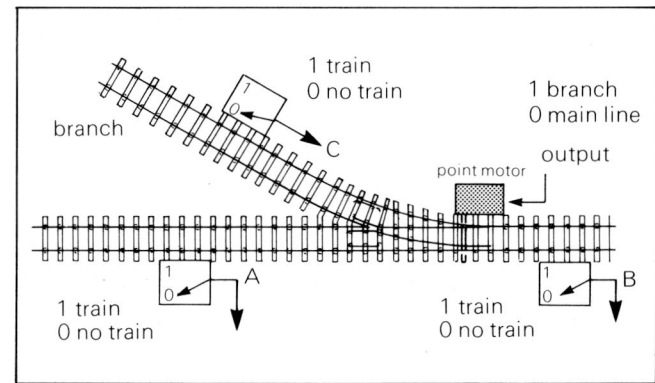

Figure 360

DEDUCTIONS, APPLICATIONS AND DATA ANALYSIS

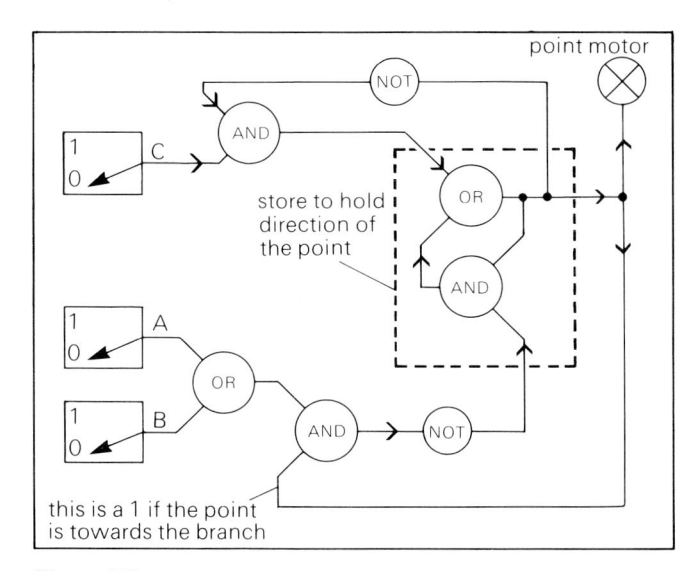

Figure 361

J. *To decode an 'address' from a microcomputer*

A microcomputer often has eight bits of data, and 16 bits which give the 'address' where the data is to be stored. Not all the addresses are taken up with internal memory locations and to control lights, motors, etc. With a computer one of the unused addresses is selected and used as a *port*. The logic circuit in figure 362 shows the

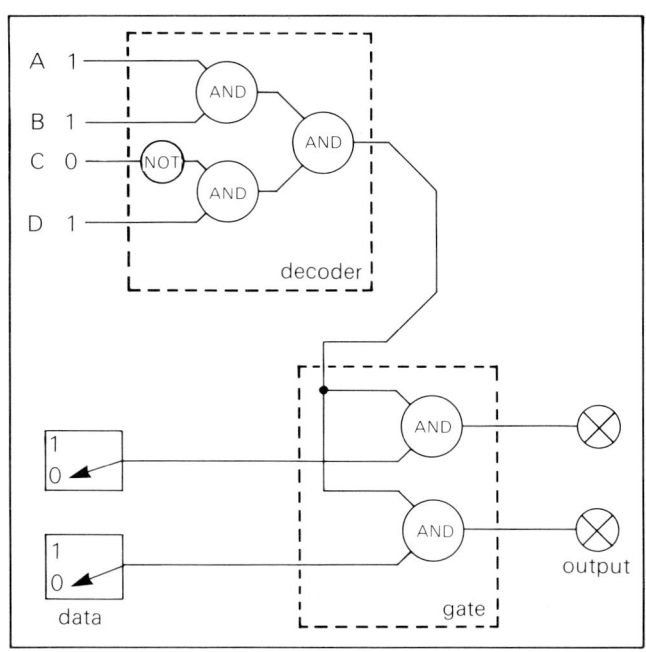

Figure 362

principle used by *decoding* a four-bit address so that two bits of data are *gated* to the output only when the particular 'address' is used. Suppose the unused address we select is 1101.

63. INVESTIGATIONS USING TTL 7400 NAND GATES AND A 7493 COUNTER

Outline

Transistor–transistor logic (TTL) is the basis behind a very widely used family of logic gates. They operate from a supply between 4.5 V and 5.5 V; so a 5 V stabilised supply is nearly always used. There are threshold voltages for each logical state. Typical values are:

logical 1 is any voltage > 2.0 V
logical 0 is any voltage < 0.8 V

The maximum current drawn by an input is 1.6 mA. The maximum current able to be drawn from the gate is 16 mA.

A one TTL load means something which draws no more than 1.6 mA. Up to ten TTL loads could be supplied, and this is called a *fan-out* of ten.

Any unconnected input to a gate is taken as logical 1, not logical 0. Logical 0 is produced by grounding an input. The circuits shown in figure 363 would be perfectly correct.

There are four two-INPUT gates in the package shown in figure 364 and 14 pin connections. The truth table below shows the output produced for all possible combinations of input for the NAND gate shown, with inputs A and B and output C.

A	B	C
0	0	1
0	1	1
1	0	1
1	1	0

This practical shows how AND, OR and NOT gates and latches can be made from NAND gates.

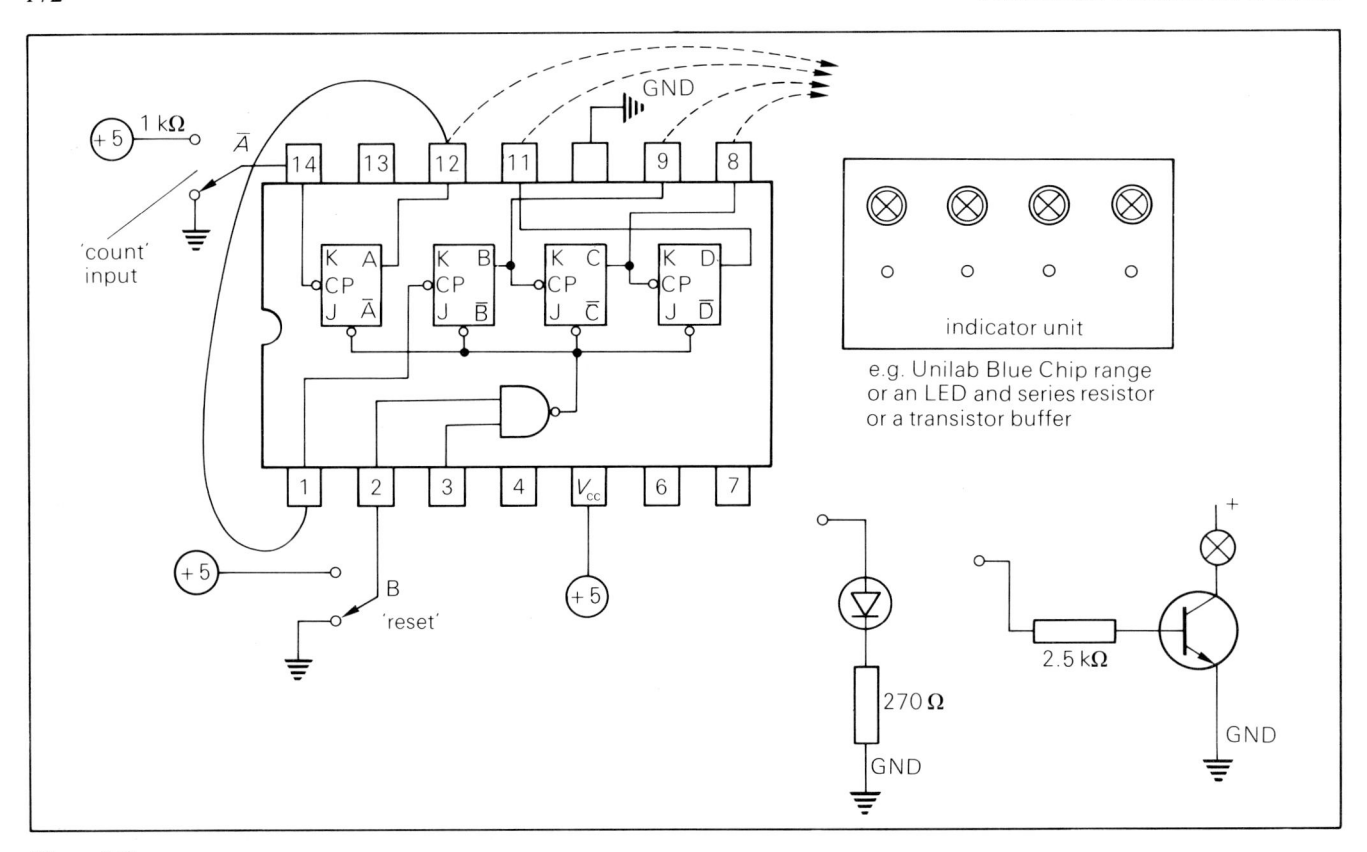

Figure 371

(a) Set up the circuit (figure 371). You may need to connect pins 1 and 12 if this is not already done for you.
(b) Find out the effect of the reset input B and whether the counter is reset for a logical 0 or a logical 1.
(c) Find out if the chip 'counts' when the input A changes from a logical 1 to a logical 0 or a logical 0 to a logical 1. What is the disadvantage of using a mechanical switch to provide the count pulses?
(d) Find out the correct order of the outputs so that the indicator display counts up in binary, i.e.

$$0\ 0\ 0\ 0$$
$$0\ 0\ 0\ 1$$
$$0\ 0\ 1\ 0$$
$$0\ 0\ 1\ 1\quad \text{etc.}$$

(e) Use two NAND gates to overcome any problems of switch bounce on the count input.
(f) If the counter is required to reset after a certain number, this can be done by using the output to operate the *reset*, e.g. to reset after 7 (i.e. on the eighth pulse) when the output would be 1000. Use two NAND gates. (See figure 372.)

The circuit in figure 373 could be used to reset after 1, 3 or 7. Any other number would need a decoding circuit, for example, to decode after 5 (i.e. when the output is 6).

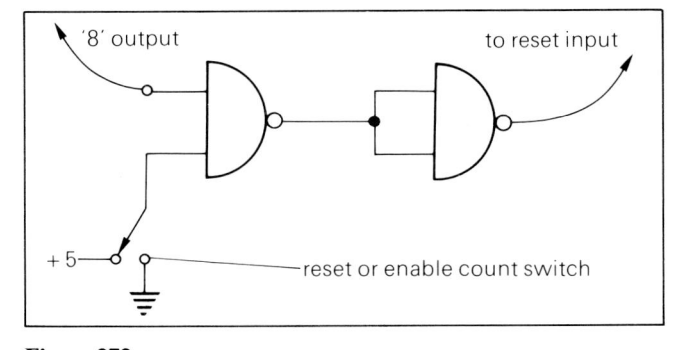

Figure 372

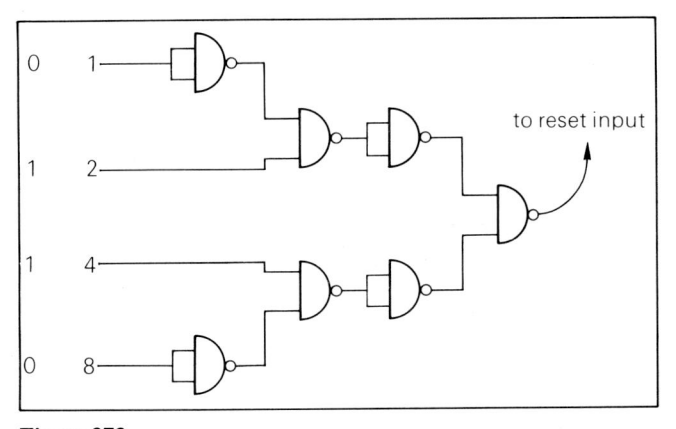

Figure 373

DEDUCTIONS, APPLICATIONS AND DATA ANALYSIS

In your report

1. Summarise your results and conclusions about the ranges of input voltages for logical 1 and for logical 0 and also the maximum resistor values.
2. Draw a diagram to show how, when a switch is open, an input of 1 is achieved and, when the switch is closed, logical 0 results.
3. Show the truth table for a NAND gate.
4. Show AND, OR, and NOT gates made from NAND gates.
5. Draw the logic diagrams of the circuits you have made from NAND gates.
6. Summarise your investigations using the counter chip.

64. PNEUMATIC CONTROL

Outline

The use of air pressure to produce linear movement by moving pistons in cylinders is a common industrial means of producing force. This practical introduces you to some of the main ideas. The pneumatics kit from the 'Control Technology' course is used. Your teacher will show you how to connect the parts together. Work through the experiments in order and read the information given.

The basic valves
The basic valve (figure 374) has two positions: either connecting the cylinder to the air supply or to the open air at the exhaust.

Single-acting cylinder
In the single-acting cylinder (figure 375) air pressure forces the piston out, and the spring returns it when the air supply is removed.

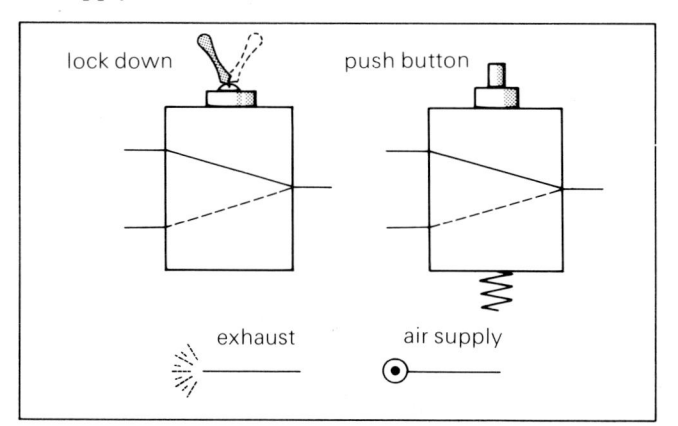

Figure 374 Basic valves

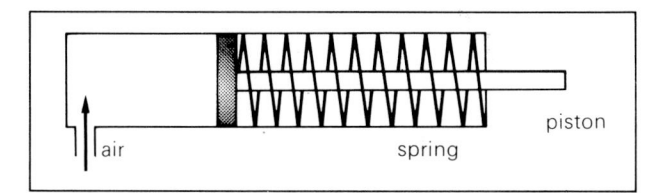

Figure 375 Single-acting cylinder

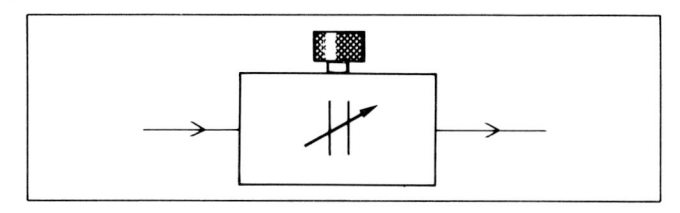

Figure 376 Slow-release valve

Slow-release valve
The slow-release valve (figure 376) produces a restriction, so altering the rate of flow of air through it.

1. THE SINGLE-ACTING CYLINDER

Connect up the arrangement shown in figure 377. The speed of piston return can be altered by adjusting the slow-release valve. Alter the arrangement so that it is operated (a) whenever one of two valves is pressed and (b) only if both of two valves are pressed at the same time.

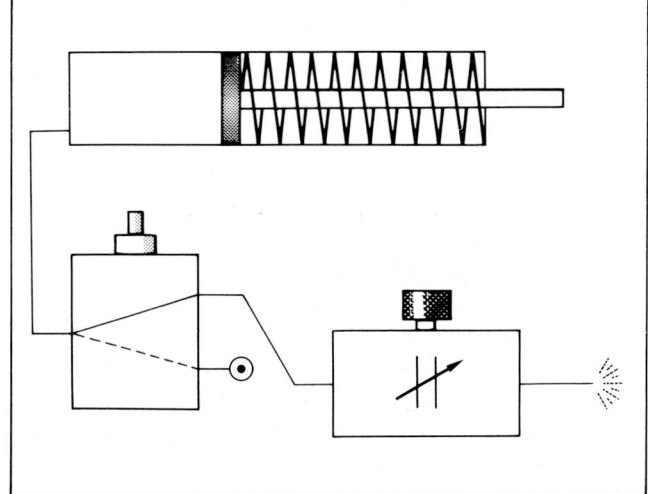

Figure 377

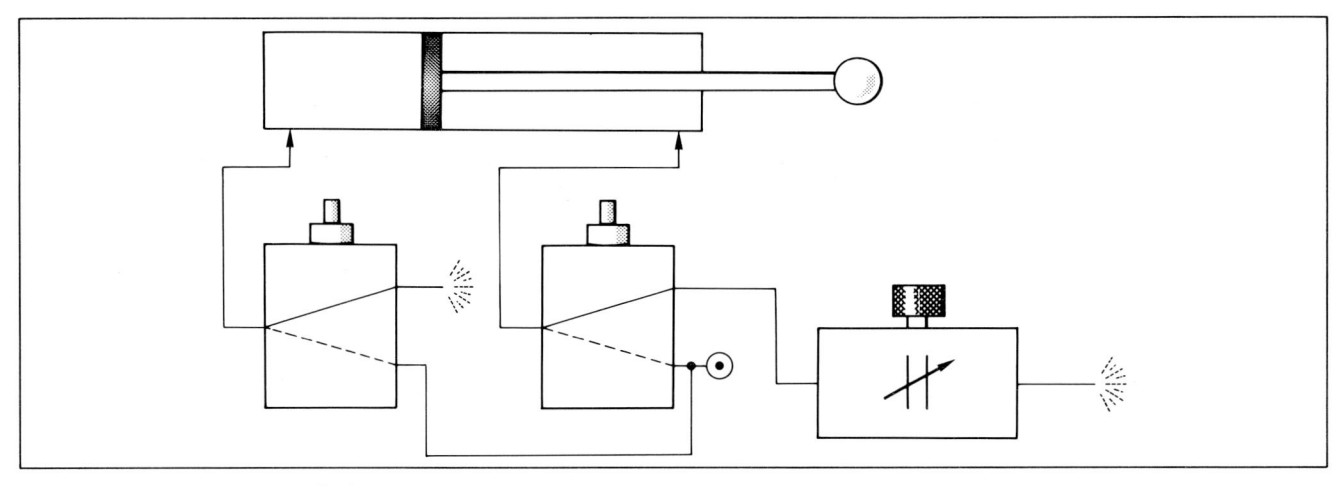

Figure 378 Double-acting cylinder

2. THE DOUBLE-ACTING CYLINDER

The arrangement shown in figure 378 uses two push-button valves and a double-acting cylinder. The piston can be moved backwards and forwards by using each valve in turn. Find the effect of adjusting the slow release valve.

Can you explain what happens when both valves are pressed at the *same* time with the piston (a) in the out position and (b) in the in position?

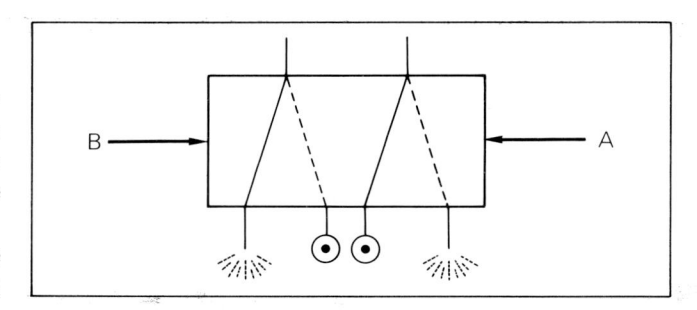

Figure 379 Pilot operated valve

3. USING AN AIR-OPERATED CHANGEOVER VALVE

An air-operated changeover valve is operated by a pulse of air. As shown in figure 379, when there is pressure on one output (from the air supply), the other is connected to the exhaust. A pulse of air on B will change the valves over and a subsequent pulse of air on A will change them back again. The advantage of this over the circuit in figure 378 is that the movement of the piston itself can be used to trigger its own return (figure 380).

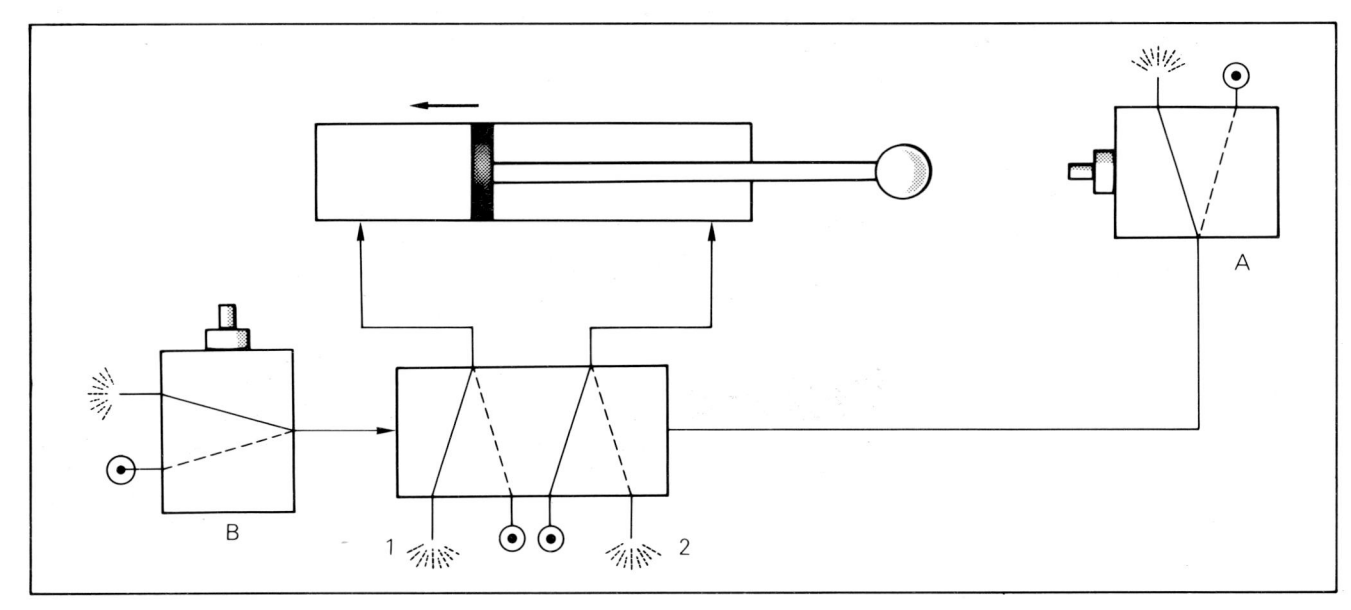

Figure 380

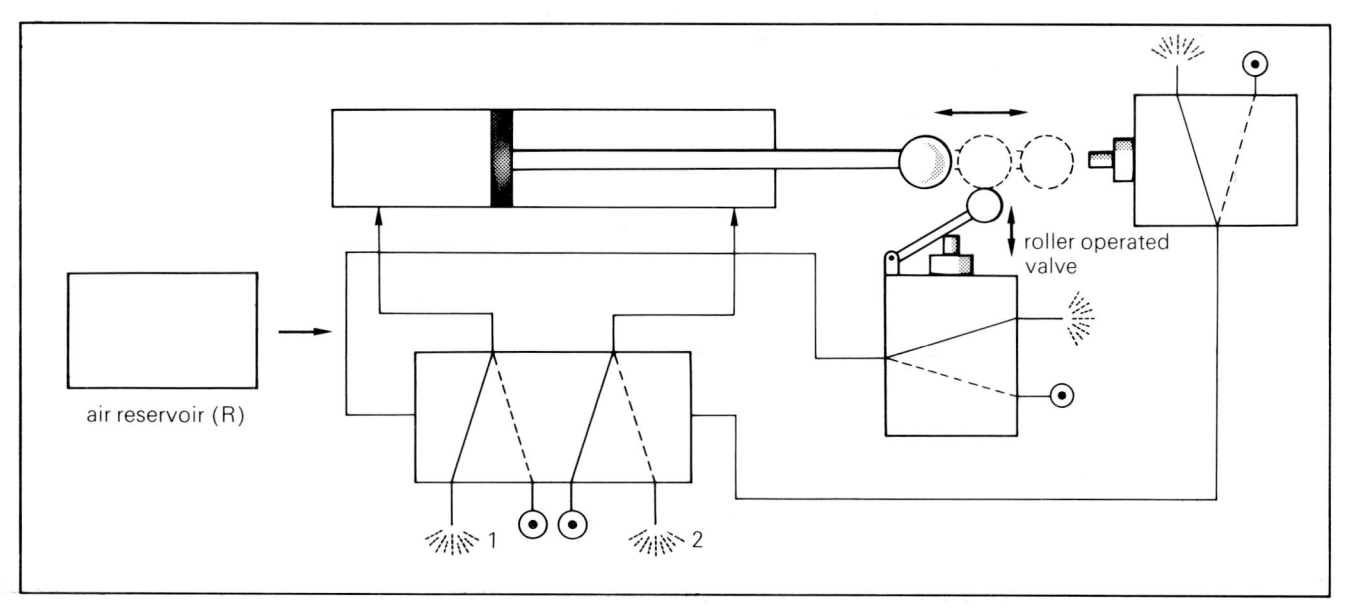

DEDUCTIONS, APPLICATIONS AND DATA ANALYSIS 175

Figure 381

On pressing the push valve B, the cylinder and piston will move because the valve has changed over. When the piston hits valve A, the changeover valve is moved back and the piston returns.

Experiment to find the effect of using a slow-release valve on the exhaust outputs 1 and 2.

This type of circuit might be used in an automatic drilling machine.

4. OSCILLATING MOVEMENT

The piston can be made to move backwards and forwards continuously if the valve B, in figure 380, is replaced by a *roller-operated valve* which is moved as the piston passes it (figure 381).

Investigate the effects of connecting a slow-release valve to the exhaust ports 1 and 2, and also the effect of connecting the air reservoir R into any of the lines.

5. AN APPLICATION

Imagine that you have to design a system to let water out of a canal lock automatically when a boat reaches the bottom gate. Some of the possible places for putting valves are shown in figure 382. Design a suitable circuit and explain how it would work. Now extend the system to

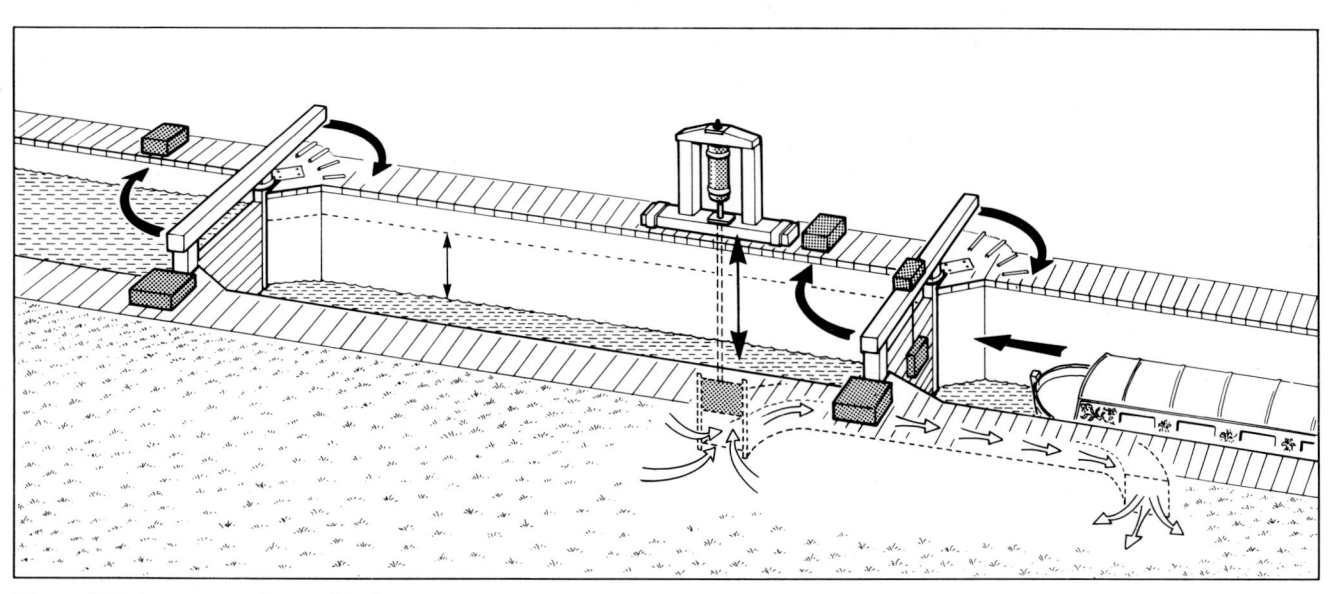

Figure 382 An automatic canal lock.

make the lock fill automatically when the boat is inside, so that it can leave by the gate at the top end of the lock.

Write a general report on what you have done, with descriptions of the circuits made, what they did, and *how* they operated. Describe any extra things you have found out. Describe your design for the canal lock.

65. INTERNAL RESISTANCE AND KIRCHHOFF'S LAWS

Outline

Every source of e.m.f. has an internal resistance. This practical measures the internal resistance of a dry cell and investigates the relationship between the internal resistance and the resistance of the load for maximum power transfer.

You have probably already investigated the rule for currents at a junction and found the rule that 'total current flowing in equals total current flowing out' and also found that the total voltage drop round a circuit equals the e.m.f. These rules are summarised as Kirchhoff's laws.

1. The algebraic sum of the currents at a junction is zero.
2. Round any closed loop the sum of the voltage drops equals the sum of the e.m.f.s: $\Sigma IR = \Sigma E$

In this practical, a dry cell is used in a simple experiment to see how well experimental results agree with the values predicted by Kirchhoff's laws.

1. MEASURING THE INTERNAL RESISTANCE OF A CELL

Equipment

A very high resistance voltmeter is needed, because at some stage the e.m.f. of the cell will be needed, and this is the 'open circuit' potential difference when no current flows. A potentiometer is the conventional choice for a voltmeter since, when a null balance point is found, *no* current flows. However, a digital voltmeter could be used or an operational amplifier used to increase the input resistance to a moving-coil meter. The potentiometer is slower and more complex to operate, but supposedly more accurate. It would be interesting to compare the accuracy of each method of measuring potential difference.

The resistor R must be capable of dissipating at least 1 W. A 0–100 Ω decade resistance box or separate resistors could be used.

Experimental details

1. Set up the apparatus as shown in figure 383, with either the operational amplifier and moving coil meter or potentiometer.
2. Open switch S and measure the e.m.f. (E) of the battery.
3. Close switch S and measure the potential difference (V) across the resistor R for values of R in the range 0.5–20 Ω.

If the current flowing through the resistor R is I, then

$E = I(R + r)$ and $V = IR$.

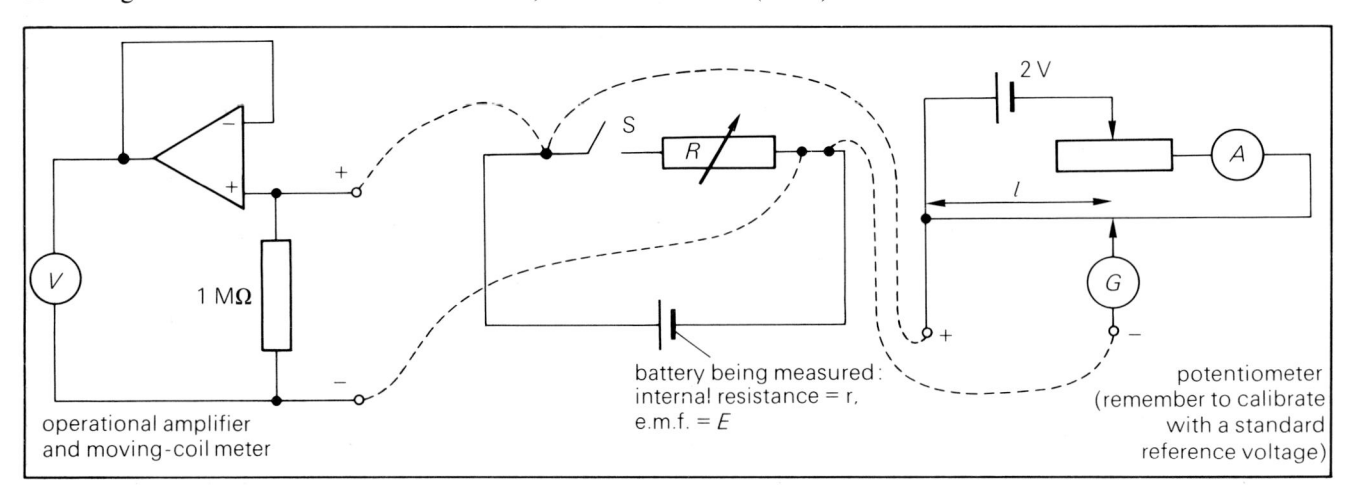

Figure 383

DEDUCTIONS, APPLICATIONS AND DATA ANALYSIS

Thus:

$$E = \frac{V}{R}(R+r) = V + \frac{Vr}{R}$$

$$\therefore \frac{E-V}{V} = \frac{r}{R}$$

$$\frac{E}{rV} - \frac{V}{rV} = \frac{1}{R}$$

$$\frac{E}{rV} - \frac{1}{R} = \frac{1}{R}$$

Rearranging gives:

$$\frac{1}{R} = \frac{E}{rV} - \frac{1}{r}$$

Plotting a graph of $\frac{1}{R}$ as ordinate and $\frac{1}{V}$ as abscissa should give a straight-line graph of gradient $\frac{E}{r}$ and negative intercept on the $\frac{1}{R}$ axis of $\frac{1}{r}$. Find a value for the internal resistance (r).

2. MAXIMUM POWER TRANSFER

Experimental details

Using the circuit shown in figure 384, start with the load at zero ohms. Record the load resistance and the readings on the voltmeter and ammeter. Work out the power being delivered to the load ($P = VI$). Increase the resistance to its maximum in $1\,\Omega$ steps and record the above readings each time.

Question

How can you be sure that the *variable* resistor has been increased by exactly $1\,\Omega$, or would it be better to use ten $1\,\Omega$ resistors?

Results

Load resistance/Ω	Current/A	Potential difference/V	Power/W

Plot a graph of power against load resistance. From it find the load resistance for maximum power transfer. How is this related to the internal resistance of the supply?

The equation for the power is $P = \frac{E^2 R}{(r+R)^2}$ and the computer program 'POWER' (package PHYS1 option 2) is available for you to investigate the power delivered to the load for other e.m.f.s, internal resistances and ranges of load resistance.

In your report

Write a summary of your findings, with results and graphs. Show how this information leads to your conclusions.

3. INVESTIGATING KIRCHHOFF'S LAWS

Use fresh 1.5 V dry cell batteries and make up a circuit similar to the one in figure 385. Resistors in the range $1\,\Omega$ to $6\,\Omega$ are suitable. Measure the current flowing at points (a), (b) and (c). Now use Kirchhoff's laws with the value for the internal resistance you have already measured and calculate the currents I_1, I_2 and I_3.

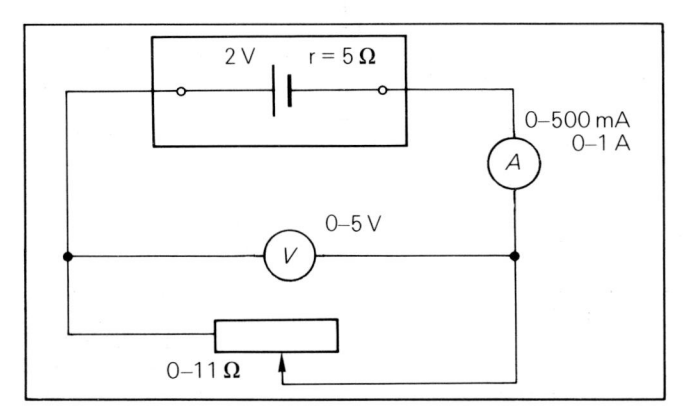

Figure 384

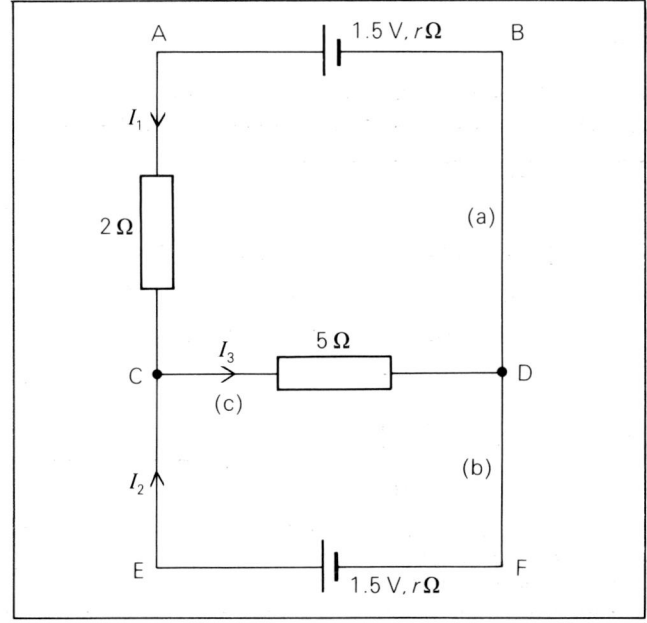

Figure 385

For the circuit shown:

in loop ACDB $\quad 1.5 = 2I_1 + rI_1$
in loop CDFE $\quad 1.5 = 5I_3 + rI_2$
at junction C $\quad I_1 + I_2 = I_3$

There are three unknowns and three equations. Solve for I_1, I_2 and I_3.

How well do your experimental values agree with the values from Kirchhoff's laws? Think in particular about:

(a) the effect of any resistance of the ammeter;
(b) the accuracy to which you know the e.m.f. of the cells;
(c) the accuracy of the resistors to their marked values.

66. ELECTRIC FIELD PATTERNS

Outline

An electric field produces a force on any charged particle placed in it. Using grains of semolina floating in a non-conducting liquid, these field line patterns can be seen in a similar way to the use of iron filings with magnetic fields.

A positively-charged particle experiences a force in the direction of the field. It follows that there should be no force acting along a direction 90° to a field line, and that if a charge is moved in this direction *no* work will be done and there will be *no* change in potential energy. The line mapped out in this way would be called an *equipotential* line. In particular, any metal surface with static charge on it must be an equipotential, otherwise charge would move along the surface.

This practical investigates the shape of the field patterns produced by different shapes and arrangements of electrodes and attempts to draw equipotential lines on these patterns. It is possible to work out the electric field and potential at any given point, but the only charges on which calculation can easily be done are point charges. The total electric field must be found using the parallelogram of vectors (figure 386).

The *electric field* due to a point charge is:

$$E = \frac{Q}{4\pi\varepsilon R^2}$$

$$\therefore E_1 = \frac{Q}{4\pi\varepsilon R_1^2}$$

and

$$E_2 = \frac{Q_2}{4\pi\varepsilon R_2^2}$$

The total electric field at point P

$$= \sqrt{(E_1 \cos y + E_2 \cos x)^2 + (E_1 \sin y + E_2 \cos x)^2}$$

and the angle θ it makes with the line joining the two charges is found from

$$\tan \theta = \frac{(E_1 \sin y + E_2 \sin x)}{(E_1 \cos y + E_2 \cos x)}$$

The potential due to a point charge is $V = \dfrac{Q}{4\pi\varepsilon R}$ and is a scalar (energy). The total potential at P is

$$V = \frac{Q_1}{4\pi\varepsilon R_1} + \frac{Q_2}{4\pi\varepsilon R_2}$$

The computer program 'EQUIPOT' (package PHYS3 option 1) uses these equations and allow you to investigate the equipotential line patterns produced by two point charges. The patterns can be traced from the screen using an acetate sheet and fine felt-tipped pens, or a copy can be produced on a suitable printer.

Experimental details

1. Set up the apparatus as shown in figure 387. The ends of the wires connected to the e.h.t. supply become charged. These charges are difficult to calculate, since the capacitance of the wire and its surroundings are not known ($Q = CV$). Start with the two wires as electrodes, which produce point charges. Use a potential difference of about 2000 V. **Take care using this high voltage.**

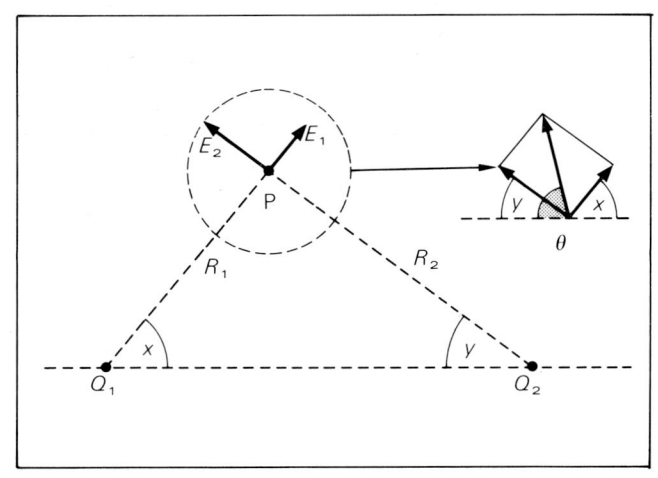

Figure 386 There is a resultant field at P.

DEDUCTIONS, APPLICATIONS AND DATA ANALYSIS

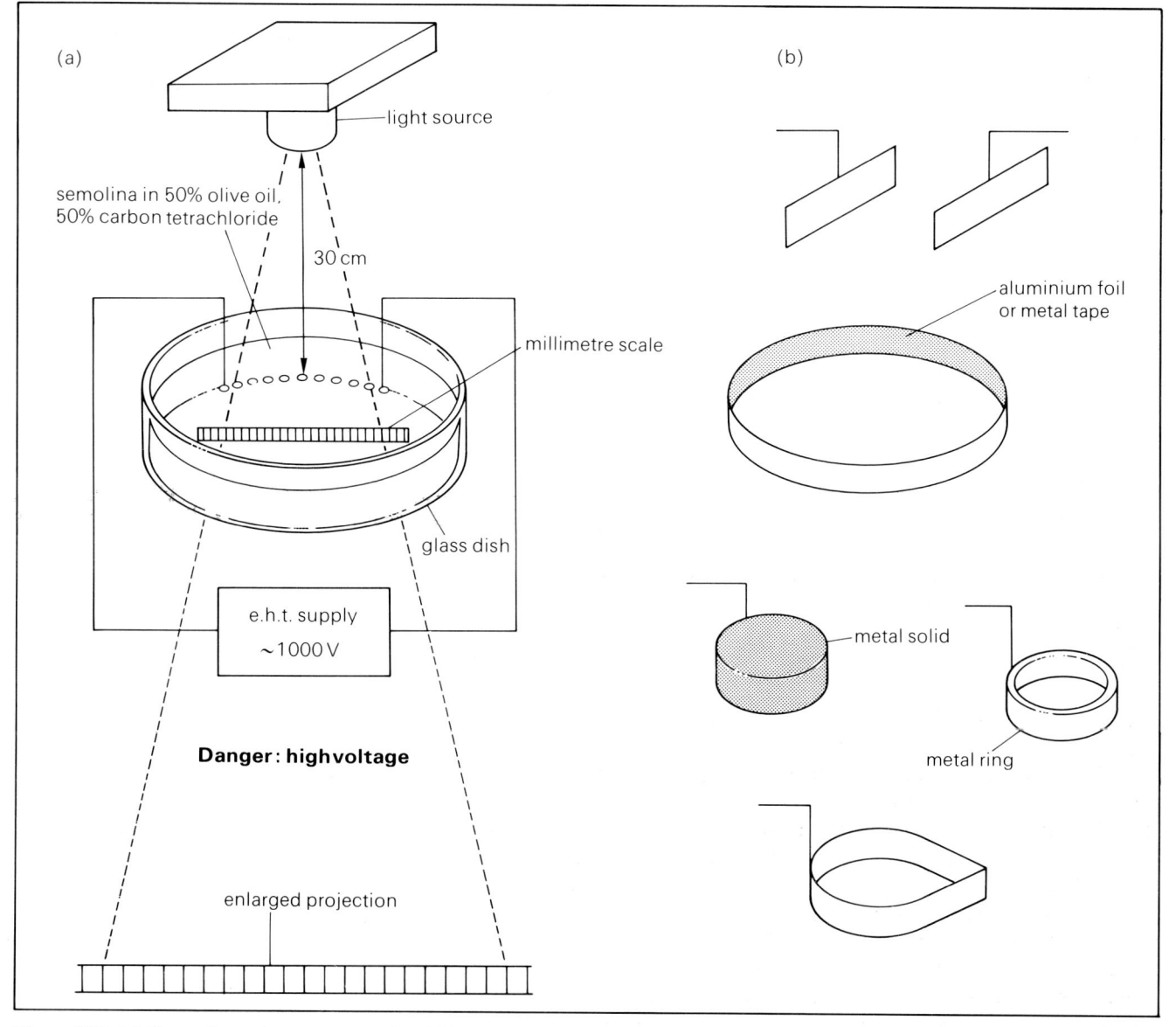

179

Figure 387 (a) Shows how the apparatus should be set up, while (b) shows the various types of electrode which can be used.

2. Project the field pattern onto the paper. Draw on the positions of the wires and the shape of the field pattern (figure 388a). Do not forget the scale.

3. If you have used the computer program, place the acetate sheet on the paper, move the lamp up or down until the positions of the wires coincide, and compare the shapes of the patterns.

4. Choose any starting point on a field line. Draw a line at 90° to the field line. Follow this through to the next field line, and so on, imagining the points drawn up with a smooth curve (figure 388b).

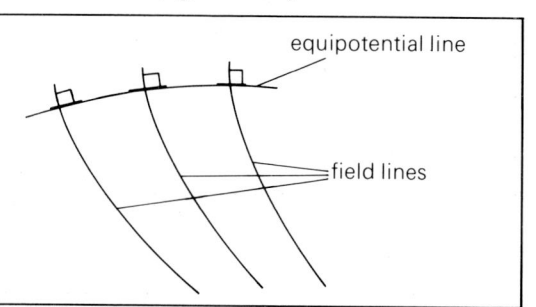

Figure 388

5. Repeat the process for the other electrode arrangements which you have available. One of the first to try is the point charges (plain wire electrodes, as before) with the same sign of charge instead of opposite charges. Use the dish with the metal tape on its sides (figure 389).
6. Use the computer program 'EQUIPOT' (package PHYS3 option 1) to investigate the shape of the electric field patterns and equipotential line patterns produced by two point charges. You are able to:

    (a) change the size of the charges;
    (b) change the sign of any charge;
    (c) change the separation of the charges.

    Record a selection of the patterns produced and comment on any observations you can make.

Figure 390 illustrates other electrode arrangements which can be used.

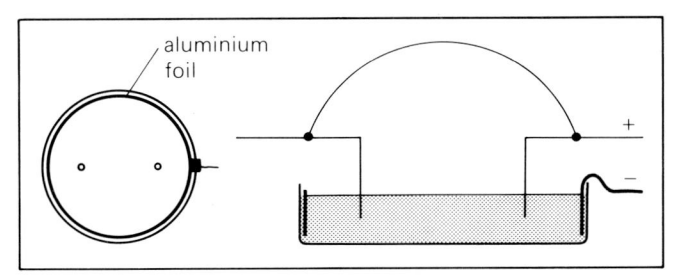

Figure 389

In your report

1. Include diagrams and sketches of the field patterns for the various arrangements.
2. Show equipotential lines on the field patterns produced by two point charges.
3. Summarise answers to the following questions and problems.

    (a) Do field lines always meet a metal surface at 90°?
    (b) Is the electric field larger near a sharp point?
    (c) How can a parallel field be produced?
    (d) How could equipment be shielded from electric fields?
    (e) What is meant by a radial field?
    (f) What is the most striking feature visible which would show if two electrodes had the same or opposite charges?

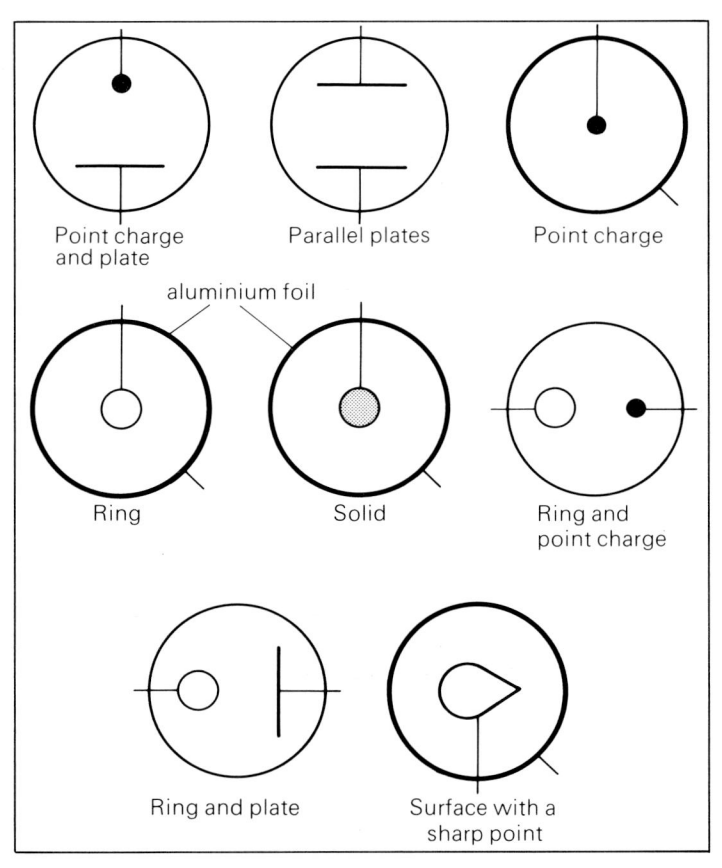

Figure 390 Other electrode arrangements which can be used.

67. ELECTRICAL FORCES

Outline

You already know the qualitative rule that like charges repel and unlike charges attract.

Coulomb suggested that the force between two point charges is proportional to:

$$\frac{\text{charge 1} \times \text{charge 2}}{(\text{distance apart})^2}.$$

We write this as:

$$F = \frac{Q_1 Q_2}{4\pi\varepsilon r^2}$$

where $Q_1 Q_2$ = charges/C
r = distance between charges/m
ε = the permittivity of the medium/F m^{-1}

Electric field is measured as the force per unit charge It is measured in newtons per coulomb (or in V m^{-1}). The field between two parallel plates is:

$$\text{electric field } (E) = \frac{\text{potential difference}}{\text{separation}}$$

and the force (F) on a point charge (Q) is $F = EQ$.
This experiment investigates both these relationships.

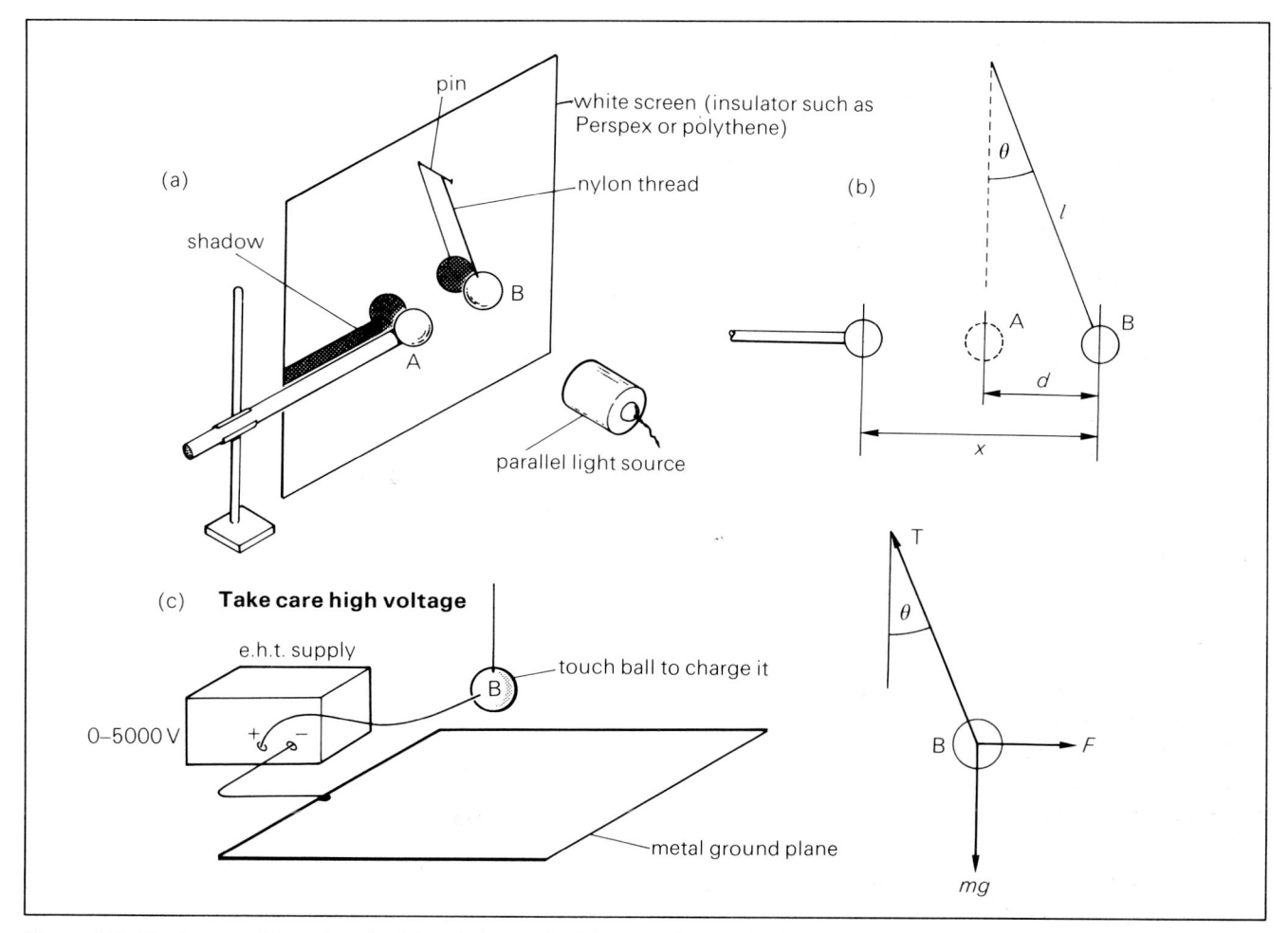

Figure 391 Equipment. There is a fixed insulating rod with a metal-coated polystyrene sphere (A) fixed to the end. B is a similar sphere fastened to an insulating nylon thread so that it can move.

1. TWO SMALL CHARGES

From figure 391b:
resolving vertically, $T \cos \theta = mg$;
resolving horizontally, $T \sin \theta = F$.

Combining these two equations gives $\tan \theta = \dfrac{F}{mg}$.

If θ is small, i.e. less than 20°, we can use the rule for small angles 'angle θ in radian $\simeq \tan \theta$' because the agreement is within the range of probable error for the experiment (see the table below):

$$F = mg \tan \theta \simeq \frac{mgd}{l} \text{ if angle } \theta \text{ is small}$$

$$\therefore F \propto d$$

Force is proportional to displacement from the vertical.

$\theta/°$	θ/rad	$\tan \theta$	Error/%
0	0	0	0
5	0.0873	0.0875	0.2
10	0.1745	0.1763	1
15	0.2618	0.2679	2.2
20	0.3491	0.3640	4.2

Experimental details

1. The whole experiment must be done quickly, in about five minutes (why?).
2. Using the apparatus in figure 391a, attach ball B on its thread to the pin. Allow it to come to rest and mark its position on the paper behind.
3. Charge each ball separately, using an e.h.t. supply at about 2000 to 3000 V, as shown in figure 391c.
4. Move the fixed ball A towards B and mark on the positions of the two balls over a series of steps until the angle θ is a maximum of 20° (it may not be possible to reach 20°). Be as quick as you can and repeat if necessary.
5. From the paper, measure the distances x and d. The force of repulsion is proportional to d. The Coulomb law of force is:

$$\text{force} \propto \frac{1}{(\text{distance apart})^2}$$

so a graph of d against $\dfrac{1}{x^2}$ should be a straight line through the origin. Plot a graph and decide if your results support the law or not.

2. FIELD BETWEEN TWO PARALLEL PLATES

Equipment

Instead of the fixed charge A, set up an arrangement of two parallel metal plates (figure 392).

Experimental details

1. Charge the ball by the same method used in the previous experiment, and suspend it from the pin by its thread. Mark the rest position of the ball, with no electric field applied.
2. Apply a voltage and steadily increase it to find the value needed to produce a deflection of about 15°. From this upper limit, decide on a convenient voltage step size which will give about five readings.
3. Recharge the ball. Start with a voltage of zero and mark the position of the ball for a series of applied voltages, increasing by the step size decided on.
4. Repeat for other separations of the plates, remembering to charge the ball at the *same* voltage each time (since the force due to the field on the ball is proportional to the charge on the ball).

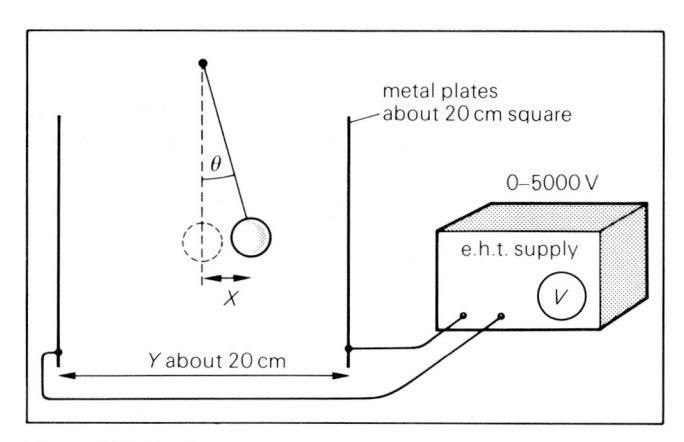

Figure 392 Equipment

Results

Tabulate your results as shown below.

From the results

If $E = \dfrac{V}{y}$ and $F = EQ$, then a graph of electric field E against 'force' x should be a straight line through the origin. Decide if your results verify the relationships or not.

Applied potential difference/V	Plate separation y/m	Electric field E/V m^{-1} or N C^{-1}	'Force' $\propto$ distance x/m

68. OPTICAL INSTRUMENTS

These practicals look at the construction and use of the camera, the astronomical telescope and the microscope. You are given practice at adjusting the instruments and observing the images produced.

1. CAMERA

The film in a camera requires a certain amount of light energy to 'expose' an image. The amount of light reaching the film is adjusted by the combined use of:

(a) the iris or aperture, which alters the size of hole in front of the lens, and
(b) the shutter, which opens and closes, determining the time of the exposure.

You probably already know that the position of the lens is adjusted either forwards or backwards to produce

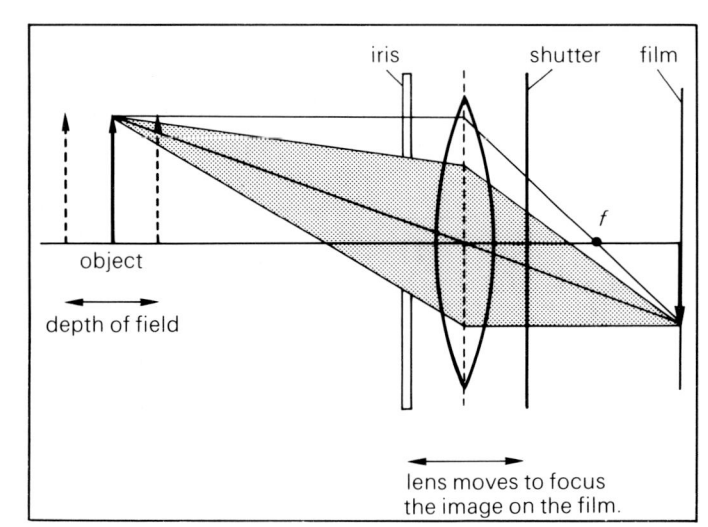

Figure 393 Camera

a sharp image of the object on the screen. Objects placed within a certain range produce acceptably sharp images. This practical looks at the effect of the iris size or f number on the depth of field. The f number has a connection with the area of lens open to light in that moving from one f number to the next alters the intensity of light falling on the film by a factor of 2.

Equipment

The *object* is an illuminated gauze in a hole approximately 1 or 2 cm in diameter.
The *lens* should have a maximum focal length of 10 cm.
The *iris* should open to the maximum diameter of the lens, or you could use a set of cards with holes in them.
The *film* is a white screen.
The shutter is not included.
Assemble the apparatus as shown in figure 393.

Experimental details

Choose an object to image distance of the maximum your apparatus allows.

1. Move the lens so that the best sharp image is formed, with the largest aperture. Record the object–image distance.
2. Move the object and find the maximum and minimum distances for which you judge the image to be acceptably sharp. Record these. The difference between these two distances is the *depth of field*.

Repeat the procedure for at least five other apertures and for smaller object–image distances.

Results

Plot two 'families' of graphs, as follows.

1. On one sheet plot depth of field against f number or hole area; one curve for each object–image distance.
2. On another sheet plot depth of field against object–image distance; one curve for each aperture size.

Conclusions

From the graphs make conclusions and observations on the way the depth of field alters with size of aperture and with distance of the object from the camera.

2. ASTRONOMICAL TELESCOPE

Refracting telescope

1. Set up the objective and eyepiece lenses with the separation of the lenses equal to the sum of their focal lengths. This is the condition for normal adjustment, with the rays to the eye parallel.
   The angular magnification

$$= \frac{\text{angle subtended by the final image to the eye}}{\text{angle subtended by the object directly to the eye}}$$

If the object distance is large compared to the distance of the objective from the eye (in practice >100 m or so),

$$\text{apparent magnification} = \frac{\beta}{\alpha}$$

$$\tan \alpha = \frac{h}{f_o}$$

If angles are less than 5°

$$\alpha = \frac{h}{f_o}$$

$$\tan \beta = \frac{h}{f_e}$$

Because the telescope is in normal adjustment

$$\beta = \frac{h}{f_e}$$

$$\therefore \text{apparent or angular magnification} = \frac{h/f_e}{h/f_o} = \frac{f_o}{f_e}$$

2. Work out the apparent or angular magnification for the lenses given you. The brightness and area of the

Diameter of aperture mm	Sharp object–image distance/cm	Max. and min. distance/cm
20	90	95, 85

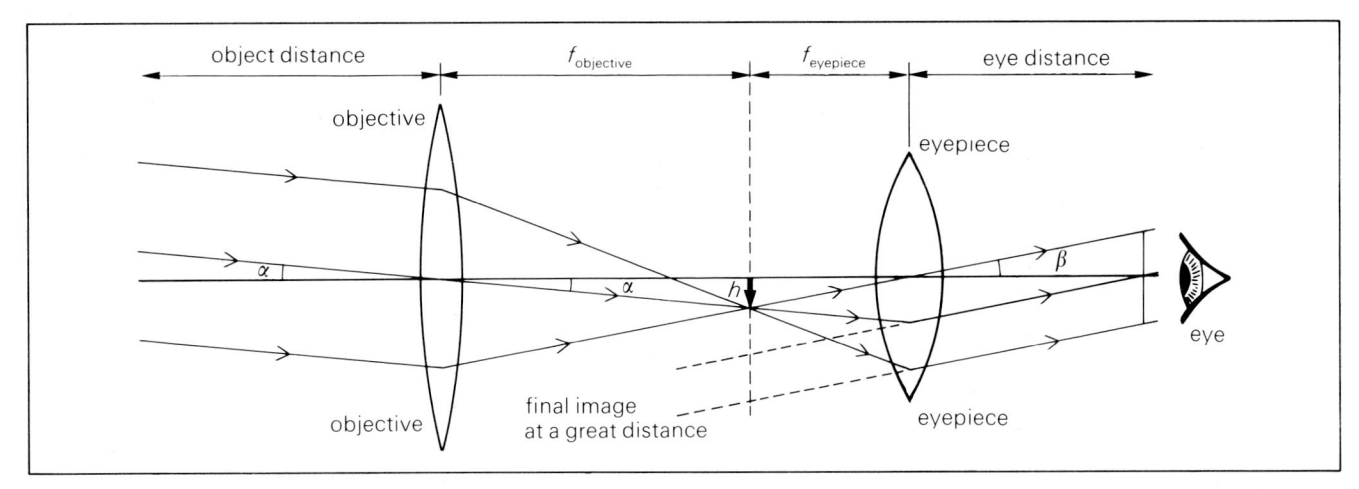

Figure 394 Refracting telescope

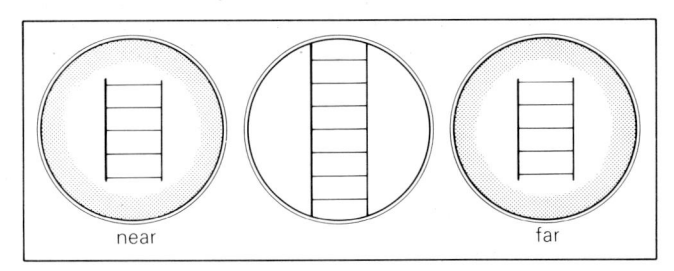

Figure 395 Looking at a distant pole with lines painted on it.

image can vary depending on the distance of the eye from the lens. If the eye is too near or too far, a 'halo' is produced, obscuring part of the image (e.g. figure 395).

3. Look at a distant object. The eyepiece may need to be moved slightly to adjust to your own eye. Move your eye and find the position of maximum image brightness. Get your partner to measure this distance or use a marker such as a card with a hole in it (figure 396). Theory indicates that the position of this 'eye ring' is the position of the image of the *objective lens itself* produced by the eyepiece. Does your measurement agree with this?

4. Measure the apparent magnification of the telescope. Can you think of a way of doing this yourself?

Reflecting telescope

The aim of this experiment is simply to set up a reflecting telescope (figure 397) so that an image can be seen. You may need shielding round it to reduce entry of stray light. Astronomical telescopes are usually used at night, so this problem does not always arise in practice.

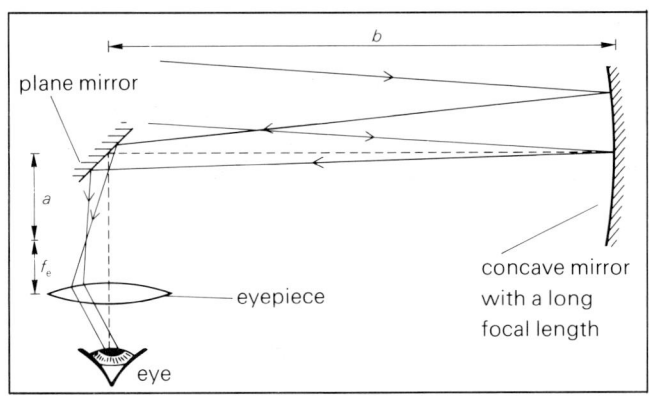

Figure 397 Reflecting microscope, the plane mirror is at 45°. $a + b = f_e$.

3. MICROSCOPE

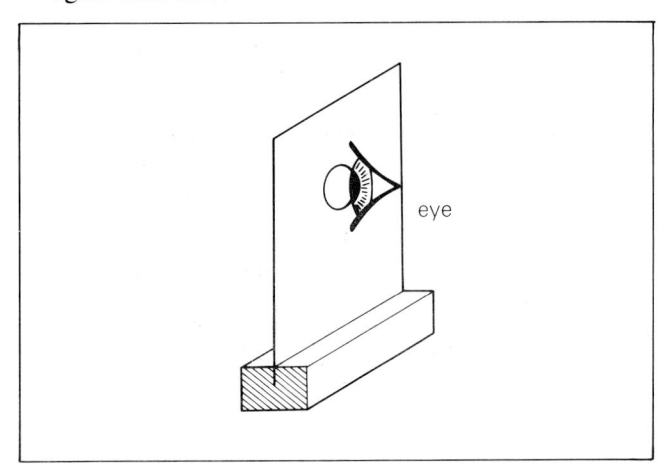

Figure 396 Eye ring

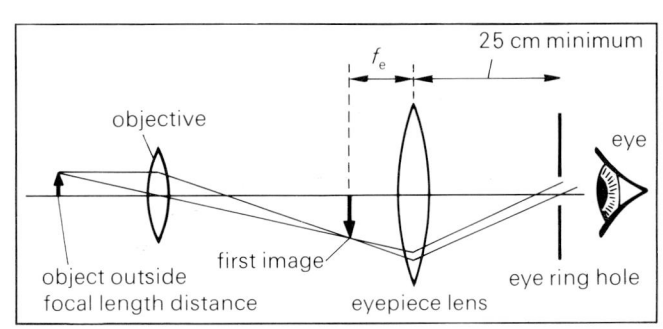

Figure 398 Microscope

DEDUCTIONS, APPLICATIONS AND DATA ANALYSIS

Experimental details

1. Set up the microscope, using illuminated 1 mm graph paper as an object. Find the position of the first image using a screen. Remove the screen and place the eyepiece lens exactly its focal length distance from this point. Look through the microscope and adjust the position of your eye to get a bright, full image. Place your 'eye-ring' hole at this point so you can reposition your eye quickly. Note its distance from the eyepiece so that it can be readjusted if the eyepiece is moved.
2. Measure the apparent magnification.
3. Alter the object distance and repeat for a sufficient number of object distances in the range f to $2f$ so that a graph of magnification against object distance can be plotted.

What do you conclude about the position of the object for maximum magnification?

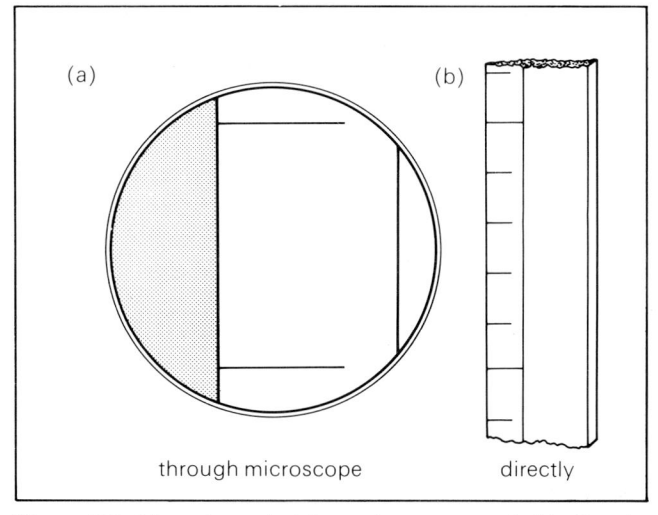

Figure 399 View through (a) a microscope and (b) directly. Apparent magnification equals 5, because 5 divisions of the scale seen directly fit into 1 division seen through the microscope

69. USING THE REFLECTION AND REFRACTION OF LIGHT

Outline

When a ray of light meets a boundary, the speed of the light wave changes and the ray can change direction. The boundary can be between different materials or where there is a change in density of the material.

$$_A n_B = \frac{\text{speed in medium A}}{\text{speed in medium B}}$$

It can be shown that the refractive index n also equals $\frac{\sin i}{\sin r}$. This is known as Snell's law.

If a ray increases its speed as it crosses the boundary, a position is reached as i increases where $\hat{r} = 90°$ and the refracted ray is along the surface of the boundary. For angles of incidence which produce $\hat{r} > 90°$ the ray is totally internally reflected. This can only happen when the wave increases its speed while moving into the second medium, and when the angle of incidence is larger than a certain angle called the *critical angle*.

The *critical angle* (c) is the angle of incidence for which the angle of refraction is 90°.

$$_A n_B = \frac{\sin c}{\sin 90} = \sin c$$

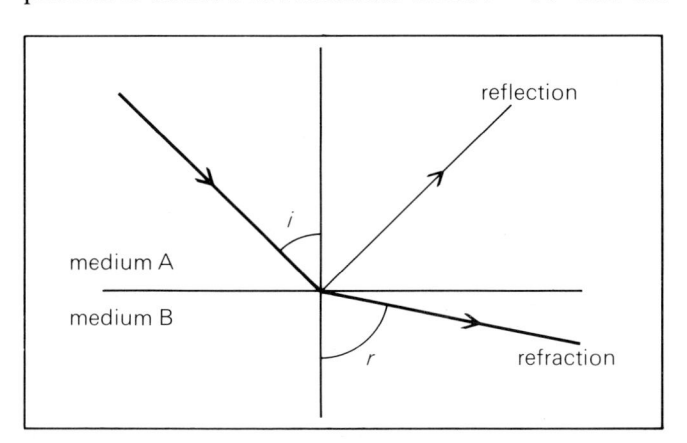

Figure 400

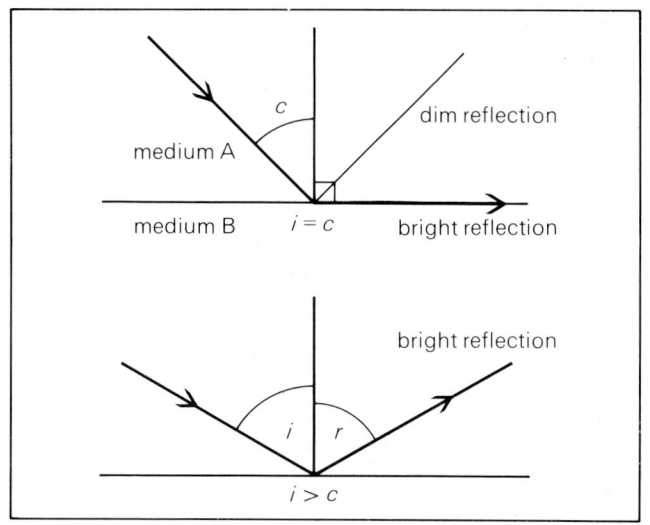

Figure 401

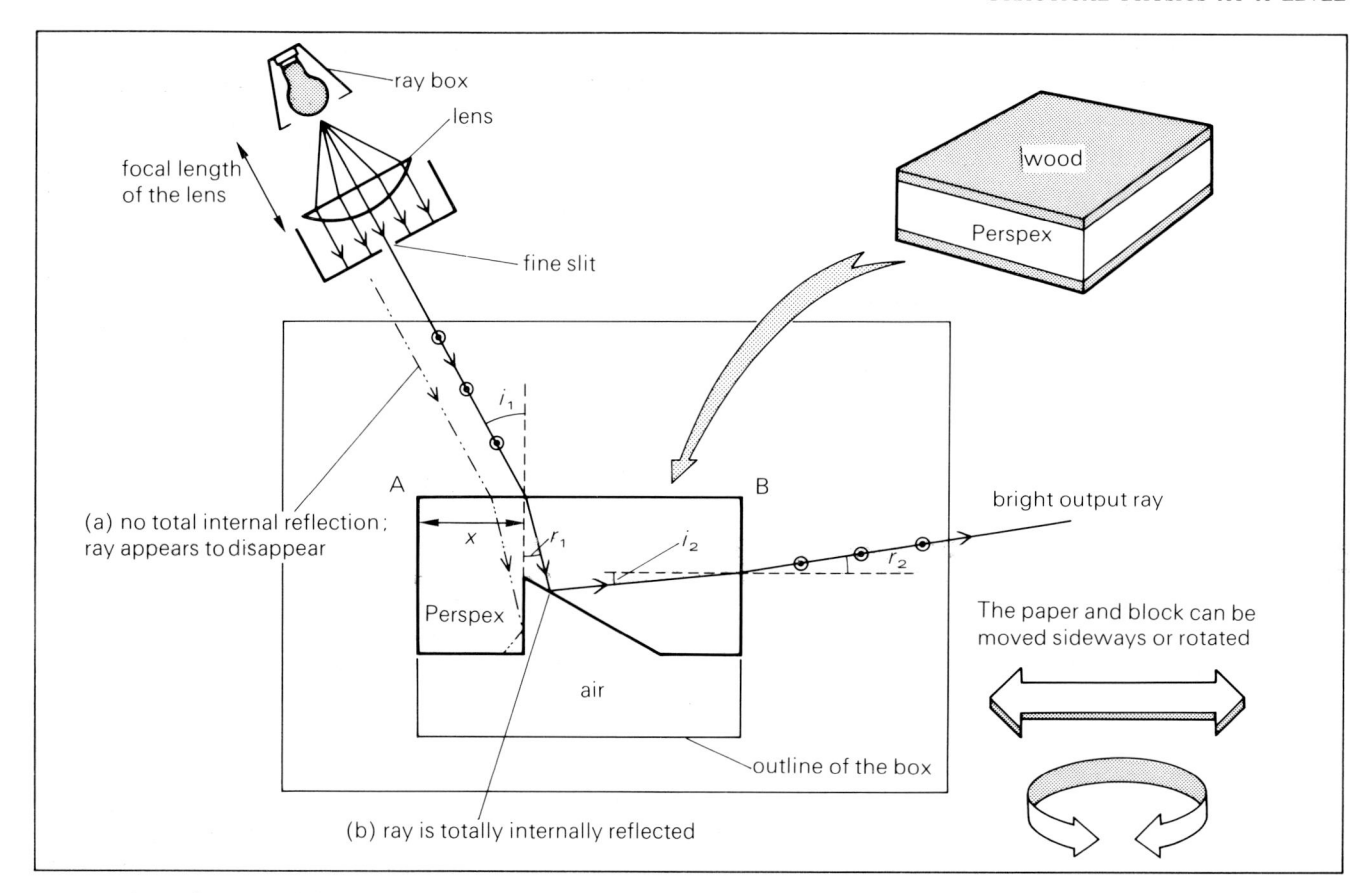

Figure 402 Equipment. Light can only pass through the plane front and sides of the box.

There is always some reflection from the surface, but it is dim in comparison to the incident beam. When total internal reflection occurs, the reflected beam is *nearly as bright* as the incident beam. (Why is it not *exactly* as bright?)

The aim of this practical is to find the size and shape of pieces of Perspex hidden inside a box (figure 402). There are three different blocks; a rectangular block with a triangular shape cut out, a semicircular block, and a shape with a hidden piece of black card in it (figures 403 and 405).

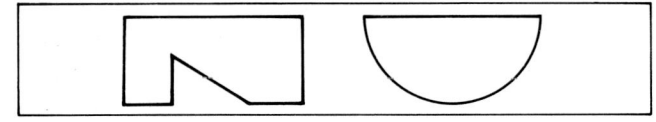

Figure 403

Experimental details

Shine the fine ray towards the block and rotate the block on the paper until total internal reflection occurs (there is a *bright* output ray). Mark at least three dots on the incident ray and three dots on the final output ray. Move the block and paper sideways and repeat for a series of positions along the front AB. Mark the front surface of the block and remove the block. Mark on normals and measure i_1 and r_2. Record distance x.

Using the refractive index of the block which you are given, calculate the angles r_1 and i_2 using Snell's law:

$$_{air}n_{Perspex} = \frac{\sin i_1}{\sin r_1}$$

$$_{Perspex}n_{air} = \frac{\sin i_2}{\sin r_2}$$

$$_{air}n_{Perspex} = \frac{1}{_{Perspex}n_{air}}$$

$$_{air}n_{Perspex} = 1.5$$

Results

x/mm	i_1/°	r_1/°	i_2/°	r_2/°

The paths of the rays can now be traced inside the block and the shape of the back surface worked out and drawn on the paper.

1. Find the shape of the triangular cut and its position relative to the front surface.

2. Find the radius of curvature of the semi-circular block. (*Hint:* see figure 404.)

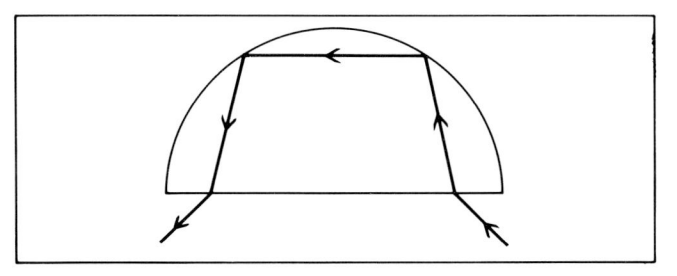

Figure 404

3. Find the position of the piece of black card sandwiched between two blocks (for example, figure 405).

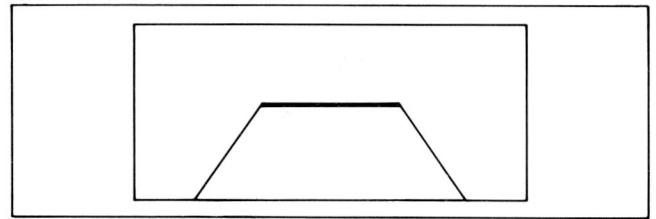

Figure 405

70. THICKNESS MEASUREMENT USING THE ABSORBTION OF RADIOACTIVITY

Outline

The aim is to investigate the way β and γ rays are absorbed by different materials, with the intention of making one thickness gauge for aluminium and one for steel. From the experimental results, calibration curves can be drawn and any limits on the thickness which can be measured decided. One problem could be that aluminium contains small quantities of copper and so it would be a good idea to compare the absorbtion of copper and aluminium.

Take all the usual precautions for using radioactive sources.

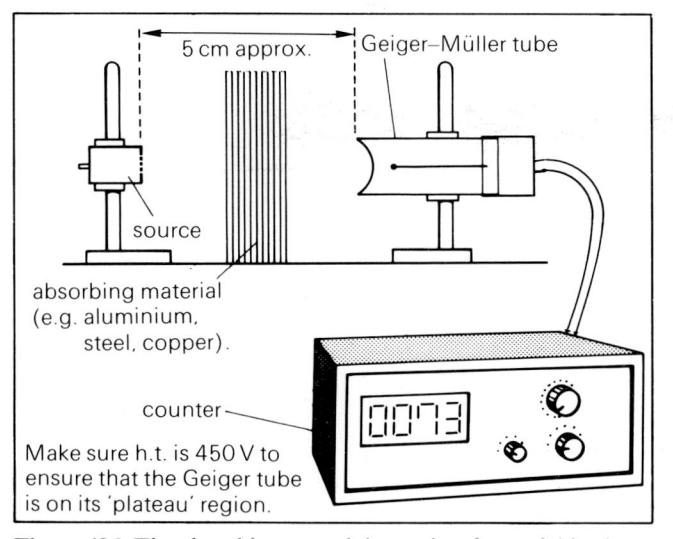

Figure 406 The absorbing materials consist of sets of thin sheets of aluminium, steel or copper, approximately 5 cm², and 0.05 cm or 0.1 cm thick, so that a range of thickness can be obtained.

Experimental details

1. Take a background count to find the level of natural radioactivity in your laboratory. The position of any boxes containing other sources will affect this, and these should not be moved during the experiment. A time of about ten minutes is suitable for measuring this count rate, and it is a good idea to repeat this measurement at the end of the experiment. The background count rate must be subtracted from all readings (or is this absolutely necessary if you are plotting a calibration curve?).

2. Take a series of counts for as many different thicknesses of the three materials as you can, up to 1 cm thickness, for both β and γ radiation. The materials are provided as sets of thin sheets (approx. 5 cm²) which are 0.05 cm or 0.1 cm thick, so that a range of known different material thicknesses can be produced, by changing the number of sheets used. Normal experimental practice would use a time of at least one minute, but this measurement gauge will be required to work much faster in operation and two, five, or ten seconds are more likely. The variation of count rate over these shorter times may be significant, and it would be a good idea to take a series of two-second and five-second readings to get some idea of the spread produced by the natural randomness of radioactive decay. From statistical theory the range of variation expected is $N \pm \sqrt{N}$ and this will give a probable error to the measurement.

Results

Tabulate your results for each material, as shown at the top of the next page.

Aluminium

Thickness/mm	Counts over 5-second periods

From the results

$$\frac{\text{corrected}}{\text{count rate}} = \text{count rate} - \frac{\text{background}}{\text{count rate}}$$

Make a second table, with the corrected count rate, the probable error and the thickness.

Corrected count rate	Error $\pm x$	Thickness/mm

Plot graphs of thickness as abscissa and count rate as ordinate. Show each 'point' as an error bar.

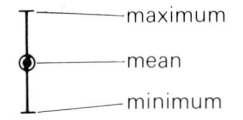

— maximum
— mean
— minimum

From the graphs

1. Decide which source is to be used for an aluminium gauge and which for a steel gauge.
2. Decide if the gauge will accept up to 10 per cent impurity of copper in the aluminium. This will involve combining readings for nine tenths of this thickness of aluminium with one tenth of this thickness of copper, working out new error bars and plotting a new graph.
3. Using the error bars, estimate the maximum resolution of each gauge. This limit is when the error bars for adjacent thicknesses overlap (figure 407).
   Does the maximum resolution change as the thickness changes?
4. Is there an upper and lower limit to the thickness which can be measured with each gauge? If so, give estimated values and explain your reasoning. At one extreme the count rate may be of the same order as the background; at the other there may be too small a change of count rate. You can only decide from *your* results.
5. What is the approximate minimum time the metal should be under the gauge?

This thickness is resolved   This thickness is not resolved

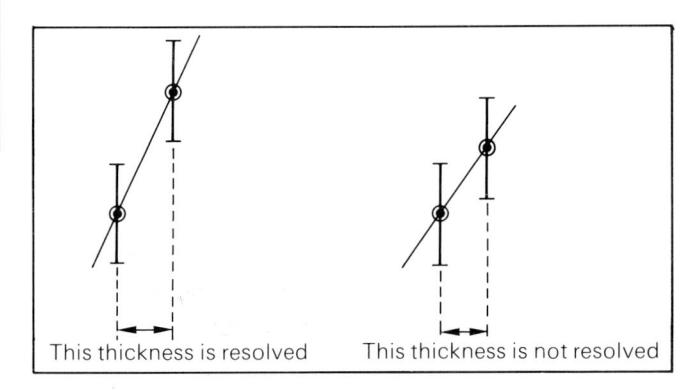

Figure 407

71. SIMULATION OF A MASS SPECTROMETER

Outline

One of the most important methods of investigating the masses of atoms is the mass spectrometer. As this is impossible to do in school, because of expense and size, you are going to use a computer simulation (Schools' Council *Computers in the Curriculum*, © Longman) to investigate the use of the mass spectrometer.

The principle of operation is as follows.

1. The atoms to be investigated are made into a beam of *ions*.

2. These ions are projected into a magnetic field where they experience a force which makes them move in a circular path.

3. The radius of this path depends on the mass, the velocity of the ions and the flux density of the magnetic field.

4. A detector is used to collect the ions and, because they are charged, a current is produced which can be measured.

DEDUCTIONS, APPLICATIONS AND DATA ANALYSIS

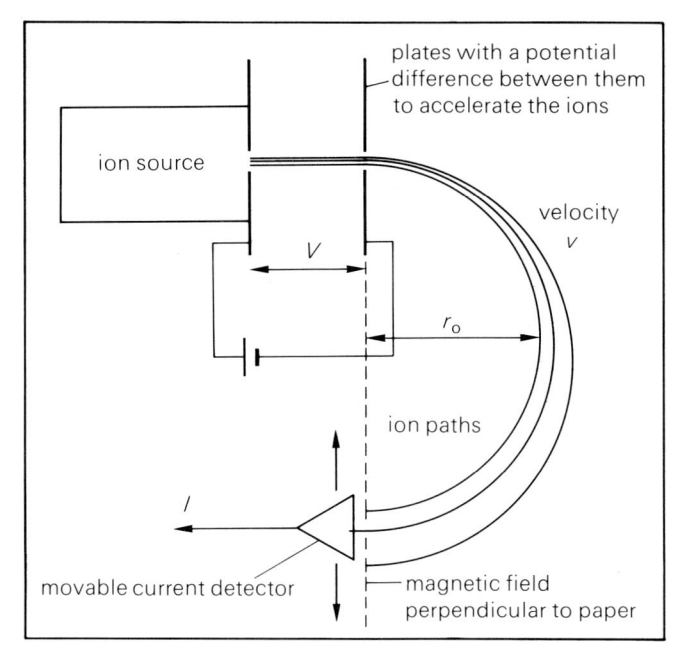

Figure 408 Mass spectrometer

5. To find the mass, the radius of the path of the ions must be found by moving the detector until a maximum current is measured. The mass can be worked out from the equation:

$$m = \frac{B^2 r_0^2 Q}{2V}$$

6. The equation is derived as follows. The ions are first accelerated by a voltage V. They gain kinetic energy from the electrical energy used, as the electric field does work on the charge.

$$QV = \tfrac{1}{2}mv^2 \qquad (1)$$

The force produced by the magnetic field $= BQv$. This provides the centripetal force needed for circular motion:

$$\therefore \frac{mv^2}{r_0} = BQv \qquad (2)$$

From (1)

$$v^2 = \frac{2QV}{m}$$

From (2)

$$v = \frac{BQr_0}{m}$$

and

$$v^2 = \frac{B^2 Q^2 r_0^2}{m^2}$$

Combining these gives:

$$m = \frac{B^2 r_0^2 Q}{2V}$$

Unfortunately, ions of the same mass do not follow *exactly* the same path. The main problems are as follows.

1. It is not certain that all ions have the same charge.
2. There will be a range of velocities in the beams.
3. The width of the detector slit has a finite width and may be too wide to resolve two ions of nearly the same mass. It is rather similar to the effect the size of the pinhole has on the image in a pinhole camera. The sharpness of the peak can be altered by changing the width of the detector slit.

By altering (a) the magnetic field strength, and (b) the accelerating voltage, the distance covered by the ions in the beam can be made larger or smaller in an attempt to get ions of different mass to give separate peaks and also to make these peaks as sharp as possible so that the separate ions can be resolved.

If the position of the detector at the maximum of the peaks is noted, the radius can be found and then the mass.

By putting values taken from the design of the mass spectrometer on which the computer model is based, the equation can be simplified* to:

$$V = \frac{n}{A} \times 1.737 \times 10^3 \qquad \text{(for 0.15 tesla field)}$$

or

$$V = \frac{n}{A} \times 6.947 \times 10^3 \qquad \text{(for 0.3 tesla field)}$$

where n is the charge on the ion and A is its mass in AMU.

A lot of time can be wasted looking for a peak in a voltage range which is completely wrong. These equations could be used to work out the approximate accelerating voltage required if the approximate mass is known. The mass number of the ion would be a sensible starting point.

The experiment involves loading different ion sources and adjusting the settings on the spectrometer to get sharp, well-resolved peaks and then to work out the mass from the voltage reading at the peak. Tables can then be used to decide which substance or which isotope of a substance is present by looking up tables and matching masses.

Computers in the Curriculum pupil notes, © Longman

Experimental details

A detailed set of investigations is given in the pupil notes which accompany the program. Alternatively, a simplified practical of about one to two hours' duration is given below.

1. Load the potassium source.
2. The atomic number of potassium is 19. A rough guide is that atoms have about the same number of neutrons as protons, and so we should expect a mass number of about 38. Use this to work out the accelerating voltage required for each size of field. Decide on the range of voltage to be used from this.
3. Using a slit width of less than 0.01 m, get a display of the detector current.
4. Continue with the program and, by changing the slit width, range of accelerating voltage and possibly the size of the magnetic field, try and get a display which best resolves the two potassium isotopes.
5. Find the voltages corresponding to the peaks and work out the masses. Decide which isotopes of potassium are present.
6. Without changing the voltage range, it might be interesting to produce a set of plots which shows the effect of changing the detector slit width.
7. Now you have mastered the controls, try and load the other sources available in turn and try to find out the isotopes present in each.

Writing a report

Write a report about the conclusions you have made about the isotopes in each source. Include the final computer outputs, the peak voltages you measured and the working out of the masses.

Question

Imagine that you have a *completely unknown* source. Describe how you would go about finding its mass.

Figure 409 shows graphs of detector current against accelerating voltage, showing the effect of changing various factors. You can use these graphs to help to decide on changes to the settings chosen on the spectrometer.

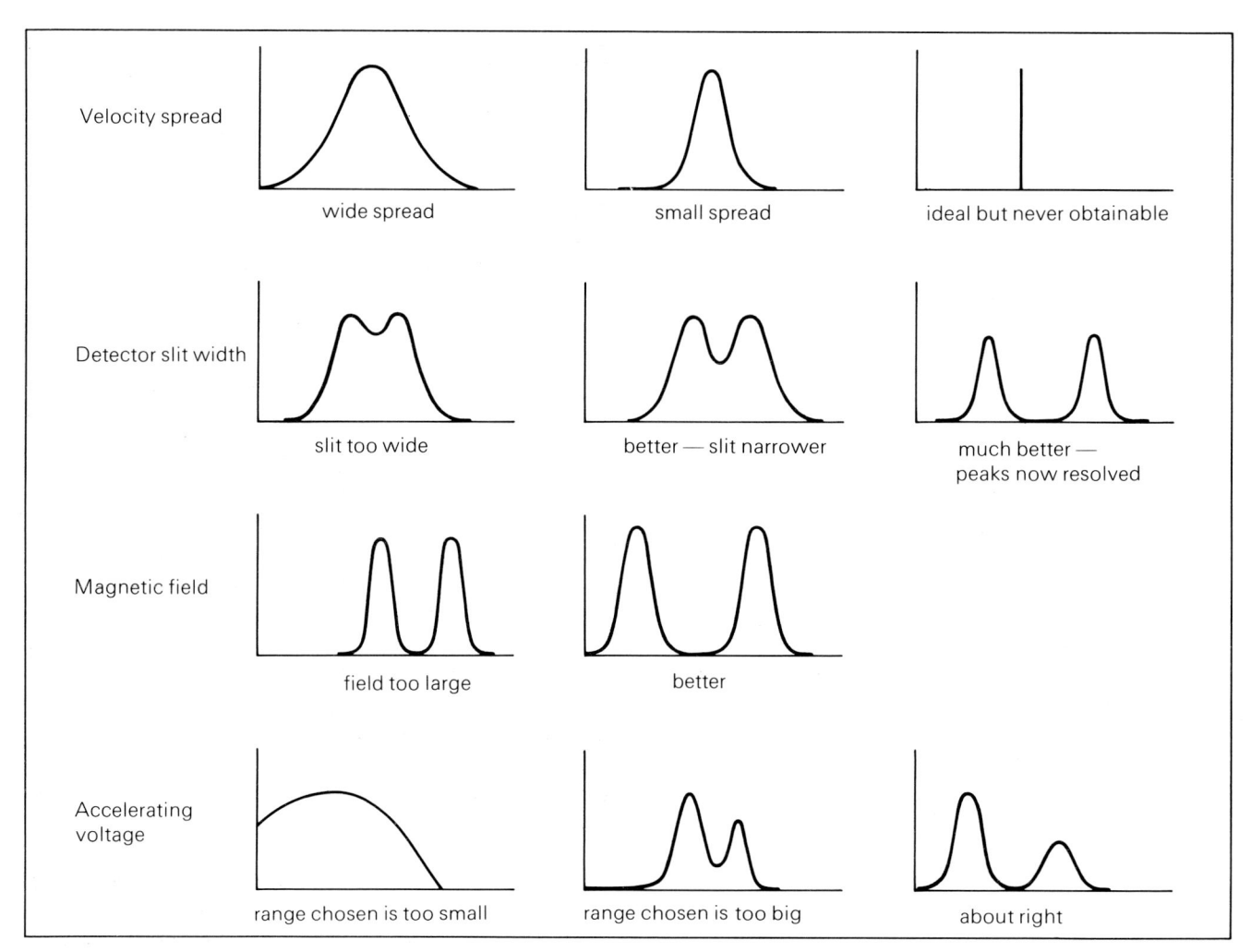

Figure 409

72. ANALOGUE COMPUTING

Outline

Analogue computing is used to solve equations which have differential terms, usually with respect to time. For example, for radioactive decay:

$$\frac{dN}{dt} = -\lambda N$$

The solution for N will vary with time. The technique can also be used to simulate situations for which component values would be difficult to change in real life, for example, when designing a suspension system (figure 410). A solution is needed for the movement x of the load after it is moved from its equilibrium position. There are four variables:

1. force constant of the spring;
2. size of load;
3. surface area of damper;
4. viscosity of damping liquid.

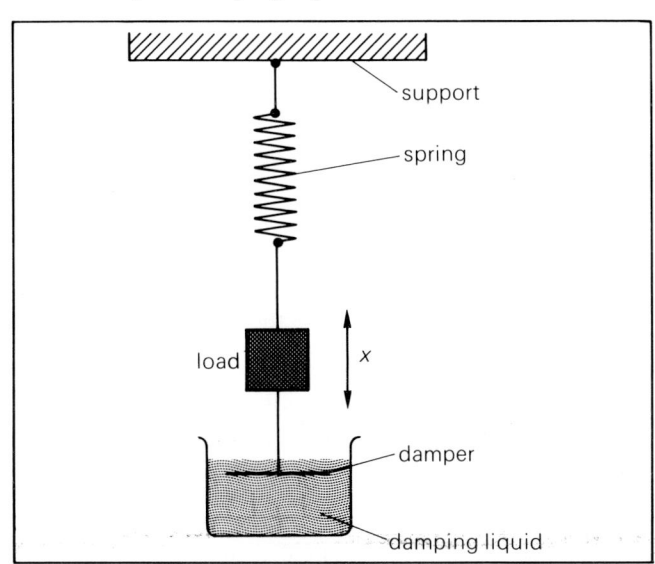

Figure 410 Damped oscillations

The electrical circuit in analogue computing makes use of operational amplifiers, because these work for changing d.c. voltages and can be wired to make the various 'building blocks' needed.

1. *Integrator* (see figure 411)

$$V_{out} = -\frac{1}{RC}\int V_{in}\, dt$$

If $R = 1\,M\Omega$, and $C = 1\,\mu F$, then

$$V_{out} = -\int V_{in}\, dt$$

since $RC = 1$.

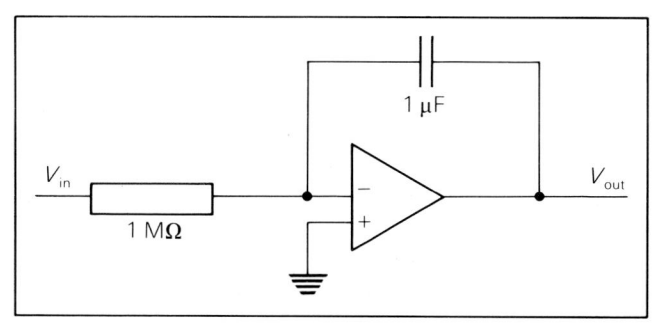

Figure 411 Integrator

2. *Invertor* (see figure 412)

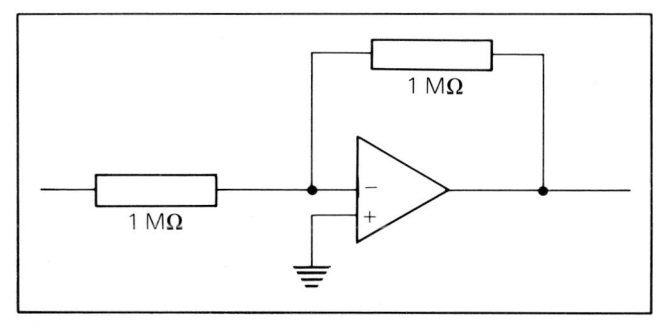

$$V_{out} = -V_{in}$$

Figure 412 Invertor

3. *Multiply by a constant k* (see figure 413)

$$k = \frac{R_f}{R_1}$$

$$V_{out} = -\frac{R_f}{R_1}V_{in}$$

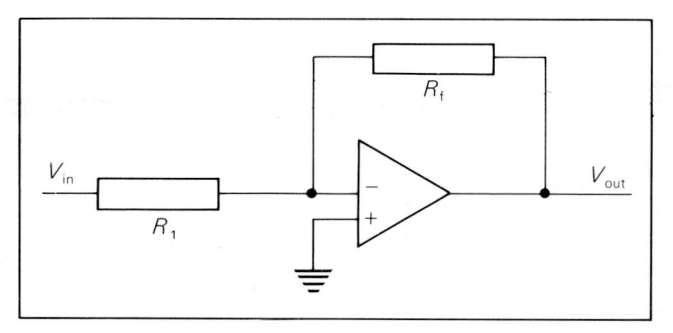

Figure 413 Multiplication by a constant

4. *Summation*

$$V_{out} = -|V_A + V_B|$$

The unit shown in figure 414 can be used to sum V_A and V_B in different proportion with optional amplification if the resistor values are altered. $100\,k\Omega$ should be regarded as the *lowest* value which should be used.

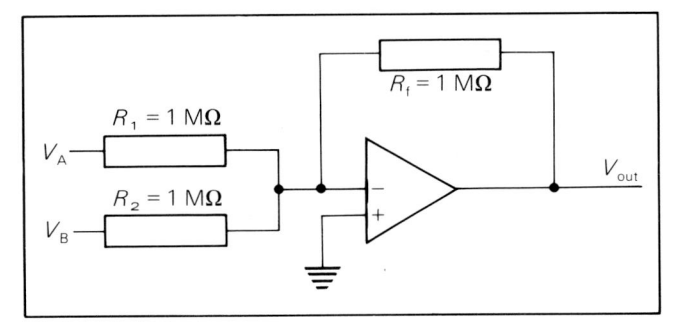

Figure 414 Summation

$$V_{out} = -\left[\frac{V_A R_f}{R_1} + \frac{V_B R_f}{R_2}\right]$$

5. *Taking a fraction*

This is done by using a voltage divider (figure 415):

$$V_{out} = kV_{in}$$

$$k = \frac{R_2}{R_1 + R_2}$$

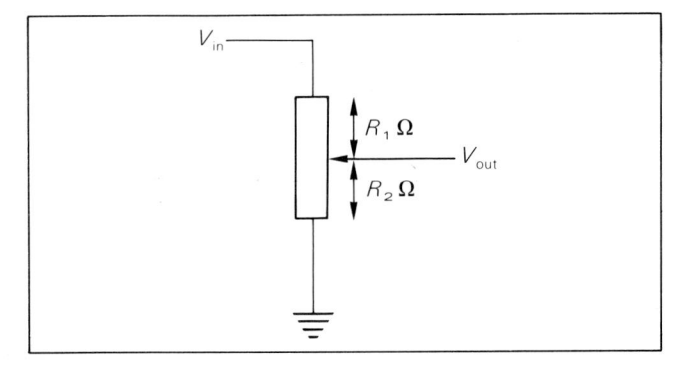

Figure 415 Taking a fraction

To display the output voltage, which is the solution to the equation, several methods are available.

1. *Moving-coil voltmeter and stopwatch*

Voltages are recorded at fixed time intervals and a graph plotted. This is only suitable for a slowly changing solution, because one reading every 10 seconds is about the maximum possible. The meter must also have a high resistance, greater than 100 kΩ, otherwise it 'loads' the circuit and can affect the voltages.

2. *Oscilloscope*

This has a high resistance, a built-in time-scale, and a permanent record can be made by taking a photograph. A time exposure is made as the spot moves across the screen.

There must be the facility to trigger the time-base externally so that the spot starts to move at a known time, and at the same instant as the integration starts. An advantage is that several successive 'runs' with different variables can be photographed on the same negative for comparison (figure 416).

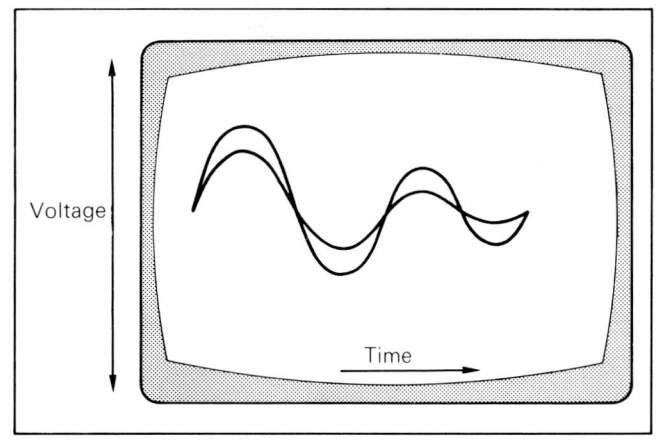

Figure 416

3. *Chart recorder*

This will produce a permanent record but can be wasteful of paper while trial runs are done, and most chart recorders do not have the facility to return to the same starting position for subsequent runs.

4. *A microcomputer with an analogue input or data gathering instrument e.g. VELA*

With a suitable program to operate it, this can have the advantages of all the other methods combined:

(a) ability to record and display the complete trace on a screen;
(b) ability to produce a printed copy;
(c) ability to display successive runs on the same screen;
(d) if a multiple analogue input is available, several voltages can be displayed at the same time.

A computer program 'DATALOG' (package PHYS2 option 5) is supplied in the teacher's pack for the BBC model B computer. There is no standard input voltage used by analogue inputs, but it is generally in the range 1 to 2.5 V. Operational amplifiers generally use a supply of ±15 V, so a voltage divider will probably be needed. A better circuit would use a voltage follower.

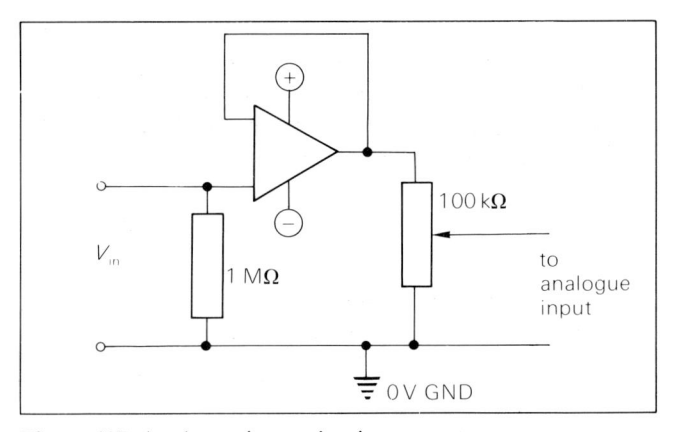

Figure 417 Analogue input circuit

DEDUCTIONS, APPLICATIONS AND DATA ANALYSIS

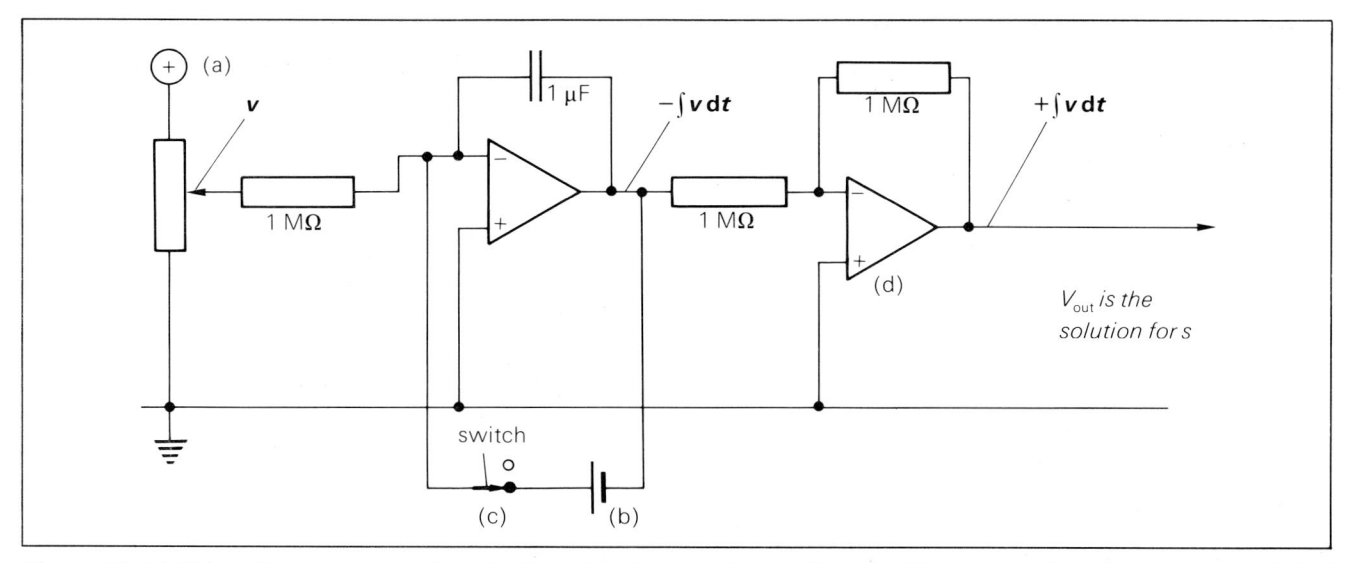

Figure 418 (a) This voltage represents the velocity and determines the gradient. (b) This voltage gives the capacitor an initial charge which represents the initial condition of the distance where $t = 0$. (c) To start the integration, move the switch to break the connection. (d) This is needed to produce the correct polarity of output.

Concepts

A. Consider the equation:

$$\text{velocity} = \frac{\text{distance}}{\text{time}}$$

$$v = \frac{ds}{dt}$$

$$s = \int v\, dt$$

If v is constant, then the solution for s is a straight line. The gradient depends on the value of v.

The intercept on the s axis depends on the initial displacement at time $t = 0$. This is called an *initial condition* (figures 418 and 419).

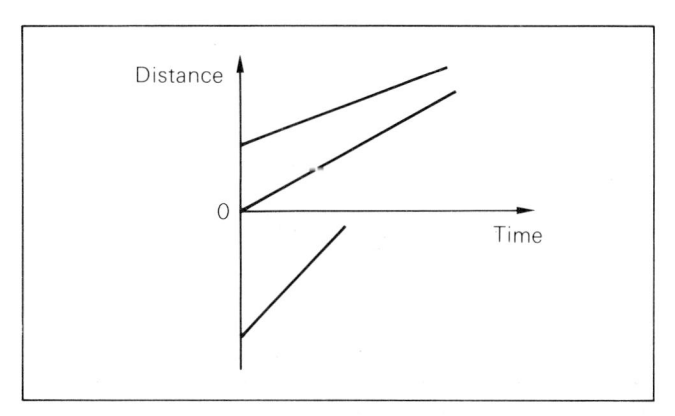

Figure 419 Example output graphs

B. Consider the equation for radioactive decay:

$$\frac{dN}{dt} = -\lambda N \quad \text{or} \quad \frac{-dN}{dt} = \lambda N$$

There is *no* constant input, only an initial condition of the initial number of atoms present (figure 420).

Because the input to the integrator depends on the output (value of N) it is continually changing, but it *always* equals λN, so the *vital connection* is to join together parts of the circuit which have the same value, in this case from the fraction output to the input.

C. Consider a system moving with s.h.m., such as a pendulum. If you wished to find out how the velocity $\left(\dfrac{dx}{dt}\right)$ varies with time, the output from P could be inverted and then displayed (figure 421).

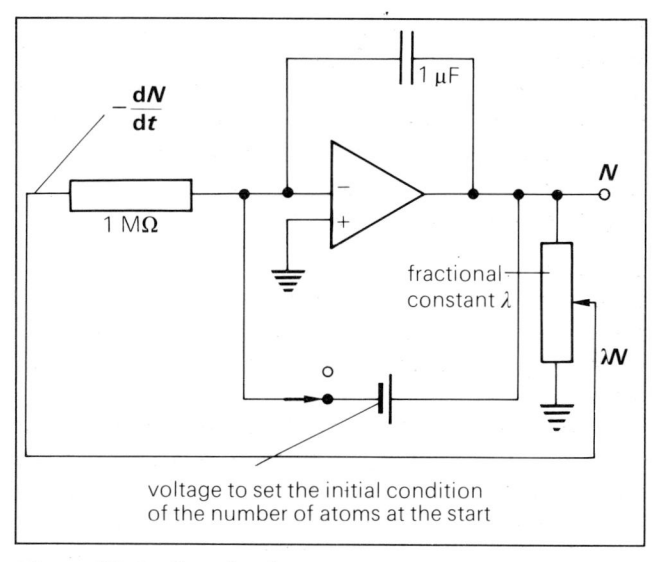

Figure 420 Radioactive decay

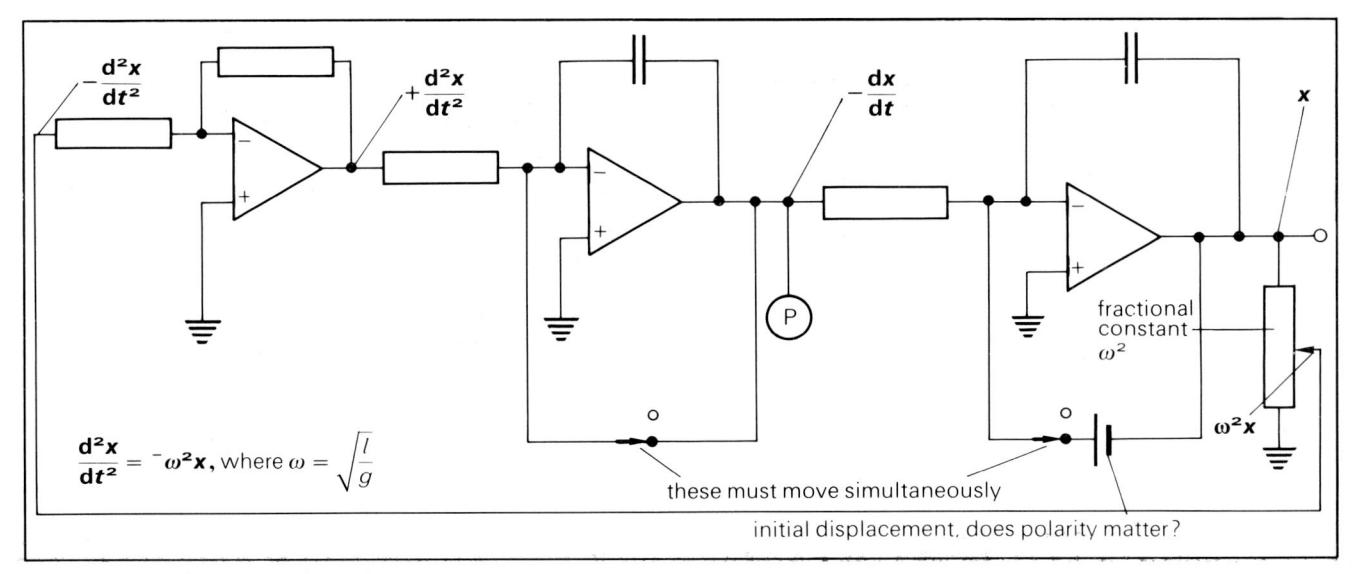

Figure 421 Simple harmonic motion

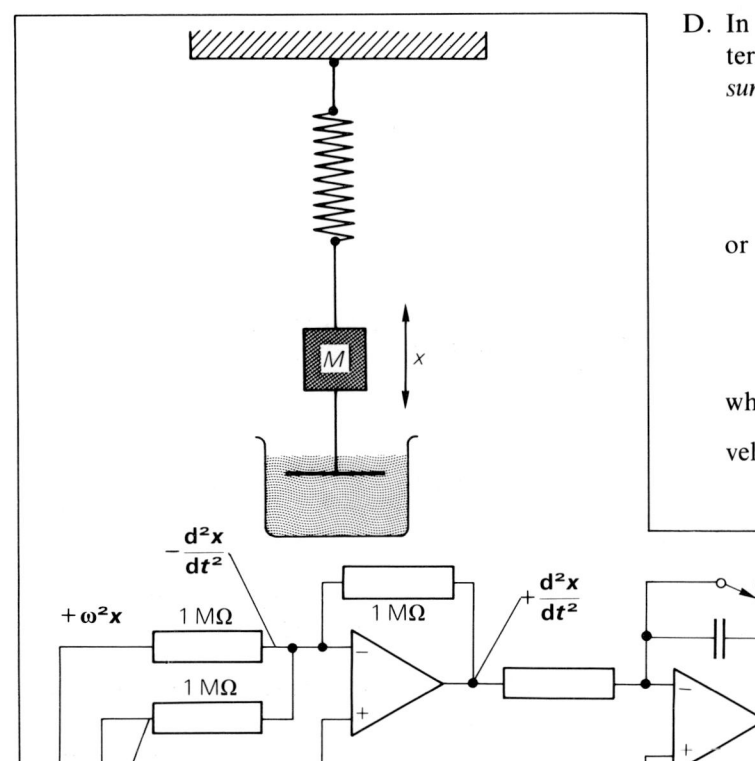

D. In the system illustrated in figure 422 there are two terms on the right-hand side of the equation, so a *summation* must be used:

$$\frac{d^2x}{dt^2} = -\omega^2 x - k\frac{dx}{dt}$$

or

$$-\frac{d^2x}{dt^2} = \omega^2 x + k\frac{dx}{dt}$$

where $\frac{dx}{dt}$ is the fluid friction term proportional to velocity; remember $F = 6\pi\eta av$ for a ball bearing.

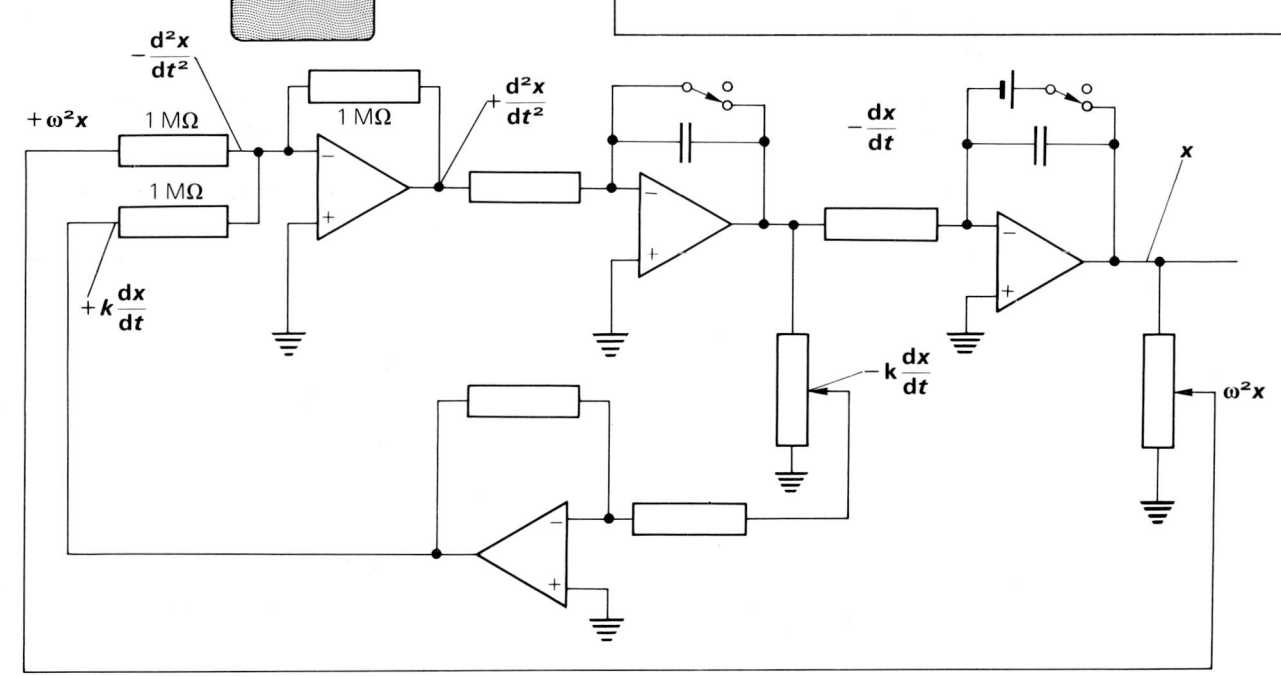

Figure 422 Damped simple harmonic motion

DEDUCTIONS, APPLICATIONS AND DATA ANALYSIS

Experimental details

1. Make sure that the *offset* of each operational amplifier used is adjusted so that the output is exactly zero with zero input.

   The position of the oscilloscope traces for both positions of the switch should match exactly, provided you are using the d.c. input of the oscilloscope.

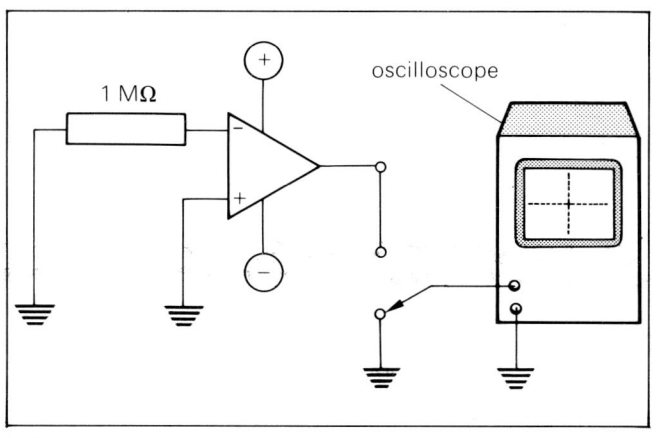

Figure 423

2. For each of the examples of analogue computing described previously in 'concepts' A–D, produce a graph to show the way in which the solution varies with time. Show how the output is altered by varying initial conditions and fractional constants. Use whatever method is available for measuring the output voltage. Your teacher will have to give you more details.

Additional experiment

Make a circuit which produces a solution for parent and daughter radioactive decay.

If the number of initial atoms is N_0 and the actual number of parent atoms at a time t is N, then:

$$\frac{dN}{dt} = -\lambda N$$

where λ is the decay constant of the parent nuclei; number of daughter nuclei $N_1 = N_0 - N$

$$\frac{dN_1}{dt} = -\lambda N_1$$

$$= -\lambda(N_0 - N)$$

73. DIGITAL CONTROL BY COMPUTER

Outline

When a number is output to the *user port* of a computer, it appears as a binary code of logical 0s and 1s, which set the wires to a voltage of between 2 and 5 V for a logical 1 and less than 0.8 V for a logical 0. These voltage levels can be used to control circuits in equipment outside the computer—for example, the number 53 would appear as

```
128 64 32 16 8 4 2 1  ← (value of each bit)
  0  0  1  1 0 1 0 1
```

Usually the maximum current which can be drawn is 10 mA. So bulbs, relays and motors cannot be connected directly because they:

(a) usually use a supply voltage other than 5 V;
(b) draw a current of more than 10 mA.

This is solved by using a transistor *buffer* stage, for example, see figure 424.

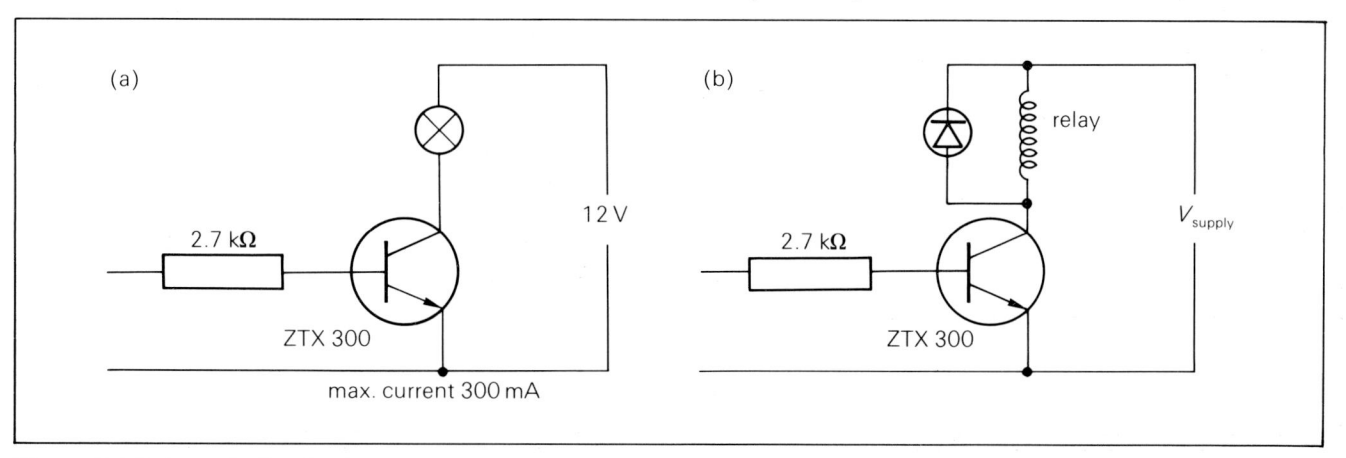

Figure 424 Drive or buffer circuits

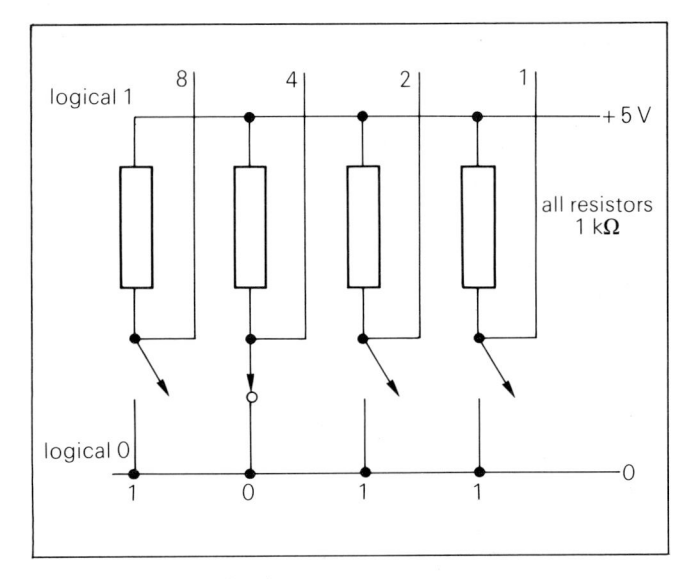

Figure 425 Input circuit

To *input* a number, voltages are placed on the eight input wires, between 2 V and 5 V for a logical 1 and less than 0.8 V for a logical 0. The computer 'reads' the accumulated value $8 + 2 + 1 = 11$ (figure 425).

Connected to your computer is a 'box' which enables you to control the numbers being read by the computer and to use the numbers output from the computer (figure 426). There are several makes of suitable interfaces available, so the one you have available may not be exactly the same as the one described here.

This practical assumes that you have some knowledge of programming in BASIC, and understand how to use the INPUT, PRINT, LET, IF...THEN, GOTO and GOSUB commands.

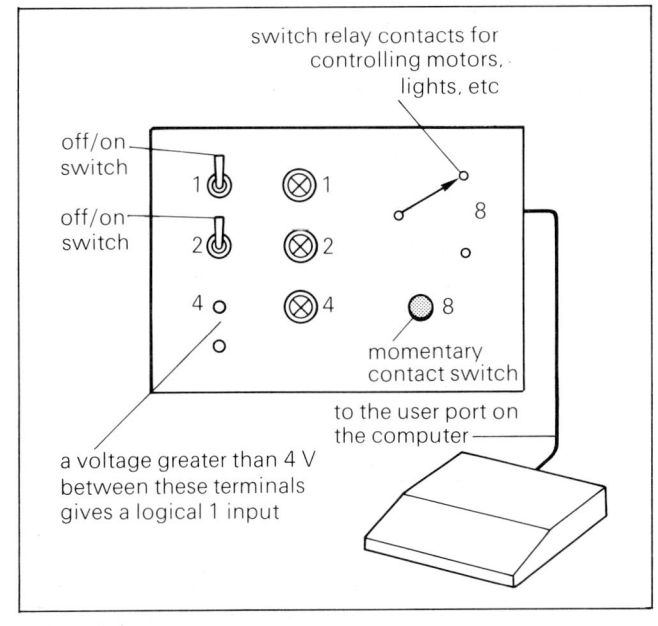

Figure 426 Example of an interface unit

The exact method used to input and output numbers to the *port* depends on the computer you are using. The simplest approach to programming is to use two *subroutines*, one for input at line 500 and one for output at line 600, with the number to be output put in variable D and the number input returned to variable C. Your teacher will probably give you these subroutines ready to load in. A third subroutine, GOSUB 700, gives a time delay of 1 second. The forth subroutine, GOSUB 800, contains any initial instructions necessary to 'set up' the user port.

In this practical you will find out how the computer can be used to:

1. input a number from the port and display it on the screen;
2. output numbers to the port;
3. turn lights on and off by typing instructions on the keyboard;
4. perform the same function as logic gates;
5. flash a light off and on, and to produce a traffic-light sequence;
6. count the number of objects passing a 'photocell';
7. act as a simple timer;
8. control the movement of a moving vehicle, e.g. Lego(TM) unit.

Experimental details

First load the subroutines into the computer:

```
499 REM BBC printer and user ports
500 C=?65120:RETURN
600 ?65121=D:RETURN
700 TIME=0:REPEAT UNTIL TIME>100:RETURN
800 C=0:D=0:?65122=0:RETURN

499 REM SPECTRUM I_pack interface
500 LET C=(IN 63)-240:RETURN
600 OUT 63,D:RETURN
700 PAUSE 50:RETURN
800 LET C=0:LET D=0:RETURN
```

A. *Input a number from the port and display it on the screen.*

Investigate the number produced by different combinations of the switches.

```
 1 GOSUB 800
10 GOSUB 500   ← Get the number from the port
20 PRINT C        and put in variable C
30 GOSUB 700   ← Wait for 1 second —
40 GOTO 10        a time delay
```

DEDUCTIONS, APPLICATIONS AND DATA ANALYSIS

B. *Output numbers to the port.*
Find the effect of outputting different numbers to the port.

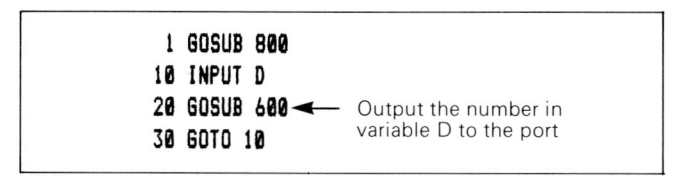

```
 1 GOSUB 800
10 INPUT D
20 GOSUB 600   ← Output the number in
30 GOTO 10       variable D to the port
```

C. *Turn a light on and off using commands typed in on the keyboard.*
Suppose light value 4 is to be controlled:

```
  1 GOSUB 800
 10 PRINT "GIVE COMMAND"  ← Decide what to do
 20 INPUT C$
 30 IF C$="ON" THEN 100
 40 IF C$="OFF" THEN 70
 50 PRINT "ERROR"
 60 GOTO 10
 70 LET D=0   ← Turn the light off
 80 GOSUB 600
 90 GOTO 10
100 LET D=4   ← Turn the light on
110 GOSUB 600
120 GOTO 10
```

D. *Perform the same functions as logic gates.*

The AND gate
Imagine two of the switches as the inputs to the AND gate and a lamp as the output.

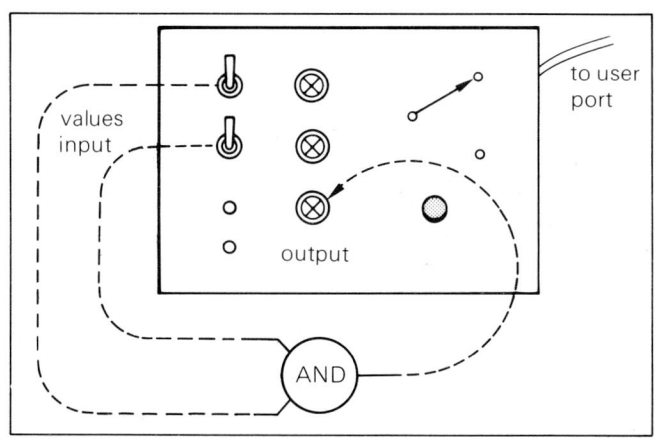

Figure 427

Truth table:

A	B	C
0	0	0
0	1	0
1	0	0
1	1	1

The flowchart is:

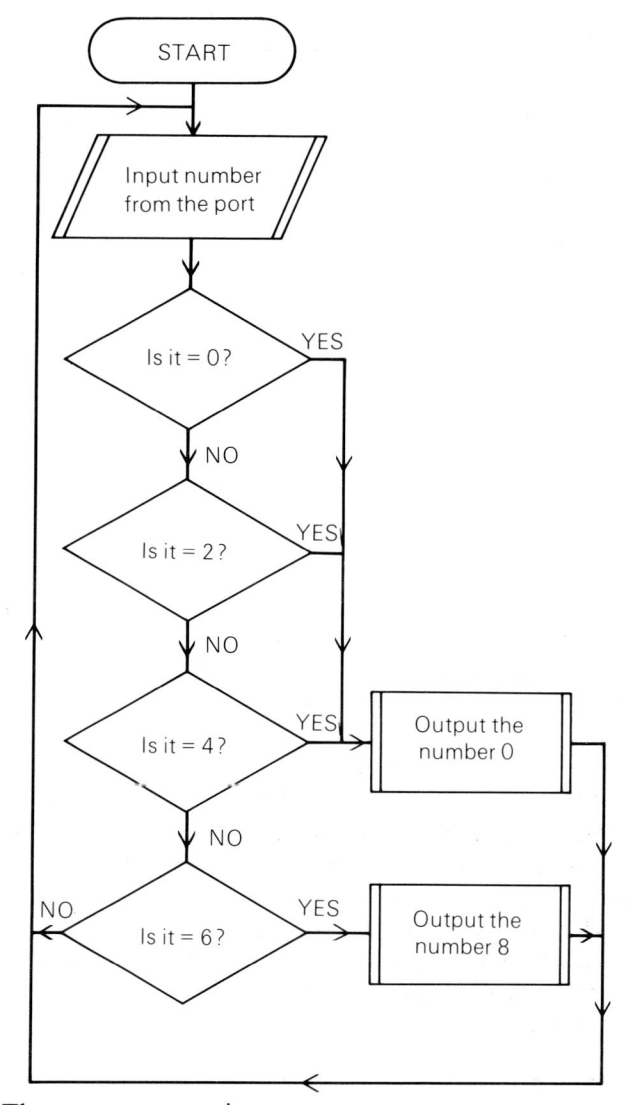

```
                START
                  ↓
         ┌─────────────────┐
    →    │ Input number    │
    │    │ from the port   │
    │    └─────────────────┘
    │             ↓
    │         ╱Is it=0?╲──YES──┐
    │         ╲        ╱        │
    │             ↓ NO          │
    │         ╱Is it=2?╲──YES──┤
    │         ╲        ╱        │
    │             ↓ NO          │
    │         ╱Is it=4?╲──YES──→ Output the
    │         ╲        ╱         number 0
    │             ↓ NO           │
    │   NO    ╱Is it=6?╲──YES──→ Output the
    └────────╲        ╱          number 8
                  ↓               │
                  ←───────────────┘
```

The BASIC program is:

```
  1 GOSUB 800
 10 GOSUB 500
 20 IF C=0 THEN GOTO 70
 30 IF C=2 THEN GOTO 70
 40 IF C=4 THEN GOTO 70
 50 IF C=6 THEN GOTO 100
 60 GOTO 10
 70 LET D=0
 80 GOSUB 600
 90 GOTO 10
100 LET D=8
110 GOSUB 600
120 GOTO 10
```

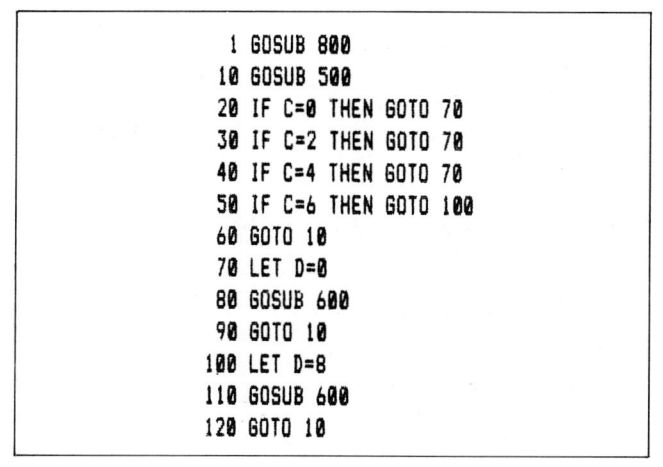

Using the same ideas, programs can be written which have the same functions as the OR gate and NOT gate. Use the following flowcharts and write programs yourself.

The OR gate

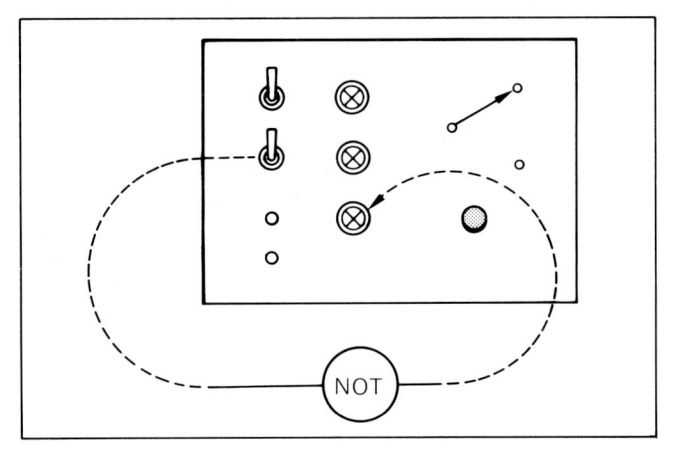

Figure 428

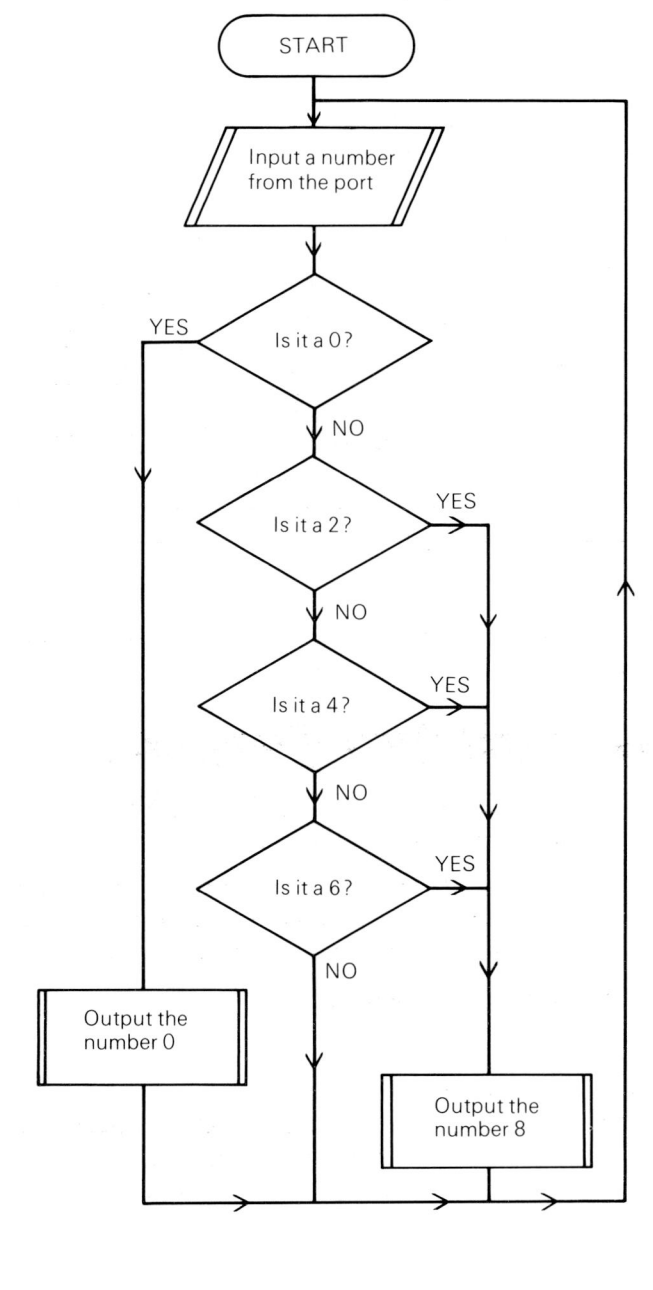

The NOT gate

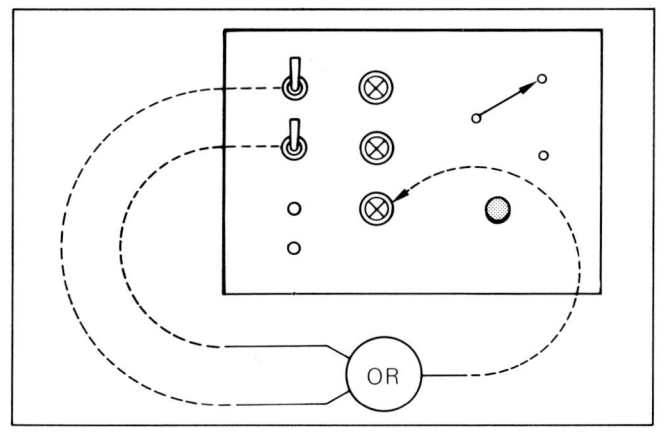

Figure 429

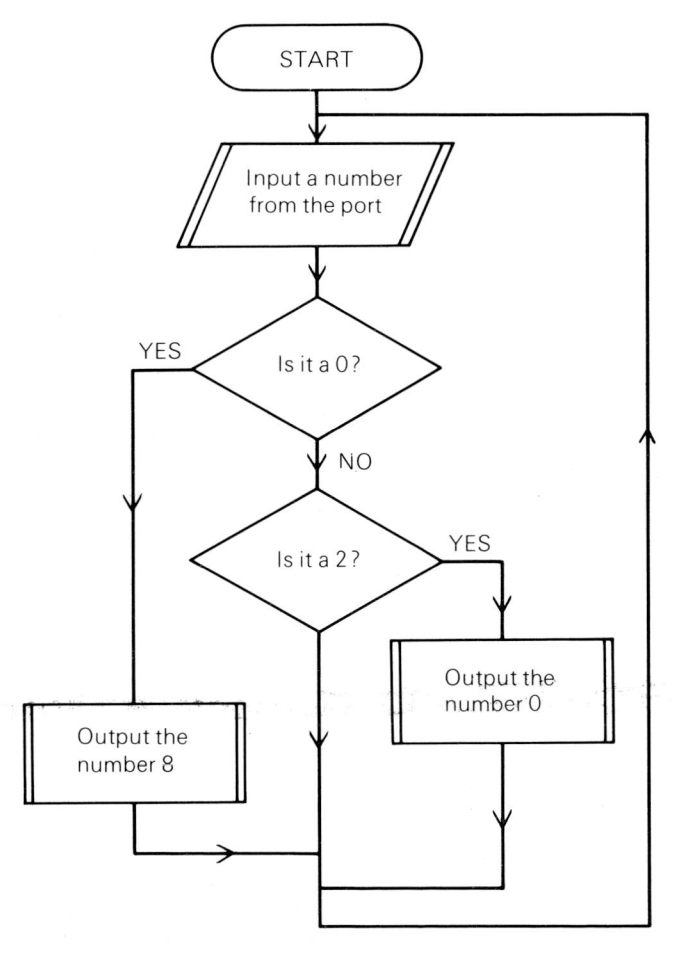

E. *Flash a light off and on.*

Write your own program from the outline flowchart given on p. 199.

Extend this idea to produce a traffic-light sequence from red to green and back to red.

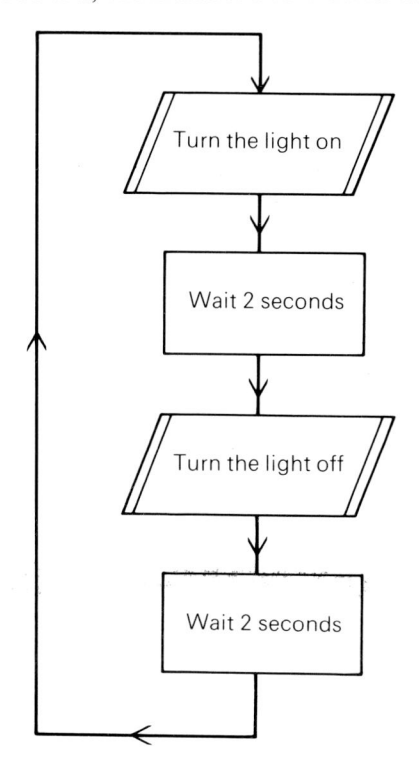

DEDUCTIONS, APPLICATIONS AND DATA ANALYSIS 199

Remember that a time delay must be used to allow the object to pass over the photocell after being detected.

G. *Act as a simple timer.*

You must first find out how long the computer takes to count up to 10 000 and then find out how many adding operations take place in one second. Time from the instant the RETURN key is pressed after typing RUN until the program stop message is displayed on the screen.

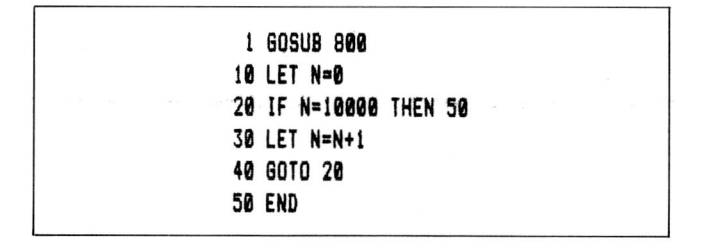

```
 1 GOSUB 800
10 LET N=0
20 IF N=10000 THEN 50
30 LET N=N+1
40 GOTO 20
50 END
```

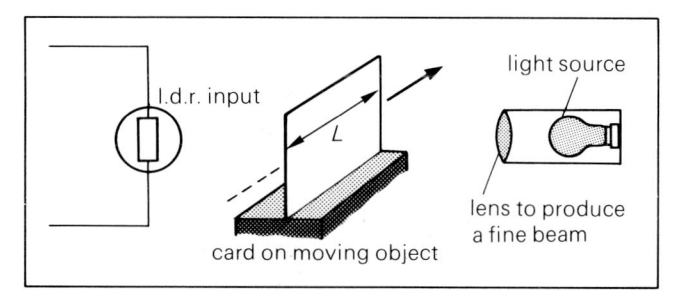

Figure 431 *Measuring speed.*

Using the equipment shown in figure 431, the program must allow you to:

(a) input the length of the card L so that the computer can be made to calculate the velocity;

(b) add 1 to a count whenever the LDR is in the dark, giving a logical 1 input;

(c) work out the real time by dividing by the number of adding operations which take place in one second, when the input changes back to 0 again;

(d) work out the velocity.

F. *Count the number of objects passing a light sensitive device.*

An l.d.r. or photodiode connected as a potential divider is used to supply a voltage to a pair of input sockets (figure 430). The resistance changes from ~1 MΩ in the dark to 10 Ω in the light. The potential at A changes from ~4.8 V to ~0.4 V, giving logical 1 in the dark and logical 0 in the light.

Whenever the input changes from 0, an object must be in front of the light and so 1 must be added to the variable in which the total is stored.

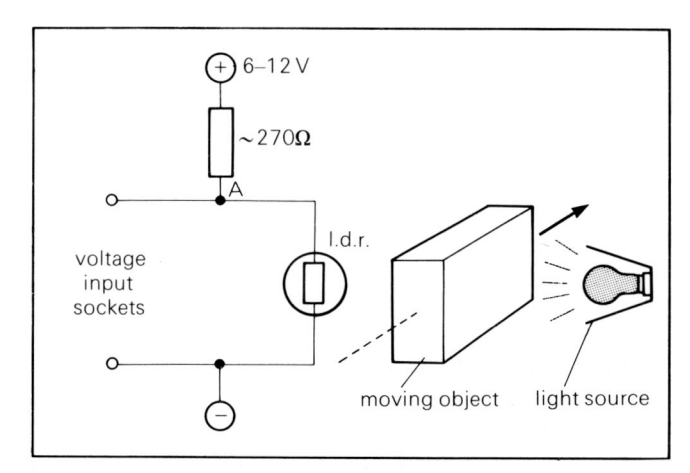

H. *Control a moving vehicle:*

In figure 432, when the push switch is pressed, the light comes on and the vehicle starts to move. When the vehicle breaks the light beam, it stops.

Figure 430 *Detecting a change in light.*

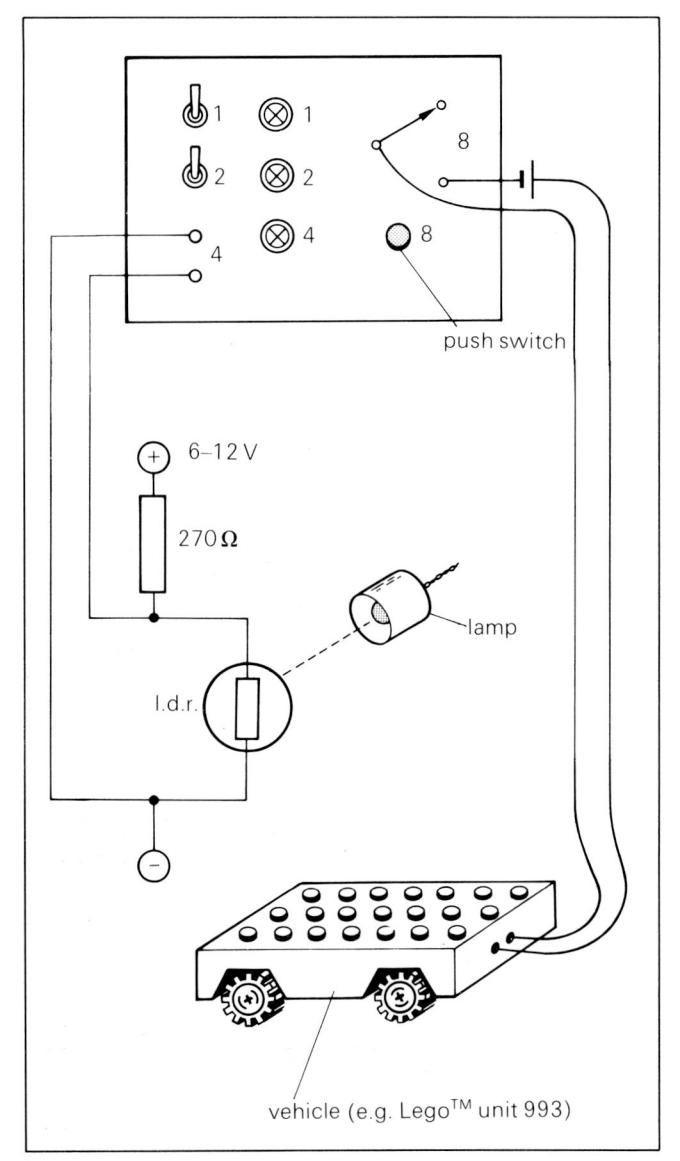

Figure 432 Controlling an electric vehicle.

74. ANALYSIS OF SPECTRA

1. DISTRIBUTION OF COLOURS IN THE SPECTRUM

When a filament lamp heats up, as the current flowing through it increases, the amount of energy produced for different colours of light alters. This experiment investigates the distribution of colours in the spectrum and their amplitudes.

Experimental details

The spectrum is continuous rather than made up of several characteristic lines.

Set up the apparatus as shown in figure 433. For a range of currents up to 2 A (why?), move the photodiode or other light detector along the line AB, at the focal length of lens Y, and take readings of the voltage produced

DEDUCTIONS, APPLICATIONS AND DATA ANALYSIS

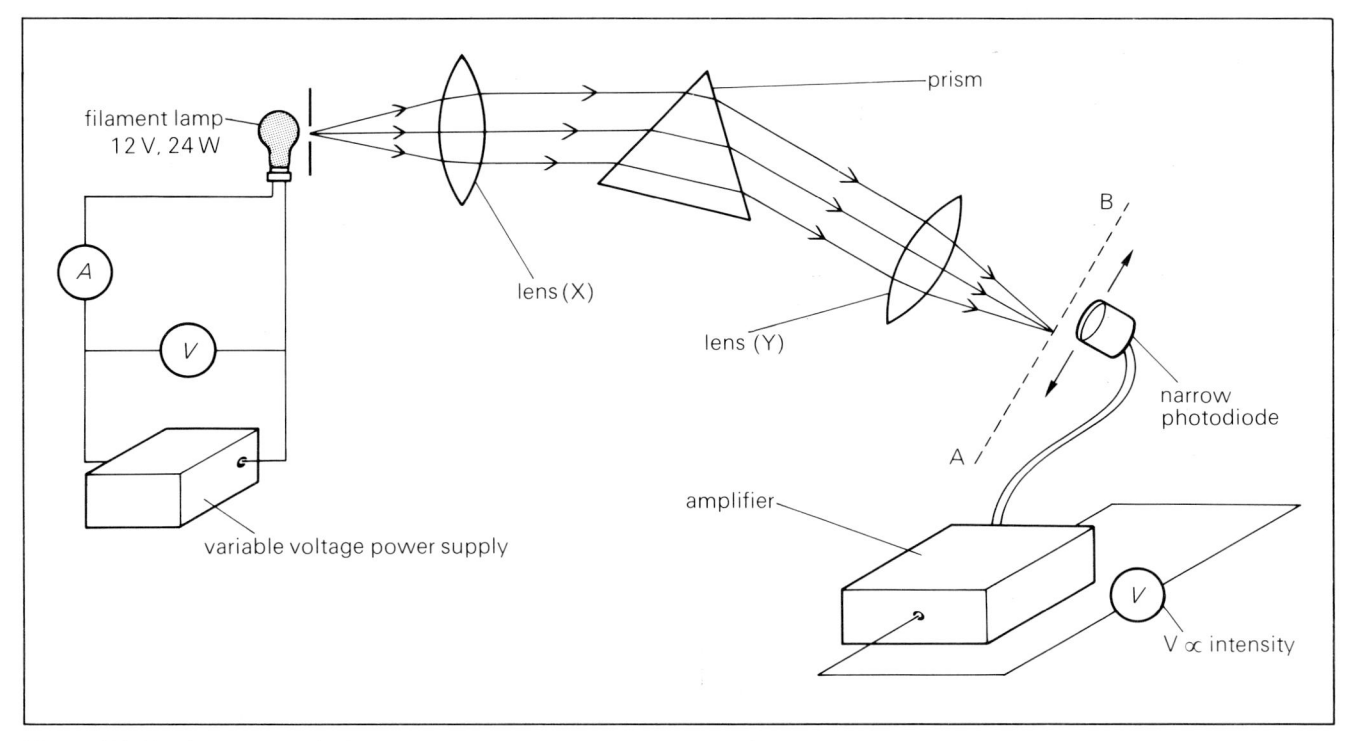

Figure 433 Equipment; producing a spectrum

by the light detector at a set of points along AB. Plot a graph of power ($V \times I$) produced by the supply against area under the intensity–distance graph.

Using a larger current, repeat the experiment so that the shapes can be compared and comments made. It would also be possible to use *data logging* packages with a computer to speed up the process of taking readings and plotting the graphs. Using a sheet of OHP plastic the shape of the trace can be marked on. This makes the process of comparing easier. The program 'DATALOG' (package PHYS2 option 5), available for the BBC model 'B' microcomputer, enables you to take a series of single readings, and to plot graphs. This can save a lot of time in recording readings and plotting the graphs. Alternatively a data gathering instrument such as the VELA could be used.

2. DATA ANALYSIS QUESTIONS

The spectrum shown in figure 434 is of the standard lines of cadmium:

red	643.84 nm
green	508.59 nm
blue	479.99 nm

The spectra shown in figure 435 are taken with exactly the same settings on the spectrometer. What element(s) are present in each? Only the major lines are given for each element. Use the information supplied on page 202 to help you.

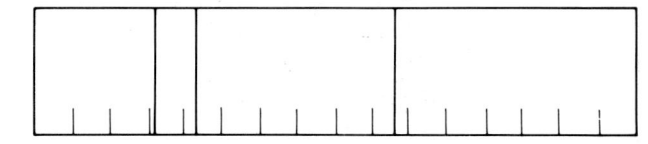

Figure 434 Spectrum of cadmium

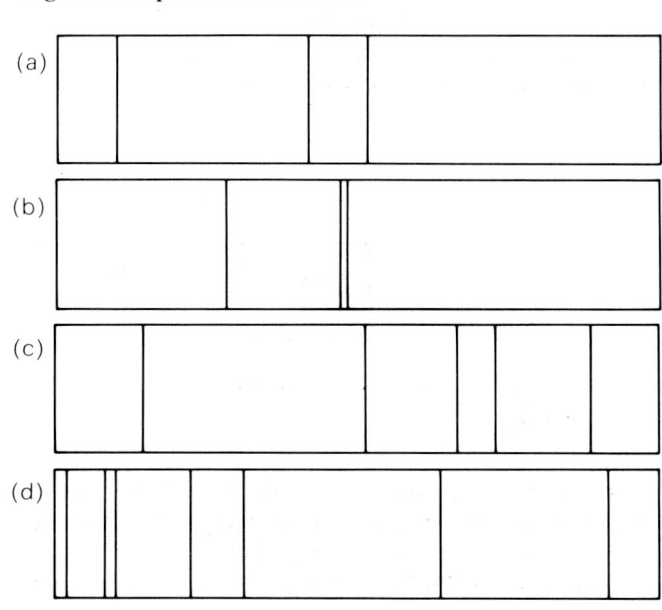

Figure 435

Information

Element	Colour	Wavelength	Element	Colour	Wavelength
K	red	766.5 nm	Fe & Ca	green	527.0 nm
O	red	759.4 nm	Mg	green b_1	518.3 nm
O	red B	687.0 nm	Mg	green b_2	517.2 nm
Li	red	670.8 nm	Mg	green b_4	516.7 nm
H_2	red	656.3 nm	Cd	green	508.58 nm
Cd	red	643.84 nm	H	blue	486.1 nm
Li	orange	610.4 nm	Cd	blue	479.99 nm
Na	orange (D_1)	589.59 nm	Sr	blue	460.7 nm
Na	orange (D_2)	590.00 nm	Li	blue	460.3 nm
He	yellow	587.56 nm	Hg	blue	435.8 nm
Hg	yellow	579.0 nm	H	blue	434.0 nm
Hg	yellow	577.0 nm	Fe & Ca	blue	430.8 nm
Hg	green	546.1 nm	Ca	blue	422.7 nm
Tl	green	535.0 nm	Hg & K	violet	404.7 nm

75. ANALYSIS OF PROJECTILES

Outline

A child's springy sucker toy can be used to investigate the effect of the angle of projection on the range (figure 436).

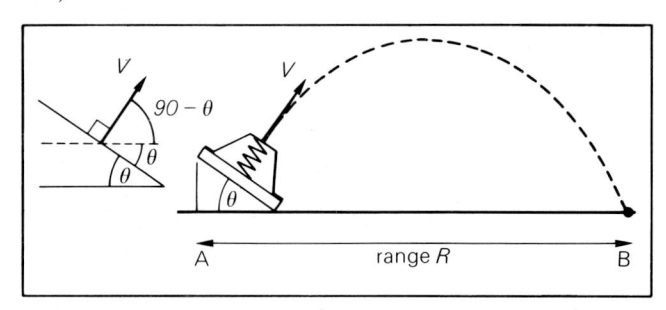

Figure 436

The vertical displacement between A and B is 0. Suppose this takes a time t:

the horizontal component of velocity $= V\cos(90-\theta)$
$= V\sin\theta$
$R = V\sin\theta \, t$

and so
$$t = \frac{R}{V\sin\theta} \quad (1)$$

the vertical component of velocity $= V\sin(90-\theta)$
$= V\cos\theta$

using $s = ut + \tfrac{1}{2}at^2$

$$0 = V\cos\theta \, t + (-\tfrac{1}{2}gt^2) \quad (2)$$

at the earth's surface $g = 10\,\text{m s}^{-2}$.

Combining equations (1) and (2):

$$0 = \frac{V\cos\theta R}{V\sin\theta} - \frac{5R^2}{V^2\sin^2\theta}$$

$$\frac{5R}{V^2\sin^2\theta} = \frac{\cos\theta}{\sin\theta}$$

so
$$R = \frac{V^2\sin^2\theta \cos\theta}{5\sin\theta}$$

$$R = \frac{V^2\sin\theta\cos\theta}{5}$$

$$\boxed{R = \frac{V^2\sin 2\theta}{10}}$$

The maximum value of a sine is 1 (at an angle of 90°). This will be when $\theta = 45°$.

Experimental details

Take a series of readings of θ and the range (R) produced. Plot a graph of $\sin 2\theta$ against R. This should be a straight line. From the graph find the velocity of projection and the angle which will produce maximum range. If this is not at 45°, explain why.

Questions

These are questions based on multiflash photographs taken of a moving object. In the first two questions the

DEDUCTIONS, APPLICATIONS AND DATA ANALYSIS

only force acting after initial projection is gravity; in the third question a frictional force acts.

1. (a) For figure 437 work out the vertical acceleration and decide if the object was photographed on the moon or the earth.
   (b) What is the initial horizontal projection velocity?

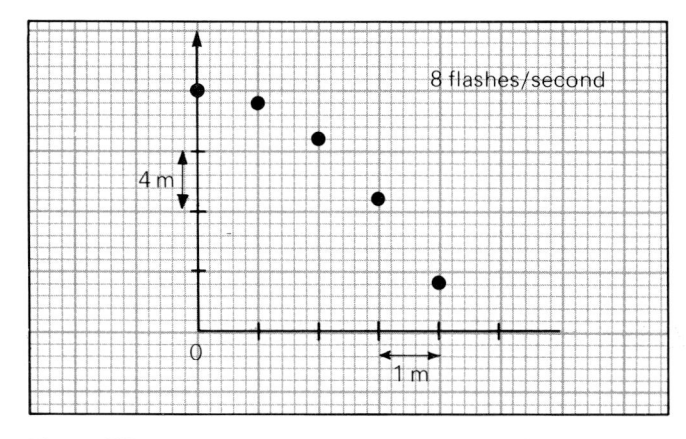

Figure 437

2. Figure 438 shows the path of a ball thrown on the earth.
   (a) What is the maximum horizontal distance reached?
   (b) What is the time of flight?
   (c) What is the horizontal velocity?
   (d) What is the angle of projection?
   (e) What is the projection velocity?

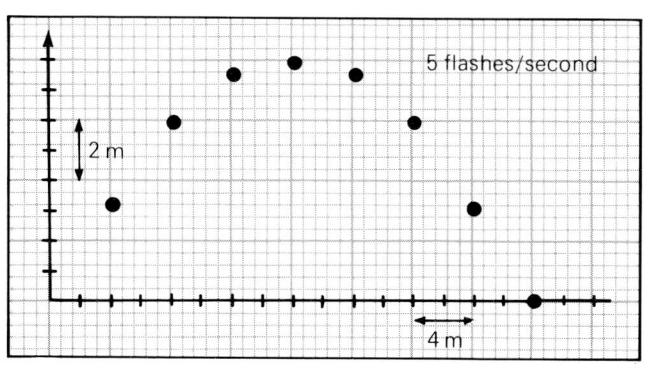

Figure 438

Figure 439 is of an object falling under gravity a few seconds from the start. The object has a mass of 2 kg and you can assume $g = 10 \, \text{N kg}^{-1}$

3. (a) What is the resultant force on the object?
   (b) Find the equation connecting the air resistance force with the velocity.

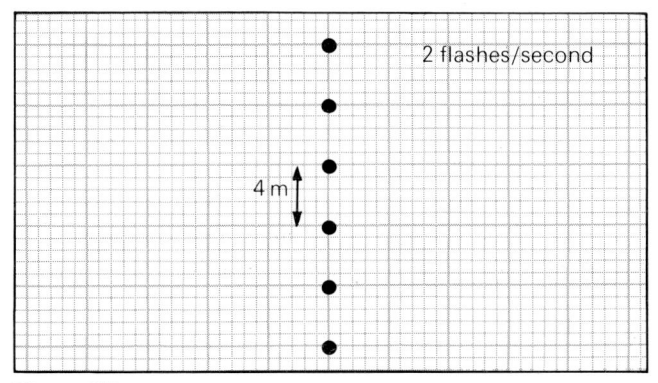

Figure 439

76. ANALYSIS OF THE COLLISIONS OF OBJECTS

1. Figure 440 represents the negative of a multiflash photograph of a collision between two vehicles on a linear air track, taken at intervals of one tenth of a second. Work out the velocities and the momenta of each vehicle. Do the results verify the law of conservation of momentum?

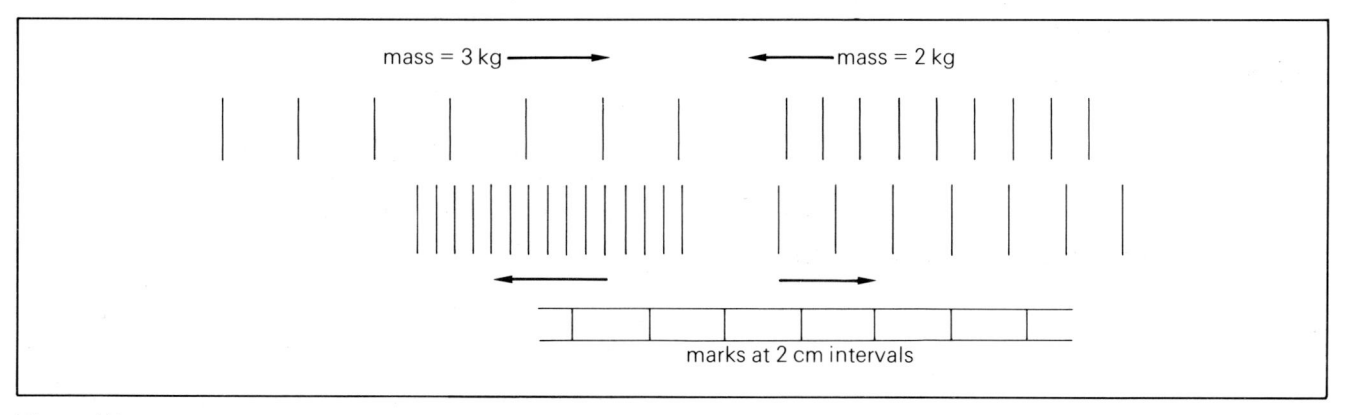

Figure 440

2. Figure 441 represents part of the negative of a multiflash photograph taken of the elastic collision between two magnetic pucks on a low-friction surface. One puck is moving and the other is initially stationary. What is the mass of the stationary puck in terms of M, where M is the mass of the moving puck? *Hint*: Measure the angles α and β. Resolve the momenta after collision (a) along the line of the incoming puck, and (b) at right angles to it.

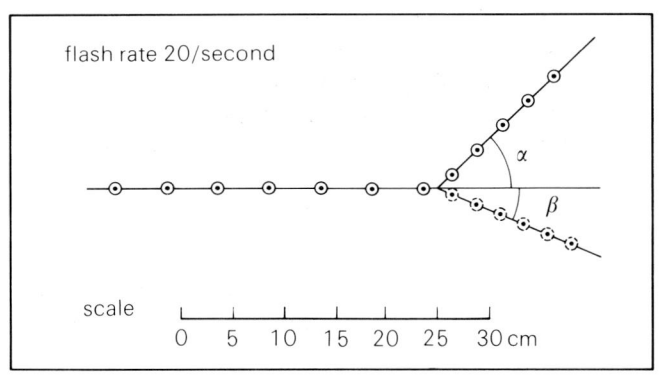

Figure 441

77. DESIGNING EXPERIMENTS

A. Describe an experiment to investigate the way in which the *rate of evaporation* of methylated spirit or alcohol depends on the *speed* of the airflow over it. Figure 442 shows the apparatus you have available, but you may include more if you need it.

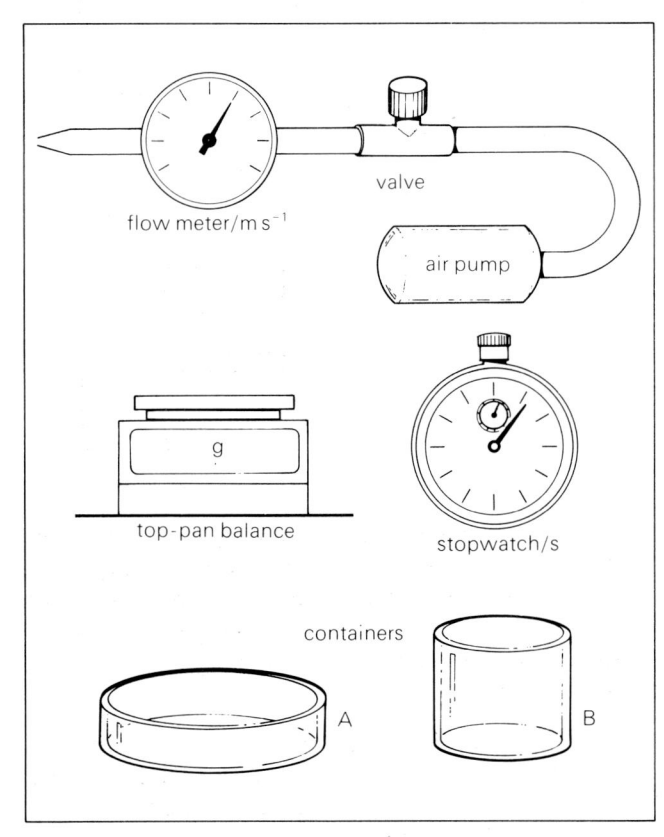

Figure 442

B. An experiment is needed to test the idea that when an object is moving in a circular path it needs a force (the centripetal force) directed towards the centre of rotation, and that the size of the force needed is given by

$$F = \frac{mv^2}{r}$$

m = mass of object
v = velocity of object
r = radius of 'orbit'

Figure 443 shows some apparatus you have available. Describe how you would use the apparatus. *Hint*: Try Hooke's law.

C. Design an experiment which will enable you to investigate the way in which the length and width of an elastic band alter as an increasing force is applied.

D. Your friend suggests that the human ear is most sensitive to sound at a frequency of about 3500 Hz, i.e. for the *same amplitude* it sounds louder than other frequencies. How would you go about investigating this? Remember that you will have to find some way of making sure that the amplitude of the sound actually produced by the speaker is constant.

E. How would you use the apparatus shown in figure 444 to find the force per metre produced by the surface tension effect between the soap film and the soap solution?

DEDUCTIONS, APPLICATIONS AND DATA ANALYSIS

F. Analysis of rock samples taken from the moon indicates that, when the craters were formed by the impact of colliding objects, material was thrown from the crater to the outside. By dropping a ball bearing from different heights onto level sand, investigate this idea. The experiment should also investigate any relationship between the speed of impact, the depth of the crater, and radius of the ball bearing used.

G. A simple 'component tester' is made from the circuit shown in figure 445, with the intention of putting an unknown component in the gap, moving the switch to 'test' and deciding on the component from the current which flows. Assuming the unknown components are a wire, nothing, a lamp, a battery or a diode, construct a flowchart to solve the problem and to make the correct deductions. An example flowchart has been started for you below.

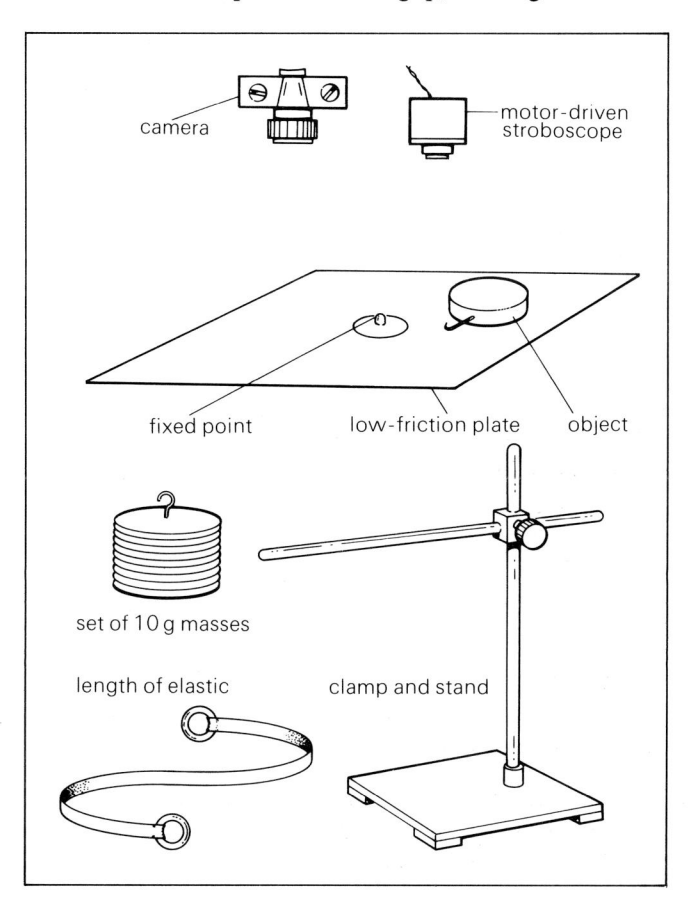

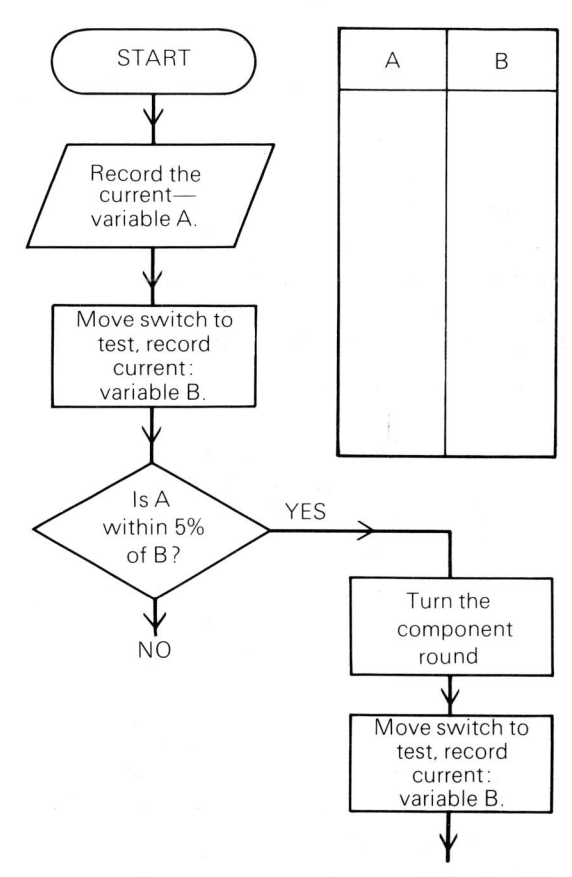

Figure 443

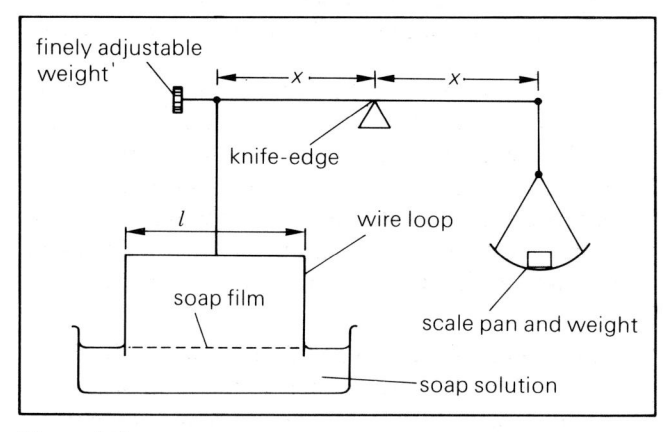

Figure 444

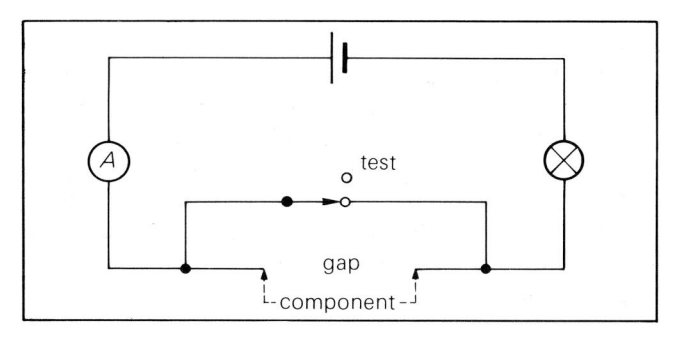

Figure 445

H. A metal bar initially at a room temperature of about 20°C is suddenly heated at one end by boiling water at 100°C and cooled at the other end by melting ice at 0°C. How would you devise an experiment which plots out how the temperature along the bar varies with time?

I. You are to decide if an α-particle source produces α-particles of one or more energies. Explain what you would do and how the correct deductions about the source can be made from the results.

78. ANALYSIS OF MELTING POINTS

You have probably done an experiment in which you have been given a quantity of material which has a melting point in the region of 70°C to 80°C and which could be inflammable, and have plotted a cooling curve in order to find the melting point. These questions are based on this type of experiment.

1. Answer the following questions concerning figure 446:

    (a) What is the melting point of the material?
    (b) How was the material heated and why?
    (c) How long did it take to lose the latent heat?
    (d) What would be the effect on the graph of:

        (i) blowing air round the container?
        (ii) using a larger mass of material?
        (iii) doing the experiment outside in a temperature of −5°C?

2. The cooling curve in figure 447 was produced by a mixture of two materials. One was known to be a wax with a melting point of 330 K and a specific latent heat of fusion of 80 J kg^{-1}.

    (a) Were there any faults with the apparatus?
    (b) What is the melting point of the other material?
    (c) Is it possible to estimate the specific latent heat of the other material from the graph? Give your reasoning.

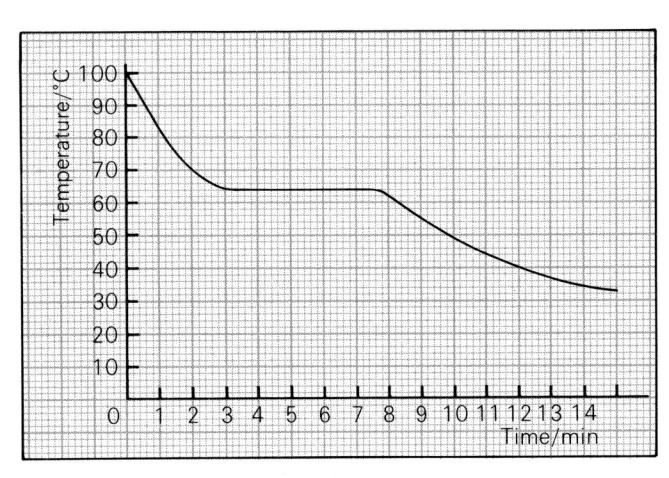

Figure 446

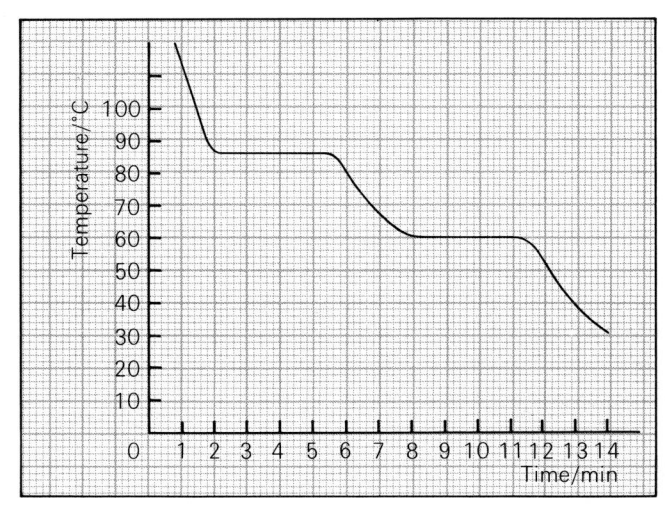

Figure 447

79. ANALYSIS OF SOUND WAVES

Outline

A wave has the general equation

$$y = A \sin(\omega t + \delta)$$

where A is the amplitude
ω is the angular frequency
δ is the phase angle (radian)

Waves of any shape can be produced by adding sine waves of different frequency, amplitude and phase. In particular:

1. The tone of musical instruments depends on the number of overtones present, their frequencies and relative amplitudes.
2. An effect called *beats* is produced when two waves of similar, but not necessarily the same, amplitude and nearly the same frequency are present together.

DEDUCTIONS, APPLICATIONS AND DATA ANALYSIS

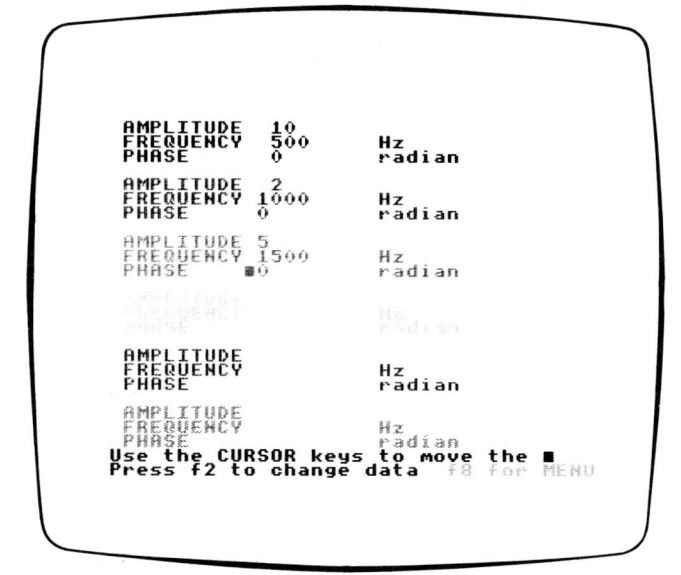

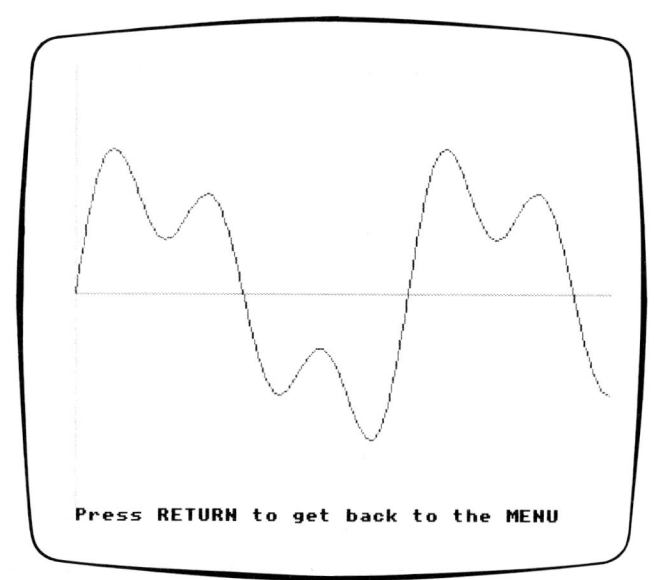

Figure 448 Entering details about a waveform (left) and the resultant waveform (right).

3. Waves do not stay still—they move. Can this movement of the wave peak (or front) be explained as a gradual change of phase angle?
4. Amplitude modulation in radio transmission involves combining a carrier wave with the frequency to be transmitted.
5. Destructive interference between two waves occurs when the phase difference is $(2n+1)\pi$. This investigation uses a computer program 'WAVES' (package PHYS3 option 4) which allows you to input the amplitude, frequency and phase of a number of waves (maximum 10) and display the resulting waveform. Alternatively, Program 10 on the VELA instrument can be used, if you have one available. (See figure 448.)

The wave pattern on the screen can be traced over using a sheet of clear acetate film (OHP transparency) or a printed copy can be produced, on a variety of printers.

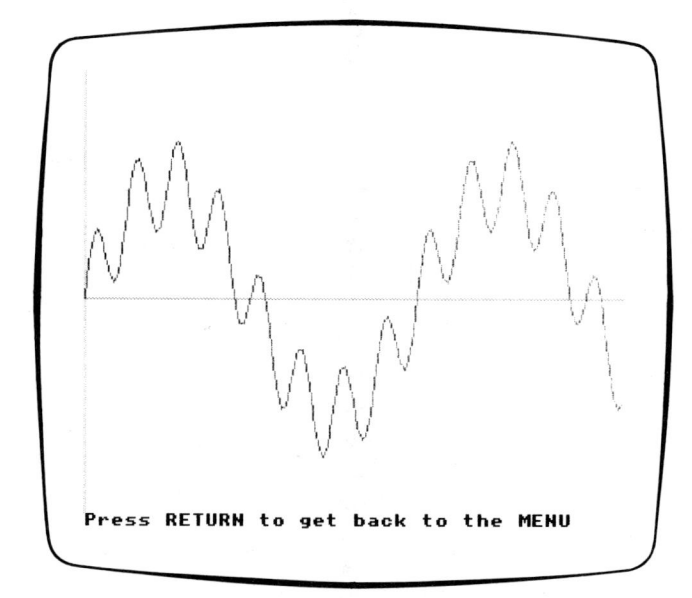

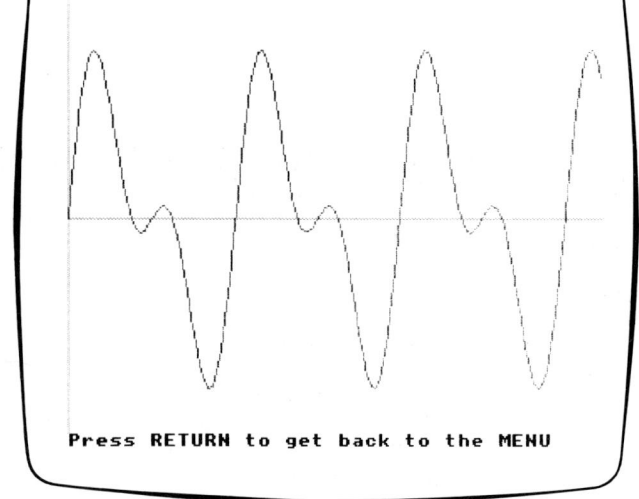

Figure 449 Two different synthesized waveforms.

Experimental details

A. Produce a 500 Hz wave with an amplitude of 10 and a phase of 0.
B. Experiment and try to find the approximate amplitudes of the overtones which make up the sound from:

   (a) two synthesized instruments (figure 449, p. 207), with only one overtone on each
   (b) a violin with a fundamental frequency of 512 Hz and with the first three overtones present (figure 450).

C. Produce a wave pattern which demonstrates *beats*.
D. Produce a pattern which demonstrates the modulation of a 5 kHz carrier wave with a 200 Hz signal.
E. Produce a series of patterns in which the phase angle is increasing. Is the movement of the wavepeak in the positive x direction or negative x direction?

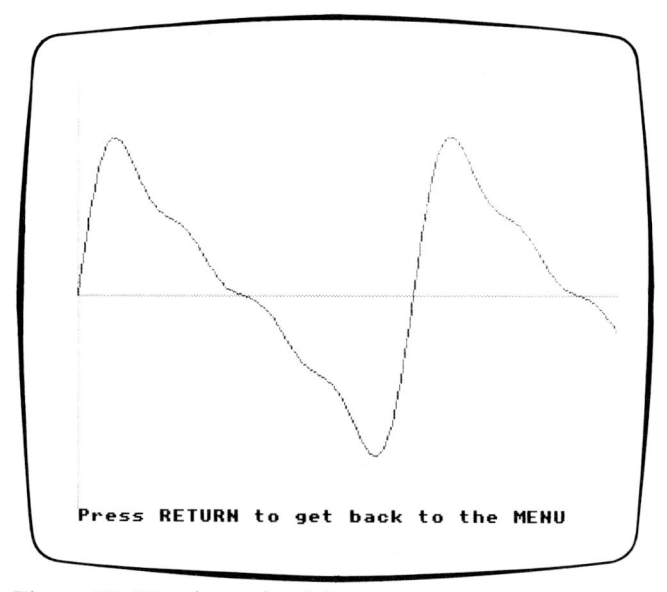

Figure 450 Waveform of a violin

80. POLARISATION OF LIGHT AND THE ANALYSIS OF STRESS

Outline

When light passes through a polaroid filter (such as polaroid sunglasses) the light emerging has only one plane of polarisation, rather than planes over the entire range of 360° (figure 451). If this plane-polarised wave is passed through another polaroid filter, the emerging light has the plane of polarisation of the second filter and will be reduced in amplitude depending on the angle through which the second filter has been turned. When the planes of the two filters are at 90° to each other, no light should emerge. The plane of polarisation can be rotated by parts of a solid under stress, and by various organic and inorganic compounds. (You have probably seen dark patches in a car windscreen when you are wearing polaroid sunglasses on a sunny day.) The angle through which the plane-polarised light has been rotated can be found by rotating the second filter until a minimum of light is again seen (ideally black). The plane of the light will then be at 90° to the second filter again and the angle through which the second filter has been turned is measured.

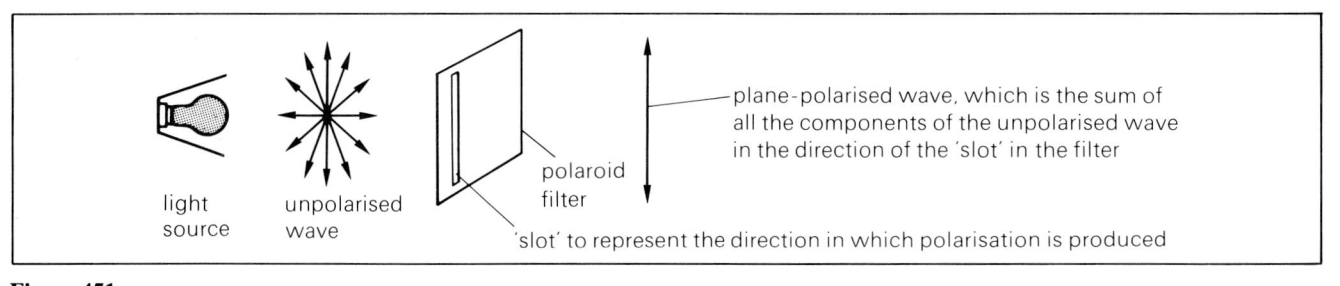

Figure 451

DEDUCTIONS, APPLICATIONS AND DATA ANALYSIS

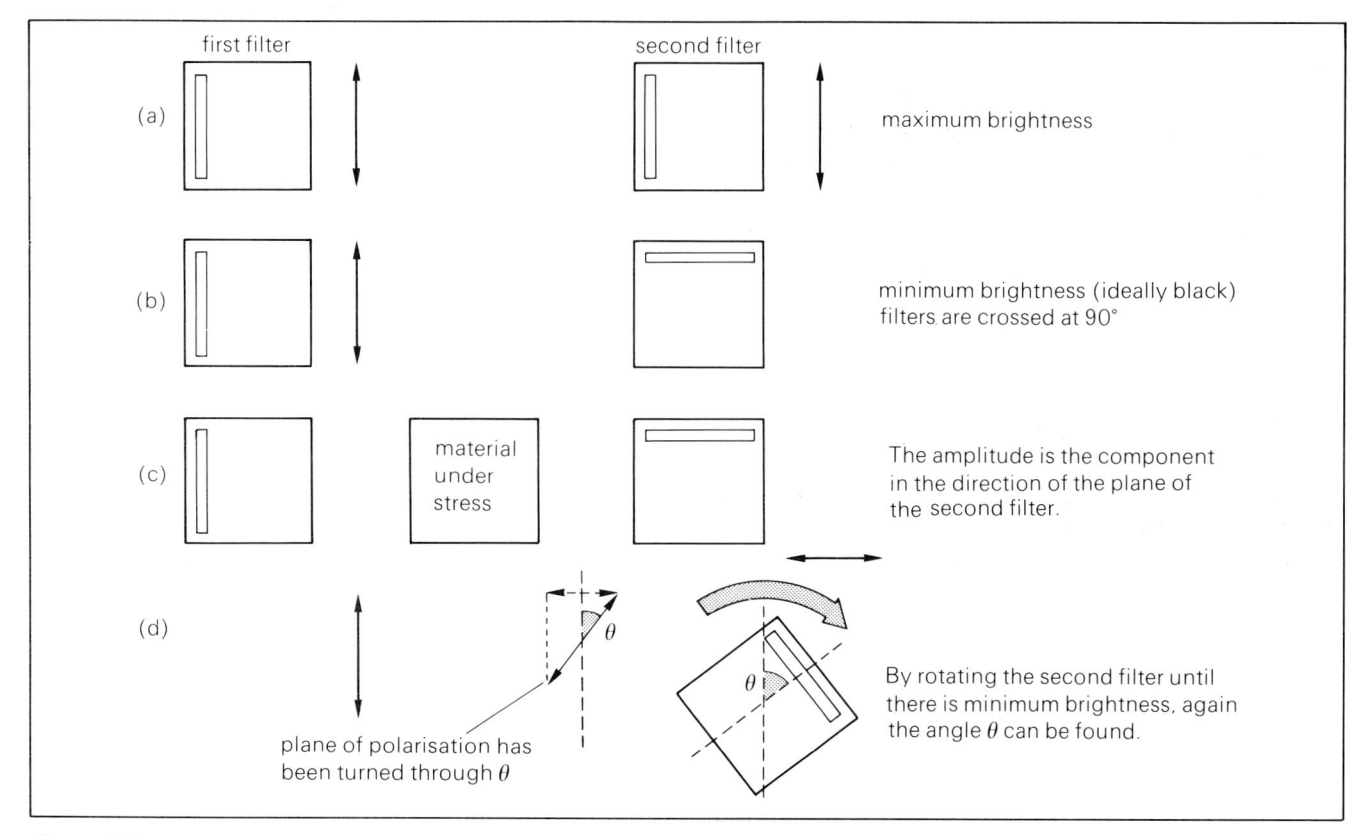

Figure 452

Experimental details

A. Set up a light source and filters as shown in figure 452. Demonstrate to yourself that the angle between the two filters is 90° when a minimum of light is seen. Use coloured filters and see if the same rule applies. Adjust the filters until a minimum of light is seen.

Fold a piece of acetate sheet (e.g. OHP transparency) so that light can pass through several layers. Place it between the two polaroid filters. Compare what is seen with (a) white, (b) red, (c) green, (d) blue light. Rotate the second polaroid filter and measure the angle through which the plane of polarisation has been turned. Can you explain the effect seen with white light? What is the effect of using more layers of acetate sheet (figure 453)?

B. Look through a polaroid filter at white light reflected from the following surfaces: (a) glass, (b) waxed wood, e.g. bench top, (c) rough wood and metal, (d) shiny metal plates, (e) Perspex sheet, and (f) polythene sheet (figure 454). If any light is polarised, there will be a position of minimum brightness as the filter is rotated. Investigate the reflections and write down your findings. Does red, green and blue light behave in the same way? What type of materials produce a plane-polarised reflected beam?

What effect does the angle of incidence have on the degree of polarisation (Brewster's law)?

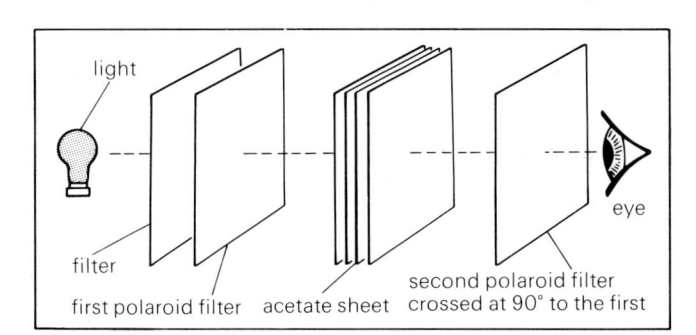

Figure 453

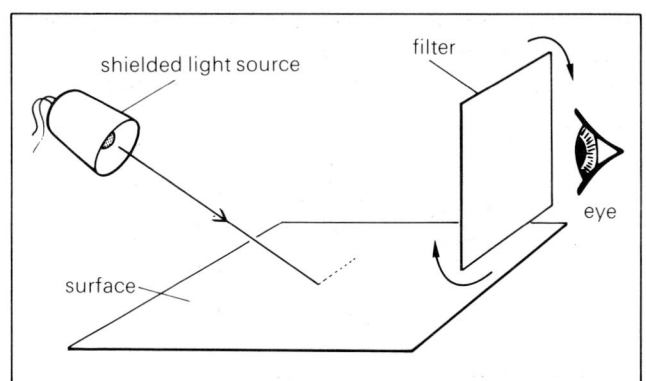

Figure 454

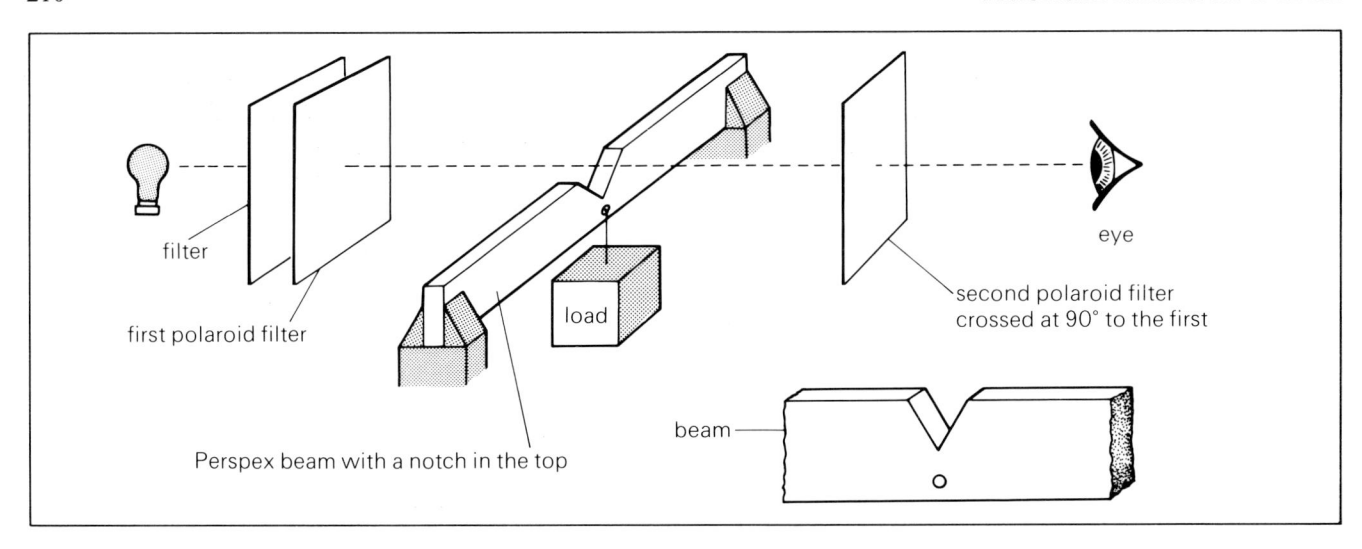

Figure 455 Looking at stress patterns.

C. *Stress patterns*
   (a) Use the equipment shown in figure 455. The second polaroid filter should be rotated until the light is a minimum. This is often referred to as 'crossed polaroid filters'.
   (b) Place the Perspex beam in position and draw diagrams of the patterns seen for different loads in the range 0 to 10 N. In what way is an increase in stress shown?
   (c) A hole is to be cut into a Perspex beam. Load the beams provided with the same weight, approximately 5 N. Draw stress patterns and use them to decide which would be the best shape to choose and to find any potential points of weakness. Some of the shapes you might have are shown in figure 456.

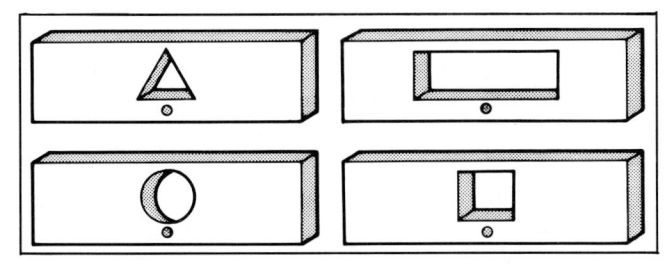

Figure 456

MEASURING QUANTITIES AND INVESTIGATING LAWS

81. FINDING INFORMATION ABOUT ATOMS AND MOLECULES

Outline

All matter is made from about 103 different atoms. Most of the first 92 are naturally occurring, the rest being man-made. It is unusual to find matter consisting of just one type of atom, because most atoms can readily combine with other atoms of a different type to form *molecules*.

Gold is unreactive and exists as uncombined atoms. This is one reason why it is a precious metal, because it does not change with age.

Iron atoms readily combine with oxygen atoms in the air, particularly when water is present, to form an oxide—*rust*.

Sodium (a very reactive metal) and chlorine (a green poisonous gas) atoms combine to form sodium chloride— a white substance called *salt* which we eat.

Hydrogen, oxygen and carbon atoms combine to form *organic* matter, which is the basis of all living things.

Plastics are long chains of hydrocarbons (made of hydrogen and carbon atoms) combined with other atoms, e.g. chlorine (PVC, polyvinyl chloride).

1. The size of all atoms is not the same, but does not increase in proportion to atomic number. The size of a single neutral atom (the *atomic* radius) is different to the size of that same atom when it is combined in a molecule (the *ionic* radius), but is of the order of 100 pm. Think! What is a pm? For example,

    $$Li(3) = 3 \times 10^{-10} \, m = 300 \, pm,$$
    $$Cs(55) = 5.2 \times 10^{-10} \, m = 520 \, pm.$$

    The figures above refer to ionic diameters *not* ionic radii.

2. Atoms and molecules are not still but are in continual random motion. This produces a gradual movement of the atoms and molecules, called diffusion, which can occur in gases, liquids and solids. Robert Brown found that large smoke particles moved randomly in air and concluded that this was due to the random collisions by air particles. This 'Brownian motion' is evidence for the idea that atoms are in continual random movement.

3. When a substance changes state, i.e. from a solid to a liquid or from liquid to vapour, energy has to be supplied to break the bonds between one atom or molecule and its neighbours. This energy is called *latent heat*. The specific latent heat is the energy needed to change the state of 1 kg of a substance at constant temperature. The equation connecting the binding energy (E) and the latent heat *per mole* is $L = \frac{1}{2}nEN$, where n is the number of nearest neighbours, E is the binding energy per molecule pair and N is Avogadro's number.

The experiments you are asked to carry out are as follows.

1. Measure the approximate size of a molecule. You can additionally investigate whether there is any connection between atomic number and atomic radius from the data supplied.

2. Investigate the processes of diffusion by:
    (a) a simple demonstration of Brownian motion using a smoke cell,
    (b) using the Schools Council *Computers in the Curriculum* package on gaseous diffusion (© Longmans).

3. Measure the specific latent heats of water and methylated spirits, in order to estimate the binding energy per molecule pair.

4. Investigate models of bombarding the atom with particles.

1. OIL-FILM EXPERIMENT

Experimental details

If a drop of oil is placed on the surface of water, the force produced because of surface tension at the boundary between the oil and water pulls the oil drop out into a very thin sheet assumed to be a few molecules thick. If the water has been dusted with a light powder first, this will be drawn back and the width of the thin sheet can be measured (figure 457). If the volume of the oil drop is known, the thickness of the sheet of oil can be worked out because the volume of the oil and the volume of the drop must be the same (assuming that the monomolecular layers have the same density as the oil).

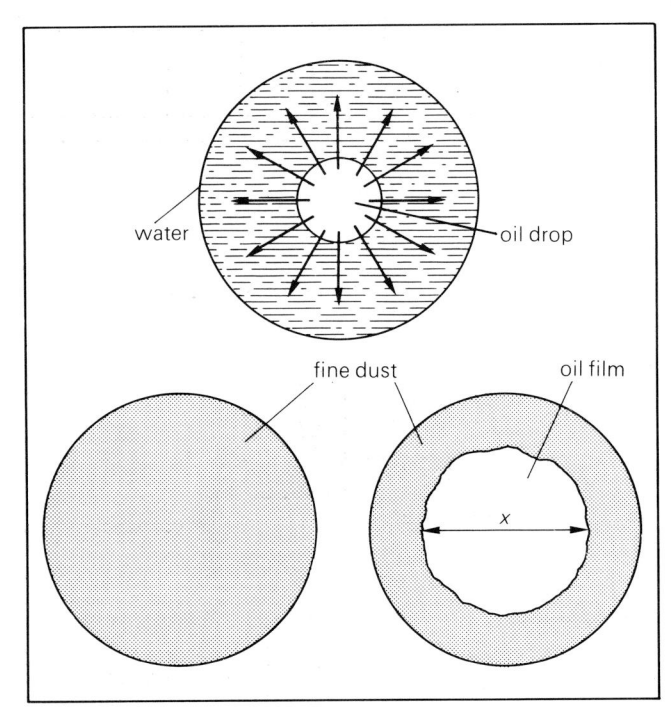

Figure 457 An oil drop spreads out on water.

1. Fill a waxed tray with water until it is just above the edge and dust it lightly with a fine powder which will be held on the surface skin, e.g. talcum powder (figure 458).

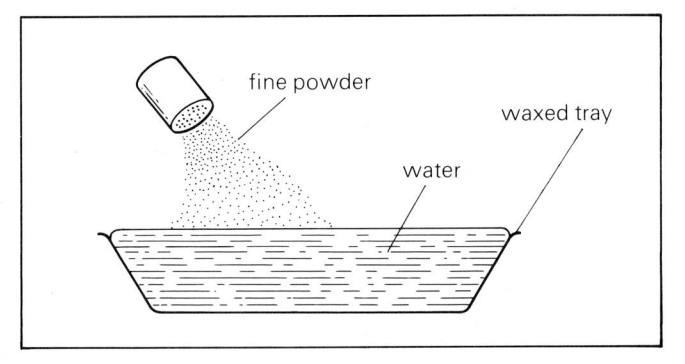

Figure 458

2. Dip a wire frame into oil so that a drop forms on the end. Use a magnifying glass and millimetre scale to find the diameter of the drop (figure 459). How accurate is this measurement?
3. Place the oil drop on the surface of the water and measure the 'diameter' (x) of the sheet of oil produced. You may need to measure several 'diameters' and find an average. Estimate the error in the measurement.
4. Calculate the thickness of the layer, which is assumed to be only a few molecules thick.

$$\text{volume of drop} = \tfrac{4}{3}\pi \left(\frac{d}{2}\right)^3$$

$$\text{volume of sheet} = \frac{\pi x^2}{4} \times \text{thickness}$$

5. Empty the tray, refill it with clean water and repeat the experiment several times. Find an average value for the thickness of the oil layer and then estimate the size of an oil molecule.

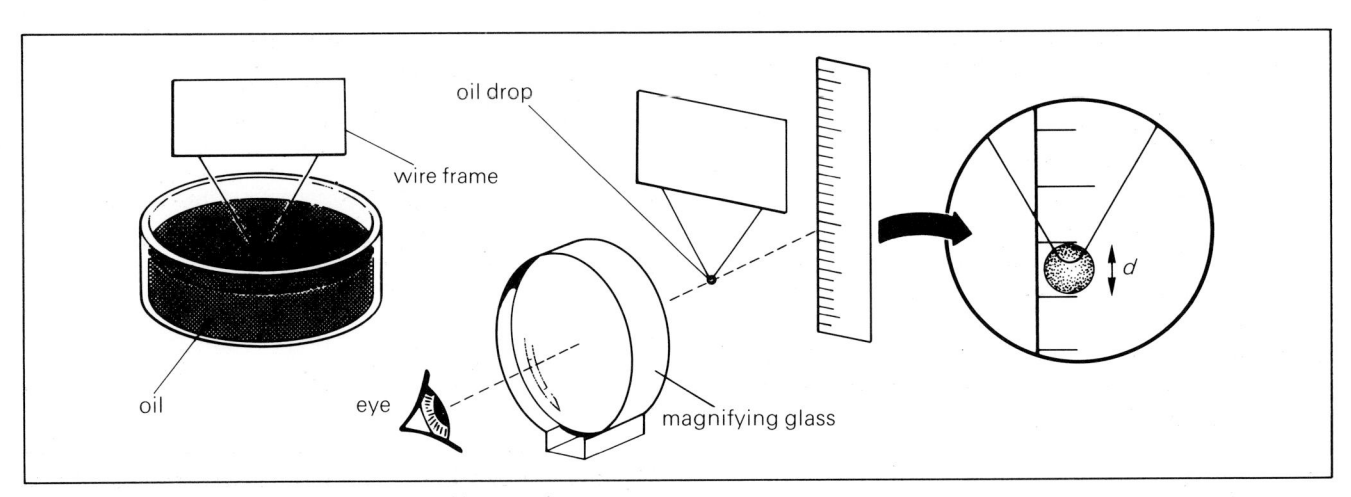

Figure 459 How to produce an oil drop of known size.

MEASURING QUANTITIES AND INVESTIGATING LAWS

1 H 46																	2 He
3 Li 152	4 Be 112											5 B 88	6 C 71	7 N 71	8 O 60	9 F 60	10 Ne 160
11 Na 185	12 Mg 160				TRANSITION ELEMENTS							13 Al 142	14 Si 118	15 P	16 S 106	17 Cl 91	18 Ar 174
19 K 231	20 Ca 196	21 Sc 160	22 Ti 146	23 V 131	24 Cr 125	25 Mn 112	26 Fe 123	27 Co 125	28 Ni 124	29 Cu 128	30 Zn 133	31 Ga 196	32 Ge 122	33 As 125	34 Se 116	35 Br 114	36 Kr 201
37 Rb 246	38 Sr 215	39 Y 131	40 Zr 160	41 Nb 143	42 Mo 136	43 Tc 135	44 Ru 133	45 Rh 134	46 Pd 137	47 Ag 144	48 Cd 148	49 In 162	50 Sn 140	51 Sb 145	52 Te 143	53 I 135	54 Xe 221
55 Cs 262	56 Ba 217	57 La 187	72 Hf 158	73 Ta 143	74 W 137	75 Re 137	76 Os 135	77 If 135	78 Pt 138	79 Au 144	80 Hg 156	81 Tl 171	82 Pb 174	83 Bi 155	84 Po 168	85 At	86 Rn
87 Fr	88 Ra	89 Ac 118															

Optional investigation—data analysis

Above is part of the periodic table, showing atomic number, chemical symbol and atomic radius (in picometres). For example:

  8 atomic number
  O symbol
  60 atomic radius/pm

Use the table to answer the following questions.
1. Is there any connection between atomic radii and the number of protons? (Try plotting a log–log graph.)
2. Does the pattern change for the transition elements?
3. What happens for the inert gases?
4. Is there any connection between the number of electrons in the outer shell and the atomic radius?

2. BROWNIAN MOTION

Experimental details

A. If you have never seen Brownian motion, set up and examine a smoke cell, as shown in figure 460. When you examine the cell under a microscope you should see white specks (smoke particles) 'jittering' around as they are bombarded in a random manner by air molecules.
B. If you have the package available, use the Schools Council *Computers in the Curriculum* (© Longman) computer program and booklet to investigate the diffusion of gases.
C. Diffusion is an example of a process called *random walk*. Statistical theory gives an expression for the resulting displacement:

$$x = \lambda \sqrt{n}$$

n is the number of moves and λ is the *mean free path*.

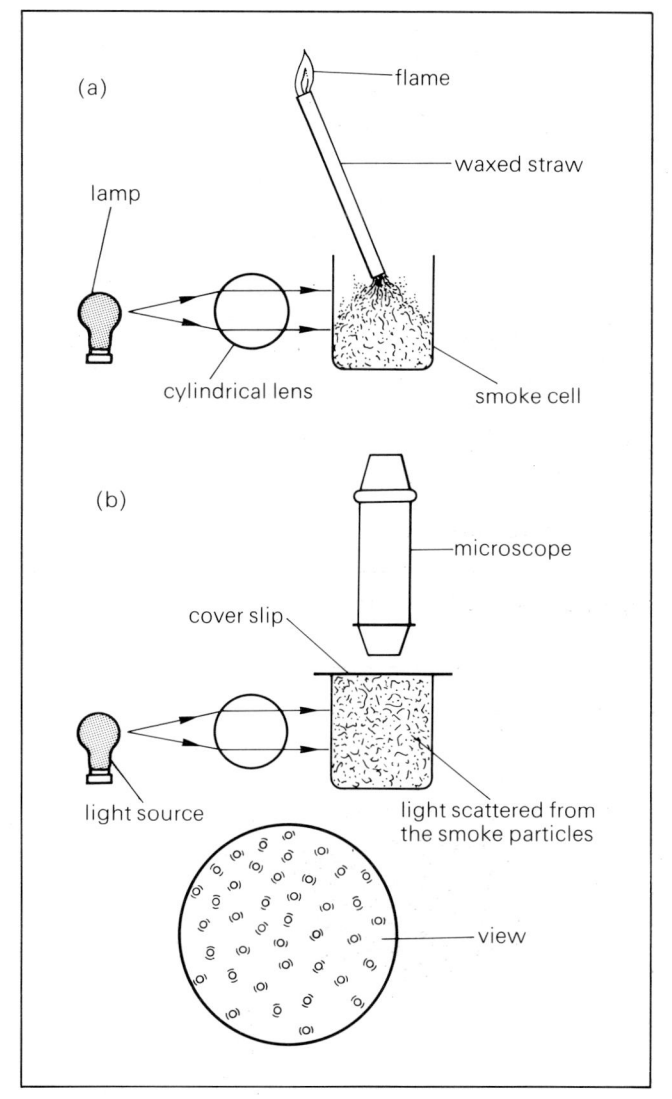

Figure 460 (a) Fill the smoke cell with smoke and immediately put the cover slip on, then (b) examine it under a microscope.

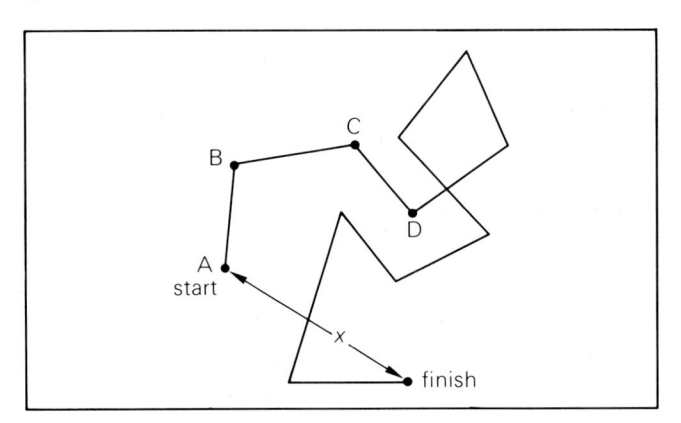

Figure 461 Path of a particle

Looking at figure 461:

$$\lambda = \frac{AB + BC + CD + \cdots}{n}$$

This means that diffusion should:

(a) increase in a low-pressure gas where the mean free path between collisions is larger than at normal atmospheric pressure.
(b) be very marked and fast in a vacuum.
(c) be slow with small distances being moved in a solid.

The principle can be tested with a die. Use 60° ruled paper (figure 462).

(a) Start from the centre.
(b) Shake the die.
(c) Draw a line one 'block' in the direction given by the number on the die.
(d) Repeat n number of times, moving on from each new position, e.g. 9, 16, 25 times.
(e) Measure the resulting displacement (x).
(f) Repeat the whole process yourself (or involve other people in your class) at least ten times.

Does $x = \lambda\sqrt{n}$? What is the spread or error?

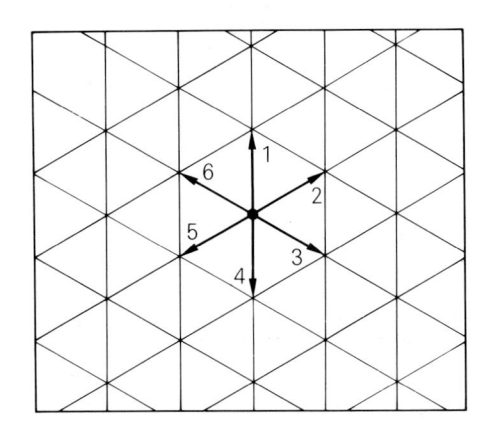

Figure 462

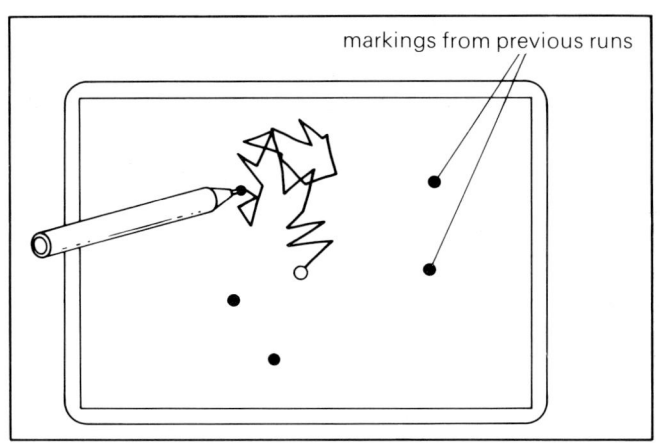

Figure 463

In this model the mean free path can only be altered by using paper ruled to a different sized grid. A more realistic model can be investigated using the computer program 'RANWALK' (package PHYS2 option 4, in the teacher's pack), in which different gases, temperatures and pressures can be chosen and a large number of moves executed each time. To record the final position, place an acetate sheet over the screen and mark with a felt-tipped pen (figure 463).

3. SPECIFIC LATENT HEAT OF VAPORISATION OF WATER AND BONDING ENERGY

Equipment

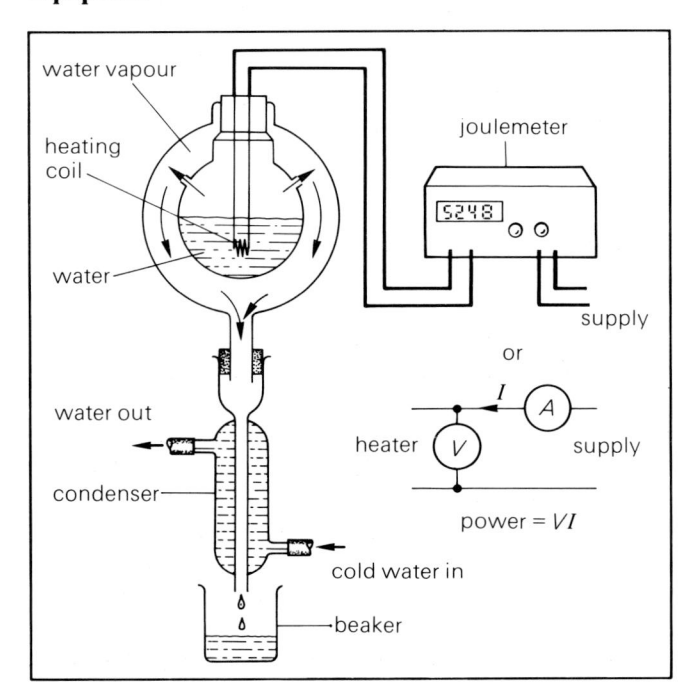

Figure 464 No energy is lost from the water to the outside because the outside of the container is at the same temperature as the water.

Experimental details

1. Using the apparatus shown in figure 464, switch on the heater and allow the water to boil. When condensed water starts to drip steadily from the end of the condenser, weigh a dry beaker and place it to collect the condensed water. At the same instant reset the joulemeter and start timing with a stopwatch.
2. After about 20 minutes, or until the water level has gone down to a level where the heater is only just covered, stop timing, remove the beaker, switch off and record the reading on the joulemeter, and reweigh the beaker.

Results and calculations

mass of beaker empty ... g
mass of beaker + condensed water ... g
mass of condensed water (m) ... g = ... kg
joulemeter reading (E) ... J
the specific latent heat (l) = $\frac{E}{m}$ J kg^{-1}

1 mole contains Avogadro's number of molecules.

Assuming that a molecule of water contains two hydrogen atoms and one oxygen atom, the molecular mass is 2 + 16 = 18. This is the mass of 1 mole of water in grams. 18 g = 0.018 kg, therefore:

$$\text{the latent heat per mole } L = \frac{\text{specific latent heat}}{0.018}$$

Work out the binding energy per molecule (E) from $L = \frac{1}{2}nEN$. (You will have to think of a sensible number to use here for n, the number of nearest neighbours.)

4. BOMBARDING THE ATOM WITH PARTICLES (A MODEL)

Outline

You have already found out that atoms produce electrical forces and that one particle contained in an atom is the electron. Because electrons are negatively charged, it would follow that in a neutral atom there must be some positive charge. If an atom is bombarded by α particles (which can be shown to have a positive charge), the particles should be repelled by the positive charge if it is in a single unit, or hardly affected if the positive and negative charge are intermixed. The way in which α particles are deflected or scattered may tell us something about the inside of the atom. Geiger and Marsden were the first to do this experiment, and they made conclusions about the existence and size of a positively charged nucleus and about the form of repulsive force produced.

To give you some idea of the way in which particles are scattered by an inverse square law scatterer $\left(F \propto \frac{1}{r^2}\right)$, a simple gravitational analogue and a computer simulation are used to investigate the shape, type and size of the scatterer inside the atom.

Experimental details

A. *Gravitational analogue*

1. Use the apparatus shown in figure 465. The height h from which the ball bearing is released determines its initial energy. As you know, α particles emerge from a given source with a particular energy and the height should therefore be kept constant.
2. Some way must be found to trace the path of the ball on the paper. One method is to dust the paper with a fine powder such as lycopodium and to mark the track with pencil dots. Another method is to place a thin sheet of carbon paper on top of the paper.
3. Record a series of tracks for different offsets p. There will probably be a fluctuation in successive paths for the same offset, so record about ten runs and then mark the central track on the paper. Measure the angle ϕ. It can be shown that if the particle moves in a $\frac{1}{r^2}$ force field $\left(\text{or } \frac{1}{r} \text{ potential field}\right)$, then:

$$\cot\frac{\phi}{2} = \frac{2p}{b}$$

where b is the distance of closest approach in a 'head-on' collision and therefore depends on the energy of the particle.

4. Plot a graph of $\cot\frac{\phi}{2}$ against p. It will be a straight line through the origin if the equation is correct. Find the distance of closest approach.
5. Repeat for two other heights (h).

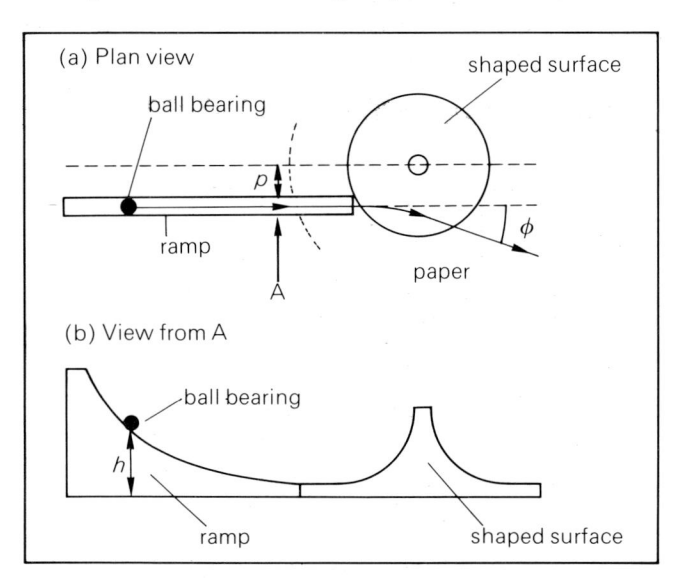

Figure 465 Apparatus

Mean $\phi/°$	p/mm	Cot $\dfrac{\phi}{2}$ /°

What conclusions can be made?

B. *Computer simulation*

One computer simulation project which could be used is 'ALPHAFOIL' from the Warwick Science Simulation Project (© Longman). This allows you to take results from an alpha scattering experiment. You can alter the foil material, the foil thickness and the alpha particle velocity. It contains its own student notes; work through these and write a summary of your 'experiments' in your report.

82. ELASTICITY AND YOUNG'S MODULUS

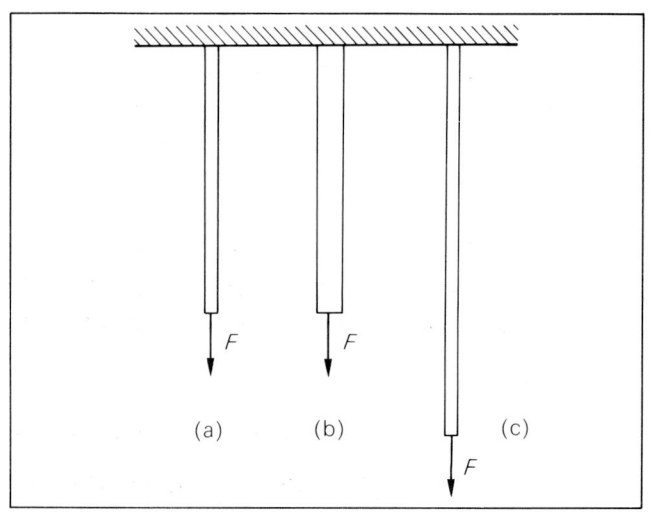

Figure 466 Three pieces of wire made from the same material

Outline

All materials change their shape when a force is applied. Consider three wires, (a), (b) and (c), of the same material (figure 466). Initial simple experimentation shows that (a) produces a larger change in length than (b), and (c) produces a larger change in length than (a).

It is reasonable to think that the cross-section area of the wire is involved and also the initial length of the wire. An equation, $\dfrac{F}{A} = \text{const.}\dfrac{\delta l}{l}$, is proposed which seems to predict these results. This experiment investigates the validity of this equation for solder, copper, steel and rubber, and a value for the constant is found. It is reasonable to assume that there is some term which is characteristic of the material used, and this may be the constant.

Equipment

The apparatus shown in figure 467 assumes that the material will stretch by at least 5 mm when the load is

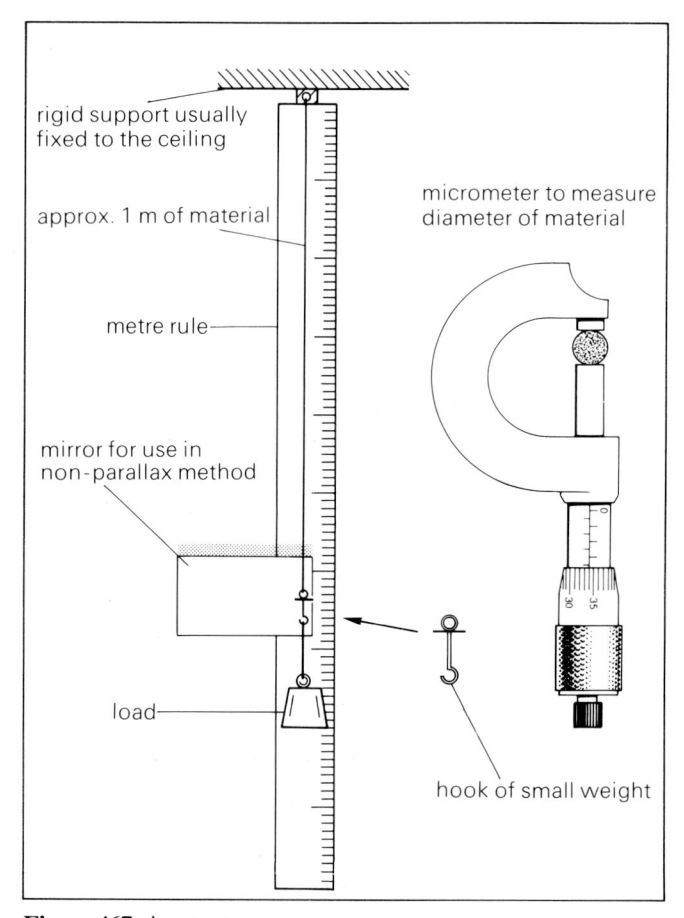

Figure 467 Apparatus

Warning: wear safety glasses in case the wire snaps.

increased. The maximum load from a safety point of view is about 200 N, so if 20 N produces stretching of less than 5 mm, a more accurate method of measuring the extension must be used. The Young's modulus apparatus, shown in figure 468, would be used.

MEASURING QUANTITIES AND INVESTIGATING LAWS

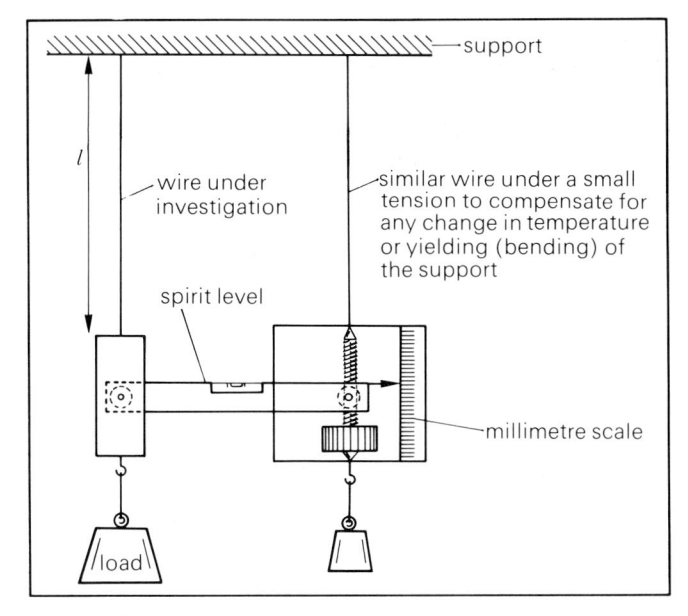

Figure 468 Young's modulus apparatus

The maximum movement is usually about 5 mm so the scale will need to be moved down, making *l* longer as the wire under investigation stretches. You will need to record the readings on the scale both before it is moved and after (see figure 469), so that the extension can be calculated.

Experimental details

Measure the length (*l*) of the wire with no load on. Ignoring the small weight of the spirit level part, this can be taken as the unextended length. For each of the wires given you need to apply a series of loads and measure the extension. About 20 results are needed and it is necessary to work out the incremental steps. To do this, keep increasing the load until (a) the wire snaps, (b) the load reaches the floor, or (c) the maximum safety load is reached. From this maximum load, work out a *sensible* incremental step for loading, which will give about 20 readings. Since the wire could have been permanently damaged by this loading, it may be necessary to use *a new piece of wire*. Apply loads by the incremental steps and record the scale readings produced. Measure the diameter of the wire with a micrometer at each loading, at four different points, so that the cross-sectional area of the wire can be found. Work out the extension from the scale readings.

Results

length = ... m

Load/N	Scale reading/mm	Diameter/mm
0	(Two columns for use alternately when the scale is moved down the wire)	

From the results

Cross-sectional area/m	$\frac{F}{A}$	Extension/m	$\frac{\delta l}{l}$

For each wire plot a graph of F/A, which is called *stress*, as ordinate against $\delta l/l$, which is called *strain*, as abscissa.

From the graph

If $\frac{F}{A} = \text{const.} \frac{\delta l}{l}$, the graph should be a straight line passing through the origin, with the constant being the gradient of the graph and the same value for all wires of the same material. Find this constant if possible; it is called Young's modulus.

If only part of the graph is a straight line, comment on the effect of

(a) the thickness of the wire and
(b) the original length of the wire,

on the stress value at this *elastic limit* (i.e. when the graph ceases to be a straight line).

Information

Material	Young's modulus $\times 10^{12}$ Pa
aluminium	71
brass	100
copper	117
solder	—
steel	210
rubber	0.02
wood: spruce (with grain)	14
wood: spruce (across grain)	0.5

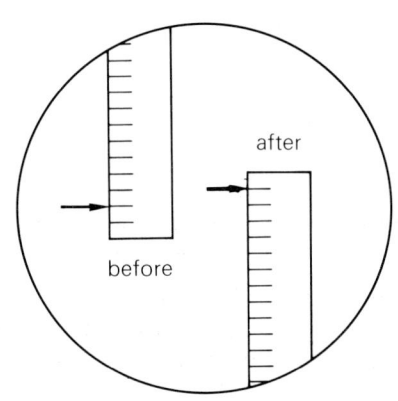

Figure 469

83. EQUILIBRIUM OF A BODY UNDER COPLANAR FORCES

Outline

This experiment aims to investigate the following two rules.

1. If only three forces act, their lines of action pass through a single point.
2. The resultant force in any direction, when three forces act, is zero. Because the lamina is not turning, it should also follow that the resultant moment about any point in the plane is zero.

Equipment

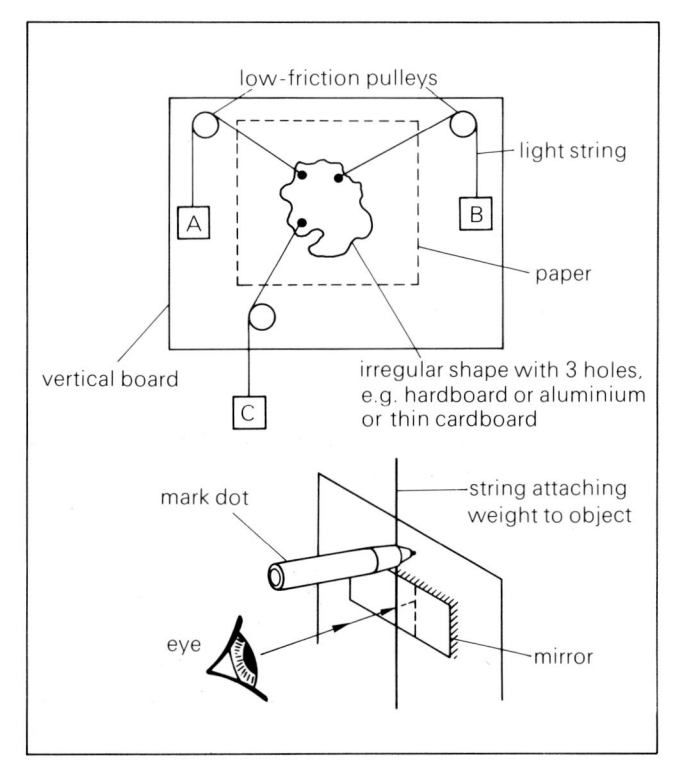

Figure 470 Apparatus. Avoid the parallax error by using a mirror and the method of no parallax, or use a 90° square, to mark the dots.

Experimental details

Cut out an irregular shape from thin cardboard and assemble the apparatus as shown in figure 470. Alter the weights A, B and C until the card is still. Mark at least three dots along the line of each string and record the forces produced by A, B and C. Repeat the procedure several times, but with the pulleys in different positions. Use a new piece of paper each time.

Repeat the experiment but with the irregular shape cut from a piece of hardboard, plastic or metal.

Results

On the pieces of paper draw lines along the 'lines of dots' and see if they meet at a point.

1. Try and estimate the accuracy from the size of the 'triangle' formed by the lines (see figure 471). The variation is approximately $\frac{x}{\theta} \times 100\%$.

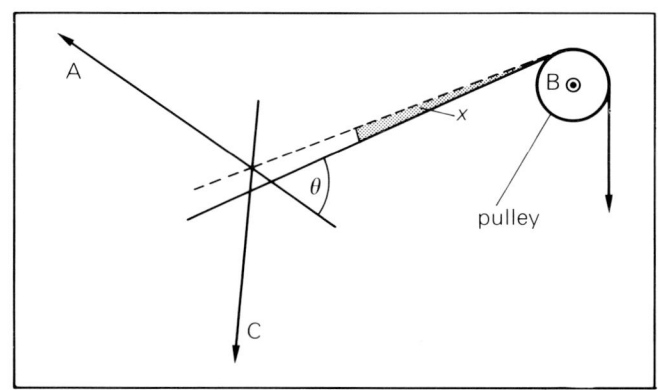

Figure 471 Measure the angle x from where the string leaves the pulley.

2. By drawing the size of the forces to scale along the lines, use the parallelogram of vectors to see if the third force is the equilibrant of the other two. Think! Will the weight of the card have any appreciable effect?
3. Choose any direction through the intersection lines of action of the three forces. Resolve each force in this direction and find the resultant force. Work out the approximate percentage variation

$$= \frac{\text{resultant}}{\text{average of the 3 forces}} \times 100\%$$

4. Choose any point on the paper at random. Work out the moment of each force about that point and the resultant moment.

Conclusions

Do you think your results support the two rules stated at the beginning of this practical?

What do you think would happen with four forces?

84. FALLING SAND: NEWTON'S SECOND LAW

Outline

Newton's second law of motion states that force is proportional to the rate of change of momentum. This experiment investigates this law. Sand or salt is allowed to fall into a container on a top-pan balance. Any force produced by the change in momentum of the sand as it hits the balance will be shown as an increase in the reading on the balance, over and above the extra mass. Readings are taken at regular time intervals. The velocity at impact is calculated from $KE_{gain} = PE_{loss}$. Therefore $\frac{1}{2}mv^2 = mgh$. As the pile of sand or salt builds up, h will vary. Can you think of a way of making the sand or salt build up as evenly as possible?

Equipment

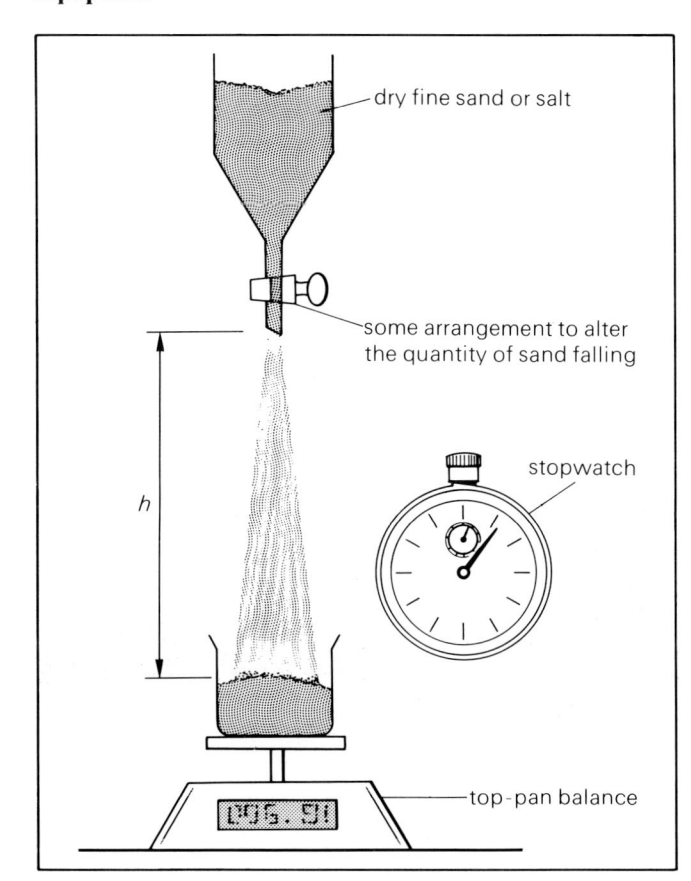

Figure 472 Apparatus. Use a digital balance or direct-reading balance.

Experimental details

1. Find the mass of the empty container.
2. Start with a height (h) of about 0.25 m. Allow sand or salt to fall, and record the balance reading every ten seconds for about one minute.
3. Find the mass of the container and sand at the end.
4. Alter the rate at which sand or salt is falling and repeat for other rates. Start with an empty container each time.
5. Alter the height h by at least 50 per cent each time and repeat for two more heights. Start with an empty container each time.

Results

Time/s	Balance reading for different rates of sand falling/g		
	A	B	C

height $h = \ldots$ m
mass of container empty $= \ldots$ g
mass of container + sand $= \ldots$ g

Processing the results

Plot graphs of balance reading against time. On the same axes mark the two points (a) mass of empty container, and (b) mass of container with sand at the end. Join these two points with a straight line. We expect it to be parallel to but below the first line (figure 473). The difference is due to the *force* produced by the sand as it was stopped when it hit the container. This difference of reading is due to the force produced. Measure it from the graph and

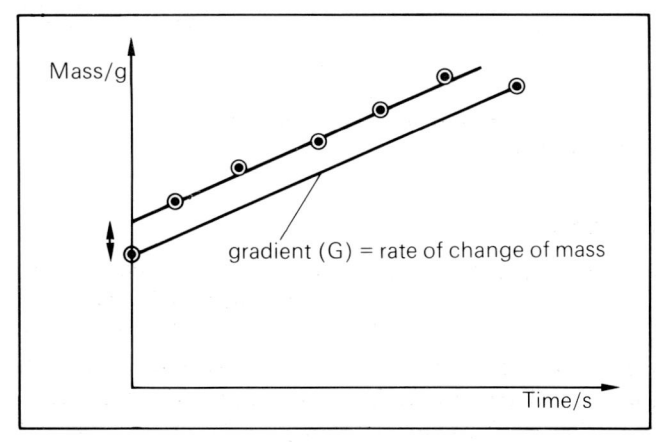

Figure 473

convert to a numerical value for the force by multiplying by the earth's gravitational field strength (g), 9.81 N kg^{-1}:

$$F = mg = m \times 9.81$$

Work out the velocity of impact, which equals $\sqrt{2gh}$. Work out the rate of change of momentum, which equals the gradient multiplied by the velocity. (Have you converted the gradient to kg s^{-1}?)

Make a second table, of force and rate of change of momentum, and plot a graph from it. You should expect a straight line through the origin at an inclination of 45° to any one axis (provided the scale on each axis is the same).

Force/N	Rate of change of momentum/kg m s^{-1}

Conclusion

Have your results supported Newton's second law? Remember to give an overall accuracy to your results and to discuss any problems you found.

85. DOES FORCE EQUAL MASS TIMES ACCELERATION?

Outline

This experiment investigates the effect of a constant force on an object initially at rest, and attempts to find out if

$$\text{acceleration} = \frac{\text{force}}{\text{mass}}.$$

A trolley is pulled along by a falling weight and its movement recorded on a ticker tape. The actual numerical acceleration is worked out from the ticker tape, and a graph of force against acceleration plotted. The expectation is that it will be a straight-line graph passing through the origin, with a gradient equal to the mass of the trolley.

The acceleration of the trolley is determined from the equation:

$$\text{acceleration} = \frac{\text{final velocity} - \text{initial velocity}}{\text{time } (t)}$$

In figure 474 the velocity is measured over a two-gap time interval, however, you could choose a three- or four-gap interval if it is more appropriate to your results.

Equipment

The apparatus should be set up as shown in figure 474.

Optional

A computer with a 'TIMING' interface and a suitable program can be used The program 'TIMER' (package PHYS2 option 7) will operate with several commercial interfaces, and will measure the times taken to cover a series of equal distances and then display the velocities and the average acceleration. Some speed–time computers could also be used, and your teacher will give you

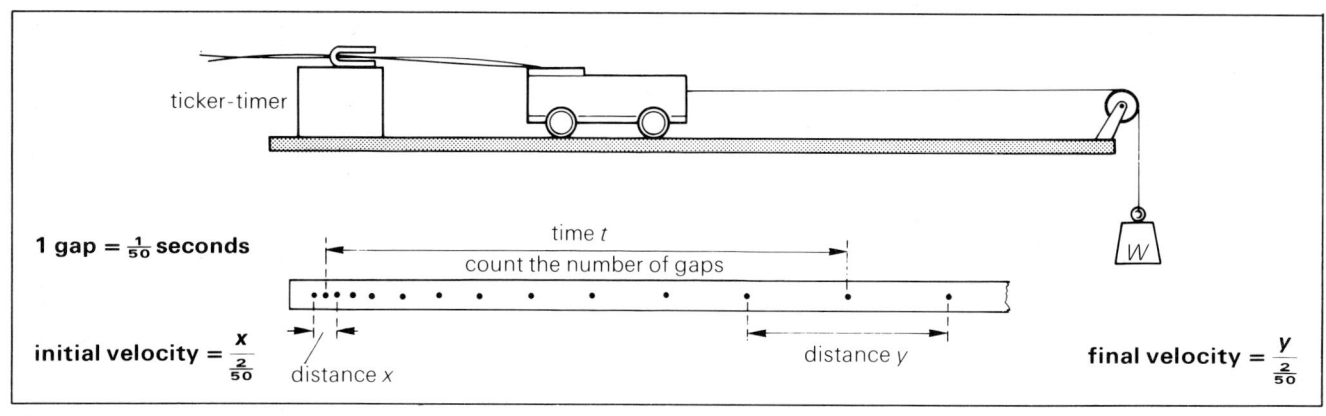

Figure 474 Apparatus

more information if you have one available. One possible method is shown in figures 475 and 476. Options exist in the program to record times when either a 'light' signal or a 'dark' signal is detected.

Experimental details

Since there will be some friction in the bearings of the wheels, the first step is to find the weight needed to keep the trolley moving at a constant velocity. (How can you check that the velocity is constant?) The weight producing the accelerating force will be in addition to this. Will this 'constant force' be different if the mass of the trolley is changed? Produce ticker tapes or direct accelerations for a range of accelerating forces ($1 \rightarrow 8$ N) and different masses of trolley. Plot suitable graphs and find the mass of the trolley from these if possible.

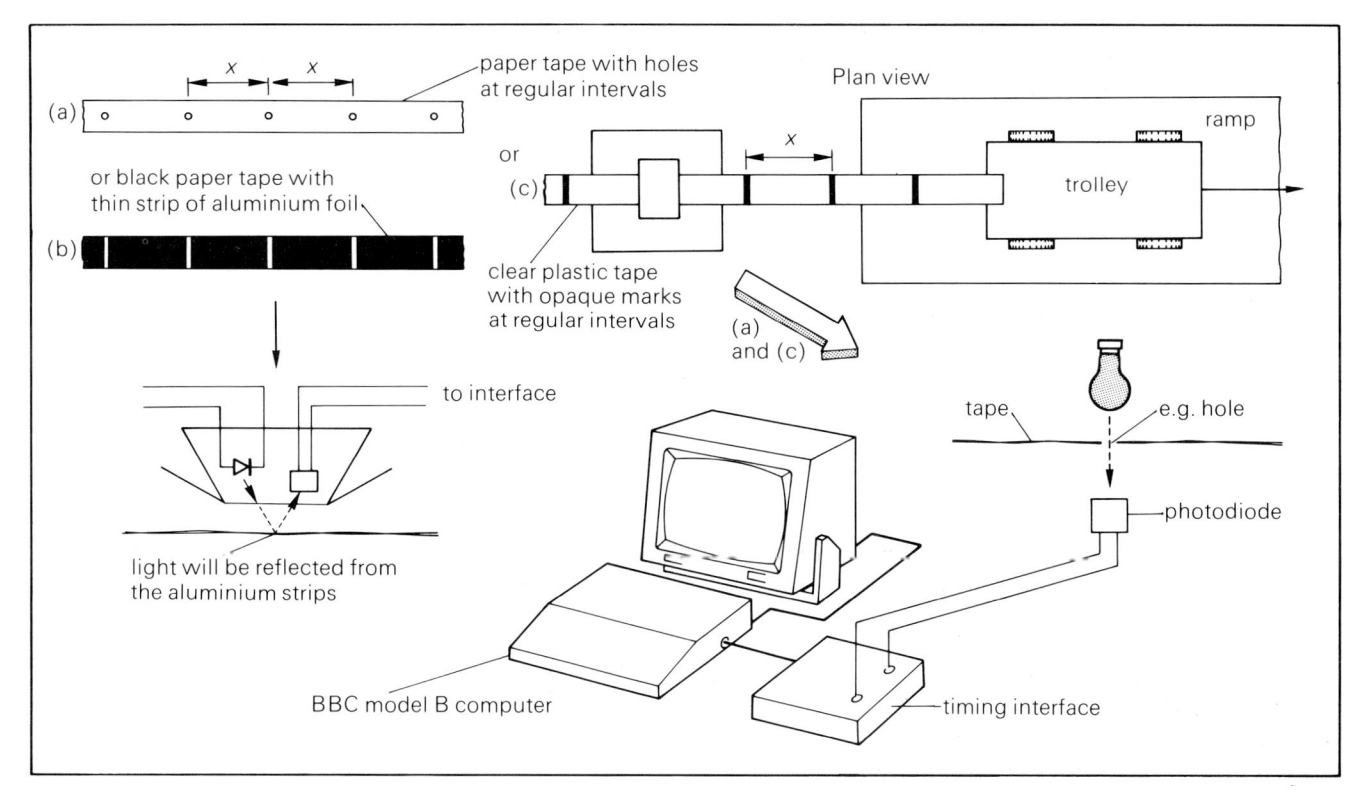

Figure 475 Methods of position sensing for computer input

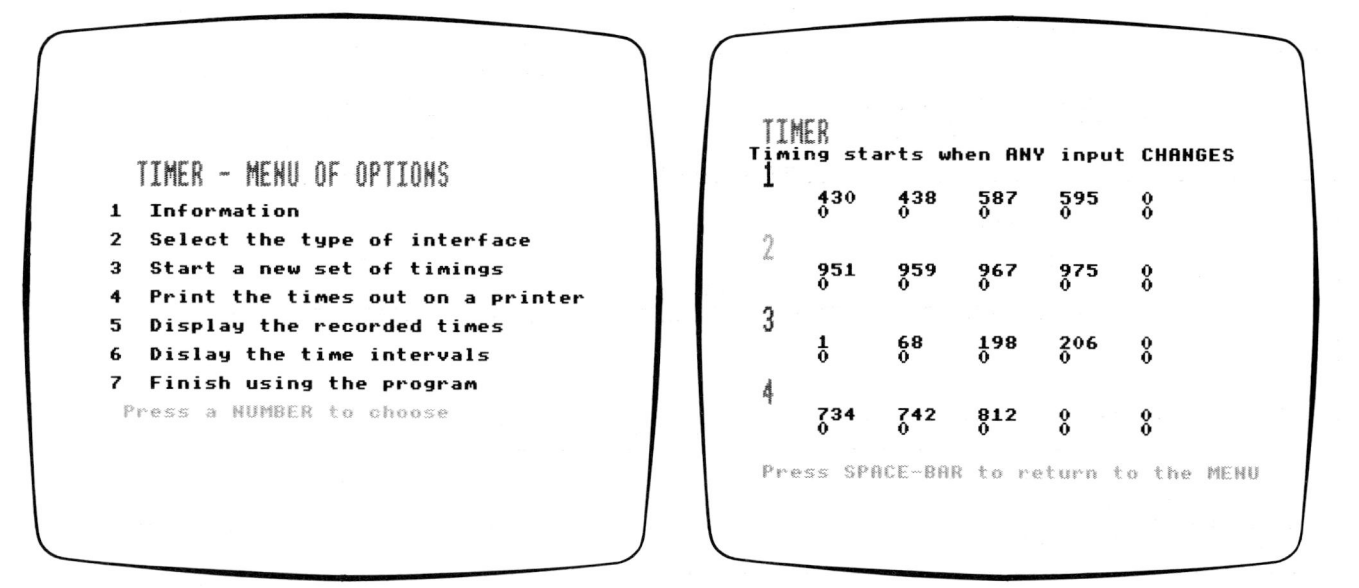

Figure 476 Typical displays from a timing program

Results

Fasten a selection of ticker tapes in your book and show how the acceleration is worked out from them. Give your table of measurements taken from the ticker tape, and the velocities and accelerations worked out from them. Plot a graph of force against acceleration. You should expect a straight-line graph passing through the origin, with the gradient equal to the mass of the trolley.

Conclusions

Does the experiment confirm that $F = ma$, and if not, can you suggest any reasons why not? What is the physical significance of any intercepts on the axes?

86. CONSERVATION OF LINEAR MOMENTUM WITH AN AIR TRACK

Outline

Newton proposed that force equals rate of change of momentum and he defined momentum as mass times velocity. He also said that an object exerting a force on another body experiences an equal but opposite force on itself. If two bodies collide, then they are in contact with each other for equal times and each will exert a force on the other, the two forces being in opposite directions.

$$\therefore F = \frac{m_1(v_1 - v_3)}{t}$$

$$= \frac{m_2(v_2 - v_4)}{t}$$

and so the numerical value of the charge in momentum of each body ought to be the same but opposite in sign, irrespective of any energy change. This means that the *total momentum* should be conserved.

In the following experiments, two objects travelling in the same straight line collide and their initial and final velocities are found (see figure 477). The aim is to investigate the validity of Newton's ideas or, since these have been proved to be true, Newton's laws.

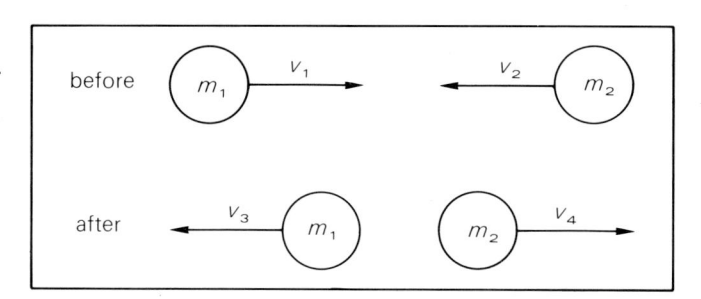

Figure 477

Equipment

In the apparatus illustrated in figure 478, the timers are operated by the cards cutting the beams of light. However, other methods of timing can be used.

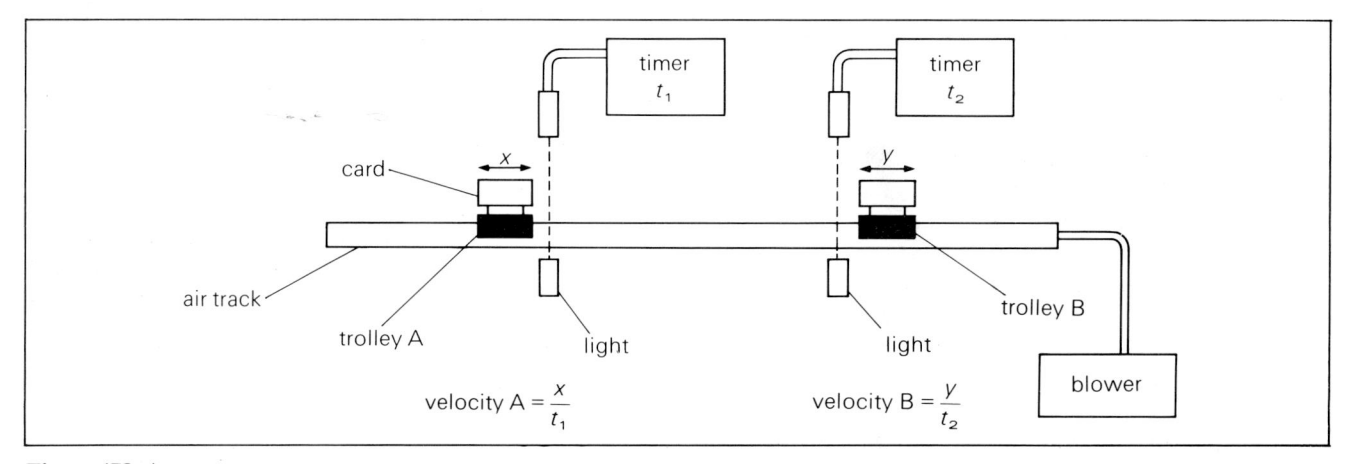

Figure 478 Apparatus

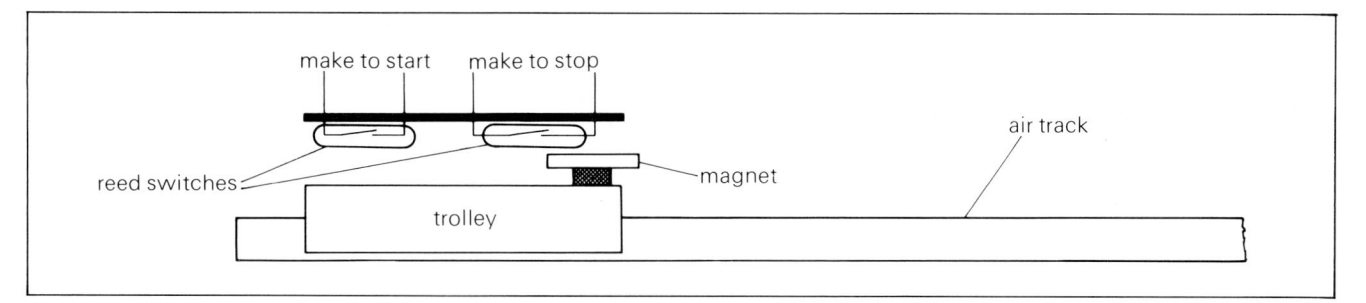

Figure 479 Using a magnet and reed switches for timing.

1. Magnet and reed switches

An alternative method of timing would be to fit reed switches to the air track and to attach a magnet to each trolley (figure 479). This has the disadvantage of being directional, since you must know which way the trolley is moving in order to connect the reed switches to the correct terminals of the timer. The distance the trolley moves between the contacts closing must also be measured. (How?)

2. Speed–time computer

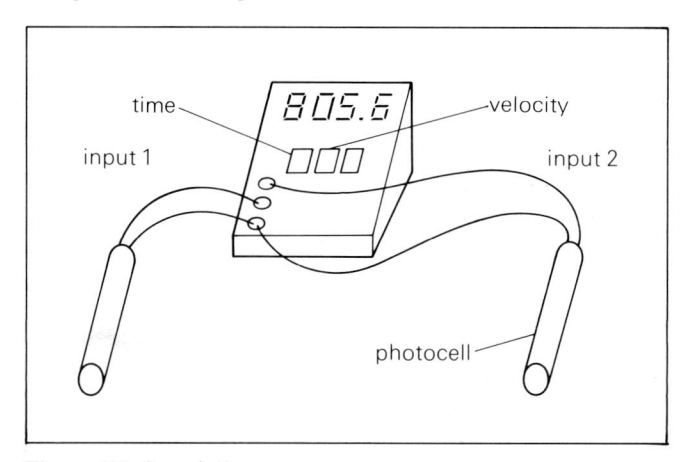

Figure 480 Speed–time computer

Speed–time computers (figure 480) are now available from at least two manufacturers and offer the ability to time two trolleys moving in the same direction, because they store the times in a series of stores. All times and velocities can be recalled afterwards. This enables experiments involving the collision of two trolleys which do not stick together on impact to be timed, which cannot easily be done using conventional timing methods. Up to four timings at each photocell can be stored.

You may be using a program in a conventional microcomputer which performs the same task or a data gathering instrument such as the VELA instead. Your teacher will give you more details.

Experimental details

The air track must be level so that a trolley placed anywhere on it will not move. The following types of collision can be investigated with two timers, as shown in figure 478.

(a) A, which is moving, collides with B, which is stationary, and they coalesce (stick together).
(b) A and B are fitted with repelling magnets and are held together, stationary, in the centre and then released. The initial momentum of each is zero.
(c) A and B initially move towards each other, and then collide and move apart.
(d) If you are using a speed–time computer, collisions can be investigated where the trolleys collide and move apart again, with the trolleys moving:

  (i) in opposite directions,
  (ii) in the same direction.

The masses of A and B can be varied depending on the apparatus available, the masses of A and B should be measured.

Record the times on the timers and the length of each card x and y so that the velocity of each trolley before and after collision can be found. Measure the mass of each trolley.

Carry out a whole series of investigations with different types of collisions (elastic and non-elastic) and different masses of trolleys.

Results

length of card (x) = ... m
length of card (y) = ... m

Type of collision	A → Time/s	← A Time/s	B → Time/s	← B Time/s
Example: A collides with B and they stick together				

From the results
For each type of collision work out:

1. velocities and momenta of A and B;
2. the change in momentum of A and the change in momentum of B (*remember* that A and B are *vectors*, so signs matter);
3. the total initial momentum;
4. the total final momentum;
5. the percentage change in momentum;
6. the total initial KE;
7. the total final KE;
8. the percentage change in KE.

Tabulate the values from (2), (5) and (8), as shown.

Conclusion

Do these results support Newton's laws?

Change in momentum of A/kg m s^{-1}	Change in momentum of B/kg m s^{-1}	% change in momentum	% change in KE

Application

In the core of a nuclear reactor, neutrons are slowed down by elastic collisions in the moderator. Theory predicts that the maximum energy occurs when the masses of the colliding particles are the same. Do your results support this statement?

87. FORCE PRODUCED BY A CURRENT-CARRYING WIRE IN A MAGNETIC FIELD

Outline

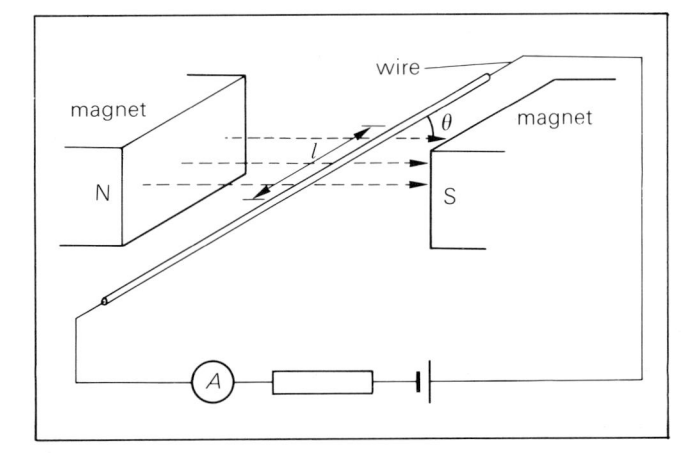

Figure 481

The force on a current carrying wire is:

$$F = BIl \sin \theta$$

where l is the length of wire in the magnetic field.

This experiment uses a top-pan electronic balance to measure the force produced, to find out if:

1. $F \propto I$ 2. $F \propto l$ 3. $F \propto \sin \theta$

Experimental details

Set up the apparatus as in figure 482, with a wire conductor of length 5 cm, at 90° to the field. This should give the maximum force. With *no* current flowing, take the reading on the balance. Switch the power supply on and adjust the current to 10 A. Record the reading on the balance and work out the force produced on the wire (and the magnet, because of Newton's third law).

1. Repeat for a range of at least five different currents between 0 and 10 A.
2. Repeat for wire frames of different lengths and a current of 5 A.
3. Using the longest wire loop possible and a current of 10 A, take a set of readings with the magnetic field at different angles to the wire over a range 0–360°. It may be helpful to draw out a set of angles on a piece of paper and a centre line on the U-core (figure 483).

MEASURING QUANTITIES AND INVESTIGATING LAWS

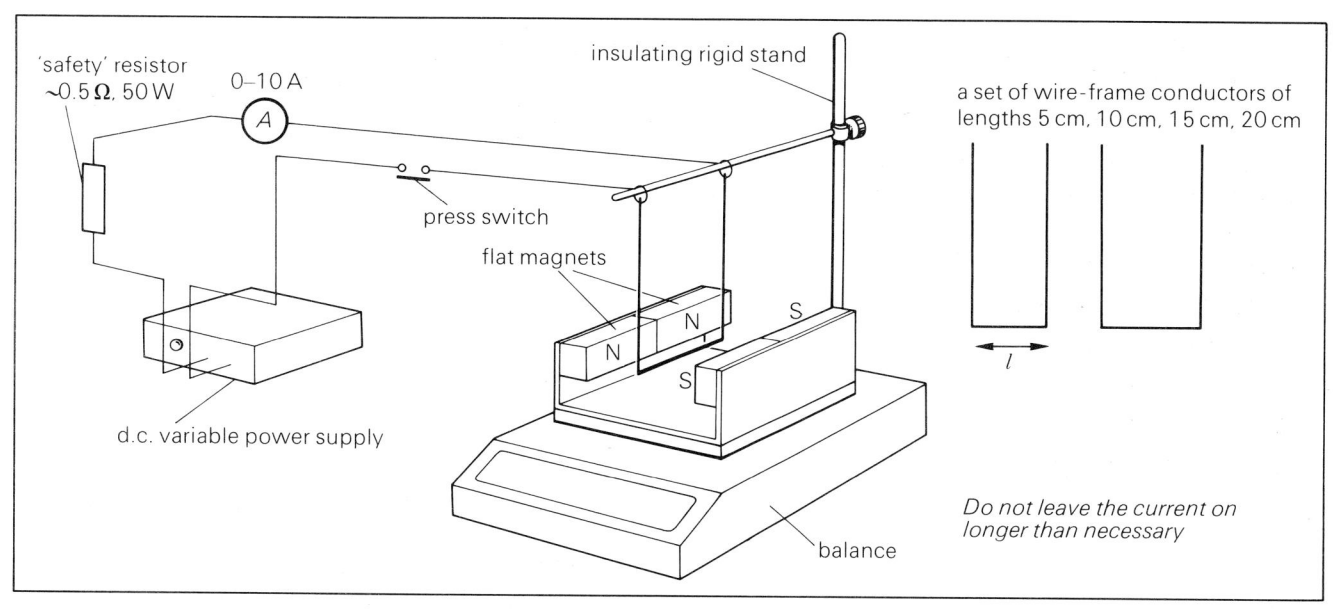

Figure 482 Apparatus. Do not leave the current on longer than necessary.

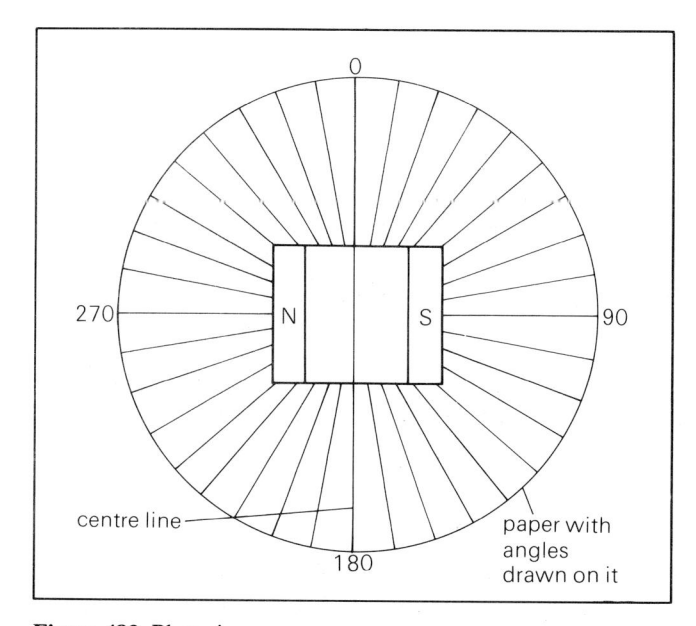

Figure 483 Plan view

Results

reading with magnet only (no current) = ... g

1. *Length of wire 5 cm*

Current/A	Balance reading/g	Change of reading/g	Force/N

2. *Current of 5 A*

Length/cm	Balance reading/g	Change of reading/g	Force/N

3. *Variation of angle θ*

Angle θ/°	Balance reading/g	Change of reading/g	Force/N

From the results
1. Plot a graph of force against current and conclude if $F \propto I$, or not.
2. Plot a graph of force against length of wire and conclude if $F \propto l$, or not. Find also the extent of the magnetic field outside the U-core.
3. Plot a graph of force against $\sin \theta$, and conclude if $F \propto \sin \theta$, or not.

88. INVESTIGATING LAWS FOR GAMMA RADIATION

Outline

Gamma radiation is electromagnetic radiation. The air absorbs very little of the electromagnetic radiation passing through it. The intensity decreases with distance simply because the radiation is spread over a large area. If the rate of emission is N particles per second then, assuming a uniform distribution, the number passing through a unit area per second at a distance r_1 equals $\frac{N}{4\pi r_1^2}$ and at a distance r_2 equals $\frac{N}{4\pi r_2^2}$ (figure 484). For any sphere radius r the number of particles per unit area per second equals $\frac{N}{4\pi r^2}$. Therefore the intensity (proportional to the number collected per second) is proportional to $\frac{1}{r^2}$, even though very little radiation is being absorbed. This effect is in addition to any absorbtion produced by a solid material and shows that the distance between the source and the detector must be kept constant in experiments investigating absorbtion. However, this does not give us a rule for the absorbtion of γ-rays by a solid. This experiment attempts to find a rule and to measure the 'half-thickness' of lead.

> **Observe all the usual safety rules for handling radioactive materials.**

1. ABSORBTION AND HALF-VALUE THICKNESS

Experimental details

1. Set up the Geiger–Müller tube and counter. The Geiger is turned, as shown in figure 485, to make the detector effectively thinner, so that the uncertainty in the distance from source to detector is less. It is not absolutely essential for this part of the experiment, but is good practice and is necessary later to investigate the inverse square law.
   Measure the background count rate. A ten-minute period should be long enough to detect sufficient particles. The error in counting N particles is $\pm\sqrt{N}$.
2. Take the γ-source from its container. **Handle it with tongs.** Place it in position.

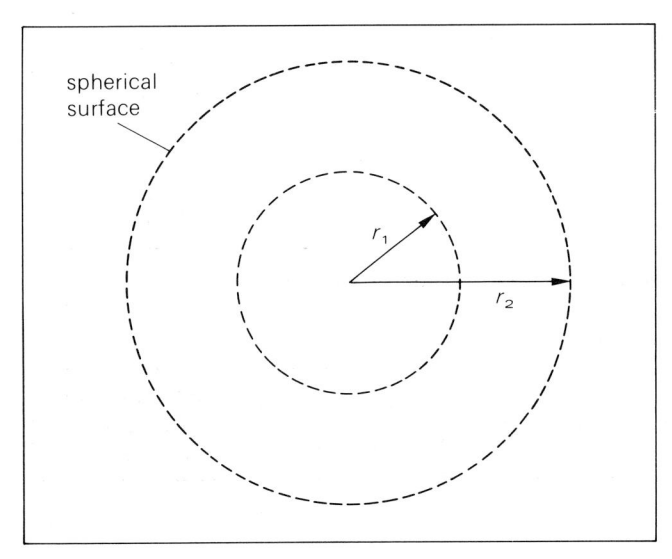

Figure 484

Equipment

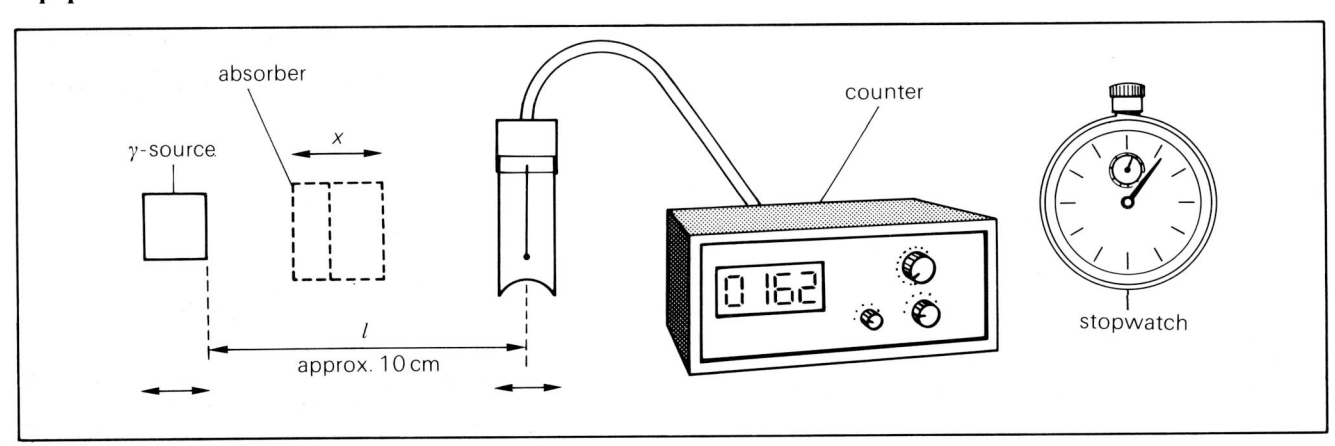

Figure 485 Apparatus. The Geiger–Müller tube is turned to make the detector effectively thinner, so that the uncertainty in the distance from source to detector is less. It is not absolutely essential for this first part of the experiment but is good practice and is necessary later to investigate the inverse square law.

MEASURING QUANTITIES AND INVESTIGATING LAWS

3. Measure the number of counts in a one-minute period for different thicknesses of lead. Calculate the corrected count per second allowing for background radiation. Avoid placing your fingers directly in front of the source when changing the thickness of lead.

Results

Background count (N) in 10 minutes			

average count per second = ...
error $\pm\sqrt{N}$ = ... per 10 minutes = ... per second

Thickness of lead x/cm	Count in 1 minute	Corrected count per second

From your results

A straight-line graph is required, if possible. Start by plotting a graph of count rate against thickness of lead. If the shape of the graph is like that shown in figure 486, the most usual relationships are

(a) count rate $\propto \dfrac{1}{\text{thickness}}$;

(b) count rate $\propto \dfrac{1}{\text{thickness}^2}$;

(c) count rate $\alpha - k \times$ thickness where k is a constant

and a graph of $\log_e$ (count rate) against thickness should be a straight line.

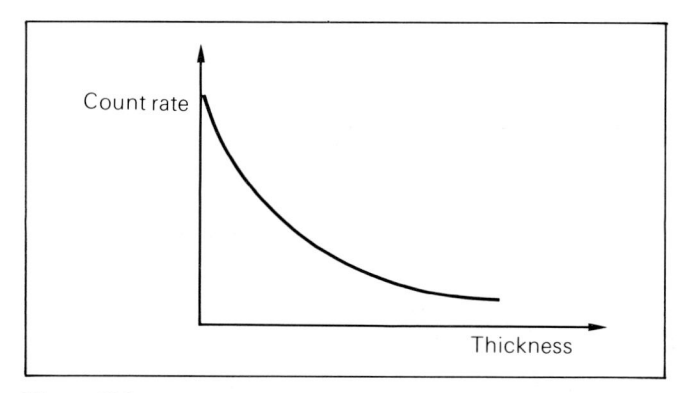

Figure 486

1. Which of these relationships fits your results?
2. Work out the 'half-thickness' of lead, that is, the thickness of lead which will reduce by half the intensity of the γ-radiation falling on it.
3. What is the physical significance of the gradient of the graph and what are its units?

2. THE INVERSE SQUARE LAW WITH NO ABSORBER

Experimental details

The detector is moved away from the source, with air in between so that there will be little absorbtion. A set of measurements is taken of counts per minute for a range of different source–detector distances (l). The problem with this experiment is the uncertainty of (a) the true position of the source material, and (b) the exact position of the detector (figure 487). The Geiger–Müller tube has been turned through 90° to reduce this. (Why is it not important for the radiation to pass through the thin mica 'window'?)

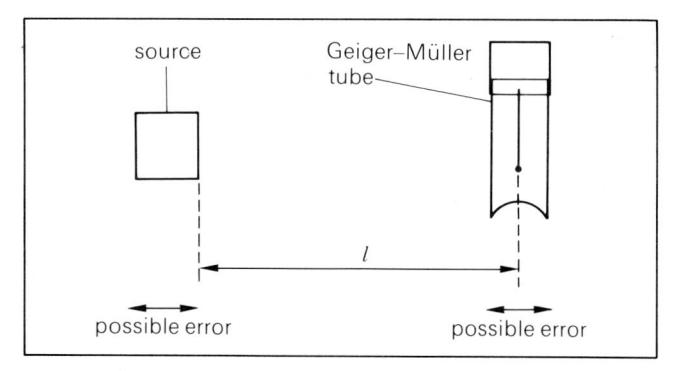

Figure 487 Position of the Geiger–Müller tube.

Results

Distance l/cm	Count in 1 minute	Corrected count per second (intensity)

If the error is y cm, then the true distance is $(l+y)$ cm. We expect intensity to be proportional to $\dfrac{1}{(l+y)^2}$, which gives:

$$l + y \propto \dfrac{1}{\sqrt{\text{intensity}}}$$

$$\propto \dfrac{1}{\sqrt{\text{corrected count/s}}}$$

A graph of l against $\dfrac{1}{\sqrt{\text{corrected count rate}}}$ should be a straight line with the gradient equal to the constant of proportionality and the intercept equal to the error, y.

What is the effect on the graph of the 'dead time' of the Geiger tube?

89. MEASUREMENT OF HALF-LIFE

Outline

The decay of any radioactive substance follows the equation $\frac{dN}{dt} = -\lambda N$. N is the number of undecayed atoms present and λ is a decay constant which is different for all substances.

The solution to this equation is $N = N_0 e^{-\lambda t}$, where N_0 is the number of atoms originally present at $t = 0$.

The *half-life* is the time taken for half the number of atoms originally present to decay.

$$\tfrac{1}{2}N_0 = N_0 e^{-\lambda t}$$
$$\log_e \tfrac{1}{2} = -\lambda t$$
$$-0.6931 = -\lambda t$$
$$\therefore \text{half-life} = \frac{0.6931}{\lambda}$$

The decay constant or disintegration constant (λ), needs to be found.

To find the *half-life*, a graph of number of atoms present against time could be plotted. By choosing any initial number of atoms, the half-life will be the time taken for this chosen number to reduce by one half. The problem is that, in the experiment, it is the *count rate* $\left(\frac{dN}{dt}\right)$ which is measured, not the number of atoms (N). However, if $\frac{dN}{dt} = -\lambda N$, then $N = -\frac{1}{\lambda}\frac{dN}{dt}$, and so $\frac{dN}{dt} \propto N$. A graph of count rate $\left(\frac{dN}{dt}\right)$ against time (t) will enable the *half-life* to be found, and from it the decay constant λ.

To find the *decay constant* (λ) directly, the following method can be used. Given that:

$$N = N_0 e^{-\lambda t}$$
$$\frac{N}{N_0} = e^{-\lambda t}$$

taking logs, $\log_e \frac{N}{N_0} = -\lambda t$

$$\log_e N - \log_e N_0 = -\lambda t$$

or $\qquad t = -\frac{\log_e N}{\lambda} + \frac{\log_e N_0}{\lambda} \qquad (1)$

Comparing with $y = mx + c$, if t is plotted as ordinate and $\log_e N$ as abscissa the gradient is $-\frac{1}{\lambda}$.

However, it is not the number of atoms present (N) which is measured, but the rate of change of N, that is $\frac{dN}{dt}$. An equation is needed which contains $\frac{dN}{dt}$ instead of N.

$$\frac{dN}{dt} = -\lambda N$$

taking logs gives

$$\log_e\left(\frac{dN}{dt}\right) = \log_e(-\lambda N)$$
$$= \log_e N - \log_e \lambda$$

Therefore

for N_0: $\qquad \log_e N_0 = \log_e\left(\frac{dN_0}{dt}\right) + \log_e \lambda$

for N: $\qquad \log_e N = \log_e\left(\frac{dN}{dt}\right) + \log_e \lambda$

substituting in (1) we get:

$$t = -\frac{1}{\lambda}\log_e\left(\frac{dN}{dt}\right) - \frac{1}{\lambda}\log_e \lambda + \frac{1}{\lambda}\log_e\left(\frac{dN_0}{dt}\right) + \frac{1}{\lambda}\log_e \lambda$$

$$\boxed{\log_e\left(\frac{dN}{dt}\right) = \log_e\left(\frac{dN_0}{dt}\right) - \lambda t}$$

A graph of $\log_e$ (count rate) against time (t) should be a straight line with gradient $-\lambda$.

Radon 220 gas has a half-life of less than two minutes and is often used for the following experiment on measuring half-life; it emits α-particles. A liquid, protactinium 234, which is a β^- emitter, can also be used.

> **Warning: Observe the usual rules for handling and using radioactive sources.**

Experimental details

1. Take a background count. A time of ten minutes should be sufficient.
2. Using the apparatus shown in figure 488, open the clip and squeeze the bottle so that gas goes into the sealed cell. Close the clip.
3. Start the counter and the stopwatch at the same time and record readings of total count every ten seconds for about five minutes, or until the count rate appears to be approaching the background count level.

MEASURING QUANTITIES AND INVESTIGATING LAWS

Equipment

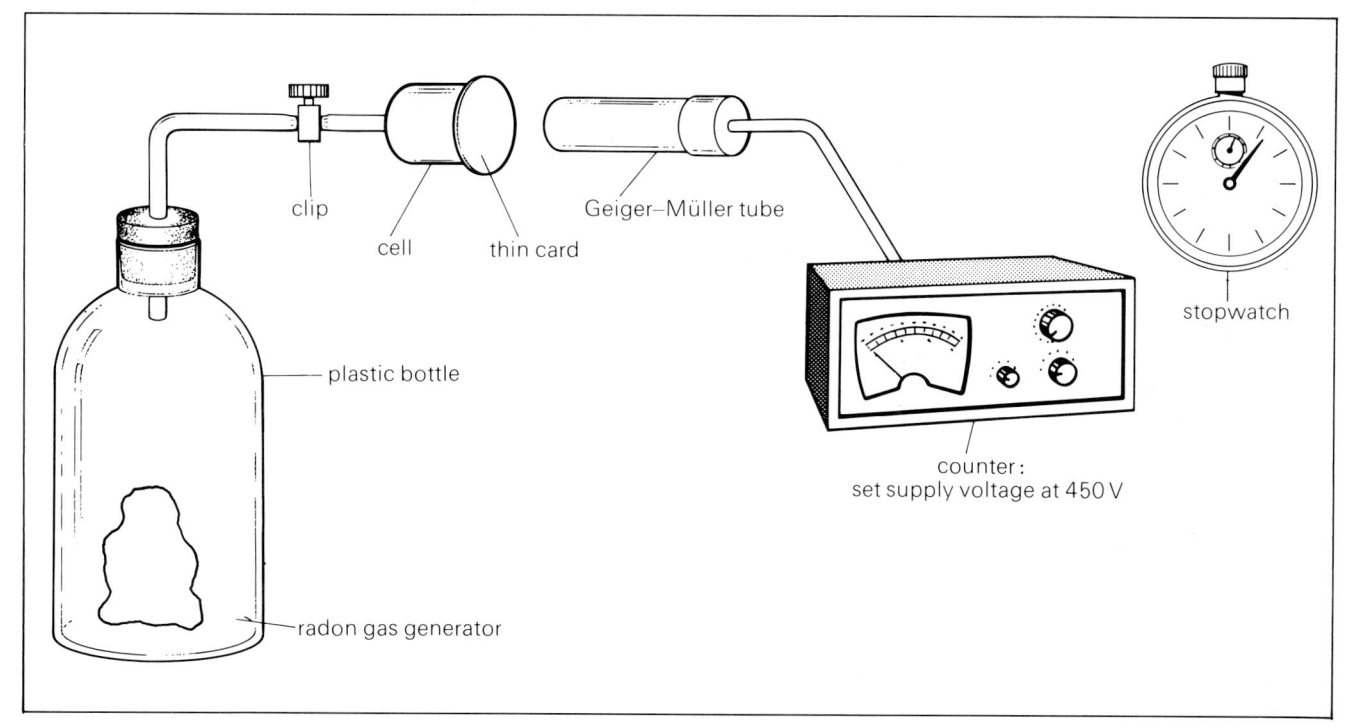

Figure 488 Apparatus

Results

background count in ten minutes = ...
background count in ten seconds = ...

Time/s	Count rate/s^{-1}	Corrected count rate/s^{-1}

What are the errors in the background count and count rate? Remember $N \pm \sqrt{N}$ is the statistically derived error.

From your results
1. Plot a graph of corrected count rate against time and find the half-life of radon.
2. Plot a graph of the log$_e$ of the corrected count rate against time and work out the decay constant λ from the gradient.

The decay constant (λ) is really a measurement of the probability of decay of an atom. Can a model based on the probability of a random process predict $\dfrac{\mathrm{d}N}{\mathrm{d}t} = -\lambda N$?

Take 100 dice, shake the dice and take out all the ones, i.e. a probability of 1/6. Count the number left. The count rate is proportional to the number of ones taken out. Repeat and make a table of the number left and the count rate. A graph of number left against an arbitrary time-scale should be the same shape as the experimental graph and should have a constant 'half life' (figure 489).

The ratio $\dfrac{\text{count rate}}{\text{number left}}$ should be constant, but in practice will vary slightly because of the randomness of the process.

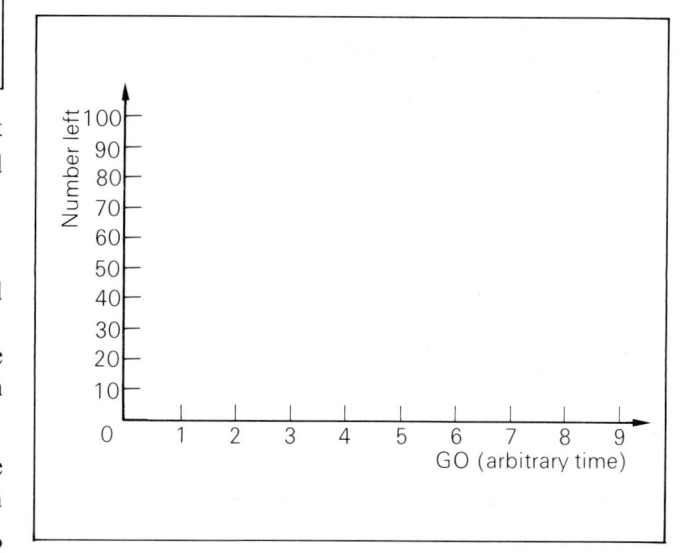

Figure 489

As an alternative, this model can be investigated using a computer program called 'DECAY' (package PHYS3 option 3, figure 490). The program allows the probability to be altered, and the decay of a number of substances into daughter and granddaughter atoms to be traced. A similar type of computer package is the Schools Council *Computers in the Curriculum* package on radioactive decay (© Longman).

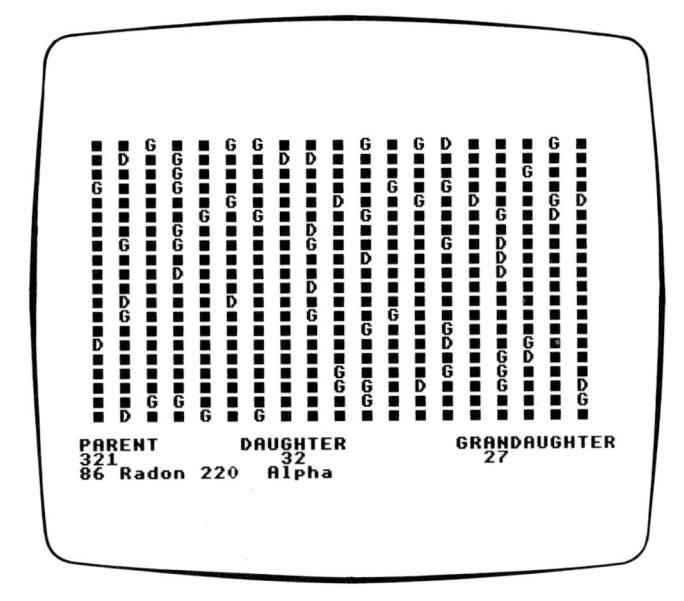

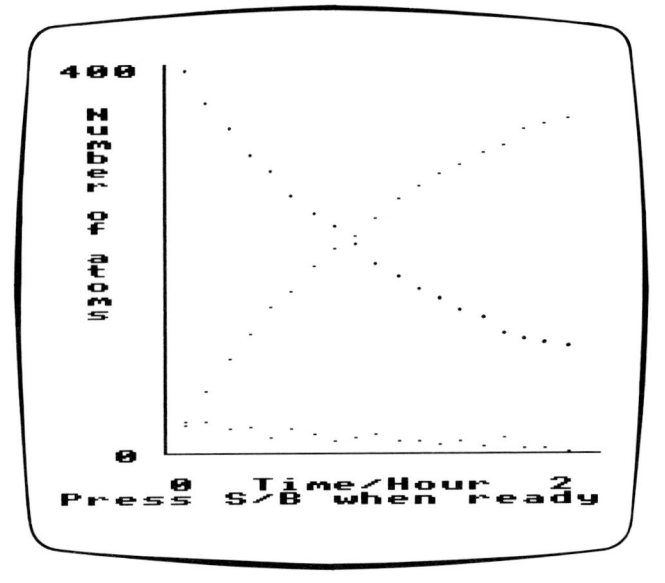

Figure 490 Display of atoms 'decaying' and graphs of the decays occurring.

90. FINDING THE ENERGY OF β^- PARTICLES

Outline

Negative beta particles (β^-) are electrons emitted from the nucleus when a neutron changes to a proton. At least, we say they are electrons, because they have identical charges and masses to electrons. The KE of the particle depends on the nucleus from which it is emitted. The aim of this experiment is to take measurements from which the range of energy of the β^- particles can be found.

The β^- particles are collimated by shielding the source (figure 491).

It is usual to use a source available commercially. If the beam is passed through a magnetic field, a force is exerted on the beam. This force is always perpendicular to the direction of movement (Fleming's left-hand rule) and produces a circular path.

For this experiment, it is necessary to determine the arc length AE (see figure 429, p. 231). The measurements taken are the angle through which the beam is deflected (α) and the width of the magnetic field (l); l is assumed to be the width of the pole, but the field will extend beyond this. How much error will this cause?

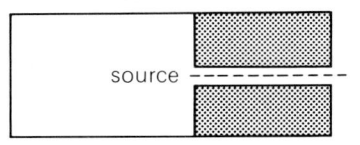

Figure 491

Deriving an expression for the radius of the path r

For figure 492
$$AB = BE$$
$$\therefore \widehat{BAE} = \widehat{BEA}$$
$$= \tfrac{1}{2}(\widehat{FBE})$$
$$= \frac{\alpha}{2}$$

in $\triangle FAE$:
$$AE = \frac{AF}{\cos \alpha/2}$$
$$= \frac{l}{\cos \alpha/2}$$

$$\widehat{EBA} = 180 - \alpha$$

Since $\triangle BDA$ and $\triangle BDE$ are congruent, it follows that:

$$\widehat{ABD} = \widehat{DBE}$$
$$= \frac{\widehat{EBA}}{2}$$
$$\therefore \widehat{DBE} = 90 - \alpha/2$$

in $\triangle CBE$:
$$\widehat{CBE} = 90 - \alpha/2$$
$$\therefore \widehat{BCE} = 180 - 90 - (90 - \alpha/2)$$
$$= \alpha/2 = \theta$$

in $\triangle DCE$:
$$DE = \frac{AE}{2}$$
$$r = \frac{DE}{\sin \theta}$$
$$= \frac{AE}{2 \sin(\alpha/2)}$$
$$= \frac{l/\cos(\alpha/2)}{2 \sin(\alpha/2)}$$
$$= \frac{l}{2 \sin(\alpha/2) \cos(\alpha/2)}$$

This simplifies to

$$r = \frac{l}{\sin \alpha}$$

$$\boxed{\therefore \text{radius of path} = \frac{l}{\sin \alpha}}$$

Deriving an expression for the kinetic energy (**KE**)

$$\text{force} = Bev$$
$$= \frac{mv^2}{r}$$

where
B = magnetic flux density
v = velocity of particle

$$\therefore v = \frac{Ber}{m}$$
$$KE = \frac{1}{2} \frac{B^2 e^2 r^2}{m^2}$$
$$= \frac{1}{2} \frac{B^2 e^2 r^2}{m}$$

$$\boxed{KE = \frac{1}{2} \frac{B^2 q^2 r^2}{m}}$$

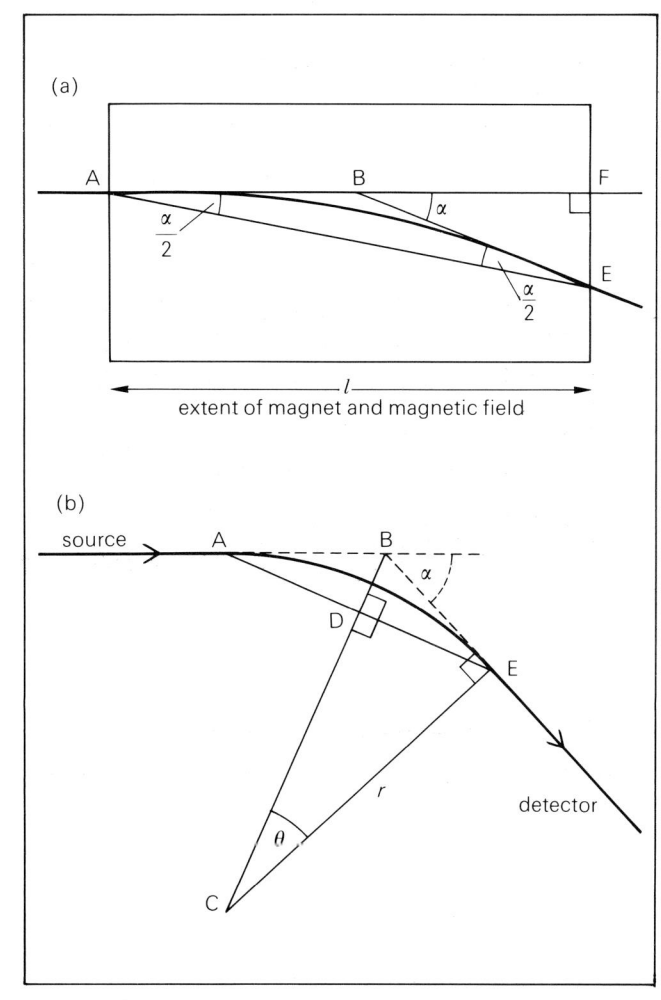

Figure 492

Observe all usual safety precautions for handling and using radioactive sources.

e and m can be found from data tables, r is measured in this experiment, B may be known for the magnet used or can be measured (see p. 88).

Always make sure that the axis of the detector is along a radial line (figure 494). This is done by aligning the pin attached to the Geiger–Müller tube with one of the lines drawn on the paper, using the method of non-parallax.

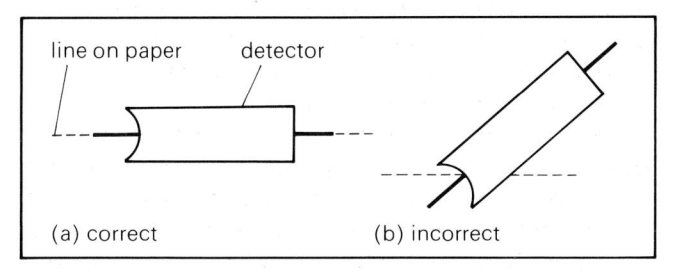

Figure 493

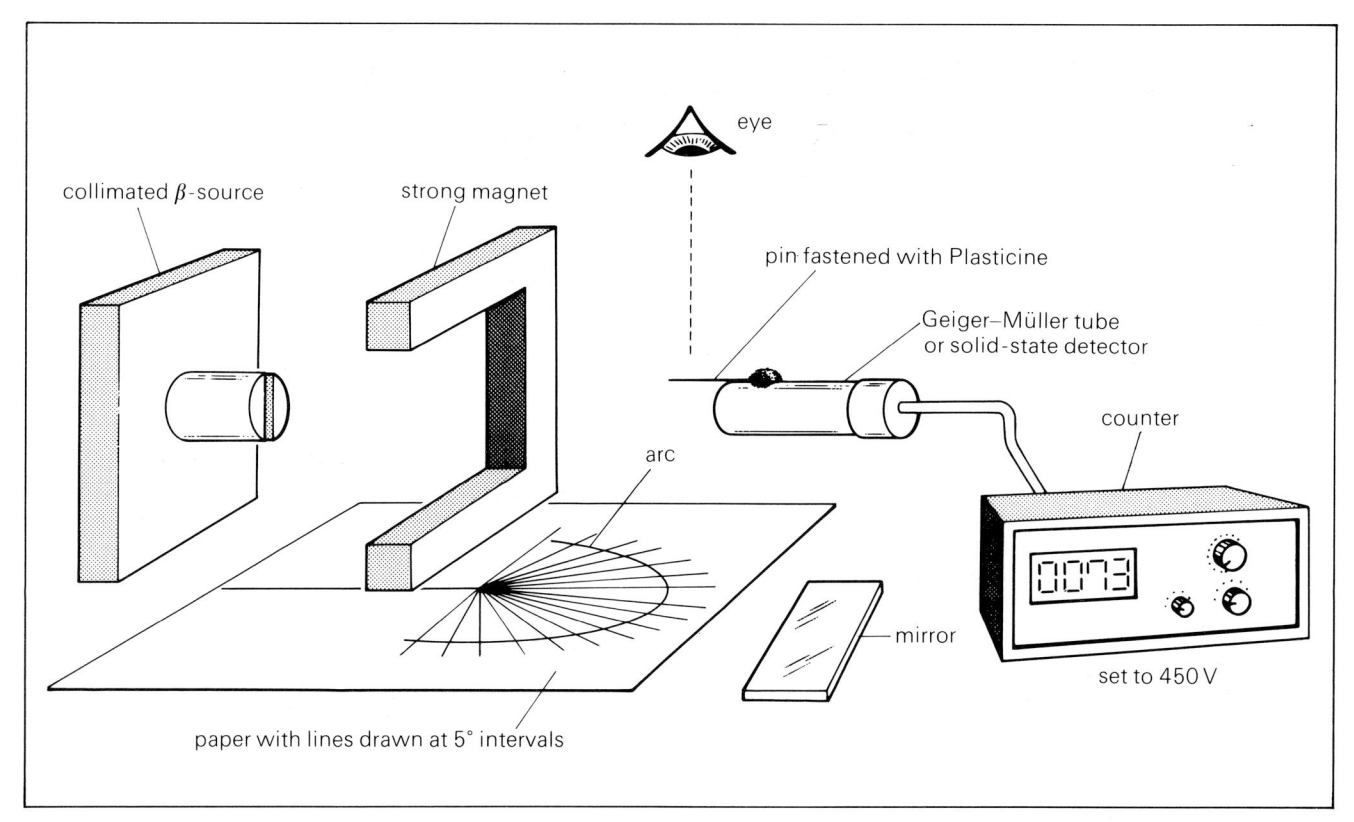

Figure 494 Apparatus (supports for items are not shown). The mirror can be placed under the pin to line the detector up with a line on the paper by the method of no parallax.

Experimental details

1. Take a background count. A time of ten minutes will be sufficient.
2. Assemble the apparatus as shown in figure 494, but without the magnet.
3. Using the arc drawn on the paper to keep the detector a constant distance from the source (why is this necessary?), find the count in one minute with the detector in line with each of the drawn lines. Tabulate the results as raw (uncorrected) count, count rate and angle of detector (+ and −, with the centre line as zero).
4. Put the magnet in place and repeat all the measurements. If you have time, experiment with the use of a slit in front of the detector to improve the discrimination.
5. If you do not know the value of the magnetic field, measure it.

Results

Tabulate your results, as shown here.

From the results

Plot two graphs of count rate as ordinate and angle as abscissa. Use the angles of the two peaks to determine the angle through which the beam has been deflected. This is α. Calculate the radius r and the approximate range of kinetic energy of the beam. Look up the energy of the β^- particles, in tables, for the source you are using. Are your results consistent with this energy, which is the maximum β^- energy?

Without magnet

Raw count	Count rate	Angle/°

With magnet

Raw count	Count rate	Angle/°

91. MEASUREMENT OF THE RATIO e/m FOR A BEAM OF ELECTRONS

Outline

When a beam of electrons enters a magnetic field which is perpendicular to the plane of movement of the electrons, the force produced on the electrons is at right angles to the direction of movement and to the field direction. Under this direction of force the electrons will travel in a circular path.

$$\text{centripetal force needed} = \frac{mv^2}{r}$$

$$\text{magnetic force produced} = Bev$$

where m = mass of electron
v = velocity
r = radius of circular path
B = magnetic flux density
e = electronic charge

$$\therefore \frac{mv^2}{r} = Bev \quad \text{giving} \quad \frac{e}{m} = \frac{v}{Br} \quad (1)$$

To find $\dfrac{e}{m}$ the following must be known:

1. radius of the circle—by direct measurement on the apparatus;

2. the velocity of the electrons—from the accelerating anode potential:

$$Ve = \tfrac{1}{2}mv^2$$

$$v = \sqrt{\frac{2eV}{m}} \quad (2)$$

3. magnetic field—either by direct measurement, or if Helmholtz coils are used, from the equation:

$$B = \frac{0.71\mu nI}{a}$$

Substituting for v in (1):

$$\frac{e}{m} = \sqrt{\frac{2eV}{m/Br}}$$

squaring

$$\frac{e^2}{m^2} = \frac{2eV}{mB^2r^2}$$

giving

$$\frac{e}{m} = \frac{2V}{B^2r^2}$$

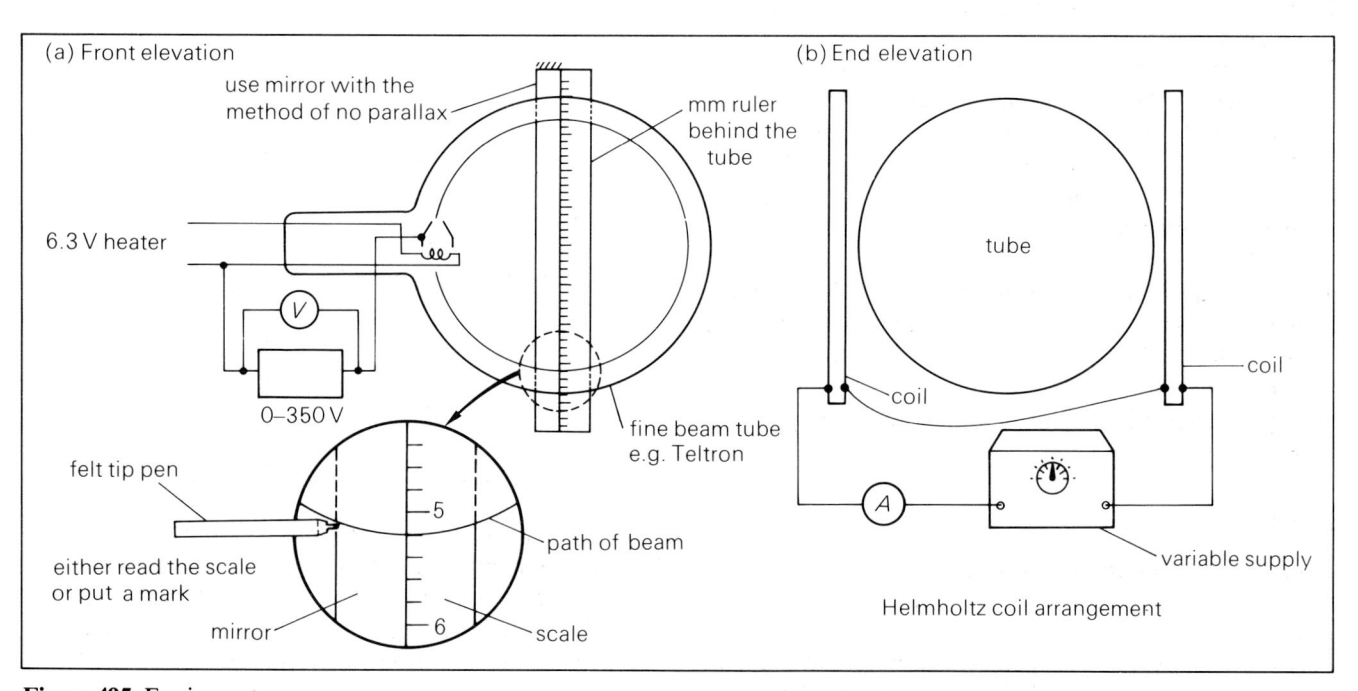

Figure 495 Equipment

Experimental details

Set up the fine-beam tube as shown in figure 495. Make sure that the current through the coils is in the same direction through each and that the separation of the coils is equal to their radius, so that a uniform field is produced.

1. Increase the accelerating voltage until a beam is produced and alter the current so that the largest possible circle is produced.
2. Use the mirror and the method of no parallax to record the upper and lower edge of the circle so that the diameter can be worked out. Make sure that the accelerating voltage is recorded, and the current through the coils is recorded.
3. Repeat for smaller diameters of circles and also for increased accelerating voltage.

Results

Accelerating potential/V	Field coil current/A	Top of circle/cm	Bottom of circle/cm

From the results
Work out:

1. magnetic field B, from $B = \dfrac{0.71\mu nI}{a}$;
2. radius of circle;
3. ratio of $\dfrac{e}{m}$, from $\dfrac{e}{m} = \dfrac{2V}{B^2 r^2}$.

Magnetic field B/tesla	Radius of circle/m	Ratio e/m

Since you may have about ten results, work out a *mean* and the *standard deviation* of the *mean* so that an accuracy for the result can be given. Remember that you can eliminate any results which give a value more than three standard deviations from the mean, but you will then have to work out a new mean and standard deviation.

In your report, give your value for e/m and quote an accuracy. Compare it with the accepted result.

92. MILLIKAN'S EXPERIMENT TO MEASURE e, THE FUNDAMENTAL UNIT OF CHARGE

Outline

This experiment can be used in a simple form to show that electric charge occurs in integral multiples of a fundamental unit. This is assumed to be the charge on an electron. A more complex experiment can measure the size of this charge.

The apparatus can be time-consuming to set up correctly. The principle is the same for apparatus from different manufacturers, but exact detail will vary. If your school does not have the apparatus, there is a computer simulation of the experiment for the BBC computer model B, or you can use the example results given at the end of this practical.

Theory
Charged oil drops or small polystyrene spheres are allowed to move between two metal plates. A voltage can be connected between the plates to produce an electric field (figure 496). The charged drops can be made to:

(a) fall freely under gravity,
(b) move upwards under the field,
(c) move downwards under the field,
(d) remain stationary, when the force produced by the field equals the gravitational force on the drop.

Symbols used:

V potential difference applied to the plates
L separation of lines on the graticule in the eyepiece
X separation of the plates
a radius of drop or sphere
g gravitational force constant
η viscosity of the air
d_{oil} density of the oil
v velocity of drop in fall with no field
M mass of drop
E electric field
Q charge on a drop or sphere

MEASURING QUANTITIES AND INVESTIGATING LAWS

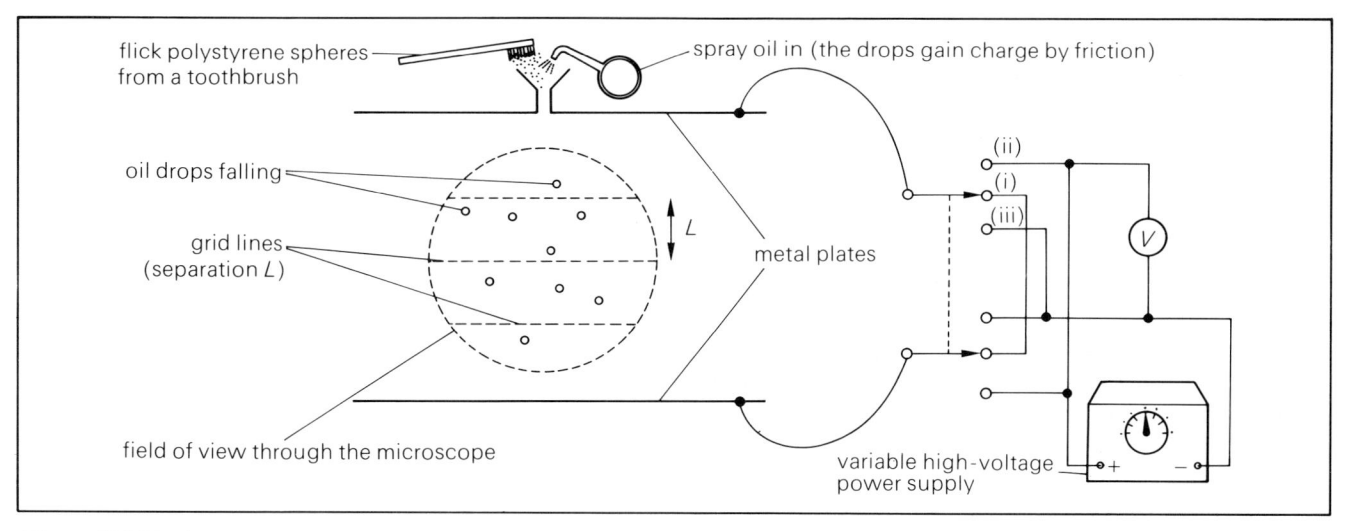

Figure 496 Equipment

1. If the voltage is adjusted until the drop is stationary:

$$EQ = mg = \frac{4\pi d_{oil} a^3 g}{3}.$$

Now,
$$E = \frac{V}{X}$$

so
$$\frac{VQ}{X} = \frac{4\pi a^3 d_{oil} g}{3}.$$

If the masses of the spheres or drops are all the same, then

$$Q \propto \frac{1}{V}.$$

If the charges Q are integral multiples of a fundamental value of charge, then all values of $1/V$ should have a highest common factor which is the value of $1/V$ when $Q = 1e$. A highest common factor for $1/V$ should also be found if the charge on the drop can be changed. This is done by using a radioactive source to ionise the drop.

2. To find the value of e, two different movements of the same drop must be measured because there are two unknowns, Q and a. This is done by (a) timing the fall of the drop between lines on the graticule with no field, and (b) finding the voltage needed to hold the drop stationary. Because of air resistance the drop very quickly reaches a terminal velocity.

(a) *No field*

$$\tfrac{4}{3}\pi a^3 d_{oil} g = 6\pi \eta a v \quad (1)$$
(weight of drop) (air friction)

(The effect of the upthrust due to displaced air is included because the density of the oil is measured in air and not in a vacuum.)

(b) *Drop held stationary*

$$\frac{VQ}{X} = \tfrac{4}{3}\pi a^3 d_{oil} g \quad (2)$$
(upward force of field) (weight of drop)

a and Q are the only unknowns.

From (1),
$$a = \sqrt{\frac{6\pi \eta v}{\tfrac{4}{3}\pi d_{oil} g}}$$

Now, $E = \dfrac{V}{X}$, so substitute into (2) for the radius a and find Q.

Equipment

Figure 496 shows the electrical connections and the view that should be seen through the microscope. The microscope is moved forward and backward to produce a sharp image of the oil drops, while the eyepiece is moved to focus the graticule.

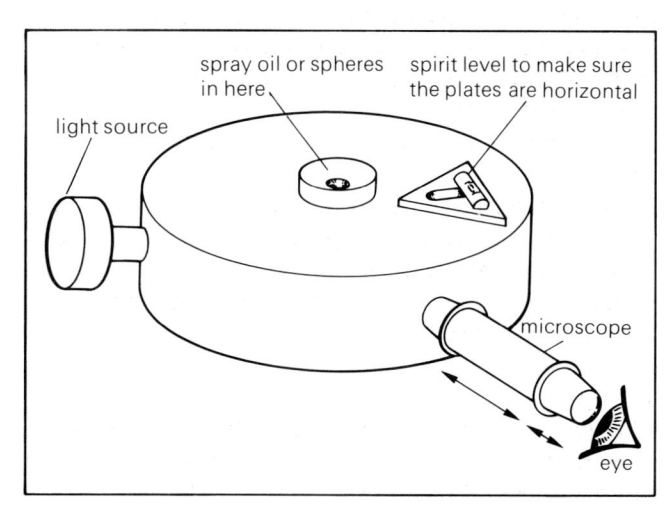

Figure 497 Equipment

Experimental details

1. After setting up the apparatus, spray in the oil or spheres. As the droplets form, they charge by friction and will acquire different charges which could be positive or negative. Hold an alpha source close to the gap between the plates for a few seconds. **Follow all the usual precautions for handling radioactive sources.**

2. To remove positively-charged particles, connect the voltage to make the bottom plate negative. Any positively-charged particles will move quickly to the bottom, and any particles with high charge values will be removed from the field of view. Reverse the polarity of the voltage several times. Do not hold the voltage on for too long or the negative drops you want to look at will hit the plates as well.

3. Reverse the polarity to move higher-charged negative particles to the top. Most of the particles now left should have a negative charge $10e$ or less. Keep reversing the polarity until all unwanted particles have cleared.

4. Choose a particular drop. Alter the voltage until that drop is stationary and record the voltage. If you are just trying to show that there is a fundamental unit of charge, go to step 8.

5. Move the drop to the top of your range of vision. Switch off the field and short the plates together. The drop will fall and quickly reach a terminal velocity. Using a stopwatch measure the time taken (t) to fall between two lines on the graticule.

6. When the drop is near the bottom of your field of view, switch the field on with the polarity such that the drop moves up. The problem here is that if too large a voltage is used the drop will move up so quickly that it moves out of vision, and if too small a voltage is used the drop falls out of vision at the bottom. About what voltage should you use?

    Steps 5 and 6 can be repeated several times, keeping the drop in vision all the time, and average values for t can be found.

7. Now choose a different drop and repeat from stage 4 to produce another set of values.

8. If you have time and suitable apparatus, select one drop and alter the voltage until it is stationary. Now try and alter the charge on it by bringing the Ra^{226} (α-source, good at ionising) near to the hole in the top of the plates. If the drop starts to move, the charge on it has been altered. You may need some patience with this part of the experiment. Find the new voltage which will hold the drop stationary. Then time its fall with no field on in the same way as before. Now try to give the drop a different charge using the radium source again and repeat the measurements.

B. *Computer simulation 'MILLIK' (package PHYS2 option 3)*

This program allows you to control the movement of 'drops' on the screen (figure 498) in exactly the same way as in the real apparatus. The potential difference applied to the plates can be altered to make a given drop stationary.

The field can be turned off and the drops timed over a given distance with a stopwatch.

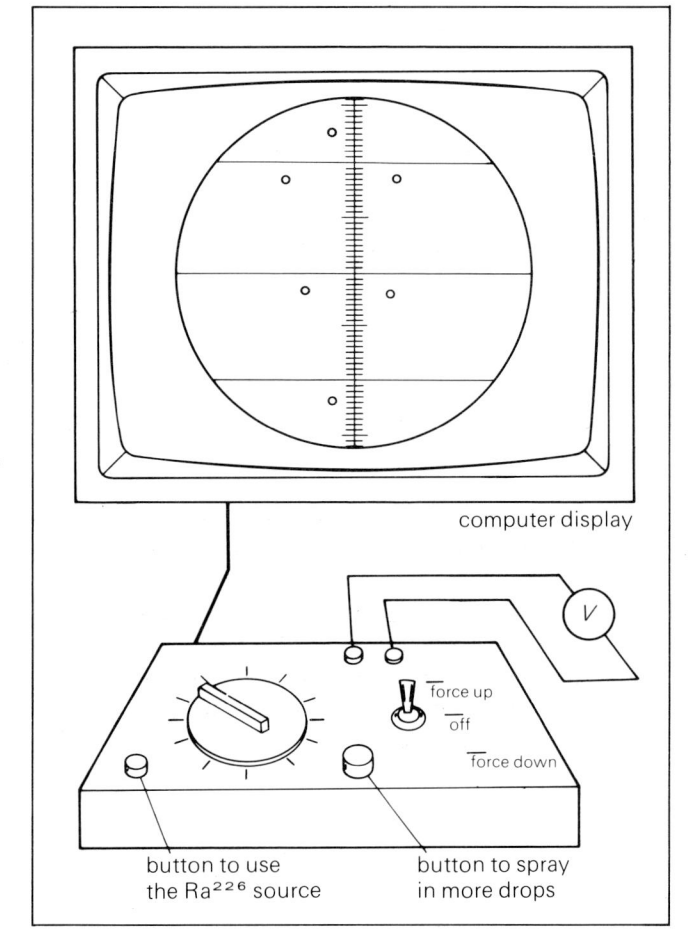

Figure 498 Equipment

Results

Several different drops

Voltage to hold drop stationary/V	Fall times with no field/s	Average time t/s

MEASURING QUANTITIES AND INVESTIGATING LAWS

A single drop with different charges

Voltage to hold drop stationary/V	Fall time with no field/s

number of graticule lines fallen = ...
distance fallen by drop = ... m

You will need to find out the following:
  viscosity of air (η)
  gravitational field constant (g)
  separation of the graticule lines (L)
  separation of the plates (X)
  density of oil

From your results

1. To investigate if charge exists in integer multiples, work out values of $1/V$ and mark each one with a line on a scale. This can only be done for measurements on a single particle whose charge is altered or if polystyrene spheres are used which are all the same size.

   Figure 499 would indicate that the value X is the highest common factor of all the others. This would only be approximate, because all drops do not have the same radius, unless the same drop were used and given different charges.

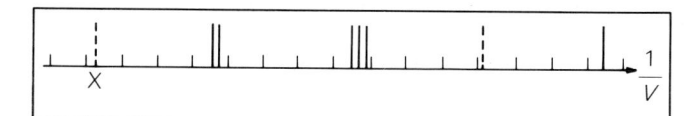

Figure 499

2. Work out the values of velocity v, radius a and the final value for the charge Q, using the equations:

$$Q \propto \frac{1}{V}$$

and

$$\frac{VQ}{X} = \frac{4\pi a^3 d_{oil} g}{3}$$

$$a = \sqrt{\frac{6\pi \eta v}{\frac{4}{3}\pi d_{oil} g}}$$

$$Q = \frac{\frac{4}{3}\pi a^3 d_{oil} g X}{V}$$

Velocity/m s^{-1}	Radius a/m	Charge on the drop/C

You may find the following program useful: it should run on most microcomputers using BASIC.

```
5 REM read in the information about the apparatus used
10 READ DO,DA,N,G,X,L
20 LET P=3.14159
25 REM input information about a single drop
30 PRINT "HOLDING VOLTAGE"
35 INPUT V
40 PRINT "FREE FALL TIME"
45 INPUT T
50 PRINT "NUMBER OF GRATICULE SPACES FALLEN"
55 INPUT H
60 LET D=4*P*DO*G/3
65 LET U=4*P*DA*G/3
67 REM work out the radius
70 LET A=SQR((6*P*N*L*H/T)/(D-U))
75 REM work out the charge
80 LET Q=D*(A^3)*X/V
85 PRINT " "
90 PRINT "CHARGE = ";Q;" COULOMB"
95 PRINT " "
100 GOTO 30
498 REM ..... position for your data
499 REM density of oil(DO) , density of air(DA)
500 DATA ..... , .....
504 REM viscocity of air(N) , gravitational field(G)
505 DATA ..... , .....
509 REM plate separation(X) , graticule line separation(L)
510 DATA ..... , .....
```

To calculate the charge on a drop

The value for the charge may not be the single electronic charge, because the drop may have more than one charge on it. From all the charge you have measured, a probable value for the highest common factor needs to be found, which should be the smallest value for a discrete charge, e.

One way is to decide on the number of charges which must have been on each drop. To do this, take the lowest charge and see if it divides into all the others nearly an integer number of times. If not, then halve the value and try again until a pattern becomes clear.

Having decided now on the number of charges on each drop, values for one charge can be found and a mean average calculated. If you have taken a large number of drops, working out the standard deviation will give a reasonable value for the probable error.

Conclusions

State whether your experiment shows that there is a fundamental unit of charge and summarise your evidence.

Give a mean average value and probable error for this charge if you measured it.

Typical results

On several drops

Drop no.	Voltage to hold drop stationary/V	Average fall time, no field/s
1	193, 195, 194	15.2 15.5 15.1
2	88, 89, 88	20.5 20.6 20.7
2	161, 163, 159	20.3 20.0 20.2
2	80	20.1
3	215, 221, 221	40.4 41.2 38.0
4	83, 83, 83	23.6 24.0 23.6
4	125, 125, 125	24.0 23.6 23.4
5	200, 198, 201	27.6 26.1 27.4
5	137, 136, 136	26.9 27.6 26.6
6	248, 255, 248	12.7 12.9 12.7
7	228, 230, 228	24.5 25.0 23.6

If you could not do the experiment, use the results given here (which are taken from the booklet Griffin and George supply with their version of Millikan's apparatus) to work out a value for e.

density of oil 973 kg m^{-3}
viscosity of air 1.83×10^{-5} N s m^{-2}
gravitational constant 9.81 N kg^{-1}
separation of plates 5×10^{-3} m
distance between lines on the graticule 4.2×10^{-4} m (0.42 mm)

On a single drop

The charge on a drop can be changed by using the radioactive source. The voltage needed to hold the drop stationary will also change.

Time t for fall over four spaces/s	Voltage to hold drop stationary/V
29.6	55
29.7	109
30.4	55
31.0	167
30.1	330
30.4	168
30.2	335
30.2	83

93. MEASURING THE PERMITTIVITY OF AIR AND PERSPEX

Outline

A parallel plate capacitor has a capacitance $C = \dfrac{\varepsilon A}{x}$.

ε = permittivity of the medium between the plates
A = area of overlap
x = separation

The charge stored on a capacitor is $Q = CV$ so that, if the charging potential is known and the charged stored on the capacitor measured, it should be possible to do an experiment to find ε. In practice, measuring charge accurately can be difficult. It is easier to measure the rate of flow of charge, because this is an electric current. The method used in this practical involves charging and discharging a capacitor very quickly at a known frequency and measuring the average current produced.

$$\text{average current} = \frac{\text{charge flowed}}{\text{time}}$$

Because the number of charge and discharge cycles per second is known, the charge flowing from each discharge can be found, assuming that all discharges are identical. If the capacitor has been fully charged and then fully discharged, this charge is the same as the value Q in the equation $Q = CV$ and ε can be worked out.

(a) How can you be sure that the capacitor is as completely discharged as it can be—say to 1 per cent of its maximum charge?
(b) How do you eliminate the effects of stray capacitance between the plates of the capacitor and surrounding objects?

Equipment

Values $R1$ and $R2$ (figure 500) must be low enough to allow the capacitor to charge and discharge fully in the time the reed contacts are closed.

MEASURING QUANTITIES AND INVESTIGATING LAWS

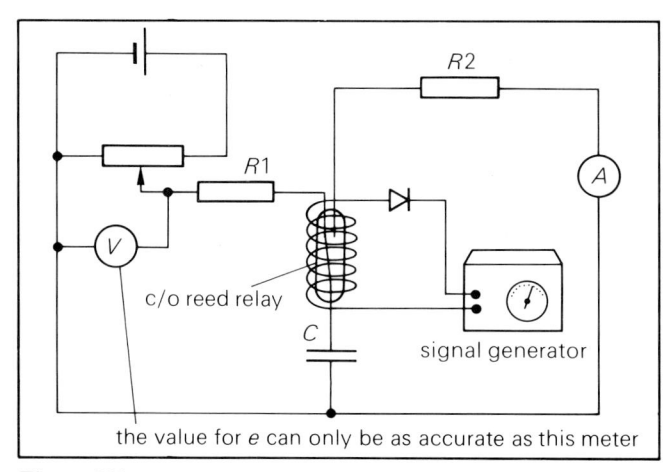

Figure 500

A typical reed switch has a maximum current of 0.5 A. If a 12 V supply was used and the maximum current was flowing initially:

$$R = \frac{12}{0.5} = 24\,\Omega$$

From this value the minimum time for which the coil contacts must be closed can be calculated. The charging equation is $V = V_0(1 - e^{-t/RC})$ and, assuming that we want to ensure that at least 95 per cent of the charge stored has flowed, the minimum time t can be calculated, and from this the frequency $\left(t = \frac{1}{2f}\right)$. (Why?) The size of the voltage V produced by the signal generator is important, since this determines for what fraction of the cycle the reed switch is turned on.

Suppose V_c is the minimum voltage required to make the reed move. (You can measure it by finding the voltage at which the lamps change over.) (See figure 501.)

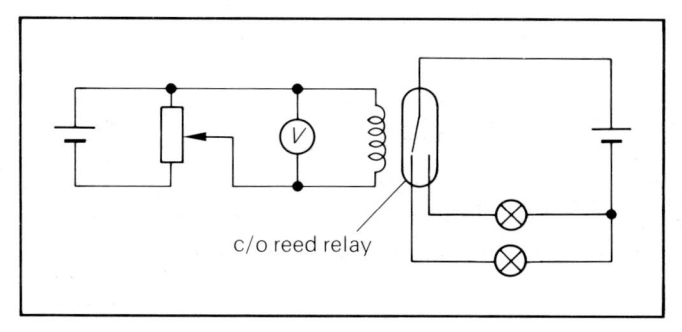

Figure 501 Measuring the voltage needed to operate the reed relay.

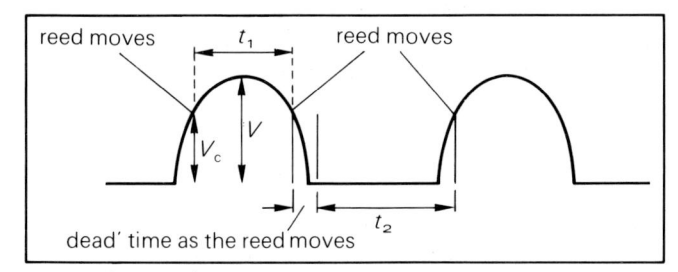

Figure 502 Half-wave rectified waveform

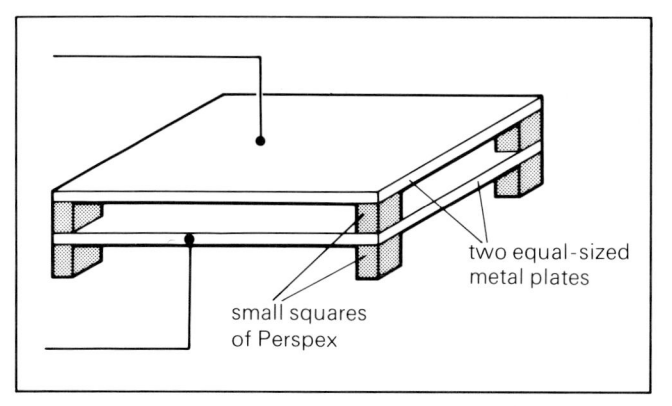

Figure 503 Construction of the parallel-plate capacitor

The half-wave rectified waveform is shown in figure 502. If $R1$ and $R2$ are similar, t_1 and t_2 should be similar and so the reed should move soon after the voltage starts to rise. A rule of thumb is that V should be about five times V_c.

Figure 503 shows the construction of the parallel plate capacitor. The two metal plates must be equal in size; their sides are measured with a pair of vernier callipers or a metre ruler if larger. The Perspex squares should be cut from the same sheet and their thickness measured with a micrometer; have sets of different thickness available.

Typical values
charging voltage 10 V
area of plates 100 cm³
separation of plates 2 mm
frequency of coil alternating supply 400 Hz
peak voltage of alternating supply to the coil 12 V

Experimental details

Decide on values for the frequency and voltage of the coil supply which are suitable for the value of parallel-plate capacitor and charging voltage being used. Justify the choices in your report.

Measure the charging voltage and average current. Repeat for several different charging voltages and separation (x) of capacitor plates. Repeat using a solid sheet of Perspex between the plates.

$$\text{average current, } I = \frac{\text{charge}}{\text{time}}$$

$$= \frac{CV}{1/f}$$

$$= \frac{\varepsilon A V f}{x}$$

$$\text{permittivity, } \varepsilon = \frac{xI}{AVf}$$

Work out a value of ε for each set of results and find the mean average. Quote a range of error.

94. THE PHOTOELECTRIC EFFECT AND THE MEASUREMENT OF PLANCK'S CONSTANT

Outline

When electromagnetic radiation falls on a metal surface, there is the possibility that electrons in the metal might absorb enough energy to escape from the surface. This poses the following questions.

1. Does the electron gradually accumulate enough energy over a period of time?
2. Does the energy in electromagnetic radiation exist in small packets and would an electron absorb the whole of a packet or *quanta*?
3. Is the force holding the electron in the metal the same for all metals, and is it a constant for each type of surface?
4. Planck's idea was that the energy of each quantum equals hf, where f is the frequency of the radiation measured in Hertz (Hz) and $h = 6.6 \times 10^{-34}$ J s, and that $KE_{electron} = hf - W$, where W is called the work function of the surface and is the energy needed to make an electron just escape. Is this so?

In the experiment, light of a certain band of frequencies is shone on a photocell; any electrons emitted cause a current to flow. The current is of the order of n A and needs to be amplified before the p.d. it causes across a resistor can be displayed on an oscilloscope. If a *negative* voltage (V) is applied to the photocell, then the current is reduced, since there is a force repelling the electrons.

When the current is zero, the trace on the oscilloscope is a minimum and $KE_{max} = Ve$. It follows that, if this voltage is measured, the maximum KE of electrons can be found. Therefore:

$$Ve = hf - W$$

If measurements of the retarding voltage V at different frequencies f are taken and a graph plotted of V against f, then the graph should be a straight line of gradient h/e and negative intercept on the V axis of W/e. A straight-line graph would support Einstein's theory.

The scope for further experimentation is limited, because surfaces open to the air quickly oxidise and stop emitting electrons. For this reason a computer model has been written for you to experiment with other aspects of photoelectric emission. This is one of the Schools Council *Computers in the Curriculum* (© Longman) packages called 'PHOTO 1' and 'PHOTO 2'. Alternatively the program 'PHOTOE' (package PHYS2 option 2) could be used.

Experimental details

Set up the apparatus and shine the light through a filter onto the photocell. For each filter find the negative voltage (V) which gives a minimum trace on the oscilloscope. Does the voltage depend on the brightness of the light? You can investigate this by moving the light further away or closer.

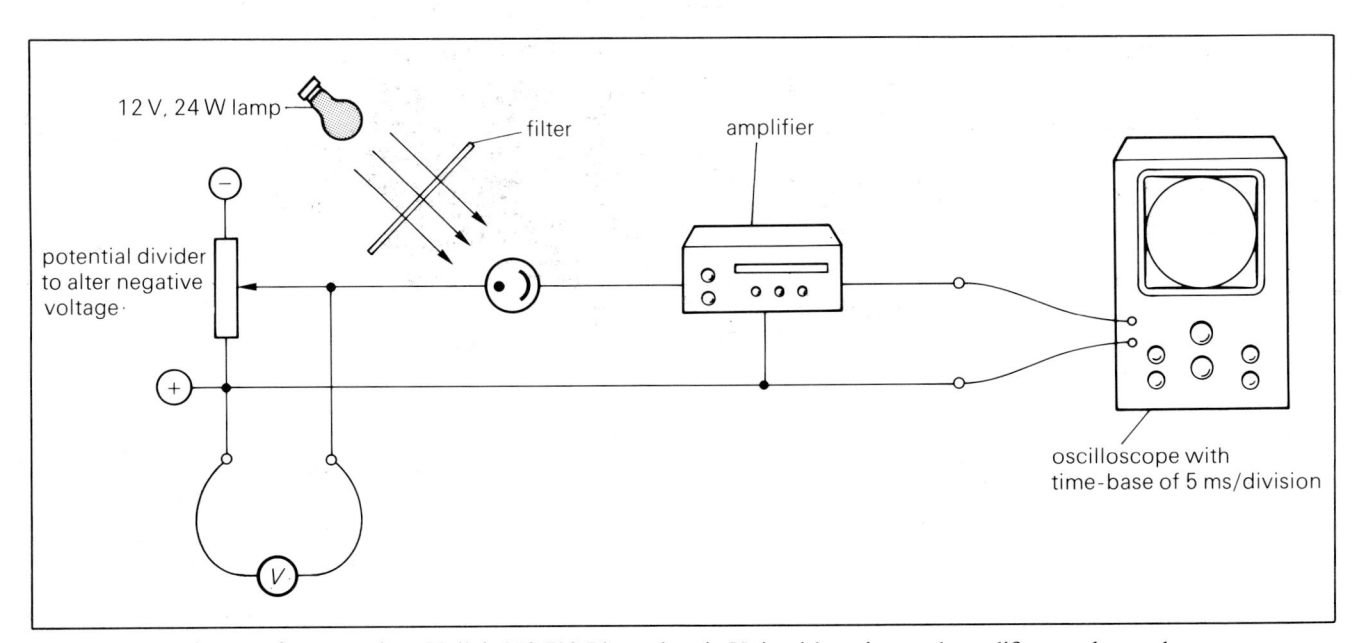

Figure 504 Equipment, for example, a Unilab 073.722 Photoelectric Unit with an internal amplifier can be used.

MEASURING QUANTITIES AND INVESTIGATING LAWS

Question
Why change the brightness by altering the current?

If the intensity of the light has no effect on V, then this supports Einstein's theory that each quantum has the same energy and is absorbed totally by one electron.

If the filters used are not marked with a mean wavelength or wavelength range, then they will need to be measured using a white light source, the filters and a spectrometer with a diffraction grating (see pp. 69).

Results

Shortest wavelength of range/λ	Voltage V/V

$$Ve = hf - W$$

Now, $c = f\lambda$, where c is the velocity of light.

Thus
$$V = \frac{hc}{e\lambda} - \frac{W}{e}$$

From the results

Plot a graph of voltage as ordinate and $\frac{1}{\lambda}$ as abscissa.

From the graph work out a value for Planck's constant h and the work function of the metal surface W.

In your report

Include your table of results, graph and values for Planck's constant and the work function. If you have used the computer simulation, summarise your conclusions about the intensity of radiation and the number of electrons produced and anything else you have found out. Have you any evidence that electromagnetic radiation is quantised?

95. MEASURING THE SPEED OF WAVES

1. SOUND IN FREE AIR

Outline

This experiment measures the speed of sound in free air by adjusting the position of two microphones so that the signals from them are a multiple of half-wavelengths out of phase. The wavelength is calculated from the separation of the microphones. The velocity is calculated from $V = f\lambda$. The speed of sound in air at room temperature is about 340 m s^{-1} so you should be able to calculate a suitable frequency to use. You should be able to fit several half-wavelengths in the length of bench on which you are working.

Either

An amplifier may be needed to make the signals from the microphones, $M1$ and $M2$, as near the same amplitude as possible. Remember that single-transistor amplifiers produce a *phase inversion*. (See figure 505.)

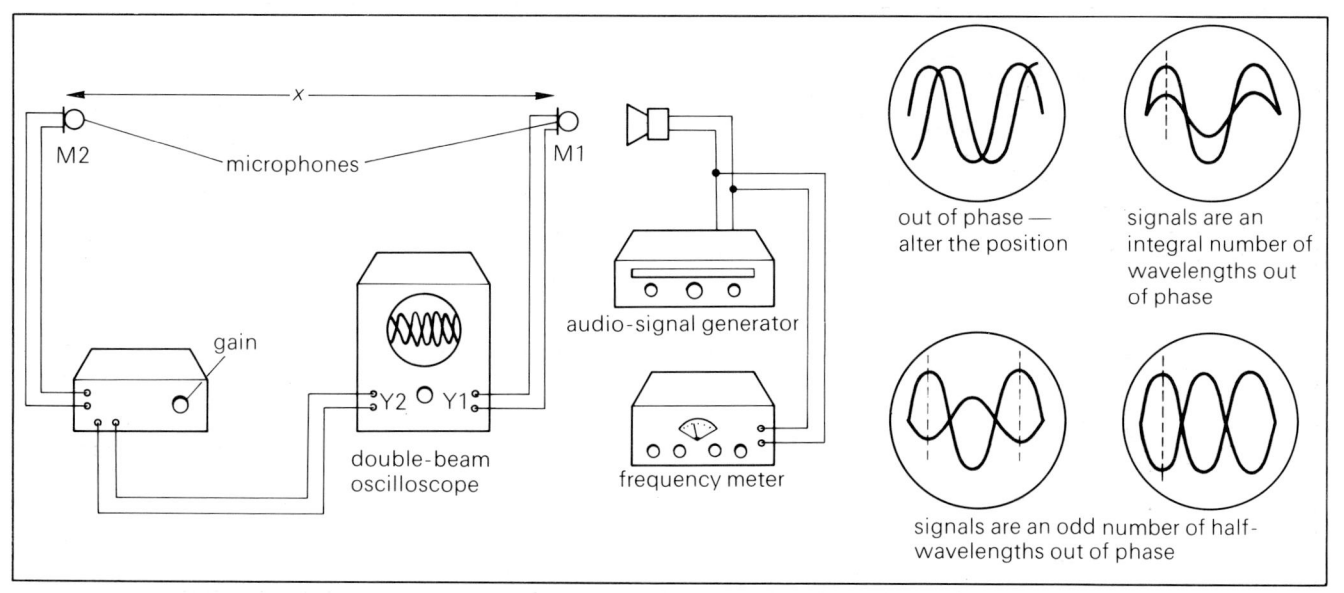

Figure 505 Equipment

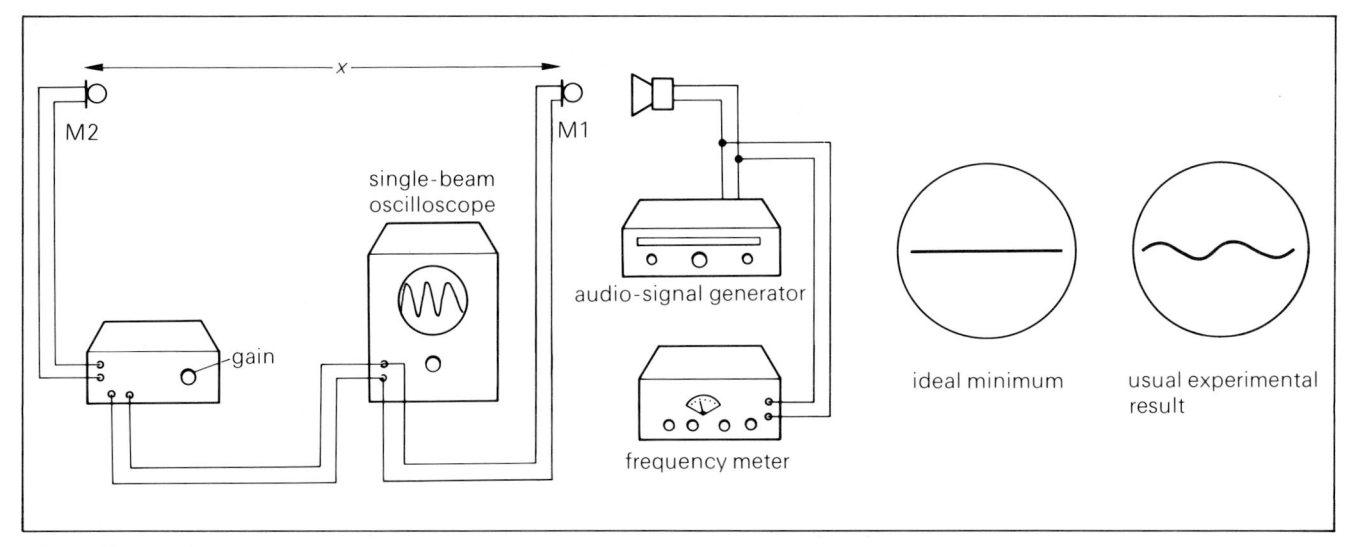

Figure 506 Equipment

Or

The signals from the microphones, M1 and M2, are summed and displayed. If the two signals are exactly an odd number of half-wavelengths out of phase, then there will be a *minimum*; if they are a whole number of wavelengths out of phase, there will be a *maximum*. (See Figure 506.)

Experimental details

The principle is the same for both types of apparatus. Only the method of deciding the position of M2 when the two signals are half a wavelength out of phase differs. Figure 507 shows the traces you should expect to see on the oscilloscope, (a) for the double beam oscilloscope and (b) for the single beam oscilloscope.

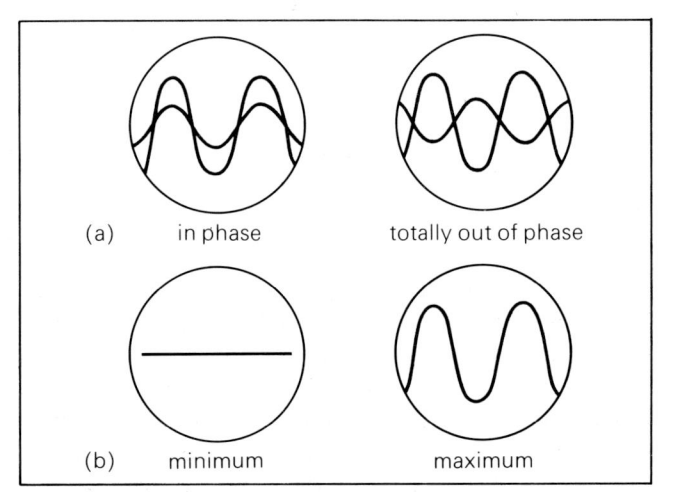

Figure 507 Traces for (a) a double beam oscilloscope and (b) a single beam oscilloscope

Start with M2 close to M1. Choose a suitable frequency and record its value. Adjust the gain of the amplifier if necessary. Move M2 away slowly until the first position is reached when the microphone has moved half a wavelength. Record the separation (x) of the two microphones.

Move M2 out again and record the distance (x) between M2 and M1 for as many $\frac{1}{2}\lambda$ 'alignments' as practical.

Work out a mean average wavelength and give a probable error. Use the frequency to calculate the velocity. Change the frequency and repeat for several different frequencies.

Results

frequency = ... Hz
mean average λ = ... m
estimated error ± ... m
velocity = frequency × wavelength = ... m s^{-1}

x/m	Error/m −	Error/m +	λ/m	Error/m −	Error/m +
$\frac{1}{2}\lambda$					
λ					

MEASURING QUANTITIES AND INVESTIGATING LAWS

Conclusions

1. Does the error get smaller if more half-wavelengths are taken?
2. Does the velocity measured become more accurate if a lower frequency is used?
3. How could you check the calibration of the signal generator for the frequency range you have chosen?
4. Design an experiment to measure the speed of sound in carbon dioxide. Discuss any problems you might encounter.

2. THE SPEED OF 3 CM MICROWAVES IN A LIQUID

Outline

When a wave crosses the boundary between two different media, or even if the density of the same medium changes, the directions of the wave can alter and refraction occurs (figure 508).

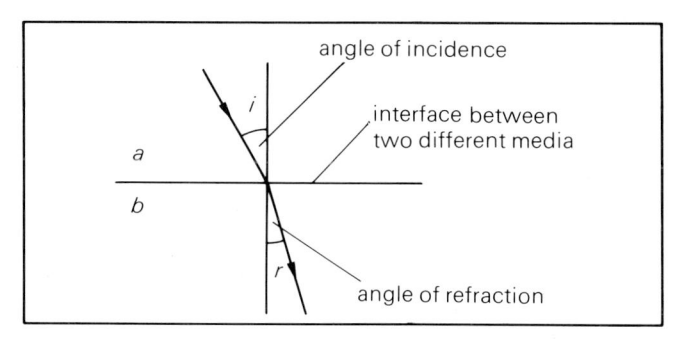

Figure 508

The refractive index $_an_b = \dfrac{\text{speed in } a}{\text{speed in } b}$

By Snell's law:

$$_an_b = \frac{\sin i}{\sin r}$$

Since the velocity of all electromagnetic waves is 3×10^8 in a vacuum and very nearly this value in air, the speed in a medium b can be found by measuring the refractive index if medium a is air.

Experimental details

Using the apparatus shown in figure 509, draw round the hollow block. Draw a line AB with an angle of incidence $i = 30°$. Align the 3 cm wave source along this line. Without the block in position, take readings on the meter as the detector moves across the arc at X, to find the maximum reading which will show the exact line of the beam. If it does not coincide with the line AB, how do you alter the apparatus so that the beam is along AB?

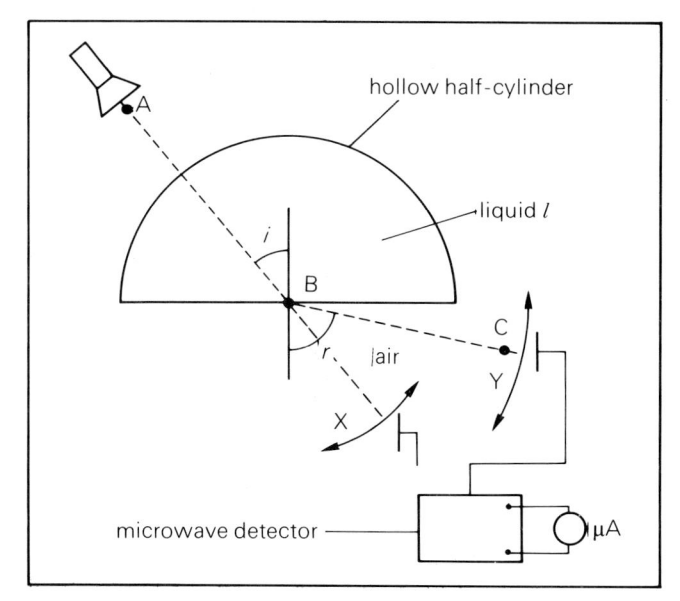

Figure 509 3 cm wave apparatus

Put the block in position and fill it with the liquid. Paraffin, meths and oil are common liquids to use initially. Move the detector to position Y and take a set of readings along the arc shown, to find the maximum (it may be useful to mark a scale along the arc drawn on the paper and note readings), so that point C can be located.

Remove the hollow box and liquid. Draw in BC and measure the angle of refraction.

From the results
Work out the refractive index for liquid–air and then calculate the speed of the microwaves in the liquid.

Questions
1. Should the speed of the microwaves in the liquid be larger or smaller than the speed in air?
2. Have you given an accuracy to your result?

3. LIGHT IN A VACUUM

Outline

The speed of light in a vacuum can be measured in your laboratory if the equipment is available, but it is expensive and not normally available. An alternative is to use a television programme from the ITV series for A-level physics 'Measuring the speed of light'. The experiment is filmed and you are asked to take readings from the television and to calculate the speed of light in air. Further details can be found in the booklet accompanying the programme.

96. MEASURING THE WAVELENGTH OF LIGHT USING NEWTON'S RINGS

Outline

Newton's rings are intereference bands produced in the air gap between two surfaces. If photographic slides are mounted between sheets of glass, an interference pattern can sometimes be seen (figure 510). This is because of a thin layer of trapped air, which alters the path difference between light reflected from the film and the glass.

If a plano-convex lens and a plane glass sheet are used, then, due to the symmetry of the air film, the shape of the interference pattern is a series of *rings* (figure 511). The formula for the nth minimum (dark ring) is:

$$(n-1)\lambda = \frac{r_n^2}{R}$$

where R is the radius of curvature of the lens. The light moving in the air film changes its phase by $2x \times \frac{2\pi}{\lambda} + \pi$ relative to light reflected at P (figure 512). The extra π is due to the phase change as a wave is reflected in an optically denser medium. From geometry, it can be shown that $r_n = 2Rx$. For a dark ring (minimum) the path difference is an odd number of $\frac{1}{2}\lambda$, i.e. a phase difference of $\pi, 3\pi, 5\pi \ldots (2n-1)\pi$. Therefore:

$$2x \times \frac{2\pi}{\lambda} + \pi = (2n-1)\pi$$

giving $(n-1)\lambda = 2x$ for $n = 1, 2, 3$ etc. ($n = 0$ gives the dark central ring); and so:

$$\boxed{(n-1)\lambda = \frac{r_n^2}{R}}$$

It is often difficult to locate the exact centre of the central minimum, and so in the experiment you measure the *diameter* of a series of rings. In this case the equation becomes

$$(n-1)\lambda = \frac{d_n^2}{4R},$$

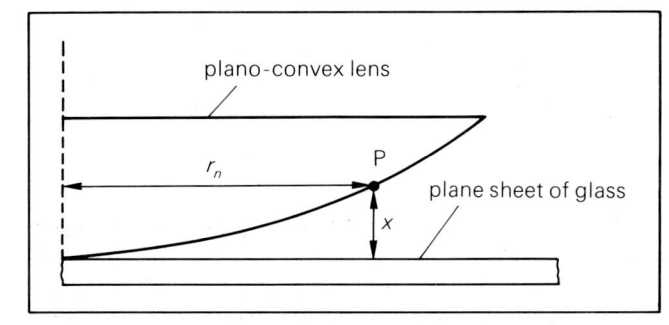

Figure 512 Section view

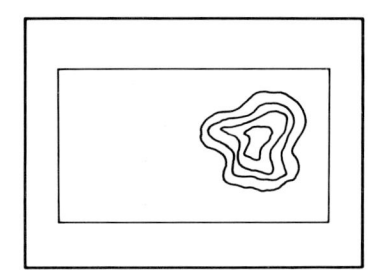

Figure 510

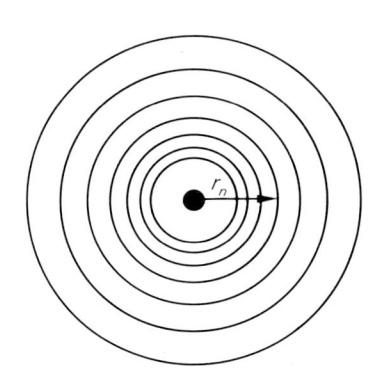

Figure 511 What you should see.

and so

$$d_n^2 = 4Rn\lambda - 4R\lambda.$$

Comparing with the equation of a straight line $y = mx + c$, a graph of d_n^2 against n should be a straight line with gradient $4R\lambda$ and intercept $4R\lambda$.

Experimental details

1. Assemble the apparatus as in figure 513. Focus the microscope on the surface of the glass plate (G). Alter the angle of the plate (M) until fringes are seen. Move the travelling microscope until it is over the central minimum.
2. Move the microscope out a number of fringes, for example 15. Measure the diameter of each ring by taking readings of the middle of each dark line as the microscope is moved back to the centre and then for the same number of fringes moving out from the centre on the other side.
3. Work out the diameter of each fringe. Plot a graph of d_n^2 against n.
4. Use a spherometer to find the radius of curvature, R, of the lens (see pp. 39).

$$R = \frac{(h_1 - h_2)^2 + x^2}{2(h_1 - h_2)}$$

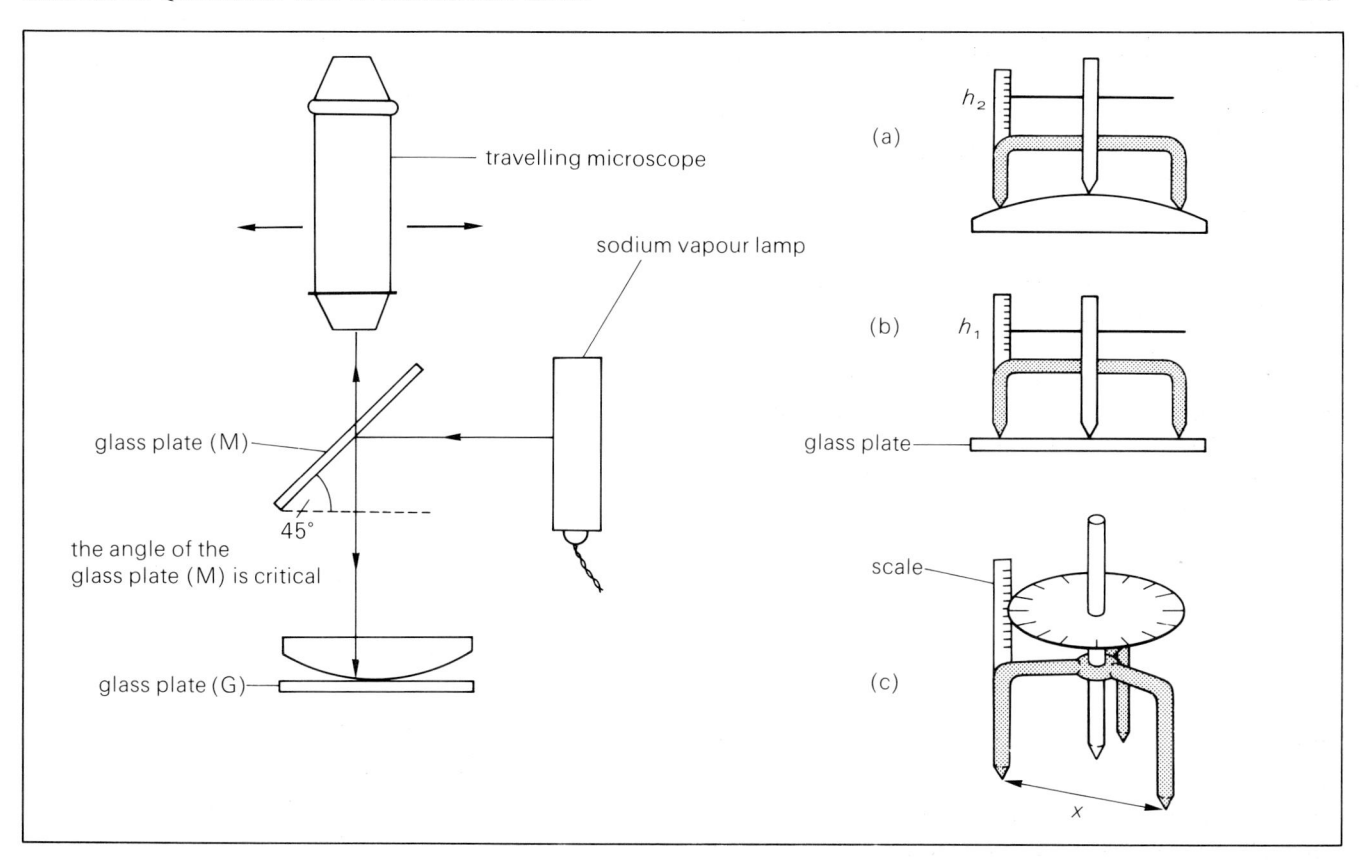

Figure 513 Equipment

From the graph
Find the wavelength, using the gradient and the intercept.

Results

Ring number n	Scale position /m × 10^{-3}	Diameter d/m × 10^{-3}	Wavelength λ/m × 10^{-9}

Questions
1. Why does sodium light have to be used rather than white light?
2. Why is the central spot dark?
3. What would be the observable effect of using a mercury vapour lamp rather than a sodium vapour lamp?

97. FOCAL LENGTH AND FOCAL PLANE OF A CONVEX LENS

Outline

The principal focus of a convex lens is defined as the point on the axis through which rays parallel and near to the axis pass through after refraction. The focal length is the distance from this point to the pole of the lens. The focal plane is the area made by the image points of parallel rays entering the lens at angles over as large a range of angles to the principal axis as possible. The following experiments map out the focal plane of various cylindrical lenses and measure the focal lengths of other convex lenses.

1. MAPPING OUT THE FOCAL PLANE

Equipment

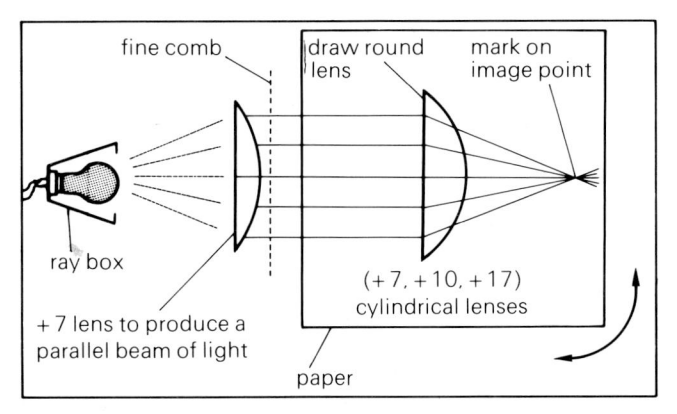

Figure 514 Equipment. Turn the paper and lens to alter the angle of the incident beam.

Experimental details

1. Choose one of the lenses given. Set the apparatus to produce a fine parallel beam of rays. How do you check that the beam is parallel? What do you do to get it parallel and why?
2. Mark on the image point. Rotate the paper through a small angle to change the angle the incident rays make with the lens and mark the image point again. Repeat for as large a range of angles as possible. From the points plotted draw in the curve of the focal plane.
3. Repeat for lenses of other focal lengths.

Questions

1. How would you describe the basic shape of the focal plane?
2. To what extent is the statement 'for incident angles of less than 10° to the axis the focal plane is flat' true?
3. What effect on the shape of the focal plane does changing the focal length have?

2. FINDING THE FOCAL LENGTH

Equipment

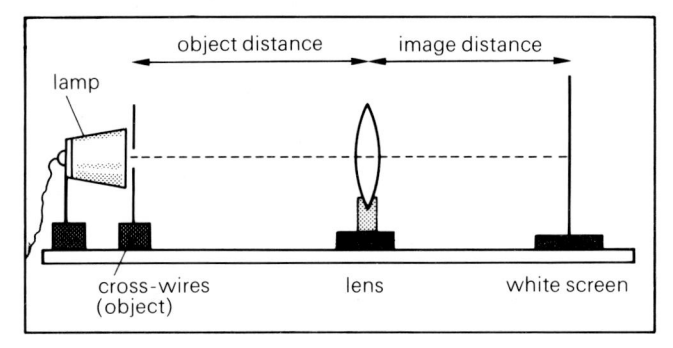

Figure 515

Experimental details

1. Set up the apparatus as shown in figure 515 (either a normal optical bench or separate apparatus). Choose a sensible object distance. Remember:
   (a) there is no real image for an object placed less than the focal length distance away,
   (b) an object just outside the focal length distance gives an image a long way away.
2. Move the screen to get as sharp an image as possible. Make a note of the range of distance for which the image is seen to be sharp.
3. Repeat for as wide a range of object distances as possible.

Results

Recorded results

Object distance/mm	Image distance/mm	Range of sharpness/mm

From the results

1. Draw a scale diagram (see figure 516) from one set of results to find the focal length. Estimate the error involved.

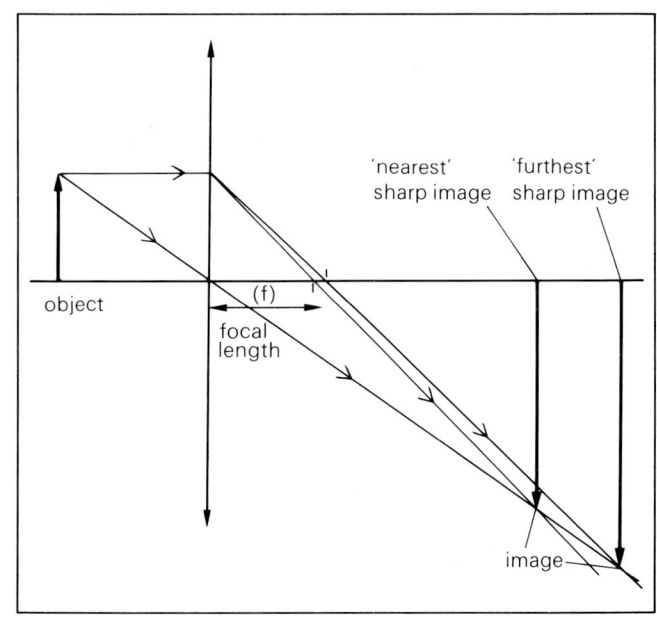

Figure 516 Scale diagram to find the focal length (f).

MEASURING QUANTITIES AND INVESTIGATING LAWS

2. Theory gives an equation:

$$\frac{1}{v} + \frac{1}{u} = \frac{1}{f}$$

where u = object distance
v = image distance
f = focal length
} all values positive

Rearrange this equation into a form with v on one side and u on the other which will enable a straight-line graph to be drawn.

Show a table of the values to be plotted. Draw a graph. What information can you deduce from (a) the intercepts, and (b) the gradient?

Questions

1. What effect does the shape of the focal plane have on the image seen on a flat screen?
2. How far do your results show that a 'wide aperture' setting on the lens of a camera gives a smaller 'depth of field' than a small aperture?

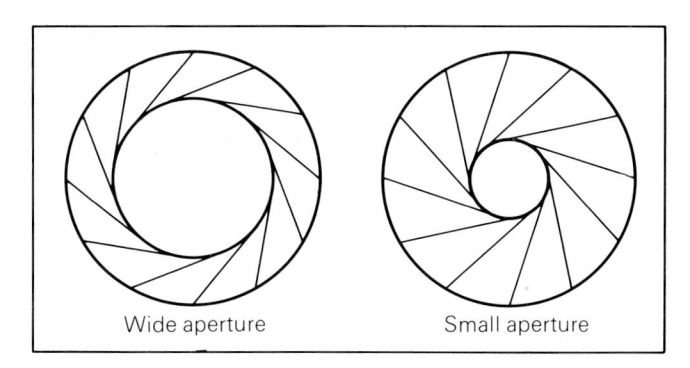

Figure 517

3. Does the accuracy of the measurements of image distance vary with the distance to be measured? Use some of your results to illustrate your answer, but remember it is percentage error which is important, i.e.:

$$\frac{\text{range of 'sharpness'}}{\text{best image distance}} \times 100\%$$

98. MEASURING THE RESOLUTION OF YOUR EYE

Outline

When light passes through any hole a diffraction pattern is produced. For example, a round source of light appears blurred at the edges, as in figure 518b. The hole in the iris of your eye, the size of the objective lens in a telescope or microscope, all produce diffraction patterns and this affects the *resolution* of the instruments.

Ideally, two small sources of light should produce the situation shown in figure 519a. In practice, they produce one of the two situations shown in figure 519b, depending on how far they are apart. Two sources are said to be resolved when the central maximum of one diffraction

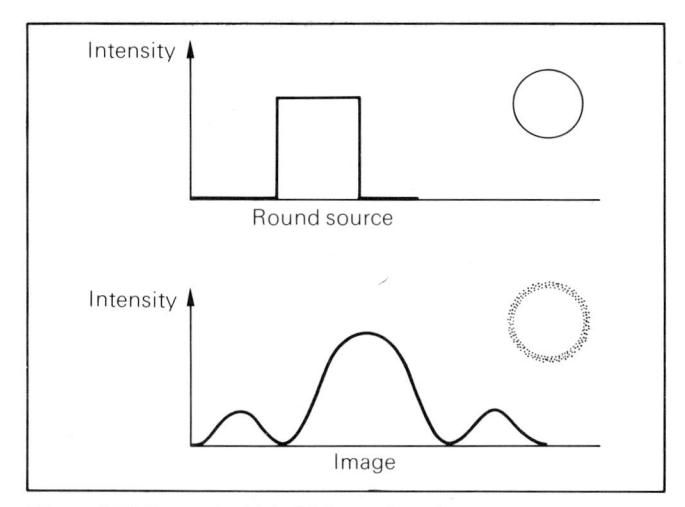

Figure 518 Instead of (a), (b) is produced.

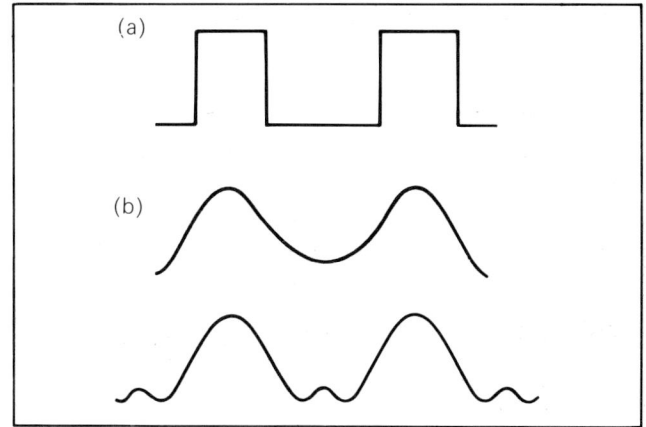

Figure 519

pattern is not closer than the first minimum in the pattern of the other (figure 520).

This experiment measures the angular resolution of your eye and investigates the effect of colour and object size.

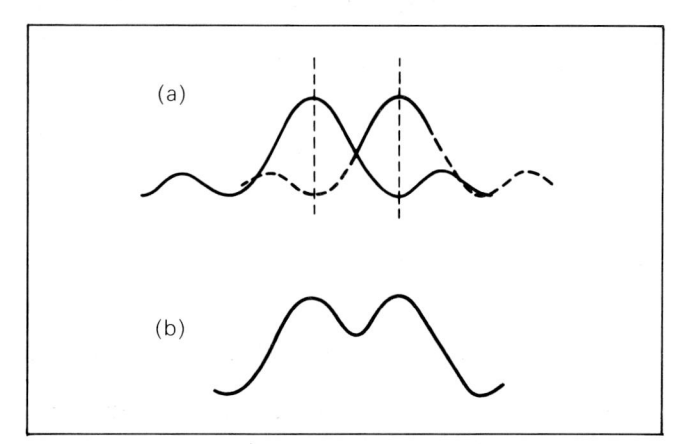

Figure 520 (a) Is seen as (b) and is just resolved.

Equipment

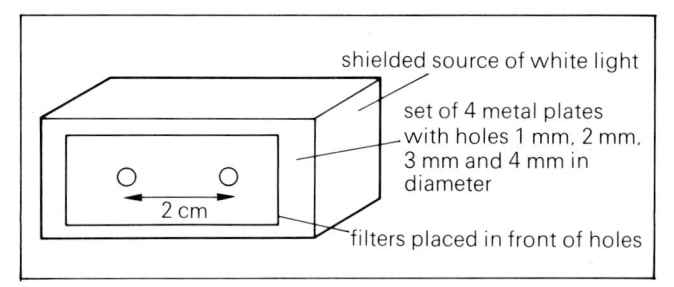

Figure 521

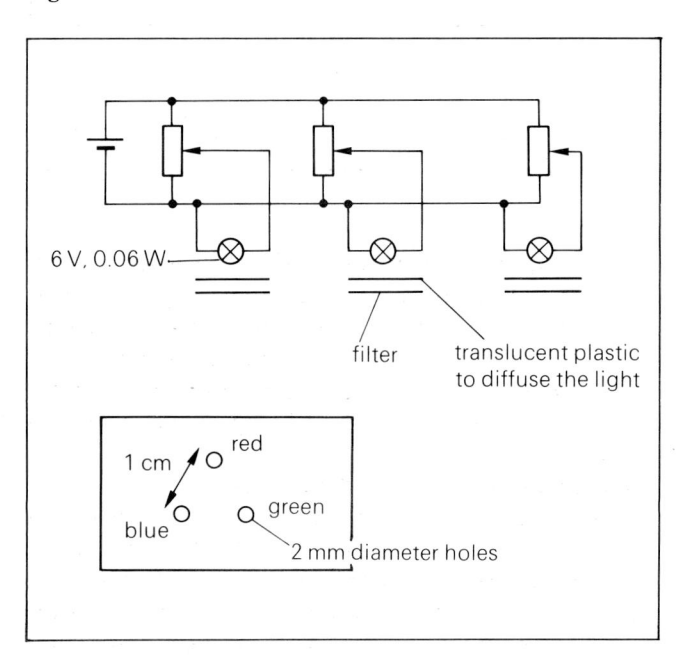

Figure 522

Experimental details

Move the source with the two holes (figure 521) away from the eye until you decide that the two holes no longer appear distinctly separate. Measure the distance from your eye. Remember to decide on an error range (+ and −). Repeat with red, green and blue filters, and then repeat with different sizes of hole, if possible.

Using the apparatus shown in figure 522, move away until the holes are no longer resolved. Alter the brightnesses to produce white, yellow, cyan and magenta. Can you produce brown?

Results

Colour	Diameter of hole			
	1 mm	2 mm	3 mm	4 mm

The numerical value for the resolution

$$= \frac{\text{separation of the holes}}{\text{distance from the eye}} \text{ radian}.$$

Conclusions

Answer these questions:

1. Does resolution depend on the colour?
2. Does resolution depend on the size of the object?
3. What approximate value would you give for the angular resolution of the eye?

$$\text{angular resolution} = \frac{\text{separation of the sources}}{\text{distance from the eye}}$$

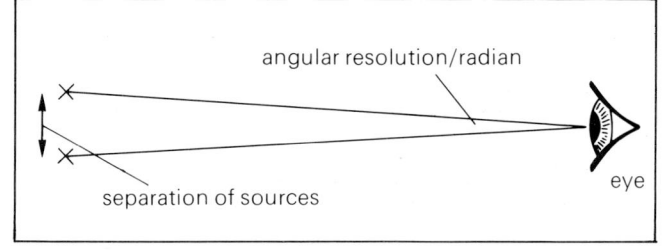

Figure 523

99. RESONANCE OF AN AIR COLUMN

Outline

Waves travelling down a tube will reflect from the end and interfere with the oncoming waves. At certain frequencies standing wave patterns are produced and the sound produced increases sharply in loudness. The tube is said to be in 'resonance'. The frequency is determined by the length of the tube and the air temperature, as players of brass musical instruments playing Christmas carols in the frosty night air will tell you. The width of the tube has a small effect, since this will determine how far the vibration spreads into the air beyond the end of the tube. The effective length of the tube will thus be slightly longer than its physical length. A tube closed at one end will resonate at different frequencies to a tube open at both ends.

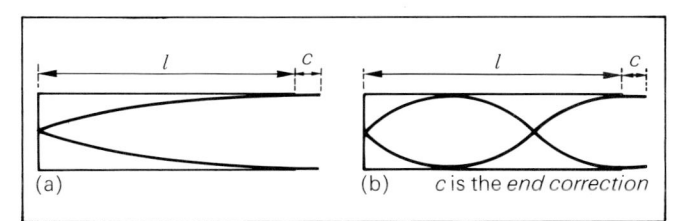

Figure 524

For figure 524:

(a) lowest frequency f_0

$$l + c = \frac{\lambda_0}{4}$$

(b) first harmonic (next higher frequency) f_1

$$l + c = \frac{3\lambda_1}{4}$$

and, since velocity = frequency × wavelength:

$$f_0 = \frac{v}{4(l+c)} \quad \text{and} \quad f_1 = \frac{3v}{4(l+c)}$$

where v is the velocity.

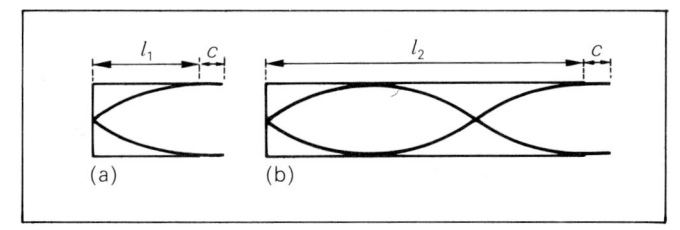

Figure 525

Alternatively, a longer tube will resonate to the same frequency when it is an overtone for that particular length. For example, for figure 525:

(a) $$l_1 + c = \frac{\lambda}{4} \quad (1)$$

and

(b) $$l_2 + c = \frac{3\lambda}{4} \quad (2)$$

Subtracting (2) from (1) gives $l_2 - l_1 = \frac{\lambda}{2}$, with the end correction cancelling out (always assuming it is the same for both lengths of tube; will it depend on the diameter?). Therefore:

$$v = 2f(l_2 - l_1)$$

For a tube open at both ends (figure 526) the lowest frequency is given by

$$\frac{\lambda}{2} = l + 2c$$

$$f = \frac{v}{2(l + 2c)}$$

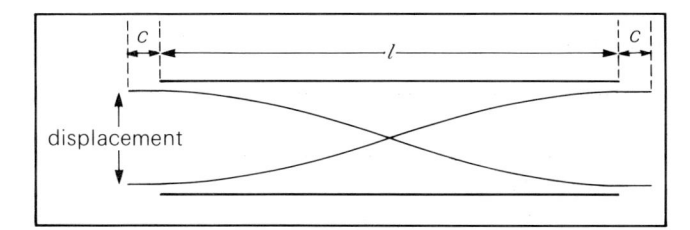

Figure 526

In this experiment you will find the frequencies to which different lengths of tube resonate, using an audio frequency oscillator and a small loudspeaker to excite the tube. You will also find the amount by which the frequency alters when you use tubes of different widths. From these measurements the velocity of sound will also be found.

The sound produced by the tube is stimulated by the speaker. We should expect the speaker to deliver a different amount of energy when the tube *resonates*, because the 'loading' on the speaker will change. This means that the current drawn by the speaker will change at resonance and this can be used to detect resonance rather than relying on your ears alone.

Equipment

A range of tubes of different lengths are needed, each length being in several different diameters if possible. You will need to be able to alter the length of the tube closed at one end by small amounts.

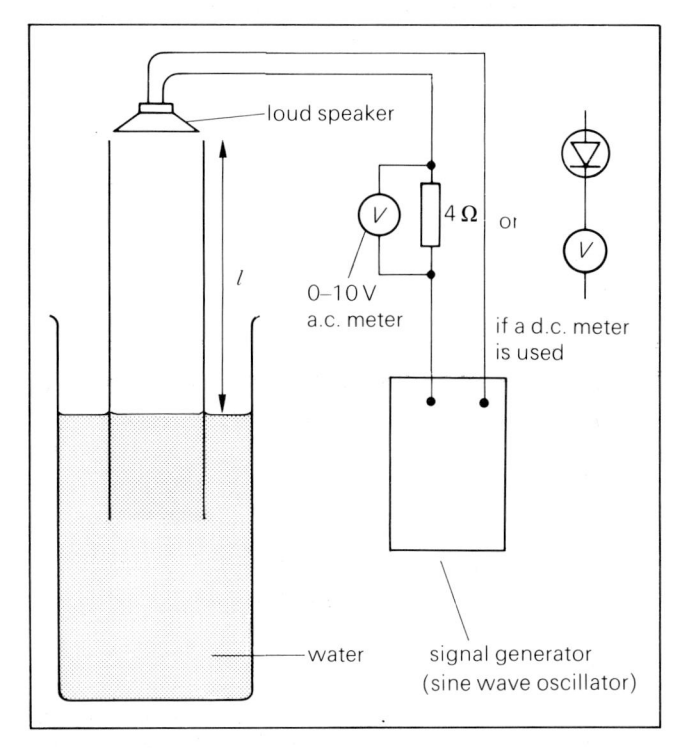

Figure 527 Tube closed at one end. Some longer lengths will also resonate at a frequency f.

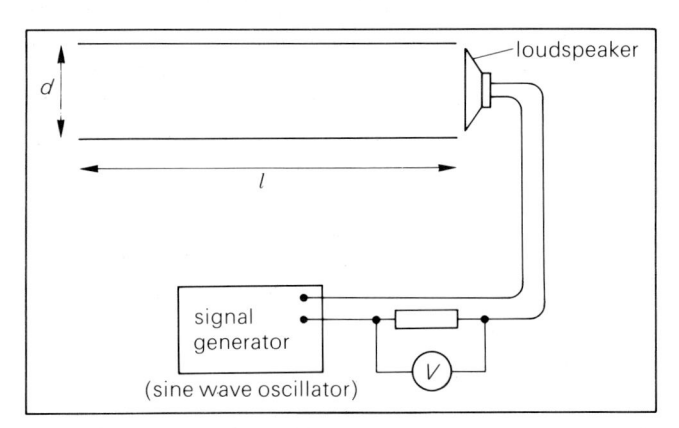

Figure 528 Tube open at both ends

1. THE LENGTHS AT WHICH A TUBE RESONATES

Experimental details

1. Using the apparatus shown in figure 527, set the oscillator to a frequency in the range 500–4000 Hz. Note the exact frequency. Your ear is most sensitive for frequencies in this range. Set the volume at a low but distinct level.
2. Start with a length, l, of about 1 cm and slowly raise the tube and speaker. Listen carefully for resonance to occur (at length l_1), when the sound will become appreciably louder and the voltmeter reading will make a sudden change. Record the length $l \to l_1$.
3. Continue to increase the length until the second resonance is heard (at length l_2). Record the length $l \to l_2$.
4. Calculate v from $v = 2f(l_2 - l_1)$.
5. Repeat for at least six different frequencies.
6. Find the mean average for v from your results, and compare it with the value calculated from the formula:

$$v = 331\left(1 + \frac{T°C}{273}\right) \text{m s}^{-1}$$

Results

Length (l)/m	Frequency/Hz					
	1	2	3	4	5	6
1st resonance						
2nd resonance						

2. THE FREQUENCIES FOR WHICH A TUBE RESONATES

Use the apparatus shown in figure 527. It is often more convenient to set the tube to a given length and then alter the frequency until resonance occurs. If you have a frequency meter available, use it to measure the exact frequency rather than to rely on the calibration of the audio frequency oscillator. Record a set of lowest resonant frequencies for different lengths of tube:

Length (l)/m	Frequency/Hz

From the results

For the lowest frequency of a tube closed at one end:

$$l + c = \frac{\lambda}{4}$$

$$\therefore v = 4f(l + c)$$

Rearranging, this gives:

$$\frac{1}{f} = \frac{4l}{v} + \frac{4c}{v}$$

MEASURING QUANTITIES AND INVESTIGATING LAWS

Comparing with the general equation for a straight line $y = mx + c$, we can see that a graph of $\frac{1}{f}$ as y (ordinate) and l as x (abscissa) should be a straight line with gradient $\frac{4}{v}$ and intercept on the $\frac{1}{f}$ axis of $\frac{4c}{v}$. Plot the graph and find v and the end correction c.

3. THE EFFECT OF THE DIAMETER OF THE TUBE

Using the apparatus shown in figure 528, find the lowest frequency at which the tubes of different diameter resonate. Can any conclusion be made about the general effect of increasing the diameter?

100. HEAT ENERGY TRANSFER

Outline

You should already be familiar with the general principles of conduction, convection and radiation. In a real situation there are a large number of factors affecting the rate of loss of heat. We can only investigate the effects of the main factors:

1. for conduction—the surface area, the temperature difference and the coefficient of thermal conductivity;
2. for convection—the temperature difference between the object and the surroundings and the effect of any flow of air;
3. for radiation—the temperature and the nature of the surface.

For example, when designing a house it is essential to reduce heat energy loss, and so the loft is insulated with a minimum of 100 mm of fibreglass, the cavity between the inner and outer layers of brick is filled with a polyurethene foam or polystyrene beads (figure 529) and sometimes the windows are double-glazed. Heat is removed from the wall by convection and radiation. This is a complex process, since:

1. the wall is a composite material, and before any calculations can be done the *coefficient of thermal conductivity* of each separate material must be known;
2. the effect of the outside temperature must be known.

The heat loss in a house can be investigated more fully using a computer simulation called HOME HEATING (published by Edward Arnold) which may be available for you to use.

1. NEWTON'S LAW OF COOLING FOR HEAT LOSS BY CONVECTION

Outline

An object can lose heat energy by conduction and/or convection and/or radiation. Newton's law of cooling applies to convection (i.e. heat energy being taken away by moving air particles). It will depend on any forced movement of air past the object, and on the surface area in contact with the air. Hot water 'radiators' used in central heating systems lose most of their energy by convection, but to produce the largest possible loss by radiation the radiator should be painted matt black. Most people do not like black radiators in their houses and so they are painted white.

This experiment investigates the rate of loss of heat by objects cooling, and also attempts to investigate the effect of colour on heat loss by radiation.

Experimental details

Record the room temperature. Using the apparatus shown in figure 530, choose one of the cans (figure 530a) and fill it about three-quarters full with water. Heat the can until the water boils (figure 530b) and then remove it from the heat. Allow the can to cool as shown in figure 530c, with the fan switched off so that the can cools by natural convection. Record the temperature at intervals. Start by taking readings every minute, since the temperature falls more rapidly at first. Gradually lengthen the time intervals between readings. You will have to decide for yourself a sensible temperature or time at which to stop taking readings.

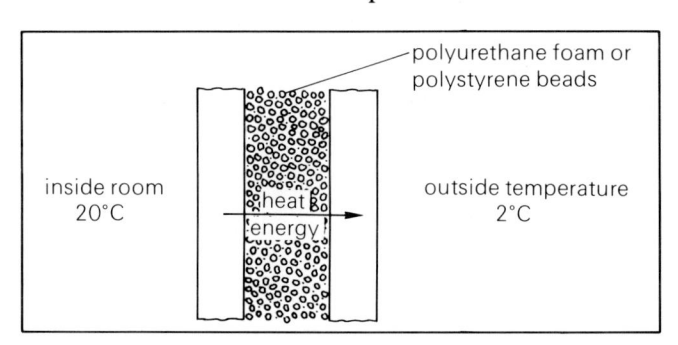

Figure 529 Section through a typical house wall

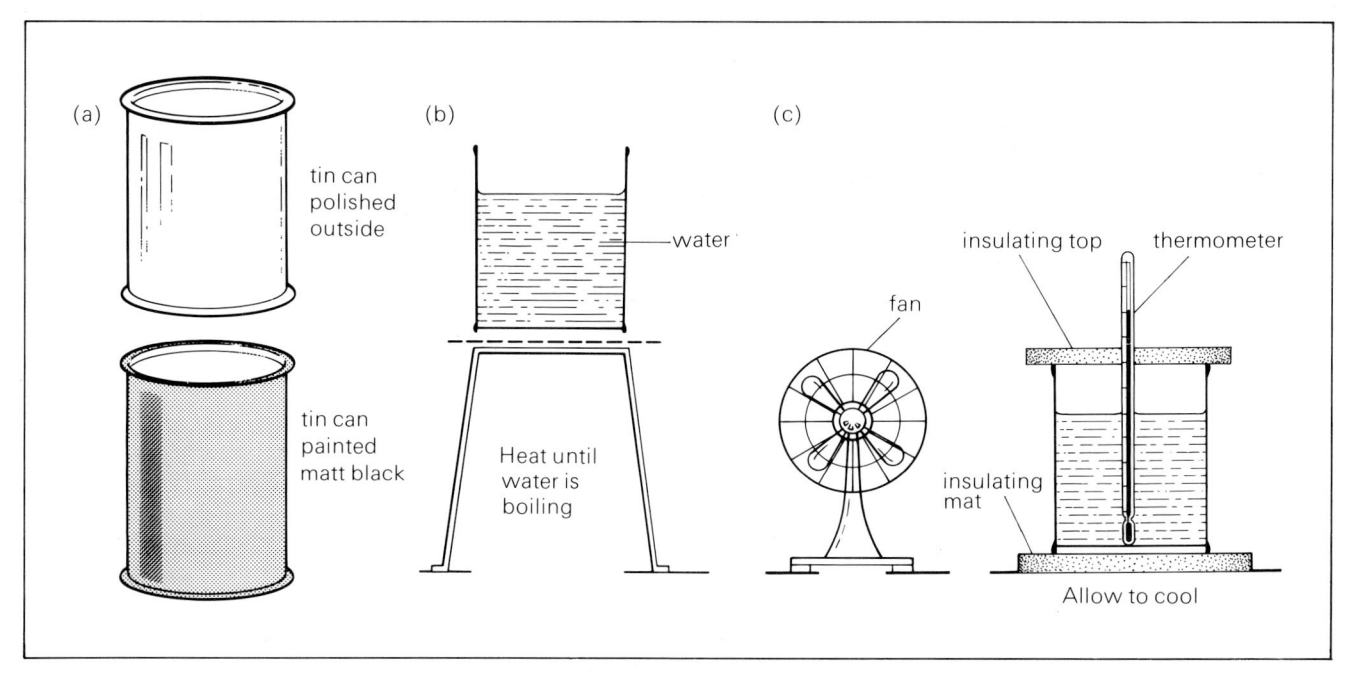

Figure 530 Equipment

Repeat the experiment, but this time use the fan to produce a flow of air so that the can cools by *forced convection*. Now repeat the whole experiment using the other can.

Plot graphs of temperature against time. Alternative methods of producing the temperature against time graphs are as follows.

1. Use a thermocouple thermometer, or other electrical temperature sensor, an amplifier and a chart recorder, assembled as shown in figure 531. The thermocouple will need to be calibrated first using melting ice and boiling water.
2. Use a computer to 'gather' the data and then display a graph, using the program 'DATALOG' (package PHYS2 option 5) for the BBC computer or other 'pack' which is available in your laboratory, e.g. VELA (VErsatile Laboratory Aid).

Use the apparatus shown in figure 532. Use boiling water and adjust the output from the amplifier and/or the range switch on the analogue input interface until the voltage (V) is just less than the maximum required by the computer input. The exact procedure will depend on the package you are using, but usually you are able to record readings for a given time and then display either the readings or a graph with optional printout on a printer. There may also be the facility to display all four graphs on the screen at the same time.

Results

From the graphs

The rate of loss of heat $\dfrac{dE}{dt}$ is proportional to the rate of fall of temperature $\dfrac{d\theta}{dt}$, since $E = mc\theta$, and so $\dfrac{d\theta}{dt}$ is the

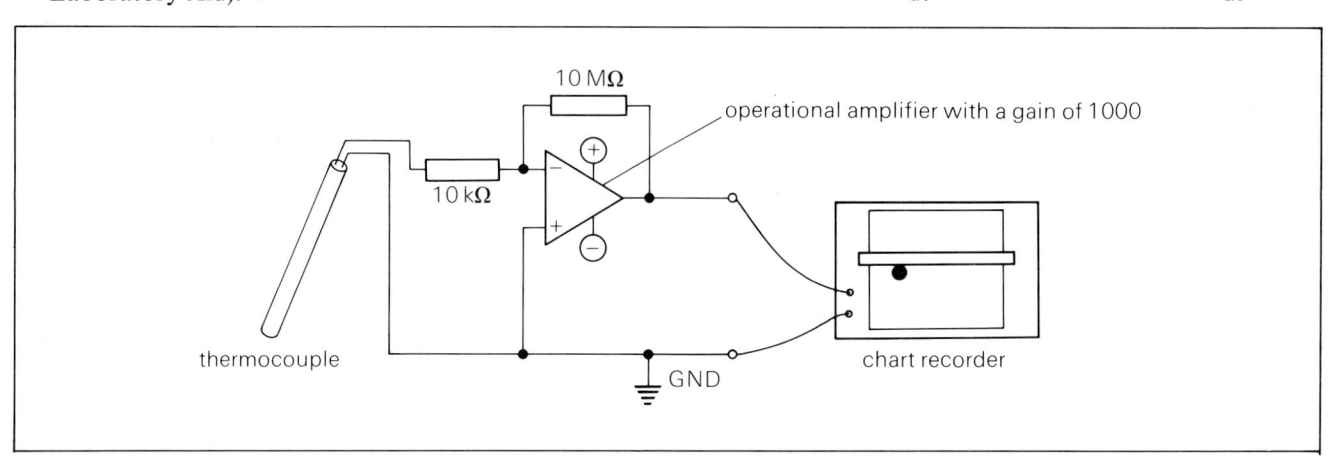

Figure 531 Equipment using a thermocouple

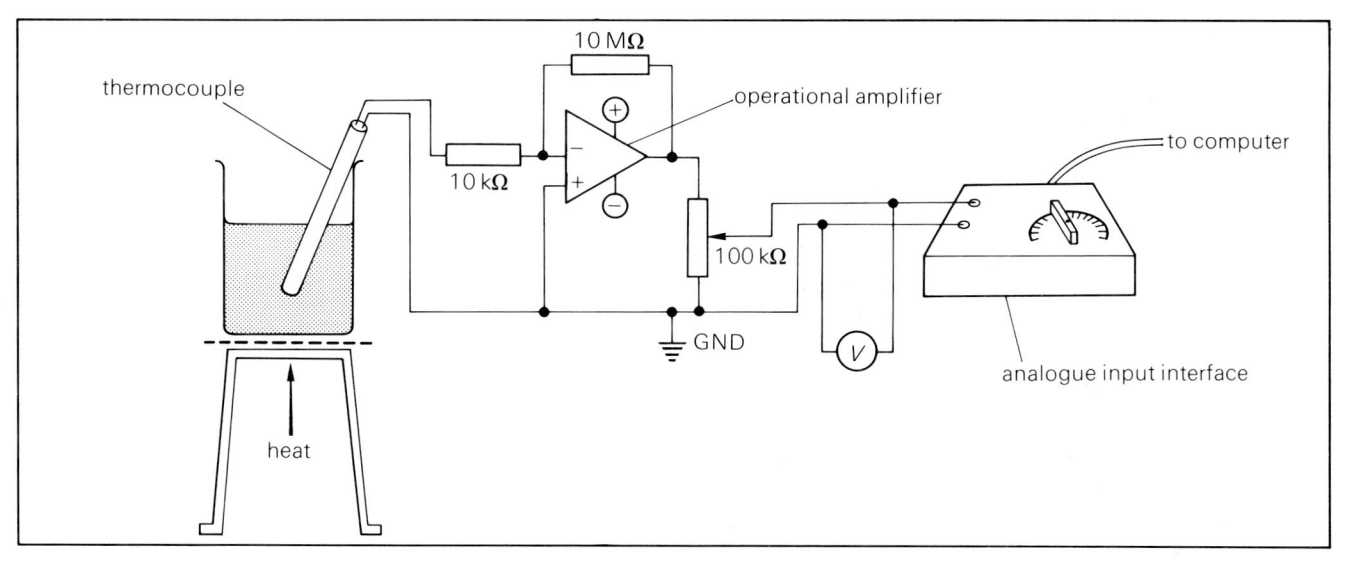

Figure 532 Datalogging; adjustment and calibration.

Polished can, natural convection $\frac{d\theta}{dt}$ /°C s^{-1}	Polished can, forced convection $\frac{d\theta}{dt}$ /°C s^{-1}	Black can, natural convection $\frac{d\theta}{dt}$ /°C s^{-1}	Black can, forced convection $\frac{d\theta}{dt}$ /°C s^{-1}	Excess temperature $(\theta - \theta_{room})$/°C

gradient of the graph at a point. Find the gradient of each graph at a series of temperatures and tabulate against the excess temperature (θ – room temperature).

Assuming that

$$\frac{d\theta}{dt} = k(\theta - \theta_{room})^n$$

where k is a constant which depends on the surface area and n is a power, then:

$$\log_e\left(\frac{d\theta}{dt}\right) = n \log_e(\theta - \theta_{room}) + \log_e k$$

Comparing with the equation for a straight-line graph $y = mx + c$, a graph of $\log_e\left(\frac{d\theta}{dt}\right)$ against $\log_e(\theta - \theta_{room})$ should be a straight line with gradient n.

1. Find a value for n in each case and summarise the rule.
2. Look at the differences between the results for the polished can and those for the black can. Work out the percentage difference caused to the total rate of heat loss by painting the can black and decide if this is sufficient reason to recommend that radiators should always be painted black.

$$\% \text{ difference} = \frac{\left(\frac{d\theta}{dt}_{black} - \frac{d\theta}{dt}_{polished}\right)}{\frac{d\theta}{dt}_{polished}} \times 100\%$$

3. Explain why reducing the temperature of a room by only about 5°C could result in a significant saving of heat.

2. THERMAL CONDUCTIVITY

Outline

When there is a temperature difference between one side of a material and another, there will be a net flow of heat energy from the surface at the higher temperature to the surface at the lower temperature. The rate of flow of heat energy $\frac{dE}{dt}$ depends on the surface area, the two temperatures and the thickness and the composition of the material.

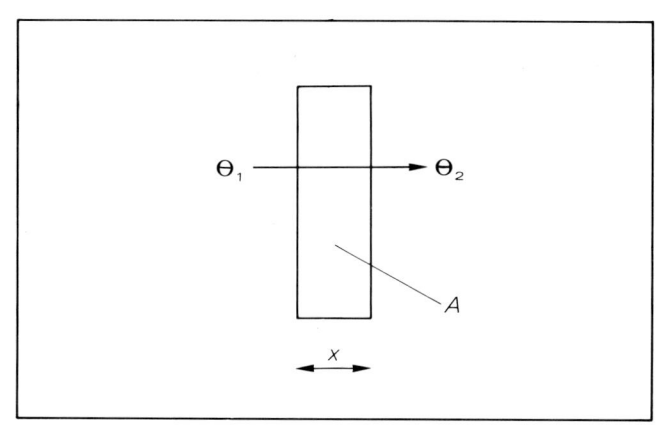

Figure 533

The equation relating to thermal conductivity through a parallel sided material (figure 533) is:

$$\frac{dE}{dt} = kA\frac{\theta_1 - \theta_2}{x}$$

k = coefficient of thermal conductivity/W m^{-1} k^{-1}
x = thickness/m
θ_1 = higher temperature/°C or K
θ_2 = lower temperature/°C or K
A = surface area of the side through which heat flows/m^2
$\frac{dE}{dt}$ = rate of flow of heat energy/W

To find k, one method would be to measure the rate of heat flow, thickness, temperatures and surface area and calculate a value for k.

If the rate of flow of heat is large enough, it may be possible to measure the rate of heat flow directly by its heating effect on something. If not, then other secondary methods must be found. In any case, some method must be found to allow for the heat energy loss through the sides. The two methods described are:

1. Searle's method for a good conductor (and presumably a larger rate of heat flow);
2. Lee's disc method for a poor conductor (and presumably a smaller rate of heat flow).

1. SEARLE'S METHOD FOR A GOOD CONDUCTOR

Notes
(a) The holes containing the thermometers contain oil to ensure good heat transfer.
(b) The copper coil is soldered to the copper bar to ensure good heat transfer.
(c) A thermocouple and galvanometer (or other suitable instrument) can be used to measure the temperature difference (only a few degrees) between the incoming and outgoing water, as shown in figure 534. The temperature difference is calculated from the e.m.f. produced. Alternatively thermometers may be used, which will be less accurate.

Experimental details

Set the apparatus up, as shown in figure 534, and switch on the heater, allowing water to flow through the coil.

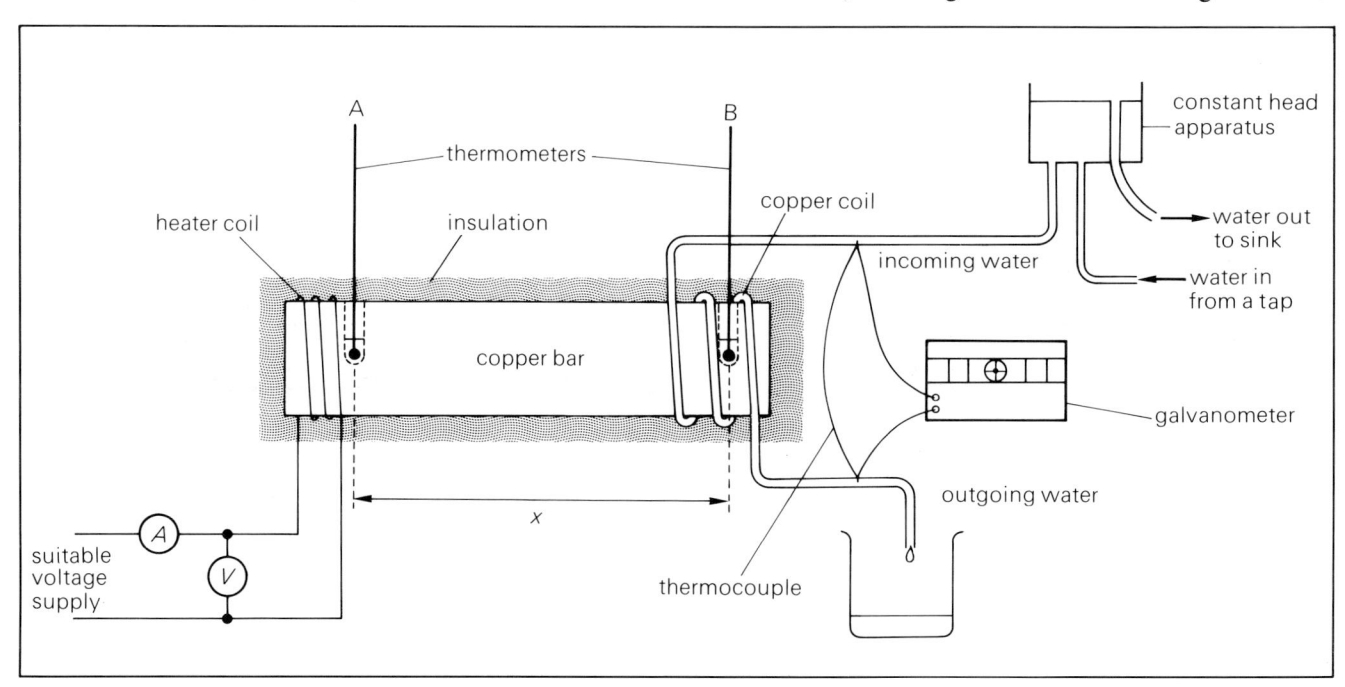

Figure 534 Equipment for a good conductor

MEASURING QUANTITIES AND INVESTIGATING LAWS

Wait until the readings on the thermometers A and B are steady (this may take 10–15 min). Then alter the rate of flow of water through the coil until a temperature difference of at least 5°C is produced between the incoming and outgoing water. This is because a mercury-in-glass thermometer is only accurate to 0.5°C and this is the measurement which limits the accuracy of the experiment. A difference of ±0.5°C would limit the overall accuracy to $\pm \frac{0.5}{5} \times 100\% = \pm 10\%$. A higher accuracy may be achieved using a thermocouple.

Find the temperature difference as accurately as you can. Measure also the mass of water flowing in a known time so that the rate of flow can be found. Record the separation of the thermometers (x) and measure the diameter of the copper-bar so that the cross-sectional area can be calculated.

Results

reading on thermometer A, $\theta_1 = \ldots °$

reading on thermometer B, $\theta_2 = \ldots °$

separation, $x = \ldots$ m

diameter of copper bar $= \ldots$ m

cross-sectional area, $A = \ldots$ m

mass of water $= \ldots$ kg in time

rate of flow $= \ldots$ kg s^{-1}

temperature difference of water, e.g. using thermocouple 3.2 mV at $\ldots$ °C^{-1} = $\ldots$ °

specific heat capacity of the water (from tables), $c = \ldots$ J kg °C

Calculations

For the water flowing through the coil, $E = mc\theta$.

$$\therefore \text{rate of flow} = \frac{E}{t} = \frac{mc\theta}{t}$$

which can be calculated, since $\frac{m}{t}$, c, and θ are known.

The coefficient of thermal conductivity k is calculated from:

$$\frac{dE}{dt} = kA\frac{(\theta_1 - \theta_2)}{x}$$

2. LEE'S DISC METHOD FOR A POOR CONDUCTOR

The disc has a large surface area and small thickness to produce as large a rate of flow of heat as possible and to reduce heat energy loss through the sides of the material.

Experimental details

Assemble the apparatus as shown in figure 535. Pass steam in (if using apparatus a) and wait until the temperatures θ_1 and θ_2 are steady, or switch on the heater (apparatus b) and adjust the voltage until a steady state is reached, where θ_1 is between 80 and 100°C. Record the values of θ_1 and θ_2.

The rate of loss of heat from the bottom plate must now be found. Do this by heating the bottom plate to about 10°C above its steady state temperature. Then remove the source of heat and cover the top with a good insulator

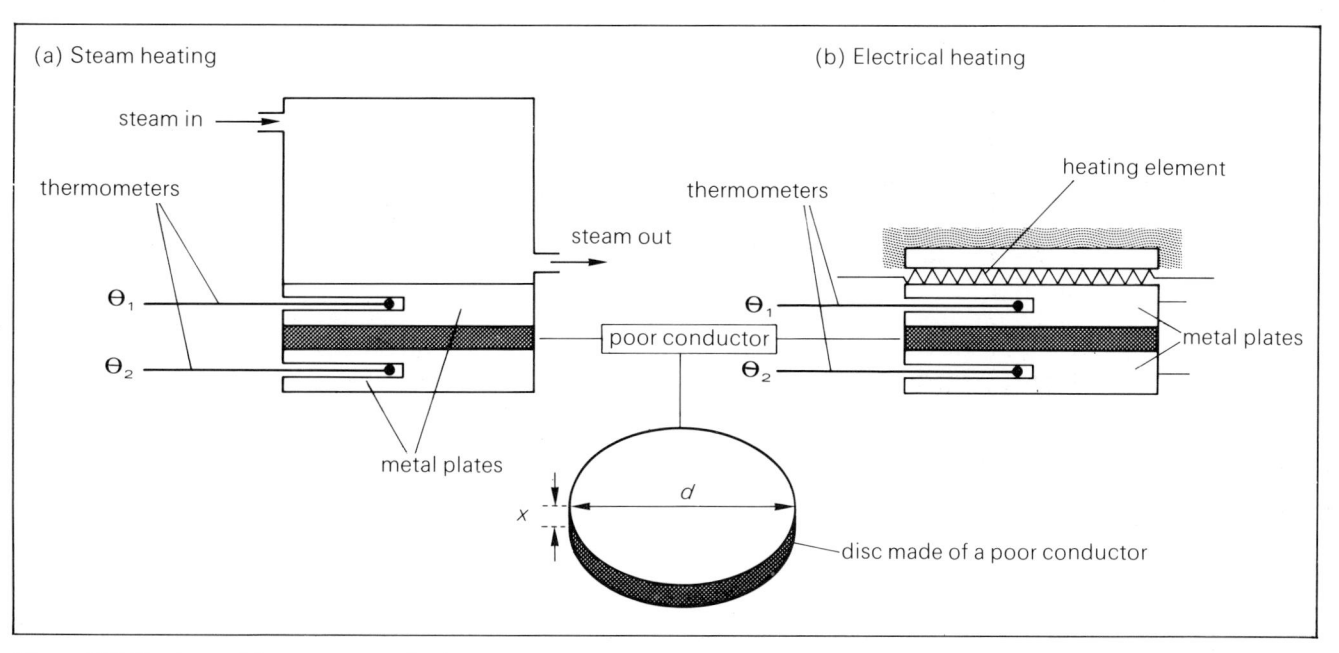

Figure 535 Equipment for a poor conductor

(figure 536). Plot a cooling curve (figure 537). Find the gradient of this curve at the steady state temperature θ_2. This equals $\dfrac{d\theta}{dt}$. If the mass (m) of the bottom plate is measured and its specific heat capacity (c) is found from tables then, since $E = mc\theta$:

$$\frac{dE}{dt} = mc\frac{d\theta}{dt}$$

where $\dfrac{dE}{dt}$ is then the rate of loss of heat energy from the bottom plate.

Calculate the thermal conductivity of the poor conductor using:

$$\frac{dE}{dt} = \frac{kA(\theta_1 - \theta_2)}{x}$$

where A is the surface area $= \dfrac{\pi d^2}{4}$.

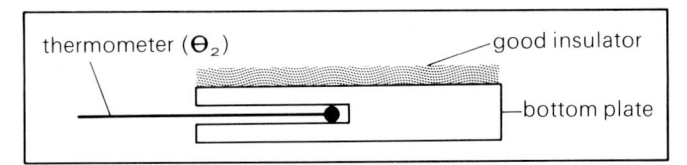

Figure 536 Finding the rate of loss of heat.

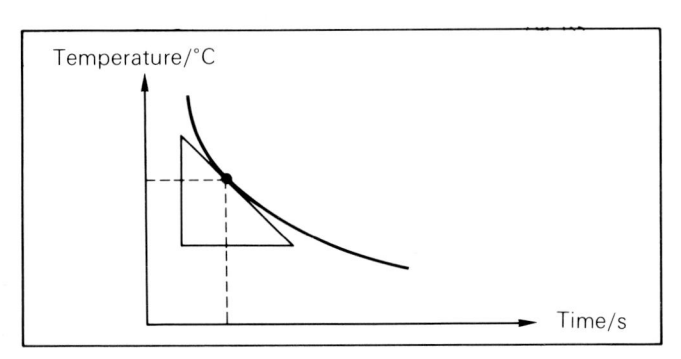

Figure 537 Cooling curve

USEFUL INFORMATION

Fundamental constants

Symbol	Constant	Value
c	velocity of light in a vacuum	$2.997 \times 10^8 \text{ m s}^{-1}$ (usually taken as $3 \times 10^8 \text{ m s}^{-1}$)
μ_0	permeability of free space	$4\pi \times 10^{-7} \text{ H m}^{-1}$
ε_0	permittivity of free space	$8.85 \times 10^{-12} \text{ F m}^{-1}$
e	elementary charge	$\pm 1.60 \times 10^{-19} \text{ C}$
h	Planck constant	$6.63 \times 10^{-34} \text{ J s}$
	electron rest mass	$9.11 \times 10^{-31} \text{ kg}$
	proton rest mass	$1.67 \times 10^{-27} \text{ kg}$
	neutron rest mass	$1.67 \times 10^{-27} \text{ kg}$
G	gravitational constant	$6.67 \times 10^{-11} \text{ N m}^2 \text{ kg}^{-2}$ ($\text{m}^3 \text{ kg}^{-1} \text{ s}^{-1}$)
N	Avogadro constant	$6.022 \times 10^{23} \text{ mol}^{-1}$
R	gas constant	$8.31 \text{ J K}^{-1} \text{ mol}^{-1}$
k	Boltzmann constant	$1.38 \times 10^{-23} \text{ J K}^{-1}$
σ	Stefan's constant	$5.669 \times 10^{-8} \text{ W m}^{-2} \text{ K}^{-4}$

Prefixes and multiplication factors used with SI units

Factor	Prefix	Symbol
10^{12}	tera	T
10^9	giga	G
10^6	mega	M
10^3	kilo	k
10^{-1}	deci	d
10^{-2}	centi	c
10^{-3}	milli	m
10^{-6}	micro	μ
10^{-9}	nano	n
10^{-12}	pico	p
10^{-15}	femto	f

Equation of a straight line

$y = mx + c$

(m = gradient; c = intercept on y axis)

Base SI units

There are seven base units:

Quantity	Unit	Symbol
length	metre	m
mass	kilogram	kg
time	second	s
electric current	ampere	A
temperature	kelvin	K
luminous intensity	candela	cd
amount of substance	mole	mol

Derived SI units

Quantity	Symbol	Unit	Symbol
mass	m	kilogram	kg
length	l	metre	m
time	t	second	s
current	I	ampere	A
potential difference	V	volt	V
charge	Q	coulomb	C
power	P	watt	W
resistance	R	ohm	Ω
inductance	H	henry	H
magnetic induction	B	tesla	T
force	F	newton	N
temperature	T	kelvin	K
energy	E	joule	J
velocity	v or u		m s^{-1}
acceleration	a		m s^{-2}
displacement	d		m
frequency	f	hertz	Hz
capacitance	C	farad	F
magnetic flux	Φ	weber	Wb
electric field strength	E	volt per metre	V m^{-1}

The Greek alphabet

Letter		Name	Letter		Name
A	α	alpha	N	ν	nu
B	β	beta	Ξ	ξ	xi
Γ	γ	gamma	O	o	omicron
Δ	δ	delta	Π	π	pi
E	ε	epsilon	P	ρ	rho
Z	ζ	zeta	Σ	σ	sigma
H	η	eta	T	τ	tau
Θ	θ	theta	Υ	υ	upsilon
I	ι	iota	Φ	φ	phi
K	κ	kappa	X	χ	chi
Λ	λ	lambda	Ψ	ψ	psi
M	μ	mu	Ω	ω	omega

Mass

electron rest mass 9.11×10^{-31} kg
proton rest mass 1.67×10^{-27} kg
neutron rest mass 1.67×10^{-27} kg
hydrogen atom 1.673×10^{-27} kg
helium atom 6.646×10^{-27} kg
α-particle 6.638×10^{-27} kg
carbon 12 atom 19.925×10^{-27} kg

the moon 7.35×10^{22} kg
the earth 5.98×10^{24} kg

The unified mass unit (u)
The mass of the isotope of carbon $^{12}_{6}C$ is defined as exactly $12.0\,u$.

1 unified mass unit $= 1.660 \times 10^{-27}$ kg.

The Avogadro constant is defined as the number of atoms in 0.012 kg of the isotope of carbon $^{12}_{6}C$ and so is the number of particles in a mole $= 6.022 \times 10^{23}\,\text{mol}^{-1}$.

hydrogen	$1.007\,u$
$^{4}_{2}$helium	$4.002\,u$
$^{12}_{6}$carbon	$12.0\,u$
$^{14}_{7}$nitrogen	$14.003\,u$
$^{16}_{8}$oxygen	$15.99\,u$
$^{20}_{10}$neon	$19.99\,u$
$^{23}_{11}$sodium	$22.9\,u$
$^{24}_{12}$magnesium	$23.9\,u$
$^{17}_{35}$chlorine	$34.9\,u$
$^{18}_{40}$argon	$39.96\,u$
$^{208}_{82}$lead	$207.97\,u$
$^{238}_{92}$uranium	$238.05\,u$

The unified mass is very nearly equal to the number of nucleons (A) in the nucleus. The difference is because of the binding energy holding the nuclei together.

Mathematical constants and formulae

1 radian $= 57.29°$

$\pi = 3.142$

If $\log_a x = y$
then $x = a^y$
In particular:
if $\log_e x = y$
then $x = e^y$

$\log(AB) = \log A + \log B$
$\log(A/B) = \log A - \log B$

$\sin(A + B) = \sin A \cos B + \sin B \cos A$
$\sin 2A = 2 \sin A \cos B$
$\cos(A + B) = \cos A \cos B - \sin A \sin B$
$\sin(A - B) = \sin A \cos B - \sin B \cos A$
$\cos(A - B) = \cos A \cos B + \sin A \sin B$
$\sin^2 A + \cos^2 A = 1$

Derivatives
If $y = x^n$
then $\dfrac{dy}{dx} = nx^{n-1}$

If $y = \sin x$
then $\dfrac{dy}{dx} = \cos x$

If $y = \cos x$
then $\dfrac{dy}{dx} = -\sin x$

Integrals
If $\dfrac{dy}{dx} = x^n$
then $y = \dfrac{x^{n+1}}{n+1} + \text{constant}$

If $\dfrac{dy}{dx} = \dfrac{1}{x}$
then $y = \log_e x + \text{constant}$

If $\dfrac{dy}{dx} = \sin x$
then $y = -\cos x + \text{constant}$

If $\dfrac{dy}{dx} = \cos x$
then $y = \sin x + \text{constant}$

Accepted values

Gravitational field strength on the earth $= 9.81\,\text{N kg}^{-1}$ (often taken as $10\,\text{N kg}^{-1}$).

Acceleration of an object in free fall under gravity $= 9.81\,\text{m s}^{-1}$ (often taken as $10\,\text{m s}^{-2}$).

Gravitation constant $G = 6.673 \times 10^{-11}\,\text{N m}^2\,\text{kg}^{-2}$
Gravitational field strength on the moon $= 1.62\,\text{N kg}^{-1}$

USEFUL INFORMATION

Wavelengths of spectrum lines

oxygen red A	759.4 nm
oxygen red B	687.0 nm
hydrogen and red	656.3 nm
*cadmium red	643.8 nm
sodium yellow (mean)	589.3 nm
(actually two lines 589.0 and 589.59 nm)	
mercury yellow and mercury green	579.0 nm 577.0 nm 546.1 nm
*cadmium green	508.5 nm
hydrogen green	486.1 nm
*cadmium blue	479.9 nm
hydrogen blue	434.0 nm

Refractive indices (n)

air n medium for sodium yellow line

glass, crown range	1.48 to 1.61
glass, flint range	1.53 to 1.96
ice	1.31
Perspex	1.49
rock salt	1.54
water	1.33
paraffin	1.43

Frequency of mains supply voltage

In Britain and Europe: 220/240 V, 50 Hz.
In North America: 110 V, 60 Hz.

Approximate e.m.f.s of cells

Daniell	1.08 V
Wet Leclanché	1.46 V
lead acid accumulator	1.85 to 2.2 V, depending on the state of charge
dry cell	1.5 V

Standard cell
Weston (cadmium cell) at 20°C = 1.0186 V

E.m.f. produced by a thermocouple

'hot' junction	100°C
'cold' reference junction	0°C
platinum–platinum/rhodium	0.64 mV
copper–constanton	4.28 mV
iron–constanton	5.40 mV
nickel cadmium	1.3 V
nickel iron 'alkaline'	1.4 V

Densities

Substance	Density
aluminium	2710 kg m^{-3}
brass	8500 kg m^{-3}
copper	8930 kg m^{-3}
gold	19300 kg m^{-3}
iron	7850 kg m^{-3}
lead	11300 kg m^{-3}
magnesium	1740 kg m^{-3}
platinum	21450 kg m^{-3}
silver	10500 kg m^{-3}
solder	9000 kg m^{-3}
steel	7860 kg m^{-3}
tin	7300 kg m^{-3}
zinc	7140 kg m^{-3}
carbon	2300 kg m^{-3}
cork	240 kg m^{-3}
glass (crown)	2600 kg m^{-3}
glass (flint)	4200 kg m^{-3}
ice	920 kg m^{-3}
marble	2600 kg m^{-3}
nylon	1150 kg m^{-3}
paraffin wax	900 kg m^{-3}
Perspex	1190 kg m^{-3}
soft wood range	500–700 kg m^{-3}
mercury	13546 kg m^{-3}
methanol	791 kg m^{-3}
alcohol	789 kg m^{-3}
olive oil	920 kg m^{-3}
paraffin	800 kg m^{-3}
water	998 kg m^{-3}
sea water (near Britain)	1025 kg m^{-3}

Gases at STP

Gas	Density
oxygen	1.429 kg m^{-3}
nitrogen	1.250 kg m^{-3}
carbon dioxide	1.977 kg m^{-3}
water vapour at 0°C (273 K)	0.800 kg m^{-3}
helium	0.179 kg m^{-3}
hydrogen	0.090 kg m^{-3}
methane	0.717 kg m^{-3}

Sizes

Object	Radius
electron	2.817×10^{-15} m
hydrogen atom	46×10^{-12} m
helium atom	176×10^{-12} m
carbon atom	71×10^{-12} m
oxygen atom	60×10^{-12} m
nitrogen atom	71×10^{-12} m
lead atom	174×10^{-12} m
uranium atom	138×10^{-12} m
earth	6.378×10^{6} m
moon	1.738×10^{6} m
mars	3.375×10^{5} m
sun	6.960×10^{8} m

Magnetic fields

Vertical component of the earth's magnetic field in Britain = 4.38×10^{-5} T

Horizontal component of the earth's magnetic field in Britain = 1.88×10^{-5} T

Relative permeabilities

Mild steel 2000

'Soft iron' range 9000–100 000 depending on the composition

μ_0 permeability of free space 4×10^{-7} H m^{-1}

Electric fields

Permittivity ε_0 of free space 8.85×10^{-12} F m^{-1}

Substance	Relative Permittivity
glass	5–10
ice	75
mica	5.7–6.7
paraffin wax	2–2.3
Perspex	3.5
PVC	4.5
ethanol	25.7
glycerine	43
water	80

Melting points at standard atmospheric pressure (101 325 Pa)

Substance	Temperature
aluminium	800 K
copper	1356 K
iron	1500 K
lead	600 K
tin	505 K
solder (50Pb/50Sn)	490 K
glass	1400 K
ice	273 K
paraffin wax	330 K
Perspex	350 K
carbon	3800 K

Boiling points at standard atmospheric pressure (101 325 Pa)

Substance	Temperature
hydrogen	20.35 K
oxygen	90.1 K
nitrogen	77.3 K
carbon dioxide	195 K
water	373 K
ethanol	352 K
methanol	337 K

Speed of sound

Medium	Temperature	Speed
air	273 K	331 m s^{-1}
helium	273 K	992 m s^{-1}
oxygen	273 K	316 m s^{-1}
water	273 K	1500 m s^{-1}
aluminium	298 K	5100 m s^{-1}
copper	298 K	3800 m s^{-1}
iron	298 K	5000 m s^{-1}

CLASSIFICATION OF EXPERIMENTS

1. EXPERIMENTAL TECHNIQUES

1 Measurement of length and mass — 38
A variety of experiments giving practice in the use of:
- Vernier calipers
- Micrometer
- Spherometer
- Balances for measuring mass and force

2. Using the travelling microscope — 42
To measure
- The pitch of a screw
- The separation of lines on a diffraction grating
- The spacings on an interference pattern
- The thickness of tracks on a microcircuit

and to take measurements so that the refractive index of a liquid can be calculated.

3. Measuring times — 44
- Using a stopwatch
- Using electronic timers
- Using microprocessor based methods

4. Timing oscillations — 47
Experiments based round measuring the periods of the following:
- Springs
- A compound pendulum
- Swinging chains
- Thin beams clamped at one end
- A Y-shaped pendulum
- A suspended beam
- Beams oscillating on a curved surface
- Coupled oscillators

5. Some experiments involving density — 51
- Deduction of the density of unknown solids hidden in Plasticine
- The identification of clear liquids
- Investigation of the pressure due to a column of liquid
- Making and using a simple hydrometer

6. Using the principle of moments — 53
- Using a balanced beam to deduce mass and to identify liquids
- Making and calibrating a simple current balance
- Investigating the angle of a force needed to support a beam

7. Detecting electromagnetic radiation — 55
- Plotting an amplitude against frequency spectrum across the frequency band of a radio
- Methods of detecting infra-red radiation
- General details about detecting other frequencies

8. Plotting rays and image positions with pins   56
   Virtual image in a plane mirror
   Path of a ray through a glass block
   Focal length of a convex lens
   Real image in a convex lens
   Maxima seen through a diffraction grating

9. Using an illuminated object with lenses and mirrors   58
   Finding a sharp image accurately and estimating the error
   Measuring the focal length of a concave mirror
   Measuring the focal length of a concave lens
   Finding the position of a hidden convex lens

10. The paths of rays through a prism   60

11. Stroboscopic and photographic methods of measuring changing position with time   61

12. Bending beams   62
    Investigation on the deflection under load of:
       A beam loaded centrally
       A cantilever

13. Measuring frequency   64
    Various experiments on the techniques of measuring frequency using:
       Beats
       The time-scale on an oscilloscope
       Lissajous' figures
       A stroboscope
       Direct electronic counting
       Resonance

14. The forced vibration of a wire   67

15. The spectrometer   69

16. Measuring potential difference   72
    Direct voltages
       A moving coil meter
       A moving coil meter with an operational amplifier as a voltage follower
       An oscilloscope
       A potentiometer
       Digital electronic methods
    Alternating voltages
       Rectification and a moving coil meter
       An oscilloscope
       A moving iron meter
       Calibration of a moving coil a.c. meter

17. Measuring the e.m.f. produced by a thermocouple   76
    Using a potentiometer with a high resistance in series
    By direct measurement using an operational amplifier to produce amplification

18. Using moving-coil ammeters and voltmeters to measure resistance   77
    An investigation into the choice of instruments, their positions in circuits and the accuracy of the value of resistance calculated

19. Wheatstone bridge and metre bridge   79

20. Finding the resistivity of a resistance wire using a metre bridge   81

21. Displaying and drawing waveforms on an oscilloscope   82

22. Measuring impedance   85

23. Methods of measuring magnetic fields   88
    Search coil and ballistic galvanometer
    Search coil and integrator
    Hall effect probe
    A.c. induction

24. Using the computer and data memories as measuring instruments   94
    Timing free fall
    Investigating the change in resistance against time after a lamp is switched on
    Damped s.h.m. of a compound pendulum
    Investigating how the temperature changes as two liquids mix

25. Detecting nuclear particles   98
    Measuring the background radiation
    Safety in the use of radioactive sources
    Adjusting the Geiger–Müller tube to measure the activities of sources
    Using a cloud chamber
    Using photographic paper

60. The effect of temperature on resistance   162
    The behaviour of various components
    The temperature coefficient of resistance

CLASSIFICATIONS OF EXPERIMENTS 263

2. SHORT OR SECTIONED EXPERIMENTS

1. Measurement of length and mass — 38
A variety of experiments giving practice in the use of:
- Vernier calipers
- Micrometer
- Spherometer
- Balances for measuring mass and force

2. Using the travelling microscope — 42
To measure
- The pitch of a screw
- The separation of lines on a diffraction grating
- The spacings on an interference pattern
- The thickness of tracks on a microcircuit

and to take measurements so that the refractive index of a liquid can be calculated.

3. Measuring times — 44
- Using a stopwatch
- Using electronic timers
- Using microprocessor based methods

4. Timing oscillations — 47
Experiments based round measuring the periods of the following:
- Springs
- A compound pendulum
- Swinging chains
- Thin beams clamped at one end
- A Y-shaped pendulum
- Suspended beam
- Beams oscillating on a curved surface
- Coupled oscillators

5. Some experiments involving density — 51
- Deduction of the density of unknown solids hidden in Plasticine
- The identification of clear liquids
- Investigation of the pressure due to a column of liquid
- Making and using a simple hydrometer

8. Plotting rays and image positions with pins — 56
- Virtual image in a plane mirror
- Path of a ray through a glass block
- Focal length of a convex lens
- Real image in a convex lens
- Maxima seen through a diffraction grating

9. Using an illuminated object with lenses and mirrors — 58
- Finding a sharp image accurately and estimating the error
- Measuring the focal length of a concave mirror
- Measuring the focal length of a concave lens
- Finding the position of a hidden convex lens

12. Bending beams — 62
Investigation on the deflection under load of:
- A beam loaded centrally
- A cantilever

21. Displaying and drawing waveforms on an oscilloscope — 81

23. Methods of measuring magnetic fields — 88
- Search coil and ballistic galvanometer
- Search coil and integrator
- Hall effect probe
- A.c. induction

25. Detecting nuclear particles — 98
- Measuring the background radiation
- Safety in the use of radioactive sources
- Adjusting the Geiger–Müller tube to measure the activities of sources
- Using a cloud chamber
- Using photographic paper

53. Circuit deductions — 149

54. Deducing hidden components — 150

55. Investigations with a magnet — 153

56. Controlling a current — 153
- Switches, thermistor, reed switch, relay, resistor

57. Diodes: junction, zener, LED and lambda — 155

58. The operational amplifier — 157
- Inverting, amplification, feedback and switching applications

59. Potential dividers — 160
- Using resistors, light dependent resistors and capacitors
- The application of potential dividers to logic gates

3. ELECTRICAL EXPERIMENTS

16. Measuring potential difference — 72
    Direct voltages
        A moving coil meter
        A moving coil meter with an operational amplifier as a voltage follower
        An oscilloscope
        A potentiometer
        Digital electronic methods
    Alternating voltages
        Rectification and a moving coil meter
        An oscilloscope
        A moving iron meter
        Calibration of a moving coil a.c. meter

17. Measuring the e.m.f. produced by a thermocouple — 76
        Using a potentiometer with a high resistance in series
        By direct measurement using an operational amplifier to produce amplification

18. Using moving-coil ammeters and voltmeters to measure resistance — 77
        An investigation into the choice of instruments, their positions in circuits and the accuracy of the value of resistance calculated

19. Wheatstone bridge and metre bridge — 79

20. Finding the resistivity of a resistance wire using a metre bridge — 81

21. Displaying and drawing waveforms on an oscilloscope — 82

22. Measuring impedance — 85

24. Using the computer and data memories as measuring instruments — 94
        Timing free fall
        Investigating the change in resistance against time after a lamp is switched on
        Damped s.h.m. of a compound pendulum
        Investigating how the temperature changes as two liquids mix

31. Efficiency of an electric motor — 107

32. Energy stored in a flywheel — 108

37. The parallel plate capacitor — 113

38. Energy stored in a capacitor — 115

39. Charge and discharge of a capacitor — 116

40. Electrical resistivity and conductivity — 119

41. Conduction in liquids and gases — 121

42. Investigating the operation and applications of a transistor — 123

43. Plotting the characteristic curves for a transistor (common-emitter mode) — 127

44. Characteristics of light sensitive devices — 129

45. E.m.f. induced as a magnet passes through a coil — 131

51. Phase angles in a.c. circuits using a capacitor and resistor in series — 144

52. Series LCR resonant circuit — 147

53. Circuit deductions — 149

54. Deducing hidden components — 150

55. Investigations with a magnet — 153

56. Controlling a current — 153
        Switches, thermistor, reed switch, relay, resistor

57. Diodes: junction, zener, LED and lambda — 155

58. The operational amplifier — 157
        Inverting, amplification, feedback and switching applications

59. Potential dividers — 160
        Using resistors, light dependent resistors and capacitors
        The application of potential dividers to logic gates

60. The effect of temperature on resistance — 162
        The behaviour of various components
        The temperature coefficient of resistance

61. Thermometers — 164
        Calibration of a thermistor thermometer and its use in temperature control
        A thermometer using resistance wire

62. Logic circuits and logical control — 166

63. Investigations using TTL 7400 NAND gates and a 7493 counter — 169

65. Internal resistance and Kirchhoff's laws — 176
        Measuring the internal resistance
        Investigating the conditions for maximum power transfer
        Investigating Kirchhoff's laws

72. Analogue computing — 191

93. Measuring the permittivity of air and Perspex — 238

4. MAGNETISM AND ELECTROMAGNETISM

6. Using the principle of moments — 53
 Using a balanced beam to deduce mass and to identify liquids
 Making and calibrating a simple current balance
 Investigating the angle of a force needed to support a beam

14. The forced vibration of a wire — 67

23. Methods of measuring magnetic fields — 88
 Search coil and ballistic galvanometer
 Search coil and integrator
 Hall effect probe
 A.c. induction

45. E.m.f. induced as a magnet passes through a coil — 131

46. Magnetic field produced by a pair of co-axial coils — 133

87. The force produced by a current-carrying wire in a magnetic field — 214

5. FORCES AND MECHANICS

4. Timing oscillations — 47
 Experiments based round measuring the periods of the following:
  Springs
  A compound pendulum
  Swinging chains
  Thin beams clamped at one end
  A Y-shaped pendulum
  Suspended beam
  Beams oscillating on a curved surface
  Coupled oscillators

5. Some experiments involving density — 51
 Deduction of the density of unknown solids hidden in Plasticine
 The identification of clear liquids
 Investigation of the pressure due to a column of liquid
 Making and using a simple hydrometer

6. Using the principle of moments — 53
 Using a balanced beam to deduce mass and to identify liquids
 Making and calibrating a simple current balance
 Investigating the angle of a force needed to support a beam

11. Stroboscopic and photographic methods of measuring changing position with time — 61

24. Using the computer and data memories as measuring instruments — 94
 Timing free fall
 Investigating the change in resistance against time after a lamp is switched on
 Damped s.h.m. of a compound pendulum
 Investigating how the temperature changes as two liquids mix

26. Frictional forces — 102
 An investigation of the static and sliding friction between two surfaces

27. Fluid friction — 103
 An investigation of the forces on ball bearings moving through a fluid

28. Springs and damping — 104

29. Energy absorbed by a bouncing ball — 105

30. Air resistance on a falling object — 106

31. Efficiency of an electric motor — 107

32. Energy stored in a flywheel — 108

36. Bernouilli's principle — 112

55. Investigations with a magnet — 153

64. Pneumatic control — 173

75.	Analysis of projectiles	202		85.	Does force equal mass times acceleration?	220
76.	Analysis of the collisions of objects	203		86.	Conservation of linear momentum with an air track	222
82.	Elasticity and Young's modulus	216				
84.	Falling sand: Newton's second law	219		87.	The force produced by a current-carrying wire in a magnetic field	224

6. WAVES, LIGHT AND SOUND

2. Using the travelling microscope — 42
To measure
- The pitch of a screw
- The separation of lines on a diffraction grating
- The spacings on an interference pattern
- The thickness of tracks on a microcircuit

and to take measurements so that the refractive index of a liquid can be calculated

7. Detecting electromagnetic radiation — 55
- Plotting an amplitude against frequency spectrum across the frequency band of a radio
- Methods of detecting infra-red radiation
- General details about detecting other frequencies

8. Plotting rays and image positions with pins — 56
- Virtual image in a plane mirror
- Path of a ray through a glass block
- Focal length of a convex lens
- Real image in a convex lens
- Maxima seen through a diffraction grating

9. Using an illuminated object with lenses and mirrors — 58
- Finding a sharp image accurately and estimating the error
- Measuring the focal length of a concave mirror
- Measuring the focal length of a concave lens
- Finding the position of a hidden convex lens

10. The paths of rays through a prism — 60

13. Measuring frequency — 64
Various experiments on the techniques of measuring frequency using
- Beats
- The time-scale on an oscilloscope
- Lissajous' figures
- A stroboscope
- Direct electronic counting
- Resonance

14. The forced vibration of a wire — 67

15. The spectrometer — 69

20. Finding the resistivity of a resistance wire using a metre bridge — 82

44. Characteristics of light sensitive devices — 129

47. Resonances of a vibrating wire — 134

48. Interference pattern produced by double slits — 137

49. The behaviour of microwaves — 139
- Width of the beam
- Reflection
- Refraction
- Double slit interference pattern

50. Interference pattern of sound waves — 142

68. Optical instruments — 182
- Camera
- Astronomical telescope
- Microscope

69. Using the reflection and refraction of light — 185

74. Analysis of spectra — 200

79. Analysis of sound waves — 206

80. Polarisation of light and the analysis of stress — 208

94. The photoelectric effect and the measurement of Planck's constant — 240

95. Measuring the speed of waves — 241
Sound, microwaves and light

96. Measuring the wavelength of light using Newton's rings — 244

97. Focal length and focal plane of a convex lens — 245

98. Measuring the resolution of your eye — 247

99. Resonance of an air column — 249

7. ATOMIC AND NUCLEAR EXPERIMENTS

25. Detecting nuclear particles — 98
    Measuring the background radiation
    Safety in the use of radioactive sources
    Adjusting the Geiger–Müller tube to measure the activities of sources
    Using a cloud chamber
    Using photographic paper

41. Conduction in liquids and gases — 121

70. Thickness measurement using the absorption of radioactivity — 187

71. Simulation of a mass spectrometer — 188

88. Investigating laws for gamma radiation — 226
    Absorption and half-value thickness
    The inverse square law with no absorber

89. Measurement of half-life — 228

90. Finding the energy of β^- particles — 230

91. Measurement of the ratio e/m for a beam of electrons — 233

92. Millikan's experiment to measure e, the fundamental unit of charge — 234

94. The photoelectric effect and the measurement of Planck's constant — 240

8. MOLECULAR MOVEMENT AND HEAT

17. Measuring the e.m.f. produced by a thermocouple — 76
    Using a potentiometer with a high resistance in series
    By direct measurement using an operational amplifier to produce amplification

33. Heat losses from a wire under different pressures — 109

34. Variation of boiling point with pressure and s.v.p. with temperature — 110

35. The general gas law — 111

61. Thermometers — 164
    Calibration of a thermistor thermometer and its use in temperature control
    A thermometer using resistance wire

78. Analysis of melting points — 206

81. Finding information about atoms and molecules — 211
    Oil film experiment
    Brownian motion
    Specific latent heat of vaporisation and bonding energy
    Bombarding the atom with particles

100. Heat energy transfer — 251
    Newton's law of cooling for heat loss by convection
    Thermal conductivity

9. EXPERIMENTS WITH DATA ANALYSIS SECTIONS

15.	The spectrometer	69
48.	Interference pattern produced by double slits	137
53.	Circuit deductions	149
54.	Deducing hidden components	150
55.	Investigations with a magnet	153
60.	The effect of temperature on resistance
The behaviour of various components
The temperature coefficient of resistance	162
69.	Using the reflection and refraction of light	185
70.	Thickness measurement using the absorption of radioactivity	187
71.	Simulation of a mass spectrometer	188
74.	Analysis of spectra	200
75.	Analysis of projectiles	202
76.	Analysis of the collisions of objects	203
77.	Designing experiments	204
78.	Analysis of melting points	206
79.	Analysis of sound waves	206
80.	Polarisation of light and the analysis of stress	208
92.	Millikan's experiment to measure e, the fundamental unit of charge	234

10. PRACTICE FOR PRACTICAL EXAMINATIONS

1. **Measurement of length and mass** — 38
   A variety of experiments giving practice in the use of:
   - Vernier calipers
   - Micrometer
   - Spherometer
   - Balances for measuring mass and force

2. **Using the travelling microscope** — 42
   To measure
   - The pitch of a screw
   - The separation of lines on a diffraction grating
   - The spacings on an interference pattern
   - The thickness of tracks on a microcircuit

   and to take measurements so that the refractive index of a liquid can be calculated

3. **Measuring times** — 44
   - Using a stopwatch
   - Using electronic timers
   - Using microprocessor based methods

4. **Timing oscillations** — 47
   Experiments based round measuring the periods of the following:
   - Springs
   - A compound pendulum
   - Swinging chains
   - Thin beams clamped at one end
   - A Y-shaped pendulum
   - Suspended beam
   - Beams oscillating on a curved surface
   - Coupled oscillators

5. **Some experiments involving density** — 51
   - Deduction of the density of unknown solids hidden in Plasticine
   - The identification of clear liquids
   - Investigation of the pressure due to a column of liquid
   - Making and using a simple hydrometer

6. **Using the principle of moments** — 53
   - Using a balanced beam to deduce mass and to identify liquids
   - Making and calibrating a simple current balance
   - Investigating the angle of a force needed to support a beam

7. **Detecting electromagnetic radiation** — 55
   - Plotting an amplitude against frequency spectrum across the frequency band of a radio
   - Methods of detecting infra-red radiation
   - General details about detecting other frequencies

CLASSIFICATIONS OF EXPERIMENTS

8. Plotting rays and image positions with pins ... 56
   - Virtual image in a plane mirror
   - Path of a ray through a glass block
   - Focal length of a convex lens
   - Real image in a convex lens
   - Maxima seen through a diffraction grating

9. Using an illuminated object with lenses and mirrors ... 58
   - Finding a sharp image accurately and estimating the error
   - Measuring the focal length of a concave mirror
   - Measuring the focal length of a concave lens
   - Finding the position of a hidden convex lens

10. The paths of rays through a prism ... 60

12. Bending beams ... 62
    Investigation on the deflection under load of:
    - A beam loaded centrally
    - A cantilever

14. The forced vibration of a wire ... 67

16. Measuring potential difference ... 72
    Direct voltages
    - A moving coil meter
    - A moving coil meter with an operational amplifier as a voltage follower
    - An oscilloscope
    - A potentiometer
    - Digital electronic methods

    Alternating voltages
    - Rectification and a moving coil meter
    - An oscilloscope
    - A moving iron meter
    - Calibration of a moving coil a.c. meter

17. Measuring the e.m.f. produced by a thermocouple ... 76
    - Using a potentiometer with a high resistance in series
    - By direct measurement using an operational amplifier to produce amplification

20. Finding the resistivity of a resistance wire using a metre bridge ... 81

21. Displaying and drawing waveforms on an oscilloscope ... 82

22. Measuring impedance ... 85

53. Circuit deductions ... 149

54. Deducing hidden components ... 150

55. Investigations with a magnet ... 153

70. Thickness measurement using the absorption of radioactivity ... 187

11. EXPERIMENTS WHICH USE A COMPUTER, A DATA MEMORY, OR A MICROPROCESSOR-CONTROLLED RECORDING INSTRUMENT

3. Measuring times ... 44
   - Using a stopwatch
   - Using electronic timers
   - Using microprocessor based methods

18. Using moving-coil ammeters and voltmeters to measure resistance ... 77
    - An investigation into the choice of instruments, their positions in circuits and the accuracy of the value of resistance calculated

19. Wheatstone bridge and metre bridge ... 79

23. Methods of measuring magnetic fields ... 88
    - Search coil and ballistic galvanometer
    - Search coil and integrator
    - Hall effect probe
    - A.c. induction

24. Using the computer and data memories as measuring instruments ... 94
    - Timing free fall
    - Investigating the change in resistance against time after a lamp is switched on
    - Damped s.h.m. of a compound pendulum
    - Investigating how the temperature changes as two liquids mix

25.	Detecting nuclear particles	98
	Measuring the background radiation	
	Safety in the use of radioactive sources	
	Adjusting the Geiger–Müller tube to measure the activities of sources	
	Using a cloud chamber	
	Using photographic paper	
28.	Springs and damping	104
39.	Charge and discharge of a capacitor	116
43.	Plotting the characteristic curves for a transistor (common-emitter mode)	127
45.	E.m.f. induced as a magnet passes through a coil	131
46.	Magnetic field produced by a pair of co-axial coils	133
51.	Phase angles in a.c. circuits using a capacitor and resistor in series	144
52.	Series LCR resonant circuit	147
59.	Potential dividers	160
	Using resistors, light dependent resistors and capacitors	
	The application of potential dividers to logic gates	
66.	Electric field patterns	178
71.	Simulation of a mass spectrometer	188
73.	Digital control by computer	195
79.	Analysis of sound waves	206
86.	Conservation of linear momentum with an air track	222
89.	Measurement of half-life	228
92.	Millikan's experiment to measure e, the fundamental unit of charge	234
94.	The photoelectric effect and the measurement of Planck's constant.	240